MW01011561

Working Toward Zion

WORKING TOWARD ZION

Principles of the United Order for the Modern World

James W. Lucas

Warner P. Woodworth

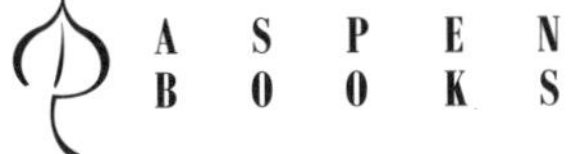

Salt Lake City, Utah

Working Toward Zion

Printed in the United States of America

10 9 8 7 6 5 4 3 2 1

Contents

Part Three: Working Toward Zion in the Modern World

Part Four: Working Toward a Zion World

Acknowledgments

Working Toward Zion is the culmination of many reflections and observations. Many close friends and associates have contributed to our collective learning. Colleagues at Brigham Young University and New York law offices have been useful critics and models of professional competence. Our dear brothers and sisters in the Third World, in far-flung missions of the Church, in U.S. inner cities, and Native American tribal reservations have shared their struggles, hopes and needs with us as they valiantly cope with regional economic disintegration. We have met dedicated individuals who possess considerable resources and skills, hearing and responding to the desperate cries of the poor. They have given us encouragement and provided wonderful examples of service and compassion.

We owe a special debt of gratitude to Don Adolphson, Leonard Arrington, Reed and May Benson, Richard Bushman, Gibb Dyer, Addie Fuhriman, Dwight Israelsen, Hugh Nibley, Clayne Pope, Fred Skousen, Bonnie Spanville, and Kaye Woodworth who read our original manuscript and offered gentle, helpful criticisms. The support staff at BYU, and especially Linda Veteto, worked cheerfully on word processors through the several iterations of this volume. Don Norton and Elizabeth Watkins were invaluable in editing early versions. Also, we benefitted from tireless efforts in our behalf by personnel at the New York Public Library and Harold B. Lee Library at BYU. Their rich collections have been invaluable and are much appreciated. Our editor, Giles Florence, and his colleagues Terry and MeLínda Jeffress, provided encouragement and wise counsel as the complex technical process of producing a book came to fruition. At the end, the tireless efforts of Aspen Books' staff, including Darla Isackson, Robert Davis, Paul Rawlins, and Jennifer Utley were critical in finally bringing the book to light. We owe a special debt of gratitude to Howard Christy of BYU Scholarly Publications, who gave us not only useful editorial advice and technical assistance, but powerful moral support as well as we have struggled to publish this atypical work.

We need to affirm that the historical interpretations, linkages between scriptures and Church leaders' pronouncements, theoretical arguments and practical suggestions—all are our views, for which we alone take full responsibility.

We dedicate the book to our parents who have given us life and taught us true principles throughout our youth. They have been marvelous examples of Christlike living and helped us avoid the materialistic values of contemporary culture.

Finally, in keeping with the spirit in which we have written, we want to inform the reader that royalties from the sale of this book will be donated to the Church's Humanitarian Services Fund, to help the poorest of the poor around the world. It is a modest attempt on our part to consecrate our financial resources by offering them to God's needy children.

Foreword

Within a few years of the pioneers' arrival in the Great Basin, the Prophet Brigham Young asked: "What does the Lord want of us up here in the top of these mountains? He wishes us to build up Zion. What are the people doing? They are merchandizing, trafficking and trading."[1] In my old age I have taken to reading the scriptures and have had it forced upon my reluctant attention, that from the time of Adam to the present day, Zion has been pitted against Babylon, and the name of the game has always been money—"power and gain."

This new book, *Working Toward Zion,* by Warner Woodworth and James Lucas, responds to Brother Brigham's criticism and his inquiry to the Saints regarding God's united order principles: "Why can we not so live in this world?" Building off the articles and speeches collected in *Approaching Zion,* this new book traces the problems of both capitalism and socialism from the rise of the Industrial Revolution to the present day. It shows how these twin economic systems diametrically oppose scriptural ideals of Zion.

According to Brother Brigham, "Elders are agreed on the way and manner necessary to obtain celestial glory, but they quarrel about a dollar. When principles of eternal life are brought before them—God and the things pertaining to God and godliness—they apparently care not half so much about them as they do about five cents."[2] "Instead of reflecting upon and searching for hidden things of the greatest value to them, [the Latter-day Saints] rather wish to learn how to secure their way through this world as easily and as comfortably as possible. The reflections, what they are here for, who produced them, and where they are from, far too seldom enter their minds."[3] Well, what was wrong with that? Isn't a comfortable living what we all want? It would be all right if we did not have our choice, but if we fail to realize that "we are engaged in a higher-toned branch of business than any merchants or railroad men, or any institution of an earthly nature,"[4] and give priority to the comfortable and respectable life after we have seen the greater light, we are in great danger. "Are their eyes single to the building up of the Kingdom of God? No, they are single to the building up of themselves."[5] "Does this congregation understand what idolatry is? The New Testament says that covetousness is idolatry; therefore, a covetous people is an idolatrous people."[6] "Man is made in the image of God, but what do we know of him or ourselves, when we suffer ourselves to love and worship the god of this world—riches?"[7]

Ancient as well as modern prophets have called us to abandon the economics of competition and inequality in favor of what President David O. McKay refers to as "the complete ideal of Mormonism."[8] The scriptures call it Zion, a place in which people live as follows:

All are "of one heart and one mind, . . . and there [are] no poor among them" (Moses 7:18), thus showing that equality extends into all fields, as it must also be in the preparation for Zion: "For if ye are not equal in earthly things ye cannot be equal in obtaining heavenly things. For if you will that I give you a place in the celestial world, you must prepare yourselves" (D&C 78:6–7). "And you are to be equal; . . . to have equal claims, . . . every man according to his wants and his needs, . . . every man seeking the interest of his neighbor, and doing all things with an eye single to the glory of God" (D&C 82:17, 19).

God recognizes only one justification for seeking wealth, and that is with the express intent of helping the poor (Jacob 2:19). One of the disturbing things about Zion is that its appeal, according to the scriptures, is all to the poor: "The Lord hath founded Zion, and the poor of his people shall trust in it" (Isaiah 14:32). Of course, once in Zion, no one suffers from poverty, for they dwell in righteousness and there are no poor among them (Moses 7:18). The law of consecration is a minimal requirement, for "if my people observe not this law, . . . it shall not be a land of Zion unto you" (D&C 119:6).

In stark contrast to the pride and power struggles of the world, true Saints have always sought the things of eternity rather than material success. They labor for a higher order, even a holy order. The question I have been asked most frequently by Saints who read or hear the pieces in *Approaching Zion* is "but what can we do? how do we do it?" Woodworth and Lucas suggest that there is much we can and must do to consecrate our lives to the blessing of others. This book is not a call to formally enter into the united order, but for each of us to do all we can to move toward Zion in this contemporary era. Drawing upon the scriptures and prophets of this dispensation, *Working Toward Zion* conveys a vision of how to apply God's temporal teachings here and now in the modern world economy.

Hugh Nibley
Provo, Utah

PART ONE

ZION AND THE MODERN WORLD

I calculate to be one of the instruments of setting up the kingdom of Daniel by the word of the Lord, and I intend to lay a foundation that will revolutionize the whole world. . . . It will not be by sword or gun that this kingdom will roll on: the power of the truth is such that all nations will be under the necessity of obeying the Gospel.

Joseph Smith, Jr., 1844[1]

Almost from the beginning of my services in Church welfare I have had the conviction that what we are doing in this welfare work is preliminary to the reestablishment of the law of consecration and stewardship as required under the united order. *If we could always remember the goal toward which we are working, we would never lose our bearings in this great work. What we are about is not new. It is as old as the gospel itself. Whenever the Lord has had a people who would accept and live the gospel, He has established the united order.*

Marion G. Romney, 1977[2]

We may not yet be the Zion of which our prophets foretold and toward which the poets and priests of Israel have pointed us, but we long for it and we keep working toward it. I do not know whether a full implementation of such a society can be realized until Christ comes, but I know . . . that the gospel of Jesus Christ holds the answer to every social and political and economic problem this world has ever faced. And I know we can each do something, however small that act may seem to be.

Jeffrey R. Holland, 1996[3]

The growth of the LDS Church around the globe has been remarkable. Above, missionaries are baptizing the Costa family from Florianopolis, a small island along Brazil's coast, in the Atlantic Ocean. This occurred in the early 1960s, shortly after the Brazilian Mission was divided into two units, having a total of approximately 3,900 members, with no stakes or wards. Today there are 23 missions, 131 stakes, and over 524,000 Latter-day Saints in Brazil.

1

It Will All Be Zion:
The Saints in the Modern World

Zion will extend, eventually, all over this earth. There will be no nook or corner upon the earth but what will be in Zion. It will all be Zion.

Brigham Young[1]

Barring catastrophic or apocalyptic intervention, on Saturday, April 6, 2030, a gathering in the Salt Lake Tabernacle will celebrate the bicentennial of the restoration of the fullness of the gospel of Jesus Christ to the earth. Counting children, a majority of members of the Church alive today can reasonably expect to witness this glorious occasion. Projecting trends decades into the future can be hazardous in retrospect. Nonetheless, conservative estimates are that, at current growth rates, the Church will have from 75 to 175 million members on April 6, 2030. Elder Neal Maxwell has estimated 90 million.[2] Approximately 70 percent of these will live in Latin America, and 15 percent will live in Asia. As few as 10 percent will live in North America and Europe combined.[3] The vast majority, possibly 98 to 99 percent, will live in areas where Latter-day Saints will still constitute a small minority of the total population.

America's leading sociologist of religion, not a Latter-day Saint, has already called the Church a "new world faith." Speaking from a secular viewpoint, he has argued that the impact of Mormonism on the world will be equal to the rise of the great world religions, such as Buddhism, Christianity, and Islam.[4] Speaking from the spiritual viewpoint, the prophet Lorenzo Snow wrote in 1901, at the beginning of the century now ending, that Mormonism "will succeed in establishing Zion, in building the holy city, in gathering out the righteous from all lands and preparing them to meet the Lord when He comes in His glory, no faithful Latter-day Saint doubts."[5]

The population of Latter-day Saints in the Third World grows dramatically each year. Chile has a higher percent of Latter-day Saints in the national population (2%) than the United States (1.7%). Nations like Mexico, the Philippines, and Brazil have displaced countries like Germany and Britain in the top ten LDS membership list since the 1970s.[6] The shift in numbers of Latter-day Saints listed below suggests growing change in the racial, cultural, and socioeconomic mix of Church members.[7]

1975		1995	
US	2,017,000	US	4,520,000
So. Pacific	73,000	Mexico	688,000
UK	73,000	Brazil	474,000
Mexico	68,000	Chile	345,000
Canada	55,000	Philippines	314,000
Asia	41,000	So. Pacific	297,000
Brazil	33,000	Peru	234,000
Argentina	19,000	Argentina	205,000
Uruguay	15,000	UK	161,000
Japan	12,000	Guatemala	140,000
Guatemala	12,000	Canada	138,000
Africa	6,000	Ecuador	115,000
Caribbean	350	Japan	103,000
		Colombia	98,000
		Bolivia	78,000
		Caribbean	77,000
		Africa	77,000
		Korea	62,000

Even more staggering is the potential growth of the Church in the Third World in decades to come. Donald Snow, a mathematician, has used United Nations and Church statistics to project LDS growth to the year 2000.[8] He calculates, for example, that Church membership in Colombia doubles every three years. Thus with current numbers of 87,000, one may project that there will be over half a million Colombian Saints by the end of this decade. For Brazil, which doubles each four years, Church membership may be 1.6 million in the year 2000. Mexico, which doubles every eight years, could have more than 1.3 million Latter-day Saints.

The impact of this dramatic growth in the Third World is awe-inspiring. For example, in 1960 there were only 22,503 LDS members in Latin America, a mere 1.3 percent of the total Church. By 1970 there were 160,355 or 5.5 percent. In 1980 there were 519,626 (11.2 percent). By 1990 those numbers had quadrupled to 2,229,000, almost 29 percent of all Latter-day Saints on the earth.[9] By the year 2000, at present growth rates, over half of all Latter-day Saints will speak Spanish or Portuguese. The days when the majority of Saints were white, English-speaking U.S. citizens are rapidly coming to a close. The "typical" LDS person of the next century will be tan or dark-skinned, urban poor or working class, from a Latin cultural background, and will not speak English.[10] To understand this new reality, we turn to the lives of several Saints in various regions of the earth.[11]

Former USSR

Natasha Stukalov, a new LDS convert, lives in Moscow, a city that was until recently the center of the Soviet empire. With the downfall of the USSR, Moscow remained the capital of Russia, the largest republic in the new Commonwealth of Independent States. Russia's current challenges are similar to those of other states in the region, including the newly independent Baltic republics and other Eastern European nations.

Under the Communist regime of past decades, Natasha and her fellow citizens lived a stifling, dreary existence in which Marxist ideology dominated education, work, and all other aspects of culture. The Cold War between East and West exacted a heavy toll on the people of the USSR. Fear, repression, KGB terror, and exorbitant expenditures to build and maintain the military machine—all sapped any glimmer of joy Natasha or her neighbors might have experienced. On the other hand, they, and virtually everyone else, had access to employment, health care, education, housing, and food. Because of the dark, authoritarian Soviet regime, Natasha had never married. She did not want to bring any children into such a depressing environment. She is now 58 years old.

Natasha lives in a cramped two-bedroom apartment with her 79 year-old mother, her brother, and her sister-in-law. The building is a huge, gray concrete structure typical of state housing projects. The elevator to their sixth-floor flat seldom works; they usually have to climb up the crumbling stairway. At night it is often dark due to theft of hallway light bulbs. Fuel shortages in Russia have left them with no hot water eight months a year.

Under the leadership of Mikhail Gorbachev beginning in 1985, *glasnost* (openness) and *perestroika* (restructuring) began. Within four short years, small gradual changes led in 1989 to a massive political tidal wave which knocked down the Berlin Wall and opened borders to the West. With the collapse of the Soviet Union in 1991 and Gorbachev's decline, Russia became a separate republic with Boris Yeltsin at the helm. Many Russians, like Natasha, had great expectations of a better life. Political democracy and movement toward a free market economy held great promise for the future.

During the growing openness of the late 1980s, the LDS Church sent a small group of missionaries to Moscow to preach the message of the Restoration. Natasha met them on the street, and their words sparked a testimony within her heart. This was what she had waited for all her life. Joseph Smith replaced the prophets of Communism, Karl Marx and V. I. Lenin. This American-based church not only brought Sister Stukalov the truths of eternity, but also hope of a better life here and now.

Several small LDS branches were established, and Natasha was called as Relief Society president only six months after her baptism. Problems, however, have grown exponentially both for her personally and for her sisters in the Church. The rubles which they earned in 1989 were traded for dollars on a one-to-one ratio then. Today it takes 4,600 rubles to get one U.S. dollar. By 1995, inflation has been as high as 2,020 percent annually, and the prospects of any change still look bleak. The monthly pension Natasha's mother receives, which used to be worth approximately $500, fell in value to under $5, while prices skyrocketed. In-fighting between Yeltsin and opposition hardliners has created much fear and uncertainty about the fragile democracy in Russia.

Some Western firms are doing joint business ventures with Russian companies, but many have been blocked by social unrest and economic instability. Corruption is rampant. Violence, street muggings, and behind-the-scenes mafia activities worry everyone. In the old days, Russia was crime-free. In harsh contrast to the guaranteed jobs and full employment of past decades, the unemployment rate now exceeds 20 percent. A quarter of the members of Natasha's branch are jobless for the first time in their lives. There is no safety net, no unemployment compensation, and no

Church Welfare Program. United Nations research predicts that old Soviet factories have 30 percent more workers than they can ever hope to use in the future, heightening the fear of rising joblessness.

The Third World

Now let us meet two families of Latter-day Saints in the Third World. Juan and Elena Flores live with their seven children on the outskirts of Mexico City. Elena became a Mormon as a child when her parents were baptized, and Juan joined the Church in his twenties, so they are essentially a second-generation LDS family. Juan has served as a bishop twice, and the family is strongly committed to building the kingdom. In contrast to Elena's life growing up, when the family was able to enjoy a relatively simple, happy existence, Mexico City today is a tough environment in which to survive.

The Flores parents both work to try to make ends meet. Juan has been laid off about a dozen times from various factory and construction jobs. Elena has worked in several markets in their *barrio* and now works three days a week at a neighborhood beauty shop. However, their combined wages are far below the minimum needed for a Mexican family to move up into the middle class. None of their three oldest children has actually graduated from high school, and the same bleak future appears before the other four.

Their LDS chapel is a twenty-minute bus ride away, and many times when Juan was bishop, he had to go to Church alone because he and Elena could not afford to pay the round-trip fare for the entire family. For the parents, Sunday was a special day when they tried to "splurge" on the children by giving them two regular meals. The rest of the week, there was enough cash for only one noon meal a day, plus a bit of rice or beans at night. However, if they did not all go to church, the family could have two meals on the Sabbath, perhaps with some fruit or *flan* dessert. Although Juan and Elena felt guilty about not taking their children to church when he was bishop, the stark struggle for survival seemed to override the luxury of Church meetings.

Half a world away, another Third World LDS family also strives to make ends meet. This is the Illagan family in Cebu, the Philippines. Missionary work in this island nation was launched in 1961. During the 1970s, Church researchers projected that the Church would grow to around 30,000 in the Philippines during the next two decades. In actuality, conversions mushroomed ten times faster than expected, to the present estimate of 300,000.

Reggie and Perla Illagan, their four children, and Reggie's aunt and uncle all live together in a five-room shack near the Cebu city dump. Smoke from burning refuse is always in the air, along with severe pollution from congested roads and factories in the area. The family speaks Cebuano at home, one of 87 native languages and dialects used in the country, but they are all fluent in English, which is often used in public. Filipinos enjoy a high literacy rate (88%) and the Illagans all have good educations.

The family's pride and joy is their 22-year-old son Ben, who recently returned from serving a mission in Manila. While on his mission, young Elder Illagan was supported financially by the Church. He wore a white shirt and tie, served in leadership positions, and had his own bed, a private room for him and his companion, and three meals a day.

But having returned home, Ben seems quite depressed because he is again forced to wear old clothes, eat only one or two meals a day, and sleep in a room with three brothers and sisters. He would like to finish high school and go on to college, but there is little opportunity to do this. On the other hand, he also cannot get a job. So he waits and looks for new possibilities. Their house is on a rich landowner's parcel, like 20 percent of Filipino Latter-day Saints who are squatters. Some 68 percent of LDS families live below the official poverty level. The Illagan family is fortunate to have any jobs, since 16 percent of Latter-day Saints are completely unemployed. The average household income of approximately $2,200 is not much for a family of eight people. Crime in the area is so great that someone must remain home, even during church, for fear the house might be broken into and completely cleaned out. Like about half of all LDS members in the Philippines, the family has no running water or indoor bathrooms.

Life is becoming increasingly hard in the Philippines. The islands used to have the second strongest economy in the Pacific Rim, but the country has slipped until now it is second from the worst. People used to think that big, American multinational companies, like Dole Pineapple, would help the country, but the jobs are few and the pay is minuscule. When Ferdinand Marcos took over as president, he promised a prosperous future, but instead he siphoned off billions of dollars to Swiss banks. While democracy has been restored, the economy only seems to get worse. Recently,

U.S. bases were closed, cutting thousands of jobs and billions of American dollars out of the country's economy. Things are so tough now that Perla has decided to seek work as a maid in Hong Kong. Some 15 other LDS mothers in their stake have done this recently, getting $400 a month pay, compared to $50 or so if they succeed at finding employment in Cebu. It would be difficult for her to leave the children, returning each year only during the Christmas season. The aunt could help out so Reggie could keep his job. But for the children it just will not be the same to sit around Monday night for home evening, and talk about how "Families Are Forever," with their mother way up north in Hong Kong.

The United States

The next illustration of current challenges facing Latter-day Saints around the globe occurs in a more familiar setting, America. Joe and Mary Brown may live in the inner city of Los Angeles, the Navajo reservation, or the old manufacturing region of Michigan. Wherever they live today, they certainly would be concerned about the problems of drugs, sex, violence, gangs, and crime. They might also be aware that some 13 percent of Americans live in poverty, roughly 30 million people. Children have become a high-risk group, with over one-fourth now living in poverty. We have seen a 30 percent rise in homeless individuals, most of whom are able to obtain only part-time work. Soup kitchens, women's shelters, welfare expenditures, and other institutions have become symbols of American life today.

But let us assume the Browns are middle-class Latter-day Saints who married in the temple and had three daughters. We'll say that Joe earned an engineering degree and worked for Boeing in the Northwest. They had a good life for several decades—an adequate home, two cars, dance and piano lessons for the girls, an Irish setter as the family pet. But suddenly the great American dream came crashing down on the Brown family when Boeing announced it was laying off 12,000 workers, including Joe Brown.

Joe searched for work elsewhere over a six-month period but found nothing comparable. Other firms with demands for technical skills have also been going through mass layoffs in the 1980s—General Motors cut 70,000, Sears 65,000, GE 100,000 and IBM 100,000. With the prospects not looking good, the family decided to move to Provo, where they thought housing and the cost of living would be lower. The plan was for Joe to seek an MBA degree and then launch a new career, not as an engineer, but as a manager.

The experience was fun in the sense that the Browns now lived in a predominantly LDS culture and BYU had a good basketball season. But the children, as teenagers, felt severely underprivileged because they could not afford the designer clothing they used to buy. The family lived in a modest rental unit in Orem and drove an aging car. To their peers the girls had to explain their circumstances in terms of "Dad's a student at the 'Y'." Mary had long prided herself on being a full-time homemaker, but with Boeing's severance pay running low, she felt forced to go to work at the local mall. Pay and benefits were miserably low for a sales clerk in Utah.

Joe struggled through the indignities of being back in the classroom at age 35, trying to recall concepts from more than a decade earlier. His fellow students seemed smarter and quicker and had skills he had never picked up. Retooling was harder than Joe ever expected, but eventually graduation came. The $40,000 investment in the MBA program appeared to pay off. He got a supervisory job at a new software firm in Utah Valley and, although the compensation was less than at Boeing, the future seemed bright. However, six months later, unable to get adequate funds for working capital, the firm laid off 20 percent of its workforce. As one of the newest hired, Joe was quickly out the door.

Throughout the next several years across America, midlevel management was hard hit by corporate downsizing. The Browns' newly purchased home was eventually repossessed by a Utah bank. Mary kept her sales clerk position at the mall while Joe spent the next year trying to get a license in order to sell real estate in the valley. The problems of a reduced lifestyle and the indignity and uncertainty of the family's future combined to force the Browns into a new realization—that the fall in their capacity to be self-sustaining was not merely a temporary aberration, but a likely prospect for the long-term future.

Our last illustration is also from the United States. It has been the subject of national news coverage, and therefore names have not been changed. Kay Whitmore had been an exemplar of the modern Latter-day Saint. A native Utahn, educated as a chemical engineer, he had moved to Rochester, New York, and worked his way up the corporate ladder at Eastman Kodak. In 1989 he became chief executive officer of this major corporation. This worldly success had not come at the expense of spiritual matters. Always active in the Church, he served as Rochester New York stake president as well as president of Kodak. Neither was his service strictly limited to Church activity. Involved in his adopted community, he had received wide notice for giving hundreds of Kodak employees paid leave to assist part-time in teaching math and science in the inner city schools of Rochester. Kodak was profitable and engaged in extensive research and development activities to preserve and advance its historical preeminence as a technology leader.

In 1993, Kay Whitmore was fired as head of Kodak. Talkative Wall Streeters on Kodak's board of directors gave frequent anonymous interviews to the press with many complaints about Kay Whitmore's performance. Kay Whitmore (at this writing serving as a mission president in England) was, and is, silent. However, his ouster was clearly rooted in large part in the new dominant thinking on Wall Street. Wall Street works on a short-term time horizon. A broker or trader focuses almost exclusively on daily, even minute-by-minute, fluctuations in the markets. Institutional fund managers generally are judged on their quarterly performances. In recent years, Wall Street has discovered a quick way to juice up a company's short-term bottom line. As Joe Brown and millions of others have found out, that method is massive layoffs of workers.[12]

It appeared that Kay Whitmore was guilty of breaking this new financial commandment. He was hardly the first. General Motors, American Express, IBM, and Westinghouse had also lost heads who had not sent enough heads rolling. His initial proposals for Kodak's future had called for only 2,000 job cuts out of a total employment of over 130,000. However, unlike the other companies, Kodak was profitable. Nonetheless, Kay Whitmore, in the view of Kodak's Wall Street directors, did not have what they required. A former Kodak executive was quoted in *The New York Times* as saying of Whitmore that "it's very difficult for him to lay off people."

None of the extensive national news coverage at the time noted that Kay Whitmore was a Mormon. Had the press investigated the matter, they may have understood why it was difficult for Kay Whitmore to lay off people. Perhaps they would have learned that a man who has served for years as a bishop and stake president has spent hundreds of hours listening to the human side of corporate "downsizing." As a million-dollar-a-year corporate president, it may have been easy enough for him to lay off thousands of workers. It is the fashion in modern American business to regard personnel as numbers, a cost component to be minimized. However, as an active priesthood holder, the day before he was fired he may well have taken groceries to an unemployed family. He may have spent the weekend with inner-city youth at a summer camp. In a hundred ways for his entire professional life, he was constantly face-to-face with, and responsible for, the *people* who would have their incomes terminated, their families disrupted and their futures put at risk by his decision to pump up those numbers.

Had they researched the matter, perhaps the press would have learned how 19th-century leaders of Mormonism, such as Joseph Smith and Brigham Young, advocated a novel economic system known as the united order. This was a system of private cooperatives which sought to combine both entrepreneurship and fraternity. Although not practiced today, they may have learned how the united order lingers deep in the Mormon cultural memory, haunting the modern Latter-day Saint with the idea that there must be a system that can combine economic reality with religious principle. Perhaps they would have been shown the Mormon scriptures relating to the united order, which denounce inequality and pride, and warn of consequences in the hereafter for those who would promote poverty in this life. It may indeed have been very difficult for Kay Whitmore to lay off people. So, instead, Kay Whitmore was laid off.[13]

However, the press did not take note of these things. The non-LDS press cannot be criticized for failing to note these matters. Even many Latter-day Saints are not aware that the restored gospel addresses all of these issues, that scripture and the labors of Saints and righteous nonmembers of many times and nations offer solutions to the dilemmas of Natasha Stukalov, the Flores, Illagan, and Brown families, and even the experience of Brother Kay Whitmore.

By the bicentennial of 2030, Zion will have become a worldwide movement.[14] Almost all Latter-day Saints in the 21st century will be a righteous minority in their larger home societies. These home societies will be challenged and distraught by economic and social turmoil. How does the gospel fit into and respond to the problems of the modern economy and society?

The Spiritual and the Temporal

This struggle to meet the physical needs of life is a universal characteristic of this mortal existence. Historically, people have responded to the terror and travails of the struggle for food, shelter, and safety in certain common ways. They have often longed for a separate "spiritual" sphere free from the toil and degraded concerns of this world. Hinduism, Buddhism, and other Asian religions have taught that heaven is the elimination of all earthly desires. Traditional Christianity made a division between the affairs of the church—a spiritual City of God interested in salvation in the next life—and the worldly or temporal city of this life, where religion was not so obviously beneficial.

The gospel restored in this dispensation denounced this dichotomy. The restored gospel does not differentiate between temporal and spiritual. Brigham Young once said, "In the mind of God there is no such thing as dividing spiritual from temporal, or temporal from spiritual; for they are one in the Lord."[15] Modern revelation defines this relationship: "That which is spiritual being in the likeness of that which is temporal; and that which is temporal in the likeness of that which is spiritual" (D&C 77:2). The Lord teaches:

> Wherefore, verily I say unto you that all things unto me are spiritual, and not at any time have I given unto you a law which was temporal; neither any man nor the children of men; neither Adam your father, whom I created. (D&C 29:34)

The Lord goes on to say that he gave to Adam to "be an agent unto himself; and I gave unto him commandments, but no temporal commandment gave I unto him, for my commandments are spiritual" (D&C 29:35).[16] Moreover, the scriptures suggest that faithfulness will result in being "blessed both spiritually and temporally" (D&C 14:11). Church president Joseph F. Smith wrote:

> It was the doctrine of Joseph Smith, the original revelator of "Mormonism," that the spirit and body constitute the soul of man. It has always been a cardinal teaching with the Latter-day Saints, that a religion which has not the power to save people temporally and make them prosperous and happy here, cannot be depended upon to save them spiritually, to exalt them in the life to come.[17]

Applying the gospel to our lives is, or ought to be, a two-way street. Going in one direction, the spiritual should flow toward the temporal aspects of life—one's education, the household, the family, the job, and the community. Conversely, the temporal ought to flow toward the spiritual—heightening the meaning of covenants, increasing dedication in one's church calling, providing service to others, contributing financial offerings, indeed, consecrating one's

Adam Smith (1723–1790), Scottish moral philosopher who is considered to be the father of free market economics. His lofty view of economic theory was based on religious and ethical values such as justice, sympathy, and benevolence.

Joseph Smith (1805–1844), American prophet who is viewed as the founder of Mormonism's spiritual and temporal ideals. His vision of Zion was based on gospel economic principles such as consecration and stewardship.

time and talents to building the kingdom of God. We cannot be whole Christians without both the temporal and the spiritual dimensions functioning in our lives. We cannot precisely split our choice of matters to obey and only focus on a narrow definition of religiosity. God's commandments involve temporal actions, from home and visiting teaching to prayer, from keeping the Word of Wisdom to temple worship. The restored gospel sees this temporal world as a setting for the highest spiritual concerns. Thus our calling, indeed our life's mission, is to integrate these two major dimensions of mortality into a congruent whole.

The Individual and Society

Beginning about two hundred years ago, humanity began to come upon a new way of dealing with the poverty and unhappiness that had theretofore been its history. Clever machines, and a new society and economy that encouraged their development, offered the possibility of producing more of the material necessities of life for each person. This gave rise to a new question: Did change come through individual actions, or through the social institutions in which the individual lives? Which was more important—one's personal will or the influence of one's environment? Was moral progress to be achieved by reform of the individual or by making a more just society?

Evangelical preachers and great men in England, following the traditional outlook of the Christian churches, taught that people should not resist the existing social order, but rather look for their rewards in the next life. In the new nation of America, it was thought that it did matter how society's institutions were organized and that it was worth making a revolution to try to do it better. A professor named Adam Smith, formerly at the university of Glasgow in Scotland, supported American self-determination and argued that the new economy that he saw developing would make people better because it would make them freer.[18]

As with the false differentiation of spiritual and temporal, the restored gospel cut through the false dichotomy between individual and social action. An ancient scripture edited for the modern age, the Book of Mormon, showed that one could not focus only on reforming either the society or the individual. Mosiah counseled against monarchical government because a wicked king could lead the entire society into much iniquity (Mosiah 29:13–36). Yet even under the government of the judges, personal iniquity and pride could arise, leading one righteous judge to resign to pursue the preaching of personal moral reform and social and economic equality (Alma 4:11–19). Society and the individual interrelate. One cannot have a good society without good individuals. A good society does not necessarily make good individuals, but an evil society can have a profoundly evil influence on individuals. The restored gospel seeks both good individuals and a good society. In the words of David O. McKay, "The betterment of the individual is only one aim of the Church. The complete ideal of Mormonism is to make upright citizens in an ideal society."[19]

The importance of the larger "temporal" society to individual spirituality and righteousness can be seen in the word of God. Many of God's commandments are social and economic in nature. For example, at least seven of the Ten Commandments relate in some way to economic activity.[20] One scholar has counted 28 percent of the lines of the Doctrine and Covenants as directly relating to economic activities.[21] Another has determined that 36 percent of the sections of the Doctrine and Covenants principally concern economic matters.[22] Of the 112 revelations that the Prophet Joseph received, some 88 deal at least partially with financial matters. At the October 1873 conference, Wilford Woodruff observed:

> Strangers and the Christian world marvel at the "Mormons" talking about temporal things. Bless your souls, two-thirds of all the revelations given in this world rest upon the accomplishment of this temporal work. . . . This is the great dispensation in which the Zion of God must be built up, and we as Latter-day Saints have it to build. We have it to do, we can't build up Zion sitting on a hemlock slab singing ourselves away to everlasting bliss; we are obliged to build cities, towns and villages, and we are obliged to gather the people from every nation under heaven to the Zion of God, that they may be taught the ways of the Lord. We have only just begun to prepare for the celestial law when we are baptized into the Church of Jesus Christ of Latter-day Saints.[23]

The celestial law to which apostle Woodruff referred is the law of consecration and stewardship. The implementation of this law is called the *united order*. While the term has sometimes been used only to describe certain specific efforts to live the law of consecration and stewardship in the 1800s, it is also applied more broadly to the entire body of divine teachings and commandments encompassed in the law of consecration and stewardship and related "temporal" matters. We will follow the latter meaning in this book.

The United Order and the Modern World

In the 19th century, the Latter-day Saints undertook an ambitious program of economic development and reform, seeking to implement the united order commandments that affect temporal affairs. The term *Zion* is used for the society which they sought to create. Today, the modern Latter-day Saint memory of this program is dominated by the rural commune of Orderville, Utah. This has yielded a current perception of the united order as a kind of Mormon socialism. Yet Church leaders have emphatically denied any connection between the united order and socialism. Seeing Orderville as the principal example of the united order also leads to the perception that the principles of the united order can only be applied in an isolated all-LDS society. Yet for over a century the Church has counseled Church members against emigrating and isolating themselves. Many Latter-day Saints therefore are confused as to their heritage and doctrine on an important range of economic and social concerns that affect the lives of every child of God every day.

Modern Latter-day Saints are confronted every day with such concerns. It is our own confrontations with these concerns that have led us to this project. We met several years ago and were intrigued to learn that each of us was writing about concepts of Zion, the united order, temporal commandments, and their meaning in today's society. These issues involve not only Natasha Stukalov and Kay Whitmore, or the Flores, Illagan, and Brown families. Both of us have been approached by numerous Latter-day Saints wanting to discuss how to practice temporal righteousness, given the structure and demands of the modern world economy. How can one truly be a Christian in today's difficult economic environment? What do the economic principles of Zion mean today? How can we truly build a Saintly community? What might be done to foster sustainable development among LDS members in Africa, Latin America, and Asia? Why is there such great inequality within industrialized nations, and how can the poor of the inner city become self-reliant? What is the future of the Church in the 21st century as it grows rapidly into a church with a majority of its members in the Third World?

What do concepts like *consecration* and *stewardship* mean for those who have an excess of material wealth? In what ways might free enterprise capitalism and love become enmeshed together? LDS managers today seek ideas about methods for creating more democratic and humane working conditions. Hourly employees raise concerns about being exploited or suffering mass layoffs. When it is universally recognized that entrepreneurs create most new jobs, LDS small employers and business founders are frustrated at receiving little support. Some wealthy Latter-day Saints have expressed frustration in having more money than they know what to do with, yet they still lack personal fulfillment. They have begun to feel guilty, or they now want to help build a better world, but they are not sure how to proceed. Parents engage us in dialogue about their affluent offspring who seem increasingly trapped in the game of material acquisition. Thoughtful colleagues seek to discuss Church history, the rise and fall of the early united order, and the theological and practical meaning of consecration and stewardship.

These issues have attracted the attention of some of Mormonism's most eminent scholars. In works such as *Great Basin Kingdom* and *Building the City of God* (with Dean May), Leonard Arrington has provided a definitive historical study of Mormon economic history.[24] Hugh Nibley has rigorously critiqued the materialism of modern Latter-day Saints and contemporary society. These essays have been collected in the well known *Approaching Zion*.[25] In *Working Toward Zion* we hope to build on these foundations to explore practical applications of the restored gospel for life in contemporary society.

Like Marion G. Romney (quoted on page 1), many Latter-day Saints look forward to the "reestablishment of the law of consecration and stewardship as required under the united order." However, it has always been understood that that ultimate event, the establishment of a sacred economic system as described in the Doctrine and Covenants, will come only by revelation. We do not know what instruction such a revelation might contain, nor do we believe that persons may presume to set up "united orders" without such authorization. Consequently, this book is not about creating a full-fledged united order, nor is it a demand for the Church's leaders to do so. What, then, is it about?

Elder John A. Widtsoe wrote that the united order "as a mode of life . . . is in abeyance" and that its full reestablishment would be "authorized through the revelation of the Lord to the President of the Church." In the meantime, tithing and "wise and earnest cooperation in all affairs of life partially take its place." He also noted that the united order has

> a practical value as an ideal by which any proposed economic system may be tested for the degree of its worthiness. The nearer

> any scheme for economic betterment conforms to the principles of the United Order, the more likely it will be to assist mankind in their efforts to attain material happiness. . . . As one studies the United Order, the more evident becomes its power for human welfare, for developing human lives, and for providing the prosperity needed on the path of progress.[26]

As suggested by President Romney, it is "the goal toward which we are working."

Our goal is to explore how, through "wise and earnest cooperation in all affairs of life," we can *work toward* being better prepared for the day when the Lord may call on us to live the full celestial law of consecration. We see temporal righteousness as a continuum along which we can progress line upon line, precept upon precept, here a little, there a little, in a continuing effort to work toward the full celestial ideal of the united order. Further, the benefits of this *working toward* are not limited to some future millennial time. The light and knowledge now available to us regarding "the principles of the United Order" can be applied to our modern world in its search for "the prosperity needed on the path of progress." Studying those principles confirms our testimonies of their divine origins and "power for human welfare [and] for developing human lives" and also can help us to test modern economic systems to determine how likely they "will be to assist mankind in their efforts to attain material happiness." Efforts inspired by these principles can do great good in the world now, even as we await a call to the full united order.

One cannot work toward something unless one knows what it is. Our approach is first to understand what the principles of the united order, the social economy of Zion, are, and then to explore how they might apply to various aspects of the life of our society and economy. In order to do so, we must place them in a real-life context. Thus, we devote Parts One and Two of the book to a review of the concurrent rise of the modern economy and the restoration of the gospel. After Part One lays the groundwork for understanding the conditions of the modern world, and historical efforts to implement the united order, Part Two studies the interplay between Zion and the world over the last two centuries. There we learn that the united order is not a historical curiosity, but rather provides dynamic principles which interrelate with the actual real lives of our brothers and sisters in our contemporary world economy and society.

Drawing on this foundation, in Parts Three and Four we then

explore what it might mean to work toward establishing Zion and living the restored gospel's principles of temporal righteousness today. Part Three looks at applications on a personal, family, and group level. Part Four then discusses implications for modern business and businessmen. Rather than abstract academic or theoretical analyses, we attempt to focus on actual specific personal, family and organizational applications, many of which have already been implemented by some Latter-day Saints or at least experimented with as partial solutions.

In doing so, we must emphasize several important caveats. The united order as a spiritual concept is a sacred doctrine, involving high ideals which challenge even the strongest of the faithful Saints. A major argument of our book is that some aspects of the Lord's economic system may be reasonably practiced in part within the context of current economic conditions. However, these same high ideals tend sometimes to generate overenthusiastic, unrealistic responses.

Taking certain principles to an extreme may lead to disaster. For instance, some well-intentioned Mormons have withdrawn from the world, physically as well as socially, to build what they considered to be a sort of quasi-united order commune. Dozens of groups have done so throughout this country. The unfortunate outcome has sometimes been that the people involved began to become a church unto themselves. Fundamentalism and other aspects of apostate offshoots have crept in.

Another word of warning regarding attempts to develop contemporary applications of united order principles is equally serious. Enthusiasm for such economic ideals has attracted certain personality types, usually very charismatic individuals, who then create authoritarian group cultures in which innocent members/investors are manipulated. The final outcome may be fraud or other forms of criminality. On occasion, victims of such activity not only lose their testimonies, but large sums of money as well. Thus we advocate that private efforts to implement any proposals of our book, or to replicate successful experiences of others, be treated with the same caution as any other business investment.

Finally, as we will see, freedom is a vital part of the united order. No private person or group should try to force others into a project because it supposedly will advance united order principles, nor arrogate to themselves the right to issue a priesthood-like "call" to participate in such a venture. Further, the *united order* designation itself is a term of holiness and ought to be used carefully. This sacred term should not be employed as a title of a firm or other form of group identification.

In this book we have attempted to bring together existing teachings relating to the economic and social concerns challenging modern Latter-day Saints, many of which are either unknown, forgotten, or buried in the mental cemeteries of the crowd. Our aim is the voluntary, practical application of these teachings in the modern world as it exists. These applications assume that we are operating within the modern free market economy. We do not attempt to describe a utopian united order system as it might exist separated from modern realities. As a practicing business lawyer and a management professor who does extensive outside consulting, we have based this book on our areas of expertise, which emphasize historical and practical current applications rather than theoretical analysis. We hope that this book will inspire, or provoke, LDS scholars in other disciplines to explore the moral dimensions of economic behavior in the light of the restored gospel. We also hope that ordinary Latter-day Saints like ourselves will find here some useful insight into understanding and practicing the glorious wisdom of the restored gospel in their temporal lives in the modern world.

The issues covered by this book have been at the heart of public debate for centuries. As we will see, this public debate usually centers on the *pros* and *cons* of government actions as solutions. Alternatively, many in the Church tend to cast the burden on the Church and its leaders and hold them responsible if the Saints do not meet the expectations found in the scriptures. Instead, we propose to look to ourselves—as individuals, families, private groups, and firms seeking together "wise and earnest cooperation in all affairs of life." Unlike with most other proposals on these issues, the applications set out here are all susceptible of implementation without any change in either current government law or policies or current Church doctrine or practices. To accomplish them, however, requires that we not simply try to do things differently. Rather, we need to begin doing different things.

The purpose of this book then is to attempt to understand how the teachings regarding the united order fit into the modern world in which we really live, and to explore how we can work toward a greater application of those teachings in the context of the worldwide Zion that is coming. As we shall see in the next chapter, this is a modern world of problems and ills, in desperate need of a cure.

2

The Perfect Prescription:
The Challenge of the Modern World

Christ's gospel is the perfect prescription for all human problems and social ills.

Ezra Taft Benson[1]

The prophets have long advocated the gospel as the means by which solutions to society's many problems may be realized. Unfortunately, such teachings have never been heeded by world leaders, opinion-makers, or, indeed, the populace as a whole. When one reflects on our world of global pain and suffering, whether in the LDS heartland of Utah and America or the growing LDS centers in the Third World, the gap between the gospel's promise and the needs of society is a great chasm. By the time you read this book specific statistics and cases cited in this chapter may have changed. However, these facts illustrate what appear to be permanent, long-term trends.

The Economy of the United States

Unemployment. As of this writing, unemployment in the United States stands at just under six percent. While this is relatively low compared to recent decades, parts of the United States are in worse condition. California, the United States' success model ever since the 1849 gold rush, collapsed in the early 1990s. Once heralded as the world's seventh largest economy, the "Golden State" has seen its real estate market disintegrate, its unemployment rise to 9.5 percent, and its manufacture decline at the rate of more than one plant closure a day for several years in a row as businesses fail or flee to other regions. The state government had to issue $2.5 billion in IOUs to pay for services and goods.

Although the American economy seems to be producing lots of jobs, economic insecurity is high and rising. This sense of insecurity may come from several factors. As illustrated by the experiences of

Joe Brown at Boeing and Kay Whitmore at Kodak, one factor is continuing massive layoffs by America's largest companies. Sears has closed over one hundred stores and its century-old catalogue business, eliminating 50,000 workers. While IBM has cut 100,000 jobs through voluntary incentives since 1986, another 50,000 will disappear as the company continues its slide from 406,000 workers worldwide to a new size of 250,000. Boeing, which used to have 149,000 workers, now employs only 110,000, while McDonnell Douglas has dropped from 132,500 to around 80,000. Even with the American economy expanding, profitable corporations continue massive layoffs.[2] To complicate matters further, in a growing number of cases, corporate downsizing affects not only the husband but his wife also, since many two-career couples are, or were, employed at the same large company. In 1992, this happened to 181,000 U.S. families. Most were whites, and nearly 120,000 of those couples had children still living at home.[3]

The ripple effect on other jobs is enormous during these periods of restructuring, and the consequence for many of those laid off will be temporary employment for the remainder of their working lives. Temporary employment through hiring agencies has mushroomed nearly 250 percent in the United States since 1982. Overall employment has increased less than 20 percent during the same time frame. In 1988, about a quarter of the workforce consisted of contingent employees. That figure is now growing toward including half of the labor force. The largest private employer in the United States in 1992 was Manpower, Inc., with 560,000 workers. General Motors was a distant second with 362,000.[4] By 1994, Manpower, Inc. employed 750,000, with displaced skilled technical workers constituting its fastest growing area of business.[5]

Increasingly there is no assurance about tomorrow, no benefits such as medical care or a retirement pension. Confidence in the ability of the industrial market economy to provide long-term economic security for families has been undermined.[6] The traditional career pattern historically consisted of starting as an apprentice and advancing over the years, according to hard work and merit. Eventually, one retired with pride and a pension as an "IBMer" or a "Sears man." There was a certain predictability and security in the job market, a social compact between employee and the company. Not so today. There is little security or permanence. Workers are becoming subcontractors who must sell themselves for the short-term, the specific situation at hand. After it is over, they are thrown away—another disposable product. Loyalty is lacking on either side. How all of this will affect the worker's sense of self-worth and family life is still not known because the phenomenon is so new. But for America as a whole, and Latter-day Saints in particular, the American Dream is harder to see than ever before. Having a home, qualifying for a mortgage loan, enjoying a predictable and stable family lifestyle—all are becoming relics of the past.[7]

Nor is the United States the only industrial nation with an employment problem. Joblessness is even worse in western Europe. Unemployment in the European Economic Community averages over 10 percent and approaches or exceeds 20 percent in Ireland and Spain. Even in the economic powerhouse of Europe, western Germany, unemployment is nine percent, and is much higher if the former East Germany is included.[8]

Income Stagnation. Not only has job insecurity increased, but even those who are employed have seen their lives deteriorate. The bulk of U.S. workers saw their wages decline in real value (constant after inflation dollars) by some 10 percent in the 1980s while they worked almost 10 percent longer hours.[9] These longer work hours have significantly reduced the time available for family and service. By 1990 the average American manufacturing worker's compensation was $14.83 per hour, below that of France, Italy, and others who enjoyed hourly compensation levels from $15.25 to $21.30 according to the U.S. Department of Labor.[10] The decline for American workers continues into the 1990s, affecting middle- as well as lower-income groups.[11] Now, it also appears doubtful that the western European economies will be able to sustain their superior wage performance.[12]

The decline in incomes exacerbates the insecurity produced by mass layoffs. Only a third of laid-off workers find new jobs at pay levels equal to or better than their old jobs.[13] One study found that victims of mass layoffs experience long-term income declines of 25 percent. It has been argued that this is because so many new jobs are in low-paying service businesses. However, even when skilled manufacturing workers found jobs in the same industry their long-term incomes declined by 20 percent.[14]

Inequality. In contrast, American executives enjoyed astronomical growth in pay and perks.[15] While "real" family income for Americans has declined over the past 15 years, CEO compensation has risen dramatically. In 1979 the ratio between the lowest paid workers in a typical Fortune 500 company and the CEO was 29 to 1.

Lately, the ratio has approached 200 to 1. *Business Week*'s analysis of total CEO compensation in major U.S. companies shows that it grew 212 percent during the 1980s, four times the increase in factory worker total pay, which was only 53 percent. Unlike Kay Whitmore, most of the corporate bureaucrats running America's large businesses focused on short-term gains through takeovers and financial manipulations, while millions of Joe Browns were laid off to pay the enormous debts incurred in this process. By 1990 average salary and bonus for top management was $1.2 million, and when stock options and other benefits are included, average total compensation rises to $1.95 million. This rose again in 1992 to the extent that average CEOs of major U.S. firms enjoyed pay increases to $3.8 million, 56 percent above 1991. For the typical U.S. factory worker at his or her compensation rate, it would take 85 years to earn as much as a CEO earns in just twelve months.[16] In contrast, the comparable ratios are 21 to 1 in Germany and 16 to 1 in Japan.[17] The trend now seems to be the normal course, with CEO compensation increasing 8.1 percent from 1992 to 1993, 11.4 percent from 1993 to 1994, and 10.4 percent from 1994 to 1995 while other employees' salaries remained comparatively flat.[18]

While increasing numbers of executives make millions annually, they are outpaced by the illegal manipulations of the Ivan Boeskys and Michael Milkens, the latter receiving $550 million in 1987. Short jail sentences have done little to punish the excesses of the superrich. American savings and loans were plundered by inside managers, while the taxpayers have been stuck with a bailout of several hundred billion dollars. Bribes at Wedtech, check-kiting at E. F. Hutton, overcharges and other illegalities in government contracts at General Dynamics, Boeing, Unisys, Hughes Aircraft, and GE, management greed at RJR Nabisco, junk bond manipulation at Drexel Burnham and Salomon Brothers, fraudulent investment sales by Prudential—all become icons of corporate America's disastrous moral and financial decline in recent years.[19]

The Poor and Needy. U.S. Census Bureau data show that the number of citizens living below the government's official poverty level jumped to a total of 36.9 million in 1992. This means that some 14.5 percent are poor, roughly one out of every seven Americans. The poor included 25 percent of all children under 6 and 22 percent of all children under 18.[20] While 34 million U.S. residents are estimated to be overweight, 5.5 million American children under age

12 are regularly hungry. Some 19 percent of us are on diets, while the caloric intake among much of the world, including millions of people in the USA, lacks sufficient nourishment for a normal life.[21]

Wealthy America has seen the emergence of a new breed, the "hyper poor."[22] This group is made up of the needy who attempt to make do on *less than half* the income which falls under the official poverty line. Translated for a family of three people, this means that they would try to survive on under $4,945 annually, which would require that each person get by on under $5 per day. Despite benefits in the form of welfare checks, food stamps, donated canned groceries, and so forth, the hyper poor are often homeless, eking out a subsistence-level lifestyle. Many become dysfunctional, lacking social support, suffering from alcoholism or mental illness. Shockingly, this group of the hyper poor grew by 52 percent during the 1980s.

While the myth is that poor Americans are simply lazy and unwilling to work, the facts are that 9 out of 10 are either handicapped, teenagers or younger, single mothers with preschool children, over age 65, or employed but receiving terribly low wages. The age-old notion that the poor are simply not motivated, and that they choose to be on "the dole," is not borne out by research evidence.[23] It may be relatively easy for many of America's upper and middle classes to admit that urban poor minority children are sadly "at risk" and then go on our merry way consuming the latest electronic games and shopping at the mall for a weekly addition to our wardrobes. What is not so appreciated is the fact that the plight of the "Have Nots" directly affects us in terms of taxpayer costs to provide education, welfare dollars, food stamps, and health care support as the very needy become less and less able to support themselves.

Inner Cities and Indians. Important areas of the United States are in a state of permanent depression. Today's urban America is a jungle of crime, racial hatred, and crushing poverty. The result is joblessness and the breakup of the family. Many residents of the inner city survive in a drug culture of addiction, family abuse, illiteracy, and nonparticipation in the workforce. The youth turn to gangs as a means of survival, as well as the illusion of self-dignity. Teenage parents, single mothers, and absentee fathers are becoming the norm in urban areas. Illegitimacy and welfare dependency are the symbols of today's inner-city family. The final outcome is often delinquency, prison, and finally violent death.

To white American Mormons, this description conjures up the image of a black inner-city stereotype. Such an assumption, however, is wrong. There are more Hispanics in the U.S. today (22.4 million) than blacks, and Hispanics are more likely to be LDS and live in the inner city than are Afro-Americans.[24] Physical density, decay of urban infrastructure, and environmental pollution seem to conspire jointly in undermining the lives of people in the inner city. The prophet Joseph Smith envisioned utopian cities of around 20,000 in population, a far cry from today's overcrowding. Thomas Jefferson foretold the plight of the urban U.S. as follows: "When we get piled upon one another in large cities, as in Europe, we shall become as corrupt as Europe."[25] Not surprisingly today, many of America's cities are *more* corrupt, more dangerous, and more criminal than the large cities of Europe, far surpassing Jefferson's dark-clouded warning.

The social pathology of inner-city America today is perhaps most graphically seen in the waves of homelessness which rose and pounded upon the pavement during the past decade. Not unlike the 2,000 year-old story of that poor, cold, tired, and unknown couple, Joseph and Mary, seeking a bed and a birthplace in the city of Bethlehem long ago, today's homeless are also turned away and abandoned. They too seek shelter and food, medical care and clothing. Many are youths, runaways or abused by parents. Others are old and abandoned by their offspring. Some are pregnant. Many are frightened. A number are addicted to drugs. Many are physically and emotionally ill. Large numbers used to be employed but lost their jobs and homes and today roam the streets, seeking only to survive. Researchers report that some three million Americans are homeless during a given year. A fourth of them are children.[26]

Perhaps even more severe is the desperate situation of the North American Indian reservations. Unemployment is over 50 percent among many tribes, problems of alcoholism and low levels of education are widespread, and the Bureau of Indian Affairs in Washington, D.C., is cutting back its funding. Suicide among young Indians is an increasing problem. The answer on a number of reservations is to create gambling industries that will attract outside whites who will pump dollars into tribal coffers. While the actual amount of revenue may increase, the side effects of corruption will, in the long run, diminish the tribes' quality of life even further.[27]

As we approach the year 2000, inequality and the number of poor and needy will increase. Research shows that incomes of the wealthiest tenth of the population rose 21 percent in the 1980s, while the poorest tenth dropped 12 percent, a gap growing faster and wider than ever before. Morality aside, such a major social problem is extremely bad in terms of economic policy and practice.[28] For Latter-day Saints, such a bifurcation can be seen as the same spiritual disease which destroyed the earlier American nation of the Nephites.

The Modern Economy of the Mormon West. Conditions in Utah, the "Zion of the Rockies," suggest that national problems are reflected in the state. Utah Valley, for example, was one of only six regions in the United States to actually *decline* in income for years in the late 1970s and early 1980s. Almost a fifth of its residents lived in poverty. A decade later, things were better, but per capita income in Utah as a whole still ranks 48th in the nation, along with West Virginia and Mississippi.[29] When looking at total household income, the national average is $35,225, while Utah's is approximately $2,000 under that amount.[30] Most of rural Utah is considerably below that amount; for instance San Juan County is $19,183, and Kane County $24,904. State officials blame Utah's poor national ranking on the large number of children per family. However, even after adjusting for the large number of children by looking at average household income, it still ranks only 34th.[31] And all those kids do not cost nothing. The unfortunate reality is that the state does have a significant problem with poverty. Regularly, 123,000 Utahns live at or below official poverty, an income for a family of four of only $1,512 per month.

Other signs of poverty, such as lack of food, correlate with low income along the Wasatch Front. In a 1990 report of the U.S. Conference of Mayors, data showed that requests for emergency food grew 20 to 25 percent over the previous year. "Despite local efforts to increase food donations, funds, and volunteers, demand always exceeds available supplies," the report declared of Salt Lake City.[32] The rise indeed has continued over the past several years. In 1992, Utah received almost $200 million in federal cash and food from the U.S. Department of Agriculture, making it a sort of welfare reservation. This was up $28 million from 1991, a rate of assistance from Washington, D.C., of $544,000 a day. The total cost of food stamps alone in Utah was $95.5 million in 1992.[33]

The Utah Community Childhood Hunger Project claims that after studying a sample of 17,000 state families, some 31,000 children are hungry each night, while 70,000 more are "at risk" because they do not receive the kind of nourishment required for growing, healthy bodies.[34] These figures translate into one of every five young Utahns. Such children suffer more health problems, miss school classes twice as often as other students, and experience other ripple effects from malnutrition.

Homelessness has also recently become a major issue for Utah. Requests for emergency shelter in Salt Lake City grow yearly by some 20 percent.[35] An estimated 1,500 to 2,000 people inhabited vacant lots, abandoned cars, and other places on any given night in Utah during 1992. Some 79 percent of the homeless are Utah residents, and 78 percent are white. The Travelers Aid Society's shelter ran at 141 percent of capacity at times during 1992. The fastest growing segment of homeless people was families headed by a mother, a sharp contrast to the 1980s stereotype of a single, alcoholic male.[36] For many active Latter-day Saints, it defies the concept of Zion in the Rockies to see groups of people living under the freeway overpass in Provo or in abandoned railcars in Salt Lake City. Even more surprising to people in the BYU community was a June 1993 front page article in the campus paper, *The Daily Universe,* which reported that three homeless men had lived the past half year in tents adjacent to the university. The shocking aspect of the story was how these homeless individuals provided various food items to an apartment of BYU students in an off-campus housing unit who were struggling financially to make ends meet during the academic year.[37] Apparently, the scriptural saying is now being fulfilled that "the last shall be first."

Utah's unemployment picture has had ups and downs over the past 10 to 15 years, ranging from a high of 9.2 percent jobless in 1983 to 3.7 percent in 1994, one of America's lowest. However, a number of small Utah towns have suffered from 15 to 26 percent unemployment for over a decade, with no improved prospects for the coming years. For a long time, a central concern about working in Utah has not been joblessness, but the quality and wages of employment. For instance, Utah worker injury and death rates are twice the U.S. average. Citations against companies which allow unsafe conditions are few. A recent study suggests that hundreds of Utah worker deaths have not even been investigated because employers did not report the incidents to state safety officials.[38] Nationally released reports cite Utah for its dangerous mines, extensive violation of child labor laws, and other problems. A *Washington Post* story on mining companies that tampered with coal dust equipment designed to protect miners from lung disease noted that Utah was the highest violator in the West and Midwest, with 16 firms breaking the law. The (Republican) U.S. Secretary of Labor accused the companies of having "an addiction to cheat" and assessed $5 million in fines and penalties.[39]

In 1992, Utah firms were required by the U.S. Department of Labor to correct abuses of the minimum wage laws by paying a total of $3.4 million to 4,667 deprived workers. Some 261 Utah firms had violated the law, making the state the leading violator in the Intermountain region. Apparently, while D&C 78:18 declares that "the riches of eternity are yours," some Mormon employers are determined that this promise should be below the minimum wage, at least during this life. The state appeared to be attempting to follow the strategy of many developing Third World countries, offering skilled low-cost labor to outside employers. While this approach has brought jobs, it has also assured continuing low wages, economic dependency, lack of self-development, and outside economic control.

Furthermore, since the 1970s Utah has consolidated its reputation for shady business dealings. Events such as the collapse of five thrifts, the AFCO fraud disaster, the Mark Hoffman forgeries, the number of bribes and kickbacks from state management of Navajo tribal oil deals, the cold fusion fiasco, Ponzi schemes, penny stock scams, and a high increase of bankruptcies all make for a poor fiscal reputation.

The Economies of the Third World

If the economies of the developed industrial nations such as the United States are in mixed circumstances, in the less developed nations (where most of humankind lives), economies are in almost unremittingly terrible circumstances. The economic situation of the Third World today is a tragic picture of pain, poverty, and pathos. In spite of billions of dollars in aid spent by industrialized nations in recent decades, the direction of most of the world's poor nations is downward.[40] Massive infusions of capital from the World Bank have built dams, bridges, and highways in Latin America, but overall economic well-being of the masses is in decline. Expensive United Nations programs in Africa to support political stability and create a new middle class have failed miserably.[41] Efforts of the U.S. Agency for International Development channeled billions of American taxpayer dollars to poor regions such as India and Egypt, but much of that wealth has ended up lining the pockets of the Haves rather than the Have-nots. Programs such as the Organization of American States and initiatives in the Caribbean have mostly benefitted U.S. firms in their effort to extract raw materials for use back home, rather than upgrading the conditions of the millions who try to survive in shantytowns.

The list below highlights some of the contrasts between rich and poor in the world:[42]

- Some forty nations of the Third World were better off in the early 1980s than the beginning of the 1990s. Per capita income in Latin America is some 9 percent under what it was a decade ago, slipping from $3,400 at the beginning of the 1980s to roughly $2,900 in 1992. Gross national product ("GNP") per capita in Sub-Saharan Africa is lower now than it was 30 years ago.

- Over a quarter of the world's total population is in absolute poverty; that is, their annual incomes are less than $500, as Table A indicates.

- Americans bemoan the wealth gap between U.S. poor and the Rockefellers, Kennedys, or Donald Trumps reflected in the fact that the richest fifth of U.S. households have 12 times the income of the poorest fifth. But in Turkey the ratio is 16:1, in Mexico the ratio is 18:1, and in Brazil the gap is even greater, at 28:1.[43]

- In most Latin American nations, one percent of landlords own some 40 percent of all arable land, transforming millions of families into tenant farmers or peasants, tilling the plantations of well-to-do elites.

- While 15 percent of all Americans are overweight and 20 percent are on diets, malnutrition has been rising in Burma, Jamaica, Nigeria, El Salvador, Paraguay, and other nations.[44] Continual hunger stalks 20 percent of all Ethiopians and Sudanese, and runs as high as 40 percent in Mozambique. Twenty percent of the world's children are malnourished.[45]

- Fourteen million of the world's children starve to death each year while Americans spend $5 billion on diet food to reduce their caloric intake. Global malnutrition

Table A

People Estimated to Be Living in Absolute Poverty

Region	Millions of People	Share of Total Population
Middle East/North Africa	75	28%
Latin America/Caribbean	150	35%
Former USSR/Eastern Europe	165	28%
Sub-Saharan Africa	325	62%
Asia	675	25%
World Total	**1.4 billion**	**23%**

kills 60,000 humans each day, two-thirds of whom are children; and females are four times more likely to be malnourished than males. Of every 1,000 children under one year of age, 172 die every year in Angola, 168 in Mali, 153 in Sierra Leone, 131 in Somalia, and 109 in Bolivia. In the developed nations only 7 to 10 out of 1,000 die in their first year.[46]

- Several hundred million adults around the globe survive childhood but live with long-term consequences of malnourishment—mental retardation, stunted bodies, and the inability to work at a job and support their families. For example, iodine deficiency in diets has caused 26 million cases of mental retardation globally.

- According to the United Nations, roughly 1.5 billion people are deprived of decent health care, resulting in millions of deaths from malaria, yellow fever, typhoid, and other diseases.

- Two billion people lack access to pure water, suffering the effects of toxic poisons and parasites for years, leading to lower life expectancies.

- In many Third World countries, 20 to 30 percent of the

population is homeless, struggling to survive by begging on the streets of Calcutta, Nairobi, La Paz, or Cairo. In many Third World cities, from 30 to 60 percent of the population has housing only by being squatters in wretched hovels and shacks. In São Paulo, officials estimate over a million children are loose on the streets, hustling passers-by, running in gangs, lean, hungry, doing hit-and-run robberies, and dealing in drugs and prostitution from age eight on up.[47]

• To cope with the crush of heavy poverty, many of the world's children are required by parents to labor in the fields or urban sweatshops 14 to 16 hours a day. According to United Nations studies, between 150 and 200 million children in 50 countries do so, in violation of international laws. They suffer abuse, exposure to dangerous pesticides, and inhumane working hours, exploited by relatives or entrepreneurs who rob them of a childhood of happiness, play or innocence.

• If the young live long enough to grow into adulthood, coping with unemployment becomes a lifelong struggle. Each year, some 40 million young people enter the labor force but are unable to secure jobs. Joblessness in Nicaragua is some 50 percent, while in Bangladesh it is 25 percent, Jamaica around 26 percent, Puerto Rico 21 percent, Romania 30 percent, etc. Underemployment, meaning one does have work but does not make enough money to live adequately, is even worse. For instance, unemployment and underemployment reach a total of some 80 percent in the Philippines. Many Third World nations suffer from a combined 50 percent in joblessness and underemployment.

• A major reason why many poor are unemployed is that they lack education, blocking their ability to qualify for hiring, even if more jobs were available. This also limits their capacity to cope with many other challenges in their lives—to competently raise their children, to manage financial problems, to write intelligently, to serve in their churches, schools, and communities, or otherwise contribute.

- Illiteracy rages in the Third World, decimating the basic quality of life for many individuals and families. In Sub-Saharan Africa, under 50 percent of the nation's children even attend school. The illiteracy rate in Jordan is 19 percent, Niger 83 percent, Nepal 70 percent, Pakistan 67 percent, India 54 percent, Burkina Faso 84 percent, Haiti 65 percent, Bangladesh 64 percent. Globally, some 900 million adults are illiterate.[48]

For many, the answer has been to try to duplicate the industrialization of the developed nations, which originally fueled the creation of mass employment. But the opposite is often true today. Automation eliminates work. Factories shut down as products are "outsourced" or factories go "offshore," building plants in locations with ever cheaper labor. The result is a phenomenon never before witnessed in modern history. Jobs do not merely shift from the farm to the factories, or from New York to Georgia, or on to Mexico. They do not simply move, they disappear. Workers have no place else to go.[49]

Megacities of the World. Whether Bombay, Mexico City, Manila, Nairobi, or Sâo Paulo, today's Third World suffering is tied to the huge influx of peasants who flood into the big cities, seeking better lives. Ten million plus people live like the Illagan and Flores families in unemployment, scavenging, and terrible pollution. They exist in squalid living arrangements, mostly in shanties, lacking basic access to toilets, sewage, and potable water. Such basics as electricity and schools are largely out of the question. The daily struggle for survival instead focuses on how to minimize violence, prostitution, AIDS, drugs and alcohol abuse. With millions homeless, having no basic medical care, longevity is measured in four to five decades at best. Desperation and fear are people's daily motivations. Scientists predict that the exodus from the rural to the urban Third World will accelerate by the year 2000 as the population increases. They estimate that within two decades, over 50 cities around the globe will each have in excess of 10 million inhabitants. A huge proportion will be unemployed, and violence will be the primary tool for survival.

The Informal Sector. With few government strategies to create jobs and with industrial downsizing occurring on a global scale, easily obtaining a job with good pay, benefits, and long-term prospects is increasingly not in the picture for most of humanity.

The response in the Third World has been the creation of the urban informal economy.

The informal economy essentially consists of people engaged in "underground" business activities—street vendors, family businesses, and other marginal jobs. They are usually not registered as formal firms. They have no payroll, no benefits or taxes. Rather they float, often moving from place to place as opportunities arise. They are small, generally composed of from one to three people, many of them women and children, who hustle, often on the streets, dealing only in cash or kind. They often supply low-cost goods and services for the majority of the populace who cannot afford the expensive imported products which are the only alternative in underdeveloped economies which do not produce enough basic goods for their people.[50] Traditional economists have tended to overlook the informal sector, assuming it to be only a short-term substitute for people during a crisis, such as a factory layoff. But the reality is that in the urban Third World, the informal sector is neither small nor temporary. Rather it is a central aspect of national survival for many nations, ranging from 20 to 60 percent of total national GNPs.[51]

While the hard work and entrepreneurial instincts of micro-enterprise participants in the Third World help put rice or beans on the family table, numerous factors interfere with achieving greater success. Inefficient government policies, legal barriers, complex and contradictory rules for registering land or other private property, lack of credit facilities, disenfranchisement of the poor—all these serve to impede the ability of the informal sector to grow or stabilize. In one study conducted by Peruvian economist Hernando de Soto, it took four law students over nine months to complete the paperwork to set up a small unincorporated clothing factory, during which process they received 10 bribe requests, had to get 11 different permits and spent 32 times the average worker's monthly salary in costs (excluding their services). To combat bureaucratic excesses, he advocates institutional reforms to create genuine, market-oriented structures. His Latin American best-seller, *The Other Path,* analyzes the plight of micro-entrepreneurs and proposes tangible solutions for strengthening informal economies. These include simplification of the process for registering one's small business, reduction in other state regulation of small businesses, establishing offices to aid the poor in becoming self-employed, providing training programs and support groups, combined with policies to encourage more bank loans to poor business people.[52] Whether his ideas receive more than lip service remains largely to be seen.

Why Underdevelopment?

While ineffective policies of Third World governments bear considerable blame for their economic plight, from the view of the Have-nots, it is still principally the Haves that are causing the growing gap between rich and poor. To illustrate, India's nearly one billion people make up 16 percent of the earth's population, yet they use only 3 percent of all energy and account for only 1 percent of the world's GNP. At the other extreme, the United States has only 5 percent of the earth's population, but uses 25 percent of all energy and accounts for 25 percent of global GNP.[53] These two extremes are not unique cases; rather, they are typical. The top one-fifth of the earth's nations consist of a group of 38 high income countries—mostly Western Europe, with some Arab, Asian, and North American additions. Annual incomes of that group are on average 65 times that of the poorest fifth—30 nations, such as Mozambique, Somalia, and so on. To illustrate, per capita GNP in Ethiopia is only $121 annually and $400 in Bangladesh, versus $17,830 in France, $19,780 in the United States, and $30,270 in Switzerland. The wealthiest 20 percent of the world's population have an average income 140 times greater than the average income of the poorest 20 percent.[54]

To exacerbate the problem, non-oil-exporting Third World nations owe $1.3 trillion in loans to the rich countries. From 1983 through 1990, these nations suffered a net capital loss of—that is, they exported to the already wealthy nations—over 220 billion dollars in wealth.[55] Extracting payments only makes attempts by Third World nations to reduce illiteracy or feed the poor less successful. Impoverished nations now spend only 12 percent of their budgets on health and education, as the World Bank and other institutions put on more pressure to pay back loans.

The reason for this massive and increasing debt is that the world economy has become structured in such a way that the Third World serves mostly as a conduit for raw materials to flow toward the developed nations. Prices of raw materials exported by these countries remain low because of overproduction. These terms of trade discourage or prevent the building of internal structures of local free enterprise, and consequently many developing nations have become dependent on foreign imports and foreign capital. They end up with huge debts and an almost addiction to the products of industrialized countries. Perhaps the obsession in Latin America with wearing U.S.-made Levi's illustrates the problem best. This process keeps the Third World in a vicious cycle of underdevelopment. This is not necessarily due to a conspiracy of the developed nations, but it is nonetheless deeply embedded in the current world economy and is abetted by the international economic policies of the developed nations and their aid organizations.[56]

Population increase is another major challenge. In 1950, 1.76 billion people, representing 70 percent of the earth's population, lived in the Third World. The less-developed nations' populations have increased to the point that by 1990, those numbers were 4.2 billion and 79 percent respectively. Human beings currently have a net increase of three new persons every second of the day—10,600 per hour, 254,000 per day, 1.8 million per week, 7.7 million each month, and 93 million per year. At present trends, by the year 2025 there will be 8.5 billion people, of whom only 1.2 billion (14 percent) will live in developed nations, and an astonishing 7.3 billion (86 percent) will make up the Third World. Over the next three decades, if present trends continue, 98 percent of the world's population growth will occur in developing nations.[57]

Foreign Aid. Many people assume that American foreign aid is reducing these inequalities, but in actuality, humanitarian aid for health projects, schools, and food has been dropping for four decades. Today the per capita aid spent per American averages only $43, about half that of the still low Japanese $73. In comparison, Scandinavian countries provide approximately $200 per person in aiding poor countries. *U.S. News and World Report* reported that in 1980, Americans spent $52 billion eating out. By 1990, the figure jumped to $236 billion. In contrast, in 1980 Americans spent a paltry $1.4 billion in food aid overseas. By 1990 that number was still a mere $1.6 billion, and millions of Third World people starved to death.[58] The World Health Organization could completely eradicate malaria if it had the amount of money spent by the world's militaries in just half a day. But the tragic reality is that over the past decade, 40 Third World countries declined in terms of education, health care, mortality, and per capita incomes.

Beyond the shortage of aid resources, many international aid agencies historically focused on assisting national governments in developing large, prestigious industrial, mining, and agribusiness projects intended to generate foreign currency income through exports. Such projects frequently proved corrupt and inefficient, and to the extent they succeeded, the foreign currency earnings went to service the debt owed to developed nations and their banks, rather than to improving goods and services for Third World consumers. Many international aid agencies developed large bureaucracies who seemed to prefer dining with the minister of finance, discussing repayment of foreign debt, to working in the *barrio*, developing a healthy self-reliant local market economy.[59]

The "Four Tigers." Even the supposed success of the so-called "Four Tigers" (Singapore, Hong Kong, Taiwan, and South Korea) has not broken the underdevelopment trap. They are merely dependent on a somewhat more successful export than most underdeveloped countries—manufactures produced by low-cost skilled labor instead of low-cost raw materials. However, the low cost remains a critical part of the equation and makes such economies dependent on suppressing personal income. The economies of the Four Tigers also remain completely export dependent. While this strategy of exporting cheap labor goods may have worked to some extent to help the relatively small populations of these four little countries, the capacity of the developed countries to absorb cheap labor imports is surfeited. This strategy cannot begin to help the vast populations of such countries as China, India, Nigeria, Brazil, or Mexico, unless the developed countries are willing to destroy their own modest wage manufacturing industries and force their own populations down to Third World living standards.[60] This, of course, would only make more people poor, the opposite of the gospel ideal of the city of Enoch, where there were "no poor among them" (Moses 7:18).

3

"He Has Not the Least Objection": The Restoration of the United Order in the Modern World

I will say, first, that the Lord Almighty has not the least objection in the world to our entering into the Order of Enoch. . . . He has not the least objection to any man, every man, all mankind on the face of the earth turning from evil and loving and serving him with all their hearts.

Brigham Young[1]

That exports alone cannot solve the Third World's economic crisis does not mean that world trade could or should be eliminated from the modern economy. Indeed, international trade was centrally important to the American economy from the earliest times. The world economy affected even the most modest Americans. In the early 1800s, Joseph Smith, Sr., invested in the export of a shipload of ginseng root to China. The voyage was very successful, but Joseph, Sr.'s partner embezzled the profits. It was financial pressures from this misadventure in international trade, and the difficult cash-poor life of a New England farmer in an economy that was becoming increasingly money based, that drove the Smiths westward toward the Hill Cumorah.[2]

Thus, it was in the midst of the foreshocks of the modern world economy that the light of the gospel dawned anew.[3] As seen in chapter 1, the restored gospel recognized the unity of the temporal and spiritual. Therefore, God gave commandments relating to humankind's temporal struggle for physical existence.[4] Shortly after the reestablishment of the Church in 1830, Joseph Smith, Jr., was told by revelation to go to Ohio, where God would "give unto you my law; and there you shall be endowed with power from on high" (D&C 38:32). In Kirtland, Ohio, a minister named Sidney Rigdon and his congregation became members of the Church. Some of Rigdon's followers, like many other Americans of the time, were attempting to live a communal life in emulation of the early Saints at Jerusalem.[5] They were joined at Kirtland by Joseph in the beginning of February 1831. Soon after arriving, Joseph received through revelation the law of consecration and stewardship.[6]

The United Orders of the 1830s

The original operation of the law of consecration and stewardship, as outlined in Section 42 of the Doctrine and Covenants and subsequent revelations, contemplates an initial consecration of properties to the bishop by "a covenant and deed which cannot be broken" (D&C 42:30). From these properties, distributions would be made "to those who have not, . . . that every man who has need may be amply supplied and receive according to his wants" (D&C 42:33, 51:3). Each participant was a steward accountable to God, whether he previously possessed property or received it from the bishop (D&C 42:32, 104:11–13). Surplus property was to be contributed to a storehouse (D&C 42:34, 51:13, 70:7) for use in assisting the poor and needy and building up the Church (D&C 42:34–35, 78:3). The implementation of this system is generally referred to as the *united order* (D&C 104:1). This operation was to be administered by the bishop. Unlike the practice in the Church today, the bishop was originally a paid manager unattached to a particular congregation (D&C 42:71–73, 51:14). The first bishop called was Edward Partridge in February 1831 (D&C 41:9–11). He was to preside over the settlement of Missouri. Later, in December 1831, Newel Whitney was called to serve as bishop at Kirtland and in the eastern United States (D&C 72:8). The original operation as set forth in the 1830s in the Doctrine and Covenants has been summarized by Ezra Taft Benson this way:

> The vehicle for implementing the law of consecration is the united order. The basic principle underlying the united order is that everything we have belongs to the Lord; and therefore, the Lord may call upon us for any and all our property, because it belongs to him. The united order was entered by a 'covenant and a deed which cannot be broken' (D&C 42:30), according to the scriptures. In other words an individual conveys his titles to all his property to the Church through the bishop. The property becomes the property of the Church. . . . The bishop then deeds back to the consecrator by legal instrument the amount of personal property required by the individual for the support of himself and his family, as the Lord declares, 'according to his circumstances and his

> wants and needs' (D&C 51:3). This becomes the private, personal property of the individual to develop as he sees fit. It is his stewardship. When the individual produces a profit or surplus more than is needful for the support of himself and his family, the surplus is then placed in the bishop's storehouse to administer to the poor and the needy.[7]

The activities of the united order were not limited to pioneer farming. A mercantile firm and publishing house were established as united order enterprises. Many of the Church leaders participated in these businesses as stewards, including Joseph Smith, who supported himself as a shopkeeper while devoting his time to the leadership of the Church.

The united order system was to be realized in Zion, a place to which "the righteous shall be gathered out from among all nations," to be "called the New Jerusalem, a land of peace, a city of refuge, a place of safety for the saints of the Most High God" (D&C 45:71, 66). At this time, Zion was conceived of as a distinct geographical locale where an all-LDS society would live in righteousness and harmony. This exclusive vision was not always well received by the Saints' nonmember neighbors.

The united order was supposed to be a means to carry out an orderly settlement of Zion. Yet, at both Kirtland and in Missouri, more poor people were interested in entering the order than could be provided for from those entering the order with property. Church leaders advised that "for the disciples to suppose that they can come to this land without ought to eat, or to drink, or to wear, or anything to purchase these necessaries with, is a vain thought. . . . The experience of almost two years' gathering, has taught us to revere that sacred word from heaven 'Let not your flight be in haste, but let all things be prepared before you.'" Where there were many poor members, local leaders were to "make preparations to send a part at one time, and a part at another."[8]

However, enthusiastic poor members ignored this advice. Providing stewardships for the poor and needy was made even more difficult by the unwillingness of better-off members to consecrate for the sake of their poorer brethren. Brigham Young recalled that when he went out to solicit surplus property for consecration, "I never knew a man yet who had a dollar of surplus property. No matter how much one might have he wanted all he had for himself, for his children, his grandchildren, and so forth."[9]

> Occasionally, some were disposed to do right with their surplus property, and once in a while you would find a man who had a cow which he considered surplus, but generally she was of a class that would kick a person's hat off, or eyes out, or the wolves had eaten off her teats. You would once in a while find a man who had a horse that he considered surplus, but at the same time he had the ringbone, was broken-winded, spavined in both legs, and had the pole evil at one end of the neck and a fistula at the other, and both knees sprung.[10]

Finally, some poorer members, anticipating an imminent Second Coming, did not always work diligently at their temporal duties. In a revelation given in June 1831, God chastised both the well-to-do who would not contribute to the poor, and the poor who coveted the wealth of others without being willing to work (D&C 56:16–19).

The united orders were beset by other problems. In Missouri the Saints were driven from their settlements several times during the 1830s. The Kirtland united order had serious financial difficulties. The long distance between Ohio and Missouri made coordination difficult. In 1834, the Kirtland and Missouri united orders were separated, and the Kirtland united order was terminated and its assets distributed among its members (D&C 104:20–53). The Missouri united order did not continue as a formal effort after the 1834 persecutions.

This persecution explains much of the failure of the first united orders. It is very hard to build an ideal society and economy when one is driven from one's home every other year. However, in revelation God pointed to faults of the Saints themselves. Zion would have been redeemed, states an 1834 revelation, but the Saints "have not learned to be obedient to the things I required at their hands, but are full of all manner of evil, and do not impart of their substance, as becometh saints, to the poor and afflicted among them; and are not united according to the union required by the law of the celestial kingdom" (D&C 105:3–4).

Tithing

Following the end of the united orders, God revealed the law of tithing, a limited and preparatory form of consecration. It is a simple "law of Moses"–like commandment designed to teach the Saints to live the higher gospel law of consecration and stewardship.[11] Initially, Church members were called on to donate all of their surplus property to the Church and then to donate "one-tenth of their interest annually" (D&C 119:2–4). Later the requirement of the initial consecration was dropped. These tithing funds were to be administered by the First Presidency and other priesthood officers of the Church (D&C 120).

Zion at Nauvoo

After being driven from Missouri, the Saints went to a new Zion at Nauvoo, Illinois. Here the Saints remained under the law of tithing and did not make a formal attempt to establish the united order. It has been suggested that at Nauvoo Joseph abandoned his efforts to realize an ideal economic system and turned the law of consecration into a strictly "spiritual" matter.[12] Such a notion contradicts a gospel that does not separate the spiritual and temporal. In fact, Joseph's interest in creating an economy that would justly and effectively provide for the temporal well-being of his people continued at Nauvoo. Although the united order was not formally reinstituted at Nauvoo, the Church continued to try to implement many of its principles. The Nauvoo Agricultural and Manufacturing Society was incorporated to raise money to start businesses "with a view of helping the poor."[13] Among other projects, efforts were made to build a pottery factory using skilled English convert immigrants. However, it was difficult to attract capital away from land speculation, especially after anti-Mormons threatened to have the Society's charter repealed by the state legislature.[14]

The Church freely gave plots of land to many of the poor. Those who had a degree of wealth were asked to purchase plots from the Church so it could pay off its debts. Many public works projects were launched to create jobs for the masses arriving in Illinois. Houses, hotels, business enterprises and the Nauvoo Temple were built primarily by projects directed by Joseph himself as chairman of the city's public works. The goal was to provide labor for every able-bodied man. Apostle Heber C. Kimball sensed the potential of Nauvoo youth. Apostle Kimball and the youth met regularly to develop service projects. One of their first efforts was to assist in constructing a cottage for a British convert who was physically handicapped. The group eventually formed an organizational structure and constitution, dedicating itself "to search out the poor of our city," so as to provide assistance.[15]

Other important developments occurred in Nauvoo. Like other Illinois cities to this day, the city of Nauvoo was divided into

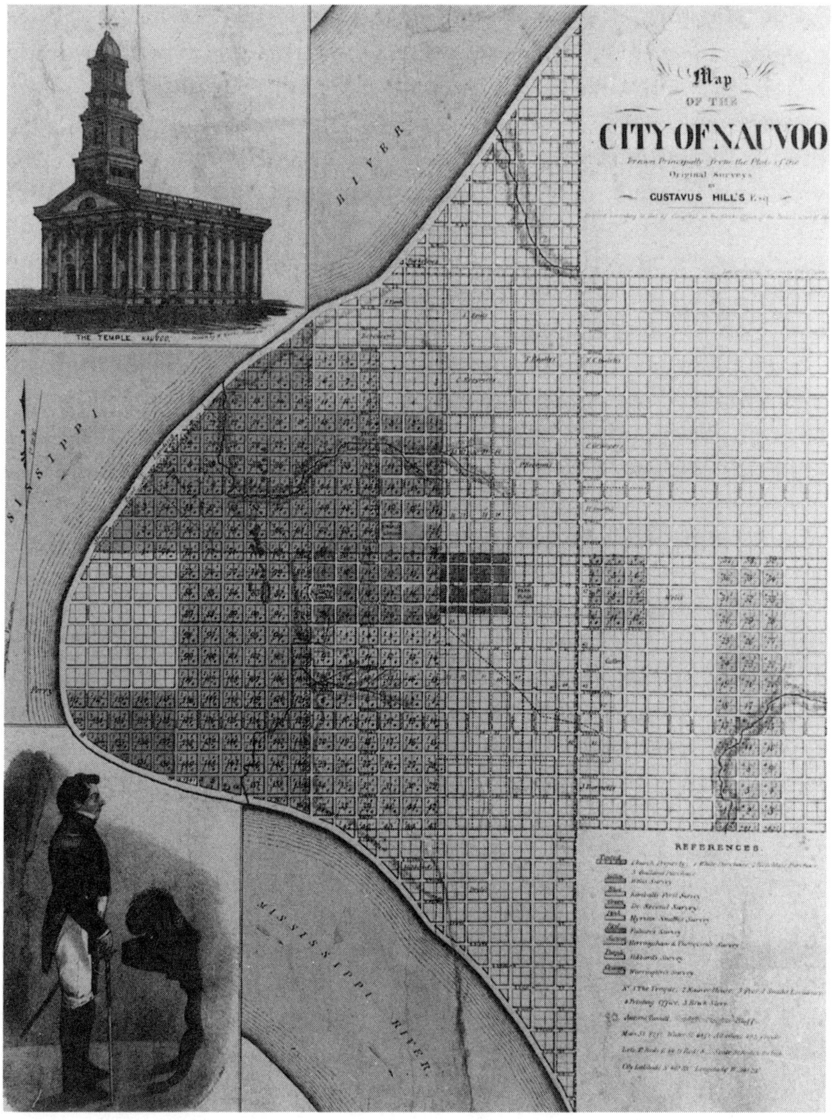

Nauvoo City Plat. The name of the city was based on a Hebrew word suggesting beauty and repose. Nauvoo consisted of a peninsula on the Illinois side of the Mississippi River purchased by the LDS Church for the building of Zion. The Prophet Joseph's design was that of a simple gridiron made up of 150 squares of four acres, each of which was divided into four equal lots. The streets were designed to run north-south or east-west and were three rods (forty-nine and one-half feet) wide.

political subdivisions called *wards*. Although not yet set up as congregations of the Church, they served as the basis for organizing relief efforts for the many impoverished immigrants who were constantly arriving. Bishops were assigned to these wards to coordinate these relief efforts, but there were no ward worship services, auxiliaries, or priesthood groups.[16] Contributions in kind were collected by early bishops, including not only agricultural produce but also participation in timber-cutting projects to keep the poor warm, fishing expeditions, and housework projects to earn compensation.

The work of looking after the needs of the new arrivals to Nauvoo gave rise to another development of vast importance to the Church, the founding of the first Relief Society. It operated on a citywide rather than a ward basis, as a means to become more aware of and offer aid to the poor. The Relief Society has been a major conduit for charitable LDS practices for over 150 years and is currently the largest women's organization in the world.[17]

Despite the Saints' willingness to participate in the local economy on a non-united order basis, hostility toward the growing Zion increased. Joseph was martyred at Carthage, Illinois, on June 27, 1844, along with his brother Hyrum. John Taylor was with them and was seriously wounded. The Zion at Nauvoo was forced to flee from the United States into the deserts of what was then northern Mexico. There Joseph's successors would continue to seek to build a righteous community where there would be "no poor among them."

The United Orders of the 1870s

For 25 years after their arrival in Utah in 1847, the Saints sought to build their western Zion. In 1869 the transcontinental railroad was completed in Utah. At first, the railroad brought prosperity to Utah, particularly through the development of the mining industry. However, in 1873 there was a national financial panic, resulting in the failure of over a third of the nation's banks. For Brigham Young, the Panic of 1873 showed the need to practice the old united order virtues of self-reliance, industry, and cooperation. As quoted at the beginning of the chapter, Brigham told the 1873 general conference that the "Lord Almighty has not the least objection in the world to our entering into the Order of Enoch."[18] With the support of the apostles, Brigham launched a new united order movement in 1874 at St. George in southern Utah.

One characteristic of the modern economy is the need for flexibility and innovation. These Brigham employed without reservation in organizing the Saints to pursue the ideals of the united order. While Brigham personally preferred a vision of the united order that came as close as possible to an extended family, he advocated any method that would promote greater equality, unity, and cooperation among the Saints. A wide variety of approaches was used, generally falling into one of four types.[19]

Community-based Cooperatives. The first method of organizing the united order preceded the formal institution of the order in 1874. In Brigham City, Lorenzo Snow had organized all of the community's businesses into cooperatives. The various businesses operated with a fair degree of autonomy, although a community board, presided over by apostle Snow, coördinated their activities. Great efforts were made to assure that everyone in the community held stock in as many of the cooperative businesses as possible. Stock ownership was not limited to participants in the particular business, but held throughout the community. Brigham City became well known for the extent to which it developed a largely self-sufficient economy, capable of supplying all of the community's basic needs, as well as producing surpluses of various goods for external sale to provide for needs that the community enterprises could not meet.

Another example along these lines was the Zion's Cooperative Mercantile Institution, or ZCMI. The largest blocks of stock were held by LDS merchants who had merged their private businesses into the ZCMI. However, the apostles attempted to promote equality by encouraging the broadest possible community-wide ownership of the stock of the united order corporations. In 1875, the First Presidency and Quorum of the Twelve issued an Apostolic Circular on ZCMI. In it they expressed the hope "that the community at large would become its stockholders" in order to combat the concentration of profits in a few hands which would lead the community to "being rapidly divided into classes, and the hateful and unhappy distinctions which the possession and lack of wealth give rise to."[20]

Unified Cooperatives. The second was the form instituted initially in St. George. A single corporation was established and stock was distributed in accordance with the amount of property consecrated to the order. Stock was also given for labor contributions, what we would today call "sweat equity."[21] Families could consecrate all or a part of their property to the order. The community's affairs were then managed by directors selected by the shareholders. The officers were usually, but not always, the local church leaders. Farming and local industries were operated as divisions of the united order corporation, with the community's resources allocated by the directors in the manner that seemed most efficient. The articles provided that withdrawals could be made only once every five years, and then for only half of contributed capital and accumulated dividends.[22]

Urban Cooperative Enterprises. In larger urban areas it was recognized that the economy was too complex to organize the entire community's efforts in a single corporation. Therefore, individual wards were encouraged to set up single enterprises capitalized by ward members. These enterprises would then provide an employment base for ward members who needed it or desired to work in a united order. This method was used particularly in Salt Lake City. One successful endeavor was a soap factory run by the Salt Lake 19th Ward.

Rural Communes. Finally, in remote newly settled areas, a more communal organization was developed in which each family held equal shares of the community corporation, which held title to all of the community's assets. Here all community economic activities were closely coordinated, and often the entire community ate together in a communal dining hall and wore similar homemade clothes. This type of united order was used in newly pioneered areas of southern Utah and Arizona. Its prototype was what is probably the best remembered of the united orders, Orderville.

Because of its place in the Mormon cultural memory as the representative united order, Orderville bears a brief, closer look.[23] Orderville was founded by pioneers who had unsuccessfully struggled to settle on the Big Muddy River in Nevada. Experienced in working together in difficult circumstances, in 1875 the pioneers moved as a group to a site on the Virgin River in southern Utah.

Initially, each family lived in its own shanty, but everyone ate together in a communal dining hall. Work was organized into departments, such as farming, cooking, working in a sawmill, and so on. Goods were distributed in accordance with a family's size. After a flood destroyed the dining hall, each family moved into a small house and ate separately. The community gradually made other adjustments. When silver mines were opened in the area in 1880, and non-order members were able to buy fancy clothes and goods from the outside, a small cash allotment was made to each family for discretionary spending. In 1883 it was decided that differential wages should be given to workers with particular skills.

Whether because of or despite these adjustments (viewpoints among the order members differed), the Orderville united order was a going concern into the 1880s, after most of the other united orders had been dissolved or converted to non-cooperative ownership. It ended only when antipolygamy persecution forced most of the men of Orderville into hiding. It is important to note that Orderville was not at all representative of the united orders. Orderville-style communes were a minority of the united orders of the 1870s. Further, even in Orderville itself, there was never one single program of operation. The Orderville community was always flexible, constantly adjusting in order to adapt to new conditions.

The Boards of Trade. For a variety of reasons discussed in chapter 10, most of the united order operations did not outlast the 1870s. However, the end of the specific united order efforts did not mean the end of the Church's concern in promoting a more cooperative economy. After Brigham Young's death in 1877, John Taylor became president of the Church. Having spent years serving the Church in such economic centers as London, Paris, and New York City, he was also very familiar with the modern industrial market economy. He endeavored to implement united order principles by establishing Boards of Trade to coordinate LDS economic activities. The rest of the national economy was evolving toward monopolistic big business, and President Taylor recognized that the Saints would also have to combine their economic clout in order to compete effectively. However, by the middle 1880s, the Boards of Trade were forced into inactivity by the same antipolygamy persecutions that ended the Orderville order.[24]

The Enterprise of Zion

It is commonplace in the Church today to regard the united order efforts as quaint stories of the last century, of only historical interest today, with no relevance perhaps until the coming of the Millennium. However, as noted at the beginning of chapter 2, Ezra Taft Benson taught that Christ's gospel "is the perfect prescription for all human problems and social ills."[25] Establishing Zion is what the Church is about *now.* Spencer W. Kimball offered this perspective to the 1978 general conference:

> For many years we have been taught that one important end result of our labors, hopes, and aspirations in this work is the building of a Latter-day Zion, a Zion characterized by love, harmony and peace—a Zion in which the Lord's children are one. . . . This day will come; it is our destiny to help bring it about! Doesn't it motivate you to lengthen your stride and quicken your pace as you do your part in the great sanctifying work of the kingdom? It does me. It causes me to rejoice over the many opportunities for service and sacrifice afforded me and my family as we seek to do our part in establishing Zion.[26]

President Kimball then notes that in "the earliest years of this dispensation the people faltered in attempting to live the full economic plan of Zion, the united order." However, the quest to live united order principles continues in the Church today. Marion G. Romney, then a counselor in the First Presidency, explained that, although Welfare Program procedures may change, "the objectives of the program remain the same. Its principles are eternal. It is the gospel in its perfection—the united order, toward which we move."[27]

In order to understand where we are moving *to,* it is necessary to understand where we are moving *from.* The next six chapters trace the rise of the modern world, its economy and society. This review includes the sharp socioeconomic insights, little known among the Saints today, of the prophets and apostles who have witnessed the course of humankind from its beginning. It also explores how "the gospel in its perfection—the united order" treats the great issues of the modern world and its economy. In view of the scope of our subject, this review is broad and sweeping, covering in sentences subjects to which others have devoted volumes. We hope that others too will find the subject of this book worthy of volumes. But now to the beginning.

PART TWO

THE UNITED ORDER AND THE RISE OF THE MODERN WORLD

Suppose that the Son of Man said to mankind in the present ages, "What seek ye?" What would be the answer? Many would say pleasure; some, wealth; others, fame and power; but the most thoughtful would answer, We are seeking the light of the ages, as mankind has ever sought. We are seeking a social Utopia. We want a society in which we may be relieved of some of the ills of mankind, free from the troubles and toils of life. With every progressive age of the world, intellectual, noble-minded leaders have sought a better way of living than that which was current. The good life, a social Utopia, has been the quest of the ages. . . . To sense the need of reform has been easy; to achieve it has been difficult and well-nigh impossible. . . . The Church, established by divine inspiration to an unlearned youth, offers to the world the solution of all its social problems.

David O. McKay[1]

Both in ancient and modern times, people have struggled with poverty and economic distress. At left: Millions of today's Third World poor suffer in squalor as squatters in temporary shantytowns until driven off by local officials. Below: Many workers in industrialized nations become victims of downsizing or closed factories like this U.S. steel mill.

4

The Sweat of Thy Face:
From Adam's Fall to Adam Smith

And unto Adam he said, . . . cursed is the ground for thy sake; in sorrow shalt thou eat of it all the days of thy life; thorns also and thistles shall it bring forth to thee; and thou shalt eat the herb of the field; in the sweat of thy face shalt thou eat bread, till thou return unto the ground; for out of it wast thou taken: for dust thou art, and unto dust shalt thou return.

Genesis 3:17–19

Since Adam and Eve were driven from the Garden, men and women have had to work to secure physical survival in this mortal existence. Then and now, this struggle for survival has been the focus of most peoples' concern and time. In the words of Lorenzo Snow, a father has had to "remain awake at night thinking what he should do for his family to keep them from begging their bread."[1] God has not ignored such a vital part of his children's lives and has always given commandments and teachings relating to this central aspect of our lives.

The Ancient Economy

Throughout human history, the struggle for physical survival has borne certain common features in every time and clime. For most of humanity, through most of its history, this has meant a hard, uncertain life of subsistence farming or herding. Usually, whatever small surplus a group of people might produce came under the control of a small minority of tribal chiefs, feudal aristocrats, priests, or traders. The ancient economy was generally quite static. One's economic position in society was based on family background. The son of a lord became a lord, the son of a farmer became a farmer, the son of a slave was a slave. Those that rose in the society sought to marry into and imitate the life of the small wealthy minority.[2]

The economy was predominantly based on farming. The landed

nobility in every society looked down on trade, commerce, and manufacture. These activities were justified only if they provided goods for consumption by the landowning elite. New ways and inventions prospered only if they served the interests of the agrarian aristocracy. China invented paper, printing, gunpowder, porcelain, the use of coins for money, the compass, stirrup and wheelbarrow, canal lock gates, cast iron, and the competitive civil service examination. In the early 1400s, half a century before Columbus's first trip to America, the government of the Ming emperors sent out naval expeditions a hundred times the size of Columbus's small fleet. However, the tradition that placed the concerns of agriculture and landowners at the center of society prevented development of these technological and commercial innovations. This stagnation led to China's subsequent weakness in facing the encroachment of European imperialism in the 19th century.[3]

No concept in the ancient economy allowed that a Hewlett and Packard, a Sam Walton, Andrew Carnegie, or Thomas Edison might leave their names in history beside those of lords and conquerors. The leisured landowning elite defined the moral values of society and became equated with them. The Roman senator and scholar Cicero wrote:

> Now in regard to trades and employments, which are to be considered liberal and which mean, this is the more or less accepted view. First, those employments are condemned which incur ill will, as those of collectors of harbor taxes and moneylenders. Illiberal, too, and mean are the employments of all who work for wages, whom we pay for their labor and not for their art; for in their case their very wages are the warrant of their slavery. . . . And all craftsmen are engaged in mean trades, for no workshop can have any quality appropriate to a free man. . . . Commerce, if it is on a small scale, is to be considered mean; but if it is large scale and extensive . . . [it] is not to be greatly censured. Indeed, it even seems to deserve the highest respect if those engaged in it, content with their profits, make their way from the harbor to the landed estate. . . . But of all things from which one may acquire, none is better than agriculture, none more fruitful, none sweeter, none more fitting for a free man.[4]

Cicero's agriculturist, of course, was not the actual tiller of the soil, but the lord of the estate who oversaw the slaves, serfs, or tenants who did the work. The idea that the wealthy, leisured landed class defined a society's moral standards is even preserved in our modern English language. Originally, words like *noble* and *gentleman* simply described a particular high socioeconomic position in English feudal society. One could say that a man was a gentleman and a scoundrel, or noble and wicked, without any contradiction, and often with accuracy.

The terms *inventor, entrepreneur,* and *businessman* are new words in the English tongue. The idea of economic "progress," that by investing in improving the means of producing things a whole society could become wealthier, was unknown until the most recent times. The notion that a wealthy man would receive prestige for working and producing, rather than the dignity of his leisurely pursuits, is modern. Wealth traditionally came from conquest, luck of discovery or taxation, not invention or investment. The Scottish philosopher David Hume observed, "I do not remember a passage in any ancient author, where the growth of a city is ascribed to the establishment of a manufacture. The commerce, which is said to flourish, is chiefly the exchange of those commodities for which different soils and climates were suited."[5] Joseph Smith eloquently described the true origins of the great fortunes and empires of human history:

> The greatest acts of the mighty men have been to depopulate nations and to overthrow kingdoms, and whilst they have exalted themselves and become glorious, it has been at the expense of the lives of the innocent, the blood of the oppressed, the moans of the widow, and the tears of the orphan. Egypt, Babylon, Greece, Persia, Carthage, Rome—each was raised to dignity amidst the clash of arms and the din of war, and whilst their triumphant leaders led forth their victorious armies to glory and victory, their ears were saluted with the groans of the dying and the misery and distress of the human family; before the earth was a paradise and behind them a desolate wilderness; their kingdoms were founded in carnage and bloodshed, and sustained by oppression, tyranny and despotism.[6]

Humankind's working life has been dominated by tradition, stagnation, and the command of the wealthy minority. Religions, rulers, and regions could vary, but the economic structure of human life did not.

God and the Ancient Economy

God's commandments relating to economic matters in all ancient societies dealt with this structure. Since these economies were generally static and seemed inevitably to tend to great inequalities, his commandments concentrated on the need for the wealthy to give to the poor and condemned the possession of great wealth in the face of the massive poverty of most of the people. God told the ancient Israelites, "The poor shall never cease out of the land: therefore I command thee, saying, thou shalt open thine hand wide unto thy brother, to thy poor, and to thy needy, in thy land" (Deuteronomy 15:11). They were commanded by the law of Moses to release all slaves and forgive all debts every seventh year and could not refrain from lending to a poor brother just because the sabbatical year of release was approaching (Deuteronomy 15:1–18). In addition, debts were forgiven and slaves released every fifty years and land returned to the families to whom it was originally given when the Israelites arrived in Palestine (Leviticus 25:23–43). Charging interest on loans was forbidden (Exodus 22:25–26, Leviticus 25:35–37). The poor received a tithe of every third year's harvest and exclusive rights every year to glean what was missed in the first harvesting (Deuteronomy 14:28–29, 24:19–21).[7]

Similarly, among the ancient Americans of the Book of Mormon, charity toward the poor was commanded. Compromise and rationalizations on the subject were not allowed. King Benjamin in his great farewell address taught that

> ye will not suffer that the beggar putteth up his petition to you in vain, and turn him out to perish. Perhaps thou shalt say: the man has brought upon himself his misery; therefore I will stay my hand, and will not give unto him of my food, nor impart unto him of my substance that he may not suffer, for his punishments are just—but I say unto you, O man, whosoever doeth this the same hath great cause to repent; and except he repenteth of that which he hath done he perisheth forever, and hath no interest in the kingdom of God. For behold, are we not all beggars? Do we not all depend upon the same Being, even God, for all the substance which we have, for both food and raiment, and for gold, and for silver, and for all the riches which we have of every kind? . . . And now, if God, who has created you, on whom you are dependent for your lives and all that ye have and are, doth grant unto you whatsoever ye ask that is right, in faith, believing that ye shall receive, O then, how ye ought to impart of the substance that ye have one to another. And if ye judge the man who putteth up his petition to you for your substance that he perish not, and condemn him, how much more just will be your condemnation

> for withholding your substance, which doth not belong to you but to God, to whom also your life belongeth. . . . I say unto you, wo be unto that man, for his substance shall perish with him; and now, I say these things unto those who are rich as pertaining to the things of this world. (Mosiah 4:16–19, 21–23)

Even a casual reader cannot miss the emphasis that appears in the Book of Mormon on the dangers of pride and sin that accompany wealth and prosperity.[8] The Book of Mormon is, in fact, somewhat unusual among ancient writings in its focus on prosperity and its consequences. The pattern recurs numerous times in the Book of Mormon record. For example, in the Book of Alma we read how many were baptized into the church at the beginning of the reign of the judges (Alma 4:4–5). Soon, however, "the people of the church began to wax proud, because of their exceeding riches, and their fine silks, and their fine-twined linen, and their gold and their silver, and all manner of precious things, which they had obtained by their industry" (Alma 4:6). The members of the church became contentious, and their pride exceeded that of nonmembers, who were led into iniquities by the bad example of the church members (Alma 4:8–11). There was "great inequality among the people, some lifting themselves up with their pride, despising others, turning their backs upon the needy and the naked and those who were hungry, and those who were athirst, and those who were sick and afflicted" (Alma 4:12). This pride and inequality would repeatedly undermine and threaten the Nephite church and nation.

When the Savior came to earth to teach humankind personally, he did not ignore the temporal issues of work and wealth. Consistent with the commandments that he had previously given to prophets of the Old Testament and the Book of Mormon, Jesus taught that those who had, had an absolute duty toward those who had not. Love of one's possessions and the failure to fulfill this duty to the poor would bar one's way to the kingdom of heaven. One cannot have two masters, he taught, "Ye cannot serve God and mammon" (Matthew 6:24). When a religious young nobleman inquired what he needed to do to inherit eternal life, Jesus told him:

> Yet lackest thou one thing: sell all that thou hast, and distribute unto the poor, and thou shalt have treasure in heaven: and come, follow me. And when he heard this, he was very sorrowful: for he was very rich. And when Jesus saw that he was very sorrowful,

THE

THEORY

OF

MORAL SENTIMENTS.

By ADAM SMITH,
PROFESSOR of MORAL PHILOSOPHY in the
Univerſity of GLASGOW.

LONDON:
Printed for A. MILLAR, in the STRAND;
And A. KINCAID and J. BELL, in EDINBURGH.
M DCC LIX.

The title page from the first edition of Adam Smith's The Theory of Moral Sentiments, *originally published in 1759.*

> he said, How hardly shall they that have riches enter into the kingdom of God! For it is easier for a camel to go through a needle's eye, than for a rich man to enter into the kingdom of God. (Luke 18:22–25)

The obligation of God's children toward each other has never been put more concisely than this:

> I was an hungered, and ye gave me meat: I was thirsty, and ye gave me drink: I was a stranger, and ye took me in: Naked, and ye clothed me: I was sick, and ye visited me: I was in prison, and ye came unto me. Then shall the righteous answer him, saying, Lord, when saw we thee an hungered, and fed thee? or thirsty, and gave thee drink? When saw we thee a stranger, and took thee in? or naked, and clothed thee? Or when saw we thee sick, or in prison and came unto thee? And the King shall answer and say unto them, Verily I say unto you, Inasmuch as ye have done it unto one of the least of these my brethren, ye have done it unto me. (Matthew 25:35–40)

The Ancient United Order

On a few brief occasions in human history, the changeless pattern of the ancient economy was changed, and the wealth of the few and the poverty of the many were overcome. The earliest of these was the great, ancient city of Enoch, where "the Lord called his people ZION, because they were of one heart and one mind, and dwelt in righteousness; and there was no poor among them" (Moses 7:18). However, it seems that such a society could not remain in our world, and God took it away into heaven (Moses 7:21).

The scriptures tell us little of how the economy of Enoch's city operated. Some time ago, Elder Neal Maxwell attempted to capture the spirit of the City of Enoch by scripting an imaginary series of letters exchanged between a resident of Zion, Mahijah, and his friend in the outside world. Mahijah reports that "our commerce must be the commerce of Christ, for the morals of the marketplace matter and do find their way into families." Months later he writes "of Enoch's telling us that there was yet another commandment we must live that many of us might find hard to bear. . . . We must give over all our goods and possessions, sharing them fully with each other, so that all may be equal in goods and substance. We who have laboriously learned not to withhold affection and esteem from each other must now no longer hold back our goods.

Enoch promises us that if we will do this, there will be no poor among us."

Later, "Enoch tells us that it is not given that one man should possess that which is above another, wherefore the world lieth in sin. . . . Those who have had their minds diverted to the care and attention of their possessions are often inclined to pride themselves on being above their neighbor. . . . When some who had been so righteous in other ways were counseled to give all they had to the poor, they went away sorrowing because their possessions were so great. . . . We now see clearly, as pertaining to our goods and possessions, that unless we are equal in earthly things, we cannot be equal in heavenly things. We can have goods in common because we first have Christ in common." The writer extols the advantages of Enoch's united order: "There is greater efficiency when people band together in love and truth. They produce more in cooperation, and there is thus more to share. The believer in the gospel of work is also more productive. Finally, there are no indolent rulers to take away the fruits of men's labor. There are no poor among us because all have a greater desire to give than to take, a stronger desire to share than to receive."[9]

After Christ's ministry in Israel and America, such ideal societies were again established. The early Saints living at Jerusalem "were of one heart and one soul: neither said any of them that ought of the things which he possessed was his own; but they had all things in common" (Acts 4:32). We do not know what became of this community other than that it disappeared in the onslaught of persecution and apostasy that was to overwhelm the early Church in the Old World.

In America, the righteous survivors of the natural disasters at the time of the crucifixion created a society in which "they had all things common among them; therefore there were not rich and poor, bond and free, but they were all made free, and partakers of the heavenly gift" (4 Nephi 3). This society endured two hundred years. As with the city of Enoch and the early church of Jerusalem, we are not told much of how this righteous economy operated. The Book of Mormon does, however, describe the fate of this society in more detail: it returned to the normal historical human economy. Mormon tells us that "they had become exceedingly rich, because of their prosperity in Christ. . . . There began to be among them those who were lifted up in pride, such as the wearing of costly apparel, and all manner of fine pearls, and of the fine things of the world. And from that time forth they did have their goods and their substance no more common among them. And they began to be divided into classes; and they began to build up churches unto themselves to get gain, and began to deny the true church of Christ" (4 Nephi 23–26). A thousand years later, when the Europeans came to the Americas, the civilizations they found were dominated by warlike, priestly elites. The origins of these elites can be seen in the proud, wealthy king-men and priestcrafts of the Book of Mormon record. For all their exoticism, the native Americans' economies were not fundamentally different from those the Europeans knew from elsewhere in the world.

The Birth of the Modern Economy

However, beginning in the 1400s in Europe, some small changes began to appear in the normal historical human economy. Trade and commerce began to assume a much larger role. More of the surplus wealth came into the hands of traders and merchants. Some began to specialize in handling these excess funds. Working from the benches (*bancos* in Italian) at their stands at trade fairs, these early bankers occasionally loaned to their fellow businessmen, although most loans went to kings and aristocrats to support wars, luxurious living, and the consumption of exotic goods imported by the traders and merchants. They traded throughout the world, providing much of the impetus for the age of European exploration and colonization. Based in the cities, the traders and merchants used their wealth to gain freedom from the feudal nobility. These landed aristocrats, pressed by the need for cash to support their lifestyles and attracted by the market offered by the growing cities, began to engage in the improvement of agricultural production. Knowledge, or "science," began to expand, and conscious efforts at invention appeared. Cities grew, and arts and literature surged into new frontiers.

However, this was still not a "free market" economy. In feudal days, one's allegiance was to a prince or family. There began to develop the idea that one's loyalty was to one's country or people, rather than to some distant feudal ruler. Politic princes used this loyalty to create stronger governments, and the modern "nation-state" was born. These newly powerful states directed and managed national economies with a view toward keeping wealth within the nation and the new colonial empires. This doctrine, called *mercantilism*, seemed the logical modern extension of the practice throughout all human history whereby the wealth of a society was controlled by a small elite.

Adam Smith and the Modern Economy

Nowhere were these economic trends more advanced than in Britain, which by the 1700s was the wealthiest nation in Europe. However, in the late 1700s, even more developments began to appear in Britain. More and more economic activity was taking place outside the bounds of either mercantilist regulation or the traditional feudal economy. The Scottish philosopher Adam Smith began to study this activity. While aristocrats looked down on the "shopkeepers mentality," in his *Theory of Moral Sentiments,* Smith proposed that this emerging market economy would better promote morality than the old aristocratic economy. "In the courts of princes, in the drawing rooms of the great, where success and preferment depend, not upon the esteem of intelligent and well-informed equals, but upon the fanciful and foolish favour of ignorant, presumptuous, and proud superiors; flattery and falsehood too often prevail over merit and abilities. In such societies the abilities to please, are more regarded than the abilities to serve." For the man in this kind of society to "figure at a ball is his great triumph, and to succeed in an intrigue of gallantry, his highest exploit. . . . But he shudders with horror at the thought of any situation which demands the continual and long exertion of patience, industry, fortitude, and application of thought."[10] In societies founded on inequality, masters will persist in such abominations as slavery, even though they are uneconomical, because of the "love of domination and authority over others, which I am afraid is naturall to mankind, a certain desire of having others below one, and the pleasure it gives one to have some persons whom he can order to do his work rather than be obliged to persuade others to bargain with him."[11]

In contrast, Smith argued for a moral philosophy whose core values were "justice," "benevolence," and "sympathy," meaning "fellow feeling,"—"that to feel much for others and little for ourselves, that to restrain our selfish, and to indulge our benevolent affections, constitutes the perfection of human nature; and can alone produce among mankind that harmony of sentiments and passions in which consists their whole grace and propriety." For Smith, "humanity, justice, generosity, and public spirit are the qualities most useful to others."[12] These are not just abstract ideals for Smith, they are central to human character. "How selfish soever man may be supposed, there are evidently some principles in his nature, which interest him in the fortune of others and render their happiness necessary to him, though he derives nothing from it except the pleasure of seeing it."[13] This altruistic sentiment is central to the human condition. Contrary to many modern understandings of his philosophy, Adam Smith did not hold cold efficiency as the highest ideal, but rather saw brotherly love as the best foundation for human actions:

> All the members of human society stand in need of each other's assistance, and are likewise exposed to mutual injuries. Where the necessary assistance is reciprocally afforded from love, from gratitude, from friendship, and esteem, the society flourishes and is happy. All the different members of it are bound together by the agreeable bonds of love and affection, and are, as it were, drawn to one common centre of mutual good offices.[14]

Of course, even without this "mutual love and affection, the society, though less happy and agreeable, . . . may subsist . . . by a mercenary exchange of good offices according to an agreed valuation."[15] Such a commercial society would still be preferable to the traditional human economy. By encouraging free human interaction, this market economy would afford more opportunity for people to develop the spirit of sympathy and other virtues. Because they are so rarely accountable to others, "they whom we call politicians are not the most remarkable men in the world for probity and punctuality." However, if politicians and nations "were obliged to treat once or twice a day, as merchants do, it would be necessary to be more precise in order to preserve their character. Wherever dealings are frequent, a man does not expect to gain so much by any one contract as by probity and punctuality in the whole."[16]

In contrast to the aristocrat or politician, to achieve in the market economy, one "must acquire superior knowledge in his profession, and superior industry in the exercise of it. He must be patient in labour, resolute in danger, and firm in distress. . . . Probity and prudence, generosity and frankness, must characterize his behaviour upon all ordinary occasions." Success depends on the "good opinion of their neighbors and equals. . . . The good old proverb, therefore, That honesty is the best policy, holds, in such situations, almost always perfectly true."[17]

These sober virtues promoted by the market economy were always to be seen in the context of the moral and religious foundation of the endeavor to build a better society, a crucial aspect of Smith's philosophy:

> The wise and virtuous man is at all times willing that his own private interest should be sacrificed to the public interest of his own particular order or society. He is at all times willing, too, that the interest of this order or society should be sacrificed to the greater interest of the state or sovereignty, of which it is only a subordinate part. He should, therefore, be equally willing that those inferior interests should be sacrificed to the greater interest of the universe, to the interest of that great society of all sensible and intelligent beings, of which God himself is the immediate administrator and director.[18]

It was within this moral context that he next formulated a description of the operation of the new economy. In 1776, he published *An Inquiry into the Nature and Causes of the Wealth of Nations.* Its most famous argument was that a market with free competition would generate national economic growth, without direction by tradition, as under feudalism, or by the state, as in mercantilism. Smith again observes that man depends on his fellows:

> In almost every other race of animals each individual, when it is grown up to maturity, and in its natural state has occasion for the help of no other living creature. But man has almost constant occasion for the help of his brethren, and it is vain for him to expect it from their benevolence only. He will be more likely to prevail if he can interest their self-love in his favour.

This "propensity to truck, barter, and exchange one thing for another," through the collective economic decisions of many relatively equal and competitive businesses seeking their own gain, would be "led by an invisible hand to promote an end which is no part of [their] intention." That end was a greater increase in the collective wealth of the nation than could be realized by any centrally directed mercantilist economic effort. "What is the species of domestick industry which his capital can employ, and of which the produce is likely to be of the greatest value, every individual can, in his local situation, judge much better than any stateman or lawgiver can do for him."[19]

Although not alone, Adam Smith could certainly compete for the dubious distinction of being one of the most frequently invoked and most regularly misunderstood of the great thinkers of our time. The argument against state economic regulation takes up only a few pages of over 900 in the *Wealth of Nations.* He condemned economic direction and control by government because, in his day, it enforced private monopoly and privilege for the elite.[20] He would have been horrified at the expression "greed is good."[21] He saw high profits as leading to both economic and moral dissolution.[22] For Adam Smith, the economy and society were better served by high wages than by high profits.[23] He did not see the market economy as being virtuous in and of itself. That the market was efficient did not make it morally self-sufficient. Benevolence, justice and sympathy were still the proper moral basis for society.[24] What justified the market economy was that as an unintended consequence of the limited and controlled pursuit of self-interest, morally worthy ends might be achieved. These ends were a general increase in the prosperity of the entire community, "that universal opulence which extends itself to the lowest ranks of the people."[25]

In the normal historical human economy, it was thought that only the elite were capable of administering wealth. Society would be disrupted if the lower orders became too comfortable. Prosperity of the poor was "luxury," which led to the social disorder produced by such notions as "all men are created equal."[26] Smith turned the old morality around. His argument that the new market economy was increasing total productive wealth was shown by

> the common complaint that luxury extends itself even to the lowest ranks of the people, and that the labouring people will not now be contented with the same food, cloathing and lodging which satisfied them in former times. . . . Is this improvement in the circumstances of the lower ranks of the people to be regarded as an advantage or as an inconveniency to the society? . . . Servants, labourers and workmen of different kinds, make up the far greater part of every great political society. But what improves the circumstances of the greater part can never be regarded as an inconveniency to the whole. No society can surely be flourishing and happy, of which the far greater part of the members are poor and miserable.[27]

Adam Smith's free market economy was justified by the democratic and Christian ideal of raising up "the lowest ranks of the people," for only then could a society "surely be flourishing and happy." To the extent that wealth remained concentrated and inequality prevailed, the market is morally deficient. The market that Adam Smith praised was one in which prudent, honest neighbors and equals sought reasonable rates of profit through diligent and steady industriousness, raising the general level of prosperity of all members of the community, thereby enabling and encouraging them to pursue the even higher virtues of sympathy and benevolence toward the greater "society of all sensible and intelligent beings."[28]

In the same year that the *Wealth of Nations* was published, a mechanic and toolmaker from Smith's old university, James Watt, patented a radically improved steam engine that was to power the modern economy then aborning. That same year saw the formal beginning of the first revolt against the mercantilist view that colonial economies should be directed by the imperial central government for its own benefit. The American Revolution was much influenced by the Scottish Enlightenment, in which Adam Smith played an important part. Indeed, Smith supported American self-determination.[29] Eventually the United States would come to symbolize the new industrial market economy. However, by the latter half of the 1800s, when this economy would acquire the name "capitalism," we will see that the moral philosophy associated with capitalism will have vastly changed from the vision first espoused by Adam Smith.[30]

5

In a Very Eventful Day:

The Industrial Revolution and the United Order

> *We are living in a very eventful day, in a time that is pregnant with great events; and it is necessary that we prepare ourselves so that we may be able to conform ourselves to the circumstances with which we are surrounded, and to fulfil the various duties that devolve upon us individually and collectively.*
>
> John Taylor[1]

Adam Smith died in 1790. Joseph Smith, Brigham Young, John Taylor, and Wilford Woodruff were born in the following decade. With the possible exception of some improvements in military and naval technology, the world of 1800 would not have been incomprehensible to a Roman senator or Lehite king, and certainly not to an ancient Chinese imperial bureaucrat. However, the generation of the first modern prophets was to see changes so vast that one historian has called it the Second Economic Revolution, equal in importance to the development of agriculture.[2]

The most obvious aspect of this revolution was the sudden acceleration of technological development. Speaking to a conference in Bountiful in 1878, President John Taylor described some of the great events to which he referred above:

> To-day we can talk of railroads and steam-boats. I remember the time, and many of you old people also remember, when there were no such things in existence. . . . The same thing applies to electricity. You remember very well when it took several months to send a message to Washington and receive an answer; now we can do it in as many minutes. . . . The art of photography has not been long known. When I was a boy people would have laughed at you if you had talked of taking a man's likeness in a minute's time; yet it is done.[3]

However, the development of modern science and technology are only part of a collection of developments that have profoundly changed our modern world and economy from what was known by our ancient ancestors. The next five chapters will attempt to summarize these developments briefly so that we can understand the circumstances with which we are surrounded, and how we can work toward fulfilling our individual and collective duty, as President Taylor concluded, "To have a heaven on earth—to be really the Zion of our God, the pure in heart, each one seeking another's welfare."[4]

The Industrial Revolution

As noted in the last chapter, the new economy first appeared in Britain.[5] British textile merchants "put out" raw cloth to self-employed, highly skilled weavers, who worked it on the looms which they owned in their homes. In the late 1790s and early 1800s, the invention of a water-powered loom and the spinning jenny, an automatic spinning wheel, permitted the location of very large looms in factories. This automation permitted cloth to be spun and woven by less skilled workers. Highly improved steam engines, developed by James Watt at the university of Glasgow, Scotland, provided new sources of power for all kinds of production. Technological inventions came to other industries such as pottery making and metal refining. What has been called the First Industrial Revolution began to spread throughout the European world. By the 1820s, textile factories were being built in France and Massachusetts, and the world began to know the promise and the travails of industrialization.[6]

By the 1850s, America and the countries of western Europe were industrializing rapidly. The American Civil War, which began in 1861, became the world's first industrial war. It demonstrated that industrialization could be used to produce repeating rifles as well as calicoes. Vast armies moved by rail and communicated by telegraph. Mass-produced, technologically advanced weapons, from ironclad ships to Gatling guns, wrought mass slaughter. One of the principal strategic objectives of the war was the capture and defense of Richmond, Virginia, as much for being the location of the Confederacy's principal ironworks as for being the Confederacy's capital.[7] A war that began with the gallant military tactics of the Napoleonic wars fifty years before was to end with the trench warfare tactics of the world war fifty years later.[8]

The bloody destructiveness of the American Civil War should have given pause to those with faith in manmade solutions to humankind's problems. However, it was not until after two horrid, worldwide industrialized wars in the 20th century that men would begin to acknowledge that learning and wealth alone would not solve humanity's age-old problems.[9] In the meantime, the 19th century's industrial powers rushed to produce the wondrous new war machines. The world wars of the 20th century were further foreshadowed by the first industrial war in Europe. In the Franco-Prussian War of 1870–1871, a newly industrialized Prussia quickly defeated France. A new era of European imperial supremacy began, enforced by the armored gunboat, the machine gun, and the telegraph.

The American Civil War not only brought victory for a strong national government and human rights, but also signaled the preeminence of the new industrial economy of the northern states over the traditional agrarian economy of the southern states. There began an era of such rapid technological and economic development as to overshadow the earlier industrialization, to the extent that the last third of the 1800s and early 1900s are referred to as the "Second" Industrial Revolution.

The Rise of Enterprise

There had always been men who had risen in society. As Adam Smith observed, the rise of men to prominence usually came through securing the favor of the ruling elite. Generally the only advancement based on pure achievement was through military conquest, which, as Joseph Smith observed, broke down and stole wealth rather than built it up. However, the Industrial Revolution and Adam Smith's new market economy introduced a new character. Men began to make large fortunes by building factories and systems for selling manufactured goods. Instead of using all one's money to imitate the luxurious lifestyle of the landed aristocracy, men began to use their money to build businesses. Eventually one could gain as much prestige for the size and productivity of one's business as for one's houses and estates. By the middle of the 1800s, even kings and aristocrats wore the dark, sober clothes of the *businessman*. For better or worse, the business suit began its now near universal dominance as the uniform of the serious person.

Such serious people began with increasing frequency to come from all levels of society. One such was the son of a skilled, self-employed Scottish weaver and political radical who was forced out of work by the textile factories. In 1848, as the Saints were settling

Salt Lake City, he and his family immigrated to America and settled in Pittsburgh. There the young man, still in his teens, moved to the forefront of the technological revolution by becoming a crack telegraph operator for the Pennsylvania Railroad. He had drive and initiative. One morning when his supervisor was out, news came of an impending crisis on the line. He quickly sent out the necessary instructions over the supervisor's name. The supervisor had nothing to say about such presumption, but was later overheard boasting about the talent of his "white haired Scotch devil." At the beginning of the American Civil War, he helped set up a communications system that permitted the movement by rail of the vast numbers and quantities of men and equipment that were vital to Union victory.

After the war, he made a fortune in stock market speculation and by helping to procure British investment for American railroads. While in Britain, he profitably made the acquaintance of Junius Morgan, an American who had made a career of placing American railroad securities in Britain. However, he wanted to build something rather than simply engage in financial manipulations. In the Panic of 1873, the stock market crashed and a third of the nation's banks failed. However, in a remarkable display of the self-confidence and courage that marked the new genus of *entrepreneur,* during the depression of the 1870s, while others despaired, Andrew Carnegie built the world's largest and most modern steelworks.[10]

It was an age of economic advance such as the world had never seen. Technological developments led to amazing increases in productivity. In the 1870s it cost Andrew Carnegie $100 to produce a ton of steel. By the end of the 1890s, the production cost had fallen to $12, and the price of a ton of steel was only $17. The cost of producing kerosene, the main method of lighting, fell by 50 percent between 1882 and 1885. Similar cost declines were seen in other industries. Overall, the wholesale price index in the United States fell 18 percent in the 1880s.[11] It would be like seeing in every industry the gains in productivity which we have seen in recent years only in the computer industry.

These productivity gains were not without a heavy toll. Declines in costs resulted in deflation, falling real prices, which caused enormous stress on businesses. The largest producers, such as Carnegie's steel operations, engaged in relentless cost control. Their size gave them the benefit of economies of scale. Employing

Andrew Carnegie (1835–1919) immigrated from Scotland and built an industrial empire in U.S. mining and steel. He eventually came to advocate the progressive idea of creating a labor-management partnership in industry and viewed his wealth as a trusteeship, eventually giving away his entire fortune.

thousands, they integrated all aspects of an industry. For example, Carnegie companies eventually owned or operated the mines from which the iron ore, coal, and other raw materials were procured; controlled most of the transportation system to Pittsburgh; performed all of the steps of refining and processing; and managed the sales to the ultimate customers. Using these advantages, the largest companies forced the railroads to give them illegal cut rates and kickbacks. They also used predatory pricing to eliminate competition. This involved cutting prices in a local competitor's market to drive him out of business and compensating by raising prices in areas where there was no competition. Through these and other methods, honest and dishonest, the drive was to monopoly, where a single firm dominated an entire industry.

The Industrial Revolution and the Enterprise of Zion

At first, after their arrival in the Salt Lake Valley in 1847, the Saints enjoyed a fair degree of autonomy. However, the Saints were soon to become involved with the modern world again after what was to become Utah was transferred from Mexican to American jurisdiction in 1848. This involvement continued to be often unhappy. After a Church-sponsored company successfully bid on the contract to carry mail to California, the former holders of the contract spread rumors that the Saints were in insurrection against the United States. Due to these and other false accusations, an army was sent to suppress this supposed rebellion in 1857. Although the "Utah War" was settled peaceably, the Saints were to be subject to continuing periodic persecution for another 40 years.

One of the founding planks of the newly formed Republican Party was opposition to the "twin relics of barbarism," slavery and polygamy. The Saints had some respite while the Republicans were occupied with a conflict that was not to be settled peacefully. However, after the end of the American Civil War, one of the most visible manifestations of the new industrial market economy pressed westward and the transcontinental railroad was completed in 1869 in Utah. Among its numerous effects was the end of whatever limited isolation the Saints had enjoyed in their Zion in the desert.

The leaders of the Church who watched the coming of that harbinger of the industrial economy were no strangers to the Industrial Revolution. In the midst of some of the most difficult times for the Church in Kirtland and Missouri, Joseph Smith had been guided to embark on a course of action that must have seemed crazy from most rational perspectives. With the Church in flight and many of its leaders in apostasy, beginning in 1837 Joseph called most of the few remaining reliable leaders to travel to distant Britain as missionaries. LDS historians are only now fully assessing the impact of the missions of the apostles and others to Europe.[12] One aspect is that the early leaders of the Church were introduced to the Industrial Revolution in its birthplace. The first missionaries went right to the heart of the industrialized regions of north and central England. Former missionaries such as Brigham Young, John Taylor, Wilford Woodruff, and Lorenzo Snow had firsthand acquaintance with the Industrial Revolution and its social, political and economic consequences.

Knowing this, one might suppose that Brigham Young and the other apostles would have opposed the encroachment of the industrial Babylon on their remote sanctuary. However, their reaction was quite the opposite. As the transcontinental railroad approached Utah, Brigham Young told the October 1868 conference that "we want to associate with men who aspire after pure knowledge, wisdom and advancement, and who are for introducing every improvement in the midst of the people, like the company who are building this railroad. We thank them and the government for it. Every time I think of it I feel God bless them, hallelujah! . . . Do we believe in trade and commerce? Yes, And by and by we will send our products to the east and to the west. . . . Let us save our money . . . to buy machinery and start more woolen factories."[13]

The Church's leaders intended Zion to be industrialized and fully capable of profitable interaction with the larger national economy. Most of us have a rather bucolic image of the 19th-century America of Joseph Smith and Brigham Young, a sort of "The Saints meet the Little House on the Prairie." However, they lived in the beginnings of the modern industrial world economy which we know today, and the united orders which they implemented in the 1870s were intended to function realistically and practically in that economy. While they rejected the world's economic or social philosophies, the Saints welcomed the scientific, technological, and economic advances of the First and Second Industrial Revolutions. This American Zion was not to be a backward, strictly agricultural society, disconnected from the world's progress, as so often has been the case with utopian communalists then and since. Even a thousand miles beyond the frontier, this Zion was involved in the larger world. At the 1862 general conference Brigham encouraged the Saints to take contracts to assist in the construction of the transcontinental telegraph:

> I now wish to say a few words about assisting the mail and telegraph companies. It has been asked, "Shall we assist these companies?" . . . I say, yes. . . . If we happen to lay in bed a little later than usual, by the aid of the telegraph wires we can read the news of the morning from Washington and New York; and by-and-by we may be favored with the news of yesterday from London, Paris, and St. Petersburg, and all the principal cities of the old world. We are among the people of this world; our bodies are of the earth, and our spirits are like the spirits of other people and from the same source, only we are trying to establish the kingdom of God on earth, to introduce righteousness, and prepare the people for the reign of Jesus Christ on the earth. . . . Fulfill your contracts and sacredly keep your word.[14]

The Church was to become a major shipping and travel concern in the course of gathering the European converts who would soon constitute the majority of the Latter-day Saints. In the 1850s, the Saints attempted to establish pottery, paper, sugar processing, iron, lead, and textile industries. Brigham Young welcomed modern industrial development and encouraged directed proselytizing in Europe of workers with useful industrial skills.[15] Wilford Woodruff and others formed a Deseret Agricultural and Manufacturing Society and through it and other organizations sought to bring scientific and technological innovations to Utah.[16]

Brigham and his fellow apostles knew that true independence for the mountain Zion lay in establishing an industrial and agricultural base which was as self-sufficient as possible and which would produce surpluses that could be traded on advantageous terms within the larger national economy. Wilford Woodruff told the 1874 general conference that "it is suicidal for any people to import ten dollars worth of products while they export only one, and it is a miracle and a wonder to me that we have lived as long as we have under this order of things."[17] How was this to be achieved? At the October 1875 conference, apostle George Q. Cannon noted that France had quickly paid a burdensome war reparations debt after her defeat in the Franco-Prussian War because she "with her wonderful industrial resources, has a stream of wealth flowing into her to-day from all nations . . . due to French skill, to their workmen of taste and ability." Another example was

Switzerland, famous for watches and clocks where "the skill of her people has made Switzerland a comparatively rich country." The same principle could be applied in Utah:

> What, then, ought to be our policy? It ought to be to bestow all the skill and labor possible upon everything we produce. Not one pound of wheat ought to go out of this Territory until it has received all the labor possible to be bestowed upon it, or in other words, until it is made into the finest of flour. . . . To send our wheat away for other men to grind and take a toll off, and then send it back to us manufactured into flour, why it is suicidal! . . . You are paying your money to sustain communities afar off, while your own people are suffering for want of labor. . . . For any portion of our people to be idle is wrong, and there is something radically wrong about a system that admits of or has a tendency to keep a portion of the community in idleness.[18]

Today, when politicians seem to be delighted with themselves for having just discovered the importance of "value-added" industry, it is sobering to note that this concept was clearly understood and preached over a hundred years ago in the western deserts. The economic security of a community depends on its ability to add significant value to a product through skilled labor. For instance, the Swiss watchmaker added more value, and received more return, from what he did to metal than the Utah miner, who dug it out of the ground and shipped the unprocessed ore away. To promote value-added enterprise and to give Utah a diverse and well-rounded economy, many different industries were started. Diversified development was an important goal of the united orders of the 1870s. Women were even encouraged to cultivate mulberry trees and raise silkworms in order to provide silk for their homemade dresses.

The Law of Stewardship and Modern Enterprise

This industriousness has been a gospel principle from the beginning. When God sent Adam and Eve out on the earth, "Adam began to till the earth, and to have dominion over all the beasts of the field, and to eat his bread by the sweat of his brow, as the Lord had commanded him. And Eve, also, his wife, did labor with him" (Moses 5:1). God told his Saints that it was his purpose to provide for them and that "the earth is full, and there is enough and to spare; yea, I, prepared all things" (D&C 104:15, 17).

> Yea, all things which come of the earth, in the season thereof, are made for the benefit and use of man, both to please the eye and to gladden the heart; yea, for food and raiment, for taste and for smell, to strengthen the body and to enliven the soul. And it pleaseth God that he hath given all these things unto man; for unto this end were they made to be used, with judgement, not to excess, neither by extortion. (D&C 59:18–20)

Humanity's dominion over the earth is that of the husbandman, who uses judgment, without excess or extortion, to cultivate and beautify the earth and, in Brigham's words, to see to "multiplying those organisms of plants and animals God has designed shall dwell upon it."[19] Adam set out to do this work. Then his son Cain discovered that one could use secret conspiracies to "murder and get gain" (Moses 5:31). By acquiring the goods that others had worked to produce, Cain and his successors could avoid the divine commandment to work. And so began, with a few exceptions, the course of human economy and history described in chapter 4.

For most of human history, wealth came only to an elite which took a heavy toll from the labors of the many. There was trading and moneylending, and Christ even used contemporary economic activities in parables such as the talents, the unjust steward, and the pounds.[20] However, these were taken as allegories, not investment counseling, and even in these parables the master is addressed as a "hard man, reaping where thou hast not sown, and gathering where thou hast not strawed" (Matthew 25:24). As seen in chapter 4, in these static and unproductive economies, God could only command periodic redistributions to the poor and oppressed.

However, the coming of the modern economy introduced a new element. The birth of entrepreneurship was as important to the Industrial Revolution as its technological advances. The possibility arose of a path to getting wealth other than theft. While capitalist entrepreneurs unfortunately showed little resistance to the temptation to use bloodshed, oppression, and tyranny to get ahead, they also introduced the concept that new wealth would be created by investing some of society's surplus in better means of production, instead of conspicuous consumption as in the ancient economy.

Unlike most of the ancient scriptures, the modern united order scriptures take into account entrepreneurial possibilities in the mission of caring for the poor. United order stewards are told that each should "improve upon his talent, that every man may gain other talents, yea, even an hundred fold" (D&C 82:18). It is contemplated that stewardships would yield money by "improving upon the properties which I have appointed unto you, in houses, or in lands, or in cattle, . . . by hundreds, or by fifties, or by twenties, or by tens or by fives" (D&C 104:68). Brigham said that "if we are the people of God, we are to be the richest people on the earth. . . . I am ashamed to see the poverty that exists among the Latter-day Saints. They ought to be worth millions and millions."[21]

However, the promise of a "universal opulence" envisioned by men like Adam Smith and Brigham Young did not follow inevitably from the Industrial Revolution, as Brigham saw when he visited Britain fifty years after the great Scots philosopher's time.

6

Who Is She Laboring For?

Wealth and Poverty in the Modern World and the United Order

The earth . . . was made for man; and one man was not made to trample his fellowman under his feet, and enjoy all his heart desires, while the thousands suffer. We will take a moral view, a political view, and see the inequality that exists in the human family. . . . It is an unequal condition of mankind. We see servants that labor early and late, and that have not the opportunity of measuring their hours ten in twenty-four. They cannot go to school, nor hardly get clothing to go to meeting on the Sabbath. I have seen many cases of this kind in Europe, when the young lady would have to take her clothing on Saturday night and wash it, in order that she might go to meeting on the Sunday with a clean dress on. Who is she laboring for? For those who, many of them, are living in luxury. And to serve classes that are living on them, the poor, laboring men and women are toiling, working their lives and to earn that which will keep a little life within them. Is this equality? No! What is to be done? The Latter-day Saints will never accomplish their mission until this inequality shall cease on the earth.

Brigham Young[1]

The technological developments which harnessed the power of steam and machine to vastly expand the output of a human worker were regarded as wonders. However, these wonders seemed perversely to create conditions for the human workers which were horrors. Women and children worked 16-hour days, seven days a week, in filthy, dangerous conditions. They dragged coal carts through narrow mine tunnels and were mercilessly discharged if injured.[2] The self-employed skilled textile weavers were slowly driven out of business. The perverse bargain whereby the gains of industrial production were purchased at the price of workers' misery was summarized in the reply of an English textile factory owner when his treatment of his workers was criticized:

"Damn their eyes, what need you care about them? How could I sell you goods so cheap if I cared anything about them?"[3] When English workers protested these conditions in 1819 at St. Peter's Fields near Manchester, they were attacked by mounted militia with drawn sabres. Over 500 were killed or wounded, including over a hundred women. The "Peterloo" massacre and other repressive policies of the British elite gradually led to the rise of a consciousness among working people in various industries and regions of Britain that they all shared common interests and needs. By the 1830s, people had first begun to speak of the "working class."[4]

Even in the United States, although an enormous amount of new wealth was created by the Industrial Revolution, it remained in the hands of a relative few. These few engaged in battles of conspicuous consumption to show off their wealth. Adam Smith observed that "with the greater part of rich people, the chief enjoyment of riches consists in the parade of riches, which in their eyes is never so complete as when they appear to possess those decisive marks of opulence which nobody can possess but themselves."[5] Railroad tycoon William Vanderbilt let everyone know that the feature of which he was proudest about his personal railroad car was that it cost more than that of his railroad rival Leland Stanford. J. P. Morgan commented that anyone who had to ask the cost of a yacht could not afford one. Newspapers reported banquets for pet dogs, hundred-dollar bills folded into dinner napkins and after-dinner cigarettes, and, of course, the symbol of proud and wasteful excess, parties at which the cigars were lighted with bills of the highest denomination possible.[6]

Even good works were drafted to the service of the parade of riches. Many a capitalist, rich with profits from low-paid workers laboring in miserable conditions, felt a high sense of responsibility to society. Patriots, they saw the building of strong industry as adding to the wealth, security and prestige of their homelands. The world today is rich with museums, schools, foundations, and other benefactions of the conspicuous philanthropy of Rockefellers, Morgans, Fords, and the most zealous of them all, Andrew Carnegie.

The "Gilded Age" of the "Robber Barons," as they came to be called, was founded on continued oppressive working conditions for most industrial workers. Even the great philanthropist Andrew Carnegie worked his men 12-hour days, seven days a week under dangerous and unhealthy conditions. Every other week the men worked a 24-hour shift, so that they could have one Sunday off every two weeks.[7] And businesses were constantly pressing to lower wages. In part this was due to the pressure of deflation, but it also assured that the benefits of increasing productivity would be enjoyed only by the owners, not by the workers. Farmers were not much better off. In many areas of the United States, increasing numbers of farmers worked as tenants, or were continually in debt to the local "furnishing" merchant.

Capital and Labor

The whole industrial and industrializing world seemed to divide into two incompatible and irreconcilable factions, Capital and Labor. By the early 1900s, after a century of industrialization in some countries, working conditions remained appalling. Unimaginable economic and technological progress seemed to have had no effect on the age-old curses of poverty and inequality. Peaceful efforts by labor to counter these conditions through unions were resisted by owners at every turn. In Pittsburgh, Andrew Carnegie's CEO, Henry Clay Frick, wanted to cut wages and decided that the union needed to be eliminated. In 1892, while Carnegie absented himself in a secluded Scottish castle, Frick sent in an army of Pinkerton security guards to seize the huge Homestead steel mill. The Homestead workers resisted, and a violent five-month strike ensued. The governor of Pennsylvania sent in the National Guard to break the strike, and the union. The use of force by the state to bust the union embittered relations between management and labor for a century to come. Frick won grudging respect when he calmly walked away from being shot and stabbed by an anarchist unassociated with the strikers. Carnegie never fully recovered the damage to his reputation from all sides for hiding away throughout the affair.[8]

Social Darwinism

It is human nature always to think of oneself as a moral and proper person, and the new industrial elite were not without a philosophy that justified their ruthless conduct. An English philosopher named Herbert Spencer taught that the development of nature was governed by the "survival of the fittest." He argued that this was also the proper and natural basis for human morality, that the survival of the fittest was not only how nature operated, but was also the morally correct way for human society to operate. Although Spencer is the chief author of this philosophy, it came to be given the name of his more famous scientific colleague, Charles Darwin, and was identified with other proponents of biological evolutionary theory such as Thomas Henry Huxley and Louis Compton Miall.[9] What came to be called "Social Darwinism" taught essentially that winning was everything and that human progress was achieved by the unrestrained triumph of those who won in the competition that was life.

Most Social Darwinists emphasized personal freedom and the progressive evolutionary improvement of humanity. They tended not to emphasize that the method of realizing this progress was the elimination of those who could not compete, the poor and the needy. However, Spencer himself did not shrink from the logical implications of his jungle morality. As in the animal world, where the weak are killed off, so the well-being of humanity is

> secured by that same beneficent, though severe discipline, . . . a discipline which is pitiless. . . . Those shoulderings aside of the weak by the strong, which leave so many "in shallows and in miseries," are the decrees of a large, far-seeing benevolence. It seems hard that an unskillfulness which with all his efforts he cannot overcome, should entail hunger upon the artisan. It seems hard that a labourer incapacitated by sickness from competing with his stronger fellows, should have to bear the resulting privations. It seems hard that widows and orphans should be left to struggle for life or death.

However, "the whole effort of nature is to get rid of such, to clear the world of them, and make room for better." To the extent that spontaneous sympathy for others interferes with this, "does it work pure evil."[10] The natural predatory instincts in mankind served civilization because they "exterminate such sections of mankind as stand in the way, with the same sternness that they exterminate beasts of prey and herds of useless animals."[11] It was forgotten that the founder of free market economics, Adam Smith, had justified the market because he thought it would bring economic progress to even the lowest levels of society.[12]

Spencer was embraced by the new elite of the industrial market economy. When Andrew Carnegie became acquainted with Spencerism, he wrote enthusiastically, "I remember that light came as in a flood and all was clear. Not only had I got rid of theology and the supernatural, but I had found the truth of evolution."[13] In 1882, his hero visited America. Spencer was delicate and something of a hypochondriac. He fled to his hotel in horror when Carnegie introduced him to the social darwinist future in the steel mills of Pittsburgh. Nonetheless, America's elite turned out to acclaim Spencer at a great dinner at Delmonico's in New York City. They competed with each other in praising the great philosopher of the new capitalist age. Perhaps most surprising to Spencer, who had no use for God or religion, was the declaration of America's foremost minister and theologian, Henry Ward Beecher, that he looked forward to meeting the great Spencer in heaven.[14] Although Herbert Spencer has disappeared into historical obscurity, every red-blooded, competitive American business champion who views life as a great contest in which the winner is the one with the most toys at the end, should acknowledge the great debt that he owes to this fey English atheist and his "scientific" morality of the jungle.

The Rise of Socialism

The "Utopian" Socialists. Many of Britain's self-described Christian elite were shocked by the conditions of the new industrial workers. One reaction was religious preaching which taught the poor that their lot in life was predestined by a God who would grant them relief in the next life if they were obedient to their betters in this life.[15] Some took other approaches. One of the first successful industrialists, Robert Owen, a Welshman who built a large textile factory in Lanark, Scotland, created humane conditions in his factory and made a fortune as well. Owen acquired a wide prominence for his ideas, which came to be called *socialism,* even if they were not copied in practice. In 1824, he visited the United States and was widely acclaimed. His lecture in the United States Capitol building was attended by the President and many members of the cabinet and Congress, and he was personally received and commended by Thomas Jefferson.[16]

Owen, like many socialists who followed him, could ably critique society's ills and stood for admirable principles. One of Owen's chief associates, John Finch, summarized the moral code of socialism in these principles:

> Man's first duty to himself is to make himself acquainted with what his nature really is. . . . This knowledge will cause him to feel pure charity for the opinions, feelings and conduct of every human being—the strongest desire to instruct the ignorant, to reform the vicious, and to place himself, his children, and the

> whole family of man in those circumstances that will make them wise, virtuous and happy. It will teach him to love his enemies, and to do good to them who hate and persecute him. It will forever banish from his mind egotism, pride, anger, contention, strife, hatred, envy, jealousy, revenge, cruelty,—and will implant there humility, gentleness, forbearance, forgiveness, love. . . .
>
> God provides liberally for the wants of every living thing; . . . therefore man's duty to God consists in imitating the divine beneficence by the unceasing practice of promoting, to the utmost extent in his power, the happiness of every man, woman, and child, without the least regard to sect, party, class, country, or colours, and in a merciful disposition towards every thing that has life and sensation.[17]

In response to the question "What think you of Christ?" Finch wrote that "He taught perfect political, civil, social, and religious liberty and equality, both for males and for females—severely reprobated the hypocrisy, tyranny and selfishness of the priesthood—taught . . . that the only criterion of true piety towards God, would be sincerity of heart, a virtuous life, and the love of our fellow men." This, he wrote, was "the Gospel of this good man—this beloved son of God" and was also "my religion—may it soon become the religion of the whole human race."[18]

The problem that has bedeviled socialists from Owen forward has never been a lack of charitable sentiments or high ideals. The problem has always been how to implement them. Owen attempted to establish an ideal community at New Harmony, Indiana, in 1826, and its progress was widely followed. Unfortunately, by 1829 it was abandoned. Too many people came too quickly without proper planning. There could be no proper planning because Owen never set out the specifics of how his ideal society was supposed to operate.[19]

Owen was hardly the first idealistic communalist to come to America from Europe. The Pilgrims had seen themselves as seeking to establish the City of God in the New World; and as early as 1663, religious exiles from Germany had established communitarian settlements in Pennsylvania. By the 1830s, the United States, and upstate New York and Ohio in particular, were the home of numerous religious communalists. Like Owen's New Harmony, these were frequently short-lived. However, many communities, such as the Shakers, were to prove quite durable. In general, those that survived tended to be small, tightly controlled, insular, and religious.

Members of successful communities often renounced normal family relationships and practiced sexual abstinence. They wore uniform clothing and limited their contact with the outside world. All aspects of their lives were regulated by the group and its leaders.[20]

Thousands flocked to these havens, for by the 1830s and 1840s, the entire world seemed to be in turmoil. This was at least in part due to the changes caused by the rise of the new industrial economy. Owen attempted to form a union of all working people. Britain came close to revolution twice, and the European continent saw major revolutions and uprisings, particularly in the early 1830s and again in 1848. French philosophers like Claude Henri Saint Simon and Charles Fourier contributed widely recognized ideas to Owenite socialism. Socialist ideas were always vague and theoretical, but they generally shared the view that the abuses of economic control by aristocrats and industrialists should be replaced by some kind of communal control in the common interest. There was no clear method suggested for producing such change other than the establishment of ideal communities as models.

In Britain, attempts were made to establish such communal control through the creation of cooperative enterprises. The most successful of these were the Rochdale consumer cooperatives. Named for the first store of this kind on Toad Lane in Rochdale, an English industrial town near Manchester, these cooperative stores gave small metal tokens with each purchase. At the end of the year, the tokens were exchanged for votes at the annual meeting which elected the store's management. They also entitled the customers to a share of any profits the store made in the year. This model was so successful that hundreds of "Rochdale" stores were set up. These stores formed a joint purchasing cooperative and opened their own factories. Eventually, the Cooperative Wholesale Society became one of the largest retail "chains" in Great Britain.[21]

Many others, however, were unsuccessful. These included many sponsored by Owen, who exhausted his fortune in efforts to create his "new moral order." In the United States, religious and secular communalists established hundreds of communities. In America in the 1840s, the ideas of the French socialist philosopher Fourier enjoyed tremendous popularity. Fourier had advocated the organization of society in self-contained communities of 1,620 members. Over 20 Fourierist "phalanxes" were formed, including Brook Farm in Massachusetts, which attracted many members of the United States' intellectual elite.

Old lithograph of the Rochdale co-op, a consumer-owned enterprise which included the right of all customers to vote in company elections and share in annual profits. The Rochdale pioneers opened the world's first cooperative store near Manchester, England, in 1844, the same year that Joseph Smith led the creation of cooperative enterprises in Nauvoo, Illinois.

Beatrice Potter Webb (1858–1943) and her husband, Sidney Webb (1859–1947), recoiled at the luxuries of wealthy Britons in the face of the grinding poverty of the masses. They were among the founders of Fabian socialism and traveled to Utah to observe Mormon cooperatives. They also founded the prestigious London School of Economics and Political Science and advocated state ownership of industry rather than privately held worker cooperatives.

The Fabians. Socialist ideals would also attract the intellectual elite in powerful Britain, including one of the most influential groups of thinkers in modern times. Although most Americans today would not recognize the name, the *Fabian socialists* were to set the tenor of acceptable political belief for most of the 20th century. They included such famous intellectual figures as George Bernard Shaw, Bertrand Russell, and H. G. Wells. However, the prototypical Fabians were a goateed, lower middle-class cockney named Sidney Webb, and his wife Beatrice.

Beatrice Webb was the daughter of a wealthy English railroad tycoon, Richard Potter.[22] Eighth daughter of a mother who preferred the company of men, Beatrice grew up privileged and neglected. Her favorite place to pass her time as a young girl was with the maids in the laundry of the family's mansion. At first her views had been typical of those of her father and his close friend, Herbert Spencer. In fact, until her marriage to a socialist, she was Spencer's literary executor. She had visited Utah with her father in 1873 as a teenager. Primly noticing the weathered faces of the frontier women, she concluded that this was a sign of their unhappiness as plural wives.[23] She even signed a petition opposing women's suffrage.

However, she also had a desire to understand and find meaning in her world. As a teenager, she had earnestly searched for religious truth, studying, visiting different churches, and inquiring of their ministers. She eventually pursued the more secular doctrines of Spencer and others after wrestling with, and being unable to find, an explanation or understanding of the Atonement. After breaking off a passionate romance with a rising young politician because she could not reconcile herself to his political principles, she set herself up as what would today be considered a sociologist. She went into the slums of London to study the sweatshops and the lives of the poor working class. She was horrified by what she saw, particularly in contrast to her own genteel and privileged background. Her older sisters, of course, had married into the intellectual and professional elite of British society. Beatrice, comparing their lives to those of the working class, came to the view that socialism offered the meaning that she was seeking. She described this conversion from the views of

> all those respectable and highly successful men, my brothers-in-law, typical of the old reign of private property and self-interested action. . . . And then I turn from the luxurious homes of these

> picked men of the individualist system, and struggle through an East End crowd of the wrecks, of the waifs and strays of this civilisation; or I enter a debating society of working men, and listen to the ever increasing cry of active brains, doomed to the treadmill of manual labour. . . . And the whole seems a whirl of contending actions, aspirations and aims, out of which I dimly see the tendency towards a socialist community, in which there will be individual freedom and public property, instead of class slavery and private possession of the means of subsistence of the whole people. At last I am a socialist.[24]

Her first major study was of the Rochdale consumer cooperatives. Raised to be a prim upper-class lady, she rather enjoyed being the only woman in a meeting of rough working men. In an influential book she concluded that worker-run cooperatives could not be self-sustaining. She argued that if they remained democratically owned and managed, they would inevitably remain small or fail. On the other hand, if they grew they would lose their cooperative nature and degenerate into ordinary private companies without significant worker ownership.[25] After she married Sidney Webb, they continued their studies and concluded that state ownership and control of industry was the most effective way to eliminate the wretched working conditions that persisted even in the most advanced industrial nations. In order for this state control to function, a professional state bureaucracy would have to be trained in the skills of the modern economy. To this end they founded the London School of Economics and Political Science.

The Fabians did not advocate change by revolutionary upheaval. Their approach was to permeate the existing ruling social class and convert it to socialism. The Webbs wrote that the goal was to "make thinking persons socialistic."[26] By the early 1900s, Fabians made up a majority of several British cabinets. Sidney was even to serve briefly as Secretary of State for Colonial Affairs (essentially chief administrator of the British Empire, which then covered a quarter of the world). He was also made a baron. More important in the long run was the fact that democratic socialism became the predominant political view of Europe's intellectual and ruling elites. Officially socialist, social democrat, or labor parties would eventually come to power in every major industrial nation other than the United States and Japan; and even in those two, social democratic ideas would be hugely influential.

European Revolutionaries. In Europe, the slowness of the permeation approach of the Fabian social democrats led many to advocate faster change. From March to May 1871, in the turmoil of the Franco-Prussian War, Paris had been taken over by a revolutionary government, the Paris Commune. The Commune's career was cut short when the Prussians released the defeated French army to suppress it. French soldiers bayoneted women and children, and over a hundred thousand Parisians were left dead, jailed, or exiled.[27] However, the memory of the "Communards" lived on. Anarchists actively assassinated government leaders, including United States president William McKinlay in 1901. Many socialists had thought that the socialist revolution would come first in the most advanced industrial nations, such as Britain and Germany. Yet even in less developed Russia, the resistance of the tsarist government to even the most elementary political reforms provided fertile ground to many radical socialist groups. These included a small party known as the Bolsheviks, led by a man who took the revolutionary code name of Lenin.

American Reformers. America was not isolated from these trends. While European-style socialism became well established in America, the most influential socialists were homegrown idealists. In 1888, Edward Bellamy published *Looking Backward: 2000 to 1887.* In this fantasy, a wealthy Bostonian is trapped in a drugged sleep in his basement in 1887 and wakes up in the year 2000. There he finds an ideal society where everyone serves in a state-directed industrial army for 24 years and then is able to retire and pursue "ease and agreeable relaxation."[28] A product of the sentimental Victorian era, it also features a maudlin romance in which the hero falls in love with the great-granddaughter and exact look-alike of his 19th-century fiancee. *Looking Backward* was an instant international bestseller. Clubs promoting Bellamy's ideas, which he called "Nationalism," spread throughout the United States. Bellamy's works were well read in the libraries of the New Dealers and inspired some of the early Israeli Zionists. Unacknowledged in a vast literature on the influences on Bellamy's influential work is his long visit with Lorenzo Snow at Brigham City in 1883.[29]

Other Americans advanced related ideas. Henry George advocated an extensive single tax on land. The Populists became politically significant in the 1890s, advocating racial harmony and the interests of poor farmers. The presence of these native socialisms limited the influence of European socialism.[30]

Marxism. In the 1800s, many different voices called themselves socialist. Originally, the world of the socialists was dominated by idealistic utopians like Owen and Fourier. However, by the 1840s the world encountered a darker vision of socialism in the analysis of a young German political exile named Karl Marx and his only friend, Friedrich Engels. Engels and Marx both came from prosperous bourgeois backgrounds. Marx gave up his family position to sit in the library of the British Museum churning out books, while being supported financially by Engels. Engels remained in his family's business and became a wealthy cotton broker in Manchester, England. A 19th-century predecessor of the limousine liberal of our time, Engels championed the working man, but preferred to pass his leisure time with his fellow gentlemen of the Manchester Shooting Club.

In 1848, the year that Andrew Carnegie's family immigrated to the United States and the year after the Saints abandoned the United States for the western deserts, the *Communist Manifesto* was first published. In it, Marx and Engels recognized that the new industrial economy of the bourgeoisie (from *burger,* or townsman) had overthrown the old aristocratic feudal economy and unleashed powerful new productive forces. However, this new economic elite would inevitably repress the rest of society into the wage slavery of the working class, or proletarians. They proclaimed that the new industrial economy had prepared the way for a workers' paradise if the workers would but abolish private property and seize "all capital from the bourgeoisie, to centralize all instruments of production in the hands of the State, i.e. of the proletariat organized as the ruling class; and to increase the total of productive forces as rapidly as possible." They concluded that Communist ends "can only be attained by the forcible overthrow of all existing social conditions. Let the ruling classes tremble at a Communist revolution. The proletarians have nothing to lose but their chains. They have a world to win. WORKING MEN OF ALL COUNTRIES, UNITE!"[31]

The Church and the Working Class

When the apostle missionaries went on their missions to Britain in the 1830s and 1840s, they observed closely all aspects of the new industrial economy. And like such contemporaries as Charles Dickens and Karl Marx, the sturdy American frontiersmen were horrified by what they saw. Viewing conditions in such cities as Liverpool and Manchester, apostle Heber Kimball wrote:

> Wealth and luxury abounded, side by side with penury and want. I there met the rich attired in the most costly dresses, and the next minute was saluted with the cries of the poor with scarce covering sufficient to screen them from the weather. Such a wide distinction I never saw before.[32]

Other missionaries shared his reaction.[33] John Taylor, himself a native Englishman, described the conditions with eloquent irony:

> Thousands of them are immured in immense factories, little less than prisons, groaning under a wearisome, sickening, unhealthy labour; deprived of free, wholesome air; weak and emaciated, not having a sufficiency of the necessaries of life. Thousands more from morning till night are immured in pits, shut out from life of day, the carol of birds, and the beauty of nature, sickly and weak, in many instances for want of food; and yet in the midst of wretchedness, gloom and misery, you will sometimes hear them trying to sing in their dungeons and prison-houses, in broken, dying accents, "Britons shall never be slaves."[34]

Most of the missionaries' converts came from the new British working class.[35] The stories of these missionaries' extraordinary successes are familiar. Wilford Woodruff alone brought over 1,800 people into the Church. What may not be so familiar is how extraordinary the impact of these converts was on the Church. Their impact may be simply put this way: they became the Church. A religious census in the United Kingdom in 1851 found at least 34,000 in attendance at Mormon church services.[36] At this time there were only 12,000 members in Utah, and already many then in Utah were British immigrants. In the early Utah years, approximately two-thirds of the population were foreign-born, a figure that does not take into account the fact that another significant part of the population would have been the American-born children of these foreign-born members.[37]

Descendants of 19th-century Latter-day Saints need only to consult their own family genealogy to learn that a large majority of converts who stayed true to the Church were not native-born Americans, but rather European converts—European working-class converts, if the working class is broadly defined, as it often was, to include agricultural as well as industrial workers. Within a few years of its foundation, The Church of Jesus Christ of Latter-day Saints, so often thought of as a typical religion of the American frontier, had instead become a religion of the international working class.

The Law of Consecration and Care for the Poor

The Lord tells us to "remember in all things the poor and needy, the sick and afflicted, for he that doeth not these things, the same is not my disciple."(D&C 52:40). In a revelation to the united order in 1834, the Lord elaborated:

> And it is my purpose to provide for my saints, for all things are mine. But it must needs be done in my own way; and behold this is the way that I, the Lord, have decreed to provide for my saints, that the poor shall be exalted and that the rich are made low. For the earth is full, and there is enough and to spare; yea, I prepared all things, and have given unto the children of men to be agents unto themselves. Therefore, if any man shall take of the abundance which I have made, and impart not his portion, according to the law of my gospel, unto the poor and needy, he shall, with the wicked, lift up his eyes in hell, being in torment. (D&C 104:15–18)

From the beginning of the Church, ministers, priests, and politicians who opposed Mormonism criticized the Church for requiring that the Saints care for the poor. In 1840, eight years before the publication of the *Communist Manifesto,* apostle Parley P. Pratt responded by suggesting that such complaints must really be faultfinding against Jesus and his disciples of old. For him a distinguishing feature of the true church is the emphasis on helping the disenfranchised. "I expect the saints to give money for the support of the poor among them, and this to the extent of all they have to spare; and I shall teach them to do so, and if they do not do it, their religion is vain. . . . We preach a religion which very materially affects men's purses; and a religion which does not affect men's purses is worse than none."[38] How does the law of the gospel teach us to "impart [our] portion . . . unto the poor and needy"?

Care for the Poor and Employment. The Doctrine and Covenants tells us that the exaltation of the poor under the united order consists of providing them with "their portions, every man equal according to his family, according to his circumstances and his wants and needs" (D&C 51:3). These portions, also referred to as "inheritances" or "stewardships," are not temporary assistance. According to Ezra Taft Benson, they are "the amount of personal property required by the individual for the support of himself and his family."[39] In the agrarian economy of the 19th century this usually meant that a family would receive land for farming. Speaking on the implementation of this scripture in the modern economy, apostle Marion G. Romney indicated that when someone is out of work and in want, "a priesthood quorum sets him up in work and tries to see that he goes along until fully self-supporting and active in his priesthood duties."[40] An "inheritance" is a situation which permits a family to be self-supporting through their own work. In the modern economy, where opportunities for self-employment are limited and most income comes from working in larger organizations, this is usually called a "job."

Care for the poor and needy under the united order is not "charity" in the sense of a "hand-out," although we are obligated to provide temporary emergency assistance if needed. Joseph F. Smith explained that the Church "has always sought to place its members in a way to help themselves, rather than adopting the method of so many charitable institutions of providing for only present needs. When the help is withdrawn or used up, more must be provided from the same source, thus making paupers of the poor and teaching them the incorrect principle of relying upon others' help, instead of depending upon their own exertions. . . . Our idea of charity, therefore, is to relieve present wants and then to put the poor in a way to help themselves so that in turn they may help others."[41] Care for the poor and needy consists principally of assisting them in getting real, self-sustaining jobs to support themselves and their families. John Taylor put the charge succinctly to the leadership and members of the stake at Kaysville, Utah, in 1879: "The presidency of this Stake ought, and all ought to unite with them, . . . in finding employment for every man and woman and child within this Stake that wants to labor."[42] This is not just a "nice thing to do" if it is convenient, the responsibility of only one of two hundred positions in the ward. It is fundamental to the restored gospel which teaches, according to Joseph F. Smith, "that a religion which has not the power to save people temporally and make them prosperous and happy here, cannot be depended upon to save them spiritually, to exalt them in the life to come."[43]

The Law of Consecration and Equality

Our responsibilities do not end with simply securing a living for the poor. God has said "if ye are not one ye are not mine," and "it is not given that one man should possess that which is above another, wherefore the world lieth in sin."[44] The united order is to be a permanent and everlasting establishment:

> To advance the cause, which ye have espoused, to the salvation of man, and to the glory of your Father who is in heaven; that you may be equal in the bonds of heavenly things, yea, and earthly things also, for the obtaining of heavenly things. For if ye are not equal in earthly things ye cannot be equal in obtaining heavenly things. (D&C 78:4–6)

This equality is not just a vague social notion—treat everyone with decency and politeness. The Book of Mormon resonates with denunciations of economic inequality as one of the great evils of any society. That some children of God should enjoy comfortable consumption when others languish in despair and need is an outrage to him.

Brigham Young's observations on economic inequality were quoted at the beginning of this chapter. Perhaps more than any early convert and leader of the church, Orson Pratt, one of the first apostles under Joseph Smith, was perceived to be the Lord's scholar and expert on doctrinal matters during most of the 1800s, the "St. Paul of Mormondom," as Tullidge referred to him. John Taylor assured him that he had earned eternal life, while Wilford Woodruff declared that only an angel would be able "to depict the glory that awaits him."[45] The apostle, in his great volume *The Seer,* wrote an article entitled "The Equality and Oneness of the Saints." It begins:

> "Be one; and if ye are not one, ye are not mine." This is the command of Jesus Christ to the Latter-day Saints, given as early as the year 1831, before the church was one year old. In what respects are the Saints required to be one? We answer: They are required to be one in things temporal and spiritual, in earthly and heavenly things. . . . The command to "be one" embraces all other commands. There is no law, statute, ordinance, covenant, or blessing, but what was instituted to make the Saints one. This is the ultimate end and aim of the great plan of salvation. . . . The saints are not only one in doctrine, but they are to be made one in temporal things without which they cannot be made equal in spiritual things.

Orson traces the problems of riches and greed down through history, contrasting the trends of materialism with New Testament church members: "Did they not sell their houses and lands and lay the avails thereof at the Apostles' feet? Did they not have all their property in common? Did not the poor rejoice in that he was exalted, and the rich in that he was made low? Were they not all considered equal and one in temporal riches? Yes; they consecrated all they had to the Lord, . . . and no part or portion of the great common stock fund was considered as belonging to some individuals to the exclusion of others." He points out the same system existed in the Nephite church and the order of Enoch. "And the same order of things must exist in the Zion of the Latter-day Saints, or else the inhabitants thereof will never be one. Anything short of a perfect equality in temporal things is a sin, hence, the Lord says, 'It is not given that one man should possess that which is above another, wherefore, the world lieth in sin.'"[46]

Equality and Arithmetic. According to Ezra Taft Benson, "it has been erroneously concluded by some that the united order is both communal and communistic in theory and practice because the revelations speak of equality. Equality under the united order is not economic and social leveling as advocated by some today. Equality, as described by the Lord, is equal[ity] according to [a man's] family, according to his circumstances and his wants and needs" (D&C 51:3)."[47] In his last general conference in April 1877, Brigham Young noted:

> The people might gather the idea that we shall be expected to divide our property equally one with another and that this will constitute the United Order. . . . Supposing that the property of the whole community were divided today equally amongst all, what might we expect? Why a year from today we should need another division, for some would waste and squander it away, while others would add to their portion. The skill of building up and establishing the Zion of our God on the earth is to take the people and teach them how to take care of themselves and that which the Lord has entrusted to their care . . . to take what we have and divide amongst or give to people, without teaching them how to earn and produce, would be no more nor less than to introduce the means of reducing them to a state of poverty. I do not wish for one moment to recognize the idea that in order to establish the United Order our property has to be divided equally.[48]

The equality in earthly things sought by the united order is more complex and realistic than a crude arithmetic division of assets. The human economy is living and dynamic, not easily reduced to the theorems and models of economic social planners. A factory has value only if it is invented and worked by human enterprise and effort, and its products have value only if designed

Zion's Cooperative Mercantile Institution (ZCMI) was established by Brigham Young and his associates in an effort to implement united order principles. The goal was to build self-reliance and a rough economic equality through broad-based ownership of the distribution system for manufactured goods.

and marketed in response to human needs and desires. Human choice and action intervene at a million points in the everyday life of sustaining our mortal existence. The recognition of this fact is the fundamental strength of the free enterprise market economy.

Equality and Class. The united order principle of equality is achieved not by mechanically dividing up assets, but by changing the human actions and attitudes that make economic life happen. Lorenzo Snow put it plainly to

> those brethren who have means and are in circumstances, to search out the mind and will of God in regard to these matters, and let us try to build up Zion. Zion is the pure in heart. Zion cannot be built except on the principles of union required by the celestial law. It is high time for us to enter into these things. It is more pleasant and agreeable for the Latter-day Saints to enter into this work and build up Zion, than to build up ourselves and have this great competition which is destroying us. Now let things go on in our midst in our Gentile fashion, and you would see an aristocracy growing amongst us, whose language to the poor would be, "we do not require your company; we are going to have things very fine; we are quite busy now, please call some other time." You would have classes established here, some very poor and some very rich. Now, the Lord is not going to have anything of that kind. There has to be an equality; and we have to observe these principles that are designed to give every one the privilege of gathering around him the comforts and conveniences of life. The Lord, in his economy in spiritual things, has fixed that every man, according to his perseverance and faithfulness, will receive exaltation and glory in the eternal worlds—a fullness of the Priesthood, and a fullness of the glory of God. This is the economy of God's system by which men and women can be exalted spiritually. The same with regard to temporal affairs.[49]

He then discusses the obligation to promote employment for all. The united order principle of equality addresses the central issues of the human economy. It calls us to exercise our economic free agency to promote full employment and the elimination of class differences. Apostle Snow explained:

> The system of union, or the Order of Enoch, which God has taken so much pains to reveal and make manifest, has been, and is, for the purpose of uniting the Latter-day Saints, the people of God, and preparing them for exaltation in the celestial kingdom, and also for the purpose of preparing them here on this earth to

> live together as brethren . . . so that there shall be no poor found in the midst of the Latter-day Saints, and no monied aristocracy in the midst of the people of God. . . . There is nothing more elevating to ourselves and pleasing to God than those things that pertain to the accomplishment of a brotherhood.[50]

As we have seen, inequality of socioeconomic classes afflicted the early Saints. Orson Pratt complained that the pioneers "have not become righteous enough to obey this law. Covetousness has taken such deep root in their hearts, . . . [so God] gave unto them another law more suited to their weakness. . . . An inequality in property is the root and foundation of innumerable evils; it tends to derision, and to keep asunder the social feelings that should exist among the people of God. It is the great barrier erected by the devil to prevent that unity and oneness which the Gospel requires; it is a principle originated in hell; it is the root of all evils. . . . Riches are not a curse, they are a great blessing; it is inequality in riches that is a great curse."[51]

Contemporary voices on Church doctrine echo the early apostles' preaching. LDS scholar *par excellence* Hugh Nibley, in a monumental collection of his work on contemporary issues, *Approaching Zion,* attacks the faulty assumption of the world "that anyone who has wealth must have earned it by hard work and is, therefore, beyond criticism; that anyone who doesn't have it deserves to suffer." "God recognizes only one justification for seeking wealth, and that is with the express intent of helping the poor" (See Jacob 2:19). "All my life I have shied away from these disturbing and highly unpopular—even offensive—themes. But I cannot do so any longer, because—from the time of Adam to the present day, Zion has been pitted against Babylon, and the name of the game has always been money—'power and gain.'"[52] Like all seemingly temporal commandments, the divine united order commandment of equality is at base spiritual. It is an aspect of the commandment to love our neighbors as ourselves. The game of "power and gain," and the class differences that are its rewards, have no place in the gospel. There should be no East Bench and "west side of the valley" in Zion.[53]

Unity and Cooperation. Like any other principle of righteousness, the united order principle of equality is not fully realized if it is only approached in the negative. "Thou shalt not" only goes so far. Commandments in the negative are guideposts on the road to exaltation, but they are not the road itself. To say that one must not commit adultery, or lust after another in one's heart, is to alert us to the soft shoulder and gully beside the road. To actually travel the road, we must work toward the eternal union of companions contemplated by the temple marriage covenants. Similarly, the warnings against power, gain, and class differences alert us to the dangers that prevent us from traveling the road to Zion. To actually travel the road toward the united order, we must work toward the sense of fraternal solidarity that permits us to regard our brothers' and sisters' interest as our own. Spencer W. Kimball told the 1978 general conference:

> We must cooperate completely and work in harmony one with the other. There must be unanimity in our decisions and unity in our actions. After pleading with the Saints to "let every man esteem his brother as himself" (D&C 38:24), the Lord concludes his instructions on cooperation . . . in these powerful words: "Behold, this I have given unto you as a parable, and it is even as I am. I say unto you, be one; and if ye are not one ye are not mine." (D&C 38:27). If the Spirit of the Lord is to magnify our labors, then this spirit of oneness and cooperation must be the prevailing spirit in all that we do. Moreover, when we do so, we are told by the Prophet Joseph Smith that "the greatest temporal and spiritual blessings which always come from faithfulness and concentrated effort, never attended individual exertion or enterprise."[54]

Equality and Enterprise. How we can freely achieve economic oneness through the application of the principles of the united order in a free market economy is the subject of much of the remainder of this book. In short, the united order calls for building up the poor by devoting the resources of the well-to-do to the development of economically viable employment for all. Because this goal has been so loudly espoused for so long by the advocates of state control of the economy, many have come to equate it with leftist economics. However, the socialists do not own the Christian united order principle of equality through full employment. It is the promise of the free market economy. The tremendous productivity unleashed by the Industrial Revolution and the free enterprise economy entrusts us with the first opportunity in human history to provide on a broad scale that universal opulence in which there shall be no more poor among us. The united order principle of equality simply demands that *all* should have the opportunity to enjoy the wealth that abounds in our time.

The prophets have understood that economic cooperation, in fact, realizes the true potential of the free enterprise system. One such was the agricultural economist Ezra Taft Benson, whose early career was spent in the agricultural cooperative system and who in the 1930s was the executive secretary of the National Council of Farmer Cooperatives. Ezra Taft Benson's biographer describes his feelings about the agricultural cooperative movement in which he spent much of his professional career by writing that "the principles basic to cooperation burned deep within Ezra. He saw them as a tool for the little man. Cooperatives, he was sure, helped the individual preserve and exercise his right of free enterprise. It was an individual's God-given right to work and have the freedom of choice."[55]

United order principles encourage equality by entrusting economic resources and possibilities to the people, not to the state or a wealthy elite. It gives the "little man," not a state bureaucrat or wealthy capitalist, the freedom to control his destiny. It gives to every child of God the freedom to make his or her own freely chosen contribution to the work of God. It was worthy of Andrew Carnegie to give away his wealth. It would have been worthier had he paid his workers a decent wage and let them have the opportunity to practice charity and philanthropy. High ideals for creating a better society led Beatrice Webb to espouse the allocation of the community's resources, through a state bureaucracy of experts, to help the disadvantaged. It is a higher ideal for society that individuals might freely so organize themselves as to enable the disadvantaged to become self-sustaining. This is the ideal of Adam Smith, a man whose name so curiously combines the names of two of the mightiest men of God, who argued that the free market was good not because it was efficient, but because it opened new possibilities for lifting the poor by providing them with wealth and means to be productive and self-reliant.[56] This is the ideal of the ancient prophet who wrote:

> Think of your brethren like unto yourselves, and be familiar with all and free with your substance, that they may be rich like unto you. (Jacob 2:17).

7

A Competence and the Conveniences of Life:

Ownership, Management, and Labor in the Modern World and the United Order

This is the spirit and aim of the United Order, and that we should endeavor to establish. We should employ our surplus means in a manner that the poor can have employment and see before them a competence and the conveniences of life, so that they may not be dependent upon their neighbors. Where is the man who wants to be dependent upon his neighbors or the Tithing Office? No! He is a man, and is the image of God, and wants to gather the means around him, by his own, individual exertions. Blessed of God, are we, who have surplus means, and we should be willing to employ those means whereby such individuals may have, as before mentioned.

Lorenzo Snow[1]

The symbol of the new industrial economy was the railroad. People had spun cloth, mined, made pottery, and sailed in trade for millennia. The First Industrial Revolution of the first half of the 1800s improved on the old means by which these activities were accomplished. However, the railroad was a thing previously unimaginable. Anyone who has observed the awe of a small child at a train or truck, or any other very big thing that goes, can perhaps guess at the impact of a mighty steam locomotive on people who had known only horse and wagon. And the great railroad called for previously unimaginable efforts. Even the largest plantation, textile factory, or sailing fleet might have employed at most a few hundred workers and usually had only a few owners. A railroad required the coordinated work of thousands to build and operate, and investment beyond even the wealthiest of individuals.

To collect the funds of numerous investors which they needed, the railroads turned to a previously rarely used legal device, the *corporation.* These collective societies had existed for hundreds of years. Corporations were creatures of the law, with a legal existence separate from their owners. They came to enjoy limited liability, which meant that their owners were not responsible for the corporation's valid debts beyond the money that they themselves had put into the venture. These strange societies were viewed with suspicion and could be chartered only by special act of the legislature. Special influence in the legislature could make or break a corporation's existence. Corporate charters were a valued perk of the politically powerful.

As the industrial economy boomed, many came to the view that these useful legal entities should not be restricted to the politically influential. States began to enact laws which provided that anyone could set up a corporation if they simply complied with certain uniform requirements and filed papers with designated state offices. A special act of the legislature was no longer necessary. Today virtually every business activity and employment in the private sector is under the auspices of a corporation. It is surprising to realize that general incorporation statutes became widely enacted and used only after the American Civil War.[2] These statutes opened possibilities of enterprise to everyone and were seen as a central element of the new industrial prosperity. Utah's territorial governor, S. A. Mann, commended the enactment of Utah's general incorporation statute in 1870 by writing to the legislature:

> The benefit arising from corporations, in the consolidation of means for the attainment of objects beyond the power of individual effort are so manifest as hardly to require, at this day, any argument to enforce the utility of such institutions. . . . Nearly all works of a public nature require the expenditure of large amounts of money, and while individuals may be induced, by public spirit or the hope of gain, to invest a portion of their means, few are found who are willing to embark all their capital in an enterprise, the management of which must, in most instances, necessarily be left to others. Through the agency of corporations, . . . all of the great works of the present are being accomplished. Through their means oceans and rivers are navigated, telegraphs are constructed, canals and irrigating ditches are dug, factories are run, mines are worked, schools and banking houses are established.[3]

Decline of Self-Employment and the Changing Nature of Work

In the new corporate industrial economy, the nature of work itself changed in important ways. In the preindustrial economy, at least in the United States, most people had been self-employed as farmers, craftsmen, or small merchants. In the economies of Ohio and Missouri of the 1830s where the Church was first reestablished, most people were farmers or small merchants. However, as industrialization progressed, larger and larger groups of organized workers came to dominate working life. In 1830, probably over two-thirds of the working population could be considered to be self-employed. However, by 1880 the rate of self-employment was under 40 percent, and by 1970, it had fallen below 10 percent.[4]

Industrialization affected work life in other ways. From the beginning of the Industrial Revolution, automation had resulted in the de-skilling and dehumanization of the workplace. Skilled craft work was replaced by routine and regimented operation of machinery. Adam Smith described the process and its results:

> In the progress of the division of labour, the employment of the far greater part of those who live by labour, that is, of the great body of the people, comes to be confined to a few very simple operations; frequently one or two. But the understandings of the greater part of men are necessarily formed by their ordinary employments. The man whose whole life is spent in performing a few simple operations . . . has no occasion to exert his understanding, or to exercise his invention in finding out expedients for removing difficulties which never occur. He naturally loses, therefore, the habit of such exertion. . . . His dexterity at his own particular trade seems in this manner, to be acquired at the expense of his intellectual, social and martial virtues. But in every improved and civilised society this is the state into which the labouring poor, that is the great body of the people, must necessarily fall, unless government takes some pains to prevent it.[5]

In the Second Industrial Revolution, the idea of "scientific management" arose. Frederick W. Taylor taught that the workers should be viewed as automatons and their work reduced to the simplest and most repetitious form possible, supposedly to increase efficiency. Taylor's view of the worker, widely shared by owners, was that he is "merely a man more or less of the type of the ox, heavy both mentally and physically."[6] Unlike Adam Smith, they did not seem to see anything wrong with this view. Another result of Taylorist industrialization was that, unlike on the farms or small businesses or shops of earlier times, work now took fathers, and often mothers also, out of the home and away from children, fundamentally changing the family experience.

The Rise of State Power

This dehumanization of work in the new industrial capitalist economy produced for many a profound sense of alienation. Capital and labor seemed permanently divided, and usually hostile. Capitalists, comfortable in their wealth and justified by Social Darwinism and their philanthropy, were content to let the system be, despite rampant corruption, vain consumption, poverty, and oppression. To those who sought reform there appeared to be only one answer: only one institution was potentially as powerful as the mighty industrial and financial capitalists. That was the state.

The socialists' constant weakness—lack of a program for the widespread implementation of their ideals—was finally addressed in the 1880s in Germany. There the autocratic "Iron Chancellor," Otto von Bismarck, had succeeded in uniting most of Germany under the rule of the emperors of Prussia. The Prussian capital, Berlin, became the center of the most powerful state on the European continent. The state had always been more important and powerful in Prussia than in the Atlantic European nations such as Britain and France. Much of industry was owned or indirectly controlled by the state. The success of the Bismarckian industrialization of Germany seemed to argue for this system. The German socialist Karl Kautsky concluded that if the government was democratically elected, and owned all of the industries, that would effectively, if indirectly, achieve the ownership by the people of the means of production—in other words, socialism. As noted in the last chapter, for most of the 20th century, democratic socialism, or social democracy, would be one of the most successful political movements in the world.[7]

Of course the socialists had always looked to the state as the solution to economic inequities. But by the turn of the century, many who would have considered being called a "red" to be worth fighting over had also turned to the state. In the United States, state intervention took the form of government regulation rather than state ownership of industry. Legislation against monopolies was first passed in 1890. Theodore Roosevelt, who became President in 1901 after William McKinlay's assassination by an anarchist, rigorously enforced these laws. Laws also limited working hours, prohibited child labor, and regulated the quality of food and drugs, insurance, alcohol, monetary policy, working conditions, labor relations, and trade practices. Moralistic capitalists such as Andrew Carnegie (a great admirer of Theodore Roosevelt) supported this trend. In 1911, Carnegie even proposed government-administered price controls: "Granted combination, there must be regulation. . . . It follows that an Industrial Court must be formed which shall fix maximum prices, that the consumer may be protected against extortion."[8]

The Democrats continued this trend after Woodrow Wilson was elected President in 1912. Between 1900 and 1916, when the United States started war mobilization, the United States government increased its number of employees by 46 percent and its budget grew by 33 percent.[9] As noted earlier, the Fabian socialists came to power in Britain at this time. In Germany, Bismarck used the state to preempt the socialists by initiating social security and other state-sponsored social welfare programs.[10] In all nations, central banks (such as the United States Federal Reserve Bank) were established and single national currencies created. With uniform currencies, the industrial economy moved from the commodity barter often used in the earlier rural economies to one in which economic transactions were almost always carried out on a cash basis.

State Power and the Great Depression. Through the beginning of the 20th century, those opposed to state economic intervention could point to the massive increase in wealth generated by industrial capitalism. However, in 1929 that wealth seemed to disappear as the entire industrial world plunged into a devastating depression. By the early 1930s, national unemployment rates in the United States reached 25 percent.

In all nations the solution appeared to be some sort of state activism. In the United States, Franklin D. Roosevelt launched the New Deal, an eclectic mixture of government relief and regulatory programs intended to pull the nation out of a depression that was beginning to appear to be far more intractable than the depressions that followed earlier Panics such as in 1873. In Germany, a new leader, Adolf Hitler, used the state to control industry and promote spending on public works and rearmament. In Russia, Lenin's successor, Stalin, created a centralized bureaucracy that mobilized the entire population in a program of rapid industrialization.[11] Stalin appeared to obtain rapid results. Many democratic socialists were impressed with the new Soviet society. The aged Sidney and Beatrice Webb (now Baron and Lady Passfield) traveled to the Soviet Union at the suggestion of their friend, playwright George Bernard

Shaw, and returned converted to the Marxist-Leninist system.[12] In 1936, the economist John Maynard Keynes introduced an economic theory that called for Adam Smith's free market to be monitored, regulated, and stimulated by the state.[13]

There were a few contrary voices. An Austrian economist, Friedrich Hayek, argued that state intervention in the economy would lead to a loss of freedom. However, Hayek, who ironically taught at the Fabians' London School of Economics and was socially friendly with the Webbs, represented the minority view.[14]

The Rise of Bureaucracy. Finally, in one of the bitter ironies that mark this temporal existence, the Great Depression was brought to an end, in the words of a prominent historian, "by Adolf Hitler with the help of a few Japanese militarists."[15] Vast wartime spending finally pulled the United States out of the Great Depression. After the Second World War, assistance from the United States in the form of aid and demand from its own prospering economy pulled the rest of the old industrial nations back. The fact that vast government wartime spending and control of the economy had finally ended the Great Depression was taken as proving the Keynesian doctrine of state economic direction. Socialist governments came to power in many nations; and even in nations without governments that identified themselves as socialist, state regulation and guidance of the economy were taken for granted. Sometimes called *dirigisme*, informal state guidance of business was widely used in successful nations such as Japan and France, which had supposedly rightist governments.

To manage the complex new industrial economy, a new phenomenon arose, soon to be far more ubiquitous than the entrepreneur. This was the *bureaucrat*. *Entrepreneur* comes from a French word meaning "to undertake, to set out on a task." *Bureaucrat* also comes from French, *bureau*, meaning "office." As the entrepreneur's task was to be out and about accomplishing things, the bureaucrat's task was to centralize and regiment operations so that they could be controlled from a headquarters office.

The Fabian and other democratic socialists saw a corps of professional government bureaucrats as the key to the operation of their socialized economy. However, increased bureaucratization was not limited to the state. In an important study published in 1933, Adolf Berle and Gardiner Means showed that the ownership and management of corporations had been separated.[16] Most large corporations were publicly held by thousands of shareholders and managed by hired executives who had little of their personal worth invested in the corporation. The days were largely gone when industry was directed by dynamic entrepreneurs like Andrew Carnegie, whose personal fortunes were tied up in the long-term success of the corporation. Instead, hired managers ran vast corporate bureaucracies.[17] Adam Smith was quite dubious about the managements of such corporations.

> The directors of such companies, however, being the managers of other people's money than of their own, it cannot be well expected, that they should watch over it with the same anxious vigilance with which the partners in a private company frequently watch over their own. . . . Negligence and profusion, therefore, must always prevail, more or less, in the management of the affairs of such a company.[18]

Even if such managers were diligent, often they saw success as being more dependent on short-term results, realized during their personal tenures in the executive suite, than on long-term growth of the corporation after their retirement. The growth of corporate bureaucracy was so extensive that it gave rise to a new field of academic study, "business administration." The master's degree offered in this field (the "M.B.A.") came to be widely sought as the primary qualification for a career as a corporate bureaucrat.

In the ultimate socialist state, the Soviet Union, state and corporate bureaucracy combined. Directed from a huge but undistinguished building on the Prospekt Marksa, a block away from Red Square, the state central planning agency, Gosplan, produced five-year plans that detailed every aspect of a continental economy. An elite corps of state bureaucrats, the *nomenklatura*, managed the economy down to the smallest detail. These *apparatchiki* were responsible only to the central state authorities and lived privileged lives, so long as they met their quotas and toadied satisfactorily to their superiors in the *nomenklatura*. This system seemed to produce enormous industrial expansion. The western nations were shocked by such technological advances as the development of the atomic bomb in the 1940s and the Soviet space program, which outstripped that of the United States in the 1950s.[19] Although by the late 1980s it had become clear that centralized management of an economy was unworkable, the institution of bureaucracy today appears to remain strong and resilient.

The Law of Stewardship, Private Property, and the Priesthood Hierarchy

How would ownership, management, and labor in our complicated modern economy function under the principles of the united order? Until recently, modern businesses and governments have been operated by highly centralized bureaucracies run in a strict, hierarchical "top-down" manner. In "top-down" management, all information, decisions, and authority are held at the top of the hierarchy. Input from farther down in the organization is discouraged and creativity is suppressed. Sometimes this management approach is even seen in the Church.[20] The influence of this approach is seen when Church members who like to think of themselves as very faithful boast that for them, "when our leaders speak, the thinking has been done."[21] When one contemplates the united order scriptures in this framework, it is logical to conceptualize the united order as a kind of Church Communism, or theocratic socialism, in which everything in a united order would be owned and controlled through the Church hierarchy and bureaucracy in Salt Lake City.

Lorenzo Snow emphatically declared that "the United Order is not *French Communism!*"[22] We can just as emphatically declare that the united order is not *Church Communism.* The first attempt at the united order in Kirtland was the establishment of a community of Saints from Colesville, New York, on a farm donated by Leman Copley. This attempt was frustrated when Copley reneged on his donation and forced the Colesville members to leave the farm. In Missouri, Bishop Partridge initially sought to deal with the problem of withdrawals by leasing rather than deeding property to the Saints. In this way the united order's property could be preserved in the event of withdrawal. However, Joseph Smith wrote him that stewards were to have legal title to and own their stewardships. Stewards were to give title to property they consecrated to the bishop, but were to retain title to property received in stewardship, even if they left the Church.

> Concerning inheritances, you are bound by the law of the Lord, to give a deed, securing to him who receives inheritances, his inheritance, for an everlasting inheritance, or in other words, to be his individual property, his private stewardship, and if he is found a transgressor and should be cut off, his inheritance is his still, and he is delivered over to the buffetings of Satan. . . . But the property which he consecrated to the poor . . . he cannot

> obtain again by the law of the Lord. Thus you see the propriety of this law, that rich men cannot have power to disinherit the poor by obtaining again that which they have consecrated.[23]

These instructions were confirmed by revelation (D&C 51:4–6). All the united orders established under Brigham Young were locally owned and managed.[24] United order surplus funds were not required to be sent to the central Church (except for tithing on behalf of order members). J. Reuben Clark, a counselor in the First Presidency from 1933 to 1961, stressed that, unlike Communism, under the united order stewardship property was privately held and controlled free of Church ownership.

> In other words, basic to the United Order was the private ownership of property, every man had his own property from which he might secure that which was necessary for the support of himself and his family. There is nothing in the revelations that would indicate that the property was not freely alienable at the will of the owner. It was not contemplated that the Church should own everything or that we should become in the Church, with reference to our property and otherwise, the same kind of automaton, manikin, that communism makes out of the individual, with the State standing at the head in place of the Church.[25]

Much confusion about the united order derives from the scriptures which place a bishop in a management role. From the beginning of the Church to the 1870s, the role of the bishop evolved from that of a paid business manager affiliated with an entire stake, to that of an unpaid leader of a congregation.[26] In Nauvoo, bishops first came to be assigned to the city political subdivisions called wards. In Utah these became the basic congregational units of the Church, and the bishop became their unpaid lay leader. By 1859, Brigham Young told the *New York Tribune* that "no Bishop, no Elder, no Deacon, or other church officer receives any compensation for his official services." They live "by the labor of their own hands, like the first Apostles. . . . We think a man who cannot make his living aside from the Ministry of Christ unsuited to that office."[27] By the 1870s, bishops often were unable to supply adequate management for the united orders because of other extensive demands upon them.[28] Therefore, management of the Utah united orders was often not the local Church priesthood leadership.[29]

Without reference to the priesthood authorities, Brigham Young and his colleagues emphasized that competent business management was a prerequisite for any successful united order. In his last general conference (after noting that the united order was not just dividing assets up equally), Brigham said that the united order was to "let those who possess the ability and wisdom direct the labors of those not so endowed, until they too develop the talents within them and in time acquire the same degree of ability."[30] Even though the priesthood authorities were fully organized with himself at the head, Brigham expressed the view that adequate management was often unavailable for the united orders and therefore declined to participate in them personally.[31]

Although the classic Doctrine and Covenants united order revealed to the rural Saints in the 1830s seemed to contemplate management by a priesthood officer, by the industrialized 1870s it was recognized that the bishop's role in the united order would be as a spiritual teacher of correct principles, while temporal management would be vested in others with the necessary technical, entrepreneurial, and business leadership skills. The united order was not to replace competent managers with whoever happened to be the presiding priesthood officer, but rather to persuade able businessmen to devote their talents to the economic building of Zion.

A closer analysis shows that the united order revelations always contemplated that the united order was to be a self-governing body independent of central Church management control. The revelations state that management of the united order is to be by common consent (D&C 51:12; 104:21, 71). Although priesthood-based management of the Church theoretically also operates pursuant to the law of common consent, in the united order management by common consent operates on a different basis than in the priesthood. The Doctrine and Covenants indicates that the managing agent of the "bishop's" storehouse was not necessarily the bishop (D&C 70:11). The revelations provide that united order management can be *replaced* by voice of the order, whereas priesthood leaders are only *sustained* by the vote of members and can only be replaced by higher priesthood authorities (D&C 104:76–77). The specific provisions relating to control of storehouse disbursements also show the distinction between priesthood leadership authority and the management of the united order. The Doctrine and Covenants states that disbursements from the united order storehouse are by the voice and common consent of the order (D&C 104:71). In contrast, the revelation on disbursement of tithing funds gives disbursement authority to the priesthood leadership without any reference to common consent (D&C 120).

The Law of Stewardship, Freedom, and the Corporate Economy

Even if the united order is to be independent of Church ownership and control, the problem remains of reconciling the united order principle of independent, privately owned stewardships with the need for larger group organization of enterprises in the modern economy. As discussed earlier, in frontier Ohio or Missouri, most people were self-employed, and the deed of some land for farming or the wherewithal to start a small business was sufficient to enable a family to support itself. In the modern economy, where opportunities for self-employment are limited and most earn their living by working in a larger organization, the concept of simply deeding some property as in the classic Doctrine & Covenants united order is largely inapplicable. As early as the 1870s, Brigham Young and other Church leaders knew that establishing an industrialized united order in the desert could not be carried out by individual efforts as in Missouri and Ohio. Apostle Orson Pratt observed:

> I do not know that the common stock operation which God commanded us to enter into in Jackson County will be suitable in the year 1874. . . . I do not know but here in Utah it may be necessary to vary materially from the principles that were commanded to be observed in Jackson County. . . . [There] every man got his stewardship, and he occupied it. . . . Here we have to labor under other circumstances. . . . Can one individual do as well as a hundred, at mining? It may require the experience of a vast amount of labor in order to develop the resources of these mountains, and in that case co-operation will be absolutely necessary.[32]

In the economy of the Second Industrial Revolution of the 1870s, Brigham Young and his colleagues addressed the matter by encouraging larger cooperative enterprises which were legally incorporated, taking advantage of Utah's then newfangled general incorporation statute. They encouraged the incorporation of all the united orders.[33] At a time when many great industrial concerns, such as Andrew Carnegie's growing steelworks, were still operated as old-fashioned partnerships, even the communalistic united order of Orderville was organized as a company incorporated under the Utah general corporation law, legal kith and kin to WordPerfect or Geneva Steel. In urging the united orders to become corporations, Brigham and the apostles sought greater legal security in the context of the new economy. Corporations also permitted a much wider shareownership than would have been possible with older legal forms of doing business, such as partnerships, joint stock companies, or individual proprietorships.

These corporations were always locally owned, usually by the participants in the united order enterprise. The central Church headquarters in Salt Lake City never owned any stock in the united order corporations and never claimed any formal management authority over them. In fact, the united orders and their members continued to pay tithing to support the Church and its activities. They were intended to be managed and controlled as corporations. When asked whether management was subject to local control or to President Brigham Young, Brigham replied that, with regard to temporal matters, the articles of incorporation clearly indicated that the management was subject to the approval or disapproval of the shareholders, and not Church leaders.[34] Thus the united order principle of independent stewardship was observed. Some recalled that under Joseph Smith, stewardships had been held as individual private property, and they questioned how the law of stewardship was preserved in these larger united order corporations. John Taylor addressed this issue at the October 1874 conference, explaining that the nature of the united order stewardship had changed to function in the new industrial economy, and now

> the voice you have in selecting your officers, and in voting for them and the stock you hold in these institutions is your stewardship. You may say—"Is not that taking away our freedom?" I do not think it is. . . . One-third, perhaps one-half, of the wealth of the world is manipulated just in the same way. . . . We have telegraph, mercantile, manufacturing and cooperative associations, which are represented by those who hold stock therein, and there are hundreds and thousands of millions of dollars throughout the world that are operated in this way by financiers, statesmen, men of intelligence—merchants, capitalists and others, in every grade and condition in life, none of whom consider that there is any coercion associated with it. These men all have their free agency.[35]

The Law of Stewardship and Equality—Employee Ownership

Setting up a united order effort as a shareholder-controlled corporation complies with the stewardship requirement that property should be privately held, independent of Church control, while permitting it to operate in an economy in which opportunities for single-family enterprise are limited. However, showing that the united order is not Church Communism or theocratic socialism does not complete the analysis. The united order must also promote equality. The Utah united orders tried to accomplish this through broad stock ownership in the community. However, these companies all gradually came into the ownership of small groups of shareholders, and Utah's economy became dependent on the larger national economy.[36] When the Church's Welfare Program was established, it still operated principally within the framework of an agrarian and self-employed economy. However, an apostle of that time saw clearly that these united order principles could be accommodated to a modern economy in which there were increasingly varied forms of livelihood and in which most were not self-employed. In his description of the united order, John A. Widtsoe explained that

> each member would receive a sufficient portion, called an "inheritance," from the common treasury, to enable him to continue in his trade, business or profession as he may desire. The farmer would receive land and implements; the tradesman, tools and materials, the merchant, the necessary capital, the professional man, instruments, books, etc. Members who work for others would receive proportionate interests in the enterprises they serve. No one would be without property—all would have an inheritance.[37]

Receiving "proportionate interests in the enterprises" where one works is usually referred to today as "employee ownership." The use of employee ownership as a way to implement united order principles applies to the majority of workers in the modern economy who work for corporations. It preserves private property, since corporations remain owned by employee shareholders, as opposed to ownership by a state or church bureaucracy. It promotes equality by broadly distributing the principal source of wealth in our society, ownership of capital stock. Elder Widtsoe's insight is also relevant because employee ownership is an application of the united order revelations which need not await the full restoration of the united order to be implemented. Elsewhere, he said that the united order "today has a practical value as an ideal by which any proposed economic system may be tested. . . . The

Apostle John A. Widtsoe (1872–1952), educator, scientist, and proponent of gospel economic principles in the early 20th century.

nearer any scheme for economic betterment conforms to the principles of the United Order, the more likely it will be to assist mankind."[38] Employee ownership meets this test.

Various forms of employee ownership are already very common in the United States and have benefitted from legal incentives which make them worthwhile temporally as well as spiritually. In the United States, over 12 million employees participate in Employee Stock Ownership Plans ("ESOPs"). As of this writing, in the United States ESOPs and other forms of employee equity participation own almost 6 percent of the total market value of all public companies. Such well-known and varied companies as Avis, Procter & Gamble, Phillips Petroleum, McDonnell Douglas, Rockwell International, E-Systems, Polaroid, Apple Computer, Merrill Lynch, Morgan Stanley, Arthur D. Little, the Kroger and Publix supermarket chains, Harcourt Brace Jovanovich, Hallmark Cards, Swank, Lilian Vernon, many airlines, and the Zions National Bancorporation have substantial employee ownership.[39] Considerable national attention has been devoted to the 1994 employee acquisition of United Airlines. Sam Walton called WalMart's employee stock ownership profit sharing plan "the single best thing we ever did." The plan now owns WalMart stock worth almost $2 billion.[40] Employee ownership is found throughout the industrial world and is a key focus of the massive privatization efforts now underway in the former Communist nations.[41]

Extensive employee ownership was advocated by such capitalist icons as Andrew Carnegie and Leland Stanford. After he sold out to United States Steel, Carnegie wrote that, while labor had made progress, "it cannot be claimed that conditions are satisfactory as they exist. In the future, Labor is to rise still higher. The joint-stock form[42] opens the door to the participation of Labor as shareholders in every branch of business. In this, the writer believes, lies the final and enduring solution of the Labor question." Leland Stanford, founder of the Central Pacific Railroad and Stanford University and Republican governor and U.S. Senator from California, said that labor "can and will become its own employer through cooperative associations. . . . What I believe is, the time has come when the laboring men can perform for themselves the office of becoming their own employers; that the employer class is less indispensable in the modern organization of industries. . . . Laboring men possess sufficient intelligence . . . to enjoy the entire benefits of their own labor."[43]

Of course, employee ownership is far from being the entirety of the united order or the law of consecration and stewardship, a celestial law that embraces the entire gospel. What this does show is that one can reconcile the united order principles of equality and individual private property in the context of the modern industrial economy by a method foreshadowed over a century ago in revelations of God and their implementation by prophets and apostles. There now exists a well-established means by which we can implement some of the principles of the united order in our current modern economy. And, this is not the only way in which the modern united order revelations are readily applicable to the modern economy.

8

All the Capital That Is Necessary:
Finance in the Modern World and the United Order

Men who are familiar with every branch of industry almost that can be named are in these mountains. But we have not capital; yet by combining our means we can obtain all the capital that is necessary, . . . and instead of seeing men walking around with their hands in their pockets, because of not having work, there would not be an idle man in the Territory. For any portion of our people to be idle is wrong, and there is something radically wrong about a system that admits of or has a tendency to keep a portion of the community in idleness.

George Q. Cannon[1]

Funds for investment are the lifeblood of an industrial economy. In the beginning of the modern economy, bankers had largely lent to princes. However, by the 19th century the financing of industry was seen as a legitimate way to invest funds. The Industrial Revolution would never have progressed beyond its earliest stages without the activities of financial institutions.

As the economy changed from one based on bartering goods to exchanges using cash, money not needed for immediate consumption was lent to bankers who would pay a rent, referred to as interest, for the use of the money. By accumulating such loans from many people, banks could aggregate substantial sums of money. These in turn could be lent to businesses for use in building and operating factories, stores, farms, railroads, and all other aspects of the modern economy. By charging a higher interest on these outgoing loans than they paid on their depositors' incoming loans, banks would make money to pay their costs and, ideally, provide a profit.

As the Industrial Revolution progressed, banks and capital markets grew rapidly in wealth and influence. "Finance" capitalism became as important as industrial capitalism. At the end of the American Civil War, 40 percent of the money in the United States was deposited in banks. By the early 1900s, over 90 percent of America's money was held in banks, which now decided how the nation's money was to be invested. A parallel method of raising money was the creation of stock exchanges, where companies could issue shares in their ownership, which were then traded by speculators. In these wild and unregulated stock markets insider trading and price manipulation (illegal today) were the norm. Indeed, the New York Stock Exchange of the 1880s probably bore a strong resemblance to the Utah penny stock market of the 1980s. Powerful banks and other financial institutions developed throughout the industrialized world.[2]

Throughout the 1800s, the influence and power of the finance capitalists grew. The Carnegie steel empire, for example, began with funding arranged by Junius Morgan. His son, Junius Pierpont, came to epitomize the finance capitalist. J. P. Morgan was never an enthusiast for free market competition, not because he loved the working man, but rather because he saw cutthroat competition as potentially disruptive to the orderly repayment of the loans and bonds which he had underwritten. To eliminate this competition, Morgan sponsored the creation of monopolies. At the turn of the century, he sponsored a wave of mergers that make the takeover mania of the 1980s seem minor.[3] One of his greatest coups came in 1901, when Andrew Carnegie agreed to sell his steel conglomerate. It was combined with the other major steel companies to make United States Steel. At a time when a steel worker made less than three dollars a day, Carnegie's share of the selling price was $225,000,000, in *1901* dollars.[4] It was an eventful day indeed when the self-made son of a poor, radical Scots weaver could become one of the world's richest men. However, the passage of control of America's steel industry from its leading industrial capitalist to its leading finance capitalist also symbolized the rising preeminence of those who controlled the industrial world's capital.

Taxation

One reaction to the expanding power of monopolistic industrial and finance capitalism was the expansion of the power of the state. Many countries adopted a program of direct socialism, in which the state owned or controlled industry and banks. In others, the state indirectly controlled the economy through regulation and social programs. In either case the state also needed funds. Governments were often seen as good credit risks and could borrow money from private banks. However, the modern nation-state has available a less expensive (to it) way of obtaining funds. Consequently, with the significant growth of the state beginning with the early 20th century, there also began a significant growth in taxation. When the modern American income tax was first enacted in 1913, the tax rate went from 1 percent to 6 percent on income over $500,000 a year (in *1913* dollars). Even at the height of the First World War, only about 8 percent of the entire population was subject to any income tax.[5] Today, of course, no adult reader of this book need be reminded of current coverage and rates of income taxation.

Financing the United Order

The Kirtland Safety Society. The united order and other Church economic efforts of the 1830s quickly confronted the rapid changes in America's economy. The old agricultural economy, which extensively used trade and barter for exchange, diminished with the increased use of cash for commercial transactions. There was a constant need for currency in the expanding, increasingly complex and cash-based economy. This need was served through money issued by local banks, since there was no national currency. In January 1837, Joseph Smith and other prominent Church members sought to establish their own bank in order to issue currency to serve the Kirtland economy, the Kirtland Safety Society Bank. Unfortunately, the Ohio state legislature had just passed into the hands of a political group which refused to grant new bank charters. Joseph then proceeded to issue currency from the "Kirtland Safety Society Anti-banking Company." The "anti-bank" was a failure. Its currency lost value. Later in 1837, a nationwide bank panic struck, sealing its doom.[6] Many leading Church members in Ohio apostatized, and Joseph had to flee from Kirtland.

Finance and the Utah United Orders. When the united order movement of the 1870s was launched, the problem of achieving successful commercial and financial interaction with the larger economy was again addressed. Apostle Erastus Snow asked, "Will our trading and trafficking with the outside world cease? Of course not. As long as we are in the world, gathering Saints, preaching to the nations and building up Zion, Zion will be as a city set on a hill, which can not be hid." However, individual Saints, confronted by the growing strength of corporate industrial and finance capitalism, would be unable to compete for income or investment, or resist "the influences of Babylon." Apostle Snow urged cooperative marketing efforts so

> instead of giving the profits to middlemen who are not of us, what we have for sale we will sell in the best markets. . . . By this combined effort we shall be able to obtain full market value of our products—the products of the farm, dairy, orchard, vineyard, the products of the woolen and cotton factory, and of our shoe shops, and every mechanical appliance, to enable us to procure all labor-saving machinery by our combined efforts, which men in their individual capacities are not able to do. We shall also be enabled to start new enterprises, and if they do not pay at first they are bound to pay in the end, if they are necessary adjuncts to the prosperity of society. Our common fund will nourish these infant establishments, instead of individuals failing and breaking down in their vain efforts to build up new enterprises in a new country, as is often the case now. And if funds are needed from abroad to aid us in any general enterprise, we shall have the combined property and credit of the community as a guarantee to capitalists abroad, instead of individuals mortgaging their inheritances to procure money to carry on individual "wild-cat" speculations by which thousands are ruined.[7]

However, this vision of a "common fund" to "nourish . . . infant establishments" and secure credit on advantageous terms from "capitalists abroad" was never implemented. Perhaps the hesitation was due to the Church's unfortunate experience with the Kirtland Safety Society's "anti-bank." The Bank of Deseret, predecessor to Zions National Bancorporation, was founded in 1871 with Church participation. However, it did not lend significantly to the united orders.[8]

The Bishop's Storehouses. In an 1831 revelation, the Lord instructed the united order managing bishop to "appoint a storehouse unto this church; and let all things both in money and in meat, which are more than is needful for the wants of this people, be kept in the hands of the bishop" (D&C 51:13). Bishop's storehouses were formed to supply food in emergency situations. However, according to the Doctrine and Covenants, the united order storehouse was to care for the poor by providing them with stewardships—permanent income-producing situations (see D&C 51:3–6). To some extent, the Church used the tithing system to fulfill this function.

Since most tithing was paid in kind or in labor, it remained at the local level rather than being sent to Church headquarters. These resources, as well as those sent to the central Church tithing office, were used for economic development as well as "religious" activities. It was considered as appropriate and spiritual to devote the tithing resources to repairing the irrigation ditches or building a needed blacksmith shop as it was to building a church or paying the stake clerk. However, the tithing resources were controlled by priesthood authorities rather than by members of the united orders and were generally spent on Church-directed community projects, not on setting individual members up in privately owned livelihoods.

The Storehouse in the United Order

The revelations on the united order commanded that the surplus residue of the people was to be placed in the storehouse, or treasury. There it is used to "administer to the poor and needy" so "that every man who has need may be amply supplied and receive according to his wants" (D&C 42:34, 33). However, the storehouse is more than a welfare fund. "Zion must increase in beauty, and in holiness; her borders must be enlarged; her stakes must be strengthened." To this end, in the storehouse

> you are to be equal, or in other words, you are to have equal claims on the properties, for the benefit of managing the concerns of your stewardships, every man according to his wants and his needs, inasmuch as his wants are just—and all this for the benefit of the church of the living God, that every man may improve upon his talent, that every man may gain other talents, yea even an hundredfold, to be cast into the Lord's storehouse, to become the common property of the whole church—every man seeking the interest of his neighbor, and doing all things with an eye single to the glory of God. (D&C 82:14, 17–19)

The storehouse resources are not only to be available for relieving poverty, but also for "managing the concerns of your stewardships," so that they could increase "even an hundredfold." In modern terminology, the storehouse is to provide investment and working capital for the stewardships. Investment capital as well as wheat storage was to be the business of the storehouse. Surpluses received from the stewardships "by improving upon the properties which I have appointed unto you, in houses, or in lands, or in cattle

. . . shall be cast into the treasury as fast as you receive moneys, by hundreds, or by fifties, or by twenties, or by tens, or by fives" (D&C 104:68–69). The storehouse took in cash as well as commodities (hundreds, fifties, or fives were worth much more in 1834 than today). These funds were then to be made available "by the voice and common consent of the order" to an individual steward "to help him in his stewardship" (D&C 104:71–73).

In discussing these scriptures, Lorenzo Snow observed, "We can easily conceive, that with a vast population of Saints acting under this celestial law, there would be an immense treasury filled after a time; and that . . . would be a pillar of financial strength, a sublime picture of holy union and fraternity, and equal to the most extreme emergencies." The purposes of such an institution would be to fulfill the purposes of the united order:

> Now, were the Saints all acting in the spirit of these revelations, what a happy community it would be! We would all be safe, and no man would need remain awake at night thinking what he should do for his family to keep them from begging their bread, or going to the Bishop, which is perhaps only one degree better. And there would be a union that would be in accordance with the union of Enoch and his people, when they were taken to the world above—a union pleasing to the Almighty, and according to the principles of the celestial world.[9]

The Storehouse and Modern Finance. As noted earlier, Lorenzo's cousin, apostle Erastus Snow, explained that the united order "designs to make the interests of capital and labor identical. . . . The combination of capital and labor in this order will enable us to promote all branches of industry which shall appear, in the judgement of the common Order, to be for the general good." The united order funds would "enable us to procure all labor-saving machinery" and "start new enterprises." This "common fund will nourish these infant establishments," and combine the "property and credit of the community as a guarantee to capitalists abroad" if outside funds are needed, "instead of individuals mortgaging their inheritances" and "breaking down in their vain efforts to build up new enterprises."[10]

The united order storehouse would thus concentrate the community's surplus assets to develop job-producing businesses. Further, by funding many enterprises from a common fund, the storehouse spreads and dilutes the risk from failure of individual enterprises. In other words, it would fulfill the function which is generally played in a free market economy by banks and other financial institutions. This is one of the most significant ways in which the modern united order revelations differ from ancient revelations on economic righteousness. In ancient economies, institutionalized moneylending for economic investment and development did not exist; the only way to achieve the righteous principles of charity and equality was to redistribute wealth from the rich to the poor through giving alms or the more elaborate redistributions prescribed by the law of Moses.

With the rise of the industrial market economy, a new possibility appeared. By combining the resources of many people, banks, brokers, and other financiers provide capital for economic development. This pooling and reinvestment of society's wealth in developing many new enterprises produces new productive wealth and jobs. Charity can for the first time be combined with self-reliance. Instead of charity consisting of the wealthy handing back to the poor part of a static, limited amount of wealth, often accumulated in the first place by oppressing the poor, new productive wealth can be created that may permit the poor to become self-supporting. The human economy does not need to be a 'zero-sum' system, in which your gain is my loss. Rather, we now have the possibility of both gaining together. While modern finance capitalism hardly arose with this objective as its main purpose, it has imperfectly and partially achieved this result in many free market nations.

Modern Revelation and Modern Finance. At a time when this role for banks and finance was only just beginning to be understood, God gave new revelations which added to the scriptural description of the celestial economic order an institution, the united order storehouse or treasury, which succinctly incorporated the functions of banking and other financing institutions. These have permitted the modern industrial economy to proffer, for the first time in human history, the hope that grinding poverty need not be the lifestyle of the vast majority of humanity. With one exception (described in chapter 19), for all that modern reformers of many different philosophies have struggled with the challenge of poverty in our times, no one has systematically recognized that the functions of modern finance capitalism could be harnessed to overcome this challenge of the ages. Yet in a few verses, given at the time of modern market finance's infancy, God outlined what is essentially a sacred commercial and investment banking system, which holds the as-yet-unrealized promise of converting the dynamism of the modern market economy to the divine purposes of eliminating poverty and inequality.

These astonishing scriptures serve as a striking example of the restored gospel's argument for the necessity of continuing revelation. However, like other aspects of the united order, the storehouse, or treasury as it is sometimes called, is not a mere variation on a worldly institution. Although it would serve the same functions as a bank, a united order inspired financial institution would operate on celestial principles. Modern scripture teaches that it is the united order storehouse or treasury and its activities, not the large personal fortunes of Church members, which are to make it possible "that the church may stand independent above all other creatures beneath the celestial world" (see D&C 78:3–14). The purpose of the united order treasury would be to establish all united order participants as self-reliant stewards, who can then advance the building of Zion.[11]

For a traditional bank, the largest concern is usually whether the loan can be secured by some kind of hard assets. In the united order, creation of productive jobs would be the principal criterion for investment decisions. Given a choice between extending funds to two businesses, say a new factory and a real estate speculation, a financial institution operating on united order principles would choose the job-producing factory, even if theoretical investment criteria suggested a larger, or even more secure, return on the real estate. This is not a theoretical issue. Banks today often do not seem to understand or care that most job growth in the modern economy comes from sectors, such as high technology, service and small business, which by their nature do not generate the land, plant, or equipment which bankers have traditionally used as loan collateral.

Some would perhaps argue that the two are not contradictory, that having hard assets for security is the best criterion for judging whether a loan will produce productive jobs. While this may be valid in theory, in practice bankers' preference for hard assets as security has tended to steer them toward investing in often quite speculative real estate instead of job-producing businesses. Too often a bank will lend to a real estate speculator buying a useless office building because there is a seemingly hard asset, and yet ignore a growing, profitable, job-producing software concern even if it has good operating results and proven prospects and reputation.[12] While it is perhaps 20-20 hindsight, few could argue that the American savings and loan industry's funds in the 1980s would have been far better invested in job-producing small businesses and modernization of the United States' manufacturing plant, rather than unnecessary hotels, office buildings, and junk bonds.[13]

Of course, many would argue that the vast funds produced by state taxation have not been any better employed. This debate has been at the center of modern politics for two centuries. The wealth of our modern age has changed the direction of human endeavor, as human thought and emotion have been seized by the great contending ideologies of capitalism and socialism. Our time has been swept by this ideological struggle to find a way to combine the interests of capital and labor in order to realize the epoch-making potential of the Second Economic Revolution. In this area yet again, the principles of the united order can enable us to approach our revolutionary times with clear thinking and sound judgment.

9

A Revolutionary Period:
Capitalism, Socialism, and the United Order in the Modern World

We are living in what may well prove to be the most epoch-making period of all time. There is ample evidence on every hand that we are witnessing one of those tidal waves of human thought and emotion which periodically sweep over the world and change the direction of human endeavor. It is a time that demands clear thinking and sound judgement. Whether we are willing to admit it or not, this is a revolutionary period.

David O. McKay[1]

In 1776, Adam Smith published *The Wealth of Nations,* James Watt patented his steam engine, and the American Declaration of Independence was issued. In 1789, the year before Adam Smith's death, the royal French government fell, driven into insolvency in part by its financial support of the Americans. The French Revolution, the Industrial Revolution, and the revolutionary rise of the market economy were all to assure that the world of the dispensation of the fullness of times would be an age of revolutions.

In the National Assembly of revolutionary France, radical delegates from the cities took to sitting on the left of the chamber of deputies, and more conservative delegates from rural areas sat on the right. Previously, men had fought for king, country, or money, and sometimes for good measure, God. Now men began to fight for ideas—ideas that were increasingly forced to fit into a straight-line, two-dimensional continuum which went from left to right, like the hall of the French chamber of deputies. What they fought about was mostly control of the rising power of the nation-state. The years 1830 and 1848, significant in Church history, saw revolutions in Europe. Born less than two decades after the French Revolution, Wilford Woodruff was to die less than two decades before the Russian Revolution.

In the late 1800s, Karl Marx came to be identified as the pre-eminent socialist thinker. During the 1860s, he published his massive *Das Kapital.* In it he analyzed and critiqued the workings of the new industrial economy, which now began to be known as *capitalism.*[2] The ideas of this dour, unpleasant man began to achieve wide acquaintance among socialists. Aided by Friedrich Engels, Marx argued that capitalism would collapse of its own success, as competition forced owners to constantly drive down wages, thereby impoverishing and radicalizing the workers. Engels carried on Marx's ideas after Marx's death in 1883. In the 20th century, variations of Marxist socialism came to dominate the majority of humankind. By 1966, apostle Marion G. Romney would tell BYU students that "notwithstanding my abhorrence of it, I am persuaded that socialism is the wave of the present and of the foreseeable future. It has already taken over or is contending for control in most nations."[3]

Certainly one of the most, if not *the* most dramatic events of our time has been the rapid collapse of European Communist governments.[4] The last decade of this century has seen the failure of systems based on state economic control. The fall of the Berlin Wall was unforeseen by any pundit, political scientist, or policy maker. Only a prophet's call for prayers that all nations might be open to the gospel might have predicted such events. Now that Spencer W. Kimball's (and Joseph's and Brigham's) vision of spreading Zion throughout the world is beginning to be realized, we can no longer say (if we ever could) that "all is well in Zion," for, as seen in chapter 2, all is definitely not well in the world. The decline of socialism alone has not ushered in the millennial day.

During the days of the struggle against Communism, Ezra Taft Benson wrote that "amid the encircling gloom, the kindly light of the Lord can lead us on—can help expose and stop evil in some places, slow it down in others, give the forces of freedom the chance to become better entrenched, provide righteous alternatives, and develop faith and hope to keep on keeping on."[5] Part of the battle to promote freedom is to "provide righteous alternatives."

In the affairs of humankind, as in the affairs of nature, a vacuum will be filled. The victory over Communism is so far a negative one. As the Communists always predicted for capitalism, Communism collapsed of its own internal contradictions, not because its peoples were converted to democratic capitalism. Central managers could not know local economic conditions, consumer preferences or

Drawing of a young Karl Marx (1818–1883), German critic of capitalism. Through works such as The Communist Manifesto *and* Das Kapital, *he sought to launch a global Communist revolution to counter the excesses of the new industrial economy.*

make an efficient allocation of resources. In the end it was the failure of the promise of the Industrial Revolution that brought down Communism. Freedom will only truly triumph when the victory is positive, when a system based on freedom and justice is solidly established in the modern world that will improve the lives of Natasha Stukalov and her neighbors. Already, former Communists have been voted back into power in a number of eastern European nations, and the rapid rise of organized crime has caused many to associate it with the coming of capitalism and democracy.[6] The fall of Communism has not replaced the modern world's obsession with the Left vs. Right frame of thinking about political, economic, and social problems. The world now needs alternatives based on righteous principles, not ideological straitjackets.

Is capitalism that righteous alternative? In general, free markets appear to be the most efficient economic arrangement and preferable to those based on state power. However, as seen in chapter 2, modern capitalism is hardly ideal. In the beginning, Adam Smith observed that merchants "have generally an interest to deceive and even oppress the public, and . . . accordingly have, upon many occasions, both deceived and oppressed it."[7] Nor are the sentiments of ruthless social darwinist competition absent from modern business. Multi-billionaire Bill Gates of Microsoft once said of a competitor "I mean I really hate this guy. This guy—you know, if it is not rape, if it is not waking up with AIDS. This guy is such an _______."[8] Is there a more righteous alternative to the great modern ideologies?

The Prophets Look at the Modern Ideologies

Scriptures teach by putting true doctrine in the context of righteous living. They tell the stories of the struggles of righteous—and wicked—people in real life. Doctrine is of little value unless we see it applied in real world settings. To us the times of Abraham Lincoln and Robert E. Lee, of cowboys and Indians and the Wild West, of Teddy Roosevelt and the Rough Riders seem quite distant. Yet, their economy was our economy. The year 1830 is as good a date as any for the take-off of the industrial, technological world economy that we live in today. Every time a coach tells his team that "winning is not the most important thing, it is the only thing," he echoes Herbert Spencer as well as Vince Lombardi. Every time a business student is urged to aggressively seek the lowest possible cost per unit, including the lowest possible labor costs, and to be proud of the wealth thus obtained if he leads a moral and generous personal life, he embarks on a path long since beaten out by Andrew Carnegie. Every time one's instinctive reaction on hearing of a new grievous social problem is "Why doesn't the government do something about this?" one is proving how successful Beatrice Webb and her fellow Fabians were at permeating not only the ruling elite, but our very way of thinking. Although their names may be forgotten today, this time was the beginning of the economy in which we now live. And these beginnings were observed at firsthand by apostles and prophets. An important legacy of the Church's economic endeavors of the 19th century was the insights left for us by the heroic first generation of the Saints in this dispensation.

Joseph Smith and the Modern Economy. Although he did not travel to Europe, the first prophet of the modern world was familiar with the issues presented by the modern industrial economy. His efforts to build Zion took full account of the larger world of his time. This is illustrated by two speeches made in 1843, the last full year of the Prophet's life.

In September 1843, Robert Owen's chief associate, John Finch, came to Nauvoo to lecture on "English socialism." He spoke for two days from a wagon in front of the temple construction site. John Taylor and Joseph introduced him and served as respondents. After hearing Joseph's commonsensical and down-to-earth views, the idealistic Finch proclaimed, "I am the spiritual Prophet—Mr. Smith the temporal." Joseph recalled his observation of Sidney Rigdon's communal "Family" at Kirtland and said that all he saw was a situation where "the big fish eat up the little"—as concise a critique of a command economy as one could ask for. Joseph indicated that he did not believe the doctrine of socialism as propounded by Finch.[9] A week later Joseph spoke on the matter again, reiterating the united order principle that "every one is steward over his own."[10]

Finch had good reason to appreciate Joseph's economic thinking, for Finch's visit to America was occasioned by his need to recuperate after leading failed efforts to create communities in Britain based on Owen's teachings. A successful Liverpool merchant, Finch had stepped in and undertaken the thankless task of actually administering utopia. Unlike the agnostic Owen, Finch was a devout Unitarian and had been so active in the temperance movement that he was dubbed the "king of the teetotallers." One can imagine that he and Joseph had much to compare of their experiences. Although they differed in their philosophies, the discussion was apparently a cordial one; Willard Richards' official journal says that "Joseph spoke and Finch replied &c. All pleasantly."[11]

Although he rejected the impractical utopian socialism of Owen, Joseph Smith, like Adam Smith, saw private economic activity as justified by its service to the prosperity of the entire community, not individual enrichment. In Nauvoo, Joseph denounced speculative ventures by the more prosperous in the community and taught them that the correct use of their wealth was to build up the poor and foster community-based enterprises. Wilford Woodruff recorded that Joseph

> prophesied in the name of the Lord, concerning the merchants in the city, that if they and the rich did not open their hearts and contribute to the poor, they would be cursed by the hand of God, and cut off from the land of the living. The main part of the day was taken up upon the business of the Agricultural and Manufacturing Society. We have a charter granted us by the legislature of the state for that purpose and the time has come for us to make use of that charter.[12]

As noted in chapter 3, the Nauvoo Agricultural and Manufacturing Society was a corporation intended to raise money to start businesses "with a view of helping the poor."[13]

For Joseph, the history of worldly systems and organizations only showed that "man's strength is weakness, his wisdom is folly, his glory is his shame. Monarchial, aristocratical and republican governments of their various kinds and grades have, in their turn, been raised to dignity, and prostrated in the dust. . . . Nation has succeeded nation, and we have inherited nothing but their folly. History records their puerile plans, their short-lived glory, their feeble intellect and their ignoble deeds. . . . Where is there a kingdom or nation that can promote the universal happiness of its own subjects, or even their general well-being?" This hard analysis applied even to the United States

> which possesses greater resources than any other, is rent, from center to circumference, with party strife, political intrigues and sectional interest; our counselors are panic stricken, our legislators are astonished, and our senators are confounded, our merchants are paralyzed, our tradesmen are disheartened, our mechanics out of employ, our farmers distressed, and our poor crying for bread, our banks are broken, our credit ruined, and our states overwhelmed in debt, yet we are, and have been in peace.

God's designs, "on the other hand, have been to promote the universal good of the universal world . . . to bring about a state of things that shall unite man to his fellow man; cause the world to "beat their swords into plowshares, and their spears into pruning hooks," make the nations of the earth to dwell in peace, and to bring about the millennial glory."[14]

Socialism. Is socialism the way to bring about this universal good? The united order and related gospel teachings on economic matters cannot remotely be construed as socialistic. Every 19th-century prophet from Joseph Smith to Lorenzo Snow was clear on this. Joseph Smith was familiar with the utopian religious groups, such as the Shakers, who filled his environment. After John Finch lectured at Nauvoo on Owenite socialism, Joseph indicated that he "did not believe the doctrine" and that "in Nauvoo, every one is steward over his own."[15]

Brigham Young, in one of his last conference talks, explained, "I do not wish for one moment to recognize that in order to establish the United Order our property has to be divided equally among the people."[16] In *The Government of God,* published in 1852, only four years after the *Communist Manifesto,* John Taylor made an insightful critique of socialist ideas:

> Another principle has many advocates on the Continent of Europe at the present time; a principle of Socialism. . . . Some of them discard Christianity altogether, and others leave everyone to do as they please. . . . If scepticism is to be the basis of the happiness of man, we shall be in a poor position to improve the world. . . . I have conversed with some who seem to think that all that is necessary to promote the happiness of man, is, that he have sufficient to eat and drink, . . . but if we cast our eyes abroad in the world, we shall find that unhappiness is not always associated with the poor: it revels in the church and state; among kings, potentates, princes and rulers. . . . There is another political party, who desire, through the influence of legislation and coercion, to level the world. To say the least it is a species of robbery; to some it may appear an honorable one, but nevertheless, it is robbery. . . . I cannot conceive upon what principles of justice, the children of the idle and profligate have a right to put their hands into the pockets of those who are diligent and careful, and rob them of their purse. Let this principle exist, and all energy and enterprise would be crushed.[17]

Lorenzo Snow thundered, "The United Order is not *French Communism!*"[18] In 1878, George Q. Cannon noted that at that time, "men are greatly concerned about the element known as Communism. . . . The working classes are becoming very dissatisfied, and men are trembling for fear of what will come upon the nation." Recognizing that Communism derived its appeal from the great inequalities in the larger society, he did not believe that Communism would be a concern in Utah, because "there is a more widespread ownership of the soil than you will find in any part of these United States." Utah was "a land [in] which men cannot . . . monopolize large bodies of land to the exclusion of their poorer neighbors."[19]

Capitalism. Apostle Cannon's insight on the social consequences of economic inequality was based on the oldest of prophetic teachings. Wealth, and pride in our wealth, are among the most serious stumbling blocks on the strait and narrow way. The modern prophets updated this insight to the circumstances of the modern capitalist economy. Like Adam Smith, Joseph Smith viewed the purpose of wealth as being to raise the position of the lowest levels of society. Brigham Young taught that simple profit maximization was not the only objective of economic activity and that economic rationality (charging the highest price that the market can bear) was not the only criterion by which economic decisions were to be made. Charging the highest price that the market will bear is an example of what is called *elasticity* in modern economics. Speaking in the 1875 general conference, Brigham Young offered his views on price elasticity:

> Our merchants have hearts that are too elastic, entirely too elastic; they are so elastic that they do not ask what they can afford to sell an article for, but what they can ask the people to pay; and as much as the people will pay, so much will the merchants take—a hundred, or a thousand per cent, if they can get it, and then thank God for their success. They put me in mind of some men I have seen who, when they had a chance to buy a widow's cow for ten cents on the dollar of her real value in cash, would then make the purchase, and then thank the Lord that he had so blessed them. Such men belong to the class of Christians referred to on one occasion by Charles Gunn; and, if you will excuse me, I will tell you what he said about them. He said that "hell is full of such Christians."[20]

Traditional capitalist economics holds that the primary objective of any business is profit maximization by any legal means. The unequal rewards of the free market, the "lifestyles of the rich and famous," are central to the functioning of the capitalist free market.[21] However, the Apostolic Circular issued in 1875, and signed by all members of the First Presidency and Quorum of the Twelve, saw matters differently:

> One of the great evils with which our own nation is menaced at the present time is the wonderful growth of wealth in the hands of a comparatively few individuals. The very liberties for which our fathers contended so steadfastly and courageously, and which they bequeathed to us as a priceless legacy, are endangered by the monstrous power which this accumulation of wealth gives to a few individuals and a few powerful corporations. . . . If this evil should not be checked, and measures not taken to prevent the continued growth of riches among the class already rich, and the painful increase of destitution and want among the poor, the nation is likely to be overtaken by disaster; for, according to history, such a tendency among nations once powerful was the sure precursor of ruin. The evidence of the restiveness of the people under this condition of affairs in our times is witnessed in the formation of societies of grangers, of patrons of husbandry, trades' unions, etc., etc., combinations of the productive and working classes against capital. Years ago it was perceived that we Latter-day Saints were open to the same dangers as those which beset the rest of the world. A condition of affairs existed among us which was favorable to the growth of riches in the hands of a few at the expense of many. . . . The growth of such a class was dangerous to our union. . . . Then it was that the Saints were counselled to enter into co-operation.[22]

Even though he died before it gained its widest influence, Brigham Young also saw and denounced the rise of Social Darwinism. Writing to one of his sons about the newly established Brigham Young Academy (later University) in Provo, he declared that he was "resolutely and uncompromisingly opposed to . . . introducing into the classroom the theories of Huxley, or Darwin, or of Miall and the false political economy which contends against co-operation and the United Order."[23]

The United Order in the 20th Century

However, the 19th century ignored the prophets. Social Darwinism permeated modern thinking until Herbert Spencer's "survival of the fittest" became a universal catch phrase even after its originator was forgotten. The world's response was not consecration and stewardship but Fabian socialism, which also permeated modern thought. As the Left and Right battled, state power rose inexorably throughout the 19th century. And even in its most benign form, the great American constitutional republic, the state crushed all who did not conform.

In 1890, the United States Supreme Court, in *The Late Corporation of the Mormon Church vs. United States,* upheld the Edmunds-Tucker Act, which dissolved the Church and provided for the escheatment to the government of most of the Church's property, including the temples. John Taylor had died in hiding in 1887, his body still carrying a bullet from the near fatal wounds he received at Carthage. The new prophet of the Church was Wilford Woodruff. Faced with the potential temporal destruction of the Church, the Lord made known to president Woodruff that the survival of the rest of the gospel was more important than plural marriage, and he issued the "Manifesto," which terminated its practice (D&C: Official Declaration 1). Zion began the long and difficult process of accommodating itself to the Babylon from which it had tried to flee.[24]

This process did not mean that the Church would abandon such fundamental principles as the united order. The Church still recognized an obligation to succor the poor and needy and to see to the temporal salvation of the Saints. To this end, the Church continued to devote its resources to economic development activities.[25] Since the Church was forced to abandon the goal of economic self-sufficiency, it became more important than ever to find a place for Utah in the modern American industrial economy. Mining was already controlled by non-Mormons, most of whom were quickly selling out to the big monopolies. It had been discovered that sugar beets grew well in the arid soils of the western United States. Efforts had been made to develop sugar beet processing as a source for sugar since the 1850s. The technology had at last been perfected.[26] On January 30, 1891, Wilford Woodruff wrote in his diary, "We spent this day in meeting the Presidency and Twelve. As the leaders of the people we had to shoulder the load and responsibility of the question of the manufacture of sugar. It was voted unanimously that the Church subscribe $50,000 and help in the first payment."[27]

As the depression that followed the Panic of 1893 hit Utah, the Church pursued these and other economic development activities despite its own difficult financial circumstances. Most of the owners of the assets of the old united orders now regarded them as strictly personal rather than cooperative property. The Church's other assets had deteriorated while under escheat to the government. Lorenzo Snow became the prophet after Wilford Woodruff's death in 1898 and called the Saints to a renewed commitment to the law of tithing. He and his successor, Joseph F. Smith, continued to remind the Saints that tithing was training for the united order and that devotion to this lesser law was necessary preparation for living the higher law of consecration.[28]

A Visit to the New State. Utah was granted statehood in 1896 and the process of adjustment was well under way by 1898, when Beatrice Potter Webb visited Utah again. The Webbs were studying local government and were very impressed with Utah and Salt Lake City's clean and orderly governments, especially in contrast to the wild, corrupt politics of the rest of America in the 1890s. Beatrice remarked on what the Saints had achieved in the 25 years since her first visit in 1873. She was especially pleased to be able to meet with Martha Hughes Cannon, who had just become the first woman elected to a state senate in the United States. Beatrice even expressed respect for Dr. Cannon's explanations of plural marriage, calling it "a loss to the world that the experiment of polygamy was not continued."[29]

She was given a tour of the new City and County Building by the head janitor, an English emigrant. Observing the orderly records at the County Recorder's office, she noted that "B. Young tried to instill in his people the doctrine of usufruct, e.g—that no man should possess more land than he could cultivate. But with the intrusion of gentiles with money to spare, came the mortgage, and with the mortgage the gradual accumulation of land in the hands of a few persons who held it as an investment." However, the initial broad distribution of land was sufficiently extensive that "even at the present time the occupier is usually the owner."[30] She also noted that the LDS cooperative enterprises, although still owned by Mormons, had lost their cooperative character. This confirmed her conclusions that no cooperative or worker-owned business could grow and remain a cooperative.

> Among other Mormon experiments was the great Zion Mercantile Cooperative Institution, established by B. Young to provide commodities for the Saints at cost price. Unfortunately he did not know of the Rochdale plan, and gave the profits and control to members as capitalists. The institution has therefore inevitably drifted into an ordinary Capitalist corporation.[31]

The Modern Church Welfare Program. By the beginning of the 20th century, the powerful central governments advocated by the Webbs had arisen in most nations. Industrialization had now spread throughout North America and Europe, and much of the rest of the world was ruled by the imperial industrial states or was otherwise integrated into their economic control. The first bloom of the military fruits of industrialization and strong central government seen in the American Civil War now came to full harvest in the massively efficient slaughter of the First World War. The 19th century's confidence in humankind's ability to better itself through science and industry was shaken. Andrew Carnegie had spent his last years promoting international peace. All his evolutionary optimism, personal fortune, and peace foundations had failed to prevent his steel from being beaten from ploughs into swords. He died disheartened in 1919.

The world seemed to recover from the "war to end all wars." The 1920s brought prosperity, democracy, and expanding state services to much of the industrial world. The prosperity was not universal, however. In Utah, growth in the mining and agricultural sectors brought by the First World War collapsed with the end of the war. The early apostles' fears about the consequences of a failure to develop an integrated and diversified economy in Utah were realized. With the end of the Church's economic development activities, Utah came to have a highly specialized and dependent economy and was especially vulnerable to economic reverses. In 1929, when the rest of the industrial world fell into depression, Utah had been experiencing one for several years.[32] By the early 1930s, national unemployment rates reached 25 percent. In Utah, they exceeded 30 percent and reached 50 percent in some areas.[33]

The Saints were in desperate straits. The presidents of the six Salt Lake City stakes coordinated a variety of relief efforts. One young stake president, Harold B. Lee, facing 50 percent unemployment in his stake, was especially innovative. He obtained permission to retain tithing funds in his stake for relief efforts. These were used to start farms and other simple projects to supply some necessities and work for the unemployed. Initially, most of the Saints relied on government relief, with the cooperation of the Church. In 1936, faced with cutbacks in federal relief programs, the Church adopted the stake presidents' program, and the Church Welfare Program was born.[34]

In an oft-repeated quote, Church president Heber J. Grant explained the purpose of the Church Welfare Program: "Work is to be re-enthroned as the ruling principle in the lives of our Church membership."[35] While President Grant objected to government relief to the idle, the intent of the Church Welfare Program was not to become a complete substitute for government assistance. President Grant did not object to government relief programs in which recipients worked for their assistance, such as the Civilian Conservation Corps and Works Progress Administration. He simply urged members who worked for the WPA "to labor with energy."[36] The Church Welfare Program was oriented to temporary relief measures. Its focus was supplying commodities to the needy, rather than establishing self-sustaining enterprises, as in the Church's united order and other 19th-century economic development programs.

The Church Welfare Program grew quickly. Over 450 projects were begun within weeks of its inception. The Beehive Clothing Mills were opened in 1937, Deseret Industries was started in 1938, and the Welfare Square complex in Salt Lake City was built in 1940.[37] By 1940, the last year of the Great Depression before the beginning of American war mobilization, the Church spent $1,597,337.69 on various welfare activities, representing 34 percent of total Church expenditures of $4,651,682.90 that year. Of a total Church membership of 862,664, over 16 percent, 137,166, received Church welfare assistance.[38] The Church Welfare Program was more than simply cans of food and resown clothes. Harold B. Lee, as an apostle, told the 1942 general conference that the welfare plan had "provided the greatest opportunities for spiritualizing this Church that perhaps have ever been given this people in our generation. . . . We have come to see therein a building for not only the temporal salvation but also the spiritual salvation of the Church as well. Priesthood quorums everywhere who have rallied to that call and have joined together as a group, have found themselves in love and unity that has blessed this Church beyond our fondest expectations."[39]

The United Order and the Modern Ideologies

J. Reuben Clark and the Rise of Socialism and State Power. Although the Church Welfare Program was clearly more limited in its scope than the united order programs of Joseph or Brigham, the establishment of the program, and the economic turmoil of the

1930s, led to a revival of interest in the united order. In particular, it seemed to many members that socialism, popular and modern in the 1930s, was substantially the same as the united order. J. Reuben Clark, Jr., second counselor in the First Presidency, noted "a growing . . . [misapprehension or] sentiment that communism and the United Order are virtually the same thing, communism being merely the forerunner . . . of a reestablishment of the United Order. I am informed that ex-bishops, and indeed, bishops, who belong to communistic organizations, are preaching this doctrine."[40] Clark was not the only one who held this view of the state of sentiments toward the united order. A non-LDS writer in 1941 described Joseph Smith as "one of America's first utopian socialists" and stated that "there are many socialists among the Mormons, who hope soon to reorganize the United Order of Enoch in order to translate their Prophet's [socialistic dream] into reality."[41] The united order was seen as a centrally directed economic system in which the Church occupied the same central position that the state did in socialism.

In his early thirties, married and with two children, Clark had gone to New York City and graduated from Columbia University's law school. He did very well and was made an editor of the school's prestigious law review. He pursued a career away from Utah, practicing international business law in New York and serving as an assistant solicitor and undersecretary of the State Department. A protege of Senator Philander Knox, who had been Andrew Carnegie's lawyer, Clark was a pioneer of the success that other Latter-day Saints were to achieve in the larger world outside the Mormon country of the western United States. He ended his public career as United States ambassador to Mexico, the first Latter-day Saint to serve in such a position.[42]

Like Friedrich Hayek, J. Reuben Clark was alarmed by the increase in state control and the threat which he perceived it presented to individual liberty. For half a century, the entire world had seemed to be undergoing a tectonic shift to the left. Andrew Carnegie ended up favoring state regulation of prices, and Beatrice Webb became an admirer of Soviet Communism. Perhaps especially attuned by his career to the dominant intellectual currents of the day, Clark was particularly alarmed that Latter-day Saints should confuse Communism with the gospel principles of the united order. At the October 1942 conference, he gave an oft-quoted talk on the differences between the united order and Communism.

He noted that the united order was founded on the principle of voluntary participation and private property, and described it as "an individualistic system, not a communal system."[43] At another time, he described Communism as "Satan's counterfeit for the United Order."[44] Clark's principled opposition to a strong state was not limited to anti-Communism. In the October 1946 conference, he denounced the United States' use of the atomic bomb against Japan. At his urging, the First Presidency also opposed the maintenance of the military draft during peacetime.[45]

Were the United Orders of the 1870s Socialistic? At this time of strong interest in the united order, a perception arose that the united orders under Joseph and Brigham were fundamentally different. Clark described the operation of the united order under Brigham Young as "more of a communal order than that set up by the Prophet Joseph Smith in Missouri and Kirtland. Under the plan set up in the West, the community owned the property and they had a common eating hall, and like matters were held in common."[46] Clark added that these organizations "got away . . . from the principles set out in the revelations."[47] Other writers in the 1940s perceived differences between the operation of the united order under Joseph Smith, as opposed to Brigham Young. An *Improvement Era* article in 1944 noted that "under Joseph Smith's Order of stewardships, each member managed his affairs as best he could," whereas under Brigham Young, "a man was assigned by the board of directors under the immediate supervision of a foreman or superintendent."[48] Another *Improvement Era* article said that "the united orders of Utah days were founded on entirely different principles from the . . . plan of Kirtland, or . . . Jackson County, Missouri. The Utah plan was much more collective in its operations."[49] This perception that Brigham's united order was collectivist resulted in confusion between the united order and socialism.

This confusion endures in reverse. While there are probably very few Mormon socialists today, at least two current writers on the united order have reacted so strongly to the impression that Brigham's united order was communalistic that they have dismissed the entire revelation of the law of consecration and stewardship as a one-time experiment of the 1830s with no relevance for today. Focusing exclusively on Joseph's teachings relating to private ownership of stewardships, they either ignore Brigham's teachings on the united order or accuse Brigham of suffering from "doctrinal drift . . . on matters affecting economics."[50] John Taylor, who was president of the Quorum of the Twelve Apostles during the 1870s, seems to have missed this, recalling that when President Young "was wrought upon to introduce co-operation and the United Order, . . . he told us that it was the word and will of God to us. I believed it then; and I believe it now."[51]

If the united order of Brigham seemed to involve larger and more elaborate organization than under Joseph, the explanation is simply that Brigham lived 33 years longer than Joseph. From 1844 to 1877, the world saw the spread of the First Industrial Revolution and the beginning of the Second Industrial Revolution. Joseph may never have ridden on a railroad; Brigham built them. Joseph lived on the American frontier and built cities; Brigham traveled extensively in industrial England and built entire states. Brigham's use of cooperative corporations, as opposed to the individual self-employed stewardships in Joseph's system, was simply a necessary adaptation of the united order to the rapidly developing new industrial market economy. Brigham's united orders were less "individualistic" than Joseph's because they had to function in an economy which as a whole was becoming less self-employed. The complex modern economy requires large organizations. Brigham and his fellow apostles were only trying to find ways to apply the principles of the united order in this context.

This misperception in the 1940s that the principles of Brigham's united orders were in some way fundamentally different from Joseph's probably arose from several factors. First, it had been over 60 years since the principal united order effort. Although a few scholars had published studies of the united order movement, these were not well known. J. Reuben Clark himself had access to little more than the scriptures, brief accounts in the *History of the Church,* and one dissertation, which he only had time to skim.[52] Second, to the extent that the Mormon community remembered the united order, those memories tended to be dominated by the more dramatic and unusual of the united orders, particularly the pioneering Orderville. Because companies such as ZCMI had evolved into noncooperatively owned capitalistic businesses, it was easy to forget that they were originally far more significant united order efforts than were remote settlements like Orderville.

Third, by the 1940s, economic, political and social thinking had become so dominated by the issue of state power that proponents of the free market had to orient their arguments almost exclusively toward combating state intrusion. All debates were basically about whether the state should or should not do a thing. It became almost impossible for defenders of the free market to discuss how things might be done more fairly or justly within the private sector. To do so might be seen as an admission of a weakness in the free market that the majority advocates of state power could use to argue for a new arena of state intervention. For the minority defenders of the free market such as J. Reuben Clark, arguing against state domination had to take priority over critiquing and improving the private free market economy.

If in 1942 J. Reuben Clark did not receive socialists with the same conviviality with which Joseph Smith had hosted John Finch in 1843, one must recognize what had become of the socialists in that 99 years. John Finch and his fellow early socialists believed in spreading their ideals by the formation of voluntary communities that would demonstrate socialist principles by example. By J. Reuben Clark's time, rare was the leftist who had not become intoxicated with the possibility of using state coercion to implement his ideas of social and economic justice. Stalin murdered millions in the pursuit of his socialist ideals, whatever they were. Even in democratic states, ever-expanding bureaucracies and state ownership seemed destined to eventually strangle freedom.

The Saints and the Modern American Economy. Such Church leaders as David O. McKay and Ezra Taft Benson (the first professional economist to be called as an apostle) joined Clark in the struggle to preserve personal freedom. J. Reuben Clark was a trailblazer in other ways. Young Latter-day Saints increasingly left the Intermountain West in what amounted to a Mormon Diaspora. Many achieved considerable success. Ezra Taft Benson was executive secretary of the National Council of Farmer Cooperatives and later, as Secretary of Agriculture, was the first Latter-day Saint to serve in a U.S. presidential cabinet.

By the mid-1900s, BYU-educated young professionals began to obtain employment in major cities. A number of LDS leaders have enjoyed significant corporate influence in North America, including N. Eldon Tanner as chairman of Trans-Canada Pipe Lines Company; Henry D. Moyle, owner of Wasatch Oil; Roy Simmons, owner and chairman of Zion's Bank; Willard Marriott, who founded and owned the huge hotel and restaurant chain; George Romney, who headed American Motors; and Lee

Bickmore, chairman of Nabisco. Other top executives and CEOs include Jay Parkinson of Anaconda, Jon Huntsman of Huntsman Chemical, Glenn Nielson of Huskey Oil, Robert Kirkwood of Woolworth, Mark Willis of General Mills and the Times Mirror Corporation, Kay Whitmore of Kodak, Stanton Hale of Pacific Mutual Life Insurance, Marriner and George Eccles of First Security Bank, Tony Burns of Ryder Truck, David Kennedy of Continental Illinois National Bank, Nolan Archibald of Black & Decker, Richard Headlee of Alexander Hamilton Life Insurance Co., Don Staheli of Continental Grain, and Stanford Stoddard of Michigan National Bank.

The business acumen of the Saints expanded as the 20th century moved on, making the Church today an economic powerhouse. The Church's Bonneville International Co. owns KSL Television and Radio and other radio stations in Los Angeles, Dallas, New York, San Francisco, and Kansas City. The Church is a major landowner in Utah and holds valuable real estate around the globe. Agribusinesses have an estimated value of $2.2 billion. This consists of nearly a million acres of land, roughly 1,500 square miles, which makes the Church the single largest farm owner in the U.S., with combined landholdings larger than the entire state of Rhode Island. Its industrial parks and commercial real estate properties have been estimated to be worth $757 million. The communication businesses may be worth over half a billion dollars, and Church insurance investments are estimated to have a market value of $118 million. Estimates in the early 1980s put the total value of all LDS Church assets at $7.9 billion.[53] In 1991, the *Arizona Republic* concluded that the Church receives some $4.3 billion from members' tithing and other donations yearly, and generates an additional $400 million in profits from its many businesses.[54] Of that amount, several hundred million dollars is plowed into investments, while the bulk of revenues are used for religious purposes. The Church issued a response acknowledging the efforts and accuracy of portions of that report, but declared there were deficiencies as well, especially with respect to the "grossly overstated" financial estimates.[55] Nonetheless, Mormonism is equated today more than ever with entrepreneurship and a business orientation.[56]

The efforts to adapt the Church to the 20th century have enjoyed considerable success. Mormonism is seen as an American success story. Part of this adaptation was a withdrawal from economic and political commentary, and the limitation of economic involvement to traditional business activities. To the extent that the Church concerned itself with the outside world, the external focus of Church teaching on temporal matters was in combatting the threat to personal freedom from Communism.

The Gospel Revolution

Whether one is discussing the developed "First World," the newly democratized nations of what used to be called the "Second World"—the former Soviet Union and eastern Europe—or the Third World, high unemployment and other economic distress generally appear to be endemic. Into this world of social, economic, and political struggle and stagnation has come the kingdom of God. The population of Latter-day Saints in the Third World grows rapidly every year. Dramatic beginnings have been made in the former "Second World." In the United States, the Church has grown significantly outside of its Intermountain West home base.

Much growth has occurred in the cities of the United States, Canada, and Europe, where the baptism of numerous poor people parallels the Church's growth in the Third World. Out of over a hundred wards in the states of Ohio and Missouri, only six inner-city wards in each have accounted for a majority of convert baptisms since 1990. Many of the new members are recent immigrants from Third World countries.[57] Significant LDS communities in Miami are Cuban and Haitian. In Los Angeles there are Tongan, Samoan, and Korean congregations. In Seattle there are Laotians and Vietnamese. The list goes on and on. Missionaries are being called and trained to speak foreign languages to teach Chinese in Australia, French-speaking Africans now in Britain, Chileans in Canada, and Turks in Germany. Baptism rates among traditional Germans or British are still quite low, but the Church is growing rapidly among refugees in the inner cities of those countries.[58]

Less than two decades after the 1978 revelation extending the priesthood to all worthy male members, many LDS wards have become the most racially integrated churches in their communities.[59] Even in its Intermountain West home base and elsewhere in America, many Church members are considerably less well-off than the popular stereotype. In the Third World, the Church has grown most rapidly in the fast-growing megacities, among working people often struggling in the informal sector.[60] Indeed, in many respects the Church is returning to its origins. It is once again becoming a church of the international working class.

In the 18th and 19th centuries, all human history was transformed by a small group of Britons. A Scottish mechanic at the university of Glasgow, James Watt, invented a steam engine that was central to launching the Industrial Revolution. A Scottish professor at the same university, Adam Smith, described a new economy which promised new freedom of individual initiative and responsibility. British-Americans, influenced by English constitutional history and the Scottish Enlightenment, made a new polity which also promised new freedom of individual initiative and responsibility. Into this setting came angels and light from heaven and the fullness of the restored gospel. Founded by British-Americans, peopled principally by immigrants from the new industrial working classes of Britain and Europe, God's church proclaimed that through the exercise of individual initiative and responsibility, humanity could overcome pride, poverty, and iniquity and join in the divine labor of exaltation. As the 20th century draws to a close, the entirety of humankind is turning to the Industrial Revolution, the market revolution, and the democratic revolution which have set our time apart from all human history.

Ezra Taft Benson argued that part of the battle to promote freedom is to "provide righteous alternatives." We believe that the united order can now provide those righteous alternatives. Even in the midst of the Church's period of adaptation to the modern 20th-century world, it did not fit into the world's neat, rigid, left-to-right ideological spectrum. Church leaders such as President Heber J. Grant cooperated willingly with government relief efforts, while urging that they should be work based rather than a dole. For them what mattered most was that the poor and unemployed should be cared for in accordance with the principles of the gospel.[61] David O. McKay also carried forward his 19th-century predecessors' view of the proper attitude toward wealth. He thought that "modern necessities and luxuries" were appropriate for the city of Zion. "On the other hand," he continued, "it is possible to have all these things and instead of reaping the blessings of Zion, suffer the very torments of hell. If the wealth, for example, from the wide acres be obtained by the oppression of the poor, . . . if in the palatial offices men sit and scheme how to prey upon their fellows, . . . then all these advantages will be but a means of making life miserable and unhappy."[62]

The Prophet Joseph declared that he intended "to lay a foundation that will revolutionize the whole world."[63] The world now awaits the gospel revolution, the worldwide Zion. The next chapter summarizes our understanding of the principles of the united order in the context of the modern world. After that, the remainder of the book discusses ways we might bring about the Gospel Revolution by working toward living, to the extent possible in our current circumstances, the celestial principles of the law of consecration.

PART THREE

WORKING TOWARD ZION IN THE MODERN WORLD

We are engaged in a work that God has set his hand to accomplish, . . . to introduce correct principles of every kind—principles of morality, social principles, good political principles; principles relating to the government of the earth we live in . . . with all our weaknesses and foibles clinging to us the Lord has called us from the nations of the earth to be his co-adjutors and co-laborers, his fellow-workmen and assistants, in rolling forth his purposes.

John Taylor[1]

Ezra Taft Benson served in the American farm cooperative movement and was appointed to U.S. President Eisenhower's cabinet in the 1950s as Secretary of Agriculture. In this photograph, he appears in Montana with officials of the U.S. Forest Service, a government organization within his administration. He was the first professional economist to be called as an apostle. As apostle and church president he worked to provide a gospel perspective on contemporary issues.

10

To Receive Celestial Inheritance:
The Principles of the United Order

The law of consecration is a celestial law, not an economic experiment. . . . I repeat and emphasize that the law of consecration is a law for an inheritance in the celestial kingdom. God, the Eternal Father, his Son Jesus Christ, and all holy beings abide by this law. It is an eternal law. It is a revelation by God to his Church in this dispensation. Though not in full operation today, it will be mandatory for all Saints to live the law in its fullness to receive celestial inheritance.

Ezra Taft Benson[1]

The law of consecration and stewardship embraces the entire gospel. It is essentially the covenant that Saints make to serve God with all their "heart, might, mind and strength" qualified by "faith, hope, charity and love, with an eye single to the glory of God" (D&C 4:2, 5). It is the devotion of all our resources to our commitment as free moral agents to join in the work of God. God has told us that his "work and his glory [is] to bring to pass the immortality and eternal life of man" (Moses 1:39). He tells us, "None are exempt from this law who belong to the church of the living God;" and "Zion cannot be built up unless it is by the principles of the law of the celestial kingdom" (D&C 70:10, 105:5). The law of consecration and stewardship and the united order are not mere 19th-century curiosities—interesting historical economic experiments with no bearing on today's world. They are at the heart of the business of the Saints, "a law for an inheritance in the celestial kingdom."

The modern Mormon image of the united order is strongly influenced by the memory of the Orderville-style rural communes. The united order is thought of as a single unchangeable form, very different from anything in our everyday experience. However, the efforts of the Church in Utah show that there is no one model or method of implementing the united order. Church leaders took the view that the organizational form for achieving the united order was flexible.[2] Nor is the united order a fixed state, which one is either "in" or "not in." Worthy and exemplary as the efforts of the Orderville communalists were, the image of the united order as an isolated, all-encompassing community is of little application in the modern economy. Rather, we can more usefully see the united order as a set of principles to be accomplished by the most effective methods in particular times and circumstances. A review of the scriptures, prophetic and apostolic statements, and Church efforts to implement the united order suggest the following as fundamental principles of the united order. (We will summarize those that have been elaborated in earlier chapters.)

Care for the Poor. In the original united order revelation, the Lord reminds us that "inasmuch as ye impart of your substance unto the poor, ye will do it unto me" (D&C 42:31). As seen in chapter 6, these consecrations are intended to be used to provide "every man" with a stewardship "as much as is sufficient for himself and his family" (D&C 42:32). As Lorenzo Snow explained, "the spirit and aim of the United Order, [is to] . . . employ our surplus means in a manner that the poor can have employment and see before them a competence and the conveniences of life."[3] The commandment to impart of our substance in ways that will provide a living for all families is not to be casually ignored. God rebuked the early Latter-day Saints because they were "full of all manner of evil, and do not impart of their substance, as becometh saints, to the poor and afflicted among them; . . . Zion cannot be built up unless it is by the principles of the law of the celestial kingdom; otherwise I cannot receive her unto myself" (D&C 105:3, 5).

Work and Self-reliance. Just as well-to-do members and the institutional Church bear a responsibility to help all become self-sustaining, conversely all have an obligation to work to become self-reliant. Self-reliance is central to one's dignity as a child of God, and helping God's children achieve self-reliance is a purpose of the gospel and the united order.[4]

The principles of work and self-reliance on one hand, and care for the poor on the other, are parallel and connected, as shown by God's warnings to both rich and poor:

> Wo unto you rich men, that will not give your substance to the poor, for your riches will canker your souls; and this shall be your lamentation in the day of visitation, and of judgement, and of indignation: The harvest is past, the summer is ended, and my

> soul is not saved! Wo unto you poor men, whose hearts are not broken, whose spirits are not contrite, and whose bellies are not satisfied, and whose hands are not stayed from laying hold upon other men's goods, whose eyes are full of greediness, and who will not labor with your own hands! But blessed are the poor who are pure in heart, whose hearts are contrite, for they shall see the kingdom of God coming in power and great glory unto their deliverance; for the fatness of the earth shall be theirs. (D&C 56:16–18)

The principal revelation setting forth the united order says that we shall "not be idle; for he that is idle shall not eat the bread nor wear the garments of the laborer" (D&C 42:42). From the beginnings of the modern Church Welfare Program, it has been emphasized that the "dole," able-bodied people receiving assistance without rendering work for it, is a great evil, corrupting to both giver and receiver. The Welfare Program was set up as a system "under which the curse of idleness would be done away with, the evils of a dole abolished, and independence, industry, thrift and self-respect be once more established amongst our people. The aim of the Church is to help the people to help themselves. Work is to be re-enthroned as the ruling principle of the lives of our Church membership."[5] The virtue of work, of supporting oneself, is a gospel principle applicable to all. There is a temptation for the economically blessed to treat this teaching in a curmudgeonly way, to browbeat "lazy" poor people. However, as Hugh Nibley has pointed out, the scripture is as applicable to the idle rich as it is to the idle poor.[6]

Beyond this, these great sibling principles of the united order go to the very heart of the gospel plan of salvation. God works. His *work* and his glory is to bring to pass the immortality and eternal life of humankind. He leads an eternal enterprise to bring exaltation to the universe's intelligences. As Saints, we have chosen to join in God's work. Upon our baptisms, we hired on to the enterprise of the eternities. We are God's children. Our journey to eternal life consists in gaining the intelligence, experience, and righteousness which permit us to make a useful contribution to the work of God. This is accomplished by helping others become useful workers for Heavenly Father, all laboring together in the joy of eternal life. In doing so, *we* are "the kingdom of God coming in power and great glory unto their deliverance" (D&C 56:18). Eternal progression is expanding our and others' capacity to serve.

Temporal salvation is part and parcel of spiritual salvation. The same principles apply. We want to be able to support ourselves and families so as to be able to contribute to the celestial endeavor. Every child of God that can come to a situation of temporal independence is that much more able to aid in this labor. Rather than the competitive and antagonistic relation that exists between capital and labor in the worldly economy, the united order principles of care for the poor, work, and self-reliance are interconnected duties which bind Haves and Have-nots in a mutual godly spirit and purpose.

Equality. This godly purpose is the equality of God's children. God has said, "In your temporal things you shall be equal, and this not grudgingly, otherwise the abundance of the manifestations of the Spirit shall be withheld" (D&C 70:14).[7] As discussed in chapter 6, this equality is not an arithmetic dead-even leveling, but rather the dynamic employment of society's assets to raise the poor to prosperity and self-sufficiency. It calls for enterprise in the service of people rather than profits, for satisfaction through broad brotherhood and voluntarily shared wealth rather than class distinctions and conspicuous consumption. For Brigham Young,

> the great duty that rests upon the saints is to put in operation God's purposes with regard to the United Order, by the consecration of the private wealth to the common good of the people. The underlying principle of the United Order is that there should be no rich and no poor, that men's talents should be used for the common good, and that selfish interests should make way for a more benevolent and generous spirit among the saints.[8]

Consecration. How do we achieve this temporal equality "not grudgingly"? How do we overcome our love of our money and substance? The law of consecration calls for the donation of all one's resources and abilities to the work of God. To consecrate literally means "to make holy." Every contribution which we make to the work of God is a consecration. In the talk quoted at the beginning of this chapter, Ezra Taft Benson went on to tell his BYU audience that they "today abide a portion of this higher law as you tithe, pay a generous fast offering, go on missions, and make other contributions of money, service and time."[9]

To abide by the fullness of this higher law is to contribute all. The Prophet Joseph taught that one "must sacrifice all to attain to the keys of the kingdom of an endless life."[10] Christ said that the widow's tiny donation to the temple was greater than the much larger contributions of the rich because "she of her want did cast in all that she had, even all her living" (Mark 12:41–44). He told the rich young man that he would have to give away all that he possessed to the poor in order to enter the kingdom of God (Mark 10:17–25). Ananias and Sapphira were struck down for keeping back a part of their consecration (Acts 5:1–11).

Consecration is not just giving money to the Church. Elder Neal Maxwell has recently commented that "we tend to think of consecration only in terms of property and money. But there are so many ways of keeping back part. One might be giving of money and time and yet hold back a significant portion of himself. One might share talents publicly yet privately retain a particular pride. One might hold back from kneeling before God's throne and yet bow to a particular gallery of peers . . . consecration may not require giving up worldly possessions so much as being less possessed by them." He voices concern over Saints "whose discipleship is casual, . . . the essentially 'honorable' members who are skimming over the surface" of church participation. Those "casual members are usually very busy with the cares and things of the world." Elder Maxwell pleads for "greater consecration" that goes beyond self-satisfaction, regular church attendance and temple work, suggesting that we become "anxiously engaged," for "only greater consecration will cure ambivalence and casualness in any of us! . . . Consecration is the only surrender which is also a victory. It brings release from the raucous, overpopulated cell of selfishness and emancipation from the dark prison of pride."[11]

Consecration extends to our thoughts, attitudes, and actions. It means acknowledging as true equals the poor or less quick who cannot get into college or the country club. It means conducting ourselves in the gospel spirit of cooperation, cheering others' progress, rather than in the worldly spirit of competition measuring our success by our defeat of others.[12] It means being willing to travel the gospel path to Zion, even though Babylon's broad highway promises us the big bucks or intellectual fashionability.

Consecration is an ongoing commitment, not a one-time act. As with all true gospel principles, we must endure to the end. In the classic united order described in the Doctrine and Covenants, consecration does not end with entry into the order. Surpluses are periodically reconsecrated to the storehouse to administer to the poor and needy. None of the Church's efforts to operate a full united order lasted long enough, or had enough assets, to put this into practice. Also, as Brigham Young noted, this was impeded by the tendency to never see any surplus in one's own balance sheet. There is always a larger boat, car, or house that needs to be bought. To consecrate our hearts to the point of sacrificing our fascination and lust for the "lifestyles of the rich and famous" may be one of the most challenging consecrations of all.

Our possession by our possessions is why it is so important to learn, according to Ezra Taft Benson, that "the basic principle underlying the united order is that everything we have belongs to the Lord," who said that "I, the Lord, stretched out the heavens and built the earth, my very handiwork; and all things therein are mine" (D&C 104:14).[13]

Stewardship. The earth and everything in it belong to the Lord, and he has entrusted it to us as stewards. As such, we are accountable for our use of it. The Lord says that in the united order, "every man shall be made accountable unto me, a steward over his own property, or that which he has received by consecration, as much as is sufficient for himself and his family" (D&C 42:32).[14] Our stewardship responsibility is to work toward fulfilling the purposes of the united order. In Zion, the responsibility of those with "surplus means" is to promote employment of those who do not yet have a "competence and the conveniences of life." John Taylor told the 1878 general conference:

> Talk about financiering! Financier for the poor, for the working man, who requires labor and is willing to do it, and act in the interest of the community, for the welfare of Zion, and the building up of the kingdom of God upon the earth. This is your calling; it is not to build up yourselves, but to build up the Church and kingdom of God. . . . Do not let us have anybody crying for bread, or suffering for want of employment. Let us furnish employment for all."[15]

As shown in chapters 5 and 7, in order to compete in the new industrial economy, Brigham Young and the apostles quickly adopted the corporation and other methodologies of modern business. The use of the corporate form promoted compliance with both of the fundamental united order principles of equality and independence. Shareownership by united order participants or others in the community preserved independence by keeping the orders, as Joseph Smith had directed, in private rather than

Church ownership. Widespread shareownership promoted equality. In this century, the increased practice of extensive (preferably majority) employee ownership offers a particularly effective method of implementing the law of stewardship in modern business. In this way owners of wealth can account to the Lord that they have used their worldly possessions to fulfill his purposes.

The Storehouse. Under the united order revelations, this accountability for our temporal stewardships is particularly manifested in the obligation for the steward to reconsecrate to the united order "profit or surplus more than is needful for the support of himself and his family."[16] This surplus is placed in the storehouse, or treasury. As shown in chapter 8, this storehouse is not intended to simply redistribute goods to the poor. Rather it is to function like a modern bank or other financial institution by funding the development of united order businesses. However, its activities would be judged by their success in generating employment, rather than the accumulation of supposedly hard, but often unproductive, assets such as real estate and bonds from corporate takeovers.

A full-fledged united order treasury would differ from a bank in an even more fundamental way. A bank derives its funds from depositors, who still own the funds and to whom the bank is liable to return the money on demand. However, in the united order treasury, God says, "let not any among you say that it is his own; for it shall not be called his, nor any part of it" (D&C 104:70).[17] Funds placed in the ultimate form of united order treasury are donations rather than deposits. The doctrine of consecration calls for Saints and enterprises in a full-fledged united order to give their surplus to the storehouse treasury, not to lend it as would be the case with placing it in a bank account. This calls for some motivation that is not a part of any aspect of the normal modern economy.

Moral motivation. Turning over one's profit or surplus by reconsecration calls for extraordinary motivation. In 1878, after the Church and the Saints had been attempting to implement the united order for several years, President John Taylor urged them to

> contrive in all our various settlements, to introduce such things, gradually and according to circumstances, as will subserve the interests of the people and make them self-sustaining. And then let the people throughout the Territory do the same thing, and we shall be progressing in the march of improvement, and get, by and by, to what is called the United Order. But I will tell you

> one thing that you can never do—unless you can get the United Order in the hearts of the people, you can never plant it anywhere else; articles and constitutions amount to very little; we must have this law, which is the law of God, written in our hearts.[18]

The spiritual and temporal are not separate. They are interwoven, each building up or pulling down the other. Apostle (later Church president) Joseph Fielding Smith wrote simply, "Keep the commandments, though temporal or spiritual they may seem. They all have a spiritual purpose."[19] The temporal environment we live in affects our spirituality. It is difficult to live a progressive spiritual life when one is starving or is surrounded by licentious living. Similarly, righteous desires are at the foundation of a righteous society. The noblest of institutions will be corrupt if the people who occupy them are corrupt. As the Prophet Joseph observed, even free democratic republican governments will falter if the people are not virtuous.

No one can be forced to be virtuous. Participation in the united order is not mandatory, it must be an act of personal free agency. Recruitment to the united order comes from the righteous example of its participants, not orders from Church leaders. Brigham Young wrote to his second counselor, Daniel Wells, that "we do not wish any one to enter upon this holy order against their own choice. . . . Such as do not wish to join, treat them with all the kindness and fellowship as though they were in the Order for many will wish to wait & see what the result of our acts will be."[20] Apostle Orson Pratt warned that those in the united order should not "begin to think that we are better than our neighbors who have not entered into the order." Instead, if order members "exercise patience, long-suffering, and forbearance with the people until they learn by experience what God is doing in our midst, many of these rich people may come into the order."[21]

A revelation to the Prophet Joseph in 1833 declared "therefore, verily, thus saith the Lord, let Zion rejoice, for this is Zion—THE PURE IN HEART; therefore let Zion rejoice" (D&C 97:21). Freely working toward the united order in a steady, "line upon line," methodical fashion, always striving to exemplify increased temporal righteousness, we can gradually get the principles of the united order "written in our hearts." This is the way to reach the condition envisioned by Ezra Taft Benson, who taught that "under the united order, idleness has no place and greed, selfishness, and covetousness are condemned. The united order may therefore operate only with a righteous people."[22]

Was the United Order a Failure?

Even if we long for the united order, can we ever hope to become such a righteous people? It is easy to despair of attaining such principles. A common reaction to discussion of the united order is, "after all, wasn't it a failure?" It is true that the united order efforts of the 19th century did not continue and that the united order is "not in full operation today." In order to understand what united order principles are and how we can work to come closer to the "gospel in its perfection," it is important to understand the reasons why those 19th-century attempts to implement the united order did not continue.

Persecution, Polygamy, and Greed. In 1862, the newly elected Republican government had passed the Morrell Act, which prohibited the practice of plural marriage in U.S. territories. Distracted by the American Civil War and post-war reconstruction, initially the government did little to enforce the law.

However, by the late 1870s, the Republicans, having triumphed over slavery, now turned their attention to the other of the "twin relics of barbarism." The Edmunds Act of 1882 made prosecution of the Saints easier by requiring only proof of cohabitation, rather than bigamous marriage. Polygamists were also barred from jury duty, public office, and the right to vote. In Idaho, all Latter-day Saints were denied the vote. Over 1,300 Saints were sent to jail, including George Q. Cannon of the First Presidency and other Church leaders. The Edmunds-Tucker Act of 1887 disincorporated the Church and the Perpetual Emigrating Fund, and permitted the federal government to seize most of the Church's property. Like the civil rights movement of our time, the Saints turned to the courts for protection from this legalized repression. However, in the 19th century the courts were more interested in protecting economic rights than human rights, and the United States Supreme Court upheld most of the anti-polygamy laws.[23]

Some defended the Saints' rights. When the eminent English philosopher and economist John Stuart Mill published his *On Liberty* in 1859, he denounced the persecution of the Mormons to illustrate his contention that people should be free to do as they wish as long as they do not harm anyone else.[24] Unfortunately, more common than the tolerant views of liberals like Mill were the countless sensationalistic books and cheap novels which had the Mormons as their subject.[25] For example, in 1888 in *A Study in Scarlet,* the very first mystery solved by Sherlock Holmes involved a tale of terror and vengeance arising from a flight from the power-mad polygamous patriarchs in Utah.[26]

It would be a mistake, however, to see the persecution of the Church as being based only on popular disapproval of the practice of plural marriage. Prosecution of the antipolygamy laws came in fits and bouts, usually started by national campaigns based on the active promotion of rumors and false accusations. Looking behind these campaigns, one usually sees that they were started by non-LDS businessmen and ministers in Utah. Underlying their activities was something more than outrage at the supposed plight of LDS women.[27]

The real basis for the promotion of the anti-LDS persecution was Babylon's most basic motive: greed.[28] Many Americans had cast covetous eyes on the wealth of the West, including Utah, since the discovery of gold in California. The Church's economic competitors were able to provoke a U.S. Army expedition to invade Utah in 1858. Great fortunes had been made by exploiting the resources of the West. While this produced a boom-and-bust culture of mining and cow towns controlled by eastern corporations, an aggressive and lucky few could take away enough wealth to permit them to enjoy the gilded life of the Robber Barons.[29] But in Utah, the economic, cultural, and political power of the Saints and their Church stood in the way of this process. To Brigham Young, Deseret was a place to make Saints and build a Christian society, not to make mining barons and boom towns.[30]

Unfortunately, the Saints themselves were not immune to the lures of late 19th-century American capitalism. As in the 1830s, the greed and selfishness of the people were seen as a primary cause of the united orders' lack of success. Brigham Young's son John saw the objective of the united order as enabling the Saints to overcome the "feeling of mine," and this seemed to be beyond most of the people. Joseph F. Smith, counselor in the First Presidency, said that "the United Order would be easily established when we were wiling to recognize the truth that we did not own what we possess, but that it was the Lord's." Brigham Young felt that even the general authorities were too committed to their own business interests, remarking "that the First Presidency and the Twelve had stood in the way of the people entering the United Order."[31]

Death of Brigham Young. Although the other brethren were also committed to the principles of the united order, there can be no doubt that the energizing spirit behind the united order program of the 1870s was Brother Brigham. He had dedicated his life to carrying forward the divine mission of the martyred Joseph. He once exclaimed, "Every time I think of Joseph, I shout hallejuah."[32] His dying words were "Joseph, Joseph, Joseph."[33] Well into his seventies, Brigham saw the reestablishment of the united order as necessary to the full implementation of the whole gospel that God had revealed to humankind through the Prophet Joseph. The establishment of the united order, the construction of temples, and the orderly continuation of the Church were the major projects of Brigham's last years. On April 6, 1877, the St. George Temple was dedicated. In July 1877, the First Presidency issued a letter of instructions that set the pattern of priesthood, ward, and stake organization which exists in the Church to this day. Among other steps, it established the bishop as the presiding priesthood officer of a ward. This completed the evolution of the office of bishop to its modern status and away from its original nature of full-time united order management.[34] The united orders, however, were still struggling when Brigham died in August 1877. Afterwards, Church leaders continued to try to implement the principles of the united order, but the need to respond to the growing antipolygamy persecutions of the 1880s became more pressing.

Ambition without Models. While persecution, materialism, and Brigham's death are the reasons most commonly given for the inability of the united orders to continue, there are other factors that were probably significant. One might be called overambition. Brigham proceeded rapidly with the united order program. Possible reasons for this may have been the press of immediate needs resulting from the depression following the Panic of 1873 and Brigham's intense desire to see the full gospel in place before his death. It was easily the most ambitious program of its kind in American history. While even the largest of the 19th-century American communes had at most one or two hundred members at one site, Brigham attempted to convert an entire economy of tens of thousands of people in over two hundred communities to a more righteous economy. While the Saints had considerable experience with many forms of cooperation during their pioneering, this still represented a major transformation of established economic arrangements.

Part of Brigham's solution to this was to be very flexible. He allowed considerable local autonomy in developing different methods of implementing the united order. While this flexibility on the part of the central Church leadership was admirable (and much needed in the Church today), it did carry certain disadvantages. In an 1882 epistle to all local Church leaders, president John Taylor and his counselors, George Q. Cannon and Joseph F. Smith, wrote that "we had no example of the 'United Order' in accordance with the word of God on the subject."[35] Lacking clear models for the organization of the united order, many faltered because the members did not have examples of how to deal with issues that would inevitably come up in cooperative management. It is understandable that even Saints might have some concerns about entrusting their families' temporal well-being to a venture without having some fairly clear idea of how it might operate and survive.

While it would have been, and would be, disastrous to have every decision unalterably dictated by central Church authorities, it is invaluable in any endeavor to have some knowledge of how others have handled similar problems. British converts and returning missionaries brought information about the Rochdale consumer cooperatives in Britain, which were probably the most successful cooperatives of the time. Some local cooperative stores were set up on this model. Yet, as Beatrice Webb noted, it does not appear that significant efforts were made to spread information about or adopt this successful example.[36] Most united orders were essentially set up in a vacuum as to how these new economic entities were to actually function.

As a consequence, there was confusion over how to apply the united order in practice. For example, decision making was supposed to be at the local level, but the habit of appealing to the general authorities on every point (a habit which persists today) could not be broken. It was thought proper that the local bishop should lead the united order; but what was to be done now that the bishop was chosen for his ability to be a "father of the ward," the spiritual leader of a congregation, rather than for his ability as a business manager? What if the existing bishop was not enthusiastic about the united order or did not have the time or experience to manage a business full-time? Or what if, as would often be the case in an industrial economy, the enterprise was on a scale larger than one ward? The question of finding management with the necessary time and ability was keenly felt and was the reason why some general authorities did not join the united order. Brigham himself noted, "I am laboring under a certain embarrassment and so are many others, with regard to deeding property, and that is to find men who know what to do with property when it is in their hands."[37]

There were also uncertainties about basic issues such as withdrawal and admission. Despite the experience in Missouri, united orders such as Orderville felt that they could not justify turning away worthy applicants. As a result, Orderville was always strained by having more poor members than resources. The scriptures seemed to imply that members could withdraw from the united order freely. This was perhaps manageable when the order stewardships were small, free-standing farms or shops. Then the withdrawal of one stewardship would not necessarily interfere with the operation of the other small, independent stewardships. However, incorporated industrial or mercantile united orders would have to pay out withdrawing members in cash or operating assets. It was a potentially unmanageable burden to subject a business to large and unpredictable drains on capital. Although the articles of the St. George united order limited withdrawals, withdrawal and terminations were to be a source of considerable conflict.[38]

The Drive for Self-sufficiency. Another difficulty encountered by the united orders was their linkage to the drive for self-sufficiency. The Lord revealed that one of the purposes of the united order was to enable the Church to "stand independent above all other creatures beneath the celestial world" (D&C 78:14). At any earlier time it would have been reasonable to expect that Utah could have a largely self-sufficient economy. Most economies in history had depended on smaller areas and resources than were available in Utah. However, this was an utterly new time in humanity's economic history. The Second Industrial Revolution brought falling prices for all types of goods. It was a time of economic development such as the earth had never seen before, nor has it seen since. With rail transportation, huge factories with significant efficiencies of scale could undercut almost any small local manufacturer; and they did. Between 1870 and 1900, American steel production quadrupled, while the number of producing units decreased by a quarter.[39] However, as noted in chapter 5, this was not all the result of fair and open competition. Large industrialists such as John D. Rockefeller got illegal preferential rail rates and kickbacks. Even the legal posted rail rates were stacked against local industries. Eastbound freight almost always had higher rates than westbound freight.[40] Whether the success of American industrial capitalism was the result of legitimate methods or not, it was difficult for local Utah industries to compete. The speeches of the general authorities of the time are full of exhortations to support local industries, rather than spend scarce cash on imported goods, even if the imported goods were less expensive.

No Treasury. Another problem of the great united order project of the 1870s was that it omitted one of the central aspects of the united order as set forth in the revelations. This was the storehouse, or treasury.[41] As noted in chapter 8, there was some effort to use tithing funds to promote economic development, but the vision articulated by apostle Erastus Snow of a "common fund" to "nourish . . . infant establishments" and secure credit on advantageous terms from "capitalists abroad" was never implemented.

Results of the United Orders of the 1870s. Although the united order institutions did not survive, this effort was not without positive benefits. Although not well known today, apostles and prophets left the valuable insights reviewed in chapter 9 on the defects of both of the great worldly economic philosophies of our times. Beyond the formal teachings of Church leaders, the effort to create a cooperative economy based on gospel brotherhood had a deeper effect. In the end, God's work is never stopped. The good ship Zion may have to tack in head winds and chart a course to the north or the south, but she always moves onward. The spirit and framework of cooperation forged in the 19th-century Church continues, even if many of the specific and insightful teachings of the apostles and prophets are not so well known among us today. If an entire Zion society could not be made, the united order principles of cooperation, equality, service, and labor can be cultivated and nurtured in families, Relief Societies, priesthood quorums, wards, and branches. The spirit of the united order remains, latent or practiced on a small scale, throughout the Church where Saints strive to live the gospel.

The United Order and the Church Welfare Program

The continued presence of the spirit and some efforts to follow the principles of the united order sometimes leads to a reaction opposite to the belief that efforts to work toward the united order are hopeless. This is the assumption that we are already there.

Some ask, "Don't we have the Church Welfare Program for that stuff?" J. Reuben Clark analyzed the Welfare Program in terms of the mandates of the united order commandments this way:

> We have, as the Welfare Plan has now developed, the broad essentials of the United Order. Furthermore, having in mind the assistance which is being given from time to time and in various wards to help set people up in business or in farming, we have a plan which is not essentially unlike that which was in the United Order when the poor were given portions from the common fund. Now, brethren, the Church has made tremendous advances in the Welfare Plan. We shall have to make still greater advances.[42]

The most significant difference between the modern Welfare Program and the united order described in the Doctrine and Covenants and practiced in the 1800s is the absence of economic development and job creation. As J. Reuben Clark noted, one could not say that the Welfare Program contained the essentials of the united order unless one took into account the "assistance which is being given from time to time and in various wards to help set people up in business or in farming" which corresponded to the united order "when the poor were given portions from the common fund." The importance of jobs was acknowledged from the beginning of the Welfare Program. Marion G. Romney told the October 1975 conference that when the First Presidency first established the Welfare Program, they "made it crystal clear that their purpose in setting up the welfare program was two-fold: first, to see that no worthy member of the Church suffers for want of the necessities of life; and second, that everyone who can work is given work to do."[43] However, under the Church Welfare program, the emphasis has been on helping members find existing jobs, rather than developing new job-producing businesses.

The Welfare Program is not the united order, but it is, in president Kimball's words, not just a program, but the "gospel in action." It seeks to move us toward the united order.[44] Pointing out differences between the two is a truism, not a criticism. That the Welfare Program is not the full united order is not due to a lack of will or sincerity on the part of its designers. It stems from the basic policy decision to have the Welfare Program focus only on providing temporary assistance.[45]

There are logical historical reasons for the absence of job

creation in the 20th-century Welfare Program. The Church was forced to give up most of its economic development activities as part of its accommodation to the larger American society at the turn of the century. Also, after Utah became integrated into the economy of the United States, the Saints, who were mostly in the United States by that time, benefitted from the general economic progress of the United States in the 20th century. With a few significant exceptions, temporary assistance was all that was needed. If an American Saint could be helped through the hard times, chances were that eventually he or she would find work again in the powerful, growing American economy.[46]

The United Order and the Future

With the rapid growth of the Church into the Third World, and into depressed areas of the developed world, it is no longer the case that most Church members can rely on American prosperity, and to be able to do so will be the rare exception in the Church of the 21st century. Sensitive observation discloses the rising concern of Church leaders at the increasing burden which the rapid growth of the Church in Third World nations will place on the Church's resources. Church membership generally does seem to encourage gradual upward economic mobility, and to some extent this individual economic advancement may help. However, the poor members seem to flood into the Church faster than the old members move up economically. Also, to the extent that the Church relies on individual economic advancement, it will remain dependent on frequently distressed local economies.[47]

Many Saints in Third World countries are poorer by orders of magnitude than the poorest American members. Even in their reduced circumstances, the Brown family is much better off on strictly material terms than the Flores or Illagan families. Concentrated in the new urban working classes, the Saints are often poor even by Third World standards. One Church-commissioned study found that 68 percent of the Church members in the Philippines, one of the areas of the most rapid Church growth, live below the official poverty levels. This is substantially higher than the already high Philippine national poverty rate of 49 percent.[48] Efforts to institute the Welfare Program in these countries are only in the initial stages.[49] Even if welfare programs are established, if they operate like the Welfare Program in the United States as non-income-producing "safety net" programs, dependent on subsidies

Women workers at the Utah Woolen Mills, one of several cooperatively owned manufacturers of cloth in 19th-century Utah. Leaders such as Brigham Young and Apostle George A. Smith urged workers to pool their money to construct buildings and buy equipment, thereby enjoying the full benefits of ownership and self-reliance.

LDS Church Welfare Program, which since 1936 has provided canned foods, such as seen here, along with clothing and other goods to help the poor.

from American tithing and fast offerings, they will eventually be overwhelmed by the unstoppable arithmetic of the Church's growth into the worldwide Zion.

One solution is for American Church members to strive more anxiously after worldly wealth in order to increase the subsidies on which the Church is dependent everywhere else in the world. Another is to look to what Spencer W. Kimball called the "full economic plan of Zion, the united order." This would call for the Church to stand independent and self-sustaining in each nation in which Zion is established. Ideally, Saints and their church should opt for Zion's strait and narrow way over Babylon's grand highway. Unfortunately, we know well the route to Babylon. It has been over a century since the Latter-day Saints have tried to follow the full economic plan of Zion. Is there any reason to think that we could be more successful than the Saints of the last century? Are there realistic ways to move toward the united order, to permit the Saints to establish Zion independent in every nook and corner of this desperate world? We believe that we can move toward increased application of the principles of the united order in the modern world and that there are ways to overcome the difficulties faced by the Saints in the 19th century. This belief is founded on two concepts.

The first is that we are not alone in this quest. John Taylor declared, "great men in every age have tried to introduce something good. . . . Is there a true principle of science in the world? It is ours. Are there true principles of music, of mechanism, or of philosophy? If there are, they are all ours. Is there a true principle of government that exists in the world anywhere? It is ours, it is God's; for every good and perfect gift that does exist in the world among men proceeds from the Father of lights."[50] We will see in the coming chapters that many good people have pioneered methods and examples which we can profitably use in building Zion.

The second is to overcome our image of the united order as a single form of utopian fixed state. This image leads to the impression that the united order can happen instantaneously by some prophetic decree. However, with no other gospel principle do we expect to achieve instant perfection. Rather, the gospel teaches faith, repentance, and progression "line upon line, precept upon precept." As John Taylor observed, it is not articles and constitutions that make the united order, but the steady work of getting the united order into the hearts of the people. This is a work in which every Saint can engage now. The principles of the united order are the Lord's way to temporal righteousness for all, a continuum along which we all can strive in many ways to move toward the gospel's celestial economic ideals, looking out for others' welfare as diligently as we do our own. The question is not "Is it the united order?" The question should be "How well does this put into effect the principles of the united order?" The question is not "When will the Church start the united order again?" That is in the Lord's hands. The question for us should be "How engaged am I today in *working toward* living the principles of the united order?" The remaining chapters will attempt to explore many ways of building paths toward Zion and its full economic plan, the united order.

11

At This Very Day:

Working Toward Zion As Individuals and Families

For behold, it is not meet that I should command in all things; for he that is compelled in all things, the same is a slothful and not a wise servant; wherefore he receiveth no reward. Verily I say, men should be anxiously engaged in a good cause, and do many things of their own free will, and bring to pass much righteousness; For the power is in them, wherein they are agents unto themselves. And insomuch as men do good they shall in nowise lose their reward. But he that doeth not anything until he is commanded and receiveth a commandment with a doubtful heart and keepeth it with slothfulness, the same is damned.

D&C 58:26–29

But while attempts to implement it [the law of consecration] come and go, the covenant remains, and those who have entered it must live by it or be cursed (D&C 104:3–5), for in this matter God is not to be mocked (D&C 104:6). I am in a perfectly viable position at this moment to observe and keep it, as I have promised, independently of any other party. I do not have to wait for permission from any other person or group to act; I do not have to join any body of protestors who feel that others are not on the right track. . . . What is there to stop me from observing and keeping the law of consecration at this very day as I *have already covenanted and promised to do without reservation? Is the foundation too broad for* us *to build on?*

Hugh Nibley[1]

The law of consecration and stewardship and principles of the united order embrace all the precepts of economic righteousness in the restored gospel. Since the restored gospel includes all truth, the principles of the united order will incorporate all concepts productive of righteous prosperity. It is not a strange economic experiment. It is simply that condition where everyone treats others as they would be treated. It is, in the words of apostle Erastus Snow, the "Godlike doctrine of raising those who are of low estate and placing them in a better condition."[2]

Like all gospel principles, it is not possible to live all the principles of the united order in an instant, like a "born-again" conversion. Rather the goal is achieved gradually through faith and works, and enduring to the end. Apostle Snow went on to note that the "minutiae of the working of the various Branches of this Order, the details of the business and relations of life," could not be covered or comprehended in a meeting, "but it will be revealed to us as we pass along, line upon line, precept upon precept, here a little and there a little, and everything necessary will appear in its time and place." Thus far we have endeavored to lay the historical, doctrinal and contemporary foundation for understanding the united order in the modern world. The rest of this book will attempt to build on this foundation to suggest some specific ways of working toward such a system in the modern world.

The plan will be to start with the most basic, everyday forms of consecration, gradually building toward increasingly more organized forms of consecration, and concluding with possible steps toward a modern economy inspired by the principles of the united order. This chapter explores ways of working as individuals and families to adhere to the fundamental principles of consecration and stewardship. Chapter 12 examines the application of these principles in groups, including wards and stakes, acting on a local level. Chapter 13 addresses ways that groups can have an international impact in advancing these principles around the world. Chapter 14 looks at many ways in which the institutional Church seeks to advance toward fulfilling the injunctions of the united order commandments. Chapter 15 examines individual and corporate responsibilities with regard to wealth. The next five chapters, 16 through 20, then explore how the principles of the united order might be applied in our current modern economy and the elements of a united order principles inspired economic system in this world. Chapter 21 then discusses the implications of a journey toward Zion for the Saints and the world.

Like other aspects of living the gospel in this life, working toward a Zion society is a journey that continues into eternity. Living the gospel principles of temporal righteousness is a part of developing the spiritual righteousness that empowers us to advance the divine enterprise of immortality and eternal life. Journeys begin with the first step, and every step along the way is progress. Every act of consecration, of Christian charity, is a step on the journey to the united order.

The Latter-day Saints are not alone in this journey. Joseph Smith said that "friendship is the grand fundamental principle of Mormonism, to revolutionize and civilize the world, and cause wars and contentions to cease and men to become friends and brothers. . . . We should gather all the good and true principles in the world and treasure them up, or we shall not come out true "'Mormons'."[3] Down through human history, the world has struggled, and continues to wrestle today, with the challenges, complexities and possibilities of economic development. What is the good life? How might a better system be created? When will massive oppression and human suffering be eliminated? Is it possible to combine socioeconomic justice with principles of democratic decision-making? Instead of prosperity being concentrated in those few at the top of the social pyramid, how might the well-being of the masses be ensured? Our exploration of the journey includes mention of a number of movements, efforts and/or projects attempted by individuals and groups "in the world." These are obviously not based directly on the Doctrine and Covenants or writings about the City of Enoch, but each case illustrates solid elements of united order principles and reflects the temporal admonitions in sacred scripture.

As authors, we do not advocate a return to the Garden of Eden. Nor do we suggest that Latter-day Saints relocate to rural regions of the Rocky Mountains and attempt to establish communal living arrangements. Experiments attempting to do so have generally led people away from the truth and out of the Church itself. Again we emphasize, this is *not* what we propose. Such practices tend to be idealized rather than pragmatic. They are sometimes proposed merely to mask a charismatic leader's drive for power and influence, forces which lead to group dependence. In other cases, seeking a rural paradise is simply a guise for practicing polygamy.

In contrast, we are interested only in substantive projects that enhance self-determination and economic well-being. Heeding the counsel of past and present prophets, we seek to strengthen Zion by becoming a stronger presence in the world, rather than by attempting to escape from it. A proactive strategy is what the restored gospel demands, not a retreat. In many cases the journey has already begun. In others it has yet to start, and we shall have to build the road as we travel. In all cases, however, the journey will never be accomplished unless we make it every day, beginning at this very day.

Personal Development for Self-reliance

The first realm of individual effort to live any gospel principle more fully is that which occurs within the walls of our own homes. This is where upright citizens are created. President Spencer W. Kimball told the October 1977 conference the priorities each Latter-day Saint ought to have:

> The responsibility for each person's social, emotional, spiritual, physical, or economic well-being rests first upon himself, second upon his family, and third upon the Church if he is a faithful member thereof.[4]

For a number of years, the Church Welfare Program has emphasized six areas in which individuals should develop self-reliance: health, education, employment, home storage, resource management, and social and spiritual strength. Each of these is highlighted in the Church's most recent guide, *Providing in the Lord's Way.*[5]

A key aspect of Church member temporal well-being has to do with family preparedness, so many Church members have organized response teams who are ready to go. They also have 72-hour emergency kits for use in disasters and a substantial amount of food storage.

Perhaps the most relevant of these areas with respect to long-term temporal welfare is education and training. Speaking on the united order in pioneer Nephi, Brigham Young urged Utahns that

> there be good teachers in the school rooms; and have beautiful gardens, and take the little folks out and show them the beautiful flowers, and teach them in their childhood the names and properties of every flower and plant. . . . When they are old enough, place within their reach the advantages and benefits of a scientific education. . . . Take, for instance, the young ladies now before me, as well as the young men, and form a class in geology, in chemistry or mineralogy; and do not confine their studies to theory only, but let them put in practice what they learn from books, by defining the nature of the soil, the composition or decomposition of a rock, how the earth was formed, its probable age, and so forth. All these are problems which science attempts to solve, although some of the views of our great scholars are undoubtedly very speculative. In the study of the sciences

> I have named, our young folks will learn how it is that, in traveling in our mountains, we frequently see sea shells—shells of the oyster, clam, etc. Ask our boys and girls now to explain these things, and they are not able to do so; but establish classes for the study of the sciences, and they will become acquainted with the various facts they furnish in regard to the condition of the earth. It is the duty of the Latter-day Saints, according to the revelations, to give their children the best education that can be procured, both from the books of the world and the revelations of the Lord. If our young men will study the sciences, they will stop riding fast horses through the streets, and other folly and nonsense which they are now guilty of, and they will become useful and honorable members of the community.[6]

Thus, the prophets have long advocated high quality education and learning to enable Latter-day Saints to become self-reliant.

Another key aspect of the Welfare Program, resource management, includes the wise and frugal use of capital to avoid unnecessary debt. In a conference address in 1876, Erastus Snow declared that "it is better for us to pay as we go . . . for debt is a yoke of bondage." The apostle decries the capitalist credit system because it exploits the working classes, declaring that while the rich profit from such institutions, since they use them for economic projects and speculation, this is not the case for the Saints. For the laboring poor of the Church, he says, "I am persuaded that the credit system is and always has been a positive evil."[7] This was not only true in early Utah, but also today, as one observes a 16 percent interest rate on credit card debt, even though all other interest rates have fallen considerably in recent years. Clearly, early pioneer apostles had a coherent understanding of the modern economy, and were critical of the barriers to our becoming self-sustaining in the contemporary world.

Individual Church Service

After looking after their own basic needs, Saints seek to relieve the pain and suffering of the poor. One means available to individual Latter-day Saints is service through LDS Church mechanisms. All Latter-day Saints have the opportunity to fast once a month and consecrate the monies saved as fast offering donations which are used to relieve the poor and needy. Referring to the needs of the growing worldwide Church, President Spencer W. Kimball observed that sometimes "we have been a bit penurious and figured that we had for breakfast one egg and that cost so many cents and then we give that to the Lord. I think that when we are affluent, as many of us are, that we ought to be very, very generous." Recognizing that "there are some who couldn't," President Kimball thought "that we should be very generous and give, instead of the amount we saved by our two meals of fasting, perhaps much, much more—ten times more where we are in a position to do it."[8] Church activity provides many more opportunities for nonmonetary consecrations of time and talents. A rich and varied range of personal service is rendered by Latter-day Saints who regularly attend Church services, do high quality home visits, assist in Church welfare programs, such as picking fruit and canning beans, and volunteer other services.

On the international scene, LDS objectives of assisting the jobless and the needy have been served by individuals and couples who volunteer to serve full-time humanitarian missions. In the mid-1970s, certain missionaries were called because of their specific ability to render practical assistance, such as agriculture, construction, public health, education, and nursing. Instead of religious preaching, the bulk of their assignments centered on raising literacy, improving employment, or increasing health through better sanitation and nutrition. These efforts focused on countries such as Bolivia and the Philippines. In the 1970s, missionaries were called to help southeast Asian refugees, many of whom were displaced because of the Vietnam War, learn English and become oriented to American culture before relocating in the United States. When numerous groups of LDS and other refugees immigrated to California, Utah, Arizona and other states, a number of those early welfare missionaries facilitated their relocation. They received housing assistance, special schooling for their children, and other community support. While the language and ethnic diversity of some groups has been immense, the situation is in many ways similar to the mass migration of European pioneers to early Utah. In both eras, many individual Latter-day Saints were ready to succor the new arrivals in both official and unofficial capacities in whatever ways were needed.

The calling of certain missionaries to do more than proselyting has continued into the 1990s. Today, even proselyting elders and sisters are to dedicate at least one-half day per week to community service, rendering help in community cleanup efforts, tutoring, working at soup kitchens, and so on. Others are assigned special roles of a nonreligious nature. For example, several married couples were sent to Hanoi, Vietnam in January 1993 to teach English to doctors and nurses at the Tran Hung Dao Hospital. Others are also serving as English teachers at a Hanoi school, and these are the first LDS missionaries to serve in that land since the outbreak of the Vietnam War in the 1960s.[9] Similarly, other older, retired couples are serving in the Canary Islands, Mexico, Zimbabwe, and Lithuania.

Individual Personal Initiatives

We next turn to personal forms of service to lift the poor and reduce their suffering. Elder Alexander Morrison of the Seventy notes that "aggregate needs may be overwhelming, but hunger and pain are experienced individual by individual. In the same way, we can relieve some needs individual by individual. To help one person is better than helping no one."[10] Elder Glenn Pace of the Seventy has taught that "the primary commandment to care for the poor is our own individual responsibility. We should give financial contributions when possible, but this alone is not complete. We must also give of ourselves. We can oftimes give of ourselves when a financial contribution is not possible."[11] Such personal giving of self has long been advocated by Church leaders, including Spencer W. Kimball.[12] He often referred to acts of individual service, such as working on production projects, giving goods and sharing talents as part of living the law of consecration. Unfortunately, many Church members think that their obligation to society is filled simply by home and visiting teaching and by paying tithing.

On the other hand, many true Saints contribute in small but significant ways to bettering society, serving not only in Church callings but with their children's parent-teacher association at school. Others "adopt" a section of highway to remove litter and keep the area ecologically beautiful. Millions of hours are donated by Church members to scout programs, youth conferences, various United Way causes, fund-raising drives to combat disease, and other worthy causes.

Below are a few activities exemplifying the spirit of the united order that dedicated Latter-day Saints are engaged in today:

- A pair of elderly women who served as missionary companions in Mexico over half a century ago have been collecting used clothing, especially white clothing for temple service, packing the goods, and driving a truck from Utah to Mexico in order to better clothe Church members across the border—they have been doing this for some 20 years. The ladies are known in Provo as the "bread ladies" because they also bake hundreds of loaves of bread during the Christmas holidays and go door-to-door in certain Provo neighborhoods, giving families freshly baked goods.

- Thousands of Church members now donate beyond regular tithes, missionary support and fast offerings, adding an amount to the Church donation slip for "other" by writing in "Church Humanitarian Fund," so that monies can go to support the Fund's numerous projects throughout the world. (Chapter 14 provides more information on the Church's international humanitarian activities.)

- Millions of members likewise donate funds at least annually to non-LDS charities such as CARE, Red Cross, Cancer Society, Catholic Relief, orphanages, literacy projects, United Negro College Fund, Africare, ACCION, Katalysis and various Utah-based development groups described in chapter 13. Many give of their time, a sacrifice which often is greater than a written check, reading to young patients at Primary Children's Hospital, serving meals at a homeless shelter, or working on the construction of a house by Habitat for Humanity. (Addresses for many of these organizations are provided in Appendix B.)

- An LDS American professional working in Nigeria helped arrange for the donation of appropriate equipment through a relief agency so that Nigerian LDS could obtain water for family use in their village. Also in Nigeria a native engineer was successful in placing a number of young returned missionaries in company jobs so that they might learn new skills and secure long term employment.

- A young Provoan, Jason Thomas, served a proselyting mission in Tennessee and returned to his Utah home after two years of preaching, determined to next serve a humanitarian cause. He ended up in India as a volunteer, working for a year in Calcutta with programs of Mother Teresa, the Nobel Prize-winning nun. Likewise, the medical relief organization Deseret International has become involved in restorative surgery services in India.

• A French Relief Society president in Paris, Cecile Pelous, mobilized her stake to create a "Drop of Water" program as members fast and donate to various causes around the globe. Bengal orphanages have benefitted from French members' funding of gardens, a fish pond, chicken coops, and a water pump project. Several dozen Indian families each obtained roosters and hens so that not only eggs but future chicks could become added to village self-sustainability. Sister Pelous organized a day care center for some 40 young children in one area. In another situation, she taught orphaned teenage girls how to print Batik designs on cloth in order to raise funds for their orphanage. Ultimately, these young women made clothing for some 800 children in other orphanages. Sister Pelous herself exemplifies the spirit of consecration by serving as a volunteer in India a quarter of each year, donating her paycheck as well as her time.[13]

• A number of LDS families have formalized their own structure for economic well-being, recognizing that the family itself can be, or should be, a united order-type organization. Some families have jointly bought land and built homes next door to one another. In certain cases, they have created an impressive pool of savings for their children to go on missions, then to attend college, or even later to provide down payments on first homes. These joint financing schemes operate like a revolving loan fund, in that the beneficiary eventually pays back the original amount so it can later be passed on to another family member. Extended family associations have acquired characteristics of tribal cultures and clans, which build strong relationships and help transmit the family values from older to younger members.

• Other wealthy families have founded their own temporal relief efforts. For example, members of the Huntsman family, one of Utah's few entries in *Forbes* 's annual list of the richest people in America, have made dozens of trips to Armenia over the last three years, offering emergency food, medical equipment and other forms of relief. The 1988 quake in that country killed 60,000 people and left half a million without shelter. The recent regional war with Azerbaijan cut off food and fuel supplies. To survive the harsh winters, some six million trees have been uprooted. So the Huntsman young adults spent early April 1993 trying to get 26,000 cases of food into Armenia from Turkey, using Armenian governmental officials and army troops to deliver and distribute the supplies to destitute cities cut off from regular channels of aid.[14]

• As noted earlier, many retired couples and younger or older individuals are serving welfare missions for the Church. Numerous others are reaching out beyond LDS Church-sponsored missions, reacting to promptings of the Spirit to bless God's children in their own personal ways. BYU student Chris Herrod took time off after completing his master's degree in organizational behavior in 1992 to spend a year living in squalid conditions in the Ukraine, teaching others. Another BYU student dropped out of school and spent a year biking across Eastern Europe and Russia in order to raise Western funds for relief and build long-term relationships with many people. He has since returned to Utah and set up an exchange program with Orem High School youth and families, linking them with counterparts he enjoyed meeting in the nations he visited. A Utah Valley medical facility packed up a few items and moved to Polynesia to spend a year in simple village conditions, providing care to area natives. Several years ago, Emma Lou Thayne, an LDS poet from a prominent Salt Lake family, traveled to the USSR to meet with Russian Mormons. Mothers and grandmothers from many countries gathered to protest nuclear proliferation around the globe, and since then other exchanges between LDS Utahns and new friends sharing common causes have occurred.

• Carol Forrest, a Latter-day Saint who used to be a foreign language teacher in Maryland, gave up her comfortable life to volunteer as a medical assistant in the wretched, increasingly dangerous conditions of Somalia in mid-December 1992. She spent six months among the sick and wounded, helping in Digfer Hospital operating rooms, its pharmacy and in-patient wards. Among injured people on crude tables soaked with blood, Carol labored with a shortage of equipment, medicine and doctors, as well as continual power outages. In one instance, she donated her own blood to save a dying victim of a gunshot, since there were no blood banks. Starvation, conflicts between native clans, and the bedlam of lawless Mogadishu itself, made for daily new horrors. Carol began each day with prayer and Book of Mormon reading, and then went out to work, hoping among other things that she would not be robbed or murdered, as some relief workers have been. Carol's conviction is that this is God's calling for her:

> I wanted to do something tough. . . . I wanted to go where I could make a difference for a long time. . . . I have a drive in me to leave a mark for good in the world, not for the personal recognition, just to do something that will help the world be a better place.[15]

- Many people we know have for years donated privately to Church members who needed groceries, medicines and other support. A number of our associates have supported young men and women who desire to serve Church missions, who otherwise could not do so. Such commitments have a long history in LDS circles, going back to pioneer days. This history is typified by a neighbor's grandfather who was orphaned a century ago at age eight in Denmark. Adult relatives took the boy's inheritance for themselves, paying a small amount to cover the passage of the child on a boat to America. In New York the boy was befriended by LDS missionaries, who eventually took him to Utah, where he was cared for and raised by the Olsen family in Ogden. He eventually served three Church missions during his life, but it was his practice of supporting others that is so impressive. As an adult he started a small business and over time became quite successful. A number of young men were hired to work in the firm, and when some of them were called on missions, Brother Simonsen continued to pay their regular salaries for the two or three years the youths were away doing missionary work, allowing many poor Ogden boys to serve who otherwise would never have been able to do so.

In addition to volunteering to serve a welfare or employment mission for the Church, nonprofit foundations and government agencies are other avenues to making a contribution. As individuals, people can dedicate a significant portion of their time and energy as volunteers to the groups mentioned above and others, such as the Benson Institute, tutoring in a Church literacy project, donating to organizations such as Katalysis and ACCION, which are described in chapter 12. Other commitments to serve might be manifest through service to needy members in countries such as Nicaragua. Traveling through Poland in 1992, author Woodworth met an LDS agri-economist from Penn State University. A stake patriarch in the eastern U.S., he and his wife decided to serve a year with a program providing technical training and counseling to Polish farmers in their efforts to turn from a command economy to free-market agriculture.

Likewise, there are the initial efforts of people like Arturo and Genevieve DeHoyos, sociology professors at BYU who recently returned from three years of mission president service in Tijuana. The couple are launching a project to establish a Cumorah University for young Mexicans who agree to abide by LDS standards. For most young people south of the border, college is not an option unless one is wealthy and has political influence to gain admission. Generating funds to establish a private alternative would offer higher education to thousands of LDS youth, including over 10,000 recently returned Mexican missionaries. It would raise their temporal well-being and that of the Church as well. The DeHoyos' dream is to build a Mexican historical theme park adjacent to the university, much like that of the Polynesian Cultural Center at BYU-Hawaii, so that year-round jobs would exist to help college students finance their higher education, as well as learn about Aztec history. Church members with an interest in Mexico, especially those with planning skills and higher education careers, would be an ideal resource in helping design and carry out the fund raising for this project.

The preceding examples do not constitute an exhaustive survey of all the types of service performed by families and individuals. Rather we are attempting to briefly highlight the kinds of consecration that exist and the rich variety of personal moral energy that has been mobilized to bless those in need. These are simply a few of many volunteer efforts we are aware of to comfort, lift and temporally bless God's suffering people, near and afar.

Creating the Spirit of Zion

In the ancient Zions described in the books of Moses, Alma, 4 Nephi, and Acts, the righteous always banded together and worked to eliminate class distinctions, laboring side by side in the field and in the community. In this dispensation, LDS pioneers pooled resources to plant crops, operate woolen mills and settle the wilderness. Between the 1930s and 1970s, Church members contributed to the welfare storehouse, hoed beats or picked peaches on stake farms. Around the globe they labored side by side to construct chapels, learning each others' weaknesses and sharing their faith and commitment.

These activities did more than supply financing for Church businesses, canned foods for Welfare Square, or new clothes in which to worship. More significantly, such activities created a sense of identity as Saints, a culture of Mormonism as real and powerful as that of many ethnic groups today. Such projects helped foster a feeling of "we-ness" in relation to other people, a shared sense of values, a social solidarity. For young people growing up in the Church, these experiences provided a process of acculturation and socialization as to who they were and what the Church really meant, and laid a foundation which combined belief with meaningful service to others.

Unfortunately, in recent years, many youth and new converts often experience the Church as merely a three-hour block of meetings on Sunday and some type of perfunctory Church calling. While they may read the scriptures and pray, many people feel that the sense of community has largely disappeared. However, determining to address this condition by beginning consciously to attempt to apply the principles of the united order through concentrated efforts for service to the poor and needy can lead to a new culture of cooperation. Through joint efforts of Saints, the lives of the poor will be improved and the quality of Christian living by many members will be enriched. A renewed identity as followers of Christ who "bear one another's burdens" will result in greater commitment to the group, and the family, quorum, or ward may become more vital units of the kingdom of God on earth.[16]

King Benjamin taught that "when ye are in the service of your fellow beings ye are only in the service of your God" (Mosiah 2:17). LDS commitments of time, money, and other means to feed the hungry, clothe the poor, and succor those in need are the very essence of the gospel. Like the Good Samaritan whom the Savior praised, we too can stop and offer aid. We can teach and provide funds for future care of those who are passed by, overlooked or ignored by the haughty and those in positions of prominence.

This summary is hardly a complete list of potential applications of the spirit of the united order in relieving the poor and needy. Consecration consists not only of financial contributions or physical property put in the storehouse, but in explicit choices to sacrifice, do without, and give of oneself to benefit others.[17] If the millions of faithful tithe payers around the globe were to "up the ante" just a bit in a righteous way by practicing the principle of "social tithing," a great rush of additional service would be forthcoming. The social tithing we advocate is the donation of ten percent of one's time, skills, and moral energy to building a better world. It means more than only carrying out one's regular Church assignments. Rather, one might rechannel a tenth of one's medical practice to a free clinic, thus serving the poor who cannot afford health care. It might be the *pro bono* services of an attorney who freely advises those unable to pay the usual fees of $75 per hour or higher. Social tithing could be offering produce from one's backyard vegetable garden to neighbors, or giving four hours a week to repairing the cars of single mothers in the ward or branch.

The great challenge for all of us today is not to rush off to create a rural Zion in the western desert or to simply pay the required offerings and thereby qualify to continue attending the temple. Our task is to better understand the principles of the gospel as they relate to wealth and service and then apply them appropriately. The varieties and possibilities are unending, if we really give of ourselves. This will not only help us to develop Christlike attributes, but can also transform our world.

12

Upright Citizens in an Ideal Society:

Working Toward Zion Through Groups Locally

The mission of the Church is to prepare the way for the final establishment of the kingdom of God on earth. Its purpose is, first, to develop in men's lives Christlike attributes; and, second, to transform society so that the world may be a better and more peaceful place in which to live. . . . The betterment of the individual is only one aim of the Church. The complete ideal of Mormonism is to make upright citizens in an ideal society.

David O. McKay[1]

Joseph Smith said that "the greatest temporal and spiritual blessings which always come from faithfulness and concentrated effort, never attended individual exertion or enterprise."[2] But what possibilities for implementing the principles of a more Christian economic system exist for those of us not engaged in positions of influence in the private sector—those of us who are homemakers or nonmanagement employees, or who work for the government or a huge corporation? Even if we are not in a position to change the larger world, we can exercise an influence toward creating Zion in our immediate surroundings. Below are several brief examples of what some Church members and others are doing to pool resources and practice cooperation, caring for one another and collectively improving the quality of life for themselves and their neighbors.

Community-based Cooperatives

Many groups around the world have bonded together to create mutual support systems. In Europe and North America, there are numerous consumer co-ops, neighborhood credit unions, and other community-based organizations. There are also electricity co-ops in rural areas. In Ottawa, Ontario, Canada there is a community organization known as the Home Energy Cooperative which provides heating oil to its members at a 10 to 15 percent savings. In many cities, neighborhoods have established health and funeral cooperatives and have organized cooperatives to provide auto repair and other types of services.

In some 28 U.S. states "Time Dollar" programs are functioning at the grassroots level. A neighborhood organization or church group, for example, operates as a kind of central bank by keeping track of volunteer worker hours donated to various projects. The computer records each 60 minutes of service, and each hour makes up a single Time Dollar. With one's credits saved up in the "bank," the volunteer may later draw on the account as needed, much like early united orders, whose members were credited for labor as well as money contributions.

The program is often run by a paid staff director who works out of donated office space with a phone and tracking system. Start-up kits and a procedures manual are currently available. When volunteers later need help themselves, the director assigns another member to fulfill the task. Examples might be tending a child, mowing a sick neighbor's lawn, or taking an elderly person to the supermarket. A program in Brooklyn, New York, for instance, called Elderplan, is a health maintenance organization (HMO) which uses service credits as purchasing power. Participants may accumulate enough credits to obtain the services of other members, or, if desired, they may use their credits to pay for their own quarterly HMO premium.

Thus one's volunteer efforts function similar to a blood bank, but the donations are in time, instead of blood, and one's service is quantified into real productivity. This form of currency operates essentially as money, matching supply with demand, linking needs with people. However, Time Dollars are not affected by recession or inflation, nor are they taxable by the IRS.[3]

Housing cooperatives have become an important tactic for many low-income citizens. A group of people incorporate for the purpose of owning, building or rehabilitating housing for its members. The corporation owns the housing, often an apartment building. The resident-members own the stock and a right to occupy their own apartment or unit. They elect from among themselves a board of directors and officers to direct the management of the building. Many such cooperatives are eligible for 100 percent financing. The corporation collects rent to cover common expenses and pays the mortgage, taxes and other bills. Some half a million families in the United States live in housing cooperatives. Housing cooperatives are especially common in Michigan, New York, and Minnesota.

Author Lucas served several years as the president of such a cooperative housing corporation in New York City and has been able to observe the effects of cooperation. New co-op owners slowly begin to lose their tenant vs. landlord mindset. Busy people volunteer to serve as directors, on committees, or to man the door or the elevators during strikes or emergencies. Residents acquire a proprietary regard for the building and a special neighborly feeling for their co-owners. It is certain that no cooperative apartment building is at any serious risk of translation to heaven like Enoch's Zion, but the changes produced by being in a cooperative environment, although very subtle, are also quite real.

Among LDS groups, similar collective efforts have been practiced with considerable success. In New York City, member and nonmember families have created a round-robin system of babysitting children while the others attend Relief Society homemaking meetings, or a couple goes out on a Friday night date or takes a weekend mini-vacation. Likewise, in a Utah Valley community, a group of neighbors facing hard economic times because of job losses organized a group buying club to make bulk purchases of food and other retail items. The effort was so successful that they continued the practice, even though their financial hard times ended and conditions improved.

Another example of joint activities grows out of Church leaders' counsel for the Saints to plant gardens and raise fresh produce. Adjacent to BYU's Wymount Terrace apartments for married students, a large parcel of vacant campus property existed. In the early 1980s, enterprising couples requested approval to till the ground and plant vegetables, making productive use of the property while cutting food expenses. Campus administrators approved the proposal, and very successful garden plots were quickly established, providing ample harvests of corn, tomatoes, peas and beans, etc. The effort became a source of pride and joy to all involved and a great example of community labor and cooperation.

Thousands of miles away, BYU-Hawaii faculty at Laie took another approach to collective action. Since the cost of living on Oahu is 15 to 20 percent higher than on the mainland, many professors and their families struggled financially. This led to the formation of a food co-op. Each participating faculty family pays a five dollar membership fee to join. Each week a food order list is given to each family to fill out for the purchases they want to make—meat, fruits and vegetables, dairy products, breads and cereals, etc. A volunteer committee compiles the list, and several men take a university truck into Honolulu to make bulk purchases. Upon their return, another group unloads the truck at a campus warehouse, and others parcel out the products to family members assigned to pick up their specific order. The process is undertaken weekly. All co-op members voluntarily spend one to two hours a week in the various roles needed to carry out this project, but it results in savings of thousands of dollars annually.

Another idea originated with LDS members in the northern United States and Europe who often experience considerable snowfall during winter. The usual method for coping with a heavy winter is that each household shovels its own sidewalks. However, many neighborhoods include elderly couples or widows who are unable to do much heavy work. Some families spend hundreds of dollars to purchase snow blowing equipment, but the cost is prohibitive for many people, particularly the elderly or single-parent households.

An alternative is for several families to make a joint purchase of such equipment. We know of two couples who did so, signing a formal contract to avoid future misunderstandings. Neither family needs the machine for more than 30 minutes after a storm in order to clear their driveways and sidewalks. They wondered why both should spend hundreds of dollars on separate machines. By cooperating they save money. They take turns getting gasoline and oil and split the cost of repairs. Further, by pooling their money, they were able to purchase a larger and better quality machine than either could afford alone. And perhaps most importantly, by doing this they began to feel more sensitivity to the needs of other families who could not so easily clear their walkways. For over a decade now, the little co-op group has removed the snow from other neighbors in the area who are elderly, widowed, or otherwise unable to do such work.

The potential implications of this simple example for LDS members around the world are enormous. Neighbors could jointly acquire such major items as rototillers for their gardens, gas-powered lawn mowers, and other expensive tools such as power saws and tree-trimming equipment. Perhaps joint purchasing of

Apostle Erastus Snow (1818–1888) organized and established numerous united order enterprises and cooperatives throughout southern Utah. Rather than assume a single model, he encouraged multiple economic experiments for implementing organizational structures in a pragmatic fashion.

high-tech items such as computers and laser printers would be practicable. Cooperative ownership of bigger, more expensive, occasionally used items would be consistent with the views of apostle Erastus Snow, who criticized salesmen who went through Sanpete County, Utah, pushing the purchase of sewing machines on every family. These machines were relatively much more expensive in those days, and the indebtedness from family purchases in the area totalled almost $50,000 in 1870s dollars. Declared the apostle:

> The irrepressible sewing machine agents have ravaged our country, imposing themselves upon every simpleton in the land, forcing their goods upon them. Tens of thousands of dollars are lying idle in the houses of the Latter-day Saints today in this article alone; almost every house you enter you can find a sewing machine noiseless and idle, but very seldom you hear it running; and all of which were purchased at enormous figures.[4]

Elder Snow went on to suggest that whether we are dealing with sewing machines or farm equipment, it is important to keep them productively used. The frugal and efficient use of big-ticket consumer and other purchases is an important aspect of provident living that promotes self-reliance. What better way to become more self-reliant than by jointly sharing the cost of big-ticket items with one's neighbors, maximizing its use in the process?

Such not-for-profit ways of working toward self-reliance in the spirit of the gospel can address needs far more pressing than snow blowers. For instance, the creation of cooperative day-care services for LDS families would greatly strengthen the quality of support given young children. In Utah, mothers are entering the labor force at a rate higher than the national average, in part due to low wages and a high divorce rate. Unfortunately, this trend has a number of negative implications, one of which is that many do not have adequate options for the care of their children. As a result, tens of thousands of Utah youngsters are either latchkey children, or are left by working parents at substandard day care centers.

However, the potential exists for ward or neighborhood families to counter this crisis. They might collectively establish high quality day care centers, using the fine facilities of local LDS chapels, which stand empty during daylight hours, five or six days each week. Compensating the ward or branch, even modestly, would provide additional revenue for local units hard pressed by budget restrictions. Or as a service to LDS members, use of the building could be free. A licensed, professional staff would be hired by the co-op, equipment purchased, licensing and insurance arranged, and a legal structure could be created to protect the Church from liability. A not-for-profit co-op could make available high quality care in pleasant, familiar surroundings near the family residence, leading to improved stewardship of parental responsibilities. After a carefully designed pilot project, such a co-op program could quickly spread to thousands of LDS meeting houses. This strategy could become a real source of support among working families, who would be assured that the children of the Church would be cared for in an effective, responsible, community-based manner.

Utopian Communities

Some groups of people have attempted to implement an ideal community comprehensively on a small scale. One of the most successful and long lasting utopian groups in America has been that of the German Community of True Inspiration which began in 1714. Its Inspirationist descendants came to America in 1842, originally settling near Palmyra, New York. They emphasized not just strict Biblical ties or a strong dependence on their priests, but rather direct spiritual experience. Personal revelation, like that of the prophets of old, suggested a communication with God by each individual—an obvious parallel to early Mormonism. Twelve years after settling in upstate New York, the movement purchased 18,000 acres of land in eastern Iowa and moved en mass. They called their home "Amana," derived from the Old Testament Song of Solomon, meaning "to remain faithful." A genuine commitment to develop a communal economy empowered them as they established several colonies. For the next nine decades all land and buildings were owned by the group. Each town was laid out in grid fashion, like Brigham Young's design for Salt Lake City. Every family was assigned its living quarters. Meals were provided in communal kitchen houses on corner lots. There the assigned women prepared three daily meals for groups of 30–40 people. A progressive program of job rotation alternated the tasks of preparing, serving, and cleaning up.

The Amana colonies moved beyond agriculture to other economic endeavors. Manufacturing enabled them to become one of America's premier makers of high-quality kitchen appliances, such as stoves and refrigerators. Today they produce exceptional freezers and microwave ovens. They also excelled in producing furniture and clothing, with woolen mills which enjoyed a worldwide reputation for superb products. These and other enterprises still exist today, with a time-honored tradition for good workmanship. Mothers of young children stayed home to care for the family, but a village "kinderschule" was available for three- to five-year-olds so their mothers could go back to work. Older youngsters attended school six days a week, and the family participated in church prayers and worship services 11 times weekly.

Eventually, during the Great Depression, economic struggles and outside influences, such as a drive for more individualism, forced the dissolution of this long-lasting utopian venture. The members abandoned their communal system and established a profit sharing corporation, the Amana Society, which issued stock to all adults who had contributed time and labor to the villages. Known as the "Great Change," the group kitchens were closed, people gained ownership of their houses or apartments, and electricity was installed. Their church was given control of chapels, schools and other religious ventures, retaining the elders' concern for devotion to God. The church continues today, with its simple worship and emphasis on personal inspiration for the individual. More liberal dress and lifestyle patterns evolved, however, including the use of modern technologies. Openness to change also is reflected in their current willingness to serve in the military. For the first time in their lives, thousands of Amana residents began to labor for wages or to function as small business entrepreneurs. Many felt they had no choice but to change. Consumerism and modernity have now combined with the search for the supernatural. Today if a person attends Sunday church in Amana, he or she will observe men dressed in dark suits, referring to themselves as "brethren." Historical sites of the past have been restructured into contemporary working villages, suggesting that among the Amana the tradition continues.[5]

Numerous other early groups attempted to create mini-societies based on ideological concepts derived from various sources. In 1774 the prophetess Ann Lee moved her band of English Shakers to America, setting up ten societies in Ohio, Kentucky, and Indiana. Believing that the Millennium had just begun, over 18,000 converts, predominantly women, joined the movement. Celibacy was viewed as the path to heaven, allowing adherents thereby to avoid the corruption of the world. Instead of the distractions of the family, the Shakers felt they could focus on pure discipleship. By the 1870s some 18 societies owned over 50,000 acres of farmland, enjoying a national reputation for superb agriculture and admirable handicrafts.[6]

At the other extreme, John Noyes' 1848 Oneida community in upstate New York was trying to become a shining example of an earthly heaven in which members "had all things common" (Acts 2:44)—including economics, child-rearing, and marriage (which functioned as a form of free love). Attempting to live like one big family, the group referred to themselves as *Perfectionists*. Enjoying considerable success, as well as enduring a great deal of persecution and ridicule, the society eventually dissolved its complex marriage structure and in 1881 transformed itself into a corporation, which today still produces high quality silverware.[7]

The Anabaptist Hutterites have enjoyed living in self-reliant economies since 1527 when the first *Bruderhof* was begun in Austria. These "brotherhood farms" were the object of violent and painful evictions by authorities, whose persecutions drove the Hutterites to the Ukraine and on to America in the 1870s. Today there are approximately 380 colonies, a huge growth from the tiny beginnings which started in America a century ago.

The typical Hutterite community consists of 100–150 members who follow the Book of Acts practice of having "all things" in common. Property is communal in every detail, from farm equipment to family houses, from land to the kitchen and the church. Unlike their Amish cousins, Hutterites are quick to adopt new equipment and technologies. Yet dressed in distinctive 1800s styles, women with headbonnets and men in beards, they appear to be straight out of early Nauvoo or pioneer Brigham City. Impressively, the *Bruderhof* have acquired a reputation for having some of the most advanced and productive farms in North American agriculture, easily outstripping the achievements of most of their neighbors.[8]

As one considers the many social and religious movements in 19th-century America, perhaps New England's famous thinker Ralph Waldo Emerson best captures the mood of the times. In 1840 he reflected, "We are all a little wild here with numberless projects of social reform. Not a reading man but has a draft of a new community in his waistcoat pocket."[9] Whether the thrust was building a New Jerusalem, creating economic equality, emphasizing the dignity of work, leading by stewardship, or consecrating one's goods to the church, elements of united order principles seem to have been manifest in many of these groups which coincided with the rise of Mormonism.

Modern Community Building

This desire to work together to create a better community continues today and is not limited to Europe and North America. The large masses of Latino rural and urban poor have suffered greatly through the centuries, and their struggles have worsened in recent decades. The image of humble Lamanites living simply, but peacefully, in an agricultural paradise, pulling fruit from trees in an Eden-like existence, is an erroneous stereotype. The reality is that millions of urban poor are crushed together in *barrio* and *favela* shantytowns. Extensive joblessness, lack of education, toxic pollution, violence, death squads, drugs, and poor health trap these victims of an ever-increasing inhuman economic holocaust.

In response to these wretched conditions, certain Catholic priests, as well as a few Protestant ministers, have begun to reformulate their church practices, moving away from the luxury of traditional worship ceremonies in elaborate cathedrals, toward simplicity and an orientation that labors in behalf of the poor. Known as "liberation theology," a radical new perspective of Jesus is being fashioned, one that views Christ through the eyes of the oppressed.[10] This view stresses consciousness-raising in which the world's injustices are critiqued and new forms of social and religious solidarity are formulated among the lower classes. Unfortunately, liberation theology became connected to certain Marxist ideologies. Thus distortions and political agendas gradually became entwined in the struggle for a better life.

However, at its core, the concept of serving others and building a self-sustaining community is valid and well-grounded in the essential message of the gospel of Jesus Christ. Grassroots initiatives are moving from the bottom up to transform churches into a force for change. Known as *communidades de base*, or base communities, these small groups of lay-led members meet informally to extract Biblical mandates for social action. Estimates are that in the past 12 to 15 years, roughly ten million participants have joined several hundred thousand such base clusters. They work intensely on problems of illiteracy, drug abuse, AIDS, alcoholism, and unemployment. Some pool money to purchase medicine for the sick among them. Others organize to combat crime in their squatter neighborhoods. Still others attempt to help create jobs for street children or the handicapped.

In today's Latin America, numerous religious, governmental, and nongovernmental organizations are laboring to raise the quality of life of the poor. Many operate under the rubric of *promoción social*, engaging in social promotion of the underclass. Professionally trained experts such as economists, lawyers, social workers, priests, and engineers often direct the drive to fuse research with action. The focus is on the poorest of the poor, whom the professionals try to serve by applying their own technical skills to the real needs and suffering of the Have Nots.

The sketches which follow suggest the range of some of these grassroots projects.[11]

- In Santo Domingo, Dominican Republic, some 5,000 tricycle riders distribute fruits, vegetables, and other items around the city. For years, they were too poor to own their tricycles, so 20 percent of their daily earnings went to a large rental company. With help from a Massachusetts foundation for development, a loan plan was devised so *tricicleros* could buy their own little vehicles on installment. They have all succeeded in doing this, becoming owners and paying off their loans, as well as building powerful "solidarity groups" into a huge association with considerable political clout. They now have a health insurance program, tools, a repair shop, a scheme for covering funeral costs of members who get hit and killed in city traffic, and other benefits.

- A new suburb of Lima, Peru, is a self-built town of urban squatters residing in very rudimentary conditions. A group of women, mostly housewives, has banded together and established the Academy for Women, holding courses to better their understanding and thereby their lives. With support from a social promotion foundation in Lima, funded by German and Dutch agencies, the academy offers classes on sewing, literacy, family health, women in politics, and other topics. Currently most of the academy's administration and course teaching is done by graduates from the program. They have learned how to participate in advocating greater support from the municipal government so that water, electricity, and other services are now provided to their simple neighborhoods.

- With funding from the Inter American Foundation in Washington, D.C., a dairy plant has been constructed in Durazno, Uruguay. Before, local farmers hauled their milk to customers by horse cart, requiring one to five hours each day. Now the milk plant sends a truck to collect milk from each farm, pasteurizes it at the plant, and delivers it to area stores. The farmers themselves are now owners of the plant, having jointly created a producer cooperative in which democracy and equality is practiced. The collective dairy now produces additional products such as butter and cheese, thereby increasing profits. And by saving thousands of hours per year of horse-drawn deliveries, dairy farmers now have more time to improve their herds, grow new crops, and devote more time to family life.

- Along the Caribbean coast of Colombia in the province of Cordoba, a group of peasants had collectively farmed a parcel of land for years. In the mid-1970s, the government sent in police to evacuate the farmers. But the people kept in communication and eventually determined that although their land and crops had been repossessed, could they not "take the sea?" Some 22 banded together and built two boats for fishing in the Caribbean. They applied for funding from an agricultural bank and enrolled in a course on cooperative economics offered by a Christian missionary program. Successful catches led next to the foundation of a marketing strategy. Increasing profits allowed for the acquisition of more boats and new outboard motors. Eventually the fishermen's cooperative was able to erect buildings on the shore—a freezer for the day's catch, a corner store, a meeting hall, and offices. Recently they have planned a fish restaurant and small hotel to attract tourists. That which began as a failed effort to obtain land has been transformed into a successful case of seizing the ocean. Instead of struggling as landless peasants, the group became fishing industry entrepreneurs. More recently, since the co-op is incorporated as a legal entity and has accumulated considerable capital, members are exploring whether to lease some agricultural property from a landowner in the region so that the earlier goal of becoming farmers may yet be fulfilled.

New Credit Mechanisms

One critical factor for the success of such grassroots self-development efforts is obtaining sources of financing. An impressive array of new approaches exists to help people obtain capital with which to build their own economic self-reliance.

Financing American Small Business. One example is among inner-city blacks. Data show that the net worth of the median white family in America is some $43,000, compared with only $4,100 for blacks. In response to these depressing statistics, a number of innovative strategies are being developed to facilitate minority economic development. One example is that of a black Methodist minister, Charles Stith, who pushed Boston banks into committing $500 million in loan money over the next decade to finance black entrepreneurs. Reverend Stith's seven-year-old Organization for a New Equality (ONE) offers neighborhood courses on economic literacy. Since the Los Angeles riots in 1992, a California minister, Cecil Murray, has obtained grants from Atlantic Richfield and Walt Disney Company to renovate black businesses and launch 35 new, small, black-owned firms. He argues, "Spiritual development cannot take place without economic development."[12] The overall goal is to transform the violent destruction of the riots into a process for reinvestment and community renewal. Through this effort, the dignity of work is emerging, rather than passive dependence on welfare.

Meanwhile, a group of inner-city business people are launching the Southside Bank in their racially mixed area of Grand Rapids, Michigan. Largely unable to secure credit from traditional lending institutions, the group seeks to show how self-determination and stewardship might become actual business practices in the urban setting. Analyzing deposits from individuals and businesses in the inner city, they found the annual total to be $508 million. However, only some $5 million came back to the community in actual loans. Creating a self-help system for achieving economic control over their destiny is beginning to be seen as an admirable objective. The federal government has taken notice of the Southside Bank, and the administration has proposed a five-year, $382 million capitalization program to create other community development banks, so that distressed people will be able to access credit and obtain technical assistance and other services required for achieving entrepreneurial success.[13]

Inner-city minorities are not the only groups who want to improve their economic situation. In impoverished Appalachia, white, rural women are also initiating a new grassroots approach. *The Wall Street Journal* recently cited the experience of 23-year-old Teresa Bowles, an eighth-grade dropout who overcame severe hardships and today owns her own T-shirt shop. Aided by loans from a nonprofit agency, Workers of Rural Kentucky, Inc. (WORK), she is one of many who for the first time in their lives hold business properties. New skills and genuine self-confidence have flowed from many projects such as Teresa's. Her town of Booneville is conservative, white, and troubled. Adult per capita income is a mere $5,791, in contrast to the national average of $14,420. Several of the town's population of 262 dwell in tar-paper shacks. Some 20 percent of the homes lack indoor plumbing, and only a third have phones. Many residents are illiterate, but through WORK they are learning new skills and becoming micro-entrepreneurs. Freeing folks from food stamps by making self-employment possible, the efforts of WORK and similar programs are having a positive impact.[14]

The Grameen Village Banking Model. Perhaps the origins of such credit projects are best traced to the Grameen Bank of Bangladesh. The name comes from a Banglai word meaning "village." Nearly 20 years ago, a young economist from Bangladesh, Muhammad Yunus, returned to his native country after earning a Ph.D. in the United States. The inconsistencies between conventional economic theory taught at the university and the painful struggle for survival in the Third World prompted him to consider more indigenous tactics for rural development. His solution was to offer micro-loans to the poor, empowering them with credit to raise from their subsistence-level existence. A set of 16 principles, including frugality, personal hygiene, and habits of personal savings, are emphasized.

Funds are provided as loans, not grants, and must be paid back with interest. The typical loan might be $20–$50 to purchase raw materials for basket weaving or other small projects. Loans are made, however, to a small group, all of whom become liable to repay the money. If one person begins to default, peer pressure tends to get the person back on track so that the group may retain its good standing. The group meets regularly and, as early small loans are paid off, members qualify for a larger pool of capital to further expand business opportunities. Since its inception in the 1970s, the Grameen Bank has loaned over $400 million, and its repayment record is an astounding 98 percent, much above that of traditional large Western banks. Millions of the poor in Bangladesh have raised their income tenfold within a year through micro-enterprise loans.[15]

The village banking model is now spreading in Asia, Africa, and Latin America. Recently it has even been applied to the poor in the United States. Tiny, home-based businesses have started up such as desktop publishing services in Denver and cut-flower cultivation in West Virginia. Other examples are jewelry designers, caterers, and beauty shops. Arkansas created the Good Faith Fund program, allotting $1200 per group member during the first year. If no defaults occur, the amount is doubled the next year. In Chicago, the Full Circle Fund is only one of six Grameen-type credit programs established to offer support for women only. On the Oglala Sioux reservation, the Lakota Fund was recently launched to encourage entrepreneurial success and self-reliance. In contrast to the typical 50 percent reservation default rate on loans through a regular bank, the Lakota Fund has had only a 7 percent average default with its peer lending and support. Sioux tribal members who never before had jobs or checking accounts are now starting up firms such as a tire repair business, an Indian crafts project, or a cafe. U.S. early success with village banking efforts has prompted the Small Business Administration to create a $15 million one-year experiment in some 35 cities for micro-loans.[16]

ACCION International, a Massachusetts-based development organization that focuses on Latin America, has likewise become a major player in the creation of credit and capital for the poor, especially in the informal economy. During the past five years, ACCION's poverty-stricken clients have increased by 13-fold, mushrooming from 54,000 to 784,000. In 1994 some $289 million in loans were allocated to small firms, resulting in some 385,000 new jobs which benefitted approximately a million family members. Recipients are given managerial training and other forms of technical assistance to make their projects more viable. Like the Grameen Bank, ACCION's cautious, well-managed program enjoys a repayment rate of 98 percent.[17]

The dramatic success of micro-lending enables recipients to avoid homelessness, hunger, and community loan sharks. It not only assists individuals and families, but boosts the local economy of a region as well. Free market entrepreneurship and a personal sense of one's dignity replace poverty, hopelessness, and passivity. The ripple effect of ACCION on other programs has spread to CARE (the world's largest private development foundation), Save the Children, and other groups. Regional banks, such as Panama's Multi Credit Bank, are entering the microcredit market. Even the U.S. Agency for International Development doubled its small enterprise budget in the early 1990s from $58 million to over $114 million.[18]

Community Building by Latter-day Saints

Latter-day Saints are also seeking to confront social problems and transform society on a local level.

United States. Salt Lake wards have organized ongoing cadres of volunteers who serve the city's homeless the evening meal at the Salvation Army. Their spokesperson reported, "In all honesty, there is no way we could handle it without LDS cooperation," since some 34,000 meals were provided in less than a three-month period.[19] Other ward groups provide food, prepare it, and serve it to the needy each Saturday of the year at the St. Vincent De Paul Center, a Utah Catholic relief organization, clear evidence of Mormonism's growing inter-church commitment to cooperative community service.

A number of years ago, the University of Utah established the Lowell Bennion Community Service Center on campus, named after the school's great professor of sociology, who also served many years as the Church's Director of the Institute of Religion adjacent to the University. Brother Bennion has become the patron saint of Christian service among LDS people throughout the United States. After retirement, he accelerated his efforts to bless the needy, the elderly, and others by creating programs to take food to Salt Lake City's suffering, gather used eyeglasses, provide free local health services, and support other humanitarian efforts. With the service center now formally incorporated, university students mobilize annually to offer significant support through various projects. To illustrate, for several years a large group of volunteers have spent the five days of spring break on the Navajo Indian Reservation, at their own expense and without college credit. They repair fences, paint houses, dig ditches for irrigation, and plant corn. Smaller groups go down monthly throughout the year to register voters, grind corn, herd sheep, weave baskets, and read to the tribe's small children. Anglos learn Navajo ways, and natives learn about urban white culture as both grow in understanding and sensitivity of the other's world views. The deep joy and satisfaction these U. of U. young people experience has spilled over to other schools such as Fordham University and USC in Los Angeles, which also have begun sending volunteers to serve.

Africa. In the Chyulu Mountains of Kenya, after two years of drought, an LDS initiative led by a missionary couple and the Chyulu branch president, bought 1500 kilos of corn and beans to give to the 40 members suffering from starvation. Lives were saved, and then an LDS agronomist from Idaho working in Kenya developed a program for members to achieve long-term self-reliance. New varieties of drought-resistant crops have been planted on six acres of Church-owned land so that Latter-day Saints and their nonmember neighbors can be trained in effective farm techniques. They have been given seed by the Church, and newly trained native experts now supervise the larger project. Members teach others who join the effort, and a bishop's storehouse is to be built that will hold some produce in reserve for future needs, similar to early united order storehouses in Utah. Greater crop yields and closer relationships with poor neighbors have already resulted from this Zion-like effort.[20]

Other grassroots member and local leader efforts have been quite effective in Kenya. For example, LDS branch officials and their membership set up a storehouse to pool their resources. It was originally predicted by some that the effort would fail because individualism tends to dominate the culture. However, the storehouse was a remarkable success as members turned over all excess material goods and occasionally took out supplies as needed. Fear that donations would soon evaporate in the mass rush of many poor to obtain needed goods was also unfounded. Years later, the practical reality is that the storehouse serves as a type of revolving resource of goods for the poor; and the ongoing replenishment by all people involved offers stability for the long-term future.

Couple missionaries and LDS experts laboring in Africa have assisted in developments as well. One branch president in Ghana has facilitated member attempts to improve their living standard by making pottery and starting small hog farms. A mission president in Nigeria helped members and their non-LDS neighbors begin an agricultural co-op, farming diverse produce and sharing the harvest.

The Americas. At a priesthood session of general conference, Presiding Bishop Victor L. Brown described how Bermejillo Branch members developed an irrigation system and planted vegetable gardens to improve their diets and reduce food cost. This and other grassroots initiatives of local Church members and congregations have emerged from stake- and ward-level needs and inspiration. These changes have resulted in spinoff efforts such as building storage units, pouring concrete floors, and buying more sophisticated stoves for cooking their food.[21] Also, some LDS groups from Mexico City have attempted to create their own mini-Zions in rural *ejidos* of the government's land reform program. Certain Mexican congregations have created micro-enterprise businesses to reduce unemployment.

In Peru, although the vast majority of LDS members are poor and many only survive by being self-employed in the informal sector, the Saints have enjoyed a certain level of aid, such as the kitchen projects described earlier. This was achieved in spite of political turmoil and guerilla attack by the violent revolutionary movement *Sendero Luminoso* (Shining Path). In Lima, quorums of priesthood brethren set up a concrete block factory in the early 1990s that has enhanced LDS members' opportunities to secure building materials to improve and expand their rudimentary houses. Bishop Glenn Pace of the Presiding Bishopric personally assisted in supplying 60 large kettles, 30 stoves, and other kitchen equipment, so that city government officials could establish several dozen additional community kitchens in the metropolitan area of ten million residents. Lima stake leaders were also involved in this public-private joint effort to relieve the poor, many of whom are Latter-day Saints.[22]

The Church and Church members from outside the country supplied emergency aid. In 1989, Church Humanitarian Services contracted with the Third World consulting firm of Technoserve to provide agricultural cooperative training in rural regions of Peru. Increasing annual inflation, up to 3,000 percent by the end of the 1980s, made the possibility of economic improvement virtually impossible. Various donations of goods and services from the Church and North American groups of professionals helped the LDS population of over 200,000 attempt to make ends meet during the crisis.

Factors such as hyperinflation, a cholera epidemic, public danger, and destruction caused by terrorist attacks, crime, national strikes, drug lord turf battles, and a state of martial law all form the context of daily life for LDS Peruvians. Yet they remain strong in the faith and have learned to integrate the spiritual side of life with the practical struggle to move beyond simply surviving another day.[23] On the Sabbath they meet in chapels for brief meetings to sing, pray, and partake of the sacrament. The rest of the meeting is then devoted to reviewing the needs of the Saints. For instance, the brother who succeeded in obtaining rice or beans during the past week offers to trade some of his quantity for meat from another person. The family with more than an adequate supply of vegetables from their community plot offers to share with neighbors who live in a tall apartment building, unable to grow anything. Thus Peruvian Latter-day Saints achieve a relative degree of having "things in common," as did fellow Saints thousands of years ago.

The Philippines. Perhaps the most extensive efforts to provide temporal help among Church members has occurred in the Philippines, where LDS growth has been phenomenal. Missionary work was first launched in Manila in the 1960s, fueled by LDS servicemen and the Vietnam War. By the early 1970s, statisticians at Church headquarters predicted that within two decades there would be 35,000 Filipino Saints. In actuality, membership today is some ten times what was anticipated. The rise of membership has been accompanied by mission expansion and construction of chapels and a temple.[24]

In the spirit of Brother Brigham, the area presidency in Manila began to read Leonard Arrington's *Great Basin Kingdom* and encouraged local leaders to do likewise as they searched to learn how LDS pioneers were able to raise their standard of living in early Utah. Various local initiatives were gradually implemented to uplift the Saints temporally and to encourage them to begin practicing principles of a Zion-like economy. A team of BYU researchers in 1989 documented a number of these activities, including the following:[25]

- Jose Tecson, a Chinese merchant and regional representative, has several handicraft stores. Approximately one-third of the items he sells are made by Church members in cottage industries—carvings, shells, dolls, and so on.

- One stake has created a consumer co-op to purchase food wholesale and distribute it to the membership.

- A group of 15 Saints in Cebu has raised 37,000 pesos and set up a stone-cutting operation, subcontracting work from a larger conventional company.

- A marketing co-op was started in Paranaque, Metro Manila, to sell products made in members' cottage industries.

- A group of Presiding Bishopric area office, temple, and Church Education System employees have formed a credit co-op, pledging 500 pesos each to join. They now contribute two percent of their monthly gross income through payroll deduction. The idea is to encourage members to save, and they have a pool of capital from which people can borrow at a reasonable interest rate of five percent.

- Two American LDS members belong to a U.S. women's club in Manila that encourages Filipinos to start up microenterprises in which they will make crafts and ship them to one of their fathers who owns a U.S. company.

- The mission president in Davao plans to remain in that part of the Philippines after his release and help new co-ops, such as the pineapple fiber co-op in Cagayen de Oro. The group has started making paper and fine material for kimonos to be marketed in Japan.

- Many members are very poor and have little, if any, income. In a number of cases they function only in the informal economy and make ends meet by bartering goods and services. Some pay tithing and fast offerings in kind only, and Church leaders have come to accept such donations.

- Pasay 1st Ward began a program several years ago to help its poor members by organizing a resource committee to serve welfare needs. All employed Saints were asked to bring a handful of rice to church each Sunday, and when they shopped for food, to buy an extra can of goods to donate. The unemployed were also invited to sacrifice by bringing items such as old clothes and broken toys to church meetings. Everyone was asked to go through their homes and take to the chapel everything they no longer used. Members without jobs would go to the chapel, repair and paint these used items, and record their time spent. With earned credits they could take out what they needed from this storehouse of goods. The result? Within the first year fast offering support was no longer needed. Those without jobs now had started little micro-businesses as self-employed people. The idea has since spread to other wards and stakes in a program called "Isang dakot na bigas"—a handful of rice.

- One bishopric arranged for a $600 loan with which to hire 60 Relief Society sisters to make shell lamp shades.

- The district presidency in Tuguegarao have established a Welfare Assistance Foundation "by inspiration of the Holy Ghost after a long and prayerful consideration by the leaders." Their feeling is that the present economic crisis in the Philippines is affecting the members adversely and severely and that something has to be done by the Church. The presidency is appealing for funds from United States LDS members to provide livelihood ventures and employment for needy Saints. "What is pulling us back is the severe dearth of capital to keep the foundation a viable pillar and instrument of the Lord," says their letter, and "time is of the essence."

Just how widespread the practices described in this chapter are or could be among Church members is difficult to ascertain, but collaborative strategies to help one another, based on reciprocal values and actions, seem to be growing in modern Mormonism. They offer a means whereby everyone can do something "to transform society so that the world may be a better and more peaceful place in which to live." And these efforts are now reaching out to build the foundation of the coming worldwide Zion.

13

More Nations Than One:

Working Toward Zion Through Groups Internationally

It is clear that all *men are invited to come unto him and* all *men are alike unto him. Race makes no difference; color makes no difference; nationality makes no difference. The brotherhood of man is literal. We are all of one blood and the literal offspring of our eternal Heavenly Father. Before we came to earth we belonged to his eternal family. We associated and knew each other there. Our common paternity makes us not only literal sons and daughters of eternal parentage, but literal brothers and sisters as well. This is a fundamental teaching of The Church of Jesus Christ of Latter-day Saints. . . . As members of the Lord's church, we need to lift our vision beyond personal prejudices. We need to discover the supreme truth that indeed our Father is no respecter of persons. . . . Do you imagine our Heavenly Father loving one nationality of his offspring more exclusively than others? As members of the Church, we need to be reminded of Nephi's challenging question: "Know ye not that there are more nations than one?" (2 Ne. 29:7).*

Howard W. Hunter[1]

Not all efforts to relieve suffering and strengthen the disenfranchised of the world occur within those nations. Thousands of projects are begun in industrialized countries and then flow to impoverished regions of the world. For example, a California builder, Jack Yager, visited Guatemala 20 years ago and, taken aback by the abject poverty and terrible lack of medical services, returned and began to raise funds for a clinic. Today that effort has grown into a 45-bed hospital in the town of Nuevo Progreso, with a pharmacy, operating and recovery rooms, eye clinic, dental clinic, and kitchens and accommodations for 40. Poverty-stricken families seeking care come not only from Guatemala, but Mexico, Honduras, and El Salvador as well. U.S. medical teams fly in for one week every few months to perform surgery. Patients pay what they can for a cataract's removal, dental work, hysterectomy, hernia repair, gallbladder surgery, or skin grafting. The surgeons treat some 1,000 patients per team's visit. Yager's Hospital de la Familia Foundation secures $125,000 through U.S. donations to operate each year, amplified with contributions from participating team physicians. It also runs a nutrition program to counter the tragic consequences of hunger.[2] Doing good, providing relief, and serving others does not require a massive reconstruction of society. In this example we see how a single individual's own consecration of resources can bless the lives of others.

Numerous other small-scale efforts also exist to help others combat the heavy toll of poverty and to cope better with the lack of health care. The list below suggests the range of services.

- Wharton School of Business M.B.A.s volunteered to spend a month in Dominica constructing a woodworking shop to be used by native craftsmen. They pooled $30,000 to cover transportation and building materials, and erected a building for village meetings as well.

- A U.S. business, One World Trading Company, has developed a partnership with a group of 80 weavers in an impoverished Quiche tribal region of Guatemala. The native group, *Artisanos Mayas,* received loans to purchase supplies and conduct training in production skills and marketing services, so that today, some 480 people have a higher standard of living because their traditional weavings are being commercially sold in North America.

- The Center for Study and Promotion of Urban, Rural and Development Alternatives developed a program at Tiradentes in northeastern Brazil to revitalize the town's economy by strengthening craftsmen and artisans. A major goal was to help young people to experience higher self-esteem and confidence in being able to provide for themselves by acquiring technical skills and raising their creative capacities. This allowed them to feel less need to flee to the huge metropolises of southern Brazil in hopes of a better life, a fantasy which for many ultimately degenerates into the reality of a horrible, violent, jobless squalor. The Tiradentes project has achieved much success, culminating in the creation of an artisans guild with a pool of capital and marketing strategies, ensuring continuing economic well-being through the next generation's craftsmanship.[3]

- Mini cement plants, supported by the Intermediate Technology Development Group, are being designed and built in rural India to produce small amounts of low-cost cement. They employ thousands of people while providing a useful product to areas that historically have not had access to this essential building material.

- Oxfam provided logistic support for small-scale water development in Ethiopia by training natives to build hand-dug wells. These provided local villages with their own water supply, making them independent from distant large-scale major water projects.

- The engineering sciences department at Oxford University responded to a request for technical assistance from the Bangladesh government, which was seeking ways to improve forms of nonmotorized transportation. The objective centered on the design of a cycle rickshaw that would have a lighter frame, more efficient transmission, and better brakes. They came up with the "Oxtrike," specifically designed for use in Third World nations where cheap but practical modes of transport are most needed. Innovative "pedal power" technologies are now spreading around the globe.

- The United Nations has turned from advocating large farms to small, one-acre agriculture units as the best way for the world's poor to become self-sustaining. UN-funded development of small-farm tools and equipment has led to the modification of traditional implements and the creation of new ones to enhance productivity during the stages of planting, raising, harvesting, and transporting produce. In countries like Zambia, a program for teaching people how to make and use this new equipment is being increasingly practiced. Do-it-yourself manuals have been prepared, published, and widely disseminated, and rural workshops are being conducted so that small farmers may become more effective. Small-scale farmers are now seen as the key to future world food production.

• Economic well-being cannot be divorced from the physical health of the poor, so a growing number of international efforts now focus on clean water supplies, sanitation, and disease prevention. Instead of the Western model of big hospitals and highly trained physicians, these efforts stress public health and education, more along the lines of China's concept of "barefoot doctors." In countries like Papua New Guinea and Tanzania, the World Health Organization has installed training programs to prepare medical assistants in skills relevant to the poor. In Kenya it provides a three-week course to village women in nutrition, child care, and hygiene. Immunization efforts to cut disease have enjoyed major successes worldwide. The main thrust of today's efforts is to place the responsibility for health care on the local community. By educating leaders and involving parents, people become more accountable for their own well-being.[4]

• LDS wards in North America have reached beyond their own boundaries to "adopt" a group of Latter-day Saints in another part of the world, taking a very real interest in the well-being of their distant brothers and sisters. They send books, Church supplies, and clothing, facilitate exchange visits by teenagers, and otherwise attempt to broaden their understanding and appreciation of God's people in other cultures.

• A number of stakes have also mobilized members to temporally assist needy Third World Saints. Youth leaders of the Pleasant Grove Utah Timpanogos Stake, for instance, accompanied adult advisors on a tour of the Deseret Industries Sort Center in Salt Lake City in late 1992 to learn about the needs of the poor in other lands. They then spent several months planning a series of stake projects to involve Mutual age members in aiding the needy. Church funds budgeted for refreshments, decorations, and stake dances were reallocated by the youth to purchase project materials. Individual young people also donated monies out of their own pockets so that ultimately they were able to raise $1,600. In May 1993, about a hundred Timpanogos Stake young men and women spent a Saturday making toy wooden cars, chalkboards, metal mirrors, and first aid

African mother and babies in the village market. The Ouelessebougou-Utah Alliance was launched in 1985 to provide humanitarian relief in southern Mali, Africa—digging wells for water, building schools for children, creating a literacy program for adults, and offering surgery and medical supplies for poor rural villagers.

items. They assembled 75 education kits containing erasers, pencils, chalk and board, and puzzles. Some 100 hygiene kits were made, each consisting of soap, washcloths, towels, shampoo, combs, buttons, thread and needles. Local firms such as The Stitching Corner donated fabric for some of the items. The youth also made 100 first aid kits with scissors, pins, gauze pads, leper bandages, burn cream, adhesive bandages, aspirin and so forth. In the end the youth learned empathy and were excited to help people far away; and all the supplies were shipped to youth in Somalia and Bosnia who suffer so greatly.

LDS Private Group Initiatives

Some groups of Latter-day Saints have mobilized their collective efforts for the specific purpose of building up Zion and making the world a better place for the poor and suffering. In the past decade a number of Utah-based, LDS-oriented nonprofit foundations have begun to extend support of various types to the less-fortunate around the globe. These include the following:

- The Andean Children's Fund and The Center for Humanitarian Outreach and Intercultural Exchange: These groups provide support for some of the poorest of the poor in Latin America, as well as other Third World nations. They provide hands-on field experience for Americans who travel at their own expense to assist indigenous groups on projects requested by the villagers, projects which are then maintained by native groups after the visitors return to the United States. CHOICE has provided health and sanitation programs, greenhouses, small farms, education, and low-tech pumps for irrigation purposes. Construction of wells and building schools are major activities. Over the past couple of years, the Andean Children's Fund has collaborated with several BYU faculty and their students in certain college courses, traveling to Latin America and spending several weeks in village projects. The outcomes have not only strengthened the rural poor overseas, but brought a greater sense of humanity, awareness, and service to LDS participants from the U.S.

- The Ouelessebougou-Utah Alliance: This organization was formed in 1985 with one of Mormondom's most well-known Good Samaritans, Lowell Bennion. The Alliance focused on Mali, West Africa, one of the poorest nations on earth. The group initially mobilized Utahns to travel there and attempt to help the natives to cope with severe drought and famine, but over the years, the effort has broadened. Medical teams have trained a local indigenous staff to strengthen health care capabilities, as well as providing direct services when Utah doctors visit Mali to help reduce disease and perform surgeries. The result is that some 17 villages now have rudimentary health clinics, some medicines, and health workers. Leprosy, malaria, and malnutrition are declining in those regions. To combat arid devastation, the Alliance members and villagers dug over 60 new wells in various villages and planted 14 gardens. Working with Laubach Literacy (whose international director is Lynn Curtis, a returned Mormon missionary) led to literacy projects and other types of educational training. Small libraries have begun to be established to provide access to reading materials for these deprived cultures.[5]

- Veterans Association for Service Activities Abroad (VASAA): Started by LDS Vietnam veterans, VASAA's purpose is to facilitate the reunification of Vietnamese and other Southeast Asian families disrupted during the 1960s–70s. Other services include locating and assisting LDS members in Vietnam, offering counseling for immigrants coming to the U.S., and providing support to military veterans and their survivors.

- Academy of LDS Dentists: Begun in the mid-1980s in Ogden, Utah, the focus of this group is to offer dental care, training, patient treatment, and education to the less fortunate around the globe. The Academy is willing to establish dental clinics and engage in the collection of used equipment and new supplies, which are then offered to needy groups to improve their welfare.

- The Norma Love Project: Focused on the impoverished condition of the Misquito Indians in Eastern Honduras, the project provides short-term assistance through collecting and shipping goods biannually, including seeds, medical supplies, clothing, toys, and education items. The long-term hope is to help build health clinics and schools, as well as teach hygiene and more efficient agricultural methods.

• Utah Medical Association International Service Committee: This group of Utah physicians encourages their peers to participate in efforts to relieve the suffering and pain of the poor who lack adequate medical care in international regions. The committee tries to provide medication needed for overseas projects. It also facilitates exchanges between Utah and overseas physicians, furthering the training and broadening the horizons of both.

• Beehive Foundation: Although based in New Mexico, this organization has strong ties to Latter-day Saints in the Intermountain region; it offers humanitarian assistance in Central America and Mexico. In addition to collecting basic necessities such as clothing, food, and medicine, the foundation also has a concern for agriculture and education of poor communities in those areas.

• Partners of the Americas: This organization seeks greater mutual understanding between Utahns and the poor of the Bolivian Altiplano, offering a broad range of services such as literacy and anti-drug education, help in preventing soil erosion, providing medical supplies, and cultural exchanges between the two mountain regions.

• Deseret International Foundation: Begun by Dr. William Jackson in 1989 while serving as mission president in the Philippines, its primary thrust is to offer surgical assistance to children in Third World nations in order to raise their quality of life and self-image. The emphasis has been on treating disfigurements such as burns, cleft lips, club feet and crossed eyes, but more recently the scope has broadened to include sending medical and dental teams, as well as supplies, overseas to provide care and teach native professionals who can continue on with critical services.

• American Indian Services: Originated at BYU to help Lamanite groups through fund-raising and collecting donated items such as farm equipment and so on, this effort is now a private, off-campus foundation that engages in relief to tribes primarily in the U.S. and Mexico.

• Brigham Young University: Various programs have been created recently to reach beyond the campus and assist groups in need. These include the David M. Kennedy Center for International Studies, which helps to arrange foreign internships for students wanting to teach English, study social relations, or otherwise learn and help other cultures, primarily in Asia and Latin America. The Zoology department has been involved in prevention and control of hydatid cysts in infested citizens of rural northwestern villages of the People's Republic of China. Students at BYU have initiated numerous efforts to aid the poor and needy. They hold a Hunger Banquet each fall, eating simple rice and beans, a diet consistent with that of the masses of hungry people around the globe. All donations are channeled to relief groups, such as Africare. In response to the economic disintegration of the former USSR, the Honor Student Council established Russian Relief, seeking donations, selling T-shirts, holding charity concerts, and soliciting Provo business sponsorships, all of which raised $7,000, which was distributed to groups in Moscow. Students and faculty participated in several efforts, such as "Have a Heart," to enable underprivileged children to obtain school supplies; "Books for Romania"; and the "Hurricane Andrew Relief" project to help south Florida. In 1993, Campus Coalition was formed to conduct a humanitarian aid drive for victims of war-torn Bosnia. Various campus organizations sponsored the drive, along with local LDS wards, so that blankets, clothing, medicine, and personal hygiene supplies could be shipped to the Balkans.

• University of Utah: A group of medical doctors at the medical school created a Pediatrics Exchange Program with the San Juan de Dios Hospital in Guatemala to promote professional development for faculty and medical students. Utahns travel to Guatemala City to train local pediatric staff workers, educate doctors, and create collaborative research efforts between the two institutions, which bring Guatemalan doctors to Salt Lake City for further training in the latest pediatric procedures—all of which is intended to raise the level of children's health in impoverished Guatemala.

This summary is hardly a complete list of potential applications of the spirit of the united order in relieving the poor and needy. Consecration consists not only of financial contributions or physical goods put in the storehouse, but in explicit choices to sacrifice, do without, and give of oneself to benefit others.

Enterprise Mentors

There is enormous potential for building temporal self-reliance by establishing nonprofit foundations through which a Zion-like economy may be approached. One case will be explored in considerable detail, that of the Enterprise Mentors International Foundation.[6]

The Startup. This foundation grew out of several individuals' concern for Third World members of the Church. One was author Woodworth, who had become involved in economic development projects with LDS Filipinos in Hawaii while spending a year there in the late 1980s as visiting professor at BYU-Hawaii. He worked with LDS and Catholic Church groups, the governor's office, and the Philippine consulate in Honolulu to create jobs through small, worker-owned co-ops. About the same time, Menlo Smith, a St. Louis businessman who was serving as president of the Philippines Baguio Mission, felt great empathy for the impoverished members of the Church there. In 1988, both happened to share their concerns with then dean of BYU's School of Management Paul Thompson, who arranged a joint meeting. As a result of the meeting, Woodworth formed a team of graduate students with the financial support of Smith and Steven Mann, vice president of a California management training firm. The team spent the summer of 1989 doing research in Manila, learning about Filipino economic issues.

The team conducted numerous interviews, met with LDS Church leaders, and visited economic development projects of the government, private voluntary organizations, and other religious groups throughout Metro Manila. Linkages were established with a number of nonprofit organizations to improve the livelihood of poor Filipinos. Factors which led to success as well as failure were identified, and various operations were analyzed. Woodworth and Reuben Lacanienta, a former native Filipino LDS leader and official with the Asian Development Bank, consulted with key government officials, including cabinet ministers of Trade and Industry, as well as the nation's minister of Finance, the LDS area presidency, and a number of top corporate and banking leaders.

Enterprise Mentors, a nongovernmental organization (NGO), was created by Latter-day Saints in the United States to develop Third World self-reliance through micro-enterprise development and job creation. Here Reggie De Aro, a micro-entrepreneur, is training one of his new employees in how to operate a lathe in their machine shop.

The team's 120-page analysis was presented to a group of concerned individuals in Manila in August 1989, including Smith, Mann, general authorities, mission presidents, Church welfare administrators from Salt Lake City and Manila, and local economic development representatives, both LDS and nonmembers. Out of several days' discussions a plan was formulated to launch a private, nonprofit foundation to help strengthen the temporal well-being of poor Filipinos, refining the model so that it might later be extended to other regions of the globe. Over the next four months a U.S.-based foundation was incorporated, and in January 1990 Enterprise Mentors officially began. It applied for tax-exempt status as a not-for-profit 501(c)(3) foundation and began with a small board of eight people. The Church Humanitarian Fund agreed to match the group's initial private fundraising of $200,000. Travel expenses and the activities of the U.S. operation are paid for out of individual board member pockets so that 100 percent of voluntary donations are channeled to worthy projects in the Philippines.

The Filipino Context. The team's 1989 research focused on both the national economic picture and the specific circumstances of the LDS population. The Philippines has some 60 million citizens scattered over some 7,000 islands, speaking 11 languages and 87 dialects. Major ethnic groups include Malay, Chinese, Spanish, and Muslim, with a strong American influence extending through most of the 20th century. At the present birth rate, the population will double within three decades. In the 1960s the Philippines was the second ranking economy in Asia, but now it is next to the lowest.

The corruption of Ferdinand Marcos and his cronies led to the outflow of billions of dollars from the country. A political dictatorship and the armed leftist movement, known as the New People's Army, have clashed in guerilla warfare for many years, with attendant problems of hostage-taking of westerners, U.S. military personnel, and upper-class natives; the bombing of buildings; and terrorist attacks on villages. The "People Power" revolution which restored democracy and installed Corazon Aquino as president created great expectations, but little solid improvement in the life of average Filipinos. In the 1980s, some 12 million people entered the ranks of the officially poor, and a third of Manila's residents were squatters. Typhoons, the eruption of Mt. Pinatubo, and other natural destruction, coupled with the withdrawal of U.S. military bases, has made life more precarious than ever.

Within this context, the research team discovered the abysmally low living standards of Church members. Filipino LDS are quite literate and well educated, in contrast to those in many Third World societies, but both unemployment and underemployment are higher among members than among nonmembers. For years the assumption was that foreign investment, the U.S. bases, and Marcos's economic plans would foster economic success. But multinational corporations were put off by societal uncertainties, ideological and armed conflicts, as well as the ravages of nature.

Some 80 percent of LDS missionaries serving in the Philippines are natives. Like Elder Ben Illagan, most have come from homes in which the family ate only one meal per day, had few clothes, and lived in crowded houses with many relatives. When they go on missions, supported by general Church funds, they get to wear nice clothes, eat three meals daily, sleep alone in their own bed, and enjoy a sense of worth, leadership, and accomplishment. But at the conclusion of the mission, the individual's Church support ends, and he or she returns to impoverished conditions at home. The pain and pathos of poverty are now greater for those who have experienced a sharply contrasting lifestyle during their missions.

Further schooling is rarely within reach, unemployment is high, and returnees often feel unable to marry and start their families. Their American companions return to the relative affluence of U.S. life, buying a car, getting university training, marrying, and going on with the "good life." The Filipino returned missionary often becomes discouraged and depressed, wondering how to proceed.

Family conditions for the Filipino returned missionary are often very troubling and stressful. LDS converts are poorer than the average Filipino and have a greater degree of joblessness. Some 60 percent lack running water in their houses, and two out of five are squatters. Many lack electricity, garbage removal, clean water, and a sufficient caloric intake to be healthy. They have a great capacity to survive in the midst of squalor and economic stress, but lack basics that Americans would consider necessitites. Approximately half of Filipino Church members attempt to make ends meet through small enterprises in the informal economy, typical of the Third World situation described in chapter 2.

Enterprise Mentors' Strategy. The foundation focuses on assisting small-scale enterprises or would-be entrepreneurs who have the potential for micro-business success, thereby generating jobs and raising the living standards of the Filipino poor, whether LDS or not. The underlying assumption is that by providing managerial training and technical assistance, the Have Nots will be able to leverage their efforts and create longer-term economic sustainability than if they simply received food aid.

Enterprise Mentors' mission is:

> To build self-reliance and entrepreneurial spirit within those who struggle for sufficiency in developing countries.
>
> We do this through the principle of a "hand up, not a hand out," for those who are committed to building their livelihood, their families and communities through micro and small scale enterprises. By training, character development, counseling and encouragement, sound business practices are established. Results created include improved livelihood, employment opportunities, hope for a better life, greater self-respect, self-sufficiency and self-realization.[7]

In contrast to huge Third World development projects which pour billions of dollars to large-scale projects such as construction of highways, bridges, and ocean ports, or international bank transfers which often end up in the pockets of governmental elites, Enterprise Mentors is a small, bottom-up effort in which resources go directly to needy recipients. It also avoids governmental red tape, and the graft and corruption which typically accompanies it. Likewise, instead of operating as an LDS Church program, with the political problems of conflicts of interest, mixing of Church and private concerns over money and its uses, Enterprise Mentors cooperates with, but operates at arm's length from, the Church.

While the Philippines supplies over ten percent of worldwide LDS converts annually, members there are unable to provide funds for their own Church programs, making them largely dependent on subsidies from the donations of the U.S. membership. The debilitating effects of poverty thus not only affect members individually and as families, but the institutional Church as well. How to enable regional centers of Mormonism to stand independent, as well as enable members to be self-reliant in their private lives, is an increasingly complex problem for the Church. Enterprise Mentors has devised a model that will empower Filipino Saints to develop and manage their own temporal well-being in a way that complements the Church's impact spiritually, and the two efforts will thus bless the whole person. Indirectly, the institutional Church will also benefit as its Third World members achieve economic well-being.

Several entities exist to facilitate this process: Enterprise Mentors International in America provides overall funding of efforts in the Philippines, offering guidelines and receiving feedback regularly. In Manila in 1990, the Philippines Enterprise Development Foundation (PEDF) was established as a nongovernmental organization (NGO) in Manila. It establishes its own budget, hires its staff, and operates programs through a technical assistance center based in Makati, a financial area of Metro Manila.

Enterprise Mentors' Operations. The center offers a variety of services to interested individuals who are needy, who want to grow an existing small firm, or who hope to do a micro-enterprise start-up. Individuals must have promise, and their projects must be economically viable. In addition, individual qualities are essential, such as high personal ethics, willingness to risk, capacity to learn business principles, ambition, and a sense of stewardship and willingness to help others in the future. Some sort of track record of past experience is also preferable.

The center offers several services: (1) training groups who already have, or want to start, small-scale enterprises, offering education in accounting, marketing, and other business essentials; (2) networking efforts which link people with others who run similar businesses or refer them to other experts such as attorneys, engineers, banks, or mentors; (3) running business clinics to provide an assessment of needs in order to provide counseling; (4) consulting by staff experts who work on site offering in-depth, long-term client services including data collection and analysis, developing business plans, and so forth; and (5) cooperative development which leads to the organization of group co-ops for credit, marketing, and other purposes.

Generally, the range of services is intended to address micro-enterprise needs for start-up, growth, productivity, and profitability, with the ultimate objective being individual and family self-reliance. All services are conducted by paid native Filipino PEDF staff members who work as trainers, consultants, secretaries, and computer technicians, led by an executive director. Assistance is provided on a "value for value received" basis so that small-scale entrepreneurs do not assume they can get something for nothing. Instead, they have a professional relationship with PEDF that encourages a financial payment of some type, at least a token fee if not the market rate for consulting. Even charging a modest fee helps create the image that PEDF is not a charity providing free services, enabling recipients of expertise to preserve their own self-respect. In other words, PEDF provides a hand up, not a handout.

At the center level, Manila's staff are all Filipinos, some LDS and some not, hired for their experience and skills. While BYU involvement was considerable at the outset and U.S. Enterprise Mentors International foundation officers visit quarterly, psychological ownership is locally based and indigenous. The expectation is that each center started with U.S. funds in a given country will become self-supporting through local contributions within five years, so that American resources can then be channeled to other regions of the globe in need.

Staff personnel typically labor with a client who has either walked into the center or who attended an introductory training seminar and expressed interest. Once a potential client is identified and his or her needs diagnosed, appropriate assistance is given, assuming that the potential success of the business is high and that the client possesses the necessary aptitudes and moral principles. The service rendered may be in the form of helping the client prepare a feasibility study to launch a new firm. Or perhaps it is to create a business plan so that he or she qualifies for a small bank loan to do a start-up. If the client is already self-employed but wants to expand, the consultant helps develop a strategy for achieving growth, better quality, or increased productivity. Eventually, the client-PEDF partnership may be dissolved as one's business objectives are accomplished and independence is reached. The individual then moves on to helping other micro-entrepreneurs in the same way as he or she had been the recipient of such support earlier, thus completing the cycle by now serving others.

The center staff and Manila executive director are hired and governed under the leadership of PEDF's board of directors. The group is made up of 10 to 12 leaders with considerable experience in business, academic, and community service. Most are Filipino, along with several U.S. multinational corporate executives who currently live in Manila.

In the Philippines, Enterprise Mentors expanded from its 1990 initial efforts in Manila, where the largest concentration of LDS members exists. In the fall of 1991, a second center was begun in

Cebu, a huge city in the center of the Philippines. Named for that region, the Visayas Enterprise Foundation (VEF) is independent from PEDF in Manila and has its own center staff and local board. It too receives funds from Enterprise Mentors International in America to deal with its particular needs and situation. In 1992, a third center was created when the Mindanao Enterprise Development Foundation (MEDF) was launched in the nation's third largest city, Davao. The three paid staffs currently employ some 20 Filipino trainers and consultants who work to help local clients start and grow entrepreneurially, thereby raising the quality of life.

Enterprise Mentors' Results. During its first three years, Enterprise Mentors International and the centers in the Philippines raised and invested over half a million dollars, all from private donations. U.S. board members cover overhead, travel, and fundraising expenses out of their own pockets, quite a contrast to many nonprofit groups. The untold hours of board member voluntary work to organize Enterprise Mentors International eventually led in late 1991 to the hiring of a full-time executive director, Chuck Cozzens, to help execute the program, implement board policies, and manage the organization's finances. By early 1993, the U.S. board had grown to some two dozen directors, including investors, corporate CEOs, past welfare missionaries and mission presidents, physicians, and academics. They serve at their own expense, traveling for meetings and projects from California, Arizona, Idaho, Texas, Michigan, Minnesota, and Missouri to Utah. Recently, Elder Marion D. Hanks, emeritus general authority, became chairman of the Enterprise Mentors International board. The results of the foundation's efforts during its first years are substantial. Summary operating results from 1990 to 1995 are:

9,432 participants in training programs
1,164 in-depth consulting projects
1,355 new jobs created
563 small businesses accessed loans
71 cooperatives received training and consulting services

These activities are just the first small steps of Enterprise Mentors, but collectively they suggest great potential for the future. They ensure the long-term vitality of hundreds of small firms. Many of the individuals who attended training seminars will eventually start up their own businesses. Approximately 6,800 Filipino Latter-day Saints have benefitted temporally, since each new job positively

The Visayas Enterprise Foundation, an affiliate of Enterprise Mentors, launched the use of LDS President David O McKay's slogan during "Family Unity Week" in the Philippines. Micro-enterprise clients of VEF sewed banners and wheel covers that were distributed by Rotary International.

affects the lives of an average of five other family members. The foundation has helped some 700 people form or expand their cooperatives, most of which are located in LDS neighborhoods where members have banded together to establish a crafts co-op or start a credit union, using the money pooled to launch new businesses.

Beyond the numbers, however, the real strength of Enterprise Mentors is most graphically seen in individual lives. Consider the case of Reggie De Aro, an LDS father who spent years working in the Persian Gulf for large foreign firms in order to obtain sufficient financial resources to support his family in the Philippines. In 1990 he returned home, having accumulated some savings with which to buy a small lathe and become a self-employed machinist. Working in a tiny shop attached to his house, he felt fortunate to feed the family once a day. Eventually, he attended a PEDF introductory training workshop. This led to the assistance of a staff consultant who helped Reggie create a business plan and marketing strategy. With these new tools, he was able to qualify for a small loan with which to purchase a larger lathe and hire a second person. Two years later his work had grown to the point that he had his own garage with various pieces of equipment, combining auto repair with machine shop activities. Today Reggie employs eight other people, including a sales manager and a bookkeeper.[8]

The experience of Reggie De Aro and hundreds like him today is solid evidence that bottom-up, grassroots development efforts can succeed. United order principles such as pooling of resources, working hard, and operating cooperatively to lift the group are able to counter the unemployment, underemployment, and temporal suffering of LDS poor. With three Philippines centers operating, and the original 1989 model refined and based on a track record of success, the foundation is now beginning new plans for expansion.

The efforts of Enterprise Mentors International and its partners increasingly are being recognized by international organizations as effective models for change. For example, PEDF was featured in the Rotary International's magazine and has been awarded a contract by the International Labour Organization to train extension workers for government and private development organizations in the Philippines. The Enterprise Mentors affiliates are also starting to have a broader impact locally. VEF helped organize and stage a major event in the Philippines, National Family Unity Week. The government, civic groups (such as the Jaycee and Rotary clubs), churches, and businesses joined to celebrate the family unit. Following a proposal by VEF, President David O. McKay's statement, "no other success can compensate for failure in the home," was adopted as the unity week's theme. The slogan was printed on posters, streamers, and banners throughout major cities. A VEF client printed the slogan in large letters on hundreds of tire jackets which are used to cover spare tires on the backs of jeepneys and trucks. The tire jackets were purchased by numerous Rotary clubs and distributed to the public.

Three more U.S.-based board councils have been established to explore launching Enterprise Mentors efforts in Mexico, Central, and South America. They are charged with carrying out the initial research, building a network of experts and influential people in those regions, raising funds and setting up in-country operations. Other individuals who so desire could undertake similar activities, focusing on areas of the globe in which they have an interest and expertise. Also, recent additional funding has permitted Enterprise Mentors to make Grameen Bank-style micro-loans.

Those so involved may begin to experience the essence of what the Prophet Joseph once said: "A man filled with the love of God, is not content with blessing his family alone, but ranges through the whole world, anxious to bless the whole human race."[9]

Other Organizational Possibilities

The world cries out for the kind of devotion, integrity, and service that Latter-day Saints could render around the globe. Critics might denigrate some of these efforts as simply a pretext to opening the political process so our missionaries can preach the faith. Thus participants would have to be grounded in their commitment to charity for its own sake, not as a means to Church proselytizing. Others might criticize such efforts as merely a chance for the giver to gain satisfaction, while the project breeds dependency in the receivers of the aid. Certainly there is always the potential for unintended consequences, but the service ought to be rendered *with* others, not merely *for* them.

Latter-day Saints who wish to serve can intervene positively, offering not only agricultural expertise or engineering skills, but models of the restored gospel in action. They can transmit the best of our culture and values to other societies, blessing them temporally as well as spiritually. And when they return home, they will have changed for the better in terms of sensitivity to global pain and suffering, and have a greater awareness and appreciation for other peoples, languages, and customs. Those changes would also be passed on to family and neighbors, creating a ripple effect that would spread our moral commitment outward to bless many others in future years.

More specifically, then, let us consider other hypothetical strategies by which Church members could organize to promote temporal self-reliance in accordance with the principles of the united order.

Nicaraguan Career and Enterprise Program. The rapid growth of the Church in many Third World nations makes it more imperative than ever to develop comprehensive grassroots programs to build local self-reliance. For example, before the 1979–1989 decade of Sandinista leftist government in Nicaragua, the Church had over 2,000 members. But when Daniel Ortega and his leadership cadre took control, Mormonism declined greatly, as did other religions. Some LDS chapels were taken over by the Sandinistas, missionary work ground to a halt, and war with the right-wing Contras devastated the economy. Now with Violeta Chamorro as a democratically elected leader, freedoms are returning. But for the Saints, life is more difficult than ever, and today national unemployment is around 60 percent. Strikes, protests, and other conflicts have given rise to increasingly repressive government measures. Foreign investment is minimal because of future political uncertainty, and many existing businesses are being considerably mismanaged.

Yet in this troubled environment Mormonism is prospering. In 1990 Church membership was only 800, but today there are over 15,000 new converts. What might be done to strengthen them temporally? One idea would be to establish a career and enterprise development center in the capital city of Managua. It would allow unemployed and needy Church members to receive training so they might engage in viable occupations and achieve personal and family self-reliance. Perhaps the LDS Welfare Department could team up with a private development organization (PDO) with considerable Central American experience. They could jointly design the project, and the PDO would act as the field-implementing agency in Nicaragua. After doing an initial assessment of needs and resources, a steering committee would be established in Managua, hiring an executive director and staff, and opening an office. The staff should build a network with other PDOs and government agencies working in Nicaragua.

The program would generate two career approaches after the individual LDS candidate completes an intake assessment of skills, interests, aptitudes and goals. One career path would be for the person who wants to find a vocation. The individual would go through occupational training to become a truck driver, seamstress, computer programmer, or other employable worker. The center would then arrange an apprenticeship with a firm interested in those specific skills, which could lead to a permanent job if that individual works well. The center might even offer the vocationalist credit for the purchase of necessary tools to secure the job, and the small loan would be paid off over time at market interest rates.

On the other hand, other candidates might seem best fitted for an entrepreneurial track. These individuals would go through a small business training program such as the one offered by Enterprise Mentors so as to either expand the micro-enterprise the person already has established or to launch a new start-up. The center would provide ongoing consulting and monitoring, and perhaps create business councils or cooperatives for groups of entrepreneurs in the same type of business. In such cases, the center would provide a Grameen Bank type of village credit system with which entrepreneurs could expand their businesses, thereby developing new products or services and creating more jobs.

Brokering Resources. A group of 3,000 returned U.S. missionaries who have served in Paraguay over the past several decades might get together and sponsor the start-up in Asuncion of a program to mentor and help LDS youth obtain jobs. Many of these Americans are now between 40 and 60 years old and have sufficient resources to donate $100 each annually to such an effort. Having over a quarter of a million dollars total would allow a center to be established in the Paraguayan capital and pay the salaries of several skilled native Paraguayans. These individuals could organize a mentoring program in which today's young, returned Paraguayan missionaries would be mentored by a seasoned LDS professional in that country. The mentor would provide counseling, encouragement, and advice during meetings with his or her protege at least monthly. The mentor could help the young person continue in schooling or perhaps obtain a job.

The center could also function as a kind of clearinghouse for job opportunities, linking returned missionaries with specific firms who desire honest, hard-working job candidates who possess important values. Such a program would gradually provide a path to self-sufficiency for young Paraguayan Latter-day Saints, leading to marital and career success, as well as personal dignity and fulfillment. Corporations that participated in this project might eventually offer financial support to such a center because it would benefit them directly, and they would have an ongoing supply of job candidates who are ethical and hard-working. Finally, the Church would benefit as well in that it would have qualified future leaders and a Paraguayan membership base that would enjoy economic well-being, at least to the point of being able to support ecclesiastical programs in Paraguay, rather than being a drain on Church coffers in Salt Lake City.

Mormon Peace Corps. Another idea that could generate a great deal of self-reliance in the world would involve a small group of retired Latter-day Saints who have experience with the U.S. State Department, embassies, and American outreach programs such as the Peace Corps or VISTA. These individuals might pool their considerable skills and help LDS youth organize a sort of Mormon Peace Corps, based in Salt Lake City or Utah Valley, or wherever else a large concentration of young Church members exists. This effort could link up with several courses taught at BYU and local colleges to train young people in international development, culture, and organizational change. Funds for overseas work could be raised through corporate or personal donations and internships arranged for college-age individuals to spend 6 to 12 months in Third World countries where service is needed, such as in Samoa working on rain forest preservation, or in Nicaragua teaching at a village school. Many candidates would be ex-missionaries who desire to return to the lands in which they served, this time to help members economically. They would already have a good grasp of people, language, and culture. Other potential candidates may be returned missionaries who served stateside but now want to go abroad. Still others could be students who never served a mission, both active and inactive LDS, as well as other Church groups who would enjoy doing some good.

A parallel effort coordinated by this "Mormon Peace Corps" would be for older retired LDS couples to do similar work. For the young, the advantage is good health and high enthusiasm and energy. For older volunteers, the advantage is experience, wisdom, and a strong skill base. Other middle-age individuals could also serve, taking a one- or two-year development leave from their firms to help the needy. We know couples who have done so and found great joy. Neighbors in their late fifties studied a year or two of Russian, for example, and then obtained a professional leave to spend a year assisting privatization efforts in Russia.[10] Others have served under the auspices of a Seventh Day Adventist program. Often companies will provide a year's salary to do such work, or at least continue health benefits and seniority, pay travel expenses, and otherwise offer support. Progressive LDS executives could create corporate policies and practices to reward community service of this type, since the firm benefits, as does the direct provider of service. There are dozens of opportunities to serve in U.S. urban areas, with programs such as the Citizens Democracy Corps, which offers consulting help to foster free market strategies in Eastern Europe. And of course numerous groups such as the LDS Humanitarian Committee, Africare, and others abound with understaffed projects and opportunities.

The accumulating impact of an LDS critical mass would be impressive. There are numerous other possibilities. Consider, for example, the huge, positive effect a hundred LDS couples could have if they worked together in the micro-loan program of ACCION in Latin America. Or what if 50 Church humanitarian missionaries were sent as a group to do rural development in Ghana? They could be a great leavening force for good over a year's time in small nations like Jamaica or Albania. Imagine if only eight to ten LDS couples were called to Santiago, Chile, to work with members there in setting up a small, enterprise finance and development system for job creation and self-determination. Members of this new group of co-ops could, within several years, become so prosperous and successful they would feel no desire to immigrate and resettle in the western U.S., but could stay and build up Zion in Chile. They would also serve as an evidence that the universal brotherhood of humankind is indeed a fundamental teaching of the restored church of Jesus Christ.

14

But A Prelude to the Establishment:

Working Toward Zion Through the Church

We must not lose sight of the fact that all we are doing now is but a prelude to the establishment of the united order, and living the law of consecration. The individual Saints must understand this.

Ezra Taft Benson[1]

Although the office of bishop evolved away from being principally concerned with united order administration, the bishop's charge to look after the temporal concerns of the Saints has remained in effect. There have been numerous programs to enhance economic conditions for members. Author Woodworth, for example, grew up in the inner city of Salt Lake. There the Liberty Stake had a soap factory at which members would labor for a few hours per month, much as rural stakes operated Church welfare farms. Making soap, shoveling chips, packaging goods, all culminated in door-to-door selling of Church products—bars of hand soap, powdered laundry detergent, bath oil, liquid detergents, and so on. During the Great Depression, Stake President Bryant S. Hinckley created a bishop's storehouse in an old, unused downtown building so that members could donate goods, receive produce, and collect firewood for distribution to members whose homes were cold. This was the first storehouse established since early Utah times.

Just west of the Liberty Stake soap factory was Pioneer Stake, where Harold B. Lee had served as president during the Depression. Several of his fellow leaders were jobless, as were approximately half of all the men in the stake. Stake President Lee implemented a sharecropping program with Salt Lake Valley farmers so that goods could be collected and stored. Warehouses were also established to store donated furniture and clothing. Vacant lands were used to grow vegetables for stake consumption. All this gave members the opportunity to work and alleviated some of the worst poverty in that area.

Meanwhile, a more agricultural stake south of Liberty Stake was presided over by Hugh B. Brown. During the Depression he launched various farm projects and established an employment and welfare committee to coordinate projects and to strategize further steps to relieve rural suffering. The stake Relief Society made quilts, repaired used clothing, and made new items which were given to the needy. The sisters also bought equipment for steam cooking so that families in the various wards could do their own canning from their gardens to get through the winter. Coal was centrally purchased by the stake and delivered to families for heating homes in the winter, and a stake food market was set up to collect in-kind tithing contributions which could then be redistributed to the hungry. Innovations such as job sharing, in which a man with employment willingly shared his hours and labor with an unemployed neighbor so that both had some income, were first started in Utah during that period. The initiative and grassroots vision of these local leaders serve as impressive reminders today that one's responsibility, as well as opportunity, derives from the promptings of the Holy Ghost rather than from administrative decree from organizational headquarters. This is the admonition in *Doctrine and Covenants* 58:26–28, in which the Lord says, "It is not meet that I should command in all things. . . . Verily I say, men should be anxiously engaged in a good cause, and do many things of their own free will."

Modern Church Welfare. The role of the institutional Church in alleviating the pain, suffering, and poverty of God's children throughout the earth continues to grow in impact.[2] President Thomas S. Monson of the First Presidency, and Chairman of the General Welfare Services Executive Committee of the Church, recently declared: "Bishops have the sacred duty to seek out and care for the poor and the needy, . . . whether those needs be spiritual, social, emotional or financial."[3] Personal time and energy of leaders are coupled with the expenditure of considerable monies to aid those who are deprived. In 1988, a former member of the Presiding Bishopric, Elder Vaughn J. Featherstone, reported that the Church had spent some $30 million in caring for the poor in the previous year, much of it administered by local Church leaders.[4]

Social services, welfare goods, and basic offerings of assistance are made available by the Church through local bishops. Originating from the Church's Utah base, a number of initiatives have been launched to enhance LDS members' temporal well-being. On a general Church level, the emphasis has been on two of the basic needs for building self-reliance: employment and education.

Employment. The Church has hired an outside company to produce a set of video tapes to advise potential job candidates on how to search, interview, and become hired so that their income level can increase. The Church has also set up employment centers to coordinate job searches and provide assistance for Church members.

Internationally, Church headquarters in Salt Lake City authorized the installation of an employment center in Mexico City in 1989 which led to job placement for hundreds of unemployed members. Native stake and regional leaders have frequently requested additional help from Salt Lake to raise the living standard of typical members in Mexico. Groups have traveled to LDS general conference and met with BYU faculty and others to plead for help, but so far little more has actually been accomplished, other than the work of the Benson Institute described below.[5]

Literacy. Beginning in 1992, the General Relief Society responded to the tremendous problems of illiteracy by launching a "gospel literacy" effort around the globe. Learning to read and improving one's ability to read, write, and communicate are essential skills in an increasingly sophisticated society. Says the general president of the Relief Society, Elaine L. Jack, "By enlarging the mind and opportunity and understanding more, we will enjoy the circumstances we live in."[6] Many projects have begun to enrich others. For instance, local sisters in Morgan Hill, California, offer literacy and tutorial services to low-income youth after school and the Relief Society in Marshalltown, Iowa, has collected books and donated them to area libraries.

Literacy has also been used as a tool for development in BYU projects. In the spring of 1992, for instance, Professor Ted Lyon led a group of Honors Spanish students to eight small villages in the state of Guanajuato, Mexico, to teach the adults who wanted to learn to read. Funding sources included several campus programs and the students themselves. In addition to tutoring the mostly female group, students also worked on the construction of a community center, built fences, worked in family gardens, and made presentations at local schools. They also attended church in a nearby town's LDS ward, and the result was that the local stake Relief Society president began organizing women from various wards to go out and continue the literacy work started by the BYU students, ensuring an ongoing development effort. A number of other literacy efforts have received LDS support in recent years, primarily through Laubach Literacy, Inc., in such nations as Nepal, Haiti, Mexico, and India.

Education. Beyond basic literacy efforts, a number of other programs have sought to provide education and training. To develop long-term employment skills in the South Pacific, BYU-Hawaii was established to accept, train, and send native graduates back to their Polynesian homes. Vocational programs were especially emphasized, such as electronics, computers, and woodwork, but this emphasis began to decline in the late 1980s.[7] In Brazil, the Church Education System offers some scholarships and other incentives to help young people, returned missionaries in particular, further their education and preparation for careers, but achieving major success is difficult.

In the spring of 1993, six couples were sent to Mongolia on 18-month service missions. One husband-wife team conducted medical training for local health care providers. The others, former business school professors, worked to set up management training, computer services, and other higher education programs for Mongolia.[8] Gradually we can expect the few thousand couples currently laboring on service missions to increase in numbers and become a significant force for Third World development, assisted by tens of thousands of proselyting missionaries now that they have been asked to devote part of their time to community service.[9] At present, the Church is looking for bilingual couples who possess math, music, social science, or high-tech capabilities for assignments in places such as the Republic of Kimbati, Poland, Bulgaria, Albania, and Nicaragua.

International Humanitarian Committee

One of the more impressive LDS institutional mechanisms for aiding the poor and improving community life and the world is the emergence of the International Humanitarian Committee of the Church.[10] The Church has a long history of responding to natural and manmade disasters, ranging from the San Francisco earthquake of 1906 to more recent events such as the Teton Dam break in Idaho, Hurricane Andrew in south Florida, and the Mississippi

River floods.[11] Significant international efforts began after the Second World War, when Elder Ezra Taft Benson, then a new apostle, was assigned to oversee relief efforts in Europe. U.S. President Harry Truman was surprised when George Albert Smith, LDS Church president at the time, proposed sending a huge amount of goods to aid the suffering in those lands. Elder Benson assessed national needs, opened missions which had been shut since the conflict began, and organized the channeling of massive amounts of food, bedding, and clothing donated and shipped by the Church.[12] By the mid-1980s, the Church saw a need to move beyond sporadic disaster relief efforts. The establishment of the International Humanitarian Committee marked the undertaking by the Church of a continuing responsibility to international relief efforts.

The committee was an outgrowth of the massive relief efforts in which the Church was involved from 1984 to 1986. As the travails of a terrible famine began to impact Ethiopia, the Church donated cash, clothes, and food supplies to international nonprofit groups such as Africare and the Red Cross. A great grassroots clamor for the Church to provide aid as a responsible Christian organization created growing pressure to respond. Not only did letters flood Church headquarters, but some members paid their tithing donations to Catholic Relief and other groups, and then told their bishops the money was to be calculated as LDS donations; they expected temple recommends and Church recognition when tax deductions were taken. In early 1985 Church leaders declared a special fast Sunday for North American Church members to aid the hungry Ethiopian victims of drought and hunger, above and beyond regular fast offerings.

After the successful 1985 fast to raise funds for the Ethiopian famine, the question arose of what to do with the outpouring of cash donations. When millions of LDS dollars were quickly expended in the purchase of wheat, corn, first aid and other forms of assistance, general authorities began to wonder if the funds would not be better spent on long-term development, rather than on emergency situations alone, which often lead to dependence. A second special fast was held in the fall of that year and the sum of LDS donations from the two events totalled over $10 million. Rather than spend the monies solely through other nonprofit relief organizations in Africa, the practice evolved of channeling small grants, not only to African famine relief groups, but to those involved in various Third World development efforts around the globe, so that eventual self-reliance might result. The Humanitarian Services Committee of the Church Welfare program directs these funds with the philosophy of encouraging local control and initiative.[13] These include:

- A Connecticut consulting firm, Technoserve, was given a grant to help 15 villages in Kenya build a culinary water system of 25 miles of pipe, which enhanced their lives, gardens, and dairy herds, while simultaneously freeing up the time of children so they could attend school instead of spending all day hauling water to their houses.

- In 1988 alone the Church donated medical equipment to a Hungarian university, channeled polio immunizations through Rotary International to the Ivory Coast, supplied relief to Mozambique, gave earthquake aid to Armenia, funded small-scale agriculture in Guatemala and village improvements in Bolivia.

- Some funds were provided in response to requests from Church members or leaders in specific geographical areas. For instance, Ghana mission leaders solicited funds to drill water wells; authorities in the Philippines sought and received education on gardening and planting techniques; Church officials in Romania requested and obtained welfare missionary couples, as well as medical, orphanage, and other aid; recycled clothing was sent in response to LDS requests in Russia and various countries of Latin America.

- A number of Utah-related nonprofit organizations have received funding from the Humanitarian Services Committee, including the Beehive Foundation, Andean Children's Fund, Benson Institute, Deseret International, and Ouelessebougou-Utah Alliance.

At the general priesthood meeting in April 1991, President Gordon B. Hinckley stressed the importance of the Golden Rule in Church Welfare efforts and suggested how fast offerings from the people of the world could impact impoverished people: "The hungry would be fed, the naked clothed, the homeless sheltered." In the same meeting, President Thomas S. Monson likewise cited the parable of the Good Samaritan and reported on the work of Humanitarian Services in funding the training of peasant farmers, purchasing medicines for Third World children, sending food and clothing to the poor of border towns in Texas and California, providing dental supplies to inner-city clinics, and so forth. At the October 1994 conference, President Monson reported that humanitarian cash donations of $23.75 million have been made to multiple groups in 109 countries around the globe and that the total value of both cash and commodity humanitarian assistance exceeded $72 million.[14]

Whether the needs of the poor derive from national disaster, economic decline, or other reasons, Humanitarian Services is a major LDS resource for blessing people's lives. When the United States and other United Nations forces launched the attacks on Iraq during the Gulf War of 1990–91, Humanitarian Services donated cash, 13,000 blankets, and tons of clothes to refugees fleeing the region. A balance was attempted in that some goods went to Kurds in the north, others to Iraqi officials for victims in Baghdad, and still others to Shiite Muslims in the south.[15]

An amazing amount of humanitarian involvement has occurred in Eastern Europe and the former USSR since the fall of the Berlin Wall in 1989. Lloyd Pendleton, a manager in Church Welfare Services, reported 17 projects in Romania so far (primarily in orphanages), 15 in the former USSR, 6 in Bulgaria, 5 in Albania (mostly medical assistance), 4 in Poland (agriculture projects), 3 in Armenia, 3 in Croatia, 2 in Hungary, and 1 in the former East Germany. The aid includes cash donations, over a million pounds of used clothing, medical equipment and supplies, medicine, and half a million pounds of food.

Humanitarian Services was involved in some 113 projects in 1991 and over 200 during 1992. The relief and development efforts have impacted some 8.5 million people in 65 countries so far—from disaster aid to refugee relief, to in-kind food and other material goods. The shipping of recycled clothing in 1990 totaled 724,000 pounds, growing to 2.2 million in 1991 and over 9 million during 1992.[16] Humanitarian Services promotes programs in self-reliance, including employment centers, social services, and other mechanisms which continue to lift people and enable them to better cope with factory closings, family concerns, homelessness, and other stresses.

Other Church-Affiliated Programs

The same is true internationally as LDS professionals, U.S. military service representatives, and government employees have taken jobs in various lands, thus paving the way for an informal Church presence which has subsequently become formalized, opening the way to full-time missionary work. Below are examples of local, regional, and Churchwide efforts to apply self-reliant steps toward raising the temporal well-being of people both in and outside the Church. We turn first to Latin America.

Brazil: Church members in this nation fight daily battles just to put bread on the table. They suffer from poor education and illiteracy, like many Third World Latter-day Saints. There are nearly half a million members currently, with thousands of native missionaries, and numerous stakes and missions. The Saints of Brazil struggle to make ends meet under conditions of great political and economic difficulty. Recently a Deseret Industries store was opened in São Paulo, and the Welfare Department in Salt Lake City began to ship cargo containers of used clothing and other supplies for Brazilian members. Employment missionaries and other temporal assistance and training are also being accelerated.

Mexico: South of the U.S. border, the Church has a long history of involvement in providing aid since the founding of the Mormon colonies of the late 1800s. Several decades ago, the Church established nearly 50 schools with over 10,000 students throughout Mexico for all ages of LDS children, but most of the schools have since been shut down. As reported in chapter 12, some LDS groups from Mexico City have attempted to create their own mini-Zions in rural *ejidos* of the government's land reform program.

Central America: This region of the Church has received considerable attention from Salt Lake City, enjoying the creation of schools and various experiments with agricultural, medical, and other types of training and relief. In spite of the dramatic decline of the Church in Nicaragua during the Sandinista regime of the 1980s, the civil wars in El Salvador, and the oppressive governments of other countries, the Church has continued to grow impressively, among both Spanish and native Indian populations. Several Church employment centers have been opened in the past three years, with relative success. Various U.S. missionaries, such as Cordell Anderson, have returned to the region to engage in services in behalf of the people they love so well. The Church has sent in large amounts of emergency relief supplies when disasters such as the major earthquakes in Guatemala and Nicaragua caused havoc in those countries. More recently, Humanitarian Services has funded several efforts in Central America to better the lives of the people. Clothing and other necessities have been donated.

Polynesia: Mormonism has grown from early missionary times in the mid-1800s to become a significant percentage of several island nations' total population. For example, 18 percent of the population of Samoa and 28 percent of the population of Tonga are LDS. The Church built many schools in the Pacific during the 20th century and established welfare farms and other projects, much like those of the Intermountain West. When hurricanes destroyed villages and farms in Tonga and Tahiti, the Church responded with large donations of emergency supplies.

The Caribbean: Recent LDS temporal relief efforts in these impoverished islands have occurred since missionary work opened after the 1978 revelation on blacks and the priesthood. For example, Humanitarian Services in 1990 supported a project to provide relief to an orphanage in the Dominican Republic and to start a rice growing project in Haiti. After a 1989 hurricane devastated sections of Puerto Rico, the Church channeled supplies through the governor's office to aid many victims.

Africa: Centuries of pain and pathos dominate today's African reality. History records exploitation by whites through ancient slave trading, inner-tribal conflicts, colonialism, and apartheid, coups and civil wars. Droughts and civil conflicts today exacerbate conditions such that agricultural production has been declining for decades while, conversely, the population grows, leading to a third of the masses now being dependent on the importation of food from other continents. With the inception of the LDS missionary thrust in the late 1970s, the bulk of Church efforts to help these nations has been the Ethiopian special fast and subsequent donations of food, clothes, emergency supplies, and cash noted earlier. A number of activities have also flowed from the LDS Humanitarian Funds to CARE, Technoserve, Red Cross, Africare, and the Ouelessebougou Alliance. These include projects such as well drilling in Nigeria, irrigation systems in Ethiopia and Chad, a demonstration farm in Ghana, a cassava processing operation in Nigeria, self-employment in Zaire, and the provision of medical care, training, and supplies to a number of nations.[17]

Many other programs are not operated by the Church Welfare Program, but are still sponsored by or affiliated with the Church.

Benson Institute. A major effort to develop local self-reliance is the Ezra Taft Benson Institute, named after the former U.S.

Secretary of Agriculture and veteran of the agricultural cooperative movement who eventually became president of the Church. The institute was established at BYU in the late 1970s. Over the past 15 years its staff has been involved in designing a series of programs to improve nutrition, health, and farming skills in the Third World, primarily in Latin America. Recent emphasis has been placed on small-scale agriculture in Mexico and Guatemala, to facilitate assisting poor rural families in supplying their nutritional requirements. Simple, labor-intensive methods are used to plant, fertilize, and harvest produce. Fish farms, animal husbandry, and other farm programs supplement the basic program of small crops. Currently, the Benson Institute has stepped back from direct implementation of its own system and begun to collaborate in more effective fashion with local, in-country schools and training programs. Latino agricultural colleges have begun to use the Institute's basic method so that it becomes their program, local ownership of the ideas thereby enhancing the likelihood that small-scale technologies will be accepted by rural peasant families.[18]

Thrasher Fund. In 1977 the Thrasher Research Fund was begun by the Church with a generous endowment from a non-LDS businessman, E. W. Thrasher, who wanted the Church to serve the health needs of children around the globe. He was willing to expend millions of dollars to achieve this goal, and gradually the criteria for doing research and providing relief have expanded. Thus, not only narrow technical studies of the causes of specific childhood diseases have been undertaken, but there is also a broader emphasis on prevention and public health as well. For instance, a group of professionals spent over a year in Africa in the 1980s working on such issues as nutrition, sanitation, and inoculation for families among certain tribes. They also studied local economic conditions and advised native women who had begun various rural cooperatives. The underlying assumption of the group was that if family economic levels could be raised, more resources could be expended on better food and medical treatment, thus improving the health of children. The Thrasher fund provided the funds to carry out this project.[19]

Katalysis. In Central America, a village banking organization called Katalysis, based in Stockton, California, has been funded by the Church and other foundations to create Grameen Bank-style groups which receive small financial loans so they can start and grow their micro-enterprises. Female participants in this program have been particularly successful in becoming self-sustaining entrepreneurs, leading the Church to propose expanding the effort throughout the region. Katalysis was founded by Bob Graham, a committed Christian who vowed to God he would spend the first 20 years of his career making as much money as he could and then spend the next two decades giving it away. Other such partnerships between the general Church and other development groups are being established.

Management of Church Efforts

In the 1990s President G. S. Gill, a BYU professor and native-born Punjab, was called to open the India, Bangalore mission in the south of that subcontinent. He declared that conversions and the building of chapels and eventually a temple were his spiritual goals. But also, his hopes were to "replace hate with love, envy with service . . . sickness with health, poverty with prosperity, illiteracy with knowledge and to give humanitarian service."[20] The new president hoped to build linkages between BYU students and faculty and the people of India, LDS members in particular, creating exchanges, learning languages, and devising strategies for achieving the temporal well-being of the poor. President Gill fully understood that conversions will be hard to maintain when suffering afflicts so many people.

However, such noble efforts must be wisely managed in the spirit of local self-government, as required by the law of stewardship. They must look to build up local self-reliance rather than using a traditional, top-down "president (general authority, Church bureaucrat, American missionary) knows best" approach. In Haiti a mission president attempted to set up agricultural cooperatives some years ago, but the lack of organizational skills, marketing, and understanding of cooperative management led to disastrous results. Some members left the Church over what happened, and missionary work itself was threatened when the government intervened and became very critical of the LDS program. Civil conflicts since then have made these problems even worse.

Such top-down efforts developed and implemented by the Church and directed from the United States were also attempted in the Philippines. In 1976, a welfare farm was set up on the outskirts of Manila, but transportation was costly, members with jobs often had to work six days a week, and water for irrigation was inadequate. For urban LDS Filipinos, the struggle to make an agricultural project succeed was impossible and the effort was abandoned. Squatters soon took over the property and established a shantytown typical of Third World metropolitan areas.

General authorities a decade ago directed the purchase of sewing machines, which were put in at least one classroom in the back of many LDS chapels. The expectation was that ward sisters would develop marketable job skills with which to obtain employment. They could also sew and repair clothes for family members. However, the outcome was that neither expectation was very successful, and the project was eventually abandoned. More recently the Humanitarian Services Committee has had considerably more success by simply funding locally based and directed training in gardening techniques for Filipino families and then getting "out of the way" so that those who were close to and familiar with the local situation could govern themselves.

In 1989, Salt Lake Church headquarters responded to the request of the area presidency in Manila by sending a husband-wife team to serve as employment specialists, and they laid the groundwork for expansion by instructing ward and stake leaders on principles and tactics for gaining member jobs. Various specialists, including author Woodworth, have been involved in training other couples as they were called to establish LDS employment centers in Cebu and Manila. They have succeeded in teaching members job skills and creating relationships with urban employers in order to offer referrals and provide counseling to local youth. They have closely coordinated their labors with bishops and other local Church leaders so that the employment efforts could be independently operated on the local level with minimal involvement from the Church in Salt Lake City.

Although success has had its ups and downs in the Philippines, overall the grassroots, locally led initiatives have had encouraging success and seem to suggest a degree of replicability in other areas of impoverished Asia, such as India, Indonesia, and Malaysia, as the Church begins to expand in those nations.

However, the work of working toward living the law of consecration is not just the domain of poor people and Third World nations. It involves the whole people. It is as important to those who can give as it is to those in need. President Kimball taught that "as givers gain control of their own desires and see others' needs in light of their own wants, then the powers of the gospel are released in their lives. They learn that by living the great law of consecration they insure not only temporal salvation but also spiritual sanctification. . . . in its purest form—in the true Zion—one may partake of both temporal and spiritual salvation."[21] Building Zion looks as well to the consecration of the wealth and talent of men of business.

PART FOUR
WORKING TOWARD A ZION WORLD

The gospel of Jesus Christ, which gospel we teach and the ordinances of which we perform, is a global faith with an all-embracing message. . . . Mormonism, so-called, is a world religion, not simply because its members are now found throughout the world, but chiefly because it has a comprehensive and inclusive message based upon the acceptance of all truth, restored to meet the needs of all mankind.

Howard W. Hunter[1]

Inside the early Zion's Cooperative Mercantile Institution (ZCMI), America's first department store. Here women employees are seen with the bolts of cloth to be sold. A major goal of ZCMI was to provide goods at wholesale prices that would serve the community interest.

15

The Talent of Men of Business:

Working Toward Zion Through Modern Business

The growth of wealth in the hands of a few individuals threaten[s] us with greater danger to-day, than anything that can be done by outsiders. . . . God does not design that there shall be classes among us, one class lifted above another, one class separated from the rest of the people. . . . Men are more disposed to compromise principle who have great monied interests at stake. . . . The time must come when the talent of men of business shall be used to benefit the whole people . . . not for individual benefit alone, not for individual aggrandizement alone, but for the benefit of the whole people, to uplift the masses, to rescue them from their poverty. That is one of the objects in establishing Zion, and anything short of that is not Zion.

George Q. Cannon[1]

The last five chapters have discussed many ways in which the spirit and principles of the united order may be promoted. However, the united order is not just good deeds in general. It purports to be the "full economic plan of Zion," a comprehensive program for the entire economy, comparable in scope to the great modern ideologies of socialism and capitalism. The next six chapters explore how we might move toward a Zion economy inspired by united order principles. This chapter begins this exploration by going into more detail as to how a fundamental goal of the united order, the elimination of poverty through viable employment, can be promoted in modern business. Then it will explore the broader issue of how the principles of consecration may be applied to the vast wealth which has been created by the Industrial Revolution. It is common to feel that these issues start applying with those who are a bit better off than we are. However, a modern American family of even modest resources enjoys vast wealth by comparison to the billions of our sisters and brothers today and historically in nonindustrialized societies. Even in his time, Adam Smith noted "that the accommodation of an European prince does not always so much exceed that of an industrious and frugal peasant, as the accommodation of the latter exceeds that of many an African king, the absolute master of the lives and liberties of ten thousand naked savages."[2]

Chapter 16 then explores how the principles of the united order can be applied in modern management—how we operate our businesses. Chapter 17 examines numerous examples of successful employee-owned companies and cooperatives where united order principles are being put into practical business application today. Chapter 18 focuses on the management of a business which has specifically undertaken to strive toward operating according to the principles of the united order. These chapters also discuss how "stewardship management" following the principles of the united order can respond to some of the criticisms of those who see the modern free enterprise economy as one which only seeks "individual aggrandizement," and examine how modern business and businessmen instead can seek "to benefit the whole people." Chapter 19 concentrates on one of the most remarkable of these cases, the Mondragon cooperative complex in Spain, where the cooperators have gone beyond a single enterprise to create an entire cooperative economic sector. Chapter 20 then discusses various issues and factors that would impact on efforts by Latter-day Saints to use these models to work toward applying the principles of the united order in the modern economy.

Corporate Outreach and Job Creation

One of the fundamental principles of the united order is care of the poor by expanding viable employment opportunities for them. Many businesses, both LDS and non-LDS, have gone beyond short-term financial considerations to make an extended effort to offer real jobs to those for whom jobs often are not readily available.

Inner-city Investment. A number of American businesses, such as Digital Equipment Company (DEC), have committed themselves to investing in the nation's inner cities, building new factories in troubled urban areas where joblessness and other problems of poverty abound. Kenneth Olsen, the founder and chairman of DEC, and an elder in his Protestant church, felt it was his Christian duty to provide employment opportunities for minority groups that are systematically excluded from the business strategies of many Fortune 500 companies. Thus in 1980, DEC built a plant in the black area of Roxbury, a neighborhood in inner-city Boston, training workers and raising their skills so the factory would be financially successful. Other facilities were later built in Washington, D.C., and St. Paul, Minnesota. Thousands of minority families were able to experience a degree of economic self-sustainability. For many of them it was the first time in their lives that there was a solid opportunity—an actual factory in their neighborhood where they could go get a job.

Other progressive firms have engaged in similar ventures. IBM hired 120 African-Americans in Brooklyn, New York's Bedford-Stuyvesant district, to recondition electronic cable. Starting in the 1960s, the plant grew to hundreds of minority employees as further new hirees were educated and socialized into the work ethic of the company culture. Eventually the work expanded to include tasks such as component assembly for several of IBM's most powerful computers. When IBM began its program of significant workforce reduction in the early 1990s, rather than simply close down the plant, IBM sold it to its employees. Today, employee-owned Advanced Technology Solutions is prospering and has almost 300 employees.[3]

Control Data Corporation, led by the innovative computer pioneer William Norris, set up a factory in a north side minority neighborhood of Minneapolis. Working with black community leaders, Norris installed the firm's most modern facility and made it Control Data's sole source for these parts so that there would be a strong management interest in achieving success. At black workers' suggestion, the plant also established an on-site day care operation for employed mothers' convenience and a flexible working hours program. The thrust of these various management efforts was clearly not philanthropy or a handout, but to create successful financial ventures in which their firms would also behave in a socially responsible fashion.

Geneva Steel. Another approach which has resulted in positive, LDS-oriented business practices is illustrated by Geneva Steel. For over 40 years after the federal government gave United States Steel ("USX") the mill on the shores of Utah Lake, the Pittsburgh company enjoyed huge profits from the work ethic of Orem and Provo Latter-day Saints. The mill's strategic location gave it access to cheap raw materials in the West and the close proximity of major California markets. A union that was nonmilitant meant peaceful labor relations and workers who trusted management. However, beginning in the mid-1970s, corporate headquarters cut investments in new technology, sped up production, and reduced its Utah workforce by half. Eventually the company forced a labor lockout which lasted over six months, and when the dispute was settled, Geneva was on a hit list for permanent closure. Unknown to innocent Utahns, Pittsburgh headquarters had secretly consummated a deal with Korea's giant steel company to ship product to the West Coast from the Pacific Rim, leaving the Utah plant obsolete.

Ultimately, a group of Latter-day Saints with Utah roots put together the capital to buy Geneva from USX, and it was resuscitated from near-death. Led by Joe Cannon, the cast-off USX facility soon began to attain high profits, and all jobs were saved, even hundreds more added. Unlike the distant, absentee-owned practices of Pittsburgh-based executives, Cannon has invested heavily in new equipment to aid productivity and cut pollution. Safe working practices and cooperative union relations began to be implemented. The mill adopted one of Utah's poorest schools, Geneva Elementary, and donated money to purchase computers and other equipment to strengthen the learning process. The company gave large amounts of money to BYU and various Utah charities and arts groups. Workers received $6,000 or more in profit sharing as the business gained strength and the fruits of their labor began to accumulate. Cannon himself spoke often of the "inspiration" that struck him when he first considered the reopening of Geneva, and he often connects his current enterprise success with that of his great-great grandfather, George Q. Cannon (quoted above), one of the early united order's most vocal advocates.[4]

International Employment Outreach. A similar strategy carried out by LDS business executives could be implemented, not only in inner-city America, but on Indian reservations and in Third World and formerly Communist countries. Some dedicated individuals are already doing so, experiencing great satisfaction as well as business success. For example, the Huntsman Company began a cement manufacturing plant in Armenia after the devastating earthquake five years ago. Likewise, the Marriott Corporation entered into a joint venture with Poland's LOT airlines in the late 1980s, a project that has benefitted both parties and created thousands of new jobs. Some of these employees have since joined the Church and served missions in the West. Today, Warsaw's tallest and finest hotel is that of Marriott, an impressive symbol of market free enterprise in the once-Communist capitol.

Huckvale/Israel Project. An LDS contractor from southern California, Fred Huckvale, is chairman of the board of Gwerdon Industries, the 35th largest home building firm in America. He became involved with the Israeli government and several contractors in Israel. This small nation has been inundated with over a million immigrants since the fall of the Iron Curtain, as Jews have streamed back to their "promised land." The most immediate question has been how to solve the housing crisis.

Huckvale proposed that prefab housing be built by his firm, which has plants in Georgia and Mississippi, and shipped to Israel. Each unit has plumbing, wiring and carpeting all intact and ready for use. Shiploads of 300 houses each, the largest ever to dock in Israeli harbors, began arriving regularly, providing new homes for Russian immigrants. Like Natasha Stukalov, most former Soviet immigrants have only lived in tall, cement apartment buildings with only one or two rooms, often shared by another family. Gwerdon has established an excellent approach for dealing with the current Israeli crisis of overcrowding. Huckvale also consulted with the Israeli housing minister, which led to the construction of a factory in Ashkalon, Israel, in which Russian immigrants themselves now construct 12 prefab homes each day, creating not only houses but jobs as well.

Russell-Newman, Inc. Another LDS businessman, Frank Martino, is chairman and CEO of Russell-Newman, Inc., a sewing company headquartered in Texas. With various plants around the United States, Martino began to consider overseas expansion in the 1980s. His son, who had served a mission in Central America, decided to return to Guatemala City and see if some of his earlier contacts might want to participate in a new business venture. One LDS fellow he located seemed a potential candidate for a new business start-up. The Martinos helped him secure a small building and several sewing machines. The budding entrepreneur hired several skilled women who began sewing to fulfill the first small sewing contract from Russell-Newman, Inc. It was a professional business arrangement, formally incorporated with a high-profile LDS flavor to everything that occurred. Top-quality products were sewn and delivered on time. Profits allowed for the acquisition of more equipment. Soon the Guatemalan enterprise purchased and moved to a larger facility. Jobs for members, and adequate profits for both the local and U.S. company, have blossomed into an impressive business.

U.S. Corporate and Latin American Partnerships. Another arena in which private enterprise initiatives could occur would be in connection with the North American Free Trade Agreement (NAFTA), which promises a significant window of opportunity in Mexico and Central America for the creation of employment and economic growth. LDS manufacturers in the United States who wish to expand operations south of the border, who are ethical and committed to progressive labor relations practices, could create joint ventures with Latino partners. Perhaps native regional representatives, stake, and mission leaders could help identify local professionals already living in those countries. They could also serve to identify and locate indigenous employees who are honest and hardworking, both LDS and of other religions, who have business aptitudes and potential. More job opportunities, expanded small factories, and a higher living standard for Church members would be likely outcomes. Although such ventures would not be official Church projects, the LDS network would be a promising resource to accomplish business goals and to serve LDS needs among Latino Saints. Whatever one's views on NAFTA, its economic results could then at least be partially turned to helping working poor Latter-day Saints to become self-reliant rather than simply enriching multinational corporations.

Perhaps some sort of "Business Development Agency" could be established by a group of North American LDS executives to coordinate and facilitate such an effort. We can envision fifty or a hundred such joint ventures begun over the next several years by LDS managers which could blossom into the creation of thousands of jobs for Church members in those countries.

Corporate Charitable Contributions

Another arena of business involvement in practicing certain united order principles is that of simple financial donations. Scott Bader Commonwealth, a British employee-owned company described in chapter 17, gives a percentage of its revenues as charitable contributions to groups around the world each year. The Mondragon cooperatives described in chapter 19 give a percentage of profits to educational and cultural groups. LDS executives could increase their participation in such areas. When a Utah company offers financial support to a community cause, such as aiding environmental preservation or donating to local arts groups, every citizen of the state becomes a beneficiary. Corporate contributions to community needs such as the Primary Children's Hospital, scout programs, literacy projects, the United Way, or shelters for battered women have blessed the lives of many. Intermountain Health Care passes on used medical equipment to groups collecting supplies for Third World hospitals. Russell's Ice Cream Company, based in Salt Lake City, donates a percentage of profits to foundations doing relief and village development in Bolivia and other nations.

Companies outside of LDS areas of the country have also been good examples. G. D. Searle Co., a pharmaceutical firm, donates heart disease drugs to poor patients. Likewise, ARCO's founder, Robert Anderson, committed his company to many social and environmental concerns in the 1970s and 1980s, even breaking with the rest of the oil industry by advocating stringent emission controls on all automobiles. Merck & Co. gives away drugs worth millions of dollars to fight the leading cause of blindness. In Chicago, business leaders organized the Corporate Responsibility Group to counter poverty, violence, and drug abuse. New York firms have adopted schools among black neighborhoods and Spanish Harlem to raise the level of education and prepare ghetto youth for college. Cleveland executives revitalized their inner city through constructive strategies of stewardship and community service. As mentioned in chapter 1, under Kay Whitmore, Eastman Kodak sent hundreds of skilled employees into the Rochester, New York, schools to teach math and science. LDS communities need to experience a greater degree of such good corporate citizenship through top management policies that strengthen needy areas, rather than ignoring them or relocating to escape them.

Wealth Sharing by Materially Blessed Saints

Not only should corporations seek to exercise what Ezra Taft Benson called a "social consciousness," but in their personal lives as well there is much that wealthy Latter-day Saints can offer the less fortunate.[5] George Meany, President of the AFL-CIO, declared, "I never met a corporation that has a conscience," suggesting that after all, it is not the organization itself, but individuals at the top who are either sympathetic or apathetic to human needs.[6] To avoid the stereotype of narrow self-interest and personal greed, the notion has emerged in some business circles that those at the top of the social pyramid have certain obligations to other members of society. Such a view is not merely an indulgence in rhetoric, but a long-standing tradition among many in the upper echelons of business. John D. Rockefeller accumulated huge amounts of money a century ago, but gave away $550 million during his lifetime and incorporated the Rockefeller Foundation, through which subsequent billions of dollars could be passed on to future generations for worthy projects.

Andrew Carnegie's famous article "The Gospel of Wealth" asserts that the duty of the person of wealth was

> to set an example of modest, unostentatious living, shunning display or extravagance; to provide moderately for the legitimate wants of those dependent upon him; and after doing so, to consider all surplus revenues which come to him simply as trust funds, which he is called upon to administer in the manner which, in his judgement, is best calculated to produce the most beneficial results for the community—the man of wealth thus becoming the mere trustee and agent for his poorer brethren. . . . The day is not far distant when the man who dies leaving behind him millions of available wealth . . . will pass away "unwept, unhonored, and unsung," no matter to what uses he leaves the dross which he cannot take with him. Of such as these the public verdict will then be: "The man who dies thus rich dies disgraced." Such, in my opinion, is the true gospel concerning wealth, obedience to which is destined some day to solve the problem of the rich and the poor, and to bring "Peace on earth, among men good will."[7]

Over 2,500 libraries and thousands of church organs, a world famous concert hall, peace foundations, pension funds for teachers and steelworkers, and more than $350 million donated to various projects attest to Carnegie's efforts to live consistent with this notion of riches as a trusteeship. In the end he literally could not give his money away fast enough and had to leave it to a foundation to carry on the task. When Herbert Spencer died in 1904, he left to Beatrice Webb a magnificent piano which Carnegie had given him. By then, Carnegie's reputation for wide-ranging philanthropy was such that even Beatrice Webb brought herself to write Carnegie asking him to exchange the piano for a contribution to the London School of Economics.[8]

That the true goal of getting is giving has another distinguished antecedent among the advocates of free enterprise. Both of his major works were international bestsellers for decades of his life, he held high paying government positions, and received a very substantial pension from a duke whose son he had briefly tutored. Yet at his death, Adam Smith left an extremely modest estate, the result of a lifetime of anonymous charity. Having lived the later Scotsman's credo, the father of modern free market economics proved by his actions, if it was ever misunderstood from his words, his belief that the wise and virtuous man always seeks first "the interest of that great society of all sensible and intelligent beings, of which God himself is the immediate administrator and director."[9]

Philanthropy thus began to be widely practiced in American social circles. The question is, where are Mormonism's captains of industry who are engaged in donations? Of course these donations may not be on the same scale as the contributions of a Carnegie or Rockefeller, but do they at least approximate the percentage of personal wealth which was donated to social causes by the most exemplary of America's earlier capitalists? Certainly a few wealthy LDS members have contributed significantly of their fortunes, such as Jon Huntsman's recent $100 million donation for cancer research at the University of Utah. However, aside from the occasional fund-raising banquet, how many have donated large sums of money to programs that attempt to lift the poverty stricken? Considering the great inequality between the world's Haves and the earth's poor, we all should remember the Biblical parable of the purple-robed rich man who barely let the crumbs from his table fall to the beggar Lazarus, leading to the "great gulf fixed" between the two after death (Luke 16:19–31). Do our lifestyles tend to exhibit an inordinate interest in "riches and . . . the vain things of the world" or are we "succoring those who stand in need of [our] succor, such as imparting [our] substance to the poor and needy, feeding the hungry, and suffering all manner of afflictions, for Christ's sake"(Alma 4:8, 13).

Overcoming Materialism

In the end, of course, strategies and programs to practice united order principles must come from within oneself and then be manifested in the family, firm, Church group, or larger community. All of this presupposes that we truly seek to become true Saints rather than merely successful Mormons. It means that we reject "Nephititis," the disease in ancient America that first

Lorenzo Snow (1814–1901), fourth president of the LDS Church and founder of the large Brigham City Cooperative Association. He was a long-time advocate of gospel principles of consecration and the creation of community and worker-owned firms throughout the Intermountain region.

destroyed individuals and families, and then progressed like a cancer to institutions, including the church and larger society, until the whole nation was destroyed. As the Book of Mormon so amply shows, righteousness led to prosperity, which led to pride and wickedness, even though prosperity continued to grow.

Many Church members today believe that capitalism is a superior system, one that encourages more righteousness and economic productivity than socialism. However, the prosperity which mainstream economics generates today also may lead to pride and wickedness. This seems to be a central theme of scriptural history, pointing to very real dangers for us today.

No wonder Spencer W. Kimball chided LDS people: "I wonder if many of us are not lusting to be rich. Are we making compromises in order to accumulate?" He challenged those who justify seeking excess farms, herds, and firms when one already possesses life's basic necessities. "Why continue to expand and increase holdings, especially when those increased responsibilities draw one's interests away from proper family and spiritual commitments, and from those things to which the Lord would have us give precedence in our lives? . . . to the point where our interests are divided and our attentions and thoughts are upon the things of the world?"[10] As President Kimball declared in his classic *Ensign* article "The False Gods We Worship," far too many LDS Church members spend their time and energy in things which they hope will "*guarantee* carnal security, throughout, it is hoped, a long and happy life."[11] The prophet labels such modern materialism as "idolatry" and calls on those who seek after many goods to fully repent.

Brigham Young warned, "The worst fear that I have about this people is that they will get rich in this country, forget God and His people, wax fat, and kick themselves out of the Church and go to hell."[12] Brother Brigham must have been viewing Church members of the late 20th century. In our time, Howard W. Hunter counseled that "this is a materialistic world, and Latter-day Saints must be careful not to confuse luxuries with necessities. . . . There are some who unwisely aspire to self-indulgent luxuries that often lead them away from complete commitment to the gospel of our Savior." Instead, priesthood holders should seek "enough income so that we may be self-sufficient and able to support our families, while leaving us enough time free to be good fathers and church workers."[13]

One of the tragedies of our time is the absentee father, working long hours making money to support his family's lifestyle of material consumption, while depriving both them and himself of the far more valuable gift of time together. Such time with the family is not only a part of joyful living, but far more critical to children's emotional health than material luxuries.[14] Can and will we cut back, live more simply, and thereby give more of what we have away? Very little in life is more satisfying than discussing principles of stewardship with our children and then having them vote in home evening to have only $25 to $30 spent on each child for Christmas, so that a matching amount can be given to Sub-for-Santa or a family project to help the needy on a neighboring Indian reservation.

Elder Dallin H. Oaks captures the problem: "Materialism is a seductive distortion of self-reliance. The corruption occurs through carrying the virtue of 'providing for our own' to the point of excess concern with accumulating the treasures of the earth."[15] Those who feel they need to acquire great sums to start their children off in life and marriage with many material possessions deprive the young of the challenges which build character. Furthermore, the next generation is crippled with the burden of status and pride, thus ensuring that the materialistic "sins of the fathers" are visited on their descendants. How much wiser to heed the counsel of the Prophet Joseph: "The faith necessary unto the enjoyment of life and salvation never could be obtained without the sacrifice of all earthy things," and "a religion that does not require the sacrifice of all things never has power sufficient to produce the faith necessary unto life and salvation."[16]

Living the simple, gospel-focused life is the greatest gift of all. Andrew Carnegie believed that one should give away wealth rather than pass it on as an inheritance, and he tried to do so during his day. Elder Oaks puts it another way: "A wealthy man died. 'How much property did he leave?' someone inquired. The wise response: 'He left all of it.'"[17] Instead of building a rich inheritance or accumulating excess goods for one's lifestyle here and now, Elder Oaks counsels that "we must also be so indifferent to material or earthly things that we are willing to give up cheerfully whatever is necessary to become 'equal' in those things . . . which is the polar opposite of aggressive and selfish materialism: 'Every man seeking the interest of his neighbor, and doing all things with an eye single to the glory of God' (D&C 82:19)."[18]

Whether rich or poor, it is our attitude and our actions which define our relationship with God. All socioeconomic classes need to overcome pride and the game of social climbing. Instead, to become true Saints we must seek equality in social regard, in our relations with all others. Belonging to exclusive clubs is not befitting of true Christians. Economic, geographical, aesthetic, or intellectual snobbery do not allow us to enjoy the presence of the Holy Ghost. Instead, we must teach our children, through precept and example, to esteem one another as God's children, integrate our neighborhoods and wards, and increase social tolerance and love, so that Zion can really be established in our hearts, minds, and the larger society, in which every person recognizes his or her calling as a steward of the greater light.

16

The Greater Light:
Stewardship Management in Modern Business

Every man shall be made accountable unto me, a steward over his own property, or that which he has received by consecration, as much as is sufficient for himself and family.

D&C 42:32

For of him unto whom much is given much is required; and he who sins against the greater light shall receive the greater condemnation.

D&C 82:3

As described in chapter 9, during the 20th century, many Latter-day Saints have achieved positions of prominence in the world of business. CEOs and chairmen of boards of directors have a major voice in company policies and new business ventures. The combination of business acumen, technical skills, availability of bank loan financing, training, and luck, have enabled certain of these individuals to launch new businesses and to achieve significant financial success. Some, like Evans and Sutherland, Novell, and the Marriott Corporation, evolved slowly but significantly. Others, such as WordPerfect, Nu-Skin, and Franklin Quest, enjoyed rapid growth and became almost overnight successes.

LDS Corporate Cultures. In certain cases these ventures have developed what a University of Massachusetts historian, Mario DePillis, thinks of as a type of contemporary corporate united order. A highly respected non-LDS scholar, DePillis feels that company cultures of such firms reflect a quasi Mormon parallel to earlier LDS Church structures.[1] A few of these companies, most of which are based in Utah, tend to have management teams which appear to function somewhat akin to stake high councils. In fact, hiring occasionally approximates a Church calling. Management meetings often begin with prayer, even scripture reading in some cases. There is a degree of organizational informality, and one's personal and family concerns often become part of business discussions.

Some of these firms allow extremely flexible working hours, at least down through supervisory ranks, so that employees may attend their children's school programs, take ill family members to the doctor, and so on. One CEO of a hundred-year-old Utah firm used to work at the office only in the morning so he could spend afternoons with his first priority, his family. Top executives in several of these companies routinely encourage employees to leave their offices by 5:00 P.M. so as to be home for family dinner and become more involved in household activities. Taking time off to lead a youth conference or to accompany a scout troop to summer camp is seen as legitimate as attending a sales conference.[2]

While these organizational cultures appear to have a number of positive features, the conduct of many LDS businesses as described in chapter 2 shows that more could be done to enable many LDS-owned or managed firms to better embody principles of the united order. The low wage levels which give Utah such a negative reputation nationally ought to be significantly raised to be commensurate with the state's much touted, highly educated workforce. Dangerous work practices and unsafe factory conditions need to be completely eliminated. Their elimination need not compromise business success. As we will see below, many non-LDS businesses and businessmen have offered excellent examples of applying united order principles in successful modern business.

Stewardship in Modern Business

However, the question goes beyond what can be done without in any way impacting the financial bottom line. The restored gospel recognizes no distinction between the spiritual and the temporal, and our conduct in business must ultimately be judged by eternal standards. The Savior himself suggests that "where much is given, much is required." It is this logic which was perhaps first articulated in the United States by Arthur T. Hadley, president of Yale University, who argued that the head of a company "is a trustee for the stockholders and creditors of his corporation. In a less obvious but equally important sense he is a trustee in behalf of the public."[3] Trusteeship and service became important values for many early business leaders, precisely because of the corporate accumulation of wealth and power.

General Robert E. Wood, the head of Sears, Roebuck and Company from the 1920s to 1954, often stressed the important social and political roles of the corporation, not just economics in the form of profits. In the 1936 Sears Annual Report, he wrote to stockholders, "In these days of changing social, economic and political values, it seems worthwhile . . . to render an account of your management's stewardship," which he goes on to define as including not just owners but customers, employees, suppliers, and the American public. Wood not only encouraged management to be active in civic affairs and donate to local charities, but he directed corporate strategy to strengthening the local economic base, helping to revive troubled firms, creating employment, and working to bring new businesses to the area.[4]

However, many LDS and non-LDS business professionals today identify with the views of economists such as Milton Friedman, who advance a very narrow view of corporate concerns. In his *Capitalism and Freedom,* he claims that the *sole* responsibility of the corporation is to maximize profits, thereby supposedly benefitting society indirectly.[5] Such exclusive logic, however, was not the view of most great corporate leaders. Decades ago, Owen Young, General Electric's chairman, declared, "The old notion . . . that the heads of business are the paid attorneys for stockholders, to exploit labor and the public in the stockholder's interest is gone—I hope forever." Likewise, *Forbes* magazine put forth the view that "the business of modern business is service."[6] LDS businessman Ray Noorda, the former head of Novell, advocated a hierarchy of priorities that put customers first, employees second, and shareholders third—and built one of the most important software companies in the world.

These broader commitments are quite a contrast to many firms today, including Sears itself, which seems to be rejecting its heritage and the very values that built its modern corporate culture. Today one reads *Deseret News* reports of unethical or illegal Salt Lake business practices—penny stock scams and fraudulent real estate deals. This includes historic Utah firms, such as the Bennett group of companies, started by a prominent early Utah family, which was mismanaged into bankruptcy when young BYU business graduates took it over. They quadrupled their own salaries, gave their wives huge clothing allowances, bought expensive company cars and a corporate jet for themselves, while at the same time slashing jobs, breaking the union, and driving the paint and glass business into the ground.

Unfortunately, certain Salt Lake banks, businesses, and government offices seem to care more for the anticipated short-term financial windfall the one-time Winter Olympics in 2002 will bring their investment deals than for enhancing new local start-up businesses. The AFCO disaster and the now unfolding story of Bonneville Pacific, a sleazy so-called energy firm of the 1980s, reinforce the sad reputation of Utah's business community. In the latter case, which government investigators have only started to explore, Bonneville top management took out over $40 million to line their pockets while the hollow shell of the corporation was collapsing, a far cry from the notion of stewardship or the CEO as a sacred trustee. It is estimated this latest fiasco cost LDS and other investors some $700 million.[7]

Spencer W. Kimball warned those who engage in deceitful business dealings: "Profit and commissions derived from worthless stock are contaminated, as is the money derived from another's deception, excessive charges, oppression to the poor," an apparent reference to the growing plethora of scams and pyramid schemes involving so many Church members. What is required by the Lord is "fair dealing in business matters, in selling, in buying, and in general representations," in contrast to the worldly capitalist dictum of *caveat emptor*—"let the buyer beware." Rather than the profit that comes from compromises, graft, and exploitation, which President Kimball calls the work of those who are "greedy for filthy lucre," he pleads for true Saints to "keep your money clean," defining it thus: "Clean money . . . is that fair profit from the sale of goods, commodities or services. It is that income received from transactions where all parties profit."[8]

The notion, advocated by leaders such as Adam Smith, Joseph Smith and Spencer Kimball, that morality should undergird the marketplace, contrasts sharply not only with the policies of many U.S. companies, but even with modern schools of business. Consider this excerpt from a management text: "Simply to make an untrue statement about a product is in itself not unethical, nor to make a shoddy product—that may be bad management, but it is not necessarily unethical."[9] Such is the logic of today's Charles Keatings, Frank Lorenzos, Ivan Boeskys, and Michael Milkens, as well as many wheelers and dealers in corporate America who have so far not yet been caught. For too many entrepreneurs and executives, whether LDS or not, Machiavelli's *The Prince* is the ethical philosophy upon which their corporate strategies are based.

Any means is justified if the end is important enough. The prince or CEO is allowed to take whatever measures are needed to accomplish his goal and preserve his power. Beating people at their own game and outplaying the cunning techniques of the competition by whatever devious strategies are possible—these are the hallmarks of Social Darwinism. By twisting scriptural truth, today's vernacular encourages executives to "Do unto others *before* they do unto you."[10]

At best, the only limitation accepted on business conduct is bare legality. If it is legal, it is OK, as illustrated by the following sworn testimony by the chief executive of a major tobacco company:

> Question: If . . . I can get together for you, any time you ask, 20 leading authorities in the world on the issue of whether or not cigarette smoke causes lung cancer, heart disease, emphysema and other diseases, . . . would you avail yourself of that opportunity?
>
> Answer: No.
>
> Question: Why not?
>
> Answer: I have no interest.
>
> Question: You never read a Surgeon General's report dealing with the issue of smoking and health, correct?
>
> Answer: No, correct. . . .
>
> Question: I assume you don't have any knowledge on the subject. . . . And basically, no interest in acquiring any knowledge?
>
> Answer: That is correct.
>
> Question: As I understand your position, generally, . . . you're going to do your thing, as long as it is legal to do it.
>
> Answer: That is correct.
>
> Question: And make as much money as you can while you're doing it?
>
> Answer: I'm a businessman.[11]

Why would an LDS businessman adhere to the philosophy espoused by the tobacco company executive—that he did not care about the social or personal damage his business caused as long as it was legal and made money? Many Church members preach the "gospel of success" which seems to equate worldly prosperity with spiritual worth. Some of these individuals enjoy a degree of fame in the Utah press and are held up as models of success in the LDS community. Bumper stickers reading "He who dies with the most toys wins," are visible not only on Rodeo Drive or Wall

Street, but on the East Bench of Salt Lake City, Bountiful, and Provo as well. Apostle Dallin Oaks accurately depicts this type of Church member:

> Those who preach the gospel of success and the theology of prosperity are suffering from "the deceitfulness of riches" and from supposing that "gain is godliness" (1 Timothy 6:5). The possession of wealth or the acquisition of significant income is not a rank of heavenly favor, and their absence is not evidence of heavenly disfavor.[12]

By the 1950s, business experts were writing about the Iron Law of Responsibility, arguing that those who do not utilize power appropriately will lose it if society concludes that they were not responsible.[13] In other words, it is in the best interest of the enlightened corporation to be responsive to the wishes and expectations of society, or its own survival will be in jeopardy. Such a view is not a statement of values or preferences, but rather a prediction that recognizes the mutual interdependence of the company and its social context. Avoiding corporate moral and social responsibility will inevitably lead to the erosion of business freedom, as shown by the increased federal regulation of corporations after the excesses of Robber Barons in the last century.

This view was taught in the October 1939 conference by apostle Stephen L Richards (later a member of the First Presidency), who argued that employers who keep wages low are both immoral and shortsighted. Low wages stifle consumers that businesses depend on. To those who would argue that businesses must push down labor costs as low as possible in order to be profitable, the apostle (who was also a successful businessman himself) said:

> I am perfectly aware that profit is the life of business, and I have no objection whatever to the profit incentive, but I do not have any sympathy with the avarice and stupidity which in the long run cut off profits and stifle prosperity. It would almost seem as if the privilege of profit should not be permitted to those who, either through ignorance or lack of humanitarian principles, are not capable of being entrusted with it. It is here that the concept of brotherhood of man plays such an important role. No one who recognizes the Fatherhood of God and mankind as his children can tolerate with equanimity the inequalities and injustices which such selfishness brings about.[14]

Implementing Stewardship in Modern Business

Do gospel principles have anything to do with our business practices? Many contemporary Utah shopping centers and food stores are busy with the hustle and bustle of shoppers on Sunday, a sharp contrast to the Salt Lake City Sabbath in the days of Brigham Young, or even David O. McKay. Such practices are at odds with the policies of some other Christian-owned firms. For example, Chick-Fil-A, Inc., a fast-food chain based in Atlanta, refuses to be open on Sunday because of Biblical commandments.[15] Many companies created tobacco-free workplaces long before most Utah firms did so. Decades ago, many firms had established codes of conduct and sponsored training in management and employee ethics. For example, J.C. Penney launched his company based on the Golden Rule, a foundation of values which has maintained a corporate conscience until the present. Johnson & Johnson's "credo" emphasizes its commitment to customers, quality, and cost reduction, so that consumers view pricing as reasonable and suppliers enjoy a fair profit. Workers are to be respected and treated with dignity, while wages are to be adequate. The company is to assist employees in the fulfilling of their family responsibilities.[16] Elsewhere, the founder of Days Inn of America, Inc. developed a very conscious gospel strategy of practices, such as not serving alcohol. Instead of seeking to maximize profits by catering primarily to society's upper echelon and business customers who would pay top dollar for executive suites, they focused on building a hotel chain that would be within reach of most middle-class American families. Days Inn even offers the services of four company chaplains to counsel and aid workers who have personal and family problems. Examples such as these suggest ways of improving LDS business practices in a number of areas.

Fair Pay. First, one may inquire about treatment of employees, working conditions, and wages. God's mandate anciently was as follows: "Thou shalt not oppress an hired servant that is poor and needy, whether he be of thy brethren, or of thy strangers" (Deuteronomy 24:14). The implication for us today seems to be that the practice of many Utah firms which pay workers the federal minimum wage or other low compensation, while legal, is not commensurate with Christian managerial actions. New Testament scriptures suggest that the appropriate attitude today's administrator might adopt is that of the apostle Peter, who admonishes those high in power and position to "feed the flock of God which is among you, taking the oversight thereof; not for filthy lucre, but of a ready mind" (1 Peter 5:1–2).

Giving workers the lowest possible pay is not only immoral, but shortsighted. Great business leaders recognize this. Sam Walton said that the single most important factor in the success of Wal-Mart was his realization that "the more you share profits with your associates—whether it's in salaries or incentives or bonuses or stock discounts—the more profits will accrue to the company."[17] Employee enterprise, energy, and loyalty are won by respect and generous compensation. As Adam Smith wrote in the *Wealth of Nations,* the "wages of labour are the encouragement of industry, which, like every other human quality, improves in proportion to the encouragement it receives. A plentiful subsistence increases the bodily strength of the labourer, and the comfortable hope of bettering his condition, and of ending his days in ease and plenty, animates him to exert that strength to the utmost. Where wages are high, accordingly, we shall always find the workmen more active, diligent, and expeditious, than where they are low."[18]

More recently, Spencer W. Kimball advocated "reasonable pay" for employees who should, in turn, provide "a full day's honest work." President Kimball practiced this in his own life. Old residents of his hometown of Thatcher, Arizona, recalled that even as a businessman struggling through the Great Depression, Spencer Kimball "always paid top wages" to his employees.[19] He taught that all of us, from the custodian to the CEO, who "do not give commensurate time, energy, devotion, and service are receiving money that is not clean."[20]

Valuing Human Resources. It may seem obvious that it is better for an enterprise to have employees who are "more active, diligent, and expeditious" than not. A firm where everyone labors with "energy, devotion, and service" would seem to be more likely to do well than one where this is not so. However, while most companies pay at least lip service to these ideas, modern American business management often seems to neglect them in practice. This may be partially explained by the inability of modern accounting principles to fully account for human resources. If a company buys a new machine it can add the cost as an asset on its balance sheet. In addition, even though the full cost was paid in cash when the machine was purchased, the company can spread the cost as a reduction to its earnings over several years. In contrast, when a company pays for additional training for a worker, it must take the full cost as an immediate reduction to its earnings. Further, it cannot add the cost of the training as an asset on its balance sheet.

The same principles operate when "disposing" of the resource as when it is "acquired." When a company incurs a loss on disposing of a machine, it must take the loss as a reduction to its earnings. However, as noted above, financial statements do not recognize employees as assets. They only appear on the financial statements as an expense for wages and benefits. Thus, when employees are subjected to low or reduced wages, or are laid off, the company generally does not have to take any reduction in earnings or assets for its depressed or depleted labor force. The only immediate effect on the financial statements is a decrease in expenses for wages and benefits, which in the very short term will increase earnings. It is only after a much longer period of time that financial statements will begin to show the results of a inadequate or demoralized workforce. In the meantime, the financial statement treatment makes it appear that disposing of employees or employment related costs gives the biggest "savings."[21]

Financial analysis is at the center of modern American business and investment management. It receives tremendous emphasis in business schools, and is the principal criteria used by stock analysts in deciding which companies' stocks to favor. There has been a marked tendency for American executives to come from financial instead of operating backgrounds. The company's chief financial officer becomes the CEO rather than the experts in manufacturing or marketing.[22] Also, as noted in chapter 1, the financial analyzing that is done tends to focus on results in the immediate present. A perhaps unintended consequence of all of this focus on short-term financial results is the inevitable devaluation of resources, such as employees, which are not fully reflected in financial statements.

Generally, one cannot blame the accounting principles. Human resources are very difficult to measure concretely. However, even though they do not appear on the balance sheet, skilled, well-motivated employees are usually a company's most important asset. The long-term journey to corporate success requires motivated human beings cooperating in joint enterprise, not labor treated as a disposable cost component on a statement of operations. If they wish to truly act on this principle, number-blinded managers and stock analysts must make a deliberate, conscious decision to see beyond the blizzard of short-term financial statement results. Executives must be willing to sacrifice the short-term paper benefits of ignoring employee motivation and development in favor of the long-term real benefits of expending resources to enhance employees' status as active, creative, contributing members of the company community. There are several ways to accomplish this in addition to fair compensation.

Employee Dignity. Many businesses have corporate constitutions, including an employee bill of rights which includes free speech, privacy, open access to information, safety practices, and due process. If one is accused by a supervisor of inappropriate behavior, a system of due process gives the individual the right to an impartial hearing before a company ombudsperson, council of peers, or outside arbitrator. Thus rights similar to those of the U.S. Constitution are being increasingly institutionalized in corporate America, to safeguard the dignity and freedom of the individual.

Another area in which LDS managers may function more ethically is industrial relations and human resource practices. The archaic assumption of authoritarian leadership with its military model and focus on control of the workers has become passé. Today's employee, well-educated and raised in the political environment of a constitutional democracy such as the United States, is becoming increasingly insistent on having a voice in workplace decisions. Progressive U.S. firms like Procter & Gamble and General Electric have responded by making organizational and cultural changes to empower the worker, thereby reaping large gains in productivity and quality. Many companies today are investing huge expenditures in developing their "human capital," not merely financial resources and factory machinery.

Great entrepreneurs have long held such views. Sam Walton predicted that "in the future free enterprise is going to have to be done well—which means it benefits the workers, the shareholders, the communities, and, of course, management, which must adopt a philosophy of servant leadership. . . . A lot of American management has bent over too far toward taking care of itself first, and worrying about everybody else later. . . . [In] the next century the way business is conducted worldwide is going to be different. . . . Good management is going to start listening to the ideas of [the] line soldiers, pooling these ideas and disseminating them around their organizations so people can act on them. . . . Great ideas come from everywhere if you just listen and look for them. You never know who's going to have a great idea."[23]

Family-Friendly Policies. With declining wages and employer pressure for longer work hours, parents are finding it increasingly difficult to fulfill their family responsibilities. This is further complicated by the large increase in the number of working mothers. While the gospel ideal is for a father to support his family on a single income so that mothers may be in the home while there are children there, exceptional circumstances in the modern economy are more than rare.[24] The ease with which men can obtain divorces, combined with lax policies toward child support payments, leave many mothers alone to support their children. Even in two-parent households, the declining incomes of the majority of workers make it often impossible to support a family in even modest circumstances on a single income. Even if one does everything "right," gets an education, pursues a promising profession, and so on, the experience of Joe and Mary Brown illustrates how corporate downsizing and other forces in the modern economy can destroy careers and family incomes, forcing the mother into the workplace.

Many modern companies are recognizing the family needs of their employees by adopting family-friendly personnel practices. Merck & Co. goes beyond legally mandated maternity leave time and allows parents six months child care leave with partial pay and full benefits. IBM allows employees to adjust the time for beginning and ending their workdays to accommodate family needs. It also has a special three-year part-time leave policy to care for a severely ill child or elderly relative. During Kay Whitmore's presidency, Eastman Kodak expanded its work policies to facilitate flexible work hours, part-time and at-home work, and job sharing (where two people agree to work part time to fill a single position). Many companies have found that these policies more than pay for themselves through increased employee productivity and reduced absenteeism and turnover.[25] Smaller companies may not have as much flexibility, but employers and managers who sincerely want to can often find many ways informally to help employees with their family situations. Often the most effective approach in any company, small or large, is to apply the united order principle of common consent management and consult with the employees about what will help them work better.

There is a tendency to see family-friendly personnel policies as a "women's issue." However, one cannot dismiss these as grudging concessions to an unrighteous world full of working mothers. These policies should be important to men as well. Howard W. Hunter taught priesthood holders that "effective family leadership, brethren, requires both quantity and quality time. The teaching and governance of the family must not be left to your wife alone, to society, to school, or even the Church."[26] Righteous employers should help fathers as well as mothers to fulfill their sacred family responsibilities by enabling them to have adequate time with their children.

Industrial Democracy. A European approach to improving lives and creating a system of economic justice is known as "Industrial Democracy." It began as an experiment after World War I and was later reinstated in the late 1940s in France and Germany. In the latter instance, the impetus came from concern about the possible rise of a future Adolf Hitler who might link with bankers and industrialists to build a Fourth Reich. *Mitbestimmung*, or "co-determination," would likely preempt such efforts because it would place working-class trade unionists on corporate boards to safeguard democracy. Through federal legislation, workers first obtained one-third of the seats on boards of directors in the steel and coal industries. The Workers Constitution Act of 1952 created a factory-level workers council, with equal numbers of labor and management representatives to make joint decisions regarding safety, personnel, disciplinary matters, and the regulating of working hours. In 1973, the law gave workers equal representation on all major company boards. As a result, management must consult with worker representatives regarding major investments in new technology, plant relocations, strategic planning, new product development, and other decisions.

Co-determination seems to be congruent with the principles of political economy espoused by philosopher John Stuart Mill, who also defended the Saints' right to religious freedom.[27] He argued that workplace democracy would not only be more productive, but lead to a "moral transformation" of industrial workers "in the pursuit of a good common to all; the elevation of the dignity of labour." Thus he theorizes that authority in industry should not be one of boss and subordinate, but the equal voice of all, with managers being elected by workers.[28]

Data on this approach to industrial democracy indicate that it correlates with increases in quality and amount of productivity, a cooperative labor relations system, and other major benefits (in contrast to the adversarial nature of American business/labor relations).[29] Indeed, some observers credit co-determination with the impressive success of the West German economy in recent decades, so much so that after watching its development, most other European nations—Austria, the Netherlands, Belgium, Spain, and others—have passed similar legislation. In Sweden, every firm with more than 25 employees must give half its board seats to workers.

Managing Corporate Downsizing. As helpful as these policies have proven to be to long-term corporate success, since the 1980s we have seen corporate policies that seem to go in the exact opposite direction, as millions of workers have been laid off as a result of the movement toward corporate "downsizing."[30] In chapters 6 through 10, we saw that a fundamental principle of the united order was that our wealth should be employed to promote employment for all. It is therefore presumptively immoral for an employer to dismiss an employee without cause.

Of course, corporate downsizers do not lay off thousands of people because of wicked delight in increasing poverty and inequality. The rationale offered for this practice is that workforce reduction is necessary for corporate efficiency and even survival. If some employees are not fired, the company will not survive, and then no one would have a job. Wall Street stock analysts also love the reduction in expenses (since financial statements only show employees as costs, not assets).[31] While clearly there are some circumstances in which a company may need to reduce the number of its employees in order to survive, managers who wish to act as stewards may want to take a closer look at the facts before following the fashionable downsizing crowd.

The first fact is that downsizing, at least as currently practiced, generally does not work. Surveys by the consulting firm Wyatt & Co. found that barely one-half to two-thirds of downsizing firms seeking to reduce expenses actually did so. And that was the best result. Less than half seeking to do so actually improved profits, productivity, customer satisfaction, competitive position, or efficiency.[32] Nor do the short-term gains in stock price endure. One survey found the stock prices of major downsized companies lagging behind the competition by 26 percent three years after the layoffs.[33]

The reasons for these failures are not hard to fathom if one remembers that corporate workforces are made of human beings rather than numbers on financial statements. The employees sent out the door take with them expertise, experience, and customer contacts. Major downsizings also devastate the morale of the remaining employees. Since many companies reduce the numbers of workers without rethinking and reducing unnecessary work, the survivors suffer from overwork and burnout doing the full workload of their fired coworkers. The survivors become fearful that they will be laid off and spend more time on office politics than productive work. An atmosphere of suspicion prevails, reducing cooperation, communication, and any sense of company culture. Further, the lack of a flow of new hires deprives the company of fresh input.[34] Exhausted, fearful, and inefficient workers weaken the company's revenues and profitability. Eventually, even the financial statements reflect the depletion in the company's most important revenue-producing asset, its people.[35]

The second important fact about downsizing is that there are alternatives to mass layoffs if company expenses must be reduced.[36]

- The number of workers can be reduced through attrition by not hiring to replace workers leaving in the normal course, such as through retirement. Also, early retirement can be encouraged.

- Companies can make greater efforts to reduce other expenses before laying off workers. Employees invited to join in the search for cost efficiencies can be very effective if they know that the alternative is layoffs.

- Also, if the alternative is layoffs, many employees will accept temporary across-the-board pay cuts or freezes. Payroll costs can be cut without reducing pay rates by encouraging voluntary unpaid leaves, eliminating overtime, shortening work hours, allowing job-sharing, having temporary plant shutdowns, or using "rolling furloughs," which are less visible to customers by keeping the business in operation full time.

- The best alternative is to put into place lean and efficient operations in the first place. An innovative way to accomplish this is found at Intel, where employees are encouraged to be self-reliant in pursuing their own careers in the company. They have access to company-funded retraining and are constantly apprised of old positions being eliminated and new ones which are opening.

- The most basic alternative is a change of attitude. Companies can decide to give value to factors which cannot be reflected in the short-term financial statements. Companies can decide that the long-term value of a skilled, loyal workforce is worth the short-term cost of keeping on workers when business slows down. Companies can decide that the potential for layoffs is a negative, rather than a positive, consideration in strategic planning.

Finally, if layoffs are unavoidable, they can be carried out humanely. The current fashion is to effect layoffs as a one-time, massive surprise attack. This is a good approach if the management's chief concern is to give the company's stock a one-time boost. However, as counterintuitive as it may seem to many of today's numbers-oriented managers, the most effective way to implement layoffs is through close and long-term consultation with the company's employees.[37] Perhaps the most important factor is whether the executives implementing the layoffs conduct themselves as stewards. In Japan, the first payroll cost to be cut is the salaries of the top managers.[38] Lorenzo Snow observed that "Jesus, brother Joseph, and brother Brigham have always been willing to sacrifice all they possess for the good of the people; that is what gives brother Brigham power with God and power with the people, it is the self-sacrificing feeling that he is all the time exhibiting."[39] One wonders what Brother Brigham would have thought of executives who award themselves large bonuses for procuring short-term cost reductions through mass layoffs.

Moral Conduct of Business

In chapters 17 and 18 we will discuss further how the principles of the united order can be used proactively to improve business management. However, in the end, managing as a steward is about more than numbers or methodologies. It is about regarding one's employees as one's brothers, as one's partners in business enterprise. It is about taking into account the well-being of those who are the business's "neighbors"—customers, suppliers, local communities, employees, as well as shareholders. It is about keeping the most important things first. At the conclusion of the talk quoted above, Lorenzo Snow reflected on the material prosperity the Saints had gained after settling in Utah.

> A person never can enjoy heaven until he learns how to get it, and to act upon its principles. Now you take some individuals, and you refer back to the circumstances that surrounded them twenty years ago, when they were living in log huts, when they had a certain amount of joy, of peace, of happiness at that time, though things were uncomfortable. Now they may have secured comfortable circumstances and temporal means that would administer to their temporal wants and necessities, but if they have not secured friends, the good feelings of their brethren, they are unhappy, and more so than they were twenty years ago.[40]

Many progressive, righteous firms today are engaged in a wide range of social and ethical concerns—truth in advertising, product warranties, pollution control, occupational safety, minority hiring and advancement, employee health and educational benefits, on-site day care services, and waste recycling programs. LDS executives as well, rather than a singular pursuit of economic ends, the "bottom line," can exemplify a philosophy that is more consistent with Church and united order teachings of stewardship and corporate service to a wider, more comprehensive arena of needs. As President Ezra Taft Benson put it:

> No fair-minded person contends that the private enterprise system is perfect. It is operated by human beings who are full of imperfections. Many of us deplore the fact that a few of our corporate entities seem to lack that social consciousness proportionate to their power and the privileges granted them by the state. Some businesses apparently still fail to recognize that there are social and spiritual values as well as profits that should be considered in their operations.[41]

Can LDS executives recognize the interdependence of various corporate stakeholders, including employees, customers, shareholders, government, community residents, creditors, and suppliers, and act on "social and spiritual values" in their operations? Can we live a higher level of managerial morality in which positive company actions are taken voluntarily simply because they are the righteous thing to do instead of due to government pressure? This follows the notion of trusteeship advocated by earlier generations of Christian owners of capital. It is also a part of the united order principle of stewardship. As President Benson suggests, LDS managers should have a "social consciousness" and strive to use their power to bless other lives and serve the interests of the larger community.

Ethical LDS executives would not be content to merely stay on the legal side of their business practices or to compensate workers as little as possible. Instead they would respond to social concerns that are clearly in their own long-term interest. Top management could invite outsiders to perform a company audit of the balance between corporate power and the firm's social responsibility. The company culture might be changed to institutionalize such values as stewardship, self-reliance, and moral motivation, utilizing united order principles. Instead of asserting that companies are amoral and respond only to unseen laws of the marketplace, society will witness the creation of a new economics founded on the scriptures, that is, an economics of cooperation which sees us all as children of God rather than materialistic automatons. Only then can we begin to truly work toward the ultimate aim and spirit of the true Church.

17

To Give Every Man Full and Proper Opportunity:

Transforming Modern Business into United Order Principles Inspired Enterprise

The united order has been suspended as a required form of life in the Church, but its spirit still remains. Those who are worthy members of the Church must accept the united order as the ultimate aim of the Church. It finds present partial expression in the practice of cooperation, under which many unite in one enterprise, in such a way that no one person dominates it, but that all concerned have a voice in it, and that the profits resulting from the enterprise are divided more or less uniformly among those connected with it. . . . To give every man full and proper opportunity is the spirit of the true Church.

John A. Widtsoe[1]

The last two chapters have discussed many ways in which the spirit and principles of Zion and the united order may be promoted in modern business in general. However, the united order challenges us to think beyond the structure of current business operations. How would a business operate that was dedicated to seeking to fulfill all of the applicable principles of the united order? How would such a firm be created? Could such businesses exist and prosper in our contemporary business environment? The next four chapters will address these questions. We must emphasize here that we are *not* discussing the creation of full-fledged united orders as dictated by the scriptures. Rather we are attempting to explore how to create and operate a business where the owners were committed to seeking to apply the *principles* of the united order in their firm as best possible in the light of our current knowledge about both the united order and modern business. From our discussion of the creation and operation of a "united order principles inspired enterprise" (hereinafter abbreviated "UOPIE"), we will then contemplate how we might move toward an economy inspired by principles of the united order. This chapter begins this exploration by examining how businesses can be made into united order principles inspired enterprises. Chapter 18 then goes into more detail regarding the management and conduct of such enterprises pursuant to the law of stewardship. Chapter 19 discusses a contemporary example of how united order principles can spread beyond individual businesses, and chapter 20 then examines the question of whether such enterprises could viably operate in the modern economy.

Early United Order Cooperatives

In seeking to build an industrial economy in Utah in the 1800s, Church leaders were well aware of the conflicts that had arisen between capital and labor in the external industrial capitalist economy. Apostle Erastus Snow told the 1874 general conference that the "United Order of Zion . . . embraces labor as well as capital, and it designs to make the interests of capital and labor identical."[2] In order to realize this identity of capital and labor, the united order industrial enterprises were conceived as worker cooperatives.

The largest of many Church organized industrial enterprises was in Utah Valley, the Provo Woolen Mills, built in 1873. The business was started with "sweat equity," such as donated materials and labor, and with cash from the Church. It was the largest such firm in the West, powered by water, and processed over a million pounds of wool annually.[3] Apostle George A. Smith, discussing the Provo Woolen Mills, said:

> If the cotton lord and the millionaire come here and hire you to build factories, . . . when the factory is erected they own it, and they set their price upon your labor and your wool or cotton—they have dominion over you. But, if by your own efforts and exertions, you cooperate together and build a factory, it is your own. . . . The profits are divided among those whose labor produced it, and will be used to build up the country. Hence, it is not capital that is, it is not so much money that is needed. It is unity of effort on the part of the bone, sinew, skill and ingenuity which we have in our midst.[4]

However, the transition to worker control was never completed. Brigham expressed concern about the ability of management.

> When this factory at Provo can go into the hands of men who know what to do with it, it will go; when my factory in Salt Lake

> County can go into the hands of men who know what to do with it, it will go. There is my beloved brother James W. Cummings, who has worked my factory ten or twelve years; he counts himself A No. 1 in all financial business. I have offered the factory to him and his workmen on the co-operative system, in the order that we wish to adopt. I said to him—"Take it and manage it, you are welcome." Said he—"If I only had plenty of money to furnish it I suppose I could do it." Have I not furnished it without money? Yes, I had not the first sixpence to start with. I furnished my factories, and I have built what I have built without asking how much they cost, or where I was to get the money to do it. When we find somebody that knows what to do with property, . . . we will give them charge of it.[5]

While Brigham may have been correct in noting the need for some entrepreneurial resourcefulness in his factory manager, Brother Cummings was not being unreasonable in wondering where he was going to get his working capital as a manager in the united order cooperative enterprise. Had the united order treasury been established as contemplated in the revelations, this issue would have been resolved, and Brigham and Brother Cummings could have proceeded with the conversion of the woolen mills into a fully worker-owned-and-operated united order cooperative.

Since Brigham Young's time, hundreds of successful cooperatives and employee-owned businesses have prospered and succeeded in responding to his concerns. This chapter explores many forms and methods that can be used to work toward the practice of united order stewardship by giving workers an equal voice and share of the profits in a united order principles inspired enterprise.

European Cooperatives and Other Worker-Owned Businesses

Britain has considerable experience in creating worker cooperatives. Perhaps the best known cooperative enterprises in history were the Rochdale cooperatives begun in the 1840s. Their cooperatively owned textile factory prospered greatly in terms of productivity and profits. In contrast to the efforts of LDS and other early American experiments, however, most of the British co-ops were secular in nature, arising from the struggle for a more equitable economy. At Rochdale, however, outsiders were allowed to purchase shares and, as worker stock was further diluted, the business eventually evolved from a worker-owned firm to a joint stock company with 1,200 outside investors. Although for the founders the Rochdale cooperative factory had degenerated into a business-as-usual operation, the dream soon gave rise to hundreds of similar ventures in worker ownership over the decades which followed. There were printers, shoe and boot producers, clothing co-ops, and cooperative bookstores.[6]

This early British legacy formed the ideological roots for cooperative drives in Britain in recent decades. A prime motivation for worker takeovers in the UK has been to combat mass layoffs and preserve not only family income but community economic stability and self-reliance as well. The latest research shows 1,200 co-op firms with 8,500 workers throughout the nation.

Beyond co-ops, a parallel program toward a higher-order economy has been the Industrial Common Ownership Movement (ICOM), which has grown out of progressive middle-class managers, often inspired by their Quaker roots. The largest example is the John Lewis Partnership, a department store chain that has grown from 1,500 to 23,000 worker-owners with annual revenues of over a billion dollars. Products and services of ICOM firms include plastic moldings, furniture, jewelry, and coffee and tea production. These businesses have prospered as they have switched from traditional ownership to "partnerships" in which all employees participate in profit sharing. People are considered to be as important as profits; and the firms employ enlightened labor relations policies, pay higher than average wage rates, and distribute company stock to all employees.[7]

The firm of Scott Bader Commonwealth perhaps most clearly demonstrates the vitality of ICOM. It was incorporated in 1920 by a young Swiss immigrant to the UK, Ernest Bader, who began from scratch to build a polyester resin factory. Three decades later the enterprise had become a solid medium-sized firm with 161 employees. Although generating millions of dollars and known as an entrepreneurial success story, Ernest was dissatisfied with the gap between himself and the employees. Profit sharing was generous from the beginning, but he felt that it was not sufficient. His biography records that eventually "light came. . . . He suddenly said, What am I doing? I'm playing the game of all these others. . . . Well, I'm not going to face my maker having done that. . . . The most simple order came from Christ—'As Christ said to the young ruler, give everything away.'"[8]

In 1951 Bader restructured his firm into a commonwealth and placed 90 percent of the stock in the hands of the workers. The other 10 percent was vested in worker accounts in 1963. Together Bader and his employees created a constitution that would limit compensation to a seven-to-one ratio from top management to lowest paid workers. Sixty percent of profits were allocated for taxes or reinvestment in the firm for new equipment, expansion, or other business needs. Of the remaining 40 percent, half was given in bonuses to all partners, while the other 20 percent would be donated to charitable causes in the larger society. The firm has been a resounding success, illustrating how enterprise growth and achievement can be consistent with stewardship and democratic management. Instead of becoming inordinately wealthy, Bader and his descendants have found great joy in building a new "social order," a working community in which all are responsible for the well-being of one another. As Ernest later put it, the motivation for this radical change in business was "to raise employees to the status of responsible owners; or in other words, to liberate them from the wage nexus, as I had already liberated myself." For him, "common ownership means the economic and social fulfillment of the Lord's Prayer, 'Thy will be done on earth as it is in heaven.'"[9]

Beyond the British experience, other Europeans also have impressive co-op economies. France's co-sector, for instance, is some ten times larger than Britain's—many French co-ops are over a century old. There are several hundred artisan cooperatives in crafts and construction. Over a hundred firms are comparable to conventional mid-sized French businesses and are leaders in their markets. Recently, much of the co-op growth in France has come as a result of the closure of traditionally owned companies.[10] Smaller producer co-ops exist in the Netherlands and Scandinavia, but their growth rate is increasing.

The Italian experience is perhaps the most significant in Europe. Worker co-ops there enjoyed huge gains after the world wars, and another growth spurt in the 1970s. Italy has over 200,000 full-time co-op jobs in over 3,000 worker-owned firms, which are affiliated with different leagues or federations. With 3,000 owners, the Bricklayers' and Cement Workers' Co-op is the nation's largest. In addition, many other cooperative associations—housing, agriculture, retail, and credit—collaborate in building a strong, self-reliant cooperative sector.[11]

The Israeli Kibbutz

A different strategy for developing a healthy, self-reliant society started in Palestine in the early 1900s—the kibbutz. Strongly impacted by the dream of making Zion, a homeland for Jews from around the world, the early settlers created a path for many to follow. Thousands flowed to their "promised land," especially from Eastern Europe. In many respects they were not unlike Mormon pioneers of 60 years earlier in that both groups consisted largely of urban dwellers attempting to farm in dry deserts.[12]

The *kibbutz*—"the group" in Hebrew—developed on the philosophy that the collective good should be the concern of every individual. Land and other resources were to be owned communally, much like at the Orderville united order. "From each according to his abilities, to each according to his needs" became the motto of this movement. Approximately 270 kibbutzim have been established in Israel, each with an average membership of some 400 residents. While only 3 to 4 percent of the national population live in kibbutzim, economic output from kibbutz farms and factories makes up roughly 7 to 8 percent of Israel's gross national product.

Kibbutz members enjoy a high standard of living and per capita consumption. However, the community determines how much and what is to be consumed. Members live in separate housing units, much like our condominiums, except for one's offspring, who live, study, and sleep in the children's house. Meals for all are communal.

A major cultural value is general equality within the community's means. Some discretionary income is available to allow for individual tastes, but it must also be congruent with real kibbutz income. Each kibbutz has a mechanism for allocating resources and goods, functioning to some extent like the earlier united order storehouse. Unlimited medical care, high priority on education, and an emphasis on high quality child rearing are important values as well. The dignity of work and the right to rotate jobs so that no one is constantly stuck with boring, repetitive labor are also important.

The kibbutz organization is extremely participative, having a general assembly of members which meets weekly to evaluate progress, determine investments, and decide the future. A smaller council manages the day-to-day business and coordinates citizen task forces that are responsible for labor, housing, culture, and

Workers on agricultural co-op at Kibbutz Afikim (1995) in southern Galilee, Israel. The system of collective ownership and production is widely recognized for its communal structure and economic successes.

other issues. Most members feel a genuine commitment to the goals of the kibbutz and spend much time and energy attempting to fulfill them. While agriculture was the original basis for most kibbutzim, currently manufacturing and new high-tech businesses are the norm.[13] Today's kibbutzim are a fascinating mix of old, traditional communities. Some are nonreligious and socialist, some are Jewish orthodox, and still others consist of young, professional kibbutzniks. Recent settlers, such as 25,000 Ethiopians, 100,000 Russians, and other groups, have formed fascinating new ethnic and linguistic subcultures in the kibbutz experience.

As with the Mondragon cooperatives in Spain that we explore in chapter 19, the kibbutzim have shown the ability to be flexible and adapt to changing economic circumstances, reducing their allegiance to socialist ideology. On the Givat Brenner kibbutz, a salaried manager was hired in 1991 to provide professional management skills at the commune's orange juice factory, attempting to make the firm more entrepreneurial and financially successful. In 1993, Kibbutz Kinneret, the second oldest in Israel, began to sell shares in its plastics factory through the Tel Aviv stock exchange. Other kibbutzim are hiring outside workers, paying overtime, and giving members greater freedom in their choice of home appliances, clothing purchases, and so on. The Ein Zivan kibbutz even shut down its communal kitchen and made it into a private restaurant. These and other reforms suggest how responsive the Israeli system can be to shifting economic realities and free market demands.[14]

North American Worker-Owned Businesses

Application of united order principles in the contemporary corporate economy is perhaps most relevant for today's urban Latter-day Saints. Experience in attempting to create a system that is both more egalitarian and more productive is considerable. The primary vehicle for doing so is worker ownership, whereby company employees function not merely as laborers who receive a wage, but as actual owners of the firm's stock.

Employee Participation in American Business History. Worker ownership and participation are neither new nor rare in U.S. economic history. During the 1830s, when the Church was in its infancy, there were over 200 producer cooperatives in which master craftsmen collaborated to share profits. The broad array of enterprises included shoemakers, printers, construction firms, furniture makers, and book binders. In 1791, the Carpenters Union led the first labor strike in U.S. history. In order to conquer their oppressors, they initiated their own construction co-op, one of the nation's first worker-owned firms. Another of America's earliest co-ops was the Martha Washington Cooperative Association, a producer of high-quality clothing. The company's female union members even voted on who would occupy the positions of management, quite a radical method for executive selection in that day. Philadelphia's most honored citizen, Benjamin Franklin, helped found several cooperatives, including a fire insurance co-op which still exists today. He believed that co-ops were the path to social reform and a major means for advancing the good society.

Even when ownership of stock by workers was not the objective, many recognized the economic benefit of more democratic management. By the late 1800s and early part of the 20th century, a number of capitalists, trade unionists, and government officials were advocating the creation of "shop councils" as a mechanism to improve organizational efficiency. Hart, Schaffner and Marx, perhaps the most famous tailors in America, created a worker's council to improve corporate decision making. The Philadelphia firm of Nelson Valve established an industrial congress, consisting of a senate for managers and a house of representatives for workers. The two groups would separately debate how to improve company competitiveness, increase sales, and improve working conditions, and then meet together to hammer out a resolution of the best proposals.[15]

Between 1900 and 1925, in an effort to overcome the abuses of the era of the Robber Barons, over two hundred firms created similar shop committees involving more than a million workers. The companies included Bethlehem Steel, DuPont, Eastman Kodak, Westinghouse, General Electric, Goodyear, Procter & Gamble, Swift, Union Pacific, and Standard Oil. During his administration, President Woodrow Wilson declared:

> Those who really desire a new relation between capital and labor can readily find a way to bring it about. . . . The object of all reform in this essential matter must be the genuine democratization of industry based upon a full recognition of those who work, in whatever rank, to participate in some organic way in every decision which affects their welfare.[16]

This fundamentally American ideal of a participative political and economic system has been widely shared. During certain eras of U.S. history, experiments with various structures of democratic management and worker ownership have been carried out. Even in the midst of the Robber Barons' rise, in the 1870s (while the LDS Church was creating united orders throughout the Great Basin) some industrialists in the East were sharing power and ownership with factory workers. The dreams and visions of greater economic justice have characterized both Latter-day Saints and the larger society.

Such efforts appear congruent with core American values. Political participation and workplace participation are both derived from the basic notion of democracy. The constitutional right to own property fits with the idea of workers owning stock in their company. Personal ambition and the pursuit of happiness are both consistent with the idea of prosperity through employee ownership. The strong motivation to work hard so that through personal effort one will be rewarded parallels the practice of workers sharing in the profits of the business they help to succeed. The early, anticolonial views of the nation's founders who claimed there should be "no taxation without representation" is the equivalent of today's worker opposition to the huge corporate profits and executive compensation for distant, absentee owners and management. Both the American economy of the past and the recent movement toward worker ownership are based on free market principles. Our original Bill of Rights is increasingly replicated to some extent by progressive corporate mission statements, charters, and the in-company constitutions of worker-owned enterprises.

There are several structures for worker ownership in the United States. A number of firms have provided company shares to employees as an outright gift. Others sell employees stock at a discount. As a result, for instance, the hundreds of thousands of Sears Roebuck employees now own 20 percent of all corporate stock. Many other firms have done the same as an incentive beyond the paycheck, to create greater loyalty and reduce turnover.

Cooperatives. Worker cooperatives are another approach to democratic ownership. These modern firms tend to be somewhat small in size and heavily egalitarian in nature. "One person-one vote" is the method for allocating power. Workers usually elect managers, and they typically have a voice on the job. This gives them a sense of dignity and self-respect that many workers in traditional firms do not experience. Business productivity and quality are also higher in many co-ops because working harder and smarter positively affects the year-end dividends workers receive as owners. This translates into less absenteeism and turnover, better productivity, higher product quality, and more profits.

The mix of American co-ops is considerable today, including worker-owned supermarkets, sewing factories, migrant worker farms, and a sector of the plywood industry.[17] In the Pacific Northwest a number of plywood cooperatives have existed since the 1930s, with a long track record of 30 percent higher profits and productivity than their conventional counterparts. Many large U.S. cities, such as Los Angeles and Chicago, are served by taxi co-ops. San Francisco's largest solid waste removal companies, such as the San Francisco Scavengers, are worker-owned cooperatives. Many small print shops, like the Salsedo Press in Chicago, are co-ops in which employees not only enjoy the increased value of stock ownership, but a wage of $10 per hour plus benefits. The Hoedad's Co-op, Inc., a reforestation firm of 250–300 worker-owners, operates in the timber-rich region of the Pacific Northwest. Under contract with the U.S. Forest Service and other agencies, workers plant and thin trees, collect seeds, and rebuild mountain trails. Since 1970 it has become a very successful and productive venture, providing jobs over the years for hundreds of worker owners and doing several million dollars of business annually.[18]

Employee Stock Ownership Plans. Another mechanism for creating U.S. worker ownership is the Employee Stock Ownership Plan (ESOP).[19] This particular approach was legislated by Congress in 1974 as part of the Employee Retirement Income Security Act (ERISA). It was supported by both Republicans and Democrats—the conservatives because it promised greater business performance and the spreading of wealth in America, and the liberals because it would preserve jobs and lift the lower classes.

The ESOP is a legal device that allows a special company pension plan to borrow money from a lender and use it to advance company concerns, such as purchasing new equipment, land or facilities, or buying out old owners. In return the ESOP receives company stock, which is held in worker accounts. The company pays off the loan incrementally to the ESOP, which in turn repays the original lender. All parties to these transactions may benefit from the ESOP. Within certain limits the company is allowed to deduct from taxes principal as well as interest as the loan is paid off. If the ESOP owns a majority of the company, the bank pays taxes on only half the interest from its loan to the ESOP, which leads many lenders to give reduced interest rates on ESOP loans. When an ESOP is used to put ownership in the hands of local workers, both they and their communities may enjoy greater job security and a higher standard of living because of business improvements, owner dividends, and so on. Unlike with Sears or many of the other approaches to making workers owners, the ESOP trust functions as a block of votes and rights, empowering workers with a potentially greater voice in the company. The individual employee cannot access or trade her or his stock at will, but rather the stock accrues interest and dividends, until the person quits or retires. At that point, the stock can be cashed out, often giving the worker hundreds of thousands of dollars in addition to whatever other pension and retirement benefits he or she may have.[20]

The growth rate of ESOPs has been impressive, from a handful of companies in 1975 to 9,500 firms by 1993, employing over 11 million worker-owners. From only a few million dollars 15 years earlier, some $24 billion was invested in ESOPs during 1989 alone. Research evidence suggests that firms with both participative decision-making systems and substantial employee ownership tend to enjoy higher growth in productivity, profits, sales and the creation of new jobs than do conventional firms.[21] Historically, most ESOPs were installed in privately owned companies, but in the past several years, large public companies have also adopted ESOPs. Some of today's largest ESOPs include Health Trust (30,000 employees), Publix Supermarkets (43,000), Avis (11,000), Parsons engineering firm (10,000), and Science Applications (11,000), as well as United Airlines, U.S. Sugar, Polaroid, Dunkin' Donuts, and the *Milwaukee Journal*.[22]

Perhaps the steel industry furnishes a prime example of how worker buyouts can rescue thousands of threatened jobs. Plant closures have been blocked and potential community economic disasters have been reversed by instituting ESOPs at the following firms: Pittsburgh Forging, a steel firm in business since 1871, bought for $187 million by 2,500 workers; Oremet Titanium, acquired in 1987 from Owens Corning; LTV's Republic Container Co. in West Virginia, sold to workers in 1985; Michigan's Copper Range, purchased by 900 worker owners, with each worker receiving $18,000 worth of stock; Cyclops Steel, sold to 1,200 workers in

1989; McLouth Steel, purchased by a union-organized ESOP in 1988; and LTV's new $220 million steel bar mill in Ohio.

Weirton Steel in West Virginia served as the path-breaking buyout which became a model for the cases mentioned above. When the parent company, National Steel, decided a decade ago not to invest further in its Weirton mill, the town banded together to explore the feasibility of an ESOP. The plant's fortunes had eroded gradually, with operating losses and 2,600 layoffs. A feasibility study was carried out which showed that the firm might succeed if workers took a 32 percent cut in income. The union spent strike fund monies and the town held bake sales to rally support and contributions. The deal was clinched in 1983 when an ESOP was launched that owned 100 percent of the business. New top management, and a new structure which included worker seats on the company board of directors, were put in place. Weirton became the largest ESOP in America and was ranked 336 on the *Fortune 500* list of America's largest corporations. Within the first year, Weirton gained 190 new customers. New products were created, modern equipment was installed, worker teams began to function to raise production, and all laid-off workers were back on their jobs. This gave a boost to the region's economy, resulting in rising house sales and retail activity. Over the next four years after the buyout, workers received $75 million in profit sharing, some getting as much as $9,000 yearly, and their ESOP accounts accumulated a total of $160 million in stock. Although, like other steel companies, Weirton has had to struggle in recent years, the examples of these ESOP companies demonstrate collectively that sharing power, giving people information, and using other united order practices do not have to be a distant dream. They can work in very applicable ways in today's modern economy.[23]

Current Economic Cooperation Among the Latter-day Saints

Economic strategies for building temporal well-being through cooperation have also been fostered among Latter-day Saints. For example, a small sewing factory in central Utah has come quite a way in implementing features of the united order together with sound business practices. It is located in the small rural town of Mt. Pleasant, where unemployment has been high and few manufacturing jobs are available. However, there was this one small sewing plant run by a male entrepreneur who hired local women to fill subcontracts with California clothing companies. For several years, the business went well, but then things started to go sour, and the owner fled the state. For the workers, many of whom were female heads of their households, the loss of their jobs was devastating.

PEIR. They sought help from a group of faculty and students at BYU who had created the Program on Economic Innovation and Revitalization (PEIR). This School of Management group had done considerable research, authored books, and provided technical assistance to firms, unions, and communities suffering from plant closures. They had used their model for economic revitalization with several local factories in Lindon, Nephi, and Salt Lake County, so the request for help from Mt. Pleasant in the late 1980s was consistent with past efforts.

PEIR helped design and carry out a feasibility study of the sewing plant's present and future capabilities, including an assessment of equipment, market opportunities, and human skills. A business plan was prepared, and the women were trained in entrepreneurial skills and running a business collectively and democratically. With donated legal expertise, the group incorporated as a Utah industrial cooperative, called Sew Fantastic, which was equally owned by all workers. Complications arose because the original owner had taken the company-owned vehicle and left the factory owing several hundred thousand dollars in unpaid taxes. But the new co-op members succeeded in resolving those problems, gaining major new customer contacts, and for the first time in their lives, controlling their own economic future. They retained their jobs, owned equal shares of stock, made decisions by common consent, and used democratic methods of leadership in order to become fully self-reliant.

Likewise, within the BYU community, PEIR applied united order principles with a group of students and faculty from different academic disciplines—sociology, engineering, law, technology, accounting, organizational behavior, and business management. Begun in 1987, this effort centered on learning to integrate concepts and practices from different fields into an effective managerial and entrepreneurial experience. The means for doing this was a new course at BYU which would enable participants in a seminar to learn theory and concepts, and then create a micro-factory in which they could apply course principles and engage in actual production processes. A worker-owned enterprise named Equitech was established. It used the shops, equipment, and facilities of BYU's Crabtree Foundry to engage in factory production. This manufacturing operation was inspired by the Mondragon student firm, Alecoop, described in chapter 19.[24]

A number of products have been made over the past six years, including metal bars and parts for weight machines, innovative snow removal equipment for an Idaho entrepreneur, and the prototype for manufacturing wheat grinders to be used by poor, rural peasants in Latin America for the Benson Institute. The major line of manufacturing has been the graphic design and casting of commemorative bronze plaques for various BYU departments as they provide awards to donors, outside speakers, students, and conference participants. Equitech has been self-sustaining throughout the years, providing students with experience and a decent income as well, since they are paid for factory work. Many Equitech students are from other countries, such as Hong Kong, Taiwan, People's Republic of China, South Korea, Peru, Mexico, and Jordan. Because of visa limitations they are not able to be employed off-campus, so Equitech became the means by which they could earn sufficient income to attend BYU. Operating as a worker cooperative with an equal number of students and faculty on the board of directors, this self-sustaining team provides a valuable opportunity to learn united order principles and apply them in an American setting. Some of the students have been involved in this cooperative enterprise two to three years and plan to establish similar egalitarian ventures when they return to their homelands.[25]

Moroni Feed Cooperative. We next turn to an impressive case that improved the circumstances of LDS families by practicing united order principles for private sector economic development. It was founded by Utah farmers living near the town of Moroni during the Great Depression. A number of LDS sugar beet farms in central Utah were near disaster; some were already repossessed, and the people's hard but tolerable lifestyle was threatened. Several local banks in Sanpete County collapsed, and the community began to search for a new economic base. Inspiration came to a few who advocated that the only path to survival was to band together collectively and leverage their revenues to create a new structure. This they did, and the outcome was the incorporation of a farmer's cooperative called Moroni Feed.

This modern attempt to implement a collaborative joint venture between independent Utah farmers by using certain principles from the united order succeeded in a remarkable way. The central ideas in establishing Moroni Feed are remarkably similar to a 1924 Deseret News Press book by J.A. Geddes, *The United Order Among the Mormons: An Unfinished Experiment in Economic Organization.* This volume, published a decade before the Moroni co-op was begun, maintained that in a cooperative setting, equality and shared control are both possible and desirable through equal ownership of shares of stock and equality of "votership," so that each person's voice carries the same weight in the enterprise.[26] According to Geddes, the united order sought to give "the wage earner a property stewardship, thus making each man a capitalist as well as a worker, and then to use a noninterested board whose policy and methods tend to build up a specialized arbitration body, to adjust disputes that occur."[27]

The farmers in Moroni incorporated themselves according to cooperative laws in Utah, each holding his own farmland as private property, but jointly creating a "non-interested board" to manage the use of their resources. They turned to collectively raising turkey chicks, purchasing them together and growing them to adult birds. Feed and other necessary items were at first jointly purchased, until they decided to build a feed-producing plant to make products for turkey consumption. They also built a slaughterhouse to process some five million turkeys each year. The pricing, marketing, and distribution of turkey meat are also handled by the co-op, all integrated under one management system. Breeding farms, hatchery, feed production, service stations, farm supplies, and disease-control laboratories were thereby all coordinated, evolving slowly as the need arose and capital to do so became available. Membership capital was pooled and, as profits grew, new business growth could be financed directly by the farmers.

The Moroni case has been remarkably successful. Local farmers participate as co-owners of the business with $100 million in sales annually and an outstanding reputation for high-quality turkey products. Not only were the Depression-era farm families saved economically, but they were able to provide a legacy of financial soundness through working together. Today, the company has an annual payroll of some $10 million, is the economic foundation of Sanpete County, and has operations in several other Utah counties as well. It has created its own financing program,

"70-30," to help young farmers get into the turkey growing business, and co-op consultants provide advice and expertise in new start-up situations. Economic multiplier effects impact not only farmers and Moroni Feed employees, but other local businesses and government as well.

Navajo Reservation Cooperatives. Many other possibilities exist for cooperating toward temporal salvation in Mormon country. One example would be a strategy of helping the Navajo Nation cope with economic and social problems by creating a system of worker-owned co-ops, like that of Mondragon (described in chapter 19) or the kibbutz. Today's reality is that federal aid to Native Americans is drying up. The Bureau of Indian Affairs is a troubled agency, and U.S. oil and mineral companies likewise are not turning out to be the bearers of reservation salvation as originally hoped. Perhaps a combination of some federal and state monies could be pooled with Church Humanitarian funds and oil-lease revenues to create a federation of small, worker-owned Indian enterprises. Through training and management development, tribal members would learn to work and experience the financial results of their labor. The group would benefit, rather than just a few isolated members. Instead of hoping that the gambling industry and other ploys for simply pouring cash into reservation bank accounts will solve Indian problems, the focus would be on sweat, labor, and self-sufficient economic endeavors, thus enhancing the quality of life for all.[28]

Working Toward the United Order through Employee Ownership

Beyond this example, Zion-like principles could be further implemented at firms owned or managed by Latter-day Saints by offering all workers company shares, thus creating common stock funds such as may have existed in the City of Enoch or among New Testament Saints. But unfortunately, involvement with some Utah business founders and owners suggests that the very idea of creating industrial cooperatives like those of Brigham City is a far cry from the limited vision of some LDS owners today.

For example, in attempting to help a group of Mormon managers and hourly employees in Utah County in 1988 rescue their troubled business from near bankruptcy, it was curious to see top executives and state officials counter the effort as strongly as they could, preferring to turn the business over to non-LDS outside investors from Pennsylvania with a very negative track record rather than allow the 130 workers to become stockholders through a worker buyout. Similarly, when an old Salt Lake firm, started by Mormon converts from Germany in the 1870s, began to experience business difficulties 120 years later, the family heirs fought a joint worker and upper-management committee that was exploring the feasibility of transforming the enterprise into an industrial co-op. The two major stockholders, brothers, declared that they would rather see the state lose hundreds of thousands of dollars in back taxes and all the workers lose their jobs than sell the business to employees. Their rigidity eventually pushed the firm into bankruptcy, and after a year the workers and their families did lose their source of income when the firm totally collapsed.

On the other hand, consider what might result if companies owned by LDS families were to take the initiative and offer workers stock without the pressure of business decline or other factors which make a buyout so much more complicated. What if there were a Mormon Ernest Bader? Or LDS owners equivalent to W. L. Gore, Sam Walton, or the family which founded Lincoln Electric? The precedent of one or two prominent LDS-influenced companies sharing all or a significant block of stock with their workers, and creating systems of participation like common consent and other democratic principles, could have an important economic and religious impact throughout the Church and eventually the entire world as the worldwide Zion rises.

If LDS founders of existing companies would consider passing on their shares to long-term employees who have labored throughout their lives to help build company success, they could preserve a congenial LDS type of culture rather than succumb to the demands of outside shareholders for higher and higher profits each quarter, regardless of long-term consequences. The layoffs and downsizing, reduced advertising, research and development and other long-term investments, and the decline of LDS inspired family-friendly corporate culture that come from outside ownership could be reduced or avoided.

Too many times, the founder of a privately held firm, perhaps as a family business, discovers on approaching retirement that one's heirs have little interest in maintaining the firm and passing it on to the next generation. Unfortunately, the typical response to this type of situation is to sell one's firm to a larger company, usually from outside the area. This often results in new owners only acquiring the smaller firm in order to increase market share or reduce competition. Many times the founder's assets are stripped away, equipment is sold or removed, lifetime employees lose their jobs, and the factory is padlocked shut. Even the founder's name is taken down, and his or her reputation disappears from history.

How much better would it be to sell a viable asset to one's workers? Doing so enables the original owners to obtain market value for their shares and a local source through which to pass the stock. Loyal, lifetime employees thus obtain a second source of income to enhance their future retirement, and the LDS-type culture of the organization is maintained. The community's economic base would also be preserved through job retention and the payment of corporate taxes in order to provide government services.

Bestowing a "manna from heaven" gift of corporate stock to one's workers at one or several prominent LDS-connected companies would open the path to more egalitarian economics among Church members throughout the western U.S., if not around the world. New, young LDS entrepreneurs who are in the early stages of establishing their small firms would be emboldened to seek more creative ways to share their success, not just keep it for themselves and their families. After all, structuring a new business from the start so that it conforms to gospel temporal and economic principles is much more likely to succeed than attempting to convert an older conventional firm to participative employee ownership.

By establishing firms with substantial employee ownership, LDS managers can create more united order-like business practices. Entrepreneurs could declare from the start that they are committed to including all people they hire in the stock ownership of the enterprise. Setting up a system of greater economic justice, democratic decision making, and more equal allocation of the fruits of one's labor is much easier and more effective if done correctly at the outset. Some states, like New York, have laws and technical assistance centers to provide advice and consulting on how to establish employee ownership when a new firm is incorporated. Not only might individual LDS entrepreneurs consider starting their businesses as an ESOP or co-op, but groups could join forces to do so. We have recently been approached by several networks of entrepreneurs who are seeking to do just this. In one case, Utah Valley businessmen requested that BYU management faculty organize a group tour of the Mondragon cooperatives (described in chapter 19), so that they could observe their system of ownership and productivity, interview managers and workers, and then return and begin to design a similar structure among their firms.

In May 1993 a group of LDS professionals met with professors to explore how early united order principles and processes could be implemented in the start-up of new businesses. They hope to integrate Zion concepts of early Mormonism under Brigham Young with present Church welfare practices and the effective, proven example of the Mondragon cooperatives. Participants include accountants, engineers, and contractors who now run small factories, construction firms, and other small or mid-sized businesses. Some families are farmers. Together they are building a collective system that will generate economic security while they function as true Christians. Key values include equality, liberty, and a union between capital and labor as they create a system of political, economic, and social well-being. Worker-owned businesses will be the productive engine to drive the whole effort so that the group may achieve independence and not be so vulnerable to waves of economic recession or depression. "Common councils" will govern the new venture, and their overarching philosophy will be to have one heart and one mind, and no contention among members. A manufacturing research institute is planned to educate all participants so that necessary skills are acquired within the group, ensuring that long-term success will be more likely. They hope to establish a Zion's Board of Trade structure that will govern the system through democratic participation and develop a pool of capital to provide consulting and fund future business start-ups. They consider what they are doing to be a kind of "cooperative free enterprise" that will lift everyone and bless the lives of all in the group, not just a select few, leading to long-term self-reliance.

Private economic initiatives such as these are congruent with Andrew Carnegie's vision nearly a century ago—that managers ought to move from profit-sharing to ownership as the final step up the ladder of economic progression:

> The joint-stock form opens the door to the participation of Labor as shareholder in every branch of business. In this, the writer believes, lies the final and enduring solution of the Labor question. . . . "Every employee a shareholder" would prevent most of the disputes between Capital and Labor, and this chiefly because

> of the feeling of mutuality that would be created, now alas! generally lacking. . . . We may look forward with hope to the day when it shall be the rule for the workman to be Partner with Capital, the man of affairs giving his business experience, the working-man in the mill his mechanical skill, both owners of the shares and so far equally interested in the success of their joint efforts, each indispensable, and without whose cooperation success would be impossible. . . . We are just at the beginning of profit-sharing, and the reign of working-men proprietors, which many indications point to as the next step forward in the march of wage-paid labor to the higher stage of profit-sharing—joint partnership—workers with the hand and workers with the head paid from profits—no dragging of the latter down, but the raising of the former up.[29]

Carnegie advocated "the progress of Labor upward under present conditions from slavery to partnership with Capital," a system that stressed the common interests of both parties to coincide with each other like a fishing fleet: "Every man in the ship from the captain down is a partner, paid by sharing in the profits of the catch, according to the value of his labor."[30]

Beyond the views of arguably the greatest entrepreneur in American business history, we might suggest the teachings of a far more important authority. One of the Savior's most challenging parables is that of the young rich man (Matthew 19:16–30, Luke 18:18–30). It is possible, of course, to rationalize it away—the young rich man really did not have to sell everything and give the proceeds to the poor; his fault was just that he loved his wealth too much. We can keep our money as long as we do not love it too much. Such clever reasoning may well be why it is easier for the camel to pass through the eye of a needle than for a rich man to enter heaven. Taken literally, the parable confronts us with a stark choice. In part, the starkness of the choice may be due to the stark nature of the economy in which the choice was presented. In the static ancient economy, in which the only way to care for the poor was wealth transfer through almsgiving, the only way to practice full consecration would have been to give everything away.

In the modern economy, the revelation of the united order offers a new approach whereby a rich man could pass through the eye of the needle. Selling one's business at a reasonable valuation and terms to one's employees through an ESOP or other form of worker ownership is a form of consecration. As long as the selling owner continues to serve in the management, he can draw an appropriate salary to support his family and thus be freed to consecrate the proceeds of the sale of the business to other charitable activities. Under the united order in the modern economy, one does not have to be a religious mendicant to enter the kingdom of heaven. Consecration can be dynamic and enterprising.

We have seen in the above cases various creative efforts to build a more humane and egalitarian existence for groups in Europe, Latin America, North America, Israel, and elsewhere. Whether rural or urban, utopian commune or worker-owned factory, industrial democracy, co-ops, or ESOPs, the quest of the ages has been a search for prosperity and the good society. Some of these efforts have been long lasting, while others were of short duration or are yet too new to fully assess. But whatever mix of systems one prefers, the preponderance of evidence suggests the great potential for designing a more equitable model of economic justice in today's world. When founded on values and processes of democratic decision making, stewardship, and the moral motivation advocated in sacred scripture, these organizational forms begin to reflect aspects of early Latter-day Saint united orders and other ethical approaches. They tend to create more jobs, provide a greater sense of the dignity of work, and build self-reliance for the long term. While none of these systems, whether secular or religious, is flawless in every detail according to God's grand eternal scheme, they suggest relevant dimensions of a better way.[31]

Whether the structure of worker economic participation is that of a co-op, ESOP, employee stock trust, or some other structure still to be developed, the key to improved labor relations is sharing profits and some form of stock distribution. Today's Avis, Weirton Steel, and Moroni Feed suggest the path that not only U.S. industry should follow, but by which LDS executives and their companies may more closely approximate principles of the united order in our day. The words of scripture and modern prophets are clear, and numerous precedents have been established in American business to justify such restructuring, both on a moral plane as well as in the economic spheres of profits and productivity. Both egalitarian and enterprising, such efforts toward a cooperative gospel economy are committed to, and able to provide, surplus resources to the poor and needy, and promise that the transformation to David O. McKay's "ideal society," the "complete ideal of

Mormonism," is not a utopian dream, but the "spirit of the true Church," and a real possibility if we will but work toward it.

In order to work toward this possibility, we must ask how a gospel economy would actually operate. The modern world has sought such a union of love and enterprise through innumerable systems and organizations. The next chapters attempt to show that it is the true life-giving principles of the united order that can supply the vital energies necessary for the ideal and spirit of a gospel economy to spread and extend.

John Taylor (1808–1887), successor as LDS prophet to Brigham Young, established and headed the Central Board of Trade to coordinate the activities of united order cooperatives in early Utah. He continually stressed the importance of collaboration in economic activity and called for the use of one's surplus in creating employment for all.

18

True Energetic Life-giving Principle:

Stewardship Management in United Order Principles Inspired Enterprise

> *The world has tried systems and organizations almost without number, and have failed in every instance. Those coming under our immediate observation, such as Socialism, Fourierism, Communism, etc. have all accomplished nothing, and have fallen to pieces; although aided by circumstances, wealth, talent, the press, philosophy and individual interest. Where are they now? What has become of "Robert Owen" and his system? What of Fourierism . . . where are they now? They are broken up; and what has caused their entire failure? They have been let alone, and have quietly fallen to pieces; and why? Because they have not the elements of strength within them; they were devoid of those principles which impart life, light and intelligence, as the human system when lacking some of its vital energies so dwindles and decays, so a social or philosophic system when destitute of the true energetic life-giving principle. It is so with all the rest, they have not been persecuted, they have been left unmolested and let alone and yet they are broken up, whilst the Mormons, although driven by mobs of ruthless savages, have increased, and still continue to spread and extend.*
>
> John Taylor[1]

Many systems and organizations have been proposed to make a more just and prosperous economy. However, they have quietly and not so quietly "fallen to pieces," both in 1856 when John Taylor spoke and in our times. How would UOPIEs (united order principles inspired enterprises) be run differently than regular businesses, and would any such differences really make a difference? This chapter goes into more detail regarding those principles "which impart life, light and intelligence" in the management and conduct of united order principles inspired enterprises and how the vital "philosophic system" of the law of stewardship can enable UOPIEs to increase, "spread and extend" as businesses. It also discusses how the "true energetic life-giving" principles of the united order respond in particular to some of the critiques of free enterprise put forth by the worldly systems and organizations mentioned by President Taylor.

Stewardship, Equality, and Self-reliance—Personal Development, Participation, and the Management of the United Order Principles Inspired Enterprise. In chapters 7 and 17, we saw that an effective method of implementing the law of stewardship in the modern economy is employee ownership. However, giving stock to employees only begins the transformation of a company into a united order principles inspired enterprise. The united order revelations state that the united order is managed by the "commo consent of the order." As we have seen, this differs from the hierarchical, top-down, bureaucratic management method found in many corporations and governments today. Running a business by "common consent" implies a participatory, "bottom-up" operating method.

Clearly, everyone has different skills, ability, and training, and not all are qualified to manage a business. In his discussion of equality at the 1877 general conference, Brigham Young noted that this diversity of ability would prevent the successful operation of a united order based on a simple arithmetic dead-level equalization. The principal reason was

> that for the lack of opportunity they are not able to develop the talents and ability that are within them. This is the condition of the peoples of most of the nations of the earth. . . . [Jesus] requires, absolutely requires, of us to take these people who have named his name through baptism, and teach them how to live, and how to become healthy, wealthy and wise. This is our duty.[2]

Lorenzo Snow told the same conference that the united order would need to draw on the abilities of all the members, including those "with great financiering abilities," and not just the bishop. This is what "the United Order designs to do for all, namely, to afford opportunity to develop the gift that nature has endowed us with."[3] Erastus Snow taught that the united order was "no agrarian doctrine, to level those who are exalted, down to the mean level of those who are in the mire, but it is the Godlike doctrine of raising those who are of low estate and placing them in a better condition."[4]

The UOPIE must work to help its participants to develop their talents, abilities, and gifts. This can be accomplished by providing job training and assistance with expenses for further education. Mentoring programs, in which more experienced people help less experienced workers improve their job skills and understanding of business, can give the less experienced confidence and boost their spirit of entrepreneurship.[5]

Once workers have gained experience and skills, they should be able to function as business partners of their fellow employees, including management. In the words of John Widtsoe, "many unite in one enterprise, in such a way that no one person dominates it, but that all concerned have a voice in it."[6] This bottom-up, participative management is sometimes referred to as "employee empowerment." There are numerous methodologies for accomplishing this. The scope of this book does not allow detailed descriptions of these.[7] However, several principles are common to all of these methods.

First, both the responsibility *and the authority* to make decisions must be vested with the workers who actually do the work. Rigid, bureaucratic rules and procedures have to replaced with wide discretion in the hands of front-line workers. Store managers must be able to put items on sale on their own initiative, customer service reps must be able to tailor work orders and refunds to suit the particular customer's circumstances, production workers must be able to decide what parts and materials they need and to order them without a lot of supervisory sign-offs. The particulars will vary widely from company to company and industry to industry. In all cases the hardest part is not giving employees responsibility, nor is it getting employees to accept responsibility. The hardest part is for management to delegate the real power and authority to the workers to do what they have been charged to do. This is not because UOPIE managers would be insincere about making employee empowerment work. It is because treating a "subordinate" as your partner and equal is completely contrary to the traditional top-down habits developed by generations of executives trained in the command-and-control management doctrines of Frederick Taylor. Such inbred habits are not changed without constant, deliberate, and well-thought-out effort.

Second, there will always be some need for central coordination and decision making. However, such decision making must be accessible to input from the front-line workers. The people who actually design and make the products and the people who directly interface with the customers should be regarded as the UOPIE's most valuable experts. Modern companies have long had ways to get quantitative data from the front—all those numbers and reports that ultimately go into the financial statements. However, methods must be developed to get qualitative data also—the kind of information that can only be passed on in human language and most effectively face-to-face. What were the customers' real reactions to the new, improved gizmatron? Is the new, improved gizmatron really as easy to manufacture as the outside design firm said it would be? Top executives and headquarters bureaucrats cannot remain unseen and isolated from their co-workers. Whether by putting regular workers on management committees, holding frequent discussion sessions with them, or just walking around the shop or plant a lot, the front-line worker in a UOPIE has to feel that he or she can speak frankly to the UOPIE's managers.

Third, in order to make bottom-up management by common consent effective, workers have to be given information about the business and the opportunity to learn how to understand and use that information. UOPIE management is accountable to the employees, and accessing and understanding the enterprise's accounting data are essential if they are to be able to assess management's performance. Access to and understanding of ongoing comprehensive information about the enterprise also helps individual workers do their jobs better. They can see their role in the big picture and are enabled to figure out ways to increase their contribution to the whole.

These united order principles have been proven in modern business. The old Taylorist concept of workers as cogs in a machine, working at routine standardized jobs carefully controlled from above, no longer works. Meeting global competition requires the full talent, energy, and creativity of every worker.[8] This is not just true of new knowledge-based industries like computers and biotechnology. After the massive Algoma steelworks in Ontario, Canada, was converted to employee ownership, there were significant improvements in operating results when workers were empowered to take charge of improving the operations on which they worked. One steelworker said, "Before, you left your brains at the gate. Now you take your brains through the gate and are allowed to use them. That's the big difference."[9]

At Springfield ReManufacturing Corporation in Missouri, employees bought a factory which was to be closed and turned it into a successful machinery refurbishing operation which produces goods of such quality that their best customers are German luxury car companies. Critical to their success was the "great game of business" strategy, in which all of the machinists were trained in accounting and supplied with detailed cost and financial information. Viewing their company's bottom line like the score in a game, they generated numerous operating efficiencies that would have been invisible to even the most trained managers.[10] The "great game of business" is so successful that Springfield ReManufacturing has been able to set up a consulting business to teach it to other companies. Such "open-book" management has now been profitably implemented at many different firms.[11]

Most of Wal-Mart founder Sam Walton's rules for success revolved around employee empowerment. The first of these was not to consider workers as employees, but rather to call and treat them as "associates." His principles included sharing profits and ownership with the associates, communicating everything possible to the associates, listening to everyone in the company, and emphasizing associate motivation and appreciation. Wal-Mart associates get weekly and monthly data on their store's performance and on such items as profit margins per product, delivery times, and so forth.[12] A review of growing companies in many different industries in *Inc.* magazine concluded that successful businesses emancipated their workers from the manager/worker mindset by enabling workers to make decisions controlling their work, providing them the information to make intelligent decisions, and giving them a stake in the outcome of the decision through ownership.[13] In fact, because of the spirit of personal and collective responsibility developed by employees in such circumstances, less management is needed, which frees up resources for more productive investment. Joseph Smith's management philosophy of "teach them correct principles and let them govern themselves" can be as effective in business as in other fields of human endeavor.[14]

Economic self-government with a minimum of management hierarchy can lead to more profound effects than increased productivity. Adam Smith noted that in highly hierarchical organizations, advancement came through sycophancy, where "the abilities to please are more regarded than the abilities to serve." Is there anyone who has not known too many cases of someone advanced for fawning to the boss rather than for their work or skill? In the employee-controlled enterprise, management by the esteem of intelligent and well-informed "neighbors and equals" encourages instead "patience, fortitude and application of thought."[15] A work environment in which we are judged by our co-workers, who see how we lead our lives every day, will encourage steadier and truer conduct than one in which we need only impress our superiors. Developing these prudent virtues not only realizes Adam Smith's moral vision of the free market society, it can help us develop character better able to devote "heart, might, mind and strength" to the enterprise envisioned by Joseph Smith: "to promote the universal good of the universal world, . . . unite man to his fellow man, . . . make the nations of the earth to dwell in peace, and to bring about the millennial glory."[16]

Stewardship and Equality—Cults and Accounting. The use of employee ownership and participative management to implement the law of stewardship also promotes the united order principle of equality in an indirect way. It is an unhappy but constant feature of human nature that decisions about where resources are to flow tend to cause them to flow toward the decision maker. When regulation of the American savings and loan industry was reduced, many unwise loans were made to bank managers, directors, and their friends. One of the features of the communes that Joseph Smith observed in his time was that "the big fish eat up the little."[17] Cult leaders always seem to do well financially. One study of a short-lived Utah united order, run by a bishop, even found that the level of inequality seemed to increase during the united order.[18] John Taylor observed, "We find little institutions they call Co-ops in most of our settlements, but when you inquire into affairs connected with them we generally find, that, instead of their being run in the interest of the community, and with a view to build up the kingdom of God, a few individuals represent the Co-op, who are the ones who are benefitted by it."

However, when a UOPIE is owned and managed by its employees in the spirit of common consent and the law of stewardship, decisions about the flow of resources are made or monitored by the entire group. Resource allocations will be made on neutral business grounds, and any contrary tendency for resources to flow to the leaders will be minimized. Then, as President Taylor continued, when the order members obey God and look to "the building up of his Zion on the earth, and take themselves and their individual interests out of the question, . . . they will become the wealthiest of all people, and God will bless them and pour out wealth and intelligence and all the blessings that the earth can afford."[19]

In order for resource allocation decisions to be made or monitored by common consent, the order participants must have access to accurate information. In the original Doctrine & Covenants united order the Lord required "of every steward, to render an account of his stewardship, both in time and eternity. For he who is faithful and wise in time is accounted worthy to inherit the mansions prepared for him by my Father. Verily I say unto to you, the elders of the church in this part of my vineyard shall render an account of their stewardship unto the bishop" (D&C 72:3–5). These accounts were to be used by the bishop to "keep the Lord's storehouse" and administer to the poor and needy. How this would function in a full-fledged united order in the modern economy is unknown, but in a UOPIE the equivalent administrative functions would be handled by managing bodies selected by the voice and common consent of the UOPIE participants. This is yet another reason then that a sincere UOPIE must make complete financial data available to all of its worker/participants.

One of the most important but unheralded aspects of the rise of the free market economy has been the development of the science (or art, as some practitioners would call it) of accounting. A major element in the success of the Carnegie steel business was the development of rigorous internal accounting systems, which permitted close monitoring of costs and results. Another major element in that success was that promotions were strictly by merit, based on the results disclosed by these accounting systems. Access to impartial and accurate information is necessary for the free market economy to function efficiently. For this reason, all publicly owned corporations in the United States are required to have their financial statements audited annually by independent accountants. Even though modern accounting does not always give full valuation to human resources, UOPIEs would still have just as much need for good accounting systems as any other enterprise in the modern economy.

While it may seem incongruous to find generally accepted accounting principles in holy writ, modern scripture's requirement of accountability in the united order is very necessary. As noted above, a common feature of cults and communes is the control, and often fraudulent use of, common funds by a charismatic leader. As the Prophet Joseph made clear, the united order has nothing to do with cults and communes. UOPIEs are intended to be honestly and well-managed businesses, credibly functioning in a free market economy. Honest and accurate financial accounting is one of the surest methods of assuring that UOPIEs do not violate the principle of equality by drifting into the control of a cult-style leader.

Stewardship, Self-reliance, and Alienation. As an employee-owned and managed enterprise creates jobs, it helps the poor and needy to work and become self-reliant. This application of the law of stewardship also addresses the united order principle of work and self-reliance in our modern economy in a more profound way. One peculiar and unfortunate aspect of the modern economy is that work and self-reliance have become disconnected. In a self-employed economy, such as the early United States or the modern Third World informal sector, the connection between one's labor and resourcefulness and one's survival is fairly obvious. However, with the coming of the Industrial Revolution and large corporate employers, this connection became less obvious. A worker's survival came to depend more and more on the resourcefulness of those who directed the corporation rather than on the resourcefulness of the worker himself. Marx used this "alienation" of the workers from the means of their sustenance to justify his theories. While his theories were no cure, the phenomenon is real enough to millions of diligent, well-trained workers such as Joe Brown, who are laid off in corporate "downsizings" to which they feel powerless to respond no matter how hard they are willing to work. It is also real to entrepreneurs, who for all our glorification of them, often lead lonely lives struggling to "meet the payroll."[20]

This disconnection led to the separation of labor and capital in industrial society. Displaced from influence over their fates, laborers could only look to improve their situation by opposing capital through unions and state controls. Owners and corporate managers responded in kind, adopting union-busting and Taylorist management practices to control and manipulate workers. Workers pressed for increases in wages and benefits without regard for the economic consequences to the company. "That's management's job," they would say. Even worse, the inability to see or control the products of their labor undermined the laborers' work ethic, the spirit of the united order principle of work and self-reliance. Management in turn treated the human beings whose labor and energy are at the heart of their enterprises as simply another cost factor, to be driven down by oppression, automation, Taylorist mechanization of work, and export of jobs to cheaper labor environments. The attitudes developed in such conditions were even carried into Zion, as apostle Erastus Snow described in 1877:

> They cling to the habits and customs of Babylon that they have learned abroad—the laborer wishing to eat up the capitalist, and the capitalist constantly guarded for fear he should be drawn into close quarters, and then to succumb to the demands of operatives. This is the way of the world, and the warfare that is going on all the time.[21]

As a result of this warfare, workers were deprived of the opportunity to develop the characteristic which most embodies the spirit of self-reliance in the industrial free market economy—entrepreneurship. The new industrial working class was prevented from seeing the big picture. The resulting attitudes stood in the way of building united order enterprises. According to apostle Snow:

> The great difficulty I have had to fight against has been the ignorance of the laborers, their inability to make their labor pay for itself, and their unwillingness to be put to the test. They prefer someone to raise the capital to be invested in the enterprises, and employ them and pay them big wages. . . . They will say, "Let us work by the day or piece, and be paid our wages every Saturday night; and then let us have a store to spend our money at, that we might do as our fathers used to do in the old countries we came from." This is the spirit of the working classes of the old world, and I said before, unfortunately we brought ourselves with us when we emigrated to the new world.[22]

Self-reliance implies responsibility. Apostle Snow said that the "United Order is designed to help us to be self-reliant and to teach us to understand what it costs to produce that which we consume."[23] One cannot be truly self-reliant unless one understands and accepts responsibility for the full economic ramifications of one's actions. In a UOPIE, workers have to accept personal stewardship responsibility for the risks and labor necessary to keep a business viable. Managers, on the other hand, must also act as stewards, not autocrats, and treat workers as brothers and sisters, and not as a cost component.

Apostle Snow told the 1874 general conference that the "United Order of Zion . . . embraces labor as well as capital, and it designs to make the interests of capital and labor identical."[24] Modern businesses and scholars now acknowledge the harm done by the separation of the interests of labor and capital. As noted above, involving workers in a broader understanding of and participation in the business is seen as vital to the success, or even survival, of businesses in the modern "post-industrial" economy. A study of companies that had made initial public offerings found that 92 percent of the companies that applied such practices and rewarded workers well were still in business five years later, whereas only 34 percent of the companies without these policies were still around.[25] Companies that combine extensive employee participation with significant employee ownership have been particularly successful in attaining a competitive advantage.[26] When workers have a capital stake in a business and receive the means to exercise personal entrepreneurial self-reliance by having real influence and control over how they do their work, they will work harder and smarter. Also, the division between ownership and management, first studied by Berle and Means, is reduced because employee owners are close at hand to monitor management's conduct of its stewardship. Enterprises owned and managed by employees have also been successful at resisting the short-term mentality of absentee owners and bureaucratic executives.[27] A UOPIE, operated in accordance with the law of stewardship, will implement the features which are now recognized as critical to the success of any business in the economy of the 21st century.

Stewardship and Moral Motivation. However, the united order is about more than simple business success. Mere human efforts inevitably fall subject to human error and weakness. After reviewing humanity's many frustrated efforts to improve society, John Taylor observed that "man never could and never will be able to govern his fellows, except the power, the wisdom and the authority be given from heaven." He then recalled a conversation with Joseph:

> When you get the Spirit of God, you feel full of kindness, charity, long-suffering, and you are willing all the day long to accord to every man that which you want yourself. You feel disposed all the day long to do unto all men as you would wish them to do unto you. What is it that will enable one man to govern his fellows aright? It is just as Joseph Smith said to a certain man who asked him, 'How do you govern such a vast people as this?' 'Oh,' says Joseph, 'it is very easy.' 'Why, says the man, 'but we find it very difficult.' 'But,' said Joseph, 'it is very easy, for I teach them correct principles and they govern themselves'; . . . How easy it is to govern the people in this way![28]

A righteous moral foundation is the basis for the successful operation of the united order principle of independent, self-governing stewardship.[29]

All economic systems have moral foundations. Capitalism is predicated on the ideals of freedom and honesty. For a free market to function, its participants must be free to contract with others and then adhere to those commitments. Socialism espouses concern for others—working for the common good over individual interests. The united order incorporates all these virtues, because it is founded upon the most basic gospel virtue, love. The fundamental revelation on the united order repeats as its basis the most fundamental of Christ's teachings: "for inasmuch as ye do it unto the least of these, ye do it unto me" (D&C 42:38). The united order is about nothing less than using Christian morals as the moral foundation of an economic system. Speaking of the Church's efforts to implement some of the united order principles through the Church's Welfare Program, president Spencer W. Kimball said, "We can see that Welfare Services is not a program, but the essence of the gospel. *It is the gospel in action.*"[30] The united order is essentially a gospel economy.[31]

Morality and Enterprise. Those experienced in the worldly economy are apt to react quickly that, while we may try to act honestly in our economic dealings in the world, some amount of realism is necessary. Morality alone is not going to get you ahead in the real world. Certainly modern economics, with its lust for quantification, has never much taken such matters into account in its theories. However, some have recognized that the human endeavor of temporal survival involves more than the mechanical input of land, capital, and raw material. Adolf Berle concluded that successful economies were characterized by a "transcendental margin" which "is the product of a value system that causes effort and expenditure beyond that calculated as conducive to the personal advantage of an individual or his immediate family group."[32] Berle's principal illustration of this is a comparison of Utah and Nevada. Settled about the same time and with comparable geographical endowments, Utah he found to have a stable, solid economic history, compared with the boom and bust of Nevada's past. He attributed the difference to the two states' differing value systems. The devotion of Church members in Utah lead every productive individual "to put more into the economic system than he took out." In contrast, in Nevada's mining and gambling mentality success means staking a small contribution and, without further work, winning a larger prize. On the cold economic side, this does not add to useful capital, make for greater production, or occasion great distribution or growth.[33]

It can be fairly argued that much of Nevada's prosperity in recent years can be attributed to the adoption of a Utah-like family orientation to its economy, and the influence of its large LDS communities.[34]

Other writers have tried to account for human motivations in economic prosperity. One economist, Harvey Leibenstein, has even attempted to factor it into economic theory, dubbing it "X-efficiency."[35] Other recent writers have observed that trust, social cohesion, and cooperation are far more central to successful economies than competition. Like Adolf Berle, they cite the Latter-day Saints as a primary example.[36]

In the end it is human motivation that makes an economy operate. Articles and constitutions for a UOPIE will be effective only if those who run it adopt the gospel principles of the united order as their value system as well as their methodology. The gospel does not oppose business ability; it seeks to transform the hearts of those who possess it. Lorenzo Snow referred to the Doctrine and Covenants where we are told:

> If we are not equal in temporal things, we cannot be equal in spiritual things. Men on whom God has bestowed financeering ability are the men that are wanted at this time. . . . Persons who have the ability are the ones who should step forward in things that would lead the Latter-day Saints to this union. It would be of more value to them than all the things of earth. The blessings of God upon them in time and eternity would well repay them to step forth and labor for the Zion of God. . . . What a lovely thing it would be if there was a Zion now, as in the days of Enoch! that there would be peace in our midst and no necessity for a man to contend and tread upon the toes of another to attain a better position, and advance himself ahead of his neighbor.[37]

President Spencer W. Kimball told the 1978 general conference:

> Unfortunately we live in a world that largely rejects the values of Zion. Babylon has not and never will comprehend Zion. . . . Zion is "every man seeking the interest of his neighbor, and doing all things with an eye single to the glory of God." (D&C 82:19.) As I understand these matters, Zion can be established only by those

> who are pure in heart, and who labor for Zion, for the "laborer in Zion shall labor for Zion; for if they labor for money they shall perish." (2 Nephi 26:31.)[38]

President Ezra Taft Benson carried forward this emphasis on preparing our hearts to realize the ideal of Zion, telling the 1986 general conference that "it takes a Zion people to make a Zion society, and we must prepare for that."[39]

The principles of the united order are for wealthy bankers, accountants and go-getter entrepreneurs as well as poor Third World peddlers and inner-city welfare recipients. They are as important to the spiritual well-being of the Haves as they are to the temporal welfare of the Have-nots. We believe that the principles of the united order are the solution to humankind's economic, social, and moral concerns and that they can be the basis for a Zion economy that can function realistically in the modern world. Such a righteous economy can be made when Saints of means, ability, and talent are as seized and propelled by Zion's vision of love and unity as the world's ambitious are by Babylon's allures. In one place such an economy already may have begun.

19

One Principle of Love:
The Mondragon Cooperatives

In reality and essence we do not differ so far in our religious views, but that we could all drink into one principle of love. One of the grand fundamental principles of "Mormonism" is to receive truth, let it come from whence it may.

Joseph Smith, Jr.[1]

One becomes a cooperator through education and the practice of virtue. . . . We need each other; we are called upon to complement each other. The man who can stand solitude is either a god or a beast, as a celebrated philosopher has stated. And this means that social classes need each other and should collaborate; this means that the people and the authorities must not live divorced from each other. This means that institutions must offer mutual aid, that we must sincerely pursue what we claim, that is the common good, there is no reason for exclusivity. . . . For this purpose it is not enough that the bosses undertake and do good things. It is necessary that the workers participate in these things, so that a real communion among them exists. It is not enough that the workers dream of great reforms, if the bosses or entrepreneurs do not contribute to their realization, providing their zeal, their technical knowledge and skills, their experience. . . . Where this fusion and spontaneous and generous collaboration has not been achieved, there is no real social life, and . . . peaceable relations will be superficial or fictitious.

Jose Arizmendiarrieta[2]

One of the most remarkable attempts to achieve both economic justice and prosperity in the modern world is little known to most Americans and to almost all Latter-day Saints. In February 1941, as Harold B. Lee and Marion G. Romney were completing the fifth year of the Church's Welfare Program, a young Catholic priest was assigned to a small industrial town named Mondragon in the Basque country of northern Spain.[3] Like the stake presidents in Salt Lake City, Father Jose Maria Arizmendiarrieta, referred to as

Father Jose Maria Arizmendiarrieta (1915–1976) drew upon the Bible, Catholic social teachings, the ideas of British utopian Robert Owen, and extensive practical efforts in creating the Mondragon industrial system of worker-owned cooperatives.

Don Jose Maria for short, also felt that he had an ecclesiastical responsibility to respond to the effects of depression and war that went beyond simply preaching unquestioning endurance and faith in justice in the next life. Mondragon had been devastated by the Spanish Civil War, in which Don Jose Maria had fought and almost been executed by the fascist victors. Don Jose Maria reflected on and discussed with his parishioners the problem of how to achieve both economic prosperity and justice. He studied socialist thought ranging from Owen to Marx, as well as Catholic social teaching. However, his predilection was more for practical and flexible action than dogmatic theorizing. One of his favorite phrases was "We build the road as we travel."[4]

Assigned to teach religion classes to the town's young workers, he founded a soccer league. With the popular support generated by the soccer league, he next raised funds from the community to start a small technical school to permit young workers to improve their job skills. He then arranged for its graduates to pursue college-level engineering degrees on an extension basis. Five of these young graduates got excellent jobs at the town's largest manufacturing firm. However, the company proved uninterested in their desire to implement some of Don Jose Maria's ideas for improving justice in the workplace. In 1956, these five decided to start a small manufacturing business as a cooperative, following Don Jose Maria's ideas and guidance.

The Mondragon Complex. This small business has now grown into a complex of over 170 cooperative enterprises employing more than 23,000 workers. Revenues in 1990 were almost $3 billion.[5] Exports make up roughly a third of revenues. Not only does it constitute the largest group of affiliated cooperative enterprises in the world, it is extremely successful in simple business terms. Research has shown that the enterprises of the Mondragon cooperative complex are more efficient, more profitable, better capitalized, and have grown faster than any comparable Spanish private firms.[6] Retained earnings, levels of job creation, and productivity are also higher than in comparable Spanish private firms.[7] Turnover and absenteeism are far lower than national or regional averages.[8] "Mondragon" cooperatives, now found throughout northwestern Spain, produce home appliances, electrical equipment, machine tools, ships, furniture, publications, and many other products.[9] They include consumer retail, custodial services, and agricultural cooperatives. They have their own highly regarded schools, research and development laboratory, and social security system. They also operate one of the largest banks in Spain. They survived the severe economic crisis of the late 1970s and early 1980s, in which Spain was particularly hard hit, without laying off a single worker. In almost 40 years of operation, out of more than one hundred separate enterprises, only three have ever had to be closed because they were not financially viable. The Mondragon cooperative complex has been admired and studied throughout the world for over a quarter of a century. And it has never been replicated.

One key aspect of the Mondragon cooperative complex is that it is complex, as befits a complex modern economy. Its structure has evolved over decades of efforts to create a business organization that would be true to its fundamental values. These values are basically to maximize job creation and to accord to every worker both the benefits and the responsibilities of being an owner. The Mondragon method profoundly reflects the fact that its leaders were trained as practical engineers rather than as abstract social theorists. Its business focus has been on high value-added jobs in sophisticated, capital intensive industries. The broad principles and goals are implemented by carefully detailed structures and procedures. However, despite its elaborate organization, it has little bureaucracy and the rules are revised or thrown out if they are not effective in achieving the objectives. Even Don Jose Maria, who taught the ideals that underlie the Mondragon system, was not above nitty-gritty technical work. At first the working folk of Mondragon could not afford sophisticated legal assistance, so their well-educated padre would roll up his sleeves and plunge into the law books to find an obscure statute or regulatory loophole that would facilitate the legal construction of this novel venture.

Mondragon enterprises are cooperative corporations owned by their employees. All employees are owners, and nonemployees cannot be owners. They are governed on a one-person, one-vote basis. General assemblies of workers, like shareholders meetings, are held annually. Management is elected by the worker assembly and usually given a multiyear contract to promote long-range planning. Management has most of the authority found in a private firm, but subject to the knowledge that reappointment depends on the support of a majority of the workers. In addition to the workers assemblies, social councils represent the workers in such matters as benefits, working conditions, and grievances.

There is a strong institutional, cultural thrust toward "bottom-up" management, and steps have been taken to institute some of the latest methods for promoting worker involvement in production decisions.[10] The organizational structure of a Mondragon cooperative is outlined in Appendix A.

One American visitor to a Mondragon cooperative factory was "impressed with the relative informality of the workplaces" and found that "conversation among workers, and between them and supervisors in the cooperatives, was easy and relaxed." This was in contrast to comparable American and Spanish firms where workers "stood silently . . . casting only sidelong glances towards us as we passed."[11] As with wards and stakes in the Church, there is a strong policy toward dividing enterprises after they reach a certain size, to the extent that this is consistent with maintaining economies of scale and overall efficiency. In this way the individual worker does not become submerged in a large and unresponsive bureaucratic environment. The cooperative enterprises are also organized in subgroups on industry and geographical lines.

Workers who are hired by a Mondragon enterprise are required to pay a substantial entry contribution to the cooperative, which can equal several months' pay. It can be financed in part through the cooperative bank and is credited toward the worker's account. New employees are also evaluated for a period of time in both work skills and personal attitudes compatible with the cooperativist corporate culture. Each worker has an individual capital account. A majority of enterprise earnings are allocated to these accounts. The remainder is divided among benefit and social security costs and a collective corporate surplus account according to a preset formula. "Salaries" and "wages" as such are not paid. Instead every worker from shop floor to management is paid a monthly *anticipio,* which is a draw against their capital account. Surplus earnings left over at the end of the year are credited to the capital accounts. The individual accounts accumulate interest and are also periodically adjusted for inflation. Normally, individual worker accounts cannot be withdrawn until retirement. Earlier withdrawals are subject to a penalty unless the worker is transferring to another enterprise within the complex of cooperative companies. In the meantime the funds in the individual accounts are available for general use by the cooperative.[12]

The rate of payment of the draw for the lowest paid workers is generally set at locally prevailing wage rates. Differentials between the lowest and highest paid workers are limited to a six-to-one ratio (which has been gradually increased from an original ratio of three-to-one). This results in management personnel generally receiving lower than prevailing salaries. However, there has not been a significant problem with loss of management talent, perhaps due to a strong bias toward internal promotion.[13]

The Mondragon Bank. Of the supplemental institutions mentioned above—schools, social security fund, etc.—the most significant is the bank, the Caja Laboral Popular.[14] It was begun at Don Jose Maria's initiative in 1959, at the very beginning of the Mondragon cooperative business, to act as a depository and source of financing for the cooperative enterprises, and as a credit union for the workers. One of the founders described their reaction to the good father's new scheme: "We told him, yesterday we were craftsmen, foremen, engineers. Today we are trying to learn how to be managers and executives. Tomorrow you want us to become bankers. That is impossible."[15] The Caja Laboral Popular (CLP) has grown into one of the largest banks in the Basque country and one of the twenty largest banks in Spain. It is owned and managed by the participating cooperatives, with a minority interest held by individual depositors and the bank's employees. It provides financing for the existing enterprises, invests in housing cooperatives, and runs an active economic research organization. The latter is so highly regarded that the Spanish national and Basque regional governments use the bank's reports on economic activity in its region rather than producing their own, surely a rare instance where modern government bureaucracies would forego an opportunity to produce reports.[16]

The bank has served as the central focus of the complex of cooperatives and provides the cooperatives' principal source of financing. It also coordinates the extensive intercooperative arrangements and joint operations which tie together the various Mondragon enterprises (which are otherwise theoretically independent) and mandates compliance by the enterprises with the basic cooperative rules through a "Contract of Association" with each of the cooperatives.[17] If, for example, a cooperative transgresses a fundamental principle—such as eliminating the one-person, one-vote rule in the general assembly—the bank is empowered to cut off the enterprise's credit. This power is balanced by the fact that a majority of the bank's ownership is held by the cooperatives, which checks unreasonable or arbitrary use of the bank's rights.

By the mid-1980s, the bank had grown so large that the cooperatives could not profitably employ all the bank's funds. In order to facilitate the expansion of its lending activities into other areas, its coordinating and supervisory functions were spun off to an overall cooperative board and congress.[18] These function in many respects like John Taylor's Board of Trade was intended to function, enabling independent enterprises to work together and combine their resources so as to be able to compete effectively with large noncooperative companies.[19] In the pursuit of their cooperative ideals, the Mondragon cooperatives have now created a structure which combines strong local autonomy on the operational level with strong central coordination—the very structure that is universally recognized as the paradigm for the successful business of the 21st century.

Mondragon and Enterprise. Most interesting of the functions recently spun off to independent status is the Entrepreneurial Division.[20] This is a cooperative consulting firm of over a hundred professionals which provides management assistance and funding from the CLP to new start-up cooperatives. When a cooperative or group of workers in the Mondragon conglomerate have an idea for a new business, they present a business plan and proposed management to the Division. The Division carefully evaluates the plan and, if it deems it feasible, provides a wide range of professional market research, financial analysis, site selection, strategic planning, legal, scientific, and technical services in developing the business launch. A "godfather" is assigned from the Division staff to shepherd the process from the evaluation through the first year or two of operations. The founding members are required to put up some financing. Other funds are loaned by the CLP. The CLP not only provides start-up funding but covers losses through the first years of operation if they are in line with the business plan. More recently, the CLP has also launched new enterprises on its own initiative, based on a need to rationalize operations among the cooperatives or to exploit inventions from the cooperative research and development laboratory, which also does contract research for outside companies such as IBM and Mercedes Benz.

The Division has achieved an impressive record of successful start-ups by helping new cooperative enterprises in overcoming two of the principal problems of start-up businesses—inadequate financing and incomplete management know-how. Anyone who has tried to start a business is keenly aware of how difficult it is to obtain funding for a start-up venture. Equally difficult is the task of becoming a master of all fields. A good engineer may be quite inexperienced in marketing, a good salesman may be mystified by cost control and accounting, and even the most knowledgeable entrepreneur never has enough time to do everything. For all our society's praise of the entrepreneur, the silence can be deafening when the crunch comes and real assistance is needed. Instead, the entrepreneur has to beg and borrow, and often ends up in the embrace of a venture capitalist who will dribble in money and criticism in exchange for the lion's share of the equity.

Although a Mondragon entrepreneur must sacrifice the dream of being the next Bill Gates or Steve Jobs billionaire, the Mondragon method of entrepreneurship offers real financial and technical assistance, as well as friends and solidarity, in the lonely struggle of launching a new enterprise. This appears to be a trade-off that many ambitious, bright workers in the Mondragon cooperatives have found worthwhile. The Mondragon method enables entrepreneurial individuals to pursue their dreams and ideas while providing for the cooperative complex the benefit of the entrepreneurial energies that are the key to maintaining the growth and dynamism of any enterprise. This activity also enables the Mondragon cooperatives to fulfill one of their central corporate cultural values, which is the constant expansion of economically viable employment.

Mondragon in Recession. Of course, noncooperative firms also produce new jobs with good management and financing, and a strong economy. What is perhaps the most impressive feature of the Mondragon cooperatives is their record of no job loss in a weak economy. In the late 1970s to mid-1980s, Spain suffered a significant recession, produced in part by the overall world recession of the time and also by the shock of opening the protected Spanish market to free trade following the restoration of democracy after the death of Franco in 1975. Unemployment rates approached 20 percent in the areas where the Mondragon cooperatives are located.

The solution was not to prohibit layoffs. Cooperatives that had to reduce their workforces were permitted to do so. However, the cooperative, the bank, the general cooperative congress, and the cooperatives' private social security fund worked together to place those workers at other cooperatives in the group. Relocation

A view of the Mondragon worker-owned bank (CLP) and nearby industrial co-ops in the Basque country of northern Spain.

and retraining costs were funded by the cooperatives. Workers who were cooperating with the program were guaranteed partial wages while on layoff. Job loss was also limited by early intervention in cooperatives that were in difficulty. In exchange for reductions in their workers' draws, the CLP provided emergency funding and the Entrepreneurial Division developed workout plans for cooperatives in loss positions. New cooperatives in growing sectors were also launched. Although the Mondragon cooperatives did not expand their employment during this period, their record of no net job loss stands in sharp contrast to the practices of other businesses, where pink slips to nonexecutive employees seem to be viewed as the easiest way out of the red.[21]

Why Only One? In light of these successes, writers on Mondragon almost inevitably ask why other cooperative ventures have not succeeded like Mondragon and whether the Mondragon model can be replicated elsewhere. One frequent argument is that the success of Mondragon is peculiar to the Basque culture and is therefore not readily transferrable. However, researchers have found that the cooperatives' Basque members identify much more strongly among themselves than with other Basque workers.[22] Another argument is that the cooperatives were fortunate in starting just at the time when Spain was beginning a period of rapid and protected economic growth. But other cooperatives have existed in booming economies and not succeeded. This argument also overlooks the subsequent relative prosperity of the Mondragon cooperatives during economic recession. Others note such factors as relatively low turnover and absenteeism and high per worker efficiency, although research is unclear on possible explanations for these facts. Many have admired the dynamic role of the bank in fostering entrepreneurship by providing capital and management assistance. However, this role only developed over time and was possible only because the economic success of the earlier cooperatives provided the bank with the strong capital and asset foundation which enabled it, indeed forced it, to expand its established client base by starting new cooperative enterprises.[23]

Many commentators feel that these factors are not conclusive explanations for the Mondragon success and are mystified by the failure of efforts to duplicate the Mondragon model elsewhere. Frequently writing from a leftist perspective, they are proud to point to Mondragon as an alternative to capitalist enterprise. However, when they examine Mondragon more closely, there are aspects which disturb them, aspects which are often omitted from efforts to apply the Mondragon model in other settings. One of these is the preoccupation on the shop floor as well as in the (modest) executive suites with operating efficiently, staying competitive, expanding markets, and making profits.[24] Another is the focus on engineering education as the principal training for Mondragon executives and workers. This has been more recently supplemented by a management training cooperative which teaches substantive fields such as accounting, marketing, finance, international business, etc.[25] The elaborate, theoretical, socialist-oriented analyses of capitalist society and economy which are the professional pursuits of many of these commentators are noticeable by their complete absence from Mondragon curricula.[26]

Perhaps most disturbing to these commentators is the attitude toward labor unions in the Mondragon cooperatives. Basically, there are none. This is not because of any ideological opposition to unions. Indeed, unions are free to organize Mondragon workers if they can. However, the general attitude of Mondragon workers toward unions is that they are unnecessary where workers own and manage the business. Further, strikes are prohibited, and there has in fact been only one strike in the entire history of the Mondragon cooperatives. This was in 1974, a protest against job classification changes in a rapidly growing factory. In response, the policy of dividing up cooperatives to maximize individual worker involvement was adopted, and the social councils were considerably strengthened. Also, the strike leaders were fired, and all the other participants were fined. These sanctions were upheld by the general workers' assembly.

Mondragon and Beatrice Webb

This incident did little to reduce organized labor's traditional hostility to employee ownership and worker cooperatives.[27] Labor unions have preferred Fabian state ownership or regulation of industry. In contrast, at least two prominent labor scholars have argued that Mondragon, far from being a socialist inspiration, is actually the definitive refutation of Beatrice Webb's contention that state control was necessary because worker cooperative and employee-owned businesses could not work and still retain their cooperative character.[28] (As noted in chapter 9, this was also her conclusion regarding the Zion's Co-operative Mercantile Institution she observed on her visit to Salt Lake City in 1898).

Webb argued that in addition to whatever other difficulties all businesses might face, such as lack of capital, competition, and so on, self-managed, employee-owned businesses would not work because of four factors inherent to that form of organization:[29]

- inadequate internal discipline
- lack of knowledge of the market
- slowness in adjusting to new conditions
- discouragement of creativity

Inadequate internal discipline. Webb wrote, "Experience seems to indicate that, with human nature as it is at present," workers will not obey a manager whom they employ, and production will suffer as a result. In fact, the Mondragon enterprises have higher productivity and lower absenteeism than comparable firms. There are several possible reasons for this sense of responsibility on the part of Mondragon cooperators. First, they have a significant personal stake in the business through their initial entry fee and the share of the profits accumulating in their personal capital accounts. Second, they are screened for their willingness to abide by the cooperative ideals.[30] Third, the availability of workers assemblies and the social councils with real authority to work out disputes reduces the need to protest through passive aggressions, such as slowdowns and sick-outs.

Lack of knowledge of the market. The regular factory worker might not have ready access to market research and consumer surveys. However, the Mondragon system recognizes the need for technically proficient management and rewards it with higher salaries. The CLP, Entrepreneurial Division, and various groups of cooperatives use professional marketing resources and otherwise provide a network of technical support which effectively gives each cooperative enterprise the technical and information resources of companies many times their size.[31]

Slowness in adjusting to new conditions. The tendency for those who are used to making and doing things a certain way to keep on doing so is overcome in the Mondragon cooperatives by oversight by the CLP and quick intervention with assistance from the Entrepreneurial Division in case of institutional sluggishness. Also, the organization of cooperative businesses into industry and geographic groups gives the individual cooperative a source of constant independent, but friendly, critique from the other cooperatives in the group (who may buy outside the group if their Mondragon suppliers are not competitive).

Discouragement of creativity. Webb maintained that "invention, like artistic production, must be the work of an individual mind; or, very occasionally, of the free interplay of the minds of two or three co-workers, untrammelled by any 'management,' whether co-operative or governmental or capitalistic." However, in the Mondragon system, the ability of a cooperator or group of cooperators to independently present a plan for a new cooperative to the Entrepreneurial Division for development and funding may be one of the best existing means for permitting a creative entrepreneurial individual to produce new products and services. It certainly seems to offer better possibilities than trying to push a new idea through a bureaucracy that has other things to do, or trying to scrounge venture capital from uncertain sources.[32]

As noted in chapter 17, many other employee-owned-and-operated businesses have proven to be competitive and successful in the modern market economy. The John Lewis department store chain in Britain has grown faster than, and has capital and labor productivity superior to, comparable British firms such as Marks and Spencer.[33] The John Lewis Partnership also was the source of ideas about employee empowerment which Sam Walton considered to be vital to the success of Wal-Mart.[34] Even if Beatrice Webb and other socialists were correct in judging that 19th-century workers needed a bureaucratic elite to guide them, the well-educated workers in today's employee-owned-and-operated companies have shown that they understand and can contribute to the long-term "big picture" success of their companies.[35]

Reflecting on the prospects for replicating the Mondragon model, a prominent British expert on workers' cooperatives, Robert Oakeshott, has observed:

> Perhaps the real problem is that the attitudes and values of which the Mondragon co-ops are both cause and effect—of collective and individual self-reliance, of collective and individual responsibility and of hard work—are so out of tune with the predominant attitudes in the welfare state, trade union and class struggle dominated societies of the Atlantic world, that a genuine experiment could never be launched. Perhaps it would be too strongly opposed by the bureaucratic socialists; perhaps it

> would be seen as too much of a threat by the trade unions. In the end it may be factors of this kind, rather than the non-replicability of Basque culture, which will determine whether 'other Mondragons' have any real chance of getting off the ground and of emulating the Mondragon success.[36]

Mondragon and the United Order

"Collective and individual self-reliance, collective and individual responsibility and hard work" are the attitudes and values of which the Mondragon cooperatives are both the cause and effect. These attitudes and values should have a familiar ring to the reader of this book. True principles are true wherever they are found. The fundamental principles of the united order should be effective wherever they are applied. It is our view that the true explanation for the success of the Mondragon cooperators is that they have independently discovered ways to apply, at least in part, God's principles for economic prosperity and justice, the united order. Let us analyze Mondragon in light of the principles of the united order outlined in chapter 10.

Care for the Poor. The Mondragon enterprises provide successful "inheritances" in the form of jobs with excellent job security, social security benefits better than those offered by the Spanish national government, and individual profit-sharing accounts that can become quite substantial. In 35 years, the Mondragon cooperatives have gone from fewer than 50 jobs to over 23,000. It could be said that the original Mondragon "stewards" have literally returned many times more than a hundredfold their original stewardship. In addition, the cooperatives' private social security organization acts as more than a simple pension fund. It also provides workers with extensive job retraining and relocation services and pays partial salaries to workers in its program if they are laid off before retirement.

Of course, Mondragon does not create the fully comprehensive system that seems to have been contemplated by the classic united order described in the Doctrine and Covenants. Distributions are on a normal salary basis and are not adjusted to take into account individual needs and family circumstances of the workers. Also, the Mondragon cooperatives are not in a position to do much to help the unemployable poor or meet the emergency assistance needs of the general community.

Work and self-reliance. The Mondragon cooperatives provide real, viable, self-sustaining jobs. The division between work and self-reliance, between capital and labor, has been largely eliminated in the Mondragon system. Every worker knows that he is an owner and is responsible for the enterprise's success, and the means are provided for the workers to apply self-reliance, responsibility, and hard work in directing the enterprise.[37] This is concretely reflected in low absenteeism and turnover.

Equality. Mondragon enterprises do permit salary differentials. However, the rules limiting salary differentials to six-to-one and the application of the one-person, one-vote principle in enterprise governance substantially promote a much more egalitarian work environment than is normally found in commercial enterprises. This environment is further enhanced by a student-run cooperative in which students at the technical college pay for their education by working as part-time factory laborers in the other cooperatives, thus helping future managers relate to regular factory workers.

Consecration. While Mondragon workers are not required to donate all that they possess to the cooperative, the entry fee does require them to make a contribution. The availability of financing of the entry contribution from the bank prevents this from discriminating against job applicants who cannot afford the fee. However, the entry fee is the same regardless of the prior economic circumstances of the applicant. The Mondragon system also provides for a form of "reconsecration." While workers and cooperatives are not required to donate their surpluses back into the system, by depositing their funds with the CLP they make their surplus assets available to further the work of improving other cooperatives and new job creation. Workers of one of the Mondragon cooperatives have even decided that their pensions will be sufficient and have voted to leave their capital surplus accounts in the cooperative when they retire.[38]

Stewardship. The Mondragon cooperatives have worked out over time a very practical method of reconciling the demands of workplace self-government with those of efficient management by providing for mutual accountability. Management supervises workers and workers elect management. The bank will intervene in an enterprise in economic difficulty and engage in extensive rescue efforts. However, ultimately the bank will let an enterprise fail if it is not wisely managed or salvageable. On the other hand, the bank is owned by the cooperatives and is in turn accountable to them for fulfilling its agreed-upon responsibilities. The passage of many of these responsibilities to a general cooperative coordinating body is a necessary adaptation to permit the cooperative complex to act in a global economy, and follows in many respects the role contemplated for the Board of Trade under John Taylor.

The Mondragon system also suggests a solution to another aspect of how to implement the law of stewardship in the modern economy. Although he was the undeniable spiritual leader, backstage booster, and conceptual creator of the Mondragon system, Don Jose Maria never held any official position in any of the Mondragon cooperatives.[39] Instead, in essence, he taught correct principles and let the cooperatives govern themselves. The nature of Don Jose Maria's involvement could serve as a useful model for the role of a bishop or other priesthood leaders in any modern efforts to work toward implementing the principles of the united order.

The Storehouse. As noted in chapter 8, one of the principal differences between the modern economy and that of 1831 is that the modern economy operates basically on a purely cash basis. In a cash economy, there is no closer analogy to a storehouse for the surplus from economic activity than a bank. The united order revelations clearly make the storehouse a central institution. Similarly, many researchers have agreed that the role played by the Caja Laboral Popular has been central to the impressive success of the Mondragon endeavor. The CLP has marshalled the assets of the community to promote economic development and job creation, which is one of the principal functions of the united order storehouse or treasury.

Moral Motivations. The workers and managers of Mondragon attribute much of their success to the teachings of Don Jose Maria. In surveys, the reason most frequently given by workers for working at a Mondragon enterprise is belief in cooperativist principles.[40] The Mondragon enterprises, while maintaining their status as profit-making businesses, have extensive records of community service. While these factors may not amount to the "perfecting of the Saints," they do show that the Mondragon model can encourage long-term allegiance to principles beyond simple profit maximization.

The importance of nonmonetary motivation is particularly significant in the case of better educated, more able, and more entrepreneurial workers. Even with the six-to-one pay differential, managers and top technical people in the Mondragon cooperatives make significantly less than they could in noncooperative private firms. Yet, in general, they stay. It is hard not to hear echoed, in Basque, John Taylor's call for those with business ability to "financier for the poor, for the working man, who requires labor and is willing to do it, and act in the interest of the community, for the welfare of Zion."[41]

Thus, while the Mondragon model cannot be said to be the complete united order, it may approach the united order more closely in many "broad essentials" than any other available proven models. In addition, in many respects it complements the Welfare Program in that it focuses on permanent job creation while the Welfare Program focuses on temporary and emergency assistance for the unemployed or unemployable.[42]

Perhaps the most significant aspect of the Mondragon experience is its ability to achieve these united order principles in the context of a modern industrial economy. The world has searched throughout the ages for economic justice and prosperity. In some significant cases, such as certain ESOPs, the Israeli kibbutzim, and particularly Mondragon, many of the principles of the united order have been discovered and astonishing success realized. However, in the world's search for the system or organization that would realize these desires, the need to apply the true, energetic, life-giving principles of the united order generally has not been recognized. There have been no "other Mondragons." The Latter-day Saints have been blessed with revelation of the principles of the united order. Can they show the way toward the realization of the "full economic plan of Zion, the united order"? The next chapter attempts to explore several critical issues that would arise if the Saints were to begin to work toward an economy inspired by the principles of the united order.

20

Building the Holy City:

Working Toward a Modern Zion Economy

That [Mormonism] will succeed in establishing Zion, in building the holy city, in gathering out the righteous from all lands and preparing them to meet the Lord when He comes in His Glory, no faithful Latter-day Saint doubts. To this end it aims to institute what is known as the United Order, a communal system inaugurated by the Prophet Joseph Smith as early as February 1831, but which owing to the Church's frequent migration and other causes has never been fully established. The purpose of the Order is to make the members of the Church equal and united in all things, spiritual and temporal, to banish pride, poverty and iniquity, and to introduce a condition of things that will prepare the pure in heart for the advent of the world's Redeemer.

Lorenzo Snow[1]

Having reviewed numerous systems and organizations that have been used by both Latter-day Saints and others in the quest to banish pride, poverty, and iniquity, we now examine what the essential elements might be in a comprehensive move toward applying the principles of the united order in the modern world, a world that desperately needs the economic plan of Zion. The united order is about economics and business. The establishment of righteous temporal self-reliance for all in accordance with the principles of the united order ultimately depends on the achievement of personal and collective economic viability in the modern world. The current Church Welfare Program generally assumes the context of a prosperous First World economy in which only temporary, subsidized assistance is required.[2] The modern Church and Saints are now challenged to achieve righteous temporal self-reliance at a time when most of the Saints will no longer be able individually to rely on a prosperous external economy to secure their temporal well-being. Further, even economically blessed

Saints continue to be confronted by the moral challenges of materialism and selfishness.

Could an economy or economic sector which was based on the principles of the united order be made to work in the modern world? Could the aspects of economic development and job creation in the united order again be successfully activated? Could full employment for all those who are willing to labor as contemplated by the united order be realized through the devotion of our surplus to the creation of viable cooperative businesses along the lines of models such as Mondragon? Could such united order principles inspired enterprises (UOPIEs) succeed in the difficult economies in the Third World, where the need is greatest? Could similar principles and methods also be applied in developed nations?

These questions are raised not as dreamy ideological issues. Such cooperatives would only be worthwhile if they could function as successful businesses which supply viable employment in the context of the modern market economy. There are several key factors to a successful business—capital, effective corporate governance, technical and management skill, entrepreneurial energy, and business opportunity. The principles of the united order provide the means as well as the purpose for achieving these.

Capital. Central to the modern economy is the organized accumulation of capital and its efficient deployment to productive investment. Junius Morgan's financing was as essential to launching the Carnegie steelworks as Andrew Carnegie's entrepreneurship. Most observers consider the Caja Laboral Popular to be one of the essential elements in the Mondragon success story. A bank is always at the center of the most successful industrial organizations of modern time, the Japanese *keiretsu*. But before all these, the Lord himself taught the importance of the financing function in this dispensation by revealing (in contrast to prior dispensations) that a storehouse or treasury was to be at the center of the economic plan of Zion. The united order is no genteel charity, no philanthropic sideshow. The restored gospel is serious business, and its economic manifestation, the united order, encompasses all aspects of the modern economy. The spare change which we now devote to fast offerings ($12.61 per member annually according to the last figures released by the Church in 1983[3]) is only a pale shadow of a Zion economy. In a Zion economy, all the economy's savings and investment capital are to be consecrated to the united order's temporal and spiritual purposes.

These purposes are not otherworldly or impractically utopian. They are to a considerable extent simply those envisioned by Adam Smith for the morally based free enterprise market economy—in which prudent, honest neighbors and equals seek reasonable rates of profit through diligent and steady industriousness, raising the general level of prosperity of all members of the community and thereby enabling and encouraging them to pursue the even higher virtues of sympathy and benevolence toward the greater "society of all sensible and intelligent beings." Productive, viable, and useful employment for all, even the poor, the "lowest ranks of the people," should be the objective of capital investment, not real estate, junk bond, penny stock and other speculations. Ultimately, the united order is not about donating 12 dollars a year to the poor, as worthy as that is. It is about the transformation of the modern economy by the righteous investment of the hundreds of billions of surplus wealth created by the Industrial Revolution and the modern free enterprise market economy.

The central institution of a Zion economy is therefore a storehouse treasury, a united order principles inspired financial institution (hereinafter abbreviated "UOPIFI"). Whether it would be incorporated as a bank, savings and loan, credit union, regular or mutual corporation, finance company, investment management entity, charitable institution, foundation, or even operated on an informal basis would depend on local law and custom. In developed nations it might take the form of a venture capital fund, which would cash out its investments by selling to ESOPs or other forms of employee ownership. The Caja Laboral Popular is an obvious model, but a UOPIFI need not be so elaborate. Operating through a charitable foundation would entail less expense and fewer legalities than setting up an actual banking institution. On the other hand, setting up a banking institution permits the application of a broader range of resources. Deposits from the cooperatives and members of the community could significantly increase the amount of capital available over what might be expected from charitable donations. The young engineers who founded the Mondragon cooperatives were incredulous when Don Jose Maria proposed that they start a bank, but if faith can move mountains, it should support a bank as well.[4]

The initial capital for such institutions might be supplied by a small endowment. Such endowments need not be large. Even in the United States, most small businesses start with capital of under

$50,000.[5] Even less would be required to establish micro-enterprises in developing countries. Implementation of this united order principle in a developed economy might require a larger investment pool. However, the investment in UOPIFIs of even a minuscule part of the wealth now found in the developed nations' banks, credit unions, savings institutions, finance companies, pension and mutual funds could have a significant impact when increased a "hundredfold" through united order principles inspired enterprise.

A common assumption is that this financing should come from the Church. However, the demands on general Church funds are already extensive. As will be discussed further below, we are here suggesting instead private consecration of such funds.[6] That the Saints are capable of making significant consecrations in addition to their tithing donations is shown by the experience of the special fast days in 1985. These special fast days for donations to relieve poverty in Africa raised more than $10 million.[7] Much of the proceeds from the special fasts were used for development projects rather than direct food aid.[8]

UOPIFIs need not be strictly charitable endeavors. They could be banks, such as the Southside Bank or Caja Laboral Popular, credit unions, venture capital mutual funds, as mentioned above, or other vehicles still to be developed.[9] We know of nothing in the united order revelations that prohibits reasonable profit, widely shared.

Governance of United Order Principles Inspired Enterprises and Financial Institutions. The law of stewardship requires that the control and allocation of the start-up investments be made by local participators, the "voice and common consent of the order" (D&C 104:71). The principle of equality would require that the recipients be employee-owned enterprises.[10] The importance of local self-management cannot be overemphasized. Someone sitting in a developed nation can never be qualified to identify the best entrepreneurial opportunities in Cuzco, Quezon City, or Queens, or to make them work. Even natives based in the country cannot generally do so if they are controlled by a developed country-based bureaucracy, even the Church's.[11]

Another advantage of following the law of stewardship by setting up UOPIEs and UOPIFIs as self-governing is that it makes it possible for nonmembers of the Church to participate in them. At first, the concept of bringing nonbelievers into efforts toward a holy order which has been thought to be beyond even most Saints

A meeting of workers and managers on a Mondragon co-op board of directors. They are elected by co-op members through democratic voting (one person/one vote) and equally share decision-making power in governing the enterprise.

may seem contradictory. When the united order was first revealed, the mission of the Church was to gather the believers to a geographically centralized Zion. A minuscule minority in the world, the seedling of the restored Church had to germinate in an environment relatively free of worldly influence.

However, now the gospel tree of life has begun to grow into the forest of the worldwide Zion. Zion now expands to fill every nook and corner of this world. Ensconced in the midst of the world, the Church and Saints must now have the strength to reach out to embrace and save the world. This process began as early as the 1890s, when Wilford Woodruff told LDS businessmen to join chambers of commerce with non-LDS business people. Organizations inspired by the principles of the united order could accommodate any nonmember who is willing to accept the operating principles of the united order: care for the poor through increasing employment, work, self-reliance, equality, consecration (as implemented through deposits with a UOPIFI and UOPIE entry contributions), collective self-government, responsibility, and morality. The cooperators of Mondragon have shown that non-LDS can acknowledge and adhere to these principles of economic righteousness. By welcoming nonmembers into their operations, the Saints would be fulfilling their mission of extending the blessings of the gospel to all peoples.

If there was to be external funding of UOPIFIs, it should be in the form of a one-time "endowment" rather than annual allocations. This would enhance local control and responsibility and reduce the bureaucratic temptation to expend the funds rapidly, and perhaps unwisely, simply in order to qualify for further allocations.[12] Also, this would require the UOPIE to practice the united order principle of self-reliance and limit the possibility of outsiders, including even well-meaning Church officials, impinging on local stewardship self-governance through their control of future appropriations.

Funds from a UOPIFI should be distributed in the form of loans. The Doctrine and Covenants seems to imply that worthy order members would have open access to storehouse assets (D&C 104:72–75). However, in this mortal and imperfect life, common sense dictates that we have not yet reached the point at which everyone can be trusted to manage a stewardship wisely without some outside review, nor where others are so generous as to put up their hard-earned surplus to be taken by others without restriction.[13] Giving loans rather than grants maintains financial discipline.[14] The "affinity" group model developed by the Grameen Bank and used by ACCION, Katalysis, and other credit organizations holds that the loans should bear interest at rates close to local prevailing commercial rates of interest so that their small entrepreneur clients will develop from the beginning the ability to function in a real market environment.[15] Lending with interest also provides an automatic method by which "surplus" can be "reconsecrated" to the UOPIFI, in that way eliminating the potentially contentious exercise of determining what stewards' surpluses really are. In this way additional poor could be cared for by recirculating and increasing the funds available to help establish new "inheritances" by making loans to new participants or otherwise funding new or expanded UOPIEs. This would follow in modern form the idea of the Perpetual Emigrating Fund, where those who went before paid back to help those who followed. Such Grameen Bank-style small business loans in developing countries have excellent repayment records.[16]

Further, basic economic responsibility was part of the original revelation of the united order in the Doctrine & Covenants: "Thou shalt not take thy brother's garment; thou shalt pay for that which thou shalt receive of thy brother" (D&C 42:54). Accountability is a part of the law of stewardship. If necessary, an unsuccessful UOPIE must be permitted to fail. Structuring UOPIFI outlays as loans with set credit criteria provides a well-developed method of enforcing the united order principle of stewardship accountability. Employment must be based on the needs of the enterprise and personal qualifications. Church membership alone cannot be seen as giving one the right to employment in a UOPIE. The observance of these principles would help to avoid overwhelming the available resources, as happened in Missouri in the 1830s.

Of course, these principles would be difficult for good-hearted Church leaders to observe. Perhaps the most important reason to set up UOPIFIs as self-governing, non-Church controlled lending institutions is a negative one. The Church's 19th-century experience with economic development produced some tremendous burdens. A primary example is the sugar beet industry. Church involvement in the sugar beet industry, while not started as a united order program, was motivated by the commendable goal of helping LDS farmers improve their livelihoods.[17] Although initially successful, it eventually turned into a major cash drain which resulted in the

Church having to engage in several expensive bailouts.[18] Brigham Young illustrated the dilemma produced by the Church's direct involvement in business activities by recalling Joseph Smith's experience as a storekeeper:

> Let me just give you a few reasons . . . why Joseph could not keep a store, and be a merchant. . . . Joseph goes to New York and buys 20,000 dollars worth of goods, comes into Kirtland and commences to trade. In comes one of the brethren, 'Brother Joseph, let me have a frock pattern for my wife.' What if Joseph says, 'No, I cannot without the money.' The consequence would be, 'He is no Prophet.' . . . Pretty soon Thomas walks in. 'Brother Joseph, will you trust me for a pair of boots?' 'No, I cannot let them go without the money.' 'Well,' says Thomas, 'Brother Joseph is no Prophet; I have found *that* out, and am glad of it.' After a while, in comes Bill and sister Susan. Says Bill, 'Brother Joseph, I want a shawl, I have not got the money, but I wish you to trust me a week or a fortnight.' Well, brother Joseph thinks the others have gone and apostatized, and he don't know but these goods will make the whole Church do the same, so he lets Bill have a shawl. Bill walks off with it and meet a brother. 'Well,' says he, 'what do you think of brother Joseph?' 'O he is a first rate man, and I fully believe he is a Prophet. See here, he has trusted me this shawl.' . . . Another comes in the same way to make a trade of 25 dollars, and so it goes. Joseph was a first rate fellow with them all the time, provided he never would ask them to pay him.[19]

There would also be a danger that, despite all declarations to the contrary, Church members would expect the Church to save UOPIEs in difficulty. The observance of the united order principles of self-reliance and stewardship self-government, by separating the priesthood leadership from the management of UOPIFIs and UOPIEs, would make it much less likely that priesthood leaders and the Church would be seen as responsible for not supporting a failing enterprise, or not getting a deserving member a job.

Management Skill. While self-management would be left in the voice and common consent of the UOPIE cooperators, as required by the law of stewardship and the principle of equality, professional quality management and technical assistance should be made available. Most small business failures in the United States are attributed to management deficiencies rather than to capital or market problems.[20] The primary importance of management skill and competence, as opposed to simply having lots of capital, has been confirmed in studies of small producer cooperatives in Third World countries.[21]

Legal, accounting, technological, financial analysis, and marketing assistance could be organized through the UOPIFIs. In a Church well supplied with MBAs and Amway salesmen, it should not be difficult to find qualified volunteers to advise young UOPIEs. Again, these specialists would need to be strongly cautioned that they are advisors and that they must respect the self-management of the UOPIEs. In Third World situations it would also be important for them to be trained in appropriate technologies. For example, it is not necessary to have a computer and a spreadsheet program to keep the accounts for a Third World informal sector micro-enterprise. Old-fashioned paper ledgers can be quite adequate and are far less expensive. The training approach developed by the IEDF Enterprise Mentors, in which expertise is transferred and operations turned over to skilled locals as rapidly as possible is an excellent model.

The goal would be for the UOPIFIs and other institutions inspired by the principles of the united order to develop self-reliance in management and technical education. Perhaps, as a complex of such institutions developed, they would be able to sponsor local training institutions funded by the UOPIEs and UOPIFIs. Such centers and training institutions, along with the UOPIFIs themselves, could promote and coordinate joint marketing and supply arrangements, mutual research and development, and technology cross-licensing or patent pooling. In particular, perhaps BYU could become an international center for training and supporting successful, righteous cooperative enterprises and educational institutions. Among other advantages, this could help provide new purpose for the Church's massive expenditures on BYU.[22]

The difference that strong managerial backup and assistance can make to the success of small businesses can be seen not only in the special experience of Mondragon, but also in the success of franchises in the American economy. While over 80 percent of small businesses in general do not survive after ten years, a similar proportion of franchises, usually backed by professional management programs and assistance from the franchisor, are still in business after that time.[23]

Entrepreneurship. Entrepreneurial energy can be supplied only by UOPIE cooperators. Systems and organizations, articles and constitutions cannot assure that the united order principle of work and self-reliance will be followed. However, one can structure the system to encourage and reward hard work and self-reliance, and to penalize their absence. Membership is voluntary, and expulsion of idlers is permitted (D&C 42:42). This institutes a certain amount of self-screening. Another way to ascertain whether sufficient energy and will is present is for local participants to exercise the primary initiative in establishing a UOPIE. Also, in our observation, for most successful entrepreneurs, at one point or another a principal motivation has been simple financial pressure and fear of failure. While the UOPIFIs should be generous and supportive, an advantage of financing by loans rather than grants is the maintenance of this motivation.[24] Some sort of "consecration" in the form of an entry contribution to the UOPIE, as in Mondragon, would provide another strong personal motivation and commitment to make the UOPIE successful.

On the positive side, there are good reasons to believe that UOPIE cooperators would devote entrepreneurial energy to achieving collective rather than individual success. Athletes will work as hard to achieve team success as individual success. All successful modern corporations are based on a culture of cooperative team endeavor. Modern management theory now holds Tayloristic management approaches in disrepute. A cooperative work environment in which each participant is encouraged and empowered to contribute to their full abilities is regarded as essential to corporate success in the 21st century. Entrepreneurship under traditional capitalism has been seen as an individual characteristic because the nature of capitalistic property ownership gave all the financial rewards of success to the owners. Modern research has shown that when employees become owners and receive the means to make a difference in how they do their jobs, the entrepreneurial spirit can be found in all workers. Everyone contributes their energy, creativity, and diligence, not just the boss. The united order spirit of collective team entrepreneurship can be as successful or even more successful, as many of our examples illustrate, as entrepreneurship inspired by the desire for individual personal gain alone.[25]

UOPIEs should have a distinct advantage in at least one area important to being competitive. The spirit of the united order calls on us to look out for others' welfare as we do our own. For a UOPIE, one of the principal groups of "others" would be its customers. Superlative, selfless customer service would be integral to the mission of a UOPIE. It would offer the best quality products at the lowest reasonable prices, and the enterprise's culture would encourage the UOPIE cooperators to give their customers the best possible assistance. Shoddy goods and surly service are incompatible with the gospel in action. Strong, positive attitudes toward quality and service would be further enhanced by a sense of personal and collective responsibility and ownership, promoted by participative management and employee ownership. Obviously, such a strong spirit of customer service should also help sales.[26]

Of course, developing this successful spirit of individual and collective responsibility and ownership does call for some adjustment in personal motivation. Individuals, particularly skilled and able managers, would have to be able to learn the principle of equality: to measure their success in the number of co-workers who can buy new pickups and minivans rather than that they personally can buy a Porsche; in the number of co-workers who can have a boat or a cabin in the mountains rather than that they personally can buy a huge home in Vail or Aspen.[27] Workers would have to be able to learn the united order principle of personal and collective self-reliance and work: to measure their success by the increased number of their co-workers and the cooperative bottom line, rather than achieving rigid union work rules and extravagant, uncompetitive wages and benefits.

Business Opportunity. Even with all these elements in place, a business has to fill an economic need and make money. Almost by definition, this could be most difficult where the need is greatest, in shaky Third World economies. However, in many respects the best opportunities are in such economies because they are often full of inefficiencies and artificial barriers. The elimination of such barriers provides excellent economic opportunities. External businessmen often do not recognize such opportunities because their exploitation does not yield profits in hard currencies. However, the goal of UOPIE cooperatives would be building up local Zions, not yielding hard currency profits (although some are always helpful).

An example may illustrate. One of the more interesting modern implementations of united order principles was established in the southern Sudan by Gordon Wagner, an LDS African relief worker. Using simple united order principles (a storehouse, pooling of surplus, etc.), he produced what was called one of the most successful of all African relief efforts. However, some of the success was also due to good, simple business opportunity arising from the exploitation of a market inefficiency. External trade in the area had long been dominated by Arab traders who charged enormous markups. By pooling resources, the Sudanese "united orders" were able to obtain outside trade goods directly, undercut the Arab traders' prices, and capture the region's external trade.[28] Such opportunities increasingly present themselves in Third World countries as governments attempt to remove the economic barriers created under earlier statist economic development theories.[29]

The successful record of Utah-based entrepreneurial ventures in the computer business suggests that opportunities also exist in developed economies.[30] Many contend that Utah is second only to California's Silicon Valley in its activity in this important industry, particularly with regard to software. Yet the utter paucity of venture capital available for the development of this potential is astonishing, especially when compared to the resources and sophisticated assistance available to their California counterparts.[31] Surely if there was ever a situation that cried out for apostle Erastus Snow's vision of the united order treasury as a "common fund [to] nourish . . . infant establishments" and "to start new enterprises," this is it.[32] Giving extensive stock participation to employees is already a well-established practice in the computer industry. In exchange for their agreement to be majority employee-owned and to conduct their business in accordance with good ethical standards (and presentation of a viable business plan), young entrepreneurs could receive the funding that would permit this industry of the future to not only grow and prosper, but also to help realize that equality and union which prepare for the future of the eternities.

Potential Problems. One reaction of readers of this book may well be "The united order didn't work before; why should we think that it could work now?" We believe that available models take into account and respond to the difficulties of the 19th-century united orders reviewed in chapter 10.

One problem that plagued the early united orders would also be a potential risk today—political opposition and persecution, particularly in the Third World. While there can be no guarantee against political risk, self-management in accordance with the law of stewardship provides part of a solution. A primary potential reason for local political opposition would possibly be the identification of the UOPIEs with American business interests. To the extent that the UOPIEs were openly self-managed by ordinary local people on a democratic cooperative basis, they could reasonably defend themselves against charges of being agents of "Yankee capitalism."[33] Further, involvement of nonmembers in united order principles inspired projects would do much to combat any indigenous anti-Mormonism.

Another difficulty which confronted the 19th-century united orders was resistance to the idea of converting the entire Church to the united order essentially at once. While joining the order was voluntary, many Church members hesitated because of its unfamiliarity and precipitousness.[34] An evolutionary approach, "line upon line," building in logical steps with a relatively small number of private united order principles inspired efforts initially, would permit the development of practical working systems with which potential participants could become comfortable. Also, at least initially such modern UOPIEs would not carry the burden of attempting to create an entirely self-sufficient regional economy, as was the case in 19th-century Utah. In the worldwide Zion, members live and work in the midst of their nonmember neighbors. Working with, rather than against, the host economy, such UOPIEs would at least initially only have to be concerned with creating a successful business, not an entire economy.

The lack of workable, successful models for a righteous economy no longer needs to be the impediment that it was to the Utah united order effort. From simple village micro-enterprise development foundations to the elaborate modern industrial cooperatives of Mondragon, many models now exist. There can be less confusion about procedure and structure and how to deal with issues such as withdrawal, admission, and administration. Take, for example, the question of withdrawal from the cooperative. The revelations seem to imply that order members may withdraw and take with them all properties that have been given to them as an "inheritance." While this may be feasible where the order properties are distinct, like farms, it can wreak havoc where the order property is a claim on the capital account of a business. Some researchers attribute part of the success of the Mondragon cooperatives to low turnover, which has limited the pressures to make large payouts from capital.[35] Even in the Utah united orders there were limitations on withdrawals from the order to prevent such adverse effects. Modern versions of such regulations, such as those developed in the Mondragon cooperatives, would probably be advisable in new UOPIEs, particularity in light of the personnel volatility that often occurs before start-up businesses become well established.

Whether Church members and leaders have reached a point of moral development to permit moving closer to living the principles of the united order probably cannot be answered until it is tried. However, well-developed, gradual efforts based on successful modern models would help eliminate much of the confusion and hesitancy of the 19th-century members and leaders. We believe that the Latter-day Saints can do it.

Why Bother? Indeed, in light of the rapid growth of the Church in Third World nations, the Latter-day Saints may soon have no choice but to build up the resources available to Church members and the Church in the emerging nations. UOPIE cooperatives could create the economic resources to enable the Church to stand independent in these new Zions. However, increasing local tithing revenues is not the only reason we need to build up resources in the new Zions of the Third World. While the scriptural injunction to institute the full united order may be currently in partial suspension, the commandment to care for the poor and needy has never been suspended. Many Saints in Third World countries are far poorer than the poorest American members. The Church Welfare Program as it is currently set up in North America is only designed for temporary relief and is dependent on subsidies from American tithing and fast offerings. The support and survival of both the poor of the Church and the Church itself in these nations is dependent on building up their "inheritances" by building economically viable cooperative businesses. It has been noted that such a model does not replace the current Church Welfare Program. Rather it complements the Welfare Program to realize more fully the principles of the united order.[36]

Such cooperative complexes also offer the possibility of providing significant benefits to nonmembers of the host countries, particularly in less-developed nations. They would provide reasonably priced goods and efficient services to economies that are frequently marked by significant economic distress and inefficiency. They could underwrite schools and community services. Most modern development experts have now started to free themselves of their old Fabian bureaucratic, big industry, statist development bias and now recognize that building the private small business sector is fundamental to establishing solidly based economic growth.[37] Also, to the extent that a sufficiently extensive complex of UOPIEs is developed, the prospect would exist of making inter-cooperative payments at negotiated values, unconnected to the local currency, through accounts maintained by the UOPIFIs (perhaps using computerized electronic funds transfer technology). Using such cooperative "credits" could free the cooperative economic sector from the debilitating effects of the hyperinflation that afflicts so many Third World national currencies.

Church Sponsorship. We must address here a potentially complicated and delicate issue. A common reaction of Church members who hear the concepts expressed in this book is "those are good ideas, the Church ought to start doing them." While that determination would ultimately be made by the Church's general leaders, we respectfully suggest a few thoughts on this issue.

The first is the point just made. The united order is sacred doctrine of the restored gospel. The commandment to begin living some form of full-fledged united order as set forth in modern revelation can only come from he who gave those revelations, the true head of The Church of Jesus Christ through the prophetic priesthood channels which he has established. We have tried to make clear throughout that this book is not about *establishing* the united order, it is about *working toward* the united order. We have written not of "united orders," but of efforts *inspired by the principles* of the united order. We do not possess, nor do we claim, any authority to tell our fellow Saints what they *should* do. We wish only to suggest what we *could* do to move closer to being "equal and united in all things" free of "pride, poverty and iniquity," striving to be more pure in heart and more prepared for the day such a commandment might come.

Indeed, our review in this book of teachings about the united order suggests that a popular image of such a day among Latter-day Saints may not be accurate. This image has members called into the bishop's office and asked to sign all of their property over to the Church, to thereafter be managed by a great central Church Economic Correlation Department. However, as we have seen earlier in this chapter, there are good policy reasons for the Church to avoid control of economic activities. Moreover, fundamental to the principles of the united order is the law of stewardship, which calls for private ownership and management of property. In the modern corporate economy, this would often mean ownership and management through private groups (such as employee-owned businesses) rather than individually. However, the united order is never a kind of centrally controlled Church Communism.

Linked to this popular image of the restoration of the united order is the powerful and inspiring memory of the great Orderville commune. Useful in pioneering the remote frontier deserts of southern Utah and Arizona, we are unlikely to need Orderville-type communes in the 21st century. And even the Orderville-type communes were always owned and managed by the local members. However, the efforts of the Saints of Orderville should be remembered, for they show that when Saints of God endeavor to be "anxiously engaged in a good cause, and do many things of their own free will," they can "bring to pass much righteousness; For the power is in them, wherein they are agents unto themselves" (D&C 58:27–28).

The fraternal relations established through local Church units could provide the trellis upon which cooperative businesses could first get started.[38] The well-developed Church organization in the midst of the poor of the Third World, as well as both the economically distressed and economically blessed of the developed nations, should offer the strongest potential foundation for temporal as well as spiritual progress. There is something instinctively right and sensible about cooperative, worker-owned businesses that seems to be universally recognized, even if it is not understood or practiced. Thinkers from Beatrice Webb to Andrew Carnegie have felt that cooperative businesses were the right way, if they could be made to work. (Carnegie thought that they could, Webb did not.) The establishment of UOPIEs in the midst of the world would be a highly visible way of testifying to the coming of Zion to the world. It would demonstrate the benefits of the restored gospel in host countries even to those who may not yet appreciate the value of its religious message. Further, we have already noted that such enterprises could supply the economic wherewithal to permit members to be self-reliant and to sustain the Church in their native lands without being dependent on subsidies from the Church in North America.

Greater practice of the principles of united order enterprise in developed nations and the development of UOPIE cooperatives among the Saints of the Third World would both remind us that we have all committed ultimately to consecrate all that we have to building up the modern Zion. Unlike most people in developed nations, the soon-to-be retired folks from Bountiful can look forward to their Church missions to Bolivia, Botswana, or Belarus, rather than spending their children's inheritance in Las Vegas. The fortunes of the good Saints of Panguitch are now bound to those of the good Saints of the Philippines. The united order principles of economic righteousness offer temporal and spiritual salvation on the East Bench of Salt Lake City as well as South Central Los Angeles. The great temple in the little city of Manti is now linked by the powers of heaven to the great temple in the world's largest, the city of Mexico. Zion and the united order will not be created by cowering in the mountains or deserts waiting for Armageddon. Zion is now outbound, engaging every nook and corner of this world. Using wisdom and order, we Saints can work toward the prophets' vision—the worldwide Zion, the united order, the holy city, the ideal society, the perfect prescription, the brotherhood and sisterhood of all humankind.

21

One Great Family of Heaven:
Zion and the New Millennium

I have looked upon the community of the Latter-day Saints in vision and beheld them organized as one great family of heaven, each person performing his several duties in his line of industry, working for the good of the whole more than for individual aggrandizement; and in this I have beheld the most beautiful order that the mind of man can contemplate, and the grandest results for the upbuilding of the kingdom of God and the spread of righteousness upon the earth. Will this people ever come to this order of things?

Brigham Young[1]

The great family of Brigham's vision now spreads to fill every nook and corner upon the earth. Both the Saints and the world need and yearn for the practice and principles of the restored gospel's full economic system, the united order. Natasha Stukalov of Moscow, who suffered so greatly during the Communist times, struggles today with the crises of Russia's post-Soviet economy. It is hard to see any prospect of real improvement in the crushing unemployment, rampant crime, and political chaos. In Mexico, Juan and Elena Flores might have anticipated some improvement in their family's well-being with the approval of the North American Free Trade Act (NAFTA). However, as of this writing, Mexico's economy reverses several years of improvement and threatens to return to the deterioration characteristic of Third World economies.[2] What prosperity has come to the nation that is home to the second largest group of Saints in the world remains concentrated in the upper levels of society.

In the Philippines, Ben Illagan, the young returned missionary, did marry his girlfriend, but having no job the couple was forced to move in with the rest of his family, making a total of ten relatives under one roof. Actually there are nine now, because Ben's mother did secure a job as a maid in Hong Kong and is only able to return to Cebu once a year. Ben and his new wife, Sandra, are expecting a child soon, so the tiny house will again have ten residents. Ben is unable to enroll in a program to finish high school, so his education is basically terminated. He does hope to find a job in the next few months that will offer at least the distant hope of having a house someday for his new little family.

Back in Utah, Joe and Mary Brown continue to work for a better life. The daughters are growing up fast and will soon be off on their own. This may cut the family's expenses a bit, but the Browns will still need every penny. And there is little prospect of being able to help their daughters with college expenses. So Mary assumes she will have to spend the rest of her years working at the local mall as a sales clerk, rather than being the homemaker she used to be. Joe's real estate business is benefitting right now from lower interest rates, but interest rates will inevitably climb again, and competition is cutthroat. Kay Whitmore has moved on to missionary service in England, but thousands of Kodak employees now join the Browns' situation, unprotected by a CEO who finds it difficult to lay people off.

The latter days are a cruel and wondrous age. Unimagined advances in science and art, and the restoration of the fullness of the gospel, encounter unimaginable iniquity, depravity, and degradation. The greatest human freedom in history confronts the ultimate in proud and unholy power, in Joseph's words, "founded in carnage and bloodshed, and sustained by oppression, tyranny and despotism."[3] Unprecedented wealth generated by the Industrial Revolution and the free market economy is still confounded by continuing and growing poverty and misery. Prophets of God have declared that the gospel of Jesus Christ in action is the perfect prescription for overcoming poverty, pride, and iniquity. Part of that prescription is the economic plan of Zion—the united order.

One of the great heros of the free enterprise system, Andrew Carnegie, saw the problem plainly. "The unequal distribution of wealth . . . was bound to force itself to the front, because, exhibiting extremes unknown before, it has become one of the crying evils of our day. In the world's progress, scientific discoveries and mechanical inventors appeared and adapted the forces and materials of nature to the use of man, followed by the commercial and industrial age in which we live, in which wealth has been produced as if by magic, and fallen largely to the captains of industry. . . . The extremes in the distribution of wealth have never been so great as they are to-day, although salaries and wages have never been so high."[4] For two hundred years, humanity's quest has been for a system or organization to employ the wealth of the Industrial Revolution to realize David O. McKay's complete ideal of Mormonism—upright citizens in an ideal society.

The World's Quest—Capitalism and Socialism. Two great systems have arisen in the world to answer this quest in the latter days. One is socialism. Socialism has focused on the persistence of poverty and inequality in the latter-day industrial age. Beatrice Webb noted that the Industrial Revolution had driven out self-employed craftsmen and small businesses and

> substituted for them a relatively small body of capitalist entrepreneurs employing at wages an always multiplying mass of propertyless men, women and children, struggling, like rats in a bag, for the right to live. . . . Commodities of all sorts and kinds rolled out from new factories at an always accelerating speed with ever falling costs of production, thereby promoting what Adam Smith had idealized as *The Wealth of Nations*. . . . On the other hand, that same revolution had deprived manual workers—that is, four-fifths of the people of England—of their opportunity for spontaneity and freedom of initiative in production. It had transformed such of them as had been independent producers into hirelings and servants of another social class; and, as the East End of London in my time only too vividly demonstrated, it had thrust hundreds of thousands of families into the physical horrors and moral debasement of chronic destitution in crowded tenements in the midst of mean streets.[5]

Millions have been and are horrified by what Beatrice Webb observed. If the slums of London's East End of her time have now been replaced by public housing estates, it is principally the work of the Webbs' British welfare state. However, even under the welfare state, this housing is filled with young unemployed people subsisting on the dole. Do their lives have that much more dignity or that much less alienation than those of their forebears? Her description is still completely accurate for the lives of billions of residents of Bombay, Lagos, Lima, and other cities of the Third World. And what of the young couples of Sandy, Utah, overmortgaged and with large families, desperately trying to keep up the middle-class lifestyle expected of them on the lowest wages in America? Although the numbers tell us that Joe and Mary Brown are wealthier than Juan and Elena Flores by multiples, do the Browns know that much more security and hope than the Flores family?

The other great system is that of the free market—capitalism. If socialists would point to the Illagans to condemn capitalism, capitalism's response would be Natasha Stukalov. The advocate of the free market admits that there are serious problems in the world, but asks how one proposes to solve them. The socialist solution is state control and management of the economy. A century and a half after the *Communist Manifesto,* its record shows little to commend it. On the other hand, despite much turmoil and mixed results, the free market has made real progress in advancing human welfare. According to Friedrich Hayek, the objective of the free market is to make "the best possible use of the forces of competition. . . . Where effective competition can be created, it is a better way of guiding individual efforts than any other." However, abstract notions of efficiency are not the only arguments for the free market:

> Competition is superior not only because it is in most circumstances the most efficient method known but even more because it is the only method by which our activities can be adjusted to each other without coercive or arbitrary intervention of authority. . . . It gives the individual a chance to decide whether the prospects of a particular occupation are sufficient to compensate for the disadvantages and risks connected with it.[6]

Andrew Carnegie saw this as the principal argument for what he called the "Individualistic system." For humankind to advance, individuals of ability must be able to come to the fore. "Under our present Individualistic system, which breeds and develops the needed leaders, there is no State official to interpose—no communism, no uniformity, no commission to consider respective claims of the exceptionals and decide upon their destinies. All are left in perfect freedom and in possession of glorious liberty of choice, free 'by the sole act of their own unlorded will' to obey the Divine call which consecrates each to his great mission."[7]

Freedom to pursue one's divine call and mission is especially important to Latter-day Saints. Despite almost a hundred years of persecution by self-righteous capitalists, Latter-day Saints believe that a democratic free market society offers the greatest possibility for freedom to follow their religion. J. Reuben Clark called Communism "Satan's counterfeit for the United Order" and did not hold a much better view of democratic socialism. Counterfeits are evil in two ways. First, they trade on the good reputation of the authentic article. Thus, in our present context, one would argue that concern for poverty and inequality are genuine virtues, which socialists have deceptively leveraged into support for their program of state economic control.

The other evil is indirect. When people are burned by accepting a counterfeit as authentic, they become suspicious of other articles which are in fact authentic. This debases the value of the authentic article. Having discovered that state economic control is oppressive and ineffective, many are suspicious of ideals like equality, community responsibility, and full employment, which have become associated with the socialist program. However, the socialists did not invent, and do not own, these ideals. Marx wrote "From each according to his abilities, to each according to his needs" in 1875, over four decades after the Lord revealed that united order "portions" would be granted to everyone "equal according to his family, according to his circumstances and his wants and needs" (D&C 51:3). Keynesian social planners undertook full employment as a social goal over six decades after John Taylor charged local Church leaders to "find employment for every man and woman and child within this Stake that wants to labor."[8]

The Saints' Quest—Zion. In 1831, seventeen years before the *Communist Manifesto* was published, God revealed to Joseph the comprehensive economic plan of Zion. Latter-day Saints have devoted much labor to arguing whether the united order is socialistic or capitalistic. Scholars and reformers outside of the Church have expended enormous energy on the search for a "third way" between socialism and capitalism.[9] We believe that all of these efforts are trying to drive forward with the car in reverse and pointed backwards. The united order is the "first way." It is, in John Widtsoe's words, the "ideal by which any proposed economic system may be tested. . . . The nearer any scheme for economic betterment conforms to the principles of the United Order, the more likely it will be to assist mankind."[10] The question is *not* "is the united order socialistic or capitalistic?" The proper question is "how do socialism and capitalism measure up to the principles of the united order?"

Socialism in its many forms clearly comes up short. Despite professing high ideals and principles, in practice it violates the law of stewardship, which calls for the exercise of free moral agency and the preservation of private property. And even in its most benign form, the democratic welfare state, socialism also usually undermines the principles of work and self-reliance.

Does this mean that the united order is therefore capitalistic? To answer this question, we must clarify what we mean by capitalistic. As we have attempted to show in this book, the principles of the united order can be widely applied in Adam Smith's free market system, when even the lowest ranks of the people enjoy economic freedom and opportunity to pursue their vocations relatively free from state interference. However, the preservation of economic freedom is not the ultimate end of our quest for Zion. That moral free agency was preserved after the great war in heaven did not mean that humankind would use it righteously on earth. That a people wins political freedom does not mean that they will always elect honest governments or enact wise laws. With regard to our struggle for economic freedom, Elder Dallin H. Oaks has written:

> During the past half century many Americans, including many Latter-day Saints, have been vigorously and successfully involved in defending our way of life against communism. Perhaps a preoccupation with turning communism away from the front door has made us vulnerable to the corruption of materialism slipping in through the back door. Communism is evil because it deprives people of their freedom and teaches that there is no God. Materialism is evil because it corrupts people in the use of their freedom and substitutes the god of property for the God of heaven.[11]

Like a democratic government, the free market system is only as good as the people who are in it. The free market system has the potential for efficiently maximizing "the wealth of nations." However, how we use the wealth thus produced is a moral decision. Economics may help tell us how to put such decisions into effect efficiently, but it will not tell us what the end uses of our wealth should be. For most stock analysts, profits from selling alcohol or pornography are as good as profits from selling soap or Bibles. Economists' statistics count the money spent on the mansion built with the bonus the CEO received for laying off hundreds of workers the same as the money that would have been spent building modest homes for those workers had they not been laid off.

In chapters 6 and 9, we saw how Adam Smith's concept of a moral free enterprise economy was corrupted by the materialism of the Social Darwinists. This materialistic capitalism as currently practiced also falls short of some of the principles of the united order. There is no mechanism in the market itself to see to the needs of those who cannot compete, the poor and needy. Herbert Spencer's version of capitalism held "that an unskillfulness which with all his efforts he cannot overcome, should entail hunger upon the artisan; . . . that a labourer incapacitated by sickness from competing with his stronger fellows, should have to bear the resulting privations; . . . that widows and orphans should be left to struggle for life or death. . . . The whole effort of nature is to get rid of such."[12] Private charity and government welfare are acts of individual or community moral choice that are neither encouraged nor rewarded by the market.

Further, the market operates on the basis of differential rewards and thus may violate the principle of equality. The Social Darwinist market responds to how much property a person has, not her or his value as a child of God. It gives more value, resources, and importance to a millionaire than to a pauper, thus placing love of property over love of others. Without equivocation or qualification, the Lord says "it is not given that one man should possess that which is above another, wherefore the world lieth in sin" (D&C 49:20). Unless its actors make a contrary moral choice, this kind of economy is inherently materialistic, and its god is the god of property.

Ezra Taft Benson spent a long and vigorous career denouncing the evils of Communism. Many expected that would continue to be his emphasis when he became president of the Church in 1985. It was with some surprise that members received his announcement that the principal emphasis of his prophetic ministry would be to get the members of the Church to study the teachings of the Book of Mormon. Much debate has surrounded the issue of whether the Book of Mormon is an "ancient" or a "modern" book. We believe that it is both, and that this can help us understand its importance to us.

We believe that there were indeed ancient Americans called Nephites and Lamanites. Nephi, Alma, and Mormon did live, and they actually wrote the writings attributed to them. The Book of Mormon is an "ancient" book in the sense that its contents were written long ago. However, the "Book of Mormon" itself is modern. When Mormon selected and edited the material to appear in the collection that bears his name, he could not "write the hundredth part of the things of my people" (Words of Mormon 6).[13] His editorial decisions on what records to include were "according to the knowledge and the understanding which God has given me. . . . For there are great things written upon them, out of which my people and their brethren shall be judged at the great and last day" (Words of Mormon 1:9, 11). Mormon did not assemble his book for his contemporaries. The Nephite civilization had already hopelessly collapsed when Mormon prepared his record. Other than Moroni, no Nephite ever read the Book of Mormon. By the inspiration of God, Mormon edited and assembled the collection of ancient records which bears his name, for us. If the Book of Mormon treats modern themes, it is because it was created for modern times. Like the coal and oil that have fueled it, the Industrial Revolution has received its holy scripture from out of the earth.

And out of the earth, from beginning to end, the Book of Mormon sounds this great theme:

> But behold, Jesus Christ hath shown you unto me, and I know your doing. And I know that ye do walk in the pride of your hearts; and there are none save a few only who do not lift themselves up in the pride of their hearts, unto the wearing of very fine apparel, unto envying, and strifes, and malice, and persecutions, and all manner of iniquities. . . . For behold, ye do love money, and your substance, and your fine apparel, and the adorning of your churches, more than ye love the poor and the needy, the sick and the afflicted. . . . Why do ye adorn yourselves with that which hath no life, and yet suffer the hungry, and the needy, and the naked, and the sick and the afflicted to pass by you, and notice them not? (Mormon 8:35–37, 39)

According to the Book of Mormon, failure to care for the poor and the needy, inequality, and pride—the very evils and shortcomings to which modern capitalism makes us most susceptible—are among the great evils of our times, the latter days.

If socialism and Communism are Satan's counterfeits, their most nefarious work has been to cause the defenders of economic freedom to ignore their own greatest moral perils. If one believes that only "reds" preach equality, one has lost the ability to protect oneself from being lifted up in the pride of one's heart, to protect oneself from being able to pass by the poor and needy, the sick, and afflicted and notice them not. If one thinks that it is weak to encourage cooperation over competition, one will not notice that the Book of Mormon contains the most concise summary of Social Darwinism ever penned, and that it is propounded by the antichrist, Korihor: "there could be no atonement made for the sins of men, but every man fared in this life according to the management of the creature; therefore every man prospered according to his genius, and that every man conquered according to his strength" (Alma 30:17). If one believes that poor people are generally lazy and undeserving, not worthy of our help or attention, can one truly take to heart King Benjamin's plea to remember that we are all beggars before God? (See Mosiah 4:17–19.)

Inequality, pride, and vanity are not the reasons we value economic freedom. Socialist state economic control is certainly not the solution to them. The value of economic freedom (and freedom's most potent defense against the socialist challenge) is that it permits us to freely use our material wealth, in the words of Lorenzo Snow, to "banish pride, poverty, and iniquity."[14] Economic freedom gives us the opportunity to choose to pursue the purposes of the united order. Since the beginnings of the Industrial Revolution, since 1831, we have had the choice of economic righteousness. The full economic plan of Zion, the united order, was laid out for us in holy scripture within ten months of the restoration of the Church. The restored gospel is more than attending Church, obeying the Word of Wisdom, and doing genealogy. According to John Taylor, it aims "to introduce correct principles of every kind—principles of morality, social principles, good political principles; principles relating to the government of the earth we live in."[15].

We can transcend the world's rigid, left-to-right, ideological model. Under the united order, defenders of economic freedom can promote equitable, morally founded free enterprise without having to justify the repulsive spectacle of the painful desperation of the poor, hard beside the vain ostentation of the wealthy. Those who love economic justice can implement it without having to resort to the crude and stultifying load of bureaucracy and regimentation that comes with attempts to achieve economic justice through state controls. According to Howard W. Hunter, Mormonism "has a comprehensive and inclusive message based upon the acceptance of all truth, restored to meet the needs of all mankind."[16] The gospel should be the center of all that we think and do, spiritually and temporally. It offers us hope, in this life and after. It offers the path to temporal as well as spiritual salvation.

Building the Road to Zion. "Will this people ever come to this order of things?" asked Brigham. There are several stages on the journey of moving toward the united order. First is individual understanding and practice. Do we understand how profound and universal the ideals of the united order are? Equality, consecration, stewardship, hard work, individual dignity, the brother and sisterhood of all people—do we believe in them, discuss and study them, try to apply them in our daily lives? Do we see their contrast with the principles of worldly thinking, which emphasize individual aggrandizement over others, having more goods, bigger homes, fancier cars and other toys? Do we confuse social status (even that arising from position in the Church) with our standing in the eyes of God? Do we recognize the pervasive sins of the ancient Nephites in our own lives and society—adherence to worldly philosophies and values ("conservative" as well as "liberal"), self-gratification, pride, lack of self-discipline, social and economic class stratification?[17]

Second is understanding and practice in our economic lives. We are all actors in the free market. Do we regard our worldly wealth, however great or small, as a stewardship to be consecrated to righteous purposes? Do we view the storeowner who sells liquor, tobacco, or pornography, or any businessman who pays the lowest possible wages (because, they say, of economic pressures) with the same high standards that we ask of teenagers who say they must sleep with their boyfriend or girlfriend (because, they say, of social pressures)? Do those of us who have some economic influence practice temporal righteousness? Do we acknowledge with Ezra Taft Benson that there are moral standards in our business and professional conduct that go beyond simply complying with the law? Do we recognize that because the free market is value-neutral does not mean that we have to be value-free?

Are our values those of the moral free enterprise of Adam Smith, which aims to raise the poor and the common wealth, or those of the jungle capitalism of the Social Darwinists, glorying in the "lifestyles of the rich and famous," in having servants and more and better stuff than our neighbor? Do we seek, like Spencer W. Kimball, to pay "top wages" rather than the lowest? Are we willing to so conduct ourselves even if it does not increase our profits, even if temporal righteousness has a real cost? What would we do if we were in the position of Kay Whitmore, who sought to find a way to improve profitability without massive layoffs and was fired by Wall Street directors as a result?[18]

Third is institutional movement. In an age of Big Business and Big Government, it is probably not surprising that many might think of the united order as being essentially Big Church. However, the law of stewardship does not follow the world's bureaucratic ways. The appropriate Church authorities will make decisions on the allocation of tithing and other assets of the institutional Church to endeavors promoting the principles of the united order. However, as we have seen in this book, numerous efforts of individuals, private groups, wards, stakes, companies, and nonprofit foundations are being made independently to change the world, to make "all things new."

The united order calls for union and order. Individual attitudes and efforts are important, but much more can be accomplished through private organized efforts. Institutions should be created or changed so as to incorporate the principles of the united order. Whether a new Mondragon or simply a new neighborhood cooperative child care center or food bank, well-established organizations carry on principles even when individual energy cools. Further, we need to look to building up new organizations proactively rather than simply reacting to past troubles and economic difficulties. The best time to institute employee ownership is when a company is young and its culture fresh, not when it is old and in danger of closing down.

Fourth, and most important, is the universal effort of all the Saints. Having learned correct principles, the time has come to exercise our stewardship responsibility of self-government, to be anxiously engaged in bringing to pass much righteousness of our own free will without having to be commanded in all things. With the entire world in its purview, Zion can no longer depend exclusively on a top-down approach. Knowing local circumstances and needs at first hand, each Saint must act as a moral agent of Zion, exercising her or his responsibilities as stewards to effect temporal righteousness, to move toward the united order and a Zion society.

How do we do it? Orson Pratt indicated that he did "not know anything laid down in the revelations, requiring us to take [a] particular method." Methods of implementing the united order are to be evaluated to see if they are "right according to the circumstances with which they are surrounded; [if they point] forward to unity and tend to instruct us in the preliminary ideas of being united together."[19] In chapters 11 through 20 we have discussed many possible efforts that could be undertaken. We do not have to wait for entirely new methods to be invented. More of what already exists—a hundred Mondragons, a thousand Enterprise Mentors, ten thousand babysitting or food buying co-ops—would move us far up the road toward a Zion society. And we are sure that there are many more which are not included in this book, even many others not yet conceived by anyone. With the enormous socioeconomic diversity which has come from the international growth of the Church, a uniform, "one-size-fits-all" approach will no longer work. Unity does not mean uniformity. Instead of simply cloning what others have done, learning must be generative—what the Japanese call "learning from within"—ongoing, continuous and improving. Sensible creativity is required—"we build the road as we travel," as they say in Mondragon. Individual efforts of Latter-day Saints as well as Church welfare programs will need to move toward a "menu" of a large variety of evolving approaches to be implemented by local Church leaders and members as appropriate for local conditions.[20]

In order to discover which efforts are appropriate for each time, place, and circumstance, many approaches must be tried at the grassroots. We must learn, as all successful modern enterprises have learned, Joseph Smith's management philosophy as passed on to us by John Taylor—"teach them correct principles and let them govern themselves." Gospel management must look to John Taylor, not Frederick Taylor, for its principles. Delegation does not mean abdication. Many of the most successful aspects of the Church, from Sunday School, Primary, and the Relief Society to the Church Welfare Program itself, started as local experiments. Successful local experiments can then be shared with other areas, which may adapt them as necessary to meet their local welfare needs. To build a true Zion, we all need to express our insights, learn to listen, explore needs, analyze future possibilities, and, in the words of more than one prophet, "Do it." In the end, as Adam Smith neatly put it, "the most sublime speculation of the contemplative philosopher can scarce compensate the neglect of the smallest active duty."[21]

After exhorting his listeners to "impart of your substance to the poor, every man according to that which he hath, such as feeding the hungry, clothing the naked, visiting the sick and administering to their relief, both spiritually and temporally, according to their wants," King Benjamin then urged "that all these things are done in wisdom and order; for it is not requisite that a man should run faster than he has strength. And again, it is expedient that he should be diligent, that thereby he might win the prize; therefore, all things must be done in order" (Mosiah 4:26–27). John Taylor advised the Saints, "Do not be in a big hurry; do not break your necks; go at it quietly, and start one industry and then another. . . .

Brethren, operate together, and sisters operate together, and let all act in the welfare of each other."[22] The journey to Zion calls for diligent orderly effort. All efforts should proceed carefully, and be monitored for both strengths and weaknesses. John Taylor said he did "not want to see one solitary principle that an honest, honorable man cannot sustain; but let everything be so that it can be dragged right forth to the daylight, and turned over and over and over and examined all sides up, and inside out, and see that it is true, good, honorable, upright and honest in every particular. That is the kind of thing we want."[23] We need continually to stop, reflect critically on what we are doing, identify higher possibilities, and then move on. Reflection and action, looking, thinking, planning, and doing, all integrated together, change lives.

To illustrate some of the ways of traveling the path to a Zion society inspired by the principles of the united order, let us visit again the brothers and sisters we met in chapter 1. Greater contributions to fast offerings and the Church's Humanitarian Fund could permit the shipment of extra clothing to the Flores family, and programs of the Benson Institute can teach them how to supplement their food supply by organizing a community garden. Members of Natasha's new branch can pool some of their resources and facilitate the sharing of goods through a local grassroots storehouse program, enabling those who have excess to share and those in need to receive. In the Philippines, the Illagan family participates in seminars conducted by Enterprise Mentors, and three of the family have started their own handicraft business, working cooperatively with other members' micro-enterprises to raise their income and move toward economic self-reliance.

In Utah, the LDS manager of the mall store where Sister Brown works will strive to pay her and her co-workers a more adequate wage than the present minimum level, and perhaps develop a stock ownership program as well. Instead of seeking to reduce health care and other employee benefits, the company will work to improve benefits, perhaps by assisting the employees to work better by helping with child care arrangements or tuition aid. Perhaps Latter-day Saints in the software industry in Utah Valley will join together to create a Mondragon-like cooperative complex, whose financial arm will provide Joe's old firm with the working capital it needs to realize its full business potential, and to rehire Joe as an employee-owner.

Other Latter-day Saints in Kay Whitmore's position in the future will perhaps benefit from a faith whose members are more conscious of the ideals of economic righteousness taught by their religion. Latter-day Saints will teach the world that it is only the energy of human beings that turns assets into an enterprise, and pioneer ways to avoid massive layoffs—challenging employees to come up with enough cost savings and "intrapreneurial" products to improve profitability; providing a substantial employee stock ownership program so that employee interests are aligned with those of the shareholders instead of in seeming opposition to them; giving employees the opportunity to buy their part of the company if it is going to be closed or spun off, or letting workers decide how to implement layoffs (such as voluntary part-time work or across-the-board pay reductions instead of mass dismissals).

To succeed will require years of hard work, research, and ongoing dialogue. Because we do not live it, it is easy to bathe the united order in a hazy utopian glow. Nitty-gritty programs such as these, and many others that could help us work toward the united order, will require hard work, skillful management, and an ample share of crises and tough decisions. Mistakes and failures are certain. Hazy utopian glows do not long survive the heat of the day and the harsh light of real life. However, such is the work of the eternities, "as old as the gospel itself." Working toward the united order is worthy of our greatest effort and devotion. It is the only enduring prescription for humankind's search for a system or organization to overcome its problems and social ills. As experience grows and self-reliance is achieved, LDS culture can evolve to the point at which all persons are respected, treated with dignity, have "a competence and the conveniences of life," and are able to develop their God-given talents, to pursue their divine call and mission. Their lives, families, and neighborhoods will become places of peace, purity, and joy. Eventually, there will be "no poor among them" and they will achieve a spirit of genuine community, the condition known in the scriptures as *Zion*.

The World's Quest—Zion. The Prophet Joseph said that he calculated "to be one of the instruments of setting up the kingdom of Daniel by the word of the Lord, and I intend to lay a foundation that will revolutionize the whole world, . . . not by sword or gun" but because "the power of the truth is such that all nations will be under the necessity of obeying the Gospel."[24] The world knows that only faith can deliver it from its travails. It has placed its faith in great economic and political systems, such as socialism and capitalism, but intuits that a higher vision is needed. Andrew Carnegie wrote of employee ownership, which he discovered too late in his own life to implement, in terms that are not strange to believers in eternal progression. "Let us get capital and labor into the same boat, rowing together, and all will be well, and we shall have made another great step forward in obedience to the eternal law of progress which insures the continual ascent of man by a law of his being to higher and higher stages of development on earth toward perfection."[25]

Even after she had become one of the world's leading socialists, Beatrice Webb would still quietly attend services at St. Paul's Cathedral in London, writing in her diary:

> I cling to the thought that man will only evolve upwards by the subordination of his physical desires and appetites to the intellectual and spiritual side of his nature. Unless this evolution be the purpose of the race, I despair—and wish only for the extinction of human consciousness. Without this hope—without this faith—I could not struggle on. It is this purpose, and this purpose only, that gives meaning to the constantly recurring battles of good and evil within one's own nature—and to one's persistent endeavour to find the ways and means of combating the evil habits of the mass of men. Oh! for a Church that would weld into one living force all who hold this faith, with the discipline and consolations fitted to sustain their endeavour. As it is, I find myself once or twice a week in St. Paul's—listening to the music of the psalms and repeating, with childlike fervour, the words of the old Elizabethan prayers.[26]

It is simple tragedy that she was to think that she had found the faith she was seeking in Stalinism. Many sincere seekers travel to the gospel of Jesus Christ through this search. Arthur Henry King, a prominent British scholar who joined the Church and taught at Brigham Young University, told a BYU conference,

> I first read Marx almost exactly fifty years ago. If it had not been for Marx, I should not yet be in this Church, if at all. . . . Remember the emotive appeal of wanting to raise all suffering humanity as I think the Lord wanted us to do. . . . There has been a deep emotive appeal of Marxism to several generations, and I have felt it myself.[27]

The world needs Zion. The world seeks Zion, but does not know where to find it. The mission of the Latter-day Saints is to journey not only for themselves, but to show the entire world the way to Zion.

Of course, many have claimed that the Saints' efforts to realize Zion were defeated by the end of the 19th century. Beatrice Webb saw the Mormon experiment as ended. Andrew Carnegie, a man who had an opinion about just about everything, and usually said it, had nothing to say about the Latter-day Saints. The controversial Mormons did not fit into the "Star-spangled Scotchman's" sunny picture of triumphant American capitalist democracy.[28] A modern non-LDS admirer of Joseph Smith writes that "there has been a falling away from his teaching and example in the Mormon Church and people of the last century or so."[29] At the end of his historic work on the economic history of the Latter-day Saints in the 1800s, *Great Basin Kingdom,* Leonard Arrington suggested that the Saints' cooperative efforts might have some relevance and influence in modern times.[30] An otherwise friendly non-LDS scholar scoffed at this notion.

> We know through the reading that Mormonism loses, adapts to the United States, and almost loses its soul. My own hypothesis is that the United States victory was complete. Mormonism is now simply a function of its larger society. . . . To say or to argue that the Mormon cooperative effort survived is to avoid the hard story of Mormon defeat and appropriation and the compromises that Mormon leaders did and did not make to forestall defeat. . . . The practice of a cooperative economy is long dead, except in books like this one. It may be a pity, but it is a fact. . . . The facts of Mormon history are smallness, rejection, irrelevance, marginality and persecution.[31]

Some have a different perspective. Brigham Young declared in 1859 that "Every time you kick "Mormonism," you kick it up stairs: you never kick it down stairs. The Lord Almighty so orders it."[32] President Spencer W. Kimball addressed all the people of the world at the 1976 general conference:

> The gospel of Jesus Christ is a gospel for all the world and for all people. . . . You will find so-called Mormonism to be a growing, vibrant, dynamic, and challenging church, indeed a way of life, touching upon every avenue of living, every facet of life. . . . The gospel spreads to the nations of the earth in its approach toward the promise made by God through Daniel to fill the whole earth,

Brigham Young, (1801–1877) colonizer and implementor of united orders in the Utah territory and second president of the LDS Church. His pioneer vision propelled the creation of a vast cooperative commonwealth in the Great Basin. Propounding his vision of the Saints as "one great family of heaven" he asked, "Why can we not so live in this world?"

> and numerous people of all nationalities and tongues are accepting the gospel in many nations, and the Church and kingdom [will] grow and develop, and we say to you and testify to you that it shall, in Daniel's words, "never be destroyed: and the kingdom . . . shall stand forever."(Dan. 2:44).[33]

From out of the earth, ancient Mormon has warned us against the challenges of our age of unimagined wealth and poverty. Through the veil, God has reached out to send us the answer—the challenge of building Zion through the principles of the united order. John Taylor told the Saints that, "with all our weaknesses and foibles clinging to us the Lord has called us from the nations of the earth to be his co-adjutors and co-laborers, his fellow-workmen and assistants, in rolling forth his purposes."[34] God has called us to be his co-partners in the enterprise of the eternities, not only for future eternities, but for every nook and corner of that part of the eternities that is *this* world. We believe that the Saints can move forward to this work and will come to answer Brother Brigham positively:

> We all concede the point that when this mortality falls off, and with its cares, anxieties, love of self, love of wealth, love of power, and all the conflicting interests which pertain to the flesh, that then, when our spirits have returned to God who gave them, we will be subject to every requirement that He may make of us, that we shall then live together as one great family; our interest will be a general, a common interest. Why can we not so live in this world?[35]

ZION!

Appendix A

Organizational Structure of Typical Mondragon Co-op

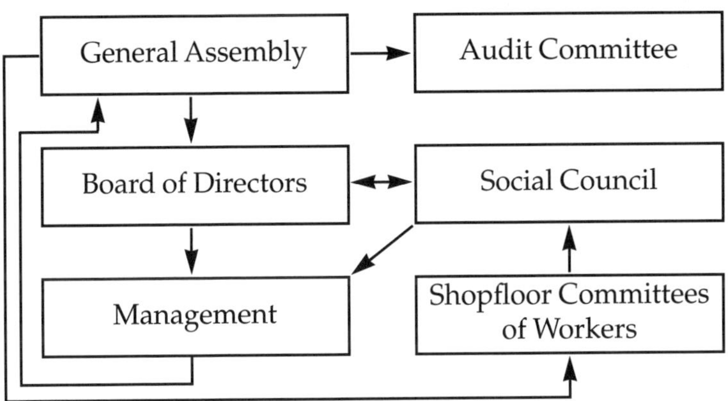

General Assembly: ultimate source of authority and decision-making in the co-op; determines major policies regarding investments, finances; reviews annual budget, profit and loss statements, productivity levels, etc.; receives reports from Audit Committee; made up of all worker-owners; the Assembly elects members to the Board of Directors; meets at least annually.

Board of Directors: develops implementation plans to carry out directives from the General Assembly; reports to the Assembly; top management attends as non-voting participants to hear concerns, responds to issues.

Audit Committee: three person watchdog group to ensure that Management and Board are fiscally responsible, and that financial transactions are appropriate and legal; may draw from co-op bank staff or other outside experts as needed; areas of concern may be conveyed directly to the workforce, or a special meeting of the General Assembly may be announced.

Management: team of top executives is appointed by the Board of Directors for a 3-4 year term; they are also members of the co-op; have administrative authority to operate day-to-day business actions such as purchasing, production, quality, accounting, marketing and so on, consistent with Board and General Assembly guidelines.

Social Council: functions somewhat like a trade union, but is more collaborative than confrontational; made up of Shopfloor Committee worker representatives; meets monthly or quarterly to consider such issues as safety, personnel matters, working conditions and so forth; rather than filing grievances, the council engages in joint problem-solving processes to improve the quality of work life.

Shopfloor Committees: teams of workers in various areas of the factory which meet monthly to discuss their needs and concerns regarding working conditions, health and safety, scheduling, and proposals for improving the workplace; representatives are chosen to voice these issues at the next level up, an overall forum known as the Social Council.

Appendix B

Charitable Organizations

Charitable organizations mentioned throughout our book are listed below, as well as several others that may be of interest.

ACADEMY OF LDS DENTISTS

109 HCEB
Brigham Young University
Provo, UT 84602
(801) 378-4851

Founded in 1977, this organization exists to instruct and support LDS dentists. Its members have also given volunteer services in Africa, China, Israel, Mexico, South America, the Republic of Georgia, Thailand, the West Indies, and the United States.

ACCION INTERNATIONAL

120 Beacon Street
Somerville, MA 02143
(617) 492-4930

Founded in 1961 as a nonprofit, private organization ACCION combats poverty and hunger by "encouraging the economic self-reliance of impoverished working women and men in the Americas." Its staff has worked in every nation of Latin America, providing credit and basic business training for the self-employed. Recently, such programs have begun to be established in poor areas of the United States as well.

ACTION AID FOR LEPERS' CHILDREN OF CALCUTTA

26, Avenue Kleber
75116 Paris
France

AFRICAN WOMEN DEVELOPMENT AND COMMUNICATIONS

PO Box 54562
Nairobi, Kenya
(254-2) 440-299

AMERICAN INDIAN SERVICES

1900 Canyon Road
Provo, UT 84604
(801) 375-1777
Dale Tingey, Executive Director

Utah-based, nonprofit organization established to raise funds, provide farm equipment, and otherwise help Native American tribes with relief efforts. Recently its goal has been to expand into Latin America as well.

APPROPRIATE TECHNOLOGY PROJECT

PO Box 4543
Sanford, CA 94305
(415) 326-8581
Ken Darrow

BEEHIVE FOUNDATION

1011 West Mermod
Carlsbad, NM 88220
(505) 885-2178
(800) 524-2799

The Beehive Foundation has volunteers who supply millions of pounds of clothes to Mexico and Central America each year. The Foundation has also planted gardens and supported orphanages and children's hospitals. Although the Foundation is not officially connected to the LDS Church, its organization was prompted by "principles of Christian charity." The Foundation seeks volunteers—"people who want to give their time, their money, their efforts, or all three in order to help wipe out poverty and sickness around the world."

BENSON INSTITUTE

110 B-49
Brigham Young University
Provo, UT 84602
(801) 378-2607
Paul Johnston, Director

Formally known as the Ezra Taft Benson Agriculture & Food Institute, the organization is affiliated with Brigham Young University. It is an outreach program attempting to provide technical assistance to small farmers, primarily in Mexico and Central America, focusing currently on small-scale farming techniques for the Third World.

BUSINESSES FOR SOCIAL RESPONSIBILITY

1850 M Street
Washington, D.C. 20036
(202) 842-5400

BSR is a national trade association for large and small companies that want to become more socially responsible on such issues as diversity, ecology, ethics, and employee relations.

CAJA LABORAL POPULAR

Consejo General
Crupo Cooperativo de Mondragon
Mondragon, Spain
Jose Maria Larranaga, Director

Center for information on the Mondragon cooperative complex in the Basque country of northern Spain. As the financial arm of this network of over a hundred worker-owned enterprises, the Caja also coordinates research, documentation, and various programs sponsored by the co-ops.

CARE

151 Ellis Street
Atlanta, GA 30303
(800) 521-CARE

Founded after the Second World War to send relief supplies to Europe and Asia, CARE has since helped more than one billion people in 121 countries to improve their lives through emergency disaster relief as well as long-term, sustainable, agriculture and environment, health and nutrition, population, and small-business development programs. One of its largest supporters is the LDS Church through the donation of surplus production from Welfare farms.

CHOICE

Center for Humanitarian Outreach and Intercultural Exchange
643 E. 400 S.
Salt Lake City, UT 84102
(801) 363-7970
Tim Evans, Founder

Organized out of the Andean Children's Foundation in 1988, CHOICE is a nonprofit, nonsectarian (though principally LDS in membership) organization dedicated to "improving people's lives through active, enduring humanitarian service." CHOICE sponsors "volunteer expeditions" in which families, organizations, groups of associates, or singles—trained or previously untrained—"work side by side with the rural poor to develop projects which the villagers request and will be able to sustain after the expedition departs." CHOICE volunteers have worked with water supply systems, greenhouses, schools and literacy, and have provided health and medical assistance.

CHURCH WELFARE DEPARTMENT

LDS Church
50 E. North Temple St., 7th Floor
Salt Lake City, UT 84150
(801) 240-3001
Keith McMullin, Director

Provides temporal relief to Latter-day Saints and others around the globe, including food, clothing, and medical supplies in response to natural disasters, civil wars, and other emergencies. Also operates farms, canneries, distribution centers, and employment services, primarily in the United States.

CO-OP AMERICA

1850 M Street, N.W.
Washington, D.C. 20036
(202) 872-20036

This nonprofit organization links consumer members and socially responsible enterprises through an annual directory, catalogues, and so forth.

COOPERATIVE LEAGUE OF THE USA

1828 L Street, N.W.
Washington, D.C. 20036

CLUSA is a professional trade federation of large consumer co-ops. It advises co-ops and sells and publishes books and pamphlets.

DESERET INTERNATIONAL FOUNDATION

890 Quail Valley Drive
Provo, UT 84604
(801) 221-0919
Arthur D. Browne, Executive Director

Started in the Philippines in 1990, and now operating in thirteen countries throughout Central and South America, Africa, Asia, and the Pacific, Deseret International "is a private, nondenominational charity whose goal is to provide surgical and dental assistance primarily for children in emerging nations." Its board of directors is composed of medical professionals who attempt to help local medical practitioners establish adequate health facilities, perform surgeries, and to keep overhead costs low by soliciting medical and dental supplies.

ENTERPRISE MENTORS

International Enterprise Development Foundation
510 Maryville College Dr., Suite 210
St. Louis, MO 63141
(314) 453-0006
Chuck Cozzens, Executive Director

Founded in 1990 by a mostly LDS group of individuals, Enterprise Mentors is a human development foundation designed "to build self-reliance and entrepreneurial spirit within those who struggle for sufficiency in developing countries." Working first in the Philippines and now expanding to Latin America, Enterprise Mentors establishes local boards of directors and indigenous staff, allowing the formation of self-reliance. Efforts are made to charge for consulting services based upon ability to pay, transforming the donor-receiver dependency relationship into a character building, consultant-client relationship. A nonprofit, tax-exempt organization, Enterprise Mentors depends on individual, foundation, and corporate donations to achieve its goals. Primary interventions include training, consulting, walk-in services, professional referrals, and access to credit.

FOUNDATION FOR INTERNATIONAL COMMUNITY ASSISTANCE
(FINCA)
901 King Street
Alexandria ,VA 22314

Non-government organization (NGO) providing access to credit for the poor in Latin America.

INTER-AMERICAN FOUNDATION
1515 Wilson Boulevard
Roslyn, VA 22209
(202) 841-3890
John Garrison

Independent agency of the government of the United States since 1969, IAF offers an alternative to traditional U.S. foreign aid programs. It provides extensive support for grassroots economic projects throughout Latin America and the Caribbean, including grants, training, and other services to cooperatives and other community-based groups. Its annual budget ranges between $30-40 million.

INDUSTRIAL COOPERATIVE ASSOCIATION
249 Elm Street
Sommerville, MA 02144

Assists in the creation and development of worker-owned and controlled industrial businesses, especially in low-income U.S. communities.

INTERMEDIATE TECHNOLOGY DEVELOPMENT GROUP
9 King Street
London WC2E 8HN
England

Associated with the pioneering work of E. F. Schumacher, ITDG is part of a worldwide movement to assist people to live more simply, using appropriate technologies and indigenous methods.

INTERNATIONAL ACTION GROUP

c/o LDS Humanitarian Services
50 E. North Temple Street, 8th Floor
Salt Lake City, UT 84105

The Salt Lake-based International Action Group, an umbrella for LDS-affiliated and other humanitarian organizations, first met in the spring of 1992. Independent of the Church—with LDS Humanitarian Services as coordinator—the group meets semiannually to discuss developments and new ideas and to consolidate resources. Beginning spring 1994, the group established a rotating chair, allowing various groups an opportunity to head the informal council.

KATALYSIS

1331 North Commerce Street
Stockton, CA 95202
(209) 943-6165
Jerry Hildebrand, President

This foundation is a North/South partnership in development that provides micro-loans of $70 to $200 to start or expand jobs in the informal economy. Its focus is on women entrepreneurs in Belize, Guatemala, and Honduras. Some 70 village banks have been established since 1989.

LDS HUMANITARIAN SERVICES

50 E. North Temple Street, 8th Floor
Salt Lake City, UT 84150
(801) 240-1201
Isaac Ferguson, Director

As an arm of the Welfare Program of the LDS Church, Humanitarian Services is heavily involved in providing aid and technical assistance to both non-Mormon as well as LDS members, especially internationally. Often working in conjunction with other NGOs, this organization has helped channel relief to crisis areas such as Ethiopia, Somalia, and Rwanda, as well as support grassroots development projects in Honduras, Guatemala, and elsewhere around the globe.

MINDANAO ENTERPRISE DEVELOPMENT FOUNDATION

Room 305, 3rd Floor, PVL Bldg.
Rizal Street
Davao City
Philippines 8,000
221-0910
Thelma Caparas, Executive Director

A sister foundation of U.S.-based Enterprise Mentors. MEDF offers hands-on consulting and managerial training to micro-entrepreneurs in the southern islands of the Philippines.

MOTHER TERESA

Missionaries of Charity
54 A Lower Circular Road
Calcutta, India

World renowned humanitarian service organization, directed by Nobel Peace Prize winner Mother Teresa.

NATIONAL CENTER FOR EMPLOYEE OWNERSHIP

2201 Broadway, Suite 807
Oakland, CA 94612-3024
(415) 272-9461
Corey Rosen, Executive Director

NCEO is a nonprofit clearinghouse which advises executives, unions, and companies on ESOP and other employee ownership systems, finances, and legal ramifications. It holds a number of conferences and workshops as well as publishing a professional journal and other materials.

OUELESSEBOUGOU-UTAH ALLIANCE

1025 South 700 West
Salt Lake City, UT 84104
(801) 978-2452
Michelle Macfarlane, Executive Director

The Alliance began in 1985 when seven Utahns traveled to Mali, a West African country, to search for a "community or group of villages with which they and the Salt Lake community could begin a long-term relationship to help and learn." The Utah group eventually forged that relationship with the Ouelessebougou region, comprised of 72 villages and 35,000 struggling people. The Alliance undertakes projects requested by the villagers, who define their own needs, contribute labor to projects, and provide their own leadership "so that when the Alliance has completed its work, the projects will continue independently." Projects include constructing wells, fencing gardens, providing basic health care training, and teaching literacy.

OXFAM—UK

274 Banbury Road
Oxford OX2 7D2
United Kingdom
Anthony Gross, Director

Humanitarian group especially focused on the needs of the poor. Originally launched in 1942 as the Oxford Committee for Famine Relief, it now has offices around the globe. It neither seeks nor accepts government funds, but raises some $13 million annually through private donations to provide seeds, irrigation systems, training, etc.

PHILIPPINES ENTERPRISE DEVELOPMENT FOUNDATION

3rd Floor, Consuelo Bldg.
1365 E. Rodriguez Sr. Street
Quezon City, Metro Manila
Philippines
722-8981
Elo Lopez, Executive Director

First overseas partner of Enterprise Mentors, engaged in small business formation, job creation, and technical assistance to cooperatives.

PHILIPPINES RURAL RECONSTRUCTION MOVEMENT

Kayumanggi Press Building
940 Quezon Avenue
Quezon City, 1103
Philippines

NGO which focuses on grassroots training and community organizing to empower peasants and rural farmers.

PROGRAMA DE ECONOMIA DEL TRABAJO

Santo Domingo 526
Santiago, Chile
632-6128
Jaime Ruiz-Tagle, Executive Director

NGO involved in workers' self-management and micro-enterprise projects in Chile.

RESULTS

236 Massachusetts Avenue, N.E. Suite 300
Washington, D.C. 20002
(202) 543-9340

International citizen advocacy group that lobbies governments to create political strategies for ending global hunger and poverty. It trains volunteers to influence public officials, media, and local communities, promoting the immunization of children, education, and micro-lending programs.

SAN DIONISIO CREDIT COOPERATIVE

0554 Quirino Avenue
San Dionisio, Paranaque
Philippines
Hermnio Hernandez, General Manager

One of the oldest and most successful credit-union type organizations which serves the many needs of its poverty-stricken members in the community of Paranaque.

SCOTT BADER COMMONWEALTH, LTD.

Wollaston, near Wellingborough
Northants, England
Godric Bader, President

British chemical company that paved the way to sharing wealth through employee ownership and worker representation on the board of directors, allowing employee input regarding the firm's corporate strategy and allocation of profits.

STUDENTS FOR INTERNATIONAL DEVELOPMENT

237 HRCB
Brigham Young University
Provo, UT 84602
(801) 378-3377

BYU student-run program which conducts charitable drives on the Provo campus, organizes international development conferences, seminars, and so on.

THRASHER RESEARCH FUND

50 E. North Temple Street
Salt Lake City, UT 84150
(801) 240-4753

In 1973, E. W. "Al" Thrasher, a non-LDS Utahn, provided a substantial endowment to be administered through the LDS Church for humanitarian, child-related research projects. Since the first grants were made in 1978, the Thrasher Fund has reviewed research proposals annually for two separate categories, the Scientific Fund and the Innovative Fund. The former exists to fund academic research focusing on "novel approaches to the solution of problems in nutrition and pediatric infectious diseases." The latter fund serves to "bridge the gap between formal research and field applications" by encouraging projects appropriate to local cultures that, through careful documentation, can be transferred to other cultures. Through these funds, Thrasher Research "will continue to support research and field applications that seek to improve the well-being of children worldwide."

VASAA

Veterans Association for Service Activities Abroad
PO Box 17815
Salt Lake City, UT 84117-0815
(801) 278-7674

Organized in 1983 by LDS Vietnam veterans and originally called Veterans Assisting Saints Abroad Association, VASAA has provided humanitarian service to LDS members and others for over a decade. With the name change in 1990, VASAA further shifted its emphasis from retrieving LDS members left behind in Vietnam to more general humanitarian service. All current and retired military personnel are eligible for membership, as are any who have served in Southeast Asia in military or civilian capacities; friends and family of veterans and others with humanitarian interests are eligible for associate membership.

VISAYAS ENTERPRISE FOUNDATION

Cinco Centrum, Room 406
Fuente Osmena
Cebu City
Philippines 6,000
219-767
Ed Siadi, Executive Director

VEF grew out of the efforts of Enterprise Mentors to expand its microenterprise strategies beyond the Metro Manila area of the Philippines. Located in the central islands, VEF has a staff and board which serves the purpose of creating jobs, assisting cooperatives, and so on.

WORLD COUNCIL OF INDIGENOUS PEOPLES

55 King Edward
Ottawa, Ontario
Canada
Donald Rojas

WORLD NEIGHBORS

4127 NW 122nd Street
Oklahoma City, OK
73120-8869

A private volunteer agency, this organization works with various local, national, and global groups to improve small farm productivity.

Notes

List of Abbreviations

EM	*Encyclopedia of Mormonism*, ed. Daniel H. Ludlow (New York: Macmillan, 1992).
JD	*Journal of Discourses*, 26 vols. (Liverpool: Latter-day Saints Book Depot, 1854–86; reprint, Salt Lake City: 1964).
HC	*History of The Church of Jesus Christ of Latter-day Saints*, 7 vols., ed. B. H. Roberts, 3rd ed. (Salt Lake City: Deseret News, 1961).

Foreword

1. *JD* 12:154.
2. *JD* 9:234.
3. *JD* 7:282.
4. *JD* 15:34.
5. *JD* 11:324–25.
6. *JD* 10:267.
7. *JD* 10:267.
8. David O. McKay, *Gospel Ideals* (Salt Lake City: Improvement Era, 1953), 104.

Part 1

1. Joseph Smith, Jr., *Teachings of the Prophet Joseph Smith*, comp. Joseph Fielding Smith (Salt Lake City: Deseret Book, 1977), 366. See also Joseph Smith, Jr., *The Words of Joseph Smith: The Contemporary Accounts of the Nauvoo Discourses of the Prophet Joseph*, comp. and ed. Andrew F. Ehat and Lyndon W. Cook (Provo, Utah: Religious Studies Center, Brigham Young University; Salt Lake City: Bookcraft, 1980), 367.
2. Marion G. Romney, "The Purpose of Church Welfare Services," *Ensign* 7 (May 1977): 92.
3. Jeffrey R. Holland, "A Handful of Meal and a Little Oil," *Ensign* 26 (May 1996): 30–31.

Chapter 1

1. *JD* 9:138.
2. Neal A. Maxwell, "The Church Can Now Be Universal with Priesthood Revelation of 1978," *Church News*, 5 January 1980, 20. Recently, some demographers have projected lower growth for the Church in the next century. However, they still concur with the projection of a significant Third World majority among the Latter-day Saints.

3. Tim B. Heaton, "Vital Statistics," in *EM,* 1520–21. As this book is published, the Church has announced that the number of members outside the United States has just exceeded the number inside the United States (John L. Hart, "Over Half LDS Now Outside U.S.," *Church News,* 2 March 1996, 3, 6).

4. Rodney Stark, "The Rise of a New World Faith," *Review of Religious Research* 26 (1984): 18–27.

5. Lorenzo Snow, "Mormonism, By Its Head," *Land of Sunshine* 15 (October 1901): 259.

6. Spanish and Portuguese are the second and third languages most frequently spoken by Latter-day Saints. Various Philippine languages now constitute seven of the 20 languages most frequently spoken in the Church. See "Top 20 Languages Spoken in the Church," *Church News,* 30 November 1991, 7. The growth of the Church in the Third World has occurred so rapidly that it has been little studied. Recent works which examine this major development are Spencer J. Palmer, *The Expanding Church* (Salt Lake City: Deseret Book, 1978); F. Lamond Tullis, ed., *Mormonism: A Faith for All Cultures* (Provo, Utah: Brigham Young University Press, 1978); F. Lamond Tullis, *Mormons in Mexico* (Logan, Utah: Utah State University Press, 1987); and Alexander B. Morrison, *The Dawning of a Brighter Day: The Church in Black Africa* (Salt Lake City: Deseret Book, 1990). A good survey of some of the issues which the Church is encountering as a result of this worldwide expansion is Lawrence A. Young, "Confronting Turbulent Environments: Issues in the Organizational Growth and Globalization of Mormonism," in *Contemporary Mormonism: Social Science Perspectives,* ed. Marie Cornwall, et al. (Urbana: University of Illinois Press, 1994), 43–63.

7. Figures from *Church Almanac, 1975* (Salt Lake City: Deseret News, 1975) and *Church Almanac, 1995* (Salt Lake City: Deseret News, 1995). See also Warner Woodworth, "Developing Innovations for Global Transformation" (keynote speech during International Week, Brigham Young University, Provo, Utah, 25 January 1993).

8. Donald R. Snow, "Models Used in Projecting Mormon Growth" (presentation at the annual Mormon History Association, Ogden, Utah, May 1982).

9. *EM,* appendix 13, 1759–60.

10. On a personal level, the experience of author Woodworth's son perhaps illustrates the explosive missionary work now occurring in Latin America. Erik served in the Chile Santiago North Mission. Reports to the missionaries indicated many pairs baptizing 12, 18, or up to 32 people per month. Certain "ripe" mission districts enjoyed 50, 70, 90, or up to 130 baptisms in a four-week period. During the three-year term of Erik's mission president, Holbrook Dupont, mission baptisms rose from 300 per month to over 600. Total annual converts increased from 2,900 to over 5,000. Many other Latin American missions have experienced similar results.

11. Names have been changed to protect personal privacy. Specific information and references providing background for most of the situations described here will be covered in chapter 2. On conditions in the former USSR, see Michael Specter, "Russia's Declining Health: Rising Illness, Shorter Lives," *New York Times,* 19 February 1995, A1, A12; Steven Erlanger, "In Russia, Success Isn't Such a Popular Idea," *New York Times,* 12 March 1995, E4;

and Celestine Bohlen, "Graft and Gangsterism in Russia Blight the Entrepreneurial Spirit," *New York Times,* 30 January 1994, A1, A12. On the Church's beginnings in Russia, see Gary L. Browning, "Out of Obscurity: The Emergence of The Church of Jesus Christ of Latter-day Saints in 'That Vast Empire' of Russia," *Brigham Young University Studies* (1993), 674–88.

12. This phenomenon has been commented on extensively. See, for example, Allan Sloan, "The Hit Men," *Newsweek,* 26 February 1996, 44–48; Floyd Norris, "You're Fired. (But Your Stock Is Way Up)," *New York Times,* 3 September 1995, E3; and Mark D. Fefer, "How Layoffs Pay Off," *Fortune,* 24 January 1994, 12. See chapter 16 under "Managing Corporate Downsizing" for a discussion on corporate downsizing from the perspective of the united order concept of stewardship management.

13. See John Holusha, "Eastman Kodak Chief Is Ousted by Directors," and Alison Leigh Cowan, "Unclear Future Forced Board's Hand," *New York Times,* 7 August 1993, 37, 49. The anonymous Kodak executive is quoted on p. 49. Kay Whitmore had more than ethical reasons to be suspicious of mass layoffs as a solution to Kodak's perceived problems. During the 1980s before he became CEO, Kodak had instituted a series of layoffs which had resulted in short-term increases in Kodak's stock price, but which had always been followed eventually by new declines in the stock price. See Don L. Boroughs, "Amputating Assets," *U.S. News & World Report,* 4 May 1992, 50–52. On Kodak's service to Rochester, including the school program, see Michael Quint, "Change Worries Kodak's Hometown," *New York Times,* 9 August 1993, D1, D8, and Milt Freudenheim, "A Doting Uncle Cuts Back, and a City Feels the Pain: Kodak Rethinks Its Civic Duties in Rochester," *New York Times,* 8 October 1995, F1, F9. Ironically, Kodak's new chairman, George Fisher, produced considerable frustration on Wall Street by announcing his intention to improve Kodak's performance through growth rather than further extensive layoffs. See John Holusha, "Kodak Chief Offers a New Vision," *New York Times,* 29 October 1993, D1, D17; John Holusha, "Kodak Joins Others in Scaling Back Expectations," *New York Times,* 16 December 1993, D1, D6; and Peter Nulty, "Kodak Grabs for Growth Again," *Fortune,* 16 May 1994, 76–78.

14. As Apostle Bruce McConkie told a Peruvian area conference, the time for gathering to one Zion in Utah and the United States had ended:

> We are in the midst of a period of change and realignment where one of the basic doctrines of the Restoration is concerned. . . . We are now engaged in gathering Israel within the various nations of the earth and in establishing stakes of Zion at the ends of the earth. . . . We are living in a new day. The Church of Jesus Christ of Latter-day Saints is fast becoming a worldwide Church. . . . The gathering place for Peruvians is in the stakes of Zion in Peru. The gathering place for Chileans is in Chile; for Bolivians it is in Bolivia; for Koreans it is in Korea; and so it goes through all the length and breadth of the earth. Scattered Israel in every nation is called to gather to the fold of Christ, to the stakes of Zion, as such are established in their nations. . . . Build up Zion, but build it up in the area where God has given you birth and nationality. Build it up where he has given you citizenship, family and friends. Zion is here in South America and the Saints who

> comprise this part of Zion are and should be a leavening influence for good in all these nations. (Bruce R. McConkie, "Come: Let Israel Build Zion," *Ensign* 7 [May 1977]: 115–18)

15. *JD* 11:18.

16. See also D&C 93:33–34, 131:7–8.

17. Joseph F. Smith, "The Truth about Mormonism," *Out West* 23 (1905): 242.

18. See discussion and notes in chapter 4 under "Adam Smith and the Modern Economy."

19. McKay, *Gospel Ideals,* 104.

20. The commandments to not make graven images (a major business activity in ancient times and a commandment which modern prophets have interpreted to include worship of money and financial success—see Spencer W. Kimball's "The False Gods We Worship," *Ensign* 6 [June 1976]: 3–6), to not work on the sabbath day, to not kill (getting gain being a primary motivation for murder since the earliest times—see Moses 5:31), to honor our parents (which includes financial support if necessary), to not steal, to not bear false witness (which includes being honest in business dealings), and to not covet our neighbor's property.

21. Dean D. McBrien, "The Economic Content of Early Mormon Doctrine," *Southwestern Political and Social Science Quarterly* 6 (September 1925): 180. While this book focuses on its economic aspects, the law of consecration involves the devotion of time, talents, and heart as well as property. See chapter 10. The economic aspects are, however, as important as these others (Luke 18:25).

22. Kent W. Huff, *Joseph Smith's United Order: A Non-Communalistic Interpretation* (Orem, Utah: Cedar Fort, 1988), 12.

23. *JD* 16:268–69.

24. Leonard J. Arrington, *Great Basin Kingdom: An Economic History of the Latter-day Saints 1830–1900* (Cambridge: Harvard University Press, 1958). Leonard J. Arrington, Feramorz Fox, and Dean L. May, *Building the City of God: Community and Cooperation among the Mormons* (Salt Lake City: Deseret Book, 1976).

25. Hugh W. Nibley, *Approaching Zion,* vol. 9 of *The Collected Works of Hugh Nibley,* ed. Don E. Norton (Salt Lake City: Deseret Book; Provo, Utah: Foundation for Ancient Research and Mormon Studies, 1986).

26. John A. Widtsoe, "Evidences and Reconciliations: Are Communism and its Related 'Isms' Preparatory to the United Order?" *Improvement Era* 43 (October 1940): 633–34. Elder Widtsoe was a member of the Quorum of the Twelve from 1921 to 1952.

Chapter 2

1. Ezra Taft Benson, *Teachings of Ezra Taft Benson* (Salt Lake City: Bookcraft, 1988), 66. In 1978 general conference, Elder Benson declared that the accomplishment of the Church's mission was "the *only* solution to the problems of the world. . . . The economic, political and social problems facing this nation, as well as other nations, will be solved only with the help of God" (Ezra

Taft Benson, "May the Kingdom of God Go Forth," *Ensign* 8 [May 1978]: 33).

2. On the broad-based and continuing decline in employment by America's largest corporations, see Louis Uchitelle and N. R. Kleinfeld, "On the Battlefields of Business, Millions of Casualties," *New York Times,* 3 March 1996, A1, A26–29. Even profitable companies such as Procter and Gamble, General Electric, Johnson & Johnson, and AT&T are reducing total employment. See Louis Uchitelle, "Strong Companies Are Joining Trend to Eliminate Jobs," *New York Times,* 26 July 1993, A1, D3; Michelle Quinn, "Job Crunch: The Slamming Doors of Silicon Valley," *New York Times,* 23 January 1994, F5 (even high-technology companies are affected); Tim Smart, "Let the Good Times Roll—and a Few More Heads," *Business Week,* 31 January 1994, 28–29; Edmund L. Andrews, "A.T.&T. Cutting Up to 15,000 Jobs to Trim Costs," *New York Times,* 11 February 1994, D1, D14 (total layoffs in the telephone companies from 1992 to the beginning of 1994 are 85,000); Steve Lohr, "Economic Recovery: Manhandle with Care," *New York Times,* 13 February 1994, E2; and Louis Uchitelle, " Job Extinction Evolving into a Fact of Life in U.S.," *New York Times,* 22 March 1994, A1, D5. See chapter 16 under "Implementing Stewardship in Modern Business—Managing Corporate Downsizing."

3. Joann S. Lublin, "Ranks of Unemployed Couples Multiply, Devastating Double-Income Households," *Wall Street Journal,* 7 May 1993, B1.

4. Lance Morrow, "The Temping of America," and Janice Castro, "Disposable Workers," *Time,* 29 March 1993, 40–47. The trend toward lower paying temporary employment has even penetrated deeply into the manufacturing sector, which previously supplied the largest number of well-paying jobs. See Louis Uchitelle, "Temporary Workers Are on the Increase in Nation's Factories," *New York Times,* 6 July 1993, A1, D2. Another trend is toward self-employment. However, this is frequently a temporary, uncertain and poor-paying alternative (Louis Uchitelle, "Newest Corporate Refugees: Self-Employed and Low-Paid," *New York Times,* 15 November 1993, A1, D2).

5. Ellen Graham, "Their Careers: Count on Nothing and Work Like a Demon," *Wall Street Journal,* 31 October 1995, B1, B10.

6. The deterioration in labor force statistics has been constant since the 1980s (Laurence Mishel and Jared Bernstein, eds., *The State of Working America, 1992–1993* [Armonk, N.Y.: Sharpe, 1993], 87–96, 129–249). Even families which are still employed and technically middle class are feeling increasingly pressured (Louis Uchitelle, "Trapped in the Impoverished Middle Class," *New York Times,* 17 November 1991, D1, D10).

7. See Matt Murray, "Amid Record Profits, Companies Continue to Lay Off Employees," *Wall Street Journal,* 4 May 1995, A1, A6. In 1994, even though corporate profits rose 11 percent, over 500,000 jobs were eliminated. Discussing Xerox's traditional "contract" with its workers after making $800 million in profits and cutting 10 percent of its workforce, a spokesman admitted that it sounded "heartless" but pronounced that there was a "new reality" which superseded the old relations with Xerox employees. Ironically, it appears that remaining employees are so fearful and fatalistic after a major layoff that productivity is reduced rather than enhanced. See also Graham, "Their Careers," and Peter T. Kilborn, "Labor Day Message No One Asked to Hear," *New York Times,* 5 September 1993, E1, E4. This has a debilitating psy-

chological as well as financial effect on heads of families. See, for example, Joseph Berger, "The Pain of Layoffs for Ex-Senior I.B.M. Workers," *New York Times*, 22 December 1993, B1, B5. Early research by Dorothea Braginsky, a Connecticut psychologist, indicates that the decline in good-paying jobs appears to affect profoundly the children of these families, leading them to cynicism about the value of hard work and other nonmonetary values, and depriving them of hope for their future (Marilyn Webb, "How Old Is Too Old?" *New York*, 29 March 1993, 71–72). The effect of this decline on families is studied in depth in Katherine S. Newman, *Falling from Grace: The Experience of Downward Mobility in the American Middle Class* (New York: Free Press, 1988). A recent summary of these trends and pessimistic evaluation of the many proposed solutions is Jeffrey Madrick, *The End of Affluence: The Causes and Consequences of America's Economic Decline* (New York: Random House, 1995).

8. Craig R. Whitney, "Western Europe's Dreams Turning to Nightmares," *New York Times*, 8 August 1993, A1, A16.

9. Mishel and Bernstein, *State of Working America*, 131–37 (wages), and Juliet B. Schor, *The Overworked American: The Unexpected Decline of Leisure* (New York: Basic Books, 1991), 29–32 (hours).

10. All these studies are summarized in "What in the World Is Happening to Workers?" *CWA News* (November 1991): 6–8.

11. Christopher Georges, "Most Americans See Their Incomes Slip Even Though the Economy Is Booming," *Wall Street Journal*, 26 October 1994, A2, A12. Overall, real annual earnings in the lowest 20 percent of workers have declined by 24 percent since 1973. Recent studies have found that real wages have declined for every group, educated or not, except college educated women (Barbara Vobejda, "Education Is No Protection from Age Squeeze, Report Says," *Washington Post*, 4 September 1994, A20). The median income of college educated male workers has fallen 17 percent since 1986 (Louis Uchitelle, "Male, Educated and Falling Behind," *New York Times*, 11 February 1994, D1, D4).

12. See Roger Cohen, "Europe's Recession Prompts New Look at Welfare Costs," *New York Times*, 9 August 1993, A1, A8, and Alan Riding, "In a Time of Shared Hardship, the Young Embrace Europe," *New York Times*, 12 August 1993, A1, A11. The trend to reduce home-country workforces and wages, or send jobs to low-wage countries, is even affecting Japan (Andrew Pollack, "Japan's Companies Moving Production to Sites Overseas," *New York Times*, 29 August 1993, A1, A16).

13. Uchitelle and Kleinfield, "On the Battlefields of Business," A26–27 citing U. S. Labor Department studies.

14. Louis Jacobson, Robert LaLonde, and Daniel Sullivan, *The Costs of Worker Dislocation* (Kalamazoo, Mich.: W. E. Upjohn Institute for Employment Research, 1996): 105–36.

15. Graef S. Crystal, *In Search of Excess: The Overcompensation of American Executives* (New York: W. W. Norton, 1991). In general, evidence shows that the economic boom of the 1980s resulted in disproportionate gains by the wealthiest Americans and a significant increase in the overall level of inequality in the United States. See Mishel and Bernstein, *State of Working America*, 203–5, 251–69; Jonathan Alter, "The 80's: A Final Reckoning," *Newsweek*, 1 March

1993, 49; Sylvia Nasar, "Fed Gives New Evidence of 80's Gains by Richest," *New York Times*, 21 April 1992, A1, A17; and Sylvia Nasar, "The 1980's: A Very Good Time for the Very Rich," *New York Times*, 5 March 1992, A1, D24.

16. John Bryne, "The Flap over Executive Pay," *Business Week*, 6 May 1991, 90–96, and John Bryne and Chuck Hawkins, "Executive Pay: The Party Ain't over Yet," *Business Week*, 26 April 1992, 56–64.

17. Crystal, *In Search of Excess*, 205–9. J. P. Morgan thought that a 20 to 1 salary differential ratio was adequate for a CEO in the companies with which he was involved.

18. Joann S. Lublin, "The Great Divide," *Wall Street Journal*, 11 April 1996, R1, R4, R15–17.

19. These and other recent business scandals have been well researched. See, for example: savings and loans: Michael Binstein and Charles Bowden, *Trust Me: Charles Keating and the Missing Billions* (New York: Random House, 1993); Kathleen Day, *S&L Hell: The People and the Politics behind the $1 Trillion Savings and Loan Scandal* (New York: W. W. Norton, 1993); L. William Seidman, *Full Faith and Credit: The Great S&L Debacle and Other Washington Sagas* (New York: Random House, 1993); junk bond manipulation by Milken, Drexel, Salomon, etc.: Mary Zey, *Banking on Fraud: Drexel, Junk Bonds, and Buyouts* (New York: Aldine de Gruyter, 1993); Michael Lewis, *Liar's Poker: Rising through the Wreckage on Wall Street* (New York: W. W. Norton, 1989); Wedtech: William Sternberg and Matthew C. Harrison, Jr., *Feeding Frenzy* (New York: Henry Holt, 1989); E. F. Hutton: James Sterngold, *Burning Down the House: How Greed, Deceit and Bitter Revenge Destroyed E. F. Hutton* (New York: Simon & Schuster, 1990); government contracts: Andy Pasztor, *When the Pentagon Was for Sale: Inside America's Biggest Defense Scandal* (New York: Scribner, 1995); RJR Nabisco: Bryan Burrough and John Helyer, *Barbarians at the Gate: The Fall of RJR Nabisco* (New York: Harper & Row, 1990); Prudential: Kurt Eichenwald, *Serpent on the Rock* (New York: HarperBusiness, 1995).

20. Robert Pear, "Poverty in U. S. Grew Faster Than Population Last Year," *New York Times*, 5 October 1993, A20; Robert Pear, "The Picture from the Census Bureau: Poverty 1993: Bigger, Deeper, Younger, Getting Worse," *New York Times*, 10 October 1993, 5; and Mishel and Bernstein, *State of Working America*, 271–314. Particularly disturbing is the large number of people who cannot lift themselves from poverty even though they work full time and more. The percentage of all full-time workers earning less than $13,000 a year has risen from 12 percent in 1979 to 18 percent in 1992, according to the Census Bureau (Jason DeParle, "Sharp Increase along the Borders of Poverty," *New York Times*, 31 March 1994, A18).

21. "Hungry World," *U.S. News and World Report*, 21 October 1991, 18.

22. David Whitman, "The Rise of the 'Hyper-Poor,'" *U.S. News and World Report*, 15 October 1990, 40–42.

23. William J. Wilson, *The Truly Disadvantaged: The Inner City, the Underclass, and Public Policy* (Chicago: University of Chicago Press, 1987).

24. Nicholas Lemann, "The Other Underclass," *Atlantic Monthly*, December 1991, 96–110.

25. Quoted in John J. Karakash (dean emeritus of the School of Engineering of Lehigh University), letter to the editor, *Time*, 1 February 1993, 4.

For a graphic description of the plight of U.S. cities, see Myron Magnet's *The Dream and the Nightmare: The Sixties' Legacy to the Underclass* (New York: Morrow, 1993).

26. David Briggs, "Look for the Face of the Prophet Elijah in the Homeless," *Provo (Utah) Daily Herald*, 21 March 1993, C1.

27. Peter Passell, "The False Promise of Development by Casino," *New York Times*, 12 June 1994, F5.

28. Aaron Bernstein, "Inequality: How the Gap between Rich and Poor Hurts the Economy," *Business Week*, 15 August 1994, 78–83, and Paul Krugman, *The Age of Diminished Expectations* (Boston: MIT Press, 1990). Even Wall Street economists are expressing concern over the long-term economic consequences of the flat or declining real incomes of the majority (Roger Lowenstein, "Will Flat Wages Beget Future Trouble?" *Wall Street Journal*, 12 October 1995, C1).

29. Joan O'Brian, "Utah Ranks 48th in Per Capita Income," *Salt Lake Tribune*, 28 April 1993, B1.

30. Tim Bovee, "Family Incomes Highest in Northeast," *Provo (Utah) Daily Herald*, 16 April 1993, A2.

31. Kenneth E. Jensen, *Utah Personal Income 1929–1985* (Salt Lake City: Utah Department of Employment Security, 1986), 17, 113–14.

32. Thomas H. Gorey, "Food Requests in S. L. Rose 20–25% in '90, Report Says," *Salt Lake Tribune*, 20 December 1990, B3.

33. Cherill Crosby, "U.S. Aid to Utah for Food $200 Million and Rising," *Salt Lake Tribune*, 8 April 1993, A1.

34. Alf Pratte, "Good Nutrition More Important Than Cholesterol," *Utah County Journal*, 23 February 1993, 1–2.

35. Gorey, "Food Requests."

36. Lois M. Collins, "Portrait of Homeless in Utah Is Changing," *Salt Lake City Deseret News*, 30 January 1993, A10.

37. John Pollard, "Students Helped by Homeless," *(Brigham Young University) Daily Universe*, 9 June 1993, 1.

38. "Utah Workplace Deaths Twice National Average," *Provo (Utah) Daily Herald*, 22 March 1993, C3.

39. See Frank Swoboda and Kathleen Day, "U.S. to Fine Coal Companies $5 Million for Safety Violations on Dust Samples," *Washington Post*, 5 April 1991, A9.

40. See generally, Purushottam Narayan Mathur, *Why Developing Countries Fail to Develop* (London: Macmillan, 1991), and Hans Singer, "Lessons of Post-War Development Experience 1945–1988," in *A Dual Economy*, ed. Willem L. M. Adriaansen and J. George Waardenburg (Rotterdam: Wolters-Noordhof, 1989).

41. See John Darnton, "'Lost Decade' Drains Africa's Vitality," *New York Times*, 19 June 1994, A1, A10.

42. Most of the data cited come from Lester R. Brown, et al., *State of the World 1990* (New York: W. W. Norton, 1990).

43. Other major countries with high inequality are South Africa, Nigeria, and Egypt. The first two, along with Mexico and Brazil, have rapidly growing LDS membership (Paul Lewis, "U.N. Lists Four Nations at Risk Because of

Wide Income Gaps," *New York Times*, 2 June 1994, A6).

44. "Hungry World," *U.S. News and World Report*, 18.

45. Joan Davidson and Dorothy Myers with Manab Chakraburty, *No Time to Waste: Poverty and the Global Environment* (Oxford: Oxfam, 1992).

46. Categories of infant mortality are taken from Sharon L. Camp and J. Joseph Speidel's *The International Human Suffering Index* (Washington, D.C.: Population Crisis Committee, 1987).

47. See Brook Larmer and Mac Margolis, "Dead End Kids," *Newsweek*, 25 May 1992, 38–40.

48. See "Erasing Illiteracy," *World Monitor Magazine* 4 (March 1991): 6–7.

49. See Richard J. Barnet, "The End of Jobs: Employment Is One Thing the Global Economy Is *Not* Creating," *Harper's* 287 (September 1993): 47–52, and Richard J. Barnet and John Cavanagh, *Global Dreams: Imperial Corporations and the New World Order* (New York: Simon & Schuster, 1994).

50. See, for example, Ian Livingstone, "A Reassessment of Kenya's Rural and Urban Informal Sector," *World Development* 16 (June 1991): 651–70.

51. See Bishwapriya Sanyal, "Organizing the Self-Employed: The Politics of the Urban Informal Sector," *International Labour Review* (1991): 39–56; Alejandro Portes, Manuell Castells, and Lauren A. Benton, eds., *The Informal Economy: Studies in Advanced and Less Developed Countries* (Baltimore: Johns Hopkins University Press, 1989), which includes studies on the informal sector in the United States, Britain, Italy, Spain, and Russia as well as Third World countries; and S. V. Sethuraman, ed., *The Urban Informal Sector in Developing Countries: Employment, Poverty and Environment* (Geneva: International Labour Office, 1981).

52. Hernando de Soto, *The Other Path: The Invisible Revolution in the Third World* (New York: Harper & Row, 1989), 132–36.

53. Philip Elmer-Dewitt, "Summit to Save the Earth," *Time*, 1 June 1992, 40–59.

54. Susan Dentzer, "The Wealth of Nations," *U.S. News & World Report*, 4 May 1992, 54.

55. United Nations Department of International Economic and Social Affairs, *World Economic Survey 1992: Current Trends and Policies in the World Economy* (New York: United Nations, 1992), 72.

56. See John Darnton, "In Poor, Decolonized Africa, Bankers Are New Overlords," *New York Times*, 20 June 1994, A1, A8; Mathur, *Why Developing Countries Fail to Develop*; Fernando Henriques Cardoso and Enzo Faletto, *Dependency and Development in Latin America* (Berkeley: University of California Press, 1979); Immanuel Wallerstein, *The Capitalist World Economy* (New York: Cambridge University Press, 1979); T. Dos Santos, "The Structure of Dependence," *American Economic Review* 60 (May 1970): 231–36; and Andre Gunder Frank, *Capitalism and Underdevelopment in Latin America: Historical Studies of Chile and Brazil* (New York: Monthly Review Press, 1967). Ronald H. Chilcote, *Theories of Development and Underdevelopment* (London: Westview Press, 1984), gives a good summary of various views on reasons for continuing underdevelopment in most of the world.

57. John W. Wright, ed., *The Universal Almanac 1995* (Kansas City: Andrews and McMeel, 1994), 355.

58. Citations from "Hungry World," *U.S. News and World Report,* 18.

59. See "The Kindness of Strangers," *Economist,* 7 May 1994, 11, 19–22; Paul Wallich and Marguerite Holloway, "More Profitable to Give Than to Receive?" *Scientific American,* March 1993, 142; and Philip Quarles van Ufford, Dirk Kruijt, and Theodore Downing, eds., *The Hidden Crisis in Development: Development Bureaucracies* (Amsterdam: Free University Press; Tokyo: United Nations University, 1988). Of course, the development community now recognizes the failure of these policies and proclaims the need to promote microdevelopment on the grassroots level. It remains to be seen whether the international development business will function any better with this approach. See John P. Lewis, ed., *Strengthening the Poor: What Have We Learned?* (New Brunswick, N.J.: Transaction Books, 1988).

60. See Mathur, *Why Developing Countries,* 204–26. The prime importance in pursuing a "Four Tigers" strategy of keeping wages down at the expense of developing an internal market economy to benefit working people was frankly admitted by the prime minister of Malaysia, Mahathir Mohamad: "We don't have a market, money, management know-how or technology. If you take our one advantage, we can't compete. . . . Once you insist workers have the right to strike, they don't know how far to go" (Quoted in Karen Elliott House, "Malaysian Premier Says U.S. Policies Hurt Chance for Global Growth, Stability," *Wall Street Journal,* 29 March 1993, A8). Prime Minister Mohamad advocated the restoration of authoritarian rule in Russia and urged the United States to stop promoting democracy in other nations.

Chapter 3

1. *JD* 16:8.

2. Richard L. Bushman, *Joseph Smith and the Beginnings of Mormonism* (Urbana: University of Illinois Press, 1984), 29–31, 39–49, 59–69.

3. The bibliography of the history of the modern Church is vast. The best single-volume history is probably James B. Allen and Glen M. Leonard, *The Story of the Latter-day Saints* (Salt Lake City: Deseret Book, 1976). Unless otherwise noted, we have followed this for basic information on modern Church history.

4. Chapter 4 discusses God's commandments on these matters in earlier dispensations.

5. See Acts 4:32–5:11. Other early American communal groups are discussed in chapter 6 under "The 'Utopian' Socialists" and in chapter 12 under "Utopian Communities."

6. Milton V. Backman, *The Heavens Resound: A History of the Latter-day Saints in Ohio 1830–1838* (Salt Lake City: Deseret Book, 1983), is the best overall history of the Kirtland period. Lyndon W. Cook, *Joseph Smith and the Law of Consecration* (Provo, Utah: Grandin Book, 1985), gives historical background on consecration and stewardship in Joseph Smith's time, although we disagree with some of his conclusions as to the fate of the law of consecration and stewardship. Joseph A. Geddes, "The United Order among the Mormons (Missouri Phase)" (Ph.D. diss., Columbia University, 1922), also covers the Joseph Smith period. Arrington, Fox, and May, *Building the City of God,* is the definitive historical work on the law of consecration and stewardship

throughout the Church's history. A good short summary is L. Dwight Israelsen, "United Orders" in *EM*, 1493–95. Gordon E. Wagner, "Consecration and Stewardship: A Socially Efficient System of Justice" (Ph.D. diss., Cornell University, 1977), gives a thorough theoretical analysis of the united order in the modern context.

7. Ezra Taft Benson, "A Vision and a Hope for the Youth of Zion," in *1977 Devotional Speeches of the Year* (Provo, Utah: Brigham Young University Press, 1978), 74.

8. *HC* 1:382–83. John Corrill said that "this regulation was not attended to, for the Church got crazy to go up to Zion. . . . The rich were afraid to send up their money to purchase land, and the poor crowded up in numbers, without having any surplus provided, contrary to the advise of the bishop" (*Brief History of the Church of Jesus Christ of Latter-day Saints*, 18–19, quoted in Geddes, *Missouri Phase*, 61).

9. *JD* 16:11.

10. *JD* 2:307.

11. Two recent works, Cook, *Joseph Smith and the Law of Consecration*, 65–95, and Huff, *Joseph Smith's United Order*, have questioned whether tithing is intended as preparation for a return to a fuller living of the law of consecration. They have sought to show that the "United Order" was nothing more than a single private firm, established one time only by Joseph Smith in the 1830s, which has been *permanently* superseded by the practice of tithing. One of these writers even argues that Brigham Young suffered from "a substantial loss of data and experience in the transition from . . . Joseph Smith's time . . . [which lead to] doctrinal drift . . . on matters affecting economics" (Huff, *Joseph Smith's United Order*, 42).

The idea that the law of tithing is finally sufficient to satisfy the law of consecration, and that after the institution of tithing in 1838 the united order would never again be established, has never been previously argued in LDS doctrine. It ignores or denies Brigham Young and his fellow apostles' authority and inspiration in setting up united order and other cooperative efforts later in the 19th century. See Dean L. May, "The Economics of Zion," *Sunstone* 14 (August 1990): 15–23. Further, it contradicts the consistent teaching of generations of prophets and apostles that tithing is a "lesser" law designed to lead the Saints to the higher law of consecration under the united order. A few references include: Brigham Young, *Millennial Star* 37:322, quoted in Edward J. Allen, *The Second United Order among the Mormons* (New York: Columbia University Press, 1936), 96; Lorenzo Snow, *JD* 19:344–46 (also found in *Latter-day Prophets Speak*, ed. Daniel H. Ludlow [Salt Lake City: Bookcraft, 1948], 335); James E. Talmage, *The Articles of Faith* (Salt Lake City: Deseret News, 1899; reprint Salt Lake City, Church of Jesus Christ of Latter Day Saints, 1975), 437–39 (page citations are to the reprint edition); Joseph F. Smith, *Gospel Doctrine*, 225; John A. Widtsoe, *Priesthood and Church Government* (Salt Lake City: Deseret Book, 1950), 60; Milton R. Hunter, *Will a Man Rob God?* (Salt Lake City: Deseret News Press, 1952), 32, 99–100; Bruce R. McConkie, *Mormon Doctrine*, 2nd ed. (Salt Lake City: Bookcraft, 1966), 796–97; Marion G. Romney, "Welfare Services," *Ensign* 5 (November 1975): 125, 127.

12. See note 11 above. The reference most frequently given is from the

minutes of comments by Joseph to the Montrose, Iowa, high council. The Prophet is addressing the need to 'keep a low profile' while the Saints pursued petitions to Congress for redress for their losses from mob persecution in Missouri. He continues:

> The law of consecration could not be kept here, and that it was the will of the Lord that we should desist from trying to keep it; and if persisted in, would produce a perfect defeat of its object, and that he [Joseph] assumed the whole responsibility of not keeping it until proposed by himself. (*HC* 4:93)

It seems hard to interpret this as anything more than a short-term practical decision by the Prophet led by inspiration applicable to particular circumstances. It seems to clearly contemplate that the law of consecration could be reproposed when Joseph found the circumstances to be appropriate. It is especially noteworthy that the rationale for the temporary suspension was that proceeding at that time would defeat the object of the law of consecration. Even if particular applications are suspended, the object and principles of the law of consecration continue to be valid.

13. Wilford Woodruff, *Wilford Woodruff's Journal,* ed. Scott G. Kenney, vol. 2 (Midvale, Utah: Signature Books, 1983), 180.

14. Robert Bruce Flanders, *Nauvoo: Kingdom on the Mississippi* (Urbana: University of Illinois Press, 1965), 144–50.

15. Additional detail is available in "A Short Sketch of the Rise of the Young Gentlemen and Ladies of the Relief Society of Nauvoo," *Times and Seasons,* 1 April 1843, 154–57.

16. On the historical development of the office of bishop, see Dale F. Beecher, "The Office of Bishop," *Dialogue* 15 (winter 1982): 103–15, and William G. Hartley, "Bishop, History of the Office," in *EM,* 119–22.

17. A recent book, *Women of Covenant: A History of the Relief Society* by Janath R. Cannon, Jill Mulvay Derr, and Maureen Ursenbach Beecher (Salt Lake City: Deseret Book, 1991), documents the founding and history of this marvelous relief organization.

18. *JD* 16:8.

19. This summary analysis of the united orders of the 1870s was first made in Allen, *Second United Order,* 92–93. The most complete description of the various united orders is Arrington, Fox, and May, *Building the City of God.*

20. Arrington, *Great Basin Kingdom,* 303–4, and Allen, *Second United Order,* 132.

21. See "Questions and Answers to Rules that Should Be Observed by Members of the United Order," in Arrington, Fox, and May, *Building the City of God,* 405.

22. Arrington, Fox, and May, "Article 13," in *Building the City of God,* 390.

23. See Arrington, Fox, and May, *Building the City of God,* 265–94, and Leonard J. Arrington, *Orderville, Utah: A Pioneer Mormon Experiment in Economic Organization* (Logan, Utah: Utah State Agricultural College, 1954).

24. See Arrington, Fox, and May, *Building the City of God,* 311–35.

25. Ezra Taft Benson, *Teachings,* 66.

26. Spencer W. Kimball, "Becoming the Pure in Heart," *Ensign* 8 (May 1978): 80.

27. Romney, "Welfare Services," 127

Part 2

1. McKay, *Gospel Ideals*, 91–92, 96.

Chapter 4

1. *JD* 20:370.

2. M. I. Finley, *The Ancient Economy*, 2nd ed. (London: Hogarth Press, 1985). T. F. Carney, *The Economies of Antiquity* (Lawrence, Kans.: Coronado Press, 1973).

3. John King Fairbank and Edwin O. Reischauer, *China: Tradition and Transformation*, rev. ed. (Boston: Houghton-Mifflin, 1989), discusses Chinese technological development (77, 111, 117, 132–33, 243), its stagnation (258–67), and the naval expeditions (197–99). The expedition of 1405–7 consisted of 62 ships and 28,000 men, in contrast to Columbus's three ships and about 90 men in 1492.

4. *De officiis*, I.150–51, quoted in Finley, *The Ancient Economy*, 41–42.

5. Quoted in Finley, *The Ancient Economy*, 21–22.

6. Joseph Smith, Jr., *Teachings*, 248.

7. Barry Gordon, "Biblical and Early Judeo-Christian Thought: Genesis to Augustine," in *Pre-classical Economic Thought*, ed. S. Todd Lowry (Dordrecht: Kluwer Academic Publishers, 1987); Martin Hengel, "Property and Riches in the Old Testament and Judaism," in *Earliest Christianity* (London: SCM Press, 1986); and Nibley, "How to Get Rich," in *Approaching Zion.*

8. A good summation on this point is Richard D. Draper, "*Hubris* and *Ate:* A Latter-day Warning from the Book of Mormon," *Journal of Book of Mormon Studies* 3 (fall 1994): 12–33.

9. Neal A. Maxwell, *Of One Heart: The Glory of the City of Enoch* (Salt Lake City: Deseret Book, 1979), 20, 37–39, 49.

10. Adam Smith, *The Theory of Moral Sentiments*, ed. D. D. Raphael and A. L. Macfie (1759; reprint, Oxford: Clarendon Press, 1976), 55–56, 63. For further discussion on Adam Smith's moral economic philosophy, see Jerry Z. Muller, *Adam Smith in His Time and Ours: Designing the Decent Society* (New York: Free Press, 1993); Patricia H. Werhane, *Adam Smith and His Legacy for Modern Capitalism* (Oxford: Oxford University Press, 1991); James Q. Wilson, "Adam Smith on Business Ethics," *California Management Review* 32 (fall 1989): 59–72; and Irving Kristol, "Adam Smith and the Spirit of Capitalism," in *Reflections of a Neoconservative* (New York: Basic Books, 1983), 139–76. A more political elaboration of Smith's views is Spencer J. Pack, *Capitalism as a Moral System: Adam Smith's Critique of the Free Market Economy* (Aldershot, U.K.: Edward Elgar Publishing, 1991). The depth and importance of Smith's thought is being increasingly rediscovered. See Sylvia Nasar, "Defending the Father of Economics: Adam Smith Was No Gordon Gekko," *New York Times*, 23 January 1994, E6. From an LDS perspective, see Lindon J. Robison, "Economic Insights from the Book of Mormon," *Journal of Book of Mormon Studies* 1 (fall 1992): 35–53. Robison uses this reading of Smith as a point of departure to argue that the Book of Mormon shows that caring is the best basis for a suc-

cessful economy.

11. Adam Smith, *Lectures on Jurisprudence,* ed. R. L. Meek, D. D. Raphael, and P. G. Stein (Oxford: Clarendon Press, 1978), 192. This lecture was originally given in 1762–63.

12. Smith, *Moral Sentiments,* 25, 190. See pp. 9–76 for Smith's full exposition on the primacy of fellow feeling as the basis of morality.

13. Smith, *Moral Sentiments,* 9.

14. Smith, *Moral Sentiments,* 85.

15. Smith, *Moral Sentiments,* 86.

16. Smith, *Lectures on Jurisprudence,* 539. This lecture was originally given in 1766.

17. Smith, *Moral Sentiments,* 55, 63.

18. Smith, *Moral Sentiments,* 235.

19. Adam Smith, *An Inquiry into the Nature and Causes of the Wealth of Nations,* ed. R. H. Campbell, A. S. Skinner, and W. B. Toad (1776; reprint, Oxford: Clarendon Press, 1976), 25, 26 (I.ii.2), 456 (IV.ii.10). This version of Smith's works, prepared at the University of Glasgow, is generally regarded as the definitive edition. However, most readers are more familiar with abridged versions of the *Wealth of Nations.* In order to facilitate readers' references to their own copies, with our page references to the Glasgow edition we also include parenthetical citations to Smith's detailed book, part, chapter, and paragraph divisions.

20. Smith makes this point repeatedly in the *Wealth of Nations.* See, for example, 84–85 (I.viii.13–14), 157–58 (I.x.c.61), 266–67 (I.xi.p.10), 471–72 (IV.ii.43–44), 584 (IV.vii.b.49), 635–41 (IV.vii.c.101–8), and 647–51 (IV.viii.17–24). He used more than simple repetition to make clear his views on business influence on government:

> But the cruellest of our revenue laws (taxes), I will venture to affirm, are mild and gentle, in comparison of some of those which the clamor of our merchants and manufacturers has extorted from the legislature, for the support of their own absurd and oppressive monopolies. Like the laws of Draco, these laws may be said to be all written in blood. (648 [IV.viii.17])

He was no libertarian. Indeed, he spent the latter part of his life as the chief of customs collection for Scotland, which, in an era before income taxes, was probably the closest equivalent in his time to being Commissioner of the Internal Revenue Service. For Smith, the purpose of the economy is not only "to provide a plentiful revenue and subsistence for the people, or more properly, to enable them to provide such for themselves," but also "to supply the state or commonwealth with a revenue sufficient for the publick services" (428 [IV.Introduction]; see also 815 [V.i.i.6] on government support of public works projects which could not be funded by user fees). Nor did he oppose *per se* the idea of government regulation. One of the sovereign's duties was "protecting, as far as possible, every member of society from the injustice and oppression of every other member of it" (708 [V.i.b.1]). He supported government action in the interests of workers and consumers as well as regulation of interest rates (157–58 [I.x.c.61], 660–62 [IV.viii.47–54], and 357

[II.iv.15]). See generally, Leslie Armour, "Smith, Morality and the Bankers," *Review of Social Economy* 34 (December 1976): 359–71.

21. Werhane, *Adam Smith and His Legacy,* offers a comprehensive book-length argument "to dispel the conclusion that Adam Smith was in any sense an egoist [or] that self-interest is or should be the motivating norm of a political economy" (vii), that the arguments for the benefit of the pursuit of private interests are subject in Smith's total philosophy to "specific conditions in which economic liberty operates in the context of prudence, cooperation, a level playing field of competition, and within a well-defined framework of justice" (viii). Although the entire book is relevant, chapters 3 and 4 particularly address this issue. See also Robert Boynton Lamb, "Adam Smith's System: Sympathy, Not Self-Interest," *Journal of the History of Ideas* 35 (1974): 671–82; Peter L. Danner, "Sympathy and Exchangeable Value: Keys to Adam Smith's Social Philosophy," *Review of Social Economy* 34 (December 1976): 317–31; and Muller, *Adam Smith in His Time and Ours,* 185–205. In contrast to the modern tendency to extreme individualism characterized by expressions like "greed is good" and "do your own thing" (which ironically essentially propound the same point of view against social responsibility, although the economic libertarian and social liberal who respectively would use such expressions probably think of themselves as opposites), Muller argues that Smith's advocacy of economic freedom presupposed a society with government regulation in "moral" areas, such as encouraging family unity and prohibiting obscenity, and in which most of the people practiced prudence and self-control. Only with the exercise of personal and social self-constraint could limited government succeed. See also note 25 below.

22. Smith, *Wealth of Nations,* 612–13 (IV.vii.c.61).

23. Smith, *Wealth of Nations,* 104 (I.viii.57), and 114–15 (I.ix.24).

24. In the 1800s, Smith's work was interpreted as supporting the economic philosophy known as *laisser faire,* which held that no government intervention in economic activities was justifiable other than the enforcement of contract and prevention of crime. As a result, British governments did little to alleviate the horrible working conditions described in chapter 6, or tragedies such as the Irish potato famine of the late 1840s. For an LDS perspective on the latter, see Alexander B. Morrison, *Visions of Zion* (Salt Lake City: Deseret Book, 1993), 103–10. In light of this interpretation, many 19th-century scholars argued that there was a fundamental inconsistency between the philosophies espoused by Smith in *The Theory of Moral Sentiments* and the *Wealth of Nations.* However, in this century, closer study of the two works has shown the supposed inconsistency to be largely illusory. First, Smith himself did not seem to see any inconsistency since he continued to publish both works simultaneously until his death without addressing the issue. Second, read as a whole rather than in "sound bite" snippets, the two works follow logically, the *Wealth of Nations* being a particular "case study" in the area of economics and politics of a larger framework set out in *The Theory of Moral Sentiments.* See A. L. Macfie, "Adam Smith's *Moral Sentiments* as Foundation for his *Wealth of Nations,*" *Oxford Economic Papers* 11 (October 1959): 209–28. Third, and perhaps most important, the use of the *Wealth of Nations* to support a rigid doctrine of *laisser faire* resulted from a serious misinterpretation of the

work as an entirety. For Smith, economies are based on social cooperation, just government, and individual self-control. Competition is of ancillary utility if, and only if, the base conditions are present. Smith's idea of self-interest is not cutthroat, anything goes, look-out-only-for-yourself selfishness. It is the ability of people endowed with the moral sentiment of sympathy to realize that promoting economic exchanges which are *mutually* beneficial will serve one's own interest. Through sympathy, one can empathize with and support what the other party will also find attractive in a transaction. This promotes honesty and cooperation, not greed. See note 21 above. If you cheat a man, you only deal with him once, whereas if you deal with him fairly and profitably for both of you, you will have long-term access to what he can offer. Thus, society is dependent on whatever institutions promote the exercise of control over one's greed, profligacy, and other antisocial impulses. Among the most significant of such institutions are disestablished religions, see *Wealth of Nations,* 794–97 (V.i.g.10–16). Finally, this sense of cooperation is dependent on there being a legal framework which is recognized as supporting justice and "natural liberty" for all participants, which necessitates some degree of constant government regulation to, as the expression goes, "level the playing field." However, this "level playing field" is not the "winner takes all" system of *laisser faire.* Smithian justice opposes rules favoring the Haves and favors government actions favorable to the Have nots, the "lowest ranks of the people." See Leonard Billet, "The Just Economy: The Moral Basis of *The Wealth of Nations,*" *Review of Social Economy* 34 (December 1976): 295–315; Nathan Rosenberg, "Adam Smith and *Laisser Faire* Revisited," in *Adam Smith and Modern Political Economy,* ed. Gerald P. O'Driscoll, Jr. (Ames: Iowa State University Press, 1979), 19–34; and notes 21, 25, and 26 herein.

25. Smith, *Wealth of Nations,* 22 (I.i.10). He favored the interests of the poor and less advantaged, and advocated free markets because he thought that the poor would be better off in free markets than under the corrupt mercantilist policies promulgated by the wealthy of his day. For example, while opposed to all forms of price fixing by business, he supported labor unions as necessary to permit workers to counteract the inherently superior bargaining power of employers (83–85 [I.viii.12–13]). See Gaston V. Rimlinger, "Smith and the Merits of the Poor," *Review of Social Economy* 34 (December 1976): 333–44.

26. "The difference of natural talents in different men is, in reality, much less than we are aware of. . . . The difference between the most dissimilar characters, between a philosopher and a common street porter, for example, seems to arise not so much from nature, as from habit, custom and education." It is "vanity" that leads the philosopher "to acknowledge scarce any resemblance" (Smith, *Wealth of Nations,* 28–29 [I.ii.4]).

27. Smith, *Wealth of Nations,* 96 (I.viii.36).

28. See generally Muller, *Adam Smith in His Time and Ours,* 63–174, and Werhane, *Adam Smith and His Legacy,* 155–75.

29. See Richard B. Sher and Jeffrey R. Smitten, eds., *Scotland and America in the Age of the Enlightenment* (Edinburgh: Edinburgh University Press, 1990). In *The Wealth of Nations,* Smith argued that the American colonies should either be integrated on an equal basis with Britain by giving them representation in Parliament or peaceably allowed to go their own way (Smith, *Wealth of*

Nations, 616–17 [IV.vii.c.65–66], 944–47 [V.iii.90–92]). After the American Revolution began, he advised that military repression of the colonists would bring no good result (*The Correspondence of Adam Smith,* ed. Ernest Campbell Mosner and Ian Simpson Ross [Oxford: Clarendon Press, 1977], 380–85).

30. See discussion and notes in chapter 6 under "Social Darwinism" and Kristol, "Adam Smith and the Spirit of Capitalism," 169–76.

Chapter 5

1. *JD* 20:130.

2. Douglass C. North, *Structure and Change in Economic History* (New York: W. W. Norton, 1981).

3. *JD* 20:130–31.

4. *JD* 20:136.

5. Phyllis Deane, *The First Industrial Revolution,* 2nd ed. (Cambridge: Cambridge University Press, 1979), is a good summary of the beginnings of the Industrial Revolution in Britain. Robert L. Heilbroner, *The Making of Economic Society,* 8th ed. (Englewood Cliffs, N.J.: Prentice-Hall, 1989), summarizes the development of the world economy and the discipline of economics. Stuart Bruchey, *The Wealth of the Nation: An Economic History of the United States* (New York: Harper & Row, 1988), gives a brief economic history of the United States, including its industrialization. Nathan Rosenberg and L. E. Birdzell, Jr., *How the West Grew Rich: The Economic Transformation of the Industrial World* (New York: Basic Books, 1986), give a distinctive overall interpretation of Western industrialization and economic growth.

6. Roger Magraw, *France 1815–1914: The Bourgeois Century* (London: Fontana, 1983), 51–62.

7. See Allan Nevins, *The War for the Union: War Becomes Revolution,* vol. 2 (New York: Charles Scribner's Sons, 1960), 42, 429, 449.

8. D&C 87 has always been somewhat problematic since, while it predicts the beginning of the American Civil War in South Carolina, it also predicts that "they shall also call upon other nations, in order to defend themselves against other nations; and then war shall be poured out upon all nations" (D&C 87:3). In fact, the American Civil War did not lead to foreign alliances or directly result in war in other nations. However, this revelation can be seen as prophetic when we see the American Civil War not as a direct cause, but as the precursor of the era of industrialized world war which has followed into our times.

9. Ezra Taft Benson put it succinctly: "The nations of the earth continue in their sinful and unrighteous ways. Much of the unbounded knowledge with which men have been blessed has been used to destroy mankind instead of to bless the children of men as the Lord intended. Two great world wars, with fruitless efforts at lasting peace, are solemn evidence that peace has been taken from the earth because of the wickedness of the people. Nations cannot endure in sin. They will be broken up but the kingdom of God will endure forever" (Ezra Taft Benson, *This Nation Shall Endure* [Salt Lake City: Deseret Book, 1977], 136–37.

10. The most recent and definitive Carnegie biography is Joseph Frazier Wall, *Andrew Carnegie,* 2nd ed. (Pittsburgh: University of Pittsburgh Press,

1989). Harold C. Livesay, *Andrew Carnegie and the Rise of Big Business* (New York: Little, Brown, 1975), is also a complete biography which highlights Carnegie's influence on the development of American business.

11. Rosenberg and Birdzell, *How the West Grew Rich,* 217–20, and Alfred D. Chandler, Jr., *Scale and Scope: The Dynamics of Industrial Capitalism* (Cambridge: Harvard University Press, 1990), 129.

12. James B. Allen and Malcolm R. Thorp, "The Mission of the Twelve to England, 1840–41: The Mormon Apostles and the Working Classes," *Brigham Young University Studies* 15 (summer 1975): 499–526. James B. Allen, David Whittaker, and Ron Esplin, *Men with a Mission: The Quorum of the Twelve in the British Isles* (Salt Lake City: Deseret Book, 1991).

13. *JD* 12:288–89.

14. *JD* 10:97.

15. Leonard J. Arrington, *Great Basin Kingdom,* 112–30.

16. Thomas G. Alexander, "Wilford Woodruff, Intellectual Progress, and the Growth of an Amateur Scientific and Technological Tradition in Early Territorial Utah," *Utah Historical Quarterly* 59 (spring 1991): 164–88.

17. *JD* 17:70.

18. *JD* 18:105, 107.

19. *JD* 9:168. See also Hugh W. Nibley, "Subduing the Earth," in *Nibley on the Timely and Timeless: Classic Essays of Hugh W. Nibley* (Provo, Utah: Religious Studies Center, Brigham Young University, 1978), 85–99; Morrison, *Visions of Zion,* 77–94; and Larry L. St. Clair and Clayton C. Newberry, "Consecration, Stewardship and Accountability: Remedy for a Dying Planet," *Dialogue* 28 (summer 1995): 93–99.

20. Matthew 25:14–30, Luke 16:1–13, Luke 19:11–27 and Luke 20:9–18.

21. *JD* 17:43–44.

Chapter 6

1. *JD* 19:46–47.

2. Robert L. Heilbroner, *The Making of Economic Society,* 8th ed. (Englewood Cliffs, N.J.: Prentice-Hall, 1989), 79–80, quotes records of a parliamentary inquiry into the textile factories. Hugh Nibley quotes parliamentary records on working conditions in the mines in *Approaching Zion,* 243–45.

3. E. P. Thompson, *The Making of the English Working Class* (London: Victor Gollancz, 1963), 685.

4. Thompson, *English Working Class,* 603–710, discusses the Peterloo massacre and political repression. The gentlemen of the Manchester militia may have fancied themselves enjoying the same glory achieved by British cavalry at Wellington's victory over Napoleon four years before. Would it be ungenerous to note that the working men and women at St. Peter's Fields were not quite the military equivalent of the elite French imperial guards that faced the Scots Greys at Waterloo?

5. Smith, *Wealth of Nations,* 190 (I.xi.c.31).

6. John Brooks, *Showing off in America* (Boston: Little, Brown, 1979), 11–21.

7. At one point, Carnegie did try to go to an eight-hour shift in one of his plants, but went back to the old schedule when his competitors did not follow suit. At all points, he pointedly rejected criticism from local clergy regarding

mandatory Sunday work. Livesay, *Rise of Big Business,* 133, and Wall, *Andrew Carnegie,* 345, 519–28, 629.

8. See Louis M. Hacker, *The World of Andrew Carnegie 1865–1901* (Philadelphia: J. B. Lippincott, 1968), 373–84, and Livesay, *Rise of Big Business,* 143–44. Years later Carnegie wrote: "No pangs remain of any wound received in my business career save that of Homestead. . . . I was the controlling owner. That was sufficient to make my name a by-word for years" (Quoted in Hacker, *The World of Andrew Carnegie,* 384). Paul Krause, *The Battle for Homestead 1880–1892: Politics, Cultures and Steel* (Pittsburgh: University of Pittsburgh Press, 1992), gives the background to and a description of the Homestead strike.

9. Richard Hofstadter, *Social Darwinism in American Thought,* rev. ed. (New York: George Braziller, 1959). Darwin and Huxley did not agree with Spencer that the theory of biological evolution could be the basis for a system of morality. For a more recent interpretation, see Robert C. Bannister, *Social Darwinism: Science and Myth in Anglo-American Social Thought* (Philadelphia: Temple University Press, 1979).

10. Herbert Spencer, *Social Statics* (New York: D. Appleton, 1866), 353–54, 414, 416. Conservatives were not the only ones who shared Spencer's disdain for the poor. John Carey, the Merton Professor of English at Oxford, has argued that the modernist literary intelligentsia were also contemptuous of the common people despite their socialist humanitarian pretensions (John Carey, *The Intellectuals and the Masses: Pride and Prejudice among the Literary Intelligentsia, 1880–1939* [New York: St. Martin's Press, 1993]).

11. Quoted in Bannister, *Social Darwinism,* 53.

12. See discussion and notes in chapter 4 under "Adam Smith and the Modern Economy."

13. Andrew Carnegie, *Autobiography of Andrew Carnegie* (1920; reprint, Garden City, N.Y.: Doubleday, Doran & Company, 1933), 327. Chapter 25 is entitled "Herbert Spencer and His Disciple."

14. The dinner at Delmonico's has been recounted numerous times. See Bannister, *Social Darwinism,* 76–78, and Wall, *Andrew Carnegie,* 387–89. On Spencer's religious views, see J. D. Y. Peel, *Herbert Spencer: The Evolution of a Sociologist* (New York: Basic Books, 1971), 127–30, 211–12. Recent historians have noted that few American capitalists overtly and consciously subscribed to Spencer's harsher views. See generally Bannister, *Social Darwinism,* and Wall, *Andrew Carnegie,* 374–97. Rather, Spencerism helped foster a general social climate which countenanced practices which were oppressive to the less advantaged.

15. Thompson, *English Working Class,* 737–42, discusses the conservative influence of Methodism.

16. Arthur E. Bestor, *Backwoods Utopias: The Sectarian Origins and the Owenite Phase of Communitarian Socialism in America 1663–1829,* 2nd ed. (Philadelphia: University of Pennsylvania Press, 1970). See Owen's reception in America (94–116).

17. John Finch, *Moral Code of the New Moral World, or Rational State of Society,* corrected, revised, and approved by Robert Owen (Liverpool: James Stewart, 1840), 5–8.

18. John Finch, *The Millennium, The Religion of Jesus and the Foolery of*

Sectarianism (Birmingham: F. B. S. Flindell, 1838), 7.

19. Bestor, *Backwoods Utopias,* 160–226.

20. Rosabeth Moss Kanter, *Commitment and Community: Communes and Utopias in Sociological Perspective* (Cambridge: Harvard University Press, 1972).

21. See Alfred D. Chandler, Jr., *Scale and Scope: The Dynamics of Industrial Capitalism* (Cambridge: Harvard University Press, 1990), 257–61.

22. On the Fabians in general see Norman and Jeanne Mackenzie, *The Fabians* (New York: Simon & Schuster, 1977). A good biography of both Beatrice and Sidney is Lisanne Radice, *Beatrice and Sidney Webb: Fabian Socialists* (London: Macmillan, 1984). A recent biography of Beatrice alone is Carole Seymour-Jones, *Beatrice Webb: A Life* (Chicago: Ivan R. Dee, 1992). Beatrice completed one volume of an autobiography, *My Apprenticeship* (London: Longmans, Green, & Co., 1926), which was completed after her death in a second volume, *Our Partnership,* ed. Barbara Drake and Margaret I. Cole (London: Longmans, Green & Co., 1948). She also kept a comprehensive diary for most of her long life, which, given her widespread influence and acquaintance, is a fascinating firsthand account of both her life and times. *Diary of Beatrice Webb 1873–1943* (original in British Library of Political and Economic Science, available on microfiche from Cambridge: Chadwyck-Healey; Teaneck, N.J.: Somerset House).

23. Her father was a wealthy railroad man and president of the Grand Trunk Railway of Canada. The 15-year-old Beatrice was impressed by some aspects of early Utah:

> We went to the Tabernacle and Temple; the latter is not nearly finished. It is built of granite and will be, as far as one can see, a very handsome building. The Tabernacle is, without exception, the most remarkable building I ever saw . . . the organ, said to be the second finest in America, was completely constructed in Utah. (Webb, *My Apprenticeship,* 68–69)

The visit to Utah is described on pp. 68–71. She was less impressed by polygamous wives and a sermon by Orson Pratt. However, as shown in chapter 9, her attitude was modified by her second visit in 1898.

24. Webb, *Beatrice Webb Diary,* 1 February 1890, quoted in Webb, *My Apprenticeship,* 408.

25. Beatrice Webb (Potter), *The Cooperative Movement in Great Britain* (London: Swan Sonnenschein; New York: Charles Scribner, 1891; reprint, London School of Economics and Political Science, 1987), 148–69. A later observer has argued that if the Rochdale worker cooperatives were unsuccessful, it was because the managers of the consumer cooperatives, which had a diffuse and compliant membership, did not like the idea of yielding power to worker-run cooperatives, where the possibility of the employee cooperators exercising real power was much greater (Peter Milford, "Worker Cooperatives and Consumer Cooperatives: Can They Be Combined?" in *Labor-Owned Firms and Worker Cooperatives,* ed. Sune Jansson and Ann-Brit Hellmark [Aldershot, U.K.: Gower Publishing, 1986], 117–39). Nonetheless, by the 1970s, worker cooperatives affiliated with the Cooperative Wholesale Society were provid-

ing the consumer cooperative stores with over half a billion dollars worth of goods annually (Sir William Richardson, *The CWS in War and Peace: 1938–1976* [Manchester, U.K.: Co-operative Wholesale Society, 1977], 355).

26. Mackenzie and Mackenzie, *The Fabians,* 230.

27. See Roger Magraw, *France 1815–1914,* 197–205, for a summary. Alistair Horne, *The Terrible Year: the Paris Commune, 1871* (New York: Viking Press, 1971), gives an illustrated book-length account.

28. Edward Bellamy, *Looking Backward 2000–1887* (1888; reprint, New York: Lancer Books, 1968). The future state is described on pp. 66–69.

29. Although the Bellamy literature does not mention it, the visit is referred to in Victor F. Calverton, *Where Angels Dared to Tread* (Indianapolis: Bobbs-Merrill, 1941), 152. The visit was also described to Leonard Arrington by Lorenzo Snow's son LeRoi, who was present at the time. LeRoi Snow showed Arrington an autographed copy of *Looking Backward* from Bellamy to Lorenzo Snow (Leonard Arrington to James Lucas, 6 July 1992, copy in possession of authors). Major works on Bellamy include Sylvia E. Bowman, *Edward Bellamy,* (Boston: Twayne Publishers, 1986), and Arthur E. Morgan, *The Philosophy of Edward Bellamy* (New York: King's Crown Press, 1945). Detailed reviews of possible sources for *Looking Backward* are Sylvia Bowman's *The Year 2000: A Critical Biography of Edward Bellamy* (New York: Octagon Books, 1979), and Arthur Morgan's *Plagiarism in Utopia: A Study of the Continuity of the Utopian Tradition* (Yellow Springs, Ohio: Arthur Morgan, 1944). On Bellamy's international influence see *Edward Bellamy Abroad: An American Prophet's Influence,* ed. Sylvia E. Bowman (New York: Twayne Publishers, 1962).

30. See Lawrence Goodwyn, *Democratic Promise: The Populist Moment in America* (New York: Oxford University Press, 1976).

31. Karl Marx and Friedrich Engels, *The Communist Manifesto* (1848), in *The Marxist Reader,* ed. Emile Burns (New York: Avenel Books, 1982), 45, 59.

32. *Journal,* 16, quoted in Malcolm R. Thorp, "The Setting for the Restoration in Britain: Political, Social and Economic Conditions," in *Truth Will Prevail: The Rise of The Church of Jesus Christ of Latter-day Saints in the British Isles 1837–1987,* ed. V. Ben Bloxham, James R. Moss, and Larry C. Porter (Solihull, U.K.: The Church of Jesus Christ of Latter-day Saints, 1987), 52.

33. Thorp, *The Setting,* 48–55.

34. John Taylor, *The Government of God* (Liverpool: S. W. Richards; London: Latter-day Saint Book Depot, 1852), 12.

35. Susan L. Fales, "Artisans, Millhands and Laborers: The Mormons of Leeds and Their Nonconformist Neighbors," in *Mormons in Early Victorian Britain,* ed. Richard L. Jensen and Malcolm R. Thorp (Salt Lake City: University of Utah Press, 1989), and James B. Allen and Malcolm R. Thorp, "The Mission of the Twelve to England, 1840–41: The Mormon Apostles and the Working Classes," *Brigham Young University Studies* 15 (summer 1975): 499–526.

36. Robert Currie, Alan Gilbert, and Lee Horsley, *Churches and Churchgoers: Patterns of Church Growth in the British Isles since 1700* (Oxford: Clarendon Press, 1977), 217–19.

37. See Tim B. Heaton, "Vital Statistics," in *EM,* 1518–37, especially 1525;

Leonard Arrington and Davis Bitton, *The Mormon Experience: A History of the Latter-day Saints* (New York: Alfred A. Knopf, 1979), 127–44, and Dean L. May, "A Demographic Portrait of the Mormons, 1830–1980," in *The New Mormon History: Revisionist Essays on the Past,* ed. D. Michael Quinn (Salt Lake City: Signature Books, 1992), 124, 129–31. The story of the migration of the British Saints is told in P. A. M. Taylor, *Expectations Westward: The Mormons and the Emigration of their British Converts in the Nineteenth Century* (Edinburgh: Oliver & Boyd, 1965).

38. *Writings of Parley Parker Pratt,* ed. Parker Pratt Robinson (Salt Lake City: Deseret News Press, 1952), 184.

39. Ezra Taft Benson, "A Vision and a Hope," 74. Marion G. Romney explained that the intent of the stewardship was for the steward "to so operate his property as to produce a living for himself and his dependents" ("The Purpose of Church Welfare Services," 93).

40. Marion G. Romney, "The Role of Bishops in Welfare Services," *Ensign* 7 (November 1977): 80.

41. Joseph F. Smith, "The Message of the Latter-day Saints on Relief for the Poor," *Improvement Era* 10 (August 1907): 832. President Smith's full explanation is succinct and illuminating:

> Belief in Jesus is well and good, but it must be of a living kind which induces the believer to work out his own salvation, and to aid others to do the same. We do not believe in charity as a business; but rather we depend on mutual helpfulness. While the gospel message requires faith and repentance, it requires, also, that temporal necessities must be met. So the Lord has revealed plans for the temporal salvation of the people. For the benefit of the poor we have the fast instituted, a leading object of which, among other things, is to provide the poor with food and other necessities until they may help themselves. For it is clear that plans which contemplate only relieving present distress are deficient. The Church has always sought to place its members in a way to help themselves, rather than adopting the method of so many charitable institutions of providing for only present needs. When the help is withdrawn or used up, more must be provided from the same source, thus making paupers of the poor and teaching them the incorrect principle of relying upon others' help, instead of depending upon their own exertions. This plan has made the Latter-day Saints independent wherever they have settled. It has prevented a constant recurring of calls for help and established permanent conditions by which the people help themselves. Our idea of charity, therefore, is to relieve present wants and then to put the poor in a way to help themselves so that in turn they may help others.

This can also be found in Joseph F. Smith, *Gospel Doctrine,* 237.

42. *JD* 20:165.

43. Joseph F. Smith, "The Truth about Mormonism," 242.

44. Quotations from D&C 38:27, 49:20. See also D&C 42:39, 51:9, 56:16, 70:14, 82:17, 104:16.

45. Wilford Woodruff, *The Discourses of Wilford Woodruff,* ed. G. Homer

Durham (Salt Lake City: Bookcraft, 1969), 7. Baptized on his 19th birthday, Orson was later confirmed by Joseph Smith himself and ordained an elder the same day. Five years later he was made an apostle at age 24, the youngest in Church history. He attended the School of the Prophets, served on the Church's first high council, helped plan Zion's Camp and was a captain on the trip to Missouri. To fulfill a prophecy, in the face of death threats and mob violence perpetrated so that "Joe Smith's prophecy" would fail, Orson and others sneaked into Far West at night and met on the temple lot, praying and ordaining Wilford Woodruff and George A. Smith as new apostles. He crossed the plains and was the first Mormon to arrive in the Salt Lake Valley. Orson created the Deseret Alphabet and published the Book of Mormon in that language.

It was he who organized the Book of Mormon and Doctrine and Covenants into chapters and verses, with references and footnotes. Orson filled eleven missions to the eastern U.S. and seven other missions to Britain, including a term as mission president, and baptized thousands. He also opened Austria to the gospel. Powerful orator, renowned debater, great scientist, University of Utah professor, LDS church historian, he also served as speaker of the Utah territorial legislature for seven terms. Apostle Orson F. Whitney, the Church's literary giant, equated Pratt with the Greek philosophers and Hebrew prophets. Understanding Orson's background as a precursor to his doctrinal teachings on Zion and the united order is important to show that these are not off-the-wall remarks by an early Church leader who is speaking outside the context of core Mormon doctrine.

46. Orson Pratt, *Masterful Discourses and Writings of Orson Pratt,* comp. N. B. Lundwall (Salt Lake City: Bookcraft, 1962), 624–28.

47. Benson, "A Vision and a Hope," 74.

48. *JD* 18:353–54.

49. *JD* 19:349.

50. *JD* 19:342, 345.

51. Orson Pratt, *Masterful Discourses,* 633–34.

52. Nibley, *Approaching Zion,* 48, 53, 58.

53. Most LDS communities in Utah are located on the western flank of a chain of the Rocky Mountains known as the Wasatch Range. Generally, the more well-to-do live on the eastern side of these valleys in the foothills of the Wasatch Range, which in Salt Lake City are referred to as the "East Bench." The less well-off live to the west on the lower valley floors.

54. Kimball, "Becoming the Pure in Heart," 79–81, quotation 81. The Joseph Smith quote is from *Teachings,* 183. Even evolutionary biologists are beginning to recognize the advantages of cooperation over competition. See Martin A. Nowak, Robert M. May, and Karl Sigmund, "The Arithmetics of Mutual Help," *Scientific American,* June 1995, 76–81.

55. Sheri L. Dew, *Ezra Taft Benson: A Biography* (Salt Lake City: Deseret Book, 1987), 149. Dew describes president Benson's career in the agricultural cooperative movement (110–12, 143–78). See also Ezra Taft Benson, "Principles of Cooperation," *Improvement Era* 48 (November 1945): 653, 710–11. Speaking at the October 1945 conference, he said that "the principles of cooperation and working together were used to develop the resources of these valleys and per-

mit people to survive. We need to adopt these same principles, which have been tried and tested by the experience of the last hundred years, to preserve and conserve these resources and to raise our economic standards" (Benson, "Principles," 653).

55. See discussion in chapter 4 under "Adam Smith and the Modern Economy."

Chapter 7

1. *JD* 19:349.

2. Rosenberg and Birdzell, *How the West Grew Rich,* 189–210, and Herbert Hovenkamp, *Enterprise and American Law 1836–1937* (Cambridge: Harvard University Press, 1991), 11–64. On the development of the business corporation in the United States generally, see Richard S. Tedlow, *The Rise of the American Business Corporation* (Chur, Switzerland: Harwood Academic Publishers, 1991).

3. S. A. Mann, "Message of S. A. Mann, Acting Governor, January 11, 1870," in *Journals of the Legislative Assembly of the Territory of Utah, Nineteenth Annual Session* (Salt Lake City: Deseret News, 1870), 13–14.

4. The lack of data makes it difficult to calculate exact numbers on self-employment in the United States before the 1940s when information in this area began to be gathered on the Census (Joseph D. Phillips, "The Self-Employed in the United States," *University of Illinois Bulletin* 59 [1962, 91]: 6–10). Nonetheless, the self-employment rate has been estimated to be 80 percent in 1780 (Jackson Turner Main, *The Social Structure of Revolutionary America* [Princeton: Princeton University Press, 1965], 271–77) and approximately 37 percent in 1880 (Spurgeon Bell, *Productivity, Wages and National Income* [Washington, D.C.: Brookings Institution, 1940], 10; Phillips, "The Self-Employed," 12–13). Since the economy of 1830 more closely resembled the economy of 1780 rather than that of 1880, it seems fair to estimate that the 1830 rate would have been closer to the 1780 rate than the 1880 rate. This decline in self-employment is found in all industrial nations (Heinz Salowsky, "The Decline of Self-Employment in Industrial Countries," *Intereconomics* [1978]: 306–8). Paralleling this development is the decline in the numbers of people engaged in agriculture. Today, agricultural employment represents a small fraction of the total available employment, a shift which is of global proportions (John Shover, *First Majority, Last Minority: The Transforming of Rural Life in America* [DeKalb: Northern Illinois University Press, 1976], 3–6, 14).

5. Smith, *Wealth of Nations,* 781–82 (V.i.f.50).

6. Frederick Winslow Taylor, *The Principles of Scientific Management* (1911; reprint, New York: Norton, 1967), 137.

7. Michael Harrington, *Socialism* (New York: Saturday Review Press, 1972), is a good overview of the many different forms of socialism up to the time that may have been the height of their influence.

8. Andrew Carnegie, "The Industrial Problem," in *Miscellaneous Writings of Andrew Carnegie,* vol. 2, ed. Burton J. Hendrick (Garden City, N.Y.: Doubleday, Doran & Company, 1933), 51. Originally published in the *North American Review,* December 1911.

9. Lewis L. Gould, *Reform and Regulation: American Politics from*

Roosevelt to Wilson, 2nd ed. (New York: Alfred A. Knopf, 1986).

10. See Lothar Gall, *Bismarck: The White Revolutionary,* trans. J. A. Underwood (London: Allen & Unwin, 1986).

11. Peter Temin, *Lessons from the Great Depression* (Cambridge: MIT Press, 1989), 89–137.

12. See Radice, *Beatrice and Sidney Webb,* 291–309, and Seymour-Jones, *Beatrice Webb: A Life,* 306–23. Sidney and Beatrice Webb published their favorable views in *The Truth About Soviet Russia* (London: Longmans, Green & Co., 1942).

13. John Maynard Keynes, *The General Theory of Employment, Interest and Money* (New York: Harcourt Brace, 1936).

14. Friedrich A. Hayek's *The Road to Serfdom* (Chicago: University of Chicago Press, 1944) is his best known exposition on this subject. Brian Lee Crowley's *The Self, the Individual, and the Community: Liberalism in the Political Thought of F. A. Hayek and Sidney and Beatrice Webb* (Oxford: Clarendon Press, 1987) is an interesting analysis and comparison of the views of Hayek and the Webbs. In 1992, the *New York Times* obituary of Hayek noted that "with the collapse of Communism in Eastern Europe, his constituency has widened. Mr. Hayek's views on the economic inadequacies and political ills of central planning are now regarded as in the mainstream" (Sylvia Nasar, "Friedrich von Hayek Dies at 92; An Early Free Market Economist," *New York Times,* 24 March 1992, A15). Thomas Sowell has argued that the *Road to Serfdom* continues to have vital importance even after the fall of Communism (Thomas Sowell, "A Road to Hell Paved with Good Intentions" *Forbes,* 17 January 1994, 60–65).

15. Bruchey, *Wealth of the Nation,* 179.

16. Adolf A. Berle, Jr., and Gardiner C. Means, *The Modern Corporation and Private Property* (New York: Macmillan, 1933).

17. See Alfred D. Chandler and Richard S. Tedlow, *The Coming of Managerial Capitalism* (Homewood, Ill.: Richard D. Irwin, 1985).

18. Smith, *Wealth of Nations,* 741 (V.i.e.18). Smith's assessment may have been particularly harsh because it was based on his acquaintance with the especially corrupt affairs of the British East India Company. However, the basic issue remains pertinent.

19. Of course, much of this progress was based on technology stolen from the West. See Antony C. Sutton, *Western Technology and Soviet Economic Development,* 3 vols. (Stanford, Calif.: Hoover Institution on War, Revolution, and Peace, 1968–73), and Robert Chadwell Williams, *Klaus Fuchs, Atom Spy* (Cambridge: Harvard University Press, 1987).

20. Like any organization in which mortal and imperfect people must work together, the Church has always had leaders and some hierarchical organization. For most of its history, the Church had very few paid employees. Administrative matters were handled directly by the general priesthood leadership. Due to the Church's relatively small size and geographic concentration, this administration could generally be carried on in a direct, personal manner. Local Church units operated with a fair degree of autonomy, and issues for the central Church could easily be handled in the frequent stake conference visits by two members of the presiding quorums. Individual Church members also had ready access to the Church's top leaders, and vir-

tually anyone could drop in to chat with an apostle, and even the president of the Church, at almost any time. There was extensive informal dialogue and exchange of views and information between the Church's top leaders and local leaders and regular Church members. In addition, the geographic concentration facilitated fairly extensive intercommunication at the local level.

With the increasing size of the Church this informal system for exchanging views and information began to break down. In the 1950s and 1960s, the "correlation" program attempted to address the administration of the growing Church by adopting the then popular methods of large corporations. A large central office staff of paid administrators was created, which closely managed local matters with a constant flow of bulletins and manuals from Salt Lake City.

It is now recognized that the 1950s model of business administration, which still drew heavily on the management ideas of Frederick Taylor, was seriously deficient. While it found a large-scale method of institutional direction from the top down (all those central office bureaucrats monitoring and regulating the local offices), it failed completely to provide a large-scale institutional means of communication from the bottom up or between parallel parts of the organization. Now, the competitive global environment of the late 20th century has forced successful corporations to recognize this defect, and they are desperately trying to correct this major deficiency by devising methods for institutionalizing communication and information flow from and between the "front-line" workers.

In mentioning the management of the Church, it is important to be very clear that what we are discussing is absolutely *not* the authority of the restored priesthood, which we fully support. We understand that some may view an exclusively "top-down" management system as appropriate for the Church. The Church is, the expression goes, a theocracy, not a democracy. Certainly, the Church ultimately should be governed by the inspired decisions of the appropriate priesthood leaders. However, the view that bottom-up and sideways communication and activity are unnecessary because the top-down communication comes directly from God misunderstands the true nature of inspired decision making. At the beginnings of the Restoration, the Lord rebuffed those who "supposed that I would give it unto you, when you took no thought save it was to ask me. But behold, I say unto you, that you must study it out in your mind; then you must ask me if it be right" (D&C 9:8). Full information flow and maximum input from every possible source is necessary for decision makers to properly study a problem out in their minds. That such means should exist in the true Church is contemplated by scripture. "And all things shall be done by common consent in the church, by much prayer and faith" (D&C 26:2). This implies more than common consent as simple rote assent, but an active engagement. For John A. Widtsoe, "Latter-day Saints who sustain their leaders, are always willing to try out debatable regulations, . . . *and then report their objections, if any, to the proper Church officers. Latter-day Saints should not and do not accept Church doctrine blindly*" ("Evidences and Reconciliations: Should Church Doctrine Be Accepted Blindly?" *Improvement Era* 51 [July 1948]: 478, emphasis added).

There are indications that Church leaders are trying to encourage more active information flow in the operation of Church units. In two recent general conference addresses, Elder Russell Ballard has advocated the increased activation of the Church's council system of government. The Taylorist military/bureaucratic organizational model glorifies and focuses on the chief. The logical extension of this model is the Nazi *fuhrer* principle and other totalitarian cults of personality where the individual subliminates himself to the personality and commands of the leader. In contrast, in Mormonism, even God works through councils to reach decisions. "God called a grand council in the premortal world to present His glorious plan for our eternal welfare. The Lord's church is organized with councils at every level, beginning with the Council of the First Presidency and the Quorum of the Twelve Apostles and extending to stake, ward, quorum, auxiliary, and family councils" (M. Russell Ballard, "Strength in Counsel," *Ensign* 23 [November 1993]: 76). These councils are not mere tools to enhance the leader's control. Each council member has a voice in conciliar deliberations as a matter of scriptural command—"let one speak at a time and let all listen unto his sayings, that when all have spoken that all may be edified of all, and that every man may have an equal privilege" (D&C 88:122). Elder Ballard notes that council participation extends to "the vital input of the sisters." Although sustaining the final decision of a council leader is important, the scriptural rule, at least at the higher levels of Church government, is that "every decision made by [the presiding] quorums must be by the unanimous voice of the same; that is, every member in each quorum must be agreed to its decision" (D&C 107:27).

When Church councils operate with the full, active participation of every member, "the cooperative effort of men and women officers in the Church . . . create[s] a spiritual synergism . . . the result of which is greater than the sum of the individual parts" (Ballard, "Strength in Counsel," 77). This full "participation broadens the base of experience and understanding, leading to better solutions." Church leaders "can lift much of the load from your shoulders through this kind of involvement. People who feel ownership of a problem are more willing to help find a solution, greatly improving the possibility of success." It is through the action of Church councils that "God can take ordinary men and women and make of them extraordinary leaders. . . . the best leaders are those who follow God's plan and *counsel* with their *councils*" (M. Russell Ballard, "Counseling with Our Councils," *Ensign* 24 [May 1994]: 26). Most of Elder Ballard's examples illustrating these principles involved getting male priesthood leaders to accept active, and even critical, discussion and to acknowledge the necessity and correctness of input from sisters.

We venture here a few suggestions about other ways of improving sideways communication to assist the Saints in magnifying their spiritual and temporal stewardships. One is direct communication between regions. Wards in the poor neighborhoods of Mexico City and Manila have much in common that does not concern members in Bountiful or Beverly Hills (although it should). Stakes in New York City and London have challenges more similar to each other than to stakes in Indianapolis or Solihull (where their respective Church administrative headquarters are located). Much could be accomplished by facilitating direct communication among units with similar situations without having to go up the hierarchical ladder to Salt Lake City and back. Another form of valuable interunit communication would be among members with common Church callings. Those with the most challenging callings, such as Primary teachers and Scoutmasters, could surely not suffer from an excess of ideas for song practice or how to prepare for wilderness treks while living in the suburbs. If the Church is to follow a uniform worldwide curriculum in Sunday School, Relief Society, and priesthood, why not make it a worldwide community endeavor by facilitating networking among teachers and students on each week's topic? Teachers could provide classes not only with their own insights, but information and perspectives from Saints throughout the world. Modern telecommunications technology suggests some tantalizing possibilities. Special forums could be established on the Internet hooked into the computers at home or in Church buildings or meetinghouse libraries, or perhaps the Church's existing broadcast system could be adapted to this use. See David Gonzalez, "The Computer Age Bids Religious World to Enter," *New York Times,* 24 July 1994, 1, 38.

Yet another way to encourage direct flows of information and activity among Latter-day Saints is for members to be "anxiously engaged in a good cause, and do many things of their own free will, and bring to pass much righteousness" (D&C 58:27). Independent organizations established by Latter-day Saints can bring together resources and talents without geographic limitation. Although one would hope that such groups would exercise wisdom and prudence, they could be more innovative and range into more areas than the institutional church, which will always have to act with a certain degree of caution. Existing examples of such independent organizations include the various LDS-founded charitable organizations described in chapter 13, the Mormon History Association, FARMS, and other LDS-oriented scholarly groups, various conservative political action groups, and the Mormon independent press in all its flavors. An as yet untried possibility is returned missionary organizations organized by country, rather than by mission or mission president, that focus on continuing temporal support for the Church and its members in the country rather than simply organizing nostalgic reunions. Organizations could be based on any important common characteristic which transcended local geographic location. Possibilities include being located in inner cities or remote rural areas, expatriate and emigrant nationality groups, common economic, agricultural, or social situations, or common Church callings (LDS software programmers; LDS former tobacco or coffee growers; LDS divorced, blended, or large families; Primary teachers in multilingual wards; etc.). Such organizations could perhaps be facilitated by a bulletin board feature in Church magazines or on some telecommunications media as mentioned above.

For further discussion of these issues in the context of the principles of the united order, see chapters 18 and 20. See note 8 in chapter 18 for references on the modern recognition of the serious deficiencies of Tayloristic management. On the growth and impact of the "correlation" centralization in the Church, see Armand L. Mauss, *The Angel and the Beehive: The Mormon Struggle with Assimilation* (Urbana: University of Illinois Press, 1994), 163–67; Frank O. May, Jr., "Correlation of the Church Administration," in *EM,* 323–25; Warner P. Woodworth, "Brave New Bureaucracy," *Dialogue* 20 (fall 1987): 25–36; Hugh W. Nibley, "Leadership Versus Management," *BYU Today* 38 (February 1984):

16–19, 45–47; and Allen and Leonard, *Story of the Latter-day Saints*, 595–616.

21. The phrase apparently originally appeared in a 1945 ward teachers' message. Church president George Albert Smith quickly repudiated it, but it nonetheless remains in use among some Latter-day Saints. See "A 1945 Perspective," *Dialogue* 19 (spring 1986): 35–39.

22. *JD* 19:349.

23. Joseph Smith to Edward Partridge, 2 May 1833, quoted in Arrington, Fox, and May, *Building the City of God*, 25–26. Arrington, Fox, and May cite Orson Whitney, "The Aaronic Priesthood," *Contributor* 6 (October 1884): 7. Cook in *Joseph Smith and the Law of Consecration*, 40, says that the original is in the Church Archives.

24. Edward J. Allen, *Second United Order*, 108–9, 122.

25. J. Reuben Clark, Jr., "Private Ownership under the United Order," in *J. Reuben Clark: Selected Papers*, ed. David H. Yarn, Jr. (Provo, Utah: Brigham Young University Press, 1984), 37. Clark's original address appears in *Improvement Era* 45 (November 1942): 688–89, 752–54.

26. See D&C 42:71–73, 51:14 on the financial support of bishoprics and other officers serving in the united order. On the historical development of the office of bishop see Beecher, "The Office of Bishop," 103–15, and Hartley, "Bishop, History of the Office," 119–22.

27. Horace Greeley, "An Overland Journey: Two Hours with Brigham Young," *New York Daily Tribune*, 20 August 1859, 5–6.

28. Dean L. May, "Brigham Young and the Bishops: The United Order in the City," in *New Views of Mormon History: A Collection of Essays in Honor of Leonard J. Arrington*, ed. Davis Bitton and Maureen Ursenbach Beecher (Salt Lake City: University of Utah Press, 1987), 130–32.

29. Arrington, Fox, and May, *Building the City of God*, 407–13.

30. *JD* 18:354. See also *JD* 17:241 (George Q. Cannon); *JD* 19:346 (Lorenzo Snow); and *JD* 17:75 (Erastus Snow). Ezra Taft Benson cautioned against going out and "in every priesthood quorum and in every ward organiz[ing] cooperative business organizations. A warning has been given, and wisely so, that cooperative enterprises, business cooperatives, require efficient business management and direction" (Ezra Taft Benson, "Principles of Cooperation," 653).

31. *JD* 17:157–58.

32. *JD* 17:33–34.

33. Leonard J. Arrington, *Great Basin Kingdom*, 329.

34. Allen, *Second United Order*, 108. See also Arrington, Fox, and May, *Building the City of God*, 150–53, 394–98; *JD* 17:75, 79 (Erastus Snow); and *JD* 17:178–79 (John Taylor).

35. *JD* 17:178–79.

36. Arrington, Fox, and May, *Building the City of God*, 334–38.

37. John A. Widtsoe, *Joseph Smith: Seeker after Truth, Prophet of God* (Salt Lake City: Bookcraft, 1957), 193.

38. Widtsoe, "Evidence and Reconciliations: Are Communism and Its Related 'Isms' Preparatory to the United Order?" 633.

39. The literature on employee ownership is quite extensive. Raymond Russell, *Sharing Ownership in the Workplace* (Albany: State University of New

York Press, 1985), and *Understanding Employee Ownership,* ed. Corey Rosen and Karen M. Young (Ithaca, N.Y.: ILR Press, 1991), gives good general overviews. Joseph R. Blasi and Douglas Kruse, *The New Owners: The Mass Emergence of Employee Ownership in Public Companies and What It Means to American Business* (New York: HarperBusiness, 1991), discuss the spread of employee ownership in large public corporations. See also issues of the *Employee Ownership Report* published by the National Center for Employee Ownership. Information on employee ownership in the named companies comes from Blasi and Kruse, *The New Owners,* 11, 58, 229, and 252–92, and the May/June and July/August 1995 issues of the Employee Ownership Report.

40. Sam Walton with John Huey, *Made in America: My Story* (New York: Doubleday, 1992), 132, 248.

41. See National Center for Employee Ownership, *Privatization and Employee Ownership: The International Experience* (Oakland, Calif.: National Center for Employee Ownership, 1992), and the fall 1995 issue of *The Journal of Employee Ownership Law and Finance.* The latter is a special issue on "Privatization through Employee Ownership" which also covers first and Third World nations.

42. Carnegie is referring to the modern corporation.

43. Andrew Carnegie, "The Final Relation Between Capital and Labor" in *Problems of To-day: Wealth, Labor, Socialism* (1908; reprint, Garden City, N.Y.: Doubleday, Doran & Company, 1933), 54. Leland Stanford in *Employee Ownership Report* (November/December 1990): 6, quoting from *Worker Coop* (summer 1990). Stanford intended for Stanford University to become a center for the propagation of worker cooperatives but died before he could institutionalize this at the school.

Chapter 8

1. *JD* 18:105, 107.

2. Deane, *The First Industrial Revolution,* 165–202, discusses the role of British finance and banking in the First Industrial Revolution. John A. James, *Money and Capital Markets in Postbellum America* (Princeton, N.J.: Princeton University Press, 1978), describes the rise of banking and capital markets in the United States. Walter Werner and Steven T. Smith, *Wall Street* (New York: Columbia University Press, 1991), covers the early development of the stock markets. John C. Carrington and George T. Edwards, *Financing Industrial Investment* (London: Macmillan, 1979), reviews how savings are transferred to investment in the major industrial nations today. Figures on bank deposits are from James, *Money and Capital Markets,* 22.

3. Ron Chernow, *The House of Morgan: An American Banking Dynasty and the Rise of Modern Finance* (New York: Atlantic Monthly Press, 1990), describes the development of finance capitalism and the role of the Morgan banks therein through the present day.

4. The story of the creation of United States Steel has been told many times. See, for example, Wall, *Andrew Carnegie,* 765–93. Figures are from Louis M. Hacker, *The World of Andrew Carnegie 1865–1901* (Philadelphia: J. B. Lippincott, 1968), 378, 434.

5. Boris I. Bittker, *Federal Taxation of Income, Estates and Gifts* (Boston:

Warren, Gorham & Lamont, 1981), 1.7–9.

6. Marvin Hill, Keith Rooker, and Larry Wimmer, "The Kirtland Economy Revisited: A Market Critique of Sectarian Economics," *Brigham Young University Studies* 17 (summer 1977): 391–475.

7. *JD* 17:77–78.

8. See Arrington, *Great Basin Kingdom,* 316–17.

9. *JD* 20:370–71.

10. *JD* 17:74–75, 78.

11. How a united order principles inspired financial institution might be set up and function is discussed further in chapter 20. See also the description of the Caja Laboral Popular in chapter 19.

12. Michael Selz and Udayan Gupta, "Lending Woes Stunt Growth of Small Firms," *Wall Street Journal,* 16 November 1994, B1, B2. Traditional venture capital firms are only a partial solution to this problem. They require that businesses have the potential for spectacular growth, and usually focus on trendy, high profile industries. There is simply no institutional source of long-term funding in our economy for solid, job-producing businesses with reasonable, but not widely speculative, growth prospects.

13. See, for example, Binstein and Bowden, *Trust Me;* Zey, *Banking on Fraud;* Seidman, *Full Faith and Credit.* The urge to engage in risky speculations instead of productive, if dull, investment services seems to continue in the financial sector, as illustrated by the spectacular collapse of Britain's Barings Bank following the losses from the activities of one trader based in Singapore. See Po Bronson "The Young and the Reckless," *New York Times,* 3 March 1995, A27, and Richard W. Stevenson, "Barings Knew of Big Gamble, Officials Assert," *New York Times,* 5 March 1995, A1, A8.

Chapter 9

1. McKay, *Gospel Ideals,* 268.

2. Karl Marx, *Kapital: A Critique of Political Economy,* trans. Ben Fowkes and D. Fernbach (New York: Vintage Books, 1977–81).

3. Marion G. Romney, "Socialism and the United Order Compared," in *Look to God and Live,* ed. George J. Romney (Salt Lake City: Deseret Book, 1971), 221.

4. Some have argued that Communism never really collapsed. See Anatoliy Golitsyn, *New Lies for Old: The Communist Strategy of Deception and Disinformation* (New York: Dodd, Mead & Company, 1984). As of this writing, "former" Communists have come to power in many East European nations and the Communist Party is in resurgence in Russia.

5. Ezra Taft Benson, *God, Family, Country: Our Three Great Loyalties* (Salt Lake City: Deseret Book, 1974), 404.

6. Bohlen, "Graft and Gangsterism in Russia," A1, A12; Steven Erlanger, "Russia's New Dictatorship of Crime," *New York Times,* 15 May 1994, E3; and Jane Perlez, "Welcome Back, Lenin," *New York Times,* 31 May 1994, A1, A9.

7. Smith, *Wealth of Nations,* 267 (I.xi.p.10).

8. Stephen Manes and Paul Andrews, *Gates: How Microsoft's Mogul Reinvented an Industry and Made Himself the Richest Man in America* (New York:

Doubleday, 1993), 448. This gives an example of the ruthless sentiments for which Gates is known. However, Microsoft's social darwinist ethos is demonstrated by more than the profanity of its founder. It is notorious for its unethical, and allegedly illegal, competitive practices and for a profoundly anti-family work environment. See Manes and Andrews, *Gates,* 200, 212–13, 226–27, 298–99, 349–51, 355, 390, 404–5, 419–21, 450–54; James Gleick, "Making Microsoft Safe for Capitalism," *New York Times Magazine,* 5 November 1995, 50–57, 64; and Kenneth C. Baseman, Frederick R. Warren-Boulton, and Glenn A. Woroch, "Microsoft Plays Hardball: The Use of Exclusionary Pricing and Technical Incompatibility to Maintain Monopoly Power in Markets for Operating System Software," *Antitrust Bulletin* 40 (summer 1995): 265–315.

9. *HC* 6:33. Also, see Joseph Smith, Jr., *An American Prophet's Record: The Diaries and Journals of Joseph Smith,* ed. Scott H. Faulring (Salt Lake City: Signature Books, 1989), 413–14, which gives the exact language appearing in Willard Richards's journal. The *History of the Church* tends to clean up grammar, phrasing, and punctuation.

10. *HC* 6:37–38. Smith, *American Prophet's Record,* 415.

11. Smith, *American Prophet's Record,* 413. For further information about Finch, see R. B. Rose, "John Finch, 1784–1857, A Liverpool Disciple of Robert Owen," *Transactions of the Historic Society of Lancashire and Cheshire* 109 (1957): 159–84. The visit to Nauvoo is mentioned on p. 179.

12. Woodruff, *Journal,* 2:179. See also *HC* 6:35.

13. Woodruff, *Journal,* 2:180.

14. Joseph Smith, Jr., *Teachings,* 248–49.

15. *HC* 6:33, 37–38.

16. *JD* 18:354.

17. John Taylor, *The Government of God* (Liverpool: S. W. Richards; London: Latter-day Saint Book Depot, 1852), 21, 22, 23.

18. *JD* 19:349. Speaking in 1878, he probably had in mind the Paris Commune of 1871.

19. *JD* 20:34. Wilford Woodruff was an active entrepreneur as well, always looking to exploit the latest scientific and technological advances.

20. *JD* 17:361–62.

21. Ivan Boesky, convicted inside trader from the glory days of the 1980s takeover boom, encapsulated capitalism in its crudest form when he told college students that "greed is good." A literary manifestation of this can be found in Ayn Rand novels, such as *Fountainhead* and *Atlas Shrugged,* which glorify the individual's personal fulfillment at the expense of all other responsibilities. Rand's books continue to be popular items in Utah bookstores. Many Latter-day Saints have been attracted by her anti-Communism and defense of individual freedom. However, while one may sympathize with some of her conclusions, the philosophy through which she reaches them contradicts fundamental Christian ethics. In *Atlas Shrugged,* Rand's hero, John Galt, states, "Do you ask what moral obligation I owe to my fellow men?—None . . . I deal with men . . . only for my own self-interest" (Ayn Rand, *Atlas Shrugged* [1957; reprint, New York: Penguin Books, 1992], 1022). In *The Virtue of Selfishness,* she illustrates her ethics by arguing that it is immoral to save a drowning stranger

unless the risk to one's own life is minimal. Even that limited "principle that one should help men in an emergency cannot be extended to regard all human suffering as an emergency . . . [a man] does not subordinate his life to the welfare of others . . . the relief of their suffering is not his primary concern, that any help he gives is an *exception*, not a rule, an act of generosity, not of moral duty, that it is *marginal* and *incidental*" (Ayn Rand, *The Virtue of Selfishness* [New York: New American Library, 1964], 45, 48, 49). Randian philosophy is also profoundly anti-religious. In fact, much of her ethical philosophy can be seen as an extended tirade against Christ's teaching that "whosoever will come after me, let him deny himself, and take up his cross, and follow me. For whosoever will save his life shall lose it; but whosoever shall lose his life for my sake and the gospel's, the same shall save it. For what shall it profit a man, if he shall gain the whole world, and lose his own soul?" (Mark 8:34–36). William F. Buckley summarized the Christian conservative view of Rand at the time of her death. "She was an eloquent and persuasive anti-statist, and if only she had left it at that—but no, she had to declare that God did not exist, that altruism was despicable, that only self-interest is good and noble. She risked, in fact, giving to capitalism that bad name that its enemies have done so well in giving it" (William F. Buckley, Jr., "Ayn Rand, RIP," *National Review*, 2 April 1982, 381). Even responsible and respected capitalist scholars such as Milton Friedman deny that companies have any social or moral responsibility other than to make as much profit as possible. See the discussion in chapter 16 under "Stewardship in Modern Business."

22. Edward J. Allen, "Appendix A: Apostolic Circular of July, 1875," in *The Second United Order*, 129–30.

23. Brigham Young to Willard Young, 19 October 1876, quoted in Brigham Young, *Letters of Brigham Young to His Sons*, ed. Dean C. Jessee (Salt Lake City: Deseret Book, 1974), 199.

24. This transition is described in depth in Thomas G. Alexander, *Mormonism in Transition: A History of the Latter-day Saints 1890–1930* (Chicago: University of Illinois Press, 1986). On the economic aspects of this transition, see also Leonard J. Arrington, "The Commercialization of Utah's Economy: Trends and Developments from Statehood to 1910," in *A Dependent Commonwealth: Utah's Economy from Statehood to the Great Depression*, ed. Dean L. May (Provo, Utah: Brigham Young University Press, 1974).

25. See Alexander, *Mormonism in Transition*, 74–92.

26. See Leonard J. Arrington, *Beet Sugar in the West: A History of the Utah-Idaho Sugar Company 1891–1966* (Seattle: University of Washington Press, 1966).

27. Woodruff, *Journal*, 9:136.

28. See Snow in *Latter-day Prophets Speak*, 335; Joseph F. Smith in *Gospel Doctrine*, 225; and James E. Talmage, *Articles of Faith*, 437–39.

29. Beatrice Potter Webb, *Beatrice Webb's American Diary, 1898*, ed. David A. Shannon (Madison: University of Wisconsin Press, 1963), 135. For further information on Martha Hughes Cannon, see Jean Bickmore White, "Dr. Martha Hughes Cannon: Doctor, Wife, Legislator, Exile," in *Sister Saints*, ed. Vicky Burgess-Olson (Provo, Utah: Brigham Young University Press, 1978).

30. Webb, *American Diary*, 129.

31. Webb, *American Diary,* 135–36.

32. Thomas G. Alexander, "The Economic Consequences of the War: Utah and the Depression of the Early 1920s," in *A Dependent Commonwealth: Utah's Economy from Statehood to the Great Depression,* ed. Dean L. May (Provo, Utah: Brigham Young University Press, 1974).

33. John F. Bluth and Wayne K. Hinton, "The Great Depression," in *Utah's History,* ed. Richard D. Poll (Provo, Utah: Brigham Young University Press, 1978), and Wayne K. Hinton, "The Economics of Ambivalence: Utah's Depression Experience," *Utah Historical Quarterly* 54 (summer 1986): 268–85.

34. Garth L. Mangum and Bruce D. Blumell, *The Mormons' War on Poverty* (Salt Lake City: University of Utah Press, 1993), 93–156, give a detailed account of the origins of the modern Church Welfare Program. Also see Glen L. Rudd, *Pure Religion: The Story of Church Welfare Since 1930* (Salt Lake City: The Church of Jesus Christ of Latter-day Saints, 1995).

35. Heber J. Grant, "Message of the First Presidency to the Church," *Conference Report* (October 1936): 3.

36. Grant, *Conference Report,* 6.

37. Alfred W. Uhrban, "Welfare in the Church," *Improvement Era* 59 (November 1956): 810.

38. "Annual Church Report," *Improvement Era* 44 (May 1941): 317. It is little known in the Church today that through the mid-1950s the Church released detailed annual financial statements.

39. Harold B. Lee, "Unity for the Welfare of the Church and Nation," *Improvement Era* 45 (May 1942): 297.

40. J. Reuben Clark, Jr., "Private Ownership," 35. On socialism in Utah see John R. Sillito and John S. McCormick, "Socialist Saints: Mormons and the Socialist Party in Utah, 1900–1920," *Dialogue* 18 (spring 1985): 121–31.

41. Calverton, *Where Angels Dared to Tread,* 147, 167.

42. Frank W. Fox, *J. Reuben Clark: The Public Years* (Provo, Utah: Brigham Young University Press; Salt Lake City: Deseret Book, 1980).

43. Clark, "Private Ownership," 39.

44. D. Michael Quinn, *J. Reuben Clark: The Church Years* (Provo, Utah: Brigham Young University Press, 1983), 190.

45. J. Reuben Clark, Jr., "Demand for Proper Respect of Human Life," *Improvement Era* 49 (November 1946): 688–89, 740. "Letter of the First Presidency Concerning Military Training," *Improvement Era* 49 (February 1946): 76–77.

46. Quoted in Quinn, *J. Reuben Clark: The Church Years,* 254.

47. Clark, "Private Ownership," 36.

48. Feramorz Fox, "United Order: Discrimination in the Use of Terms," *Improvement Era* 47 (July 1944): 461.

49. William R. Palmer, "United Orders in Utah," *Improvement Era* 46 (January 1943): 24.

50. Cook, *Joseph Smith and the Law of Consecration,* and Huff, *Joseph Smith's United Order,* 42. Cook and Huff's conclusions are symptomatic of Latter-day Saints who, in their zeal to show that the united order is not socialistic, misunderstand the history of the united order. In arguing about what the united order is not, they overreact by denying the united order entirely. This leads

them to ignore the vast body of positive teachings about the united order regarding fundamental issues of wealth, poverty, and the modern economy. That the united order is not socialistic seems a point hardly worth discussing in light of the numerous clear statements of 19th-century Church leaders summarized in this and other chapters. See also chapter 3, note 11.

51. *JD* 21:54. Like his modern successors such as Spencer W. Kimball and Ezra Taft Benson, Brigham saw the united order as an eternal celestial law:

> We have a great work before us; and that portion of it we are now trying to inaugurate is not new. The doctrine of uniting together in our temporal labors, and all working for the good of all is from the beginning, from everlasting, and it will be for ever and ever. No one supposes for one moment that in heaven angels are speculating, that they are building railroads and factories, taking advantage one of another, gathering up the substance there is in heaven to aggrandize themselves, and that they live on the same principle that we are in the habit of doing. No Christian, no sectarian Christian in the world believes this; they believe that the inhabitants of heaven live as a family, that their faith, interests and pursuits have one end in view—the glory of God and their own salvation, that they may receive more and more,—go on from perfection to perfection, receiving, and then dispensing to others; they are ready to go, and ready to come, and willing to do whatever is required of them and to work for the interest of the whole community, and for the good of all. . . . We will try to imitate in some small degree, the family that lives in heaven, and prepare ourselves for the society that will dwell upon the earth when it is purified and glorified and comes into the presence of the Father. (*JD* 17:117–18)

Chapters 3, 10, 14, 15 and 21 discuss similar views held by presidents Kimball and Benson.

52. Clark, "Private Ownership," 35.

53. These estimated dollar amounts are calculated by John Heinerman and Anson Shupe in *The Mormon Corporate Empire* (Boston: Beacon Press, 1985), especially chapter 3.

54. See a series of articles originally appearing in the *Arizona Republic*, then reprinted as "LDS Financial Empire Puts Church at Fortune 500 Level," *Salt Lake Tribune*, 30 June 1991, A1–5; 1 July, A1–5; 2 July, A1–5.

55. "LDS Church Officials Dispute Finance Report," *Provo (Utah) Daily Herald*, 30 June 1991, A1, A2.

56. On the issue of Mormonism and business, see "Business-like Saints," *Economist*, 20 January 1963, 228; Ronald J. Ostrow, "Mormon Merchants," *Wall Street Journal*, 20 December 1956, A1, A8; Jeffrey Kay, "An Invisible Empire: Mormon Money in California," *New West*, 8 May 1978, 36–41; Robert Gottlieb and Peter Wiley, *America's Saints: The Rise of Mormon Power* (New York: G. P. Puttman's Sons, 1984), especially chapter 4; and Heinerman and Shupe, *The Mormon Corporate Empire.*

57. Steven Wood, "City Wards and Branches in the LDS Church," (paper presented at 1993 Washington Sunstone Symposium, Washington, D.C., 13

March 1993).

58. See, for example, Jessie L. Embry, "Ethnic Groups and the LDS Church" and "Speaking for Themselves: LDS Ethnic Groups Oral History Project," *Dialogue* 25 (winter 1992): 81–110.

59. See Cardell K. Jacobson, et al., "Black Mormon Converts in the United States and Africa: Social Characteristics and Perceived Acceptance," in *Contemporary Mormonism*, 326–47.

60. Tullis, "Church Development Issues," 99. For example, President Ruben Torres Cruz of the Mexico City Mexico Moctezuma Stake estimated that about 60 percent of the stake members earn their livelihoods as street vendors or through micro-enterprises (quoted in John L. Hart, "Gospel's Influence Spreads from Temple," *Church News*, 24 June 1995, 8–10).

61. Leonard J. Arrington and Wayne K. Hinton, "Origin of the Welfare Plan of The Church of Jesus Christ of Latter-day Saints," *Brigham Young University Studies* 5 (winter 1964): 67–85. Although they complained about government spending, Utahns had among the highest rates of participation in government relief programs in the United States. See Hinton, *The Economics of Ambivalence.*

62. McKay, *Gospel Ideals*, 334.

63. Joseph Smith, Jr., *Teachings*, 366. See also Joseph Smith, Jr., *Words of Joseph Smith*, 367.

Part 3

1. *JD* 15:169.

Chapter 10

1. Ezra Taft Benson, "A Vision and a Hope," 74–75.

2. Arrington, Fox, and May, *Building the City of God*, 170, 317; *JD* 20:43–45 (John Taylor).

3. *JD* 19:349.

4. See generally Marion G. Romney, "The Celestial Nature of Self-Reliance," *Ensign* 12 (November 1982): 91–93.

5. Grant, "Message of the First Presidency," 3.

6. Hugh Nibley, "Work We Must, but the Lunch Is Free," in *Approaching Zion*, 241.

7. See also D&C 42:39, 49:20, 51:9, 56:16, 78:6, 82:17, 104:16.

8. Quoted in Nibley, *Approaching Zion*, 440.

9. Benson, "A Vision and a Hope," 75.

10. Joseph Smith, Jr., *Words of Joseph Smith*, 244. See also Joseph Smith, Jr., *Teachings*, 322.

11. Neal A. Maxwell, "Settle This in Your Hearts," *Ensign* 22 (November 1992): 65–67.

12. See Lindon J. Robison, *Becoming a Zion People* (Salt Lake City: Hawkes Publishing, 1992).

13. Benson, "A Vision and a Hope," 74.

14. See also D&C 72:16, 104:11–13.

15. *JD* 19:308. George Q. Cannon, counselor to four presidents of the Church, said that "the time must come when the talent of men of business shall be used for the benefit of the whole people . . . not for individual benefit

alone, not for individual aggrandizement alone, but for the benefit of the whole people, to uplift the masses, to rescue them from their poverty. That is one of the objects in establishing Zion, and anything short of that . . . is not Zion" (*JD* 23:281–82). See Part Four for a fuller discussion of this point.

16. Benson, "A Vision and a Hope," 74. See also D&C 70:7.

17. See also D&C 82:19.

18. *JD* 20:45.

19. Joseph Fielding Smith, Jr., *Answers to Gospel Questions,* vol. 4 (Salt Lake City: Deseret Book, 1963), 211.

20. Quoted in Arrington, Fox, and May, *Building the City of God*, 204.

21. *JD* 17:35–36.

22. Benson, "A Vision and a Hope," 74.

23. Gustive O. Larson, *The "Americanization" of Utah for Statehood* (San Marino, Calif.: Huntington Library, 1971), gives a thorough account of the Church's struggles at this time. Ray Jay Davis, "Antipolygamy Legislation," in *EM*, 52–53, gives a good short summary.

24. John Stuart Mill, *On Liberty* (1859; reprint, Indianapolis, Ind.: Bobbs-Merrill, 1956), 111–13.

25. See Leonard J. Arrington and Jon Haupt, "Intolerable Zion: The Image of Mormonism in Nineteenth Century American Literature," *Western Humanities Review* 22 (1968): 243–60, and Gary L. Bunker and Davis Bitton, *The Mormon Graphic Image, 1834–1914: Cartoons, Caricatures, and Illustrations* (Salt Lake City: University of Utah Press, 1983).

26. Arthur Conan Doyle, *A Study in Scarlet* (1887; reprint, London: John Murray and Jonathan Cape, 1974). Part II (83–128) purports to factually describe Utah at the time. It is an outrageous collection of falsehoods and blatant fiction. Conan Doyle scholars have been embarrassed by this mark on the introductory volume of the great detective series. Much later, in 1922, Conan Doyle visited Utah and changed his views on Mormonism. He thereafter criticized the anti-Mormon attitude of the British press. See Jack Tracy, *Conan Doyle and the Latter-Day Saints* (Bloomington, Ind.: Gaslight Publications, 1979).

27. In fact, sometimes at great personal sacrifice, most LDS women supported the practice of plural marriage, and held several great rallies to protest the government's persecution of the Saints for it. See, for example, "'Mormon' Women's Protest: An Appeal for Freedom, Justice and Equal Rights," (Full account of proceedings at the Great Mass Meeting, Salt Lake City, 6 March 1886). For accurate contemporaneous accounts, see Jessie L. Embry, *Mormon Polygamous Families: Life in the Principle* (Salt Lake City: University of Utah Press, 1987).

28. See Larson, *"Americanization" of Utah*, 243, 271–81, 300–303.

29. Richard D. Lamm and Michael McCarthy, *The Angry West: A Vulnerable Land and Its Future* (Boston: Houghton-Mifflin, 1982), 5–18, 55–56. Lamm (a former governor of Colorado) and McCarthy argue that this pattern continues to dominate the West today. See, for example, Timothy Egan, "Montana's Sky and Its Hopes Are Left Bare after Logging," *New York Times,* 19 October 1993, A1, A26, which describes the consequences to Montana after a large outside corporation logged far beyond sustainable yield on millions of acres and then sold the land to other outsiders, abandoning the area to both

economic and ecological devastation.

30. See Ronald W. Walker, "Brigham Young on the Social Order," *Brigham Young University Studies* 28 (summer 1988): 37–52.

31. Quoted in Edward J. Allen, *Second United Order,* 103.

32. *JD* 3:51, 13:216.

33. Quoted in Leonard J. Arrington, *Brigham Young: American Moses* (New York: Alfred A. Knopf, 1985), 399.

34. Allen and Leonard, *Story of the Latter-day Saints,* 370–75.

35. Quoted in Allen, *Second United Order,* 114, and Arrington, Fox, and May, *Building the City of God,* 334.

36. Arrington, Fox, and May, *Building the City of God,* 88–105. Hamilton Gardner also documented the failure to achieve fully cooperative operations in most retail and industrial enterprises while noting that they seem to have been administered to cooperative ends (Hamilton Gardner, "Cooperation among the Mormons," *Quarterly Journal of Economics* 31 [1917]: 461–99).

37. *JD* 17:157.

38. Allen, *Second United Order,* 105–6.

39. Livesay, *Rise of Big Business,* 155.

40. John F. Stover, *American Railroads* (Chicago: University of Chicago Press, 1961), 104–42, 290–91.

41. *JD* 17:179.

42. Clark, "Private Ownership," 40.

43. Romney, "Welfare Services," 127.

44. At the time that the Welfare program was first set up the issue of whether it was the reestablishment of the united order was raised and specifically answered in the negative, although the hope was expressed that the Welfare program would move the Saints in the direction of eventually being better able to live the united order. See Harold B. Lee, *Stand Ye in Holy Places* (Salt Lake City: Deseret Book, 1974), 280–81 (quoting apostle Melvin J. Ballard, who was in charge of founding the Welfare program).

45. Dallin H. Oaks, *The Lord's Way* (Salt Lake City: Deseret Book, 1991), 114–15, and Mangum and Blumell, *Mormons' War on Poverty,* 165, 206–8.

46. Mangum and Blumell, *Mormons' War on Poverty,* 161–65, 187, 203–8.

47. Tullis, *Mormons in Mexico,* 178–79, 191–95, 207–10.

48. Charlene Renberg Winters, "Project Manila Helps Third World Entrepreneurs," *BYU Today* (September 1992): 14.

49. See, for example, Mark L. Grover, "Relief Society and Church Welfare: The Brazilian Experience," *Dialogue* 27 (winter 1994): 29–38.

50. *JD* 10:51, 56–57.

Chapter 11

1. Hugh W. Nibley, "How Firm a Foundation! What Makes It So," in *Approaching Zion,* 172–73.

2. *JD* 17:76.

3. Joseph Smith, Jr., *Teachings,* 316.

4. Spencer W. Kimball, "Welfare Services: The Gospel in Action," *Ensign* 7 (November 1977): 77.

5. The Church of Jesus Christ of Latter-day Saints, *Providing in the Lord's*

Way, (Salt Lake City: The Church of Jesus Christ of Latter-day Saints, 1990).

6. *JD* 17:45. Adam Smith advocated similar views about the value of education and the community's responsibility to provide it (Smith, *Wealth of Nations*, 781–88, 796 (V.i.f.48–61, V.i.g.13–14). A study by the Census Bureau has found that increases in workers' education levels produce twice the gain in workplace efficiency as comparable increases in the value of tools and machinery (Peter Applebome, "Study Ties Educational Gains to More Productivity Growth," *New York Times*, 14 May 1995, A22). Part of this obligation rests with the youth, who have a responsibility to study and make use of their educational opportunities. This is a very current challenge in light of the decline in homework and standards in American schools. See Gabriella Stern, "Kid's Homework May Be Going the Way of the Dinosaur," *Wall Street Journal*, 11 October 1993,B1, B8.

7. *JD* 17:366–67.

8. Spencer W. Kimball, "Welfare Services Meeting Address," 7 April 1974, *Conference Report* (Salt Lake City: The Church of Jesus Christ of Latter-day Saints, 1974), 184. See also Kimball, "Becoming the Pure in Heart," 80.

9. "Couples Enter Vietnam to Teach English," *Church News*, 30 January 1993, 3.

10. Morrison, *The Dawning of a Brighter Day*, 45.

11. Glenn L. Pace, "Infinite Needs and Finite Resources," *Ensign* 23 (June 1993): 55.

12. Kimball, "Becoming the Pure in Heart," 79–81.

13. For more detail see "In True Fashion," *Ensign* 21 (September 1991): 66–67; Thierry Crucy, "Cecile Pelous: Love and Friendship in India," *Tambuli* (March 1992): 8–15; and Carri P. Jenkins, "Cecile Pelous: Rubbing away the Hurt," *BYU Today* (July 1992): 23–28.

14. Jon Ure, "Sons of Industrialist Aid Armenians," *Salt Lake Tribune*, 11 April 1993, B1, B2, and "Assistance Proffered in Armenia," *Church News*, 1 April 1995, 11.

15. George Esper, "LDS Medical Volunteer Recounts Somalia's Horrors," *Provo (Utah) Daily Herald*, 28 March 1993: A9, A10.

16. An excellent article on such ward and family service is Kathleen Lubeck Peterson, "The Ward Family: Pulling Together," *Ensign* 25 (July 1995) 22–26. Joint service projects can build significant family unity. See Clare Collins, "Families That Do Good Together Enjoy It," *New York Times*, 6 June 1991, C10. Robison, *Becoming a Zion People*, gives many good ideas on how to develop a spirit of cooperation in families.

17. See Pace, "Infinite Needs," 50–55.

Chapter 12

1. McKay, *Gospel Ideas*, 96, 104.

2. Joseph Smith, Jr., *Teachings*, 183.

3. More information on alternative currencies can be obtained by contacting Time Dollars, P. O. Box 19405, Washington, D.C. 20036, or ordering the founder's 1992 book, *Time Dollars*, by Edgar Chan.

4. *JD* 19:183.

5. Diane L. Barthel, *Amana: From Pietist Sect to American Community*

(Lincoln: University of Nebraska Press, 1984).

6. See, for instance, Robbey Edward Whitson's *The Shakers: Two Centuries of Spiritual Reflection* (New York: Paulist Press, 1983).

7. Further details are in Maren Lockwood's "The Oneida Community: A Study in Organizational Change" (Ph.D. diss., Harvard University, 1962).

8. Research on the Hutterian Brethren is considerable. The most thorough book is John W. Bennett's *Hutterian Brethren: The Agricultural Economy and Social Organization of a Communal People* (Stanford, Calif.: Stanford University Press, 1967). Other in-depth studies are John Hofer's *The History of the Hutterites* (Elie, Manitoba: James Valley Book Centre, 1982) and John A. Hostetler's *Hutterite Society* (Baltimore: Johns Hopkins University Press, 1974).

9. Quoted in Alice Felt Tyler's *Freedom's Ferment* (New York: Harper and Brothers, 1962), 166.

10. See, for example, Leonardo Boff, *Faith on the Edge: Religion and Marginalized Existence* (San Francisco: Harper and Row, 1989); Leonardo and Clodovis Boff, *Liberation Theology: From Confrontation to Dialogue* (San Francisco: Harper & Row, 1986); and Gustavo Gutierrez, *A Theology of Liberation* (Maryknoll, N.Y.: Orbis, 1973). A good scholarly overview is Arthur F. McGovern, *Liberation Theology and Its Critics: Toward an Assessment* (Maryknoll, N.Y.: Orbis Books, 1989).

11. These brief summaries are taken from Albert O. Hirschman's *Getting Ahead Collectively: Grassroots Experiences in Latin America* (New York: Pergamon, 1984).

12. Cited in Sylvester Monroe, "The Gospel of Equity," *Time*, 10 May 1993, 54–55.

13. Kenneth H. Bacon, "Inner City Capitalists Push to Start a Bank for Their Community," *Wall Street Journal*, 19 January 1993, A1, A6. Regular commercial banks are required by the Community Reinvestment Act to make loans to poor and minority people and areas. However, the banks are unable to adjust their approach to accommodate the circumstances of smaller and start-up businesses. For example, they still focus on traditional hard collateral such as real estate instead of such personal factors as credit history and cash flow which are more applicable in a small or new business. See Saul Hansell, "Banks Learning to Make Loans to Help Poor Areas," *New York Times*, 9 January 1994, A1, A18.

14. Timothy L. O'Brien, "Making Entrepreneurs of the Poor May Lift Some Off Federal Aid," *Wall Street Journal*, 22 January 1993, A1, A5.

15. Abu N. M. Wahid, ed., *The Grameen Bank: Poverty Relief in Bangladesh* (Boulder, Colo.: Westview Press, 1993); Mahabub Hossain, *Credit for the Rural Poor: The Experience of the Grameen Bank in Bangladesh* (Dhaka, Bangladesh: Bangladesh Institute for Development Studies, 1985); and Muhammad Yunus, "Credit as a Human Right: A Bangladesh Bank Helps Poor Women," *New York Times*, 2 April 1990, A17.

16. See, for instance, Wali I. Mondal and Ruth Anne Tune, "Replicating the Grameen Bank in North America: The Good Faith Fund Experience, " in *The Grameen Bank*, 223–34; Steven Balkin, "A Grameen Bank Replication: The Full Circle Fund of the Women's Self-Employment Project of Chicago," in *The Grameen Bank*, 235–66; Michael Schuman, "The Microlenders," *Forbes*, 25

October 1993, 164–66; Joe Klein, "We Can Do It for Ourselves," *Newsweek*, 29 March 1993, 31; Marguerite Holloway and Paul Wallich, "A Risk Worth Taking," *Scientific American*, November 1992, 126; Mary Ann Zehr, "Imported from Bangladesh," *Foundation News* (November-December 1992): 28–32; and Eugene Carlson, "SBA Introduces Its 'Microloan' Program," *Wall Street Journal*, 3 June 1992, B2. Somewhat similar group lending systems have been developed independently in some cultures, such as the *tontines* of Cameroon (James Brooke, "Informal Capitalism Grows in Cameroon," *New York Times*, 30 November 1987, D8).

17. ACCION International, 130 Prospect Street, Cambridge, Mass. 02139. See also *ACCION International Bulletin* 30, no. 4 (autumn 1995): 1–4; Brent Bowers, "Third World Debt That Is Almost Paid in Full," *Wall Street Journal*, 7 June 1991, B2; Michael S. Serrill, "Banker to the Poor," *Time*, 27 May 1991, 66 (international edition); and James Brooke, "Lending a Hand to the Small Latin Entrepreneur," *New York Times*, 1 August 1991, D6. On other micro-enterprise assistance for women in Latin America, see Marguerite Berger and Mayra Buvinic, eds., *Women's Ventures: Assistance to the Informal Sector in Latin America* (West Hartford, Conn.: Kumarian Press, 1989).

18. See preceding notes and Joseph Kahn and Miriam Jordan, "Women's Banks Stage Global Expansion," *Wall Street Journal*, 30 August 1995, A8.

19. Peter Scarlet, "Mormons Unite with Other Faiths to Solve Social Problems of the World," *Salt Lake Tribune*, 3 April, 1993, D1, D2.

20. Mary Mostert, "Planting with Humble Faith, Devoted Effort," *Church News*, 4 December 1992, 3–4.

21. Victor L. Brown, "The Remarkable Example of the Bermejillo, Mexico Branch," *Ensign* 8 (November 1978): 79–81.

22. "Officials in Peru Receive Supplies from Church for Community Kitchens," *Church News*, 15 December 1990, 6.

23. See John L. Hart, "'No Poor among Them' Is Ultimate Goal in Peru," *Church News*, 7 November 1981, 12.

24. For information on the Church in the Philippines generally, see Marvin Gardner, "Philippine Saints: A Believing People," *Ensign* 21 (July 1991): 32–37.

25. Warner Woodworth, "The Informal Economy and Micro-Entrepreneurs in the Philippines: Research Analysis" (unpublished technical report, Brigham Young University, 1990). Also see Woodworth's "Third World Strategies Toward Zion," *Sunstone* 14 (October 1990): 13–23.

Chapter 13

1. Howard W. Hunter, "All Are Alike unto God," *Ensign* 9 (June 1979), 72, 74.

2. Lee Green, "Jungle Doctors," *American Way* (15 April 1993): 58–100.

3. Manfred A. Max-Neef, *From the Outside Looking In: Experiences in 'Barefoot Economics'* (Uppsala, Sweden: Dag Hammarskjold Foundation, 1982), part 2.

4. These and other illustrations may be explored further in George McRobie's *Small Is Possible* (New York: Harper and Row, 1981).

5. See Pat Capson, "Utahns Extend a Much-Needed Helping Hand to

Ouelessebougou," *Salt Lake Tribune,* 25 March 1993, A8.

6. Enterprise Mentors International is a nonprofit foundation based in Missouri. Requests for further information and tax deductible contributions can be sent to Enterprise Mentors/IEDF, 510 Maryville College Drive, Suite 210, St. Louis, Mo. 63141. Telephone inquiries may be made by calling (314) 453-9700. Also see Winters, "Project Manila," 14, 16.

7. Internal Enterprise Mentors Organization Documents, "Case Statement," March 1993, 5.

8. Laura Andersen, "Foundation Helping Filipinos Establish Small Businesses," *Salt Lake City Deseret News,* 9–10, September 1992, B4.

9. *HC* 4:227.

10. An example of such efforts are a series of seminars given in Russia by American Mennonite travel agency, hotel and restaurant owners and operators to new Russian entrepreneurs in those businesses. Unlike most business consultants from the West, they paid their own way to share their know-how in successful Christian-oriented free enterprise (Alessandra Stanley, "Mission to Moscow: Preaching the Gospel of Business," *New York Times,* 27 February 1994, F4).

Chapter 14

1. Benson, *Teachings,* 123.

2. Mangum and Blumell, *Mormons' War on Poverty,* review current LDS welfare programs in the United States and Canada (183–99) and internationally (209–60). See also Stanley Taylor, "Economic Aid," in *EM,* 434–35, and Rudd, *Pure Religion,* 203–43.

3. From a speech by Thomas S. Monson in "A Sacred Duty to Help the Poor, Needy," *Church News,* 15 December 1990, 7.

4. Adilson Parrella, "Featherstone Speaks at Fireside," *(Brigham Young University) Daily Universe,* 2 March 1988, 1.

5. Mike Cannon, "LDS Volunteer Efforts Bless Lives Worldwide," *Church News,* 15 December 1990, 3, 7.

6. G. Sheridan and R. Sheffield, "Aim of Gospel Literacy Effort: Enrich Lives," *Church News,* 30 January 1993, 3, 5.

7. The full reasons for this diminished support for technical training are not clear, but the changes occurred as a new president was appointed, apparently with a mandate to recast the school in a more traditional liberal-arts fashion. Administrators at BYU in Provo had long pushed for such a restructuring of the curriculum in Laie also.

8. Peggy Fletcher Stack, "Senior Couples Lend Skills to Mormon 'Peace Corps,'" *Salt Lake Tribune,* 23 January 1993, D1, D2.

9. Giles H. Florence, Jr., "Called to Serve," *Ensign* 21 (September 1991): 13–16.

10. The Committee operates as a division of the Church Welfare department.

11. See Bruce D. Blumell, "The LDS Response to the Teton Dam Disaster in Idaho," *Sunstone* 5 (March-April 1980): 35–42, and Rudd, *Pure Religion,* 261–79.

12. This inspiring story is told in Frederick W. Babbel, *On Wings of Faith*

(Salt Lake City: Bookcraft, 1972), and Rudd, *Pure Religion,* 244–61.

13. Author Woodworth has been directly involved in various discussions, workshops, and planning meetings with Humanitarian Services staff since 1989. Additional information is covered in Mike Cannon, "Helping Hearts and Hands Span the Globe," *Church News,* 11 February 1995, 8–10; "Church's Humanitarian Efforts Provide Relief around the World," *Church News,* 13 August 1994, 3; Mary Kay Stout, "Russian Members Distribute Bales of Clothes and Shoes among LDS, Others," *Church News,* 4 September 1993, 3, 10; Peggy Fletcher Stack, "Famine, Flood? LDS Humanitarian Agency Supplies International, Local Helping Hand," *Salt Lake Tribune,* 31 August 1991, A10; "Officials in Peru Receive Supplies from Church for Community Kitchens," *Church News,* 15 December 1990, 41; Isaac C. Ferguson, "Freely Given: How Church Members, Donations, and Special Fasts are Helping Those in Need," *Ensign* 18 (August 1988): 10–15; and Isaac C. Ferguson, "Humanitarian Services," in *EM,* 662. Mangum and Blumell, *Mormons' War on Poverty,* 247–53, gives a comprehensive list of Church humanitarian services' activities through 1992.

14. Gordon B. Hinckley, "The State of the Church," *Ensign* 21 (May 1991): 51–54, and Thomas S. Monson, "A Royal Priesthood," *Ensign* 21 (May 1991): 47–51. Figures from 1994 are from Thomas S. Monson, "My Brother's Keeper," *Ensign* 24 (November 1994): 44.

15. Stack, "Famine, Flood?" A10.

16. Presentation by Lloyd Pendelton of LDS Church Welfare Services at Brigham Young University, September 1992.

17. See Morrison, *The Dawning of A Brighter Day,* 38–56, and "Caring in Africa," *Church News,* 31 October 1987, 8–10.

18. Greg Hill, "Benson Institute Program Enhances Lives of Struggling People," *Church News,* 3 June 1995, 8–10, and James P. Bell, "The Poor among Us," *BYU Today* (September 1991): 38–46.

19. Joan Dixon (Africa project team member and currently a Ph.D. student at the University of Massachusetts, Amherst), personal interview, 1992.

20. Shellie Fillmore, "LDS Mission Will Aid in Restoring Peace," *(Brigham Young University) Daily Universe,* 9 December 1992, 1.

21. Kimball, "Welfare Services," 77. See also Pace, "Infinite Needs," 50–55.

Part 4

1. Howard W. Hunter, "The Gospel—A Global Faith," *Ensign* 21 (November 1991): 18–19.

Chapter 15

1. *JD* 23:281–82.

2. Smith, *Wealth of Nations,* 24 (I.i.11).

3. Thomas J. Leuck, "Save the Business, Keep It in Brooklyn," *New York Times,* 17 July 1994, CY4.

4. On the mismanagement of USX's Geneva Mill in Utah see Warner Woodworth, "Steel Busting in the West," *Social Policy* 18, no. 3 (1988): 53–56. The story of Joe Cannon's efforts to revitalize Geneva as a Utah-owned firm is

documented in Warner Woodworth, "Capitalism with a Human Face: Social Responsibility in the Steel Industry" (paper read at the International Association of Business and Society, Sundance, Utah, 22–24 March 1991).

5. Benson, *God, Family, Country,* 309–10. The full quotation is discussed in chapter 16 under "Moral Conduct of Business."

6. George Meany, quotation in an announcement of a conference on corporate social responsibility (Chicago: Urban Research Corporation, 1973).

7. Andrew Carnegie, "The Gospel of Wealth," *The Gospel of Wealth and Other Essays* (Garden City, N.Y.: Doubleday, Doran & Company, 1933), 13, 17 (article originally published in the *North American Review,* 1889). If this seems to contradict Carnegie's professed Spencerism, all Carnegie biographers agree that his actual familiarity with Spencer's ideas was rather sparse. The Presbyterian concept of Christian stewardship and the political radicalism which he inherited from his Scottish forebears were in many respects more profoundly influential. Carnegie recognized that he was not a strict Spencerian. In a newspaper interview in 1892, he said, "I differ from my great master Herbert Spencer in regard to the duties of the State. No hard and fast line can be drawn in this matter . . . but I believe that we shall have more and more occasions for the State to legislate on behalf of the workers, because it is always the worst employers that have to be coerced into what fair employers would gladly do of their own accord if they had not to compete with the hard men" (J. Quail, *Mr. Andrew Carnegie on Socialism, Labour and Home Rule: An Interview* [Aberdeen, Scotland: Northern Newspaper, 1892], 24).

8. Beatrice Webb to Mr. Troughton, 14 January 1904, Andrew Carnegie Papers, container 102, Library of Congress. The letter was forwarded to Carnegie, who noted on the letter that "it was otherwise disposed of before I could reply." Webb had earlier referred to Carnegie as a "reptile" in response to a suggestion that he be approached to endow the London School of Economics (Beatrice Webb Diary, 15 May 1899, quoted in Webb, *Our Partnership,*185). She and Sidney had just returned from a trip to America, and, like her friend Herbert Spencer, had been horrified by the actual conditions of the new industrial world order incarnate. This sentiment shows the strength of the feelings of the age, for by any standard Carnegie was one of the most high-minded and admirable of the great industrialists. Beatrice's sentiments seemed to have mellowed by 1904. Although they shared an extensive mutual acquaintance in addition to their friendship with Herbert Spencer, there is no indication that they ever met, except for a letter dated 16 November 1908 from Sidney Webb to Carnegie. In it he thanks Carnegie for sending a copy of Carnegie's *Problems of To-day,* in which Sidney is quoted several times. Sidney then adds "my wife begs to be remembered to you" (Andrew Carnegie Papers, container 158, Library of Congress).

9. Smith, *Moral Sentiments,* 235.

10. Spencer W. Kimball, "Keep Your Money Clean," *Improvement Era* 56 (December 1953): 950.

11. Spencer W. Kimball, "The False Gods We Worship," *Ensign* 6 (June 1976): 4–5. See also Ezra Taft Benson, "Beware of Pride," *Ensign* 19 (May 1989): 4–7, and Brent L. Top, "'Thou Shalt Not Covet,'" *Ensign* 24 (December 1994):

22–26.

12. Bryant S. Hinckley, *The Faith of Our Pioneer Fathers* (Salt Lake City: Deseret Book, 1956), 13.

13. Howard W. Hunter, "Prepare for Honorable Employment," *Ensign* 5 (November 1975): 123.

14. The "work-and-spend cycle," where ever-increasing consumer desires lead to ever-longer work hours is described in Schor, *The Overworked American*, 107–38. The negative consequences of this parental time deficit are described in Sylvia Ann Hewlett, *When the Bough Breaks: The Cost of Neglecting Our Children* (New York: Basic Books, 1991), 62–88. Ironically, a recent study has suggested that all those long hours do not make much difference, that those workers who place a high value on family and marriage do as well or better financially as those who put long work hours as their priority (Judith H. Dobrzynski, "Assessing the Value of Family" and "Should I Have Left An Hour Earlier?" *New York Times*, 18 June 1995, F1, F12). For some helpful suggestions, see "How to Keep Your Career from Dominating Your Life," *Church News*, 30 July 1988, 15.

15. Dallin H. Oaks, *Pure in Heart*, (Salt Lake City: Bookcraft, 1988), 85.

16. Joseph Smith, Jr., *A Compilation Containing the Lectures on Faith*, comp. N. B. Lundwall (Salt Lake City), 58.

17. Oaks, *Pure in Heart*, 80.

18. Oaks, *Pure in Heart*, 85.

Chapter 16

1. Mario DePillis (Professor of History, University of Massachusetts, Amherst), interview, 1991. See, for example, Peter H. Lewis, "Drawing on Family Values to Fight the Software Wars: Alan Conway Ashton," *New York Times*, 3 October 1993, F8.

2. These values are held by non-LDS workers also. A recent workforce study has shown that such factors as open communication at work, effect on family life, job location, family supportive policies and control of work schedule all are considered to be more important than salary in deciding to take a job (Sue Shallenbarger, "Work-Force Study Finds Loyalty Is Weak, Divisions of Race and Gender Are Deep," *Wall Street Journal*, 3 September 1993, B1, B8.

3. Cited in Morrel Heald, *The Social Responsibility of Business: Company and Country, 1900–1960* (Cleveland: Press of Case Western University, 1970), 29.

4. James C. Worthy, *Shaping an American Institution: Robert E. Wood and Sears, Roebuck* (Urbana: University of Illinois Press, 1984), 173.

5. Milton Friedman, *Capitalism and Freedom* (Chicago: University of Chicago Press, 1962), 133–36.

6. Morrel Heald, *The Social Responsibility of Business*, 47, 97.

7. Bill Richards, "Investigators Sort Out A Mess from the Days of Alternative Energy," *Wall Street Journal*, 15 December 1994, A1, A6.

8. Spencer W. Kimball, "Keep Your Money Clean," 948–50.

9. Charles C. Walton, *Ethos and the Executive: Values in Managerial Decision Making* (Englewood Cliffs, N.J.: Prentice-Hall, 1969), 38.

10. Niccolo Machiavelli, *The Prince* (1513; reprint, New York: Mentor

Books, 1962). One publication for managers with a paid circulation of 45,000 specializes in giving advice on how to be ruthless and successfully cheat in business. See Brent Bowers, "How to Get Ahead As a Middle Manager by Being Ruthless," *Wall Street Journal*, 23 March 1993, A1, A9.

11. From sworn deposition testimony between Stanley Rosenblatt, an anti-smoking attorney representing flight attendants (questions) and Bennett S. LeBow, chairman of the owner of the Liggett Group (answers). Quoted in Michael Janofsky, "On Cigarettes, Health and Lawyers," *New York Times*, 6 December 1993, D8. Recent disclosures have shown that tobacco companies were aware of the risks of cigarette smoking since the 1950s but elected to hide them from the public. See Philip J. Hilts, "Tobacco Company Was Silent on Hazards," *New York Times*, 7 May 1994, A1, A11, and Philip J. Hilts, "Cigarette Makers Debated the Risks They Denied," *New York Times*, 16 June 1994: A1, D22.

12. Oaks, *Pure in Heart*, 75.

13. Howard R. Bowen, *Social Responsibilities of the Businessman* (New York: Harper & Brothers, 1953).

14. Stephen L. Richards, "The Gospel of Work," *Improvement Era* 43 (January 1940): 61.

15. Chick-Fil-A founder and CEO S. Truett Cathy also devotes a substantial portion of his profits to a network of foster homes. The chain has experienced increasing sales for over 25 consecutive years. See Dan McGraw, "The Christian Capitalists," *U.S. News & World Report*, 13 March 1995, 60.

16. Internal documents of Johnson & Johnson Company, 1988.

17. Walton, *Made in America*, 128.

18. Smith, *Wealth of Nations*, 99 (I.viii.44).

19. Andrew Worden, "A Prophet Touched My Life," *Ensign* 7 (February 1977): 59.

20. Kimball, "Keep Your Money Clean."

21. See. Roger H. Hermanson, Daniel M. Ivancevich, and Dana R. Hermanson, "Corporate Restructuring in the 1990s: The Impact of Accounting Incentives," *The Corporate Growth Report* 10 (February 1992): 14–18.

22. William Roth, "The Dangerous Ploy of Downsizing," *Business Forum* (fall 1993): 7.

23. Walton, *Made in America*, 253–54. Management experts are also recognizing that such moral concepts are an essential part of successful entrepreneurship. See Stephen R. Covey, *Principle-Centered Leadership* (New York: Simon & Schuster, 1991); Peter Block, *Stewardship: Choosing Service Over Self-Interest* (San Francisco: Berrett-Koehler Publishers, 1993); and Neil H. Snyder, James J. Dowd, Jr., and Dianne Morse Houghton, *Vision, Value and Courage: Leadership for Quality Management* (New York: Free Press, 1994).

24. In both Utah and the United States generally, approximately three of every five married mothers with children under 18 are in the workforce, although Utah mothers have a slightly higher tendency to work part time. The rates of employment for mothers are even higher where there is no father in the home (Jerry Mason, "Family Economics," in *Utah in Demographic Perspective*, ed. Thomas K. Martin, Tim B. Heaton, and Stephen J. Bahr [Salt

Lake City: Signature Books, 1986], 100–2). See also chapter 2 under "Inequality" and chapter 7 under "Decline of Self-Employment and the Changing Nature of Work."

25. These and other examples are found in Hewlett, *When the Bough Breaks,* 195–232. See also Schor, *The Overworked American,* 152–62, on the productivity, family, and community benefits of such policies.

26. Howard W. Hunter, "Being a Righteous Husband and Father," *Ensign* 24 (November 1994): 50.

27. See "Was the United Order a Failure?—Persecution, Polygamy and Greed" in chapter 10.

28. John Stuart Mill, *Collected Works,* ed. J. M. Robson (Toronto: University of Toronto Press, 1965), 792.

29. One of the principal methods for achieving this cooperation is legally mandated labor/management works councils. See Joel Rogers and Wolfgang Streeck, "Workplace Representation Overseas: The Works Councils Story," in *Working under Different Rules,* ed. Richard B. Freeman (New York: Russell Sage Foundation, 1994), 97–156. For further information on promoting labor/management cooperation through employee workplace representation and participation in the context of American business, see Warner P. Woodworth and Christopher B. Meek, *Creating Labor-Management Partnerships* (Reading, Mass.: Addison-Wesley, 1995); Warner P. Woodworth, "Hard Hats in the Boardroom: New Trends in Workers' Participation," in *Organization and People,* ed. J.B. Ritchie and Paul Thompson (St. Paul: West, 1988), 362–71; Scott and Barbara Hammond, "Reworking the Workplace," *BYU Today* (October 1985): 21–24; and Jaroslav Vanek, ed., *Self-Management: Economic Liberation of Man* (Baltimore: Penguin, 1975), especially sections 6 and 11.

30. See chapter 2 under "The Economy of the United States—Unemployment."

31. See James J. Cramer, "Confessions of a Limousine Neoliberal," *New York,* 11 March 1996, 34–38.

32. These surveys are reported in "Employee Morale Is Getting Worse," *Incentive* 168 (January 1994): 5, and Amanda Bennett, "Downsizing Doesn't Necessarily Bring an Upswing in Corporate Profitability," *Wall Street Journal,* 6 June 1991, B1. It should be noted that these surveys were based on self-reporting by the companies themselves. Given the natural human tendency to be defensive about failed decisions, one can reasonably expect that the actual results were even worse than reported.

33. Boroughs, "Amputating Assets," 51.

34. See Barbara Presley Noble, "Questioning Productivity Beliefs," *New York Times,* 10 July 1994, F21; Marc Levinson, "Thanks. You're Fired," *Newsweek,* 23 May 1994, 48–49; Robert M. Tomasko, *Rethinking the Corporation: The Architecture of Change* (New York: American Management Association, 1993): 23–32; "Employee Morale Is Getting Worse"; Roth, "The Dangerous Ploy"; Stephanie Overman, "The Layoff Legacy," *HRMagazine* 36 (August 1991): 28–32; and Boroughs, "Amputating Assets," 52.

35. Hermanson, et al., "Corporate Restructuring in the 1990s."

36. Good summaries of these suggestions can be found in David E.

Sanger and Steve Lohr, "A Search for Answers to Avoid the Layoffs," *New York Times,* 9 March 1996, A1, A12–A13; Helen Gracon and Maureen Clark, "Layoffs Should Come Last," *IEEE Spectrum* 31 (May 1994): 52–55; and Edmund Faltermayer, "Is this Layoff Necessary?" *Fortune,* 1 June 1992, 71–86.

37. Kim S. Cameron, "Strategies for Successful Organizational Downsizing," *Human Resource Management* 33 (summer 1994): 189–211, and Gilbert Fuchsberg, "Why Shake-Ups Work for Some, Not for Others," *Wall Street Journal,* 1 October 1993, B1, B4.

38. Ken Blanchard, "Alternatives to Downsizing," *Manage* 47 (July 1995): 11–12.

39. *JD* 4:246.

40. *JD* 4:246–47.

41. Benson, *God, Family, Country,* 309–10.

Chapter 17

1. John A. Widtsoe, *A Rational Theology: As Taught by The Church of Jesus Christ of Latter-day Saints* (Salt Lake City: Deseret Book, 1965), 147. Elder Widtsoe also notes that "Cooperative enterprises have been fostered constantly and consistently by the Church, and in the majority of instances have been extremely successful. In fact, when the Church settled in Utah, it would have been impossible to accomplish the great work before the pioneers, had they not practiced cooperation" (147).

2. *JD* 17:74.

3. Craig Witham, "Provo Woolen Mills: A Cooperative Enterprise," *Utah County Journal,* 23 September 1987, 1, 14, 22, and Leonard J. Arrington, *Great Basin Kingdom,* 317–20.

4. *JD* 14:14.

5. *JD* 17:157–58.

6. Robert Oakeshott, *The Case for Workers' Co-operatives,* 2nd ed. (London: Macmillan, 1990).

7. Chris Cornforth, et al., *Developing Successful Worker Co-operatives* (London: Sage, 1988).

8. Susanna Hoe, *The Man Who Gave His Company Away* (London: Heinemann, 1978), 105–7. See also E. F. Schumacher's *Small Is Beautiful* (New York: Harper and Row, 1973), part IV-5.

9. Hoe, *Gave His Company Away,* 226–27.

10. On the French cooperative sector, see Saul Estrin and Derek C. Jones, "The Viability of Employee-Owned Firms: Evidence from France," *Industrial and Labor Relations Review* 45 (January 1992): 323–38.

11. See Oakeshott, *The Case for Workers' Co-operatives,* chapter 9 on the Italian cooperative sector. A comprehensive survey of cooperatives in western Europe is by the Commission of the European Communities, *Programme of Research and Actions on the Development of the Labour Market: Forms of Organisation, Type of Employment, Working Conditions and Industrial Relations in Cooperatives, Any Collectiveness or Other Self-Managing Structure of the EEC* (Luxembourg: Office for Official Publications of the European Communities; Washington, D.C.: European Community Information Service, 1986).

12. Joseph Blasi, *The Communal Experience of the Kibbutz* (New Brunswick,

N.J.: Transaction Books, 1986).

13. See, for example, Warner Woodworth, "Israeli Hi Tech Co-ops Challenge Popular Myths," *Workplace Democracy* 12, no. 2 (fall 1985): 10–19.

14. On recent kibbutz economic rearrangements, see Henry Kamm, "Even in the Kibbutz, Socialism Is under Challenge," *New York Times,* 10 September 1991, A3; Amy Dockser Marcus, "Israeli Kibbutz's New Free-Market Style Defies Socialist Ideals, Sparks Debate," *Wall Street Journal,* 26 May 1993, A15; Clyde Haberman, "Reluctantly, a Kibbutz Turns to (GASP!) the Stock Market," *New York Times,* 8 July 1993, A1, A6.

15. National Industrial Conference Board, *Special Report No. 32, The Growth of Working Councils in the United States: A Statistical Summary* (New York: National Industrial Conference Board, 1932), and Derek Jones, "Historical Perspectives on Worker Cooperatives," in *Worker Cooperatives in America,* ed. Robert Jackall and Henry Levin (Berkeley: University of California Press, 1984).

16. President Woodrow Wilson's advocacy of industrial democracy appears in W. J. Lauck, *Political and Industrial Democracy* (New York: Funk & Wagnalls, 1926), 59–60. See David Brody, *Workers in Industrial America: Essays on the Twentieth Century Struggle,* 2nd ed. (New York: Oxford University Press, 1993), 48–81, for discussion of other early advocacy of such views.

17. See Daniel Zwerdling, *Workplace Democracy* (New York: Harper & Row, 1980); Robert Jackall and Henry M. Levin, eds., *Worker Cooperatives in America* (Berkeley: University of California Press, 1984); Joyce Rothschild and J. Allen Whitt, *The Cooperative Workplace* (Cambridge, U.K.: Cambridge University Press, 1980); Len Krimerman and Frank Lindenfeld, eds., *When Workers Decide: Workplace Democracy Takes Root in North America* (Philadelphia: New Society Publishers, 1992); and Derek Jones and Jan Svejnar, eds., *Participatory and Self-Managed Firms* (Lexington, Mass.: Lexington Books, 1982).

18. Christopher Gunn, *Workers' Self-Management in the United States* (Ithaca, N.Y.: Cornell University Press, 1984), chapter 3.

19. Further technical details on ESOPs may be obtained from Christopher Meek, Warner Woodworth, and W. Gibb Dyer, Jr., *Managing by the Numbers* (Reading, Mass.: Addison-Wesley, 1988); Joseph R. Blasi, *Employee Ownership: Revolution or Ripoff?* (New York: Ballinger, 1987); David P. Ellerman, *The Democratic Worker-Owned Firm: A New Model for East and West* (London: Unwin Hyman, 1990); Robert W. Smiley, Jr., and Ronald J. Gilbert, eds., *Employee Stock Ownership Plans: Business Planning, Implementation, Law and Taxation* (New York: Prentice-Hall, 1989 [with annual Yearbook updates]); and Gerald Kalish, ed., *ESOPs: The Handbook of Employee Stock Ownership Plans* (Chicago: Probus Publishing, 1989). Also interesting are the writings of the inventor of the ESOP concept, Louis Kelso. See Louis O. and Patricia Hetter Kelso, *Democracy and Economic Power: Extending the ESOP Revolution* (Cambridge, Mass.: Ballinger Publishing Company, 1986), which explores many variations on the forms and uses of ESOPs, and in chapter 3 sets out Kelso's philosophy in terms strongly reminiscent of some of the principles of consecration and stewardship; Louis O. Kelso and Mortimer J. Adler, *The New Capitalists* (New York: Random House, 1961); and Louis O. Kelso and

Mortimer J. Adler, *The Capitalist Manifesto* (New York: Random House, 1958). As of this writing, Congress has proposed repealing the exclusion of 50 percent of ESOP interest income.

20. The case of blue collar workers at Oregon Steel Mills, Inc., is illustrative. A decade ago the firm was nearly bankrupt, suffering from old equipment and high costs. It was rescued through a worker buy-out of 95 percent of the stock. By 1988 its market value had risen from $15 million to over $400 million. Workers' shares that were only valued at a few cents earlier grew to $38 by 1990. Many employees are like Jackie Williams, who was a bookkeeper living in a mobile home, but now has assets of $1.3 million and lives in a $500,000 home on the edge of a country club's golf course. Two other employees, a foreman in the mill and an office clerk, recently married, combining their shares and retiring with $2.5 million in stock. See Dana Milbank, "Here Is One LBO Deal Where the Workers Became Millionaires," *Wall Street Journal,* 27 October 1992, A1, A12. See also James P. Miller, "Some Workers Set Up LBOs of Their Own and Benefit Greatly," *Wall Street Journal,* 12 December 1988, A1, A7.

21. See Corey Rosen and Michael Quarrey, "How Well Is Employee Ownership Doing?" *Harvard Business Review* 65 (September–October 1987): 126–30; and chapter 18, note 26.

22. See Blasi and Kruse, *The New Owners.*

23. The case of Weirton and other steel examples appears in Warner Woodworth's "Weirton Steel: An ESOP Conversion," in *Worker Empowerment: The Struggle for Workplace Democracy,* Jon D. Wisman, ed. (New York: Bootstrap Press, 1991) 117–30.

24. Equitech is described in more detail in Charlene Renberg Winters, "Building a Business beyond Accounting Ledgers and Elbow Grease," *BYU Today* (July 1990), 8–9.

25. Warner Woodworth and Vernon Dillenbeck, "A New Strategy: Combining Manufacturing and Management," *Journal of Engineering Technology* 7, no. 2 (fall 1990): 32–34.

26. Joseph A. Geddes, *The United Order among the Mormons: An Unfinished Experiment in Economic Organization* (Salt Lake City: Deseret News Press, 1924), 84.

27. Geddes, *The United Order among the Mormons,* 144.

28. On the hidden costs in relying on gambling for economic development, see Passell, "The False Promise," F5, and George Judson, "Some Indians See a Gamble with Future in Casinos," *New York Times,* 15 May 1994, E5. According to the latter article, many Indians have moral objections to gambling on reservations, including the Senecas of New York, who voted down a casino proposal in part because of the prophecy of a chief in 1799 that gambling would destroy their nation. On the possibilities for non-gambling economic development of Indian reservations, see Dirk Johnson, "Economies Come to Life on Indian Reservations," *New York Times,* 3 July 1994, A1, A18.

29. Andrew Carnegie, "Final Relation," 54, 56, 57, 63.

30. Carnegie, *Problems of To-day,* 66, 63. See also Andrew Carnegie, "The Industrial Problem":

> Many a time since the writer's retirement from business he has felt

that if he were induced to return thereto, his chief aim would be to address many thousands of workmen as "fellow-shareholders." . . . [We] especially welcome the introduction of the germ which is destined to prove the best possible solution of the problem of capital and labor, workmen shareholders, no union comparable to this union of employer and employed. Let us get capital and labor into the same boat, rowing together, and all will be well, and we shall have made another great step forward in obedience to the eternal law of progress which insures the continual ascent of man by a law of his being to higher and higher stages of development on earth toward perfection. (57–58, 59–60)

31. A good summary of many different methods of implementing employee ownership in the United States is Sue Steiner, *Employee Ownership: Alternatives to ESOPs* (Oakland, Calif.: National Center for Employee Ownership, 1990). For information on approaches applicable to other nations, see Corey Rosen, Gianna Durso, and Raul Rothblatt, *International Developments in Employee Ownership* (Oakland, Calif.: National Center for Employee Ownership, 1990).

Chapter 18

1. John Taylor, "Address to the Annual Conference of the New York Conference, November 2, 1856," *The Mormon* (31 January 1857): 1.

2. *JD* 18:354.

3. *JD* 18:375.

4. *JD* 17:76. Apostle Snow continued: "It is for the strong to foster and bear the infirmities of the weak, for those who possess skill and ability to accumulate and preserve this world's goods, to use them for the common good, and not merely for their own persons, children and relatives, so as to exalt themselves in pride and vanity over their fellowmen, and sink themselves into ruin by worshipping the God of this world. . . . The word of God to us is to change our front, and to learn to love our neighbors as ourselves and so cultivate the spirit of the Gospel."

5. The importance of developing human resources is beginning to be recognized by American business. See Barbara Presley Noble, "Retooling the 'People Skills' of Corporate America," *New York Times*, 22 May 1994, F8, and Applebome, "Study Ties Educational Gains to More Productivity Growth." This importance has long been recognized by successful Japanese companies (John E. Rehfeld, "In Japan, Personnel Has a Corner Office," *New York Times*, 1 May 1994, F9.

6. Widtsoe, *A Rational Theology*, 147.

7. Good books on employee empowerment include James A. Belasco and Ralph C. Stayer, *Flight of the Buffalo* (New York: Warner, 1993); Jack Stack, *The Great Game of Business* (New York: Doubleday, 1992); Max de Pree, *Leadership Is an Art* (New York: Doubleday, 1989); Marvin R. Weisbord, *Productive Workplaces* (San Francisco: Jossey-Bass, 1987); Block, *The Empowered Manager;* and Lawler, *High Involvement Management*.

8. Taylorism began to be heavily criticized in the 1970s because of its mind-numbing routines, its transformation of the worker into a mere cog in

the factory machine, and its degradation of work itself. See Harry Braverman, *Labor and Monopoly Capital* (New York: Monthly Review Press, 1974). By the early 1980s a number of organization and management experts were criticizing the dehumanization and alienation that 'scientific' management had created, with its consequences of declining productivity, poor quality, labor-management conflicts, and the industrial sickness described as the 'blue-collar blues.' One of the most prominent voices criticizing Taylorist methods was Tom Peters, author of three New York Times bestsellers. See, for example, Thomas J. Peters and Robert H. Waterman, Jr., *In Search of Excellence: Lessons from America's Best-Run Companies* (New York: Harper & Row, 1982), 40–54, 89–103. Other major organization scholars who have written similar critiques of Taylorist management include James Belasco, *Teaching the Elephant to Dance: Empowering Change in Your Organization* (New York: Crown, 1990); Edward E. Lawler III, *High Involvement Management* (San Francisco: Jossey-Bass, 1986); Rosabeth Moss Kanter, *When Giants Learn to Dance: Mastering the Challenge of Strategy, Management and Careers in the 1990s* (New York: Simon & Schuster, 1989); Peter M. Senge, *The Fifth Discipline: The Art and Practice of the Learning Organization* (New York: Doubleday, 1990); Peter Block, *The Empowered Manager: Positive Political Skills at Work* (San Francisco: Jossey-Bass, 1987); James C. Taylor and David F. Felten, *Performance by Design: Sociotechnical Systems in North America* (Englewood Cliffs, N.J.: Prentice-Hall, 1993).

9. Clyde H. Farnsworth, "Experiment in Worker Ownership Shows a Profit," *New York Times* 14 August 1993, 33, 46. Quotation from Nick Caruso, 33.

10. Jack Stack, *The Great Game of Business.*

11. See John Case, *Open-Book Management: The Coming Business Revolution* (New York: HarperBusiness, 1995).

12. Walton, *Made in America,* 246–49. Walton said that this management approach arose on a visit to Britain where he saw a department store which listed all of its employees on a plaque prominently displayed at the front of the store:

> It is Lewis Company. J. M. Lewis Partnership. They had a partnership with all their associates listed up on the sign. For some reason that whole idea really excited me: a partnership with all our associates. As soon as we got home, we started calling our store workers "associates," instead of employees. That may not sound like a big deal to some folks, and they're right. It wouldn't have meant a thing if we hadn't taken other actions to make it real, to make it something more than window dressing. The decision we reached around that time, to commit ourselves to giving the associates more equitable treatment in the company, was without doubt the single smartest move we ever made at Wal-Mart. (131–32)

The actions taken included profit-sharing and discount stock purchase plans. J. M. Lewis is a large 100 percent employee-owned department store chain in the United Kingdom. It is described further in chapter 17.

13. John Case, "A Company of Businesspeople," *Inc.,* April 1993, 79–93.

14. See, for example, Gifford and Elizabeth Pinchot, *The End of Bureaucracy and the Rise of the Intelligent Organization* (San Francisco: Berrett-Koehler Publishers, 1993), and Carri P. Jenkins, "Empowering the People: Expanding the Role of Followers," *BYU Today* (September 1990): 28–32, 60–63. A good analysis of successful participatory firms such as Hewlett-Packard and the Mondragon cooperatives (discussed in chapter 19) is David Levine, "Participation, Productivity and the Firm's Environment," *California Management Review* 32 (summer 1990): 86–100.

15. Smith, *Moral Sentiments*, 56, 63.

16. Joseph Smith, Jr., *Teachings*, 249.

17. *HC* 6:33.

18. L. Dwight Israelsen, "An Economic Analysis of the United Order," *Brigham Young University Studies* 18 (summer 1978): 536–62.

19. *JD* 20:164. President Taylor concluded, however, that if the Saints disobeyed these principles, "you will go downward, and keep going the downward road to disappointment and poverty in things spiritual as well as temporal. I dare prophecy that in the name of the Lord. . . . Well, what shall we do? Why, do the best we can, and keep on trying to improve upon our present condition, always keeping in view the object to be gained, dealing honestly on a fair basis and correct principles, then we will succeed and things will move on pleasantly, and we shall be a united people, owned and blessed of the Lord. It was on this principle that the Nephites became a prosperous, a blessed and happy people; it was not because one was a little smarter than another, or through his smartness taking advantage of his neighbor; it was not that a man was a good financier, that he should "financier" other people's property into his own pockets and leave them without."

20. See W. Gibb Dyer, Jr., *The Entrepreneurial Experience: Confronting the Career Dilemmas of the Start-up Executive* (San Francisco: Jossey-Bass Publishers, 1992).

21. *JD* 19:186.

22. *JD* 19:184.

23. *JD* 19:186.

24. *JD* 17:74.

25. Doreen Hemlock, "I.P.O.'s: When Employee-Friendly=Investor-Friendly," *New York Times*, 25 February 1996, F4.

26. High levels of employee ownership are characteristic of the fastest growing midsized companies. Such companies also have a strong sense of corporate values, encourage experimentation and treat bureaucracy as the archenemy (Donald K. Clifford, Jr., and Richard E. Cavanagh, *The Winning Performance: How America's High Growth Midsize Companies Succeed* [New York: Bantam Books, 1985]). Early studies of employee ownership indicated significant results. Employee-owned companies generated three times as many new jobs as comparable companies (Katherine Klein and Corey Rosen, "Job Generation Performance of Employee Owned Companies," *Monthly Labor Review* 8 [August 1983]: 15–19). A survey of companies with Employee Stock Ownership Plans (ESOPs) showed them to have twice the annual productivity growth rate of comparable firms without ESOPs (Thomas Marsh and Dale McAllister, "ESOP's Tables," *Journal of Corporation Law* 3 [spring

1981]: 613–17). A linear study found that companies that set up ESOPs had annual sales increases of over 3 percent compared to their own sales growth before the ESOP was established and in comparison with similar companies without ESOPs (Michael Quarrey and Corey Rosen, *Employee Ownership and Corporate Performance* [Berkeley, Calif.: National Center for Employee Ownership, 1986]).

However, more recent studies have questioned whether employee ownership alone increases productivity or profitability. The General Accounting Office found that companies with ESOPs in general had the same performance as comparable companies without ESOPs, except when there was also participation by nonmanagerial employees in significant corporate decision-making. In the latter case, productivity was 52 percent higher than nonparticipative ESOP firms (United States General Accounting Office, *Employee Stock Ownership Plans: Little Evidence of Effects on Corporate Performance* [Washington, D.C.: United States General Accounting Office, 1987], 28–31). Another study found that employee ownership made a significant difference in corporate performance chiefly when combined with regular contributions to the ESOP, substantial level of total employee ownership and encouragement of employee participation in management (John Logue and Cassandra Rogers, *Employee Stock Ownership Plans in Ohio: Impact on Company Performance and Employment* [Kent, Ohio: Northeast Ohio Employee Ownership Center, 1989], 23–24). The most effective form of employee participation in management is "hands-on" control on the shopfloor (Michael A. Conte and Jan Svejnar, "The Performance Effects of Employee Ownership Plans" in *Paying for Productivity: A Look at the Evidence,* ed. Alan S. Blinder [Washington, D.C.: Brookings Institution, 1990], 143–81. Michael Quarrey and Corey Rosen, *Employee Ownership and Corporate Performance* (Oakland, Calif.: National Center for Employee Ownership, 1994), survey recent research on the topic.

It has been suggested that perhaps it is employee participation, not employee ownership, that makes the difference. However, a recent study of employee participation programs alone concludes that they not only do not help, but appear to hurt, efficiency (Bennett Harrison, "The Failure of Worker Participation," *Technology Review* 94 [January 1991]: 74). Another study of a wide variety of employee participation methods found "that only those also involving employee ownership appeared to increase both productivity and job satisfaction" (John L. Cotton, et al., "Employee Participation: Diverse Forms and Different Outcomes," *Academy of Management Review* 13 [January 1988]: 8–22). Other studies claim to find favorable results from participation programs alone, but the positive results are slight, and are unlikely to be widespread without significant government support and legislation (David I. Levine and Laura D'Andrea Tyson, "Participation, Productivity and the Firm's Environment," in *Paying for Productivity,* 183–243)

While further research is always needed, it appears that the synergy between ownership and participation makes the difference, amounting to superior corporate performance in a variety of measures of 12 to 17 percent annually (Rosen, "Ownership, Motivation and Corporate Performance: Putting ESOPs to Work," in *ESOPs,* ed. Kalish, 271–89). This has been confirmed by the most comprehensive studies, such as the GAO study referred to above and a more recent one of employee-owned and comparable control firms in Washington state (Peter Kardas, et al, "Employment and Sales Growth in Washington State Employee Ownership Companies: A Comparative Analysis," *The Journal of Employee Ownership Law and Finance* 6 [spring 1994]: 83–135). The key elements appear to be a substantial level of employee ownership, a management attitude that regards workers as fellow owners and partners, and methods of implementing employee participation which individual workers can directly exercise, coupled with the provision of extensive information about the business. See Quarrey and Rosen, *Employee Ownership*, 30–45. Anecdotal evidence about the success of these approaches abounds. See, for example, Susan Chandler, "United We Own," *Business Week*, 18 March 1996, 96–100; Adam Bryant, "Kiwi Seeks New Labor Ethic, End to Us Versus Them," *New York Times* 24 February 1994, D1, D5; Farnsworth, "Experiment in Worker Ownership," 33, 46; Stack, *The Great Game of Business*; Peter T. Kilborn, "Scrapping 'Us Versus Them,' Industry Is Giving Workers a Say and a Stake," *New York Times*, 22 November 1991, A23; and Steven Prokesch, "Labor Policy Aids Miller Furniture," *New York Times*, 14 August 1986, D1, D5. Advocates also include many policy analysts. See William C. Freund and Eugene Epstein, *People and Productivity* (Homewood, Ill.: Dow Jones-Irwin, 1984), and Ray Marshall, *Unheard Voices: Labor and Economic Policy in a Competitive World* (New York: Basic Books, 1987), 183–204.

27. See "Capitalism: Punters or Proprietors?" *Economist*, 5 May 1990, 65–84, and Peter F. Drucker, *Managing for the Future: The 1990s and Beyond* (New York: Penguin Books, 1993), 21–23, 293–99.

28. *JD* 10:57–58.

29. The principles of the united order are interconnected. Seen in context, this oft-quoted phrase shows the priesthood's function in a united order-inspired society. Under the principle of stewardship discussed in chapter 7, the priesthood is not to manage or administer the affairs of the Saints. Rather it teaches righteousness so that privately owned and controlled self-managing united order cooperatives can govern themselves righteously.

30. Spencer W. Kimball, "Welfare Services," 77.

31. See Robison, "Economic Insights," 35–53, for an interesting examination of this concept based upon the Book of Mormon.

32. Adolf A. Berle, *The American Economic Republic* (New York: Harcourt, Brace & World, 1963), 202.

33. Berle, *The American Economic Republic*, 199.

34. Calvin Sims, "Family Values As a Las Vegas Smash," *New York Times* 3 February 1994, D1, D7.

35. See Harvey Leibenstein's *Beyond Economic Man: A New Foundation for Economics* (Cambridge: Harvard University Press, 1976) and *General X-Efficiency Theory and Economic Development* (Oxford: Oxford University Press, 1978). See also a summary of this point in George Gilder, *Wealth and Poverty* (New York: Basic Books, 1981), 72–74.

36. Joel Kotkin, *Tribes: How Race, Religion, and Identity Determine Success in the Global Economy* (New York: Random House, 1992), 245–49, and Francis Fukuyama, *Trust: The Social Virtues and the Creation of Prosperity* (New York: Free Press, 1995), 290–93.

37. *JD* 19:346–47.

38. Kimball, "Becoming the Pure in Heart," 81. President Kimball goes on to say that Zion can only be created "through consistent and concerted daily effort by every single member of the Church. No matter what the cost in toil or sacrifice, we must 'do it.'" He then discusses the fundamental things that can be done to bring about Zion: overcoming selfishness and the practice of cooperation and consecration. The entire address is highly recommended as an excellent summary on becoming Zion.

39. Ezra Taft Benson, "Cleansing the Inner Vessel," *Ensign* 16 (May 1986): 4.

Chapter 19

1. Joseph Smith, Jr., *Teachings*, 313.

2. Quoted in William Foote Whyte and Kathleen King Whyte, *Making Mondragon: The Growth and Dynamics of the Worker Cooperative Complex* (Ithaca, N.Y.: ILR Press, 1988) 240, 243–44.

3. Several books have been written on the Mondragon cooperatives and their history. See Henk Thomas and Christopher Logan, *Mondragon: An Economic Analysis* (London: George Allen & Unwin, 1982); Keith Bradley and Alan Gelb, *Cooperation at Work: The Mondragon Experience* (London: Heinemann Educational Books, 1983); Hans Wiener with Robert Oakeshott, *Worker-Owners: Mondragon Revisited* (London: Anglo-German Foundation for the Study of Industrial Society, 1987); Whyte and Whyte, *Making Mondragon;* Oakeshott, *The Case for Workers' Cooperatives*, 165–214.

4. Whyte and Whyte, *Making Mondragon*, 237–50. "We build the road as we travel" has been adopted as something of a motto in the Mondragon cooperatives (241). Interestingly, when we mentioned this motto to a colleague who is an Israeli attorney who represents several kibbutz, he immediately identified it as a common expression and philosophy among the kibbutzim as well.

5. Shela C. Turpin-Forster, *Mondragon's Message for Employee Ownership* (paper in possession of the authors), 1.

6. Thomas and Logan, *Economic Analysis*, 96–130.

7. Thomas and Logan, *Economic Analysis*, 131–47, 158–61; Levin, "Employment and Productivity in Producer Cooperatives," in Jackall and Levin, *Worker Cooperatives in America*, 16–31.

8. Keith Bradley and Alan Gelb, "Motivation and Control in the Mondragon Experiment," *British Journal of Industrial Relations* 19 (1981): 211–31; Thomas and Logan, *Economic Analysis*, 49–52.

9. William Foote Whyte and Kathleen King Whyte, "Mondragon: A Vision Lives On," *National Catholic Reporter* 25 (3 March 1989): 2. Wiener and Oakeshott, *Worker-Owners*, 75–77.

10. Thomas and Logan, *Economic Analysis*, 71–72, 158–61, 181–186; Whyte and Whyte, *Making Mondragon*, 113–27, 204–11; Wiener and Oakeshott, *Worker-Owners*, 65.

11. Sally L. Hacker, "Gender and Technology at the Mondragon System of Producer Cooperatives," *Economic and Industrial Democracy* 9 (May 1988): 231.

12. Retention of capital funds for use in the enterprise and advance-

ment of the goal of job creation is considered by some scholars to be a very significant factor in the success of the Mondragon system. See Frank H. Stephen, *The Economic Analysis of Producer Cooperatives* (London: Macmillan, 1984), 174–202; Henk Thomas, "The Dynamics of Social Ownership: Some Considerations in the Perspective of the Mondragon Experience," *Economic Analysis and Workers' Management* 19 (1985): 147–60; and Blasi, *Employee Ownership,* 196–98.

13. Bradley and Gelb, *Cooperation at Work,* 62.

14. See Whyte and Whyte, *Making Mondragon,* 68–87, 169–87, for the most complete description of the bank and its history.

15. Quoted in Oakeshott, *The Case for Workers' Cooperatives,* 175.

16. Whyte and Whyte, *Making Mondragon,* 186.

17. An English translation of a form of Contract of Association is found at Wiener and Oakeshott, *Worker-Owners,* 69–74.

18. Wiener and Oakeshott, *Worker-Owners,* 21–24, summarizes the new structure.

19. The LDS Board of Trade is described in Arrington, Fox, and May, *Building the City of God,* 315–33. The function of enabling smaller groups to compete effectively in a Big Business economy is comparable. The circumstances which led to their adoption were different. In Utah, the Board of Trade was instituted to coordinate the activities of both cooperative and private noncooperative LDS businesses. It was instituted in part as a sort of "rear-guard" effort to try to preserve some degree of cooperation among Mormons attracted by the desire to engage in business on a capitalistic basis. In contrast, the Mondragon congress and council of groups are a result of the vibrant growth of an all-cooperative community of enterprises.

20. Good descriptions of the work of the Entrepreneurial Division are found in Oakeshott, *The Case for Worker Cooperatives,* 206–12, and Whyte and Whyte, *Making Mondragon,* 71–87.

21. See generally Whyte and Whyte, *Making Mondragon,* 129–222, and Keith Bradley and Alan Gelb, "Cooperative Labour Relations: Mondragon's Response to Recession," *British Journal of Industrial Relations* 25 (1987): 77–97. Such corporate downsizings have not in fact led to the expected increases in productivity or profitability except, ironically, when they are effected through extensive employee consultation and participation. Fuchsberg, "Why Shake-Ups Work for Some, Not Others," B1, B4.

22. See Bradley and Gelb, *Cooperation at Work,* 50, 55, and Keith Bradley and Alan Gelb, "The Replication and Sustainability of the Mondragon Experiment," *British Journal of Industrial Relations* 20 (1982): 20–33, particularly 22–23.

23. Thomas and Logan, *Economic Analysis,* 172–73.

24. Sol Encel, "Reflections on a Visit to Mondragon," *Bulletin of the International Communal Studies Association* 8 (fall 1990): 4–6.

25. Wiener and Oakeshott, *Worker-Owners,* 52–53.

26. See for example Hacker, *Gender and Technology.* Author Woodworth has argued elsewhere that the alliance of cooperative ideals to practical, 'hard' technical education is one of the important ingredients in the Mondragon success story. Christopher B. Meek and Warner P. Woodworth,

"Technical Training and Enterprise: Mondragon's Educational System and Its Implications for other Cooperatives," *Economic and Industrial Democracy* 11 (November 1990): 505–28.

27. The fullest account of the strike and its aftermath is Whyte and Whyte, *Making Mondragon,* 91–112. On labor union attitudes see also Oakeshott, *The Case for Worker Cooperatives,* 196–97, 244–48; Wiener and Oakeshott, *Worker-Owners,* 55–58; and John C. Raines and Donna C. Day-Lowen, *Modern Work and Human Meaning* (Philadelphia: Westminster Press, 1986), 139.

28. Whyte and Whyte, *Making Mondragon,* 3–4, 272–76; Oakeshott, *The Case for Worker Cooperatives,* 39, 259–60. The federal structure for interfirm cooperation is one important specific element which has permitted the Mondragon cooperatives to avoid the negative predictions of critics of worker cooperatives. See Frederick Leete-Guy, "Federal Structure and the Viability of Labour-Managed Firms in Mixed Economies," in *Ownership and Participation,* vol. 2 of *International Handbook of Participation in Organizations,* ed. Raymond Russell and Veljko Rus (Oxford: Oxford University Press, 1991), 64–79.

29. Beatrice Webb, "Appendix E: Why the Self-Governing Workshop Has Failed," in *My Apprenticeship,* 446–53. See also Connel M. Fanning and Thomas McCarthy, "A Survey of Economic Hypotheses Concerning the Non-Viability of Labour-Directed Firms in Capitalist Economies," in *Labor-Owned Firms and Workers' Cooperatives,* ed. Sune Jansson and Ann-Britt Hellmark (Aldershot, U.K.: Gower Publishing, 1986), 7–50.

30. Bradley and Gelb, "The Mondragon Cooperatives: Guidelines for a Cooperative Economy?," in Jones and Svejnar, *Participatory and Self-Managed Firms,* 162–69.

31. See Chris Cornforth, "Can Entrepreneurship Be Institutionalized? The Case of Worker Co-operatives," *International Small Business Journal* 6 (July–September 1988): 10, 15–18.

32. Cornforth, *Can Entrepreneurship Be Institutionalized?*

33. Keith Bradley, Saul Estrin, and Simon Taylor, "Employee Ownership and Company Performance," *Industrial Relations* 29 (fall 1990): 385–402.

34. Walton, *Made in America,* 131–32.

35. See discussion and notes in chapter 18 under "Stewardship, Equality and Self-reliance—Personal Development, Participation and the Management of the United Order Principles Inspired Enterprise" and "Stewardship, Self-reliance and Alienation." A recent summary of the research on this point is Derek C. Jones and Jeffrey Pliskin, "The Effects of Worker Participation, Employee Ownership, and Profit-Sharing on Economic Performance: A Partial Review," in *Ownership and Participation,* 43–63. Even sympathetic commentators have remarked on the strong elitist bias in the Webbs' advocacy of rule by a bureaucracy of professional experts insulated from control by uninformed legislators. See, for example, Barbara E. Nolan, *The Political Theory of Beatrice Webb* (New York: AMS Press, 1988), 219–53, and Thomas Clarke, "Democracy, Integration, and Commercial Survival: The Webbs on Associations of Producers," in *Ownership and Participation,* 123–34. John Carey, a professor at Oxford, has argued that many Fabian intellectuals, including Shaw and Wells, denigrated the lower and middle classes and expressed views

which were in fact compatible with those of their fascist contemporaries. The Webbs, however, are not included in this criticism (Carey, *The Intellectuals and the Masses*). The late Christopher Lasch has made somewhat similar charges against America's modern intellectual elites (Christopher Lasch, *The Revolt of the Elites and the Betrayal of Democracy* [New York: W. W. Norton, 1995]).

36. Oakeshott, *The Case for Workers' Cooperatives*, 214.

37. See Turpin-Forster, *Mondragon's Message*, 2–4.

38. Henk Thomas, "The Performance of the Mondragon Cooperatives in Spain," in *Participatory and Self-Managed Firms*, ed. Jones and Svejnar, 144.

39. Indeed, while founders of the Church Welfare program such as Harold B. Lee and Marion G. Romney were soon called to apostolic responsibilities, Don Jose Maria was never promoted in the Catholic Church. He ended his career in the Catholic priesthood as he began, a parish priest in Mondragon.

40. Bradley and Gelb, *Motivation and Control*, 219.

41. *JD* 19:308.

42. See chapter 20, note 36.

Chapter 20

1. Snow, "Mormonism, By Its Head," 259. Also quoted in William J. McNiff, *Heaven on Earth: A Planned Mormon Society* (Oxford, Ohio: Mississippi Valley Press, 1940), 47. This was probably president Snow's last writing before his death.

2. Mangum and Blumell, *Mormons' War on Poverty*, 161–65, 187, 203–8.

3. Mangum and Blumell, *Mormons' War on Poverty*, 172.

4. That is with proper legal guidance. Don Jose Maria did considerable ground work in ferreting out obscure provisions of Spanish banking law which provided a solid legal basis for the Caja Laboral Popular, and even permitted it to pay an extra point of interest above the then mandated legal rate, which gave the CLP a competitive advantage. BYU scholars who have studied the Kirtland Safety Society bank episode have suggested that it would have been preferable if Joseph had waited to obtain a legal charter from the state of Ohio. See Hill, Rooker, and Wimmer, "The Kirtland Economy Revisited," 391–475.

5. Charles Kuehl and Peggy Lambing, *Small Business Planning and Management*, 2nd ed. (Chicago: Dryden Press, 1990), 113.

6. Using one's surplus to produce employment opportunities for the poor is after all, as Lorenzo Snow said, the "spirit and aim of the United Order." See *JD* 19:349.

7. Isaac Ferguson, "Humanitarian Service," in *EM*, 661–63.

8. Ferguson, "Freely Given," 10–15; Gerry Avant, "Lifting Families from Poverty," *Church News*, 17 November 1990, 8–10.

9. One banking law expert has suggested to us that a Utah state chartered industrial bank would be an excellent vehicle for such an institution. A good summary on setting up microlending from a banking point of view is Jayne Crosby Giles, "Microbusiness Lending: Bank Services for the Smallest Companies," *Journal of Commercial Lending* 76 (November 1993): 21–31. ACCION International publishes a variety of guides for setting up and operating microlending projects. See ACCION International, *An Operational Guide*

for Micro-Enterprise Projects (Toronto: Calmeadow Foundation, 1988), and Maria Otero and Elisabeth Rhyne, eds., *The New World of Microenterprise Finance: Building Healthy Financial Institutions for the Poor* (West Hartford, Conn.: Kumarian Press, 1994).

10. To ignore this is not only contrary to the united order principle of equality, but to plead for trouble. Access to credit is one of the most powerful advantages in any economy, whether it is Wall Street or the informal market on the local plaza. A significant element of the American savings and loan scandal of the 1980s was that bank insiders used their influence to get financing for their own unsound, personal projects. Nothing could generate controversy more quickly than if UOPIFI loans were given to build up the private wealth of a few individual business owners. Lending only to employee-owned businesses assures the widest possible distribution of the benefits of a UOPIFI consistent with private ownership, and should obviate this potential source of controversy.

11. If official Church involvement was thought useful or necessary, some local Church leaders could perhaps hold a minority of Board seats *ex officio*. Otherwise, acting as unofficial spiritual advisors and supporters, in the manner of Don Jose Maria, would probably be the most effective position for Church leaders. Of course, there would be no reason to prevent individuals who also happened to have Church leadership callings from working in UOPIEs for their secular livelihood.

12. Peter Abell and Nicholas Mahoney, *Establishing Support Systems for Industrial Cooperatives: Case Studies from Third World Countries* (Brookfield, Vt.: Gower, 1988).

13. John Taylor cited this latter factor in explaining why a storehouse was not created in the Utah united order effort. See *JD* 17:179.

14. Abell and Mahoney, "The Performance of Small-Scale Producer Cooperatives in Developing Countries," in Jones and Svejnar, *Participatory and Self-Managed Firms*, 295.

15. The difference between a "Grameen"-style loan and a local bank loan is that the "Grameen" lender will lend on the basis of the affinity group's collective reputation and repayment record rather than requiring hard assets as security. Lending at a profitable interest rate is also necessary for the lender to become self-supporting rather than continually dependent on donors for funding. See Richard L. Meyer, "Financial Services for Microenterprises," in *Microenterprises in Developing Countries*, ed. Jacob Levitsky (London: Intermediate Technology Publications, 1989), 126–27.

16. See Bowers, "Third World Debt," B2, and Hossain, *Credit for the Rural Poor*, 63–71, 127. Hossain's study of the Grameen Bank's hundreds of thousands of microloans found that almost 90 percent were current and less than 2 percent ultimately defaulted.

17. Arrington, *Beet Sugar*, 11–13.

18. Arrington, *Beet Sugar*, 95–100, 124–27.

19. *JD* 1:214–15.

20. Kuehl and Lambing, *Small Business*, 17; Mary Rowland, "Why Small Businesses Are Failing," *New York Times*, 11 August 1991, F16; and Clifford Baumback, *How to Organize and Operate a Small Business*, 8th ed. (Englewood

Cliffs, N.J.: Prentice-Hall, 1988), 16–18.

21. The willingness of able managers to remain in the producer cooperative sector has been found to be a critical factor to their success. The supposed inability of cooperatives to have effective management was one of the reasons Beatrice Webb argued that they could not work. The experience of Mondragon seems to refute this, but the issue remains as to whether other worker cooperatives can secure the same management allegiance. See Peter Abell, "Supporting Industrial Cooperatives in Developing Countries: Some Tanzanian Experiences," *Economic and Industrial Democracy* 11 (November 1990): 483–504, and Peter Abell and Nicholas Mahoney, *Small-Scale Industrial Producer Cooperatives in Developing Countries* (Delhi: Oxford University Press, 1988).

22. See Gordon B. Hinckley, "Out of Your Experience Here," *BYU Today* (March 1991): 18–21, 35–37; Boyd K. Packer, "The Edge of the Light," *BYU Today* (March 1991): 22–24, 38–43.

23. Baumback, *How to Organize,* 15, 65. Franchise chains are in fact a worthwhile model to explore for developing united order businesses. They are often labor intensive, they lend themselves to independent local ownership and management, they use collective resources (such as advertising and research and development) economically, and they permit the efficient delivery of management assistance.

24. Abell and Mahoney, "Small-Scale Producer Cooperatives," 295.

25. See chapter 18, note 26.

26. One of Sam Walton's rules for success was to always exceed your customers' expectations (Walton, *Made in America,* 248).

27. Applying the principle of equality in a UOPIE would challenge executives to share more than money. As discussed in chapter 18, UOPIEs preferably would be managed with extensive worker participation. Sharing real management authority is difficult even for the management of companies with employee ownership, and is a major reason why top managers resist implementing this well-proven path to corporate success. See Aaron Bernstein, "Why ESOP Deals Have Slowed to a Crawl: Few Executives Seem Comfortable Sharing Power with Employees," *Business Week,* 18 March 1996, 101–2.

28. Gordon E. Wagner, "Stewardship in the Southern Sudan" (paper presented at the Plotting Zion conference sponsored by Sunstone Foundation and National Historic Communal Societies Association, Provo, Utah, 3–5 May 1990).

29. Sylvia Nasar, "Third World Embracing Reforms to Encourage Economic Growth," *New York Times,* 8 July 1991, A1, D3. While the best ideas should come from the potential participants, a few ideas may suggest the possible range of opportunities. One intriguing international business opportunity is the development of drugs derived from local lore about rain forest plants. One start-up pharmaceutical company, Shaman Pharmaceuticals, Inc., is already trying to exploit this possibility (Thomas M. Burton, "Drug Company to 'Witch Doctors' to Conjure Products," *Wall Street Journal,* 7 July 1994, A1, A8. The growing numbers of Latter-day Saints in tropical areas offer a natural base for such a search. Cultivating useful plants for such medical

drugs could then supply a continuing local cooperative business. In addition, to local Saints, at least one BYU botany professor, Paul Cox, has established an international reputation in this area (Charlene Renberg Winters, "AIDS Knowledge May Get Boost from Samoan Rain Forest," *BYU Today* [September 1992], 2–3, and Sheridan R. Sheffield, "Botanist's Studies Motivated by Desire to Help Sick, Afflicted," *Church News,* 5 September 1992, 7). Opportunities also exist in areas that are more urban. Cooperative Home Care Associates of the Bronx in New York City is a successful worker cooperative which trains and employs disadvantaged women in the growing field of home health care (Douglas Martin, "Hiring Welfare Recipients and Making Them Management," *New York Times,* 21 May 1994, 26). A successful cooperative in Belgium operated by former unemployed and other disadvantaged people recycles 25 tons a day of discarded clothing, shoes, and other consumer goods, and donates its profits to form worker cooperatives in developing countries (Marlise Simons, "Gold in Streets [Some Call It Trash]," *New York Times,* 4 January 1994, A4). In South Africa's large informal sector, enterprising shopkeepers built themselves a cooperative shopping mall out of shipping containers. With the coming of democratic rule and the growth of the Church among South Africa's urban blacks, organizing and financing such efforts could yield very visible benefits to local Saints and their communities (Bill Keller, "A South African Mall That Black Know-How Built," *New York Times,* 12 September 1993, L3).

30. Evans and Sutherland, a large computer graphics firm was started in Salt Lake City in 1968, and smaller, newer firms have since been spun off through the University of Utah's research park. A group of high-tech medical firms have emerged in Salt Lake City as well, engaged in leading-edge products such as the artificial heart. Further south, in Utah County, a number of entrepreneurial firms were established from BYU research and collegial networks. WordPerfect, started in the late 1970s, did its first $1 million sales in 1982 and was a half billion dollar word processing corporation with 5,600 employees at the time of its sale to Novell. In a decade Novell moved from being a tiny computer manufacturer with 14 employees to a computer network global giant doing over $1 billion in business yearly. All told, some 150 new technology-based firms employing 8,000 people have sprung up in Utah Valley, growing at about 20 percent annually. Entrepreneurial values such as a need to achieve, hard work, and optimism tend to be characteristic of many Latter-day Saints, making business start-ups a common, rather than rare, phenomenon. The following excerpt captures the linkage of resource networks derived from relationships between faculty and students in BYU's Computer Science Department and over 30 Utah Valley firms. Individuals, concepts, and financing have facilitated business growth by such occurrences as the following: "Paul Sybrowsky, the founder of Dynix, a company that specializes in computerized library systems and has annual revenues of $25 million, gained funding for his venture through Eyring Research. The connection between Sybrowsky and Eyring was made through Sybrowsky's 'home teacher'—a person in The Church of Jesus Christ of Latter-Day Saints who makes monthly visits to church members to determine and meet their needs. When Sybrowsky's home teacher, an employee at Eyring, found out that Sybrowsky needed capital to fund his struggling venture, he introduced him

to the right people at Eyring. Through the funding provided by Eyring, the company, initially a division of Eyring, has been able to grow substantially and is now an independent corporation" (Dyer, *The Entrepreneurial Experience,* 47). Carol M. Bullinger, "Utah Valley: Coming into Its Own," *BYU Today* (January 1990): 38–48, and "Technology in Utah: Software Valley," *Economist* (23 April 1994): 69–70, survey Utah Valley's booming entrepreneurial activity.

31. For example, see Bullinger, *Utah Valley,* 48, and "Technology in Utah," 69, which notes that "few of the state's software start-ups received help from the local banks, which still class venture capital alongside hard liquor."

32. *JD* 17:78. See chapter 8 for a fuller discussion of the financing function in the united order.

33. See David Knowlton, "Missionaries and Terror: The Assassination of Two Elders in Bolivia," *Sunstone* 13 (August 1989): 10–15.

34. Dean L. May, "Brigham Young and the Bishops: The United Order in the City," in *New Views of Mormon History: A Collection of Essays in Honor of Leonard J. Arrington,* ed. Davis Bitton and Maureen Ursenbach Beecher (Salt Lake City: University of Utah Press, 1987), 126.

35. Bradley and Gelb, "Replication and Sustainability," 20–33.

36. The principles of the united order outlined in chapter 10 can be used to analyze how the two could complement each other in fulfilling the objectives of the law of consecration and stewardship. *Care for the Poor, Work and Self-Reliance:* The Welfare program assists all the worthy poor and needy, including the unemployable or those who do not qualify for employment in the UOPIEs. It also takes into account their individual circumstances. On the other hand, the Welfare program is not set up for job creation and cannot always provide opportunities for recipients to work. UOPIEs would provide living "inheritances" for their workers in the form of jobs and requires that they perform real work, as required by the commandments. However, the jobs are not adjusted to take into account individual family circumstances. The UOPIEs and the Welfare program would complement each other. UOPIEs provide employment for the employable and surplus wealth which can permit the Welfare program to assist the unemployed or unemployable poor and needy. *Consecration:* The Welfare program calls for limited consecration in the form of fast offerings. UOPIEs would also likely call for only a limited consecration in the form of entry Mondragon-style contributions or perhaps using a UOPIFI for banking services. *Equality:* UOPIEs can promote equalization by constitutional restrictions on ownership and salary differentials. The Welfare program does little to make the Saints equal in earthly things. *Stewardship:* In the Welfare program accountability and management-control rest with priesthood leaders or Church officials. In UOPIEs, accountability and management control rest with the "voice and common consent of the Order." *The Storehouse:* Both pool surpluses into a common treasury or storehouse. The Welfare program's bishop's storehouse uses its resources more for the assistance of the poor than would a UOPIFI. A UOPIFI would be more actively involved in the increase of its "talents" to further expand and benefit the "Lord's storehouse" and in providing "inheritances," i.e., job creation. *Moral motivation:* Both systems seek to inculcate moral behavior beyond

that needed to achieve their immediate economic objectives.

37. See for example, Norman Uphoff, "Paraprojects as New Modes of International Development Assistance," *World Development* 18 (October 1990): 1401–11, and Raundi Halvorson-Quevedo, "The Growing Potential of Micro-Enterprises," *The OECD Observer* 173 (December 1991/January 1992): 7–11.

38. On the economic possibilities of Mormon fraternity, see Kotkin, *Tribes*, 245–49, and Fukuyama, *Trust*, 290–93. A study of a rural Mexican town where the Church was well-established found that local Latter-day Saints not only pursued more education and worked harder than their neighbors, but also were more likely to cooperate with other villagers in adopting agricultural innovations and improvements (David L. Clawson, "Religious Allegiance and Economic Development in Rural Latin America," *Journal of Interamerican Studies and World Affairs* 26 [1984]: 499–524).

Chapter 21

1. *JD* 12:153.

2. See Anthony DePalma, "Economy Reeling, Mexicans Prepare Tough New Steps," *New York Times*, 26 February 1995, A1, A8, and Geri Smith and Elisabeth Malkin, "Surveying the Wreckage," *Business Week*, 23 January 1995, 58–59. Even before the crash of the peso in early 1995, Mexico's per capita income was below the level of 1980.

3. Joseph Smith, Jr., *Teachings*, 248.

4. Carnegie, *Problems of To-day*, 2.

5. Webb, *My Apprenticeship*, 346–47.

6. Hayek, *Road to Serfdom*, 36.

7. Carnegie, *Problems of To-day*, 132.

8. *JD* 20:165.

9. See, for example, Alasdair Clayre, ed., *The Political Economy of Co-operation and Participation: A Third Sector* (Oxford: Oxford University Press, 1980).

10. Widtsoe, "Evidences and Reconciliations: Are Communism and Its Related 'Isms' Preparatory to the United Order?" 633.

11. Oaks, *Pure in Heart*, 86. The entire discussion on materialism and pride (chapters 5 and 6) is recommended.

12. Spencer, *Social Statics*, 353–54, 414.

13. See also 1 Nephi 9:2–4, Jarom 14, 3 Nephi 5:8–9, and Ether 15:33. A fuller discussion of this point can be found in Richard Dilworth Rust, "The Book of Mormon, Designed for Our Day," *Review of Books on The Book of Mormon* 2 (1990): 1–25.

14. Snow, "Mormonism, By Its Head," 259. Of the free enterprise system, Ezra Taft Benson wrote, "Are we to discard a system that has produced so much simply because it has not worked perfectly? We all admit that there are abuses. . . . all will agree that family life is not perfect . . . but our objective is not to throw the family overboard, but rather to work for the improvement of family relations" [Benson, *God, Family, Country*, 310–11]. As suggested by President Benson, our object should be to improve the free enterprise system by acting more righteously in our economic activities. We recommend all of chapter 31 of *God, Family, Country* (pp. 305–15) as an excellent short summary of the argument for the free enterprise system.

15. *JD* 15:169.

16. Howard W. Hunter, "The Gospel—A Global Faith," *Ensign* 21 (November 1991): 18–19.

17. Examples of conservative worldly philosophies are the immoral egoism of Friedrich Nietzsche and Ayn Rand or the intense individualism and anti-communitarianism that led one LDS writer on the united order to dismiss it entirely and argue that the law of consecration does not require any sacrifice on the part of the wealthy other than tithing and fast offerings and that property "producing the funds needed to support the poor would be most efficiently operated by private owners, with a *small portion* of the income donated to the support system for the poor" (Huff, *Joseph Smith's United Order,* 349, emphasis added). See also chapter 9, notes 21 and 50.

18. See references in chapter 1, note 13, and the description of Kay Whitmore's ouster in chapter 1. The references to Presidents Kimball and Benson are discussed in chapter 16.

19. *JD* 21:148.

20. This idea has been suggested in Mangum and Blumell, *Mormons' War on Poverty,* 268–71.

21. Smith, *Moral Sentiments,* 237.

22. *JD* 20:165.

23. *JD* 17:48–49.

24. Joseph Smith, Jr., *Teachings,* 366. See also Joseph Smith, Jr., *Words of Joseph Smith,* 367.

25. Carnegie, "The Industrial Problem," 60.

26. Quoted in Webb, *Our Partnership,* 366–67. In this particular passage, she was reacting to H. G. Wells' arguments in favor of "free love" (i.e., sexual promiscuity).

27. King, quoted in Tullis, *Mormonism,* 356. Many European Latter-day Saints past and present come from socialist backgrounds. See Wilfried Decoo, "Mormonism in a European Catholic Region: A Contribution to the Social Psychology of LDS Converts," *Brigham Young University Studies* 24 (winter 1984): 61–77.

28. Joseph Frazier Wall (Carnegie biographer), telephone conversation with James Lucas, 3 September 1992.

29. Harold Bloom, *The American Religion: The Emergence of the Post-Christian Nation* (New York: Simon & Schuster, 1992), 86.

30. Arrington, *Great Basin Kingdom,* 411–12.

31. Mark P. Leone, "An Anthropological View of *Great Basin Kingdom,*" in *Great Basin Kingdom Revisited: Contemporary Perspectives,* ed. Thomas G. Alexander (Logan, Utah: Utah State University Press, 1991), 91, 93, 95.

32. *JD* 7:145.

33. Spencer W. Kimball, "The Stone Cut without Hands," *Ensign* 6 (May 1976): 7, 9.

34. *JD* 15:169.

35. *JD* 12:153.

Photography Credits

The authors express their appreciation to the staffs of several organizations, as well as individuals who shared their photographs for this book. The photos throughout this volume are from the following sources and are used with their permission.

Archival material

The Daily Herald: Page 52 (steel mill)

Mondragon Cooperative Corporation: Pages 311, 318, 331

New York Public Library: Pages 14, 71, 85, 86, 128

© Utah State Historical Society. All rights reserved. Used by permission: Pages 15, 45, 96, 114, 148, 155, 166, 187, 242, 252, 296, 360.

Contemporary photographs

Chuck Cozzens: Page 214

Richard Oscarson: Page 221

Cassandra Stuart: Page 279

Warner Woodworth: Pages 2, 52 (Third World), 208

Bibliography

Abell, Peter. "Supporting Industrial Cooperatives in Developing Countries: Some Tanzanian Experiences." *Economic and Industrial Democracy* 11 (November 1990): 483–504.

Abell, Peter, and Nicholas Mahoney. "The Performance of Small-Scale Producer Cooperatives in Developing Countries." In *Participatory and Self-Managed Firms,* edited by Derek Jones and Jan Svejnar. Lexington, Mass.: Lexington Books, 1982.

———. *Establishing Support Systems for Industrial Cooperatives: Case Studies from Third World Countries.* Brookfield, Vt.: Gower, 1988.

———. *Small-Scale Industrial Producer Cooperatives in Developing Countries.* Delhi: Oxford University Press, 1988.

ACCION International. *ACCION International Bulletin* 30, no. 4 (autumn 1995).

———. *An Operational Guide for Micro-Enterprise Projects* (Toronto: Calmeadow Foundation, 1988).

Alexander, Thomas G. "The Economic Consequences of the War: Utah and the Depression of the Early 1920s." In *A Dependent Commonwealth: Utah's Economy from Statehood to the Great Depression,* edited by Dean L. May. Provo, Utah: Brigham Young University Press, 1974.

———. *Mormonism in Transition: A History of the Latter-day Saints 1890–1930.* Chicago: University of Illinois Press, 1986.

———. "Wilford Woodruff, Intellectual Progress, and the Growth of an Amateur Scientific and Technological Tradition in Early Territorial Utah." *Utah Historical Quarterly* 59 (spring 1991): 164–88.

Allen, Edward J. *The Second United Order among the Mormons.* New York: Columbia University Press, 1936.

Allen, James B., and Glen M. Leonard. *The Story of the Latter-day Saints.* Salt Lake City: Deseret Book, 1976.

Allen, James B., and Malcolm R. Thorp. "The Mission of the Twelve to England, 1840–41: The Mormon Apostles and the Working Classes." *Brigham Young University Studies* 15 (summer 1975): 499–526.

Allen, James B., David Whittaker, and Ron Esplin. *Men with a Mission: The Quorum of the Twelve in the British Isles.* Salt Lake City: Deseret Book, 1991.

Alter, Jonathon. "The 80's: A Final Reckoning." *Newsweek,* 1 March 1993, 49.

Andersen, Laura. "Foundation Helping Filipinos Establish Small Businesses." (Salt Lake City)*Deseret News,* 9–10 September 1992, B4.

Andrews, Edmund L. "A.T.&T. Cutting Up to 15,000 Jobs to Trim Costs." *New York Times,* 11 February 1994, D1, D14.

"Annual Church Report." *Improvement Era* 44 (May 1941): 317.

Applebome, Peter. "Study Ties Educational Gains to More Productivity Growth." *New York Times,* 14 May 1995, A22.

Armour, Leslie. "Smith, Morality and the Bankers." *Review of Social Economy* 34 (December 1976): 359–71.

Arrington, Leonard J. *Beet Sugar in the West: A History of the Utah-Idaho Sugar Company 1891–1966.* Seattle: University of Washington Press, 1966.

———. *Brigham Young: American Moses.* New York: Alfred A. Knopf, 1985.

———. "The Commercialization of Utah's Economy: Trends and Developments from Statehood to 1910." In *A Dependent Commonwealth: Utah's Economy from Statehood to the Great Depression,* edited by Dean L. May. Provo, Utah: Brigham Young University Press, 1974.

———. *Great Basin Kingdom: An Economic History of the Latter-day Saints 1830–1900.* Cambridge: Harvard University Press, 1958.

———. *Orderville, Utah: A Pioneer Mormon Experiment in Economic Organization.* Logan, Utah: Utah State Agricultural College, 1954.

Arrington, Leonard J., and Davis Bitton. *The Mormon Experience: A History of the Latter-day Saints.* New York: Alfred A. Knopf, 1979.

Arrington, Leonard J., Feramorz Fox, and Dean L. May. *Building the City of God: Community and Cooperation among the Mormons.* Salt Lake City: Deseret Book, 1976.

Arrington, Leonard J., and Jon Haupt. "Intolerable Zion: The Image of Mormonism in Nineteenth Century American Literature." *Western Humanities Review* 22 (1968): 243–60.

Arrington, Leonard J., and Wayne K. Hinton. "Origin of the Welfare Plan of The Church of Jesus Christ of Latter-day Saints." *Brigham Young University Studies* 5 (winter 1964): 67–85.

"Assistance Proffered in Armenia." *Church News,* 1 April 1995, 11.

Avant, Gerry. "Lifting Families from Poverty." *Church News,* 17 November 1990, 8–10.

Babbel, Frederick W. *On Wings of Faith.* Salt Lake City: Bookcraft, 1972.

Backman, Milton V. *The Heavens Resound: A History of the Latter-day Saints in Ohio 1830–1838.* Salt Lake City: Deseret Book, 1983.

Bacon, Kenneth H. "Inner City Capitalists Push to Start a Bank for Their Community." *Wall Street Journal,* 9 January 1993, A1, A6.

Ballard, M. Russell. "Counseling with Our Councils." *Ensign* 24 (May 1994): 24–26.

———. "Strength in Counsel." *Ensign* 23 (November 1993): 76–78.

Bannister, Robert C. *Social Darwinism: Science and Myth in Anglo-American Social Thought.* Philadelphia: Temple University Press, 1979.

Barnet, Richard J. "The End of Jobs: Employment Is One Thing the Global Economy Is *Not* Creating." *Harper's* 287 (September 1993): 47–52.

Barnet, Richard J., and John Cavanagh. *Global Dreams: Imperial Corporations and the New World Order.* New York: Simon & Schuster, 1994.

Barthel, Diane L. *Amana: From Pietist Sect to American Community.* Lincoln, Nebr.: University of Nebraska Press, 1984.

Baseman, Kenneth C., Frederick R. Warren-Boulton, and Glenn A. Woroch. "Microsoft Plays Hardball: The Use of Exclusionary Pricing and Technical Incompatibility to Maintain Monopoly Power in Markets for Operating System Software." *Antitrust Bulletin* 40 (summer 1995): 265–315.

Baumback, Clifford. *How to Organize and Operate a Small Business.* 8th ed. Englewood Cliffs, N.J.: Prentice-Hall, 1988.

Beecher, Dale F. "The Office of Bishop." *Dialogue* 15 (winter 1982): 103–15.

Belasco, James A. *Teaching the Elephant to Dance: Empowering Change in Your Organization.* New York: Crown, 1990.

Belasco, James A., and Ralph C. Stayer. *Flight of the Buffalo.* New York: Warner, 1993.

Bell, James P. "The Poor among Us." *BYU Today* (September 1991): 38–46.

Bell, Spurgeon. *Productivity, Wages, and National Income.* Washington, D.C.: Brookings Institution, 1940.

Bellamy, Edward. *Looking Backward 2000–1887.* New York: Lancer Books, 1888. Reprint, 1968.

Bennett, Amanda. "Downsizing Doesn't Necessarily Bring an Upswing in Corporate Profitability." *Wall Street Journal,* 6 June 1991, B1.

Bennett, John W. *Hutterian Brethren: The Agricultural Economy and Social Organization of a Communal People.* Stanford, Calif.: Stanford University Press, 1967.

Benson, Ezra Taft. "Beware of Pride." *Ensign* 19 (May 1989): 4–7.

———. "Cleansing the Inner Vessel." *Ensign* 16 (May 1986): 4–9.

———. *God, Family, Country: Our Three Great Loyalties.* Salt Lake City: Deseret Book, 1974.

———. "May the Kingdom of God Go Forth." *Ensign* 8 (May 1978): 32–34.

———. "Principles of Cooperation." *Improvement Era* 48 (November 1945): 653, 710–11.

———. *Teachings of Ezra Taft Benson.* Salt Lake City: Bookcraft, 1988.

———. *This Nation Shall Endure.* Salt Lake City: Deseret Book, 1977.

———. "A Vision and A Hope for the Youth of Zion." In *1977 Devotional Speeches of the Year.* Provo, Utah: Brigham Young University Press, 1978.

Berger, Joseph. "The Pain of Layoffs for Ex-Senior I.B.M. Workers." *New York Times,* 22 December 1993, B1, B5.

Berger, Marguerite and Mayra Buvinic, eds. *Women's Ventures: Assistance to the Informal Sector in Latin America* (West Hartford, Conn.: Kumarian Press, 1989).

Berle, Adolf A., Jr. *The American Economic Republic.* New York: Harcourt, Brace & World, 1963.

Berle, Adolf A., Jr., and Gardiner C. Means. *The Modern Corporation and Private Property.* New York: Macmillan, 1933.

Bernstein, Aaron. "Inequality: How the Gap between Rich and Poor Hurts the Economy." *Business Week,* 15 August 1994, 78–83

———. "Why ESOP Deals Have Slowed to a Crawl: Few Executives Seem Comfortable Sharing Power with Employees." *Business Week,* 18 March 1996, 101–2.

Bestor, Arthur E. *Backwoods Utopias: The Sectarian Origins and the Owenite Phase of Communitarian Socialism in America 1663–1829.* 2nd ed. Philadelphia: University of Pennsylvania Press, 1970.

Billet, Leonard. "The Just Economy: The Moral Basis of *The Wealth of Nations.*" *Review of Social Economy* 34 (December 1976): 295–315.

Binstein, Michael, and Charles Bowden. *Trust Me: Charles Keating and the Missing Billions.* New York: Random House, 1993.

Bittker, Boris I. *Federal Taxation of Income, Estates and Gifts.* Boston: Warren, Gorham & Lamont, 1981.

Blanchard, Ken. "Alternatives to Downsizing." *Manage* 47 (July 1995): 11–12.

Blasi, Joseph R. *The Communal Experience of the Kibbutz.* New Brunswick, N.J.: Transaction Books, 1986.

———. *Employee Ownership: Revolution or Ripoff?* New York: Harper & Row, 1988.

Blasi, Joseph R., and Douglas Kruse. *The New Owners: the Mass Emergence of Employee Ownership in Public Companies and What it Means to American Business.* New York: HarperBusiness, 1991.

Blinder, Alan S., ed. *Paying for Productivity: A Look at the Evidence.* Washington, D.C.: Brookings Institution, 1990.

Block, Peter. *The Empowered Manager: Positive Political Skills at Work.* San Francisco: Jossey-Bass, 1987.

———. *Stewardship: Choosing Service Over Self-Interest.* San Francisco: Berrett-Koehler Publishers, 1993.

Bloom, Harold. *The American Religion: The Emergence of the Post-Christian Nation.* New York: Simon & Schuster, 1992.

Bloxham, V. Ben, James R. Moss, and Larry C. Porter, eds. *Truth Will Prevail: The Rise of The Church of Jesus Christ of Latter-day Saints in the British Isles 1837–1987.* Solihull, U.K.: The Church of Jesus Christ of Latter-day Saints, 1987.

Blumell, Bruce D. "The LDS Response to the Teton Dam Disaster in Idaho." *Sunstone* 5 (March-April 1980): 35–42.

Bluth, John F., and Wayne K. Hinton. "The Great Depression." In *Utah's History,* edited by Richard D. Poll. Provo, Utah: Brigham Young University Press, 1978.

Boff, Leonardo. *Faith on the Edge: Religion and Marginalized Existence.* San Francisco: Harper and Row, 1989.

Boff, Leonardo and Clodovis Boff. *Liberation Theology: From Confrontation to Dialogue.* San Francisco: Harper & Row, 1986.

Bohlen, Celestine. "Graft and Gangsterism in Russia Blight the Entrepreneurial Spirit." *New York Times,* 30 January 1994, A1, A12.

Boroughs, Don L. "Amputating Assets." *U.S. News & World Report,* 4 May 1992, 50–52.

Bovee, Tim. "Family Incomes Highest in Northeast." *Provo (Utah) Daily Herald,* 16 April 1993, A2.

Bowen, Howard R. *Social Responsibilities of the Businessman.* New York: Harper & Brothers, 1953.

Bowers, Brent. "How to Get Ahead as a Middle Manager by Being Ruthless." *Wall Street Journal,* 23 March 1993, A1, A9.

———. "Third World Debt That Is Almost Always Paid in Full." *Wall Street Journal,* 7 June 1991, B2.

Bowman, Sylvia E. *Edward Bellamy.* Boston: Twayne Publishers, 1986.

———, ed. *Edward Bellamy Abroad: An American Prophet's Influence.* New York: Twayne Publishers, 1962.

———. *The Year 2000: A Critical Biography of Edward Bellamy.* New York: Octagon Books, 1979.

Bradley, Keith, and Alan Gelb. *Cooperation at Work: The Mondragon Experience.*

London: Heinemann Educational Books, 1983.
———. "Cooperative Labour Relations: Mondragon's Response to Recession." *British Journal of Industrial Relations* 25 (1987): 77–97.
———. "Motivation and Control in the Mondragon Experiment." *British Journal of Industrial Relations* 19 (1981): 211–31.
———. "The Mondragon Cooperatives: Guidelines for a Cooperative Economy?" In *Participatory and Self-Managed Firms,* edited by Derek Jones and Jan Svejnar, 153–69. Lexington, Mass.: Lexington Books, 1982.
———. "The Replication and Sustainability of the Mondragon Experiment." *British Journal of Industrial Relations* 20 (1982): 20–33.
Bradley, Keith, Saul Estrin, and Simon Taylor. "Employee Ownership and Company Performance." *Industrial Relations* 29 (fall 1990): 385–402.
Braverman, Harry. *Labor and Monopoly Capital.* New York: Monthly Review Press, 1974.
Briggs, David. "Look for the Face of the Prophet Elijah in the Homeless." *Provo (Utah) Daily Herald,* 21 March 1993, C1.
Brody, David. *Workers in Industrial America: Essays on the Twentieth Century Struggle.* 2nd ed. New York: Oxford University Press, 1993.
Bronson, Po. "The Young and the Reckless." *New York Times,* 3 March 1995, A27.
Brooke, James. "Informal Capitalism Grows in Cameroon." *New York Times,* 30 November 1987, D8.
———. "Lending a Hand to the Small Latin Entrepreneur." *New York Times,* 1 August 1991, D6.
Brooks, John. *Showing Off in America.* Boston: Little, Brown, 1979.
Brown, Lester R., et al. *State of the World 1990.* New York: W.W. Norton & Co., 1990.
Brown, Victor L. "The Remarkable Example of the Bermejillo, Mexico Branch." *Ensign* 8 (November 1978): 79–81.
Browning, Gary L. "Out of Obscurity: The Emergence of The Church of Jesus Christ of Latter-day Saints in 'That Vast Empire' of Russia." *Brigham Young University Studies* (1993): 674–88.
Bruchey, Stuart. *The Wealth of the Nation: A Economic History of the United States.* New York: Harper & Row, 1988.
Bryant, Adam. "Kiwi Seeks New Labor Ethic, End to Us Versus Them." *New York Times,* 24 February 1994, D1, D5.
Bryne, John. "The Flap Over Executive Pay." *Business Week,* 6 May 1991, 90–96.
Bryne, John, and Chuck Hawkins. "Executive Pay: The Party Ain't Over Yet" *Business Week,* 26 April 1992, 56–64.
Buckley, William F., Jr. "Ayn Rand, RIP." *National Review,* 2 April 1982, 380–81.
Bullinger, Carol M. "Utah Valley: Coming into Its Own." *BYU Today* (January 1990): 38–48.
Bunker, Gary L., and Davis Bitton. *The Mormon Graphic Image, 1834–1914: Cartoons, Caricatures, and Illustrations.* Salt Lake City: University of Utah Press, 1983.
Burrough, Bryan, and John Helyer. *Barbarians at the Gate: The Fall of RJR Nabisco.* New York: Harper & Row, 1990.
Burton, Thomas M. "Drug Company to 'Witch Doctors' to Conjure Products." *Wall Street Journal,* 7 July 1994, A1, A8.

Bushman, Richard L. *Joseph Smith and the Beginnings of Mormonism.* Urbana: University of Illinois Press, 1984.

"Business-like Saints." *Economist,* 20 January 1963, 228.

Calverton, Victor F. *Where Angels Dared to Tread.* Indianapolis: Bobbs-Merrill, 1941.

Cameron, Kim S. "Strategies for Successful Organizational Downsizing." *Human Resource Management* 33 (summer 1994): 189–211.

Camp, Sharon L., and J. Joseph Speidel. *The International Human Suffering Index.* Washington, D. C.: The Population Crisis Committee, 1987.

Cannon, Janath R., Jill Mulvay Derr, and Maureen Ursenbach Beecher. *Women of Covenant: A History of the Relief Society.* Salt Lake City: Deseret Book, 1991.

Cannon, Mike. "Helping hearts and hands span the globe." *Church News,* 11 February 1995, 8–10.

———. "LDS Volunteer Efforts Bless Lives Worldwide." *Church News,* 15 December 1990, 3, 7.

"Capitalism: Punters or Proprietors?" *Economist,* 5 May 1990, 65–84.

Capson, Pat. "Utahns Extend a Much-Needed Helping Hand to Ouelessebougou." *Salt Lake Tribune,* 25 March 1993, A8.

Cardoso, Fernando Henriques, and Enzo Faletto. *Dependency and Development in Latin America.* Berkeley: University of California Press, 1979.

Carey, John. *The Intellectuals and the Masses: Pride and Prejudice among the Literary Intelligentsia, 1880–1939.* New York: St. Martin's Press, 1993.

"Caring in Africa." *Church News,* 31 October 1987, 8–10.

Carlson, Eugene. "SBA Introduces Its 'Microloan' Program." *Wall Street Journal,* 3 June 1992, B2.

Carnegie, Andrew. *Autobiography of Andrew Carnegie.* 1920. Reprint, Garden City, N.Y.: Doubleday, Doran & Company, 1933.

———. *Collected Papers.* Washington, D. C.: Library of Congress.

———. *The Gospel of Wealth and Other Essays.* Garden City, N.Y.: Doubleday, Doran & Company, 1933.

———. *Miscellaneous Writings of Andrew Carnegie.* Edited by Burton J. Hendrick. Garden City, N.Y.: Doubleday, Doran & Company, 1933.

———. *Problems of To-day: Wealth, Labor, Socialism.* 1908. Reprint, Garden City N.Y.: Doubleday, Doran & Company, 1933.

Carney, T. F. *The Economies of Antiquity.* Lawrence, Kans.: Coronado Press, 1973.

Carrington, John C., and George T. Edwards. *Financing Industrial Investment.* London: Macmillan, 1979.

Case, John. "A Company of Businesspeople." *Inc.,* April 1993, 79–93.

———. *Open-Book Management: The Coming Business Revolution.* New York: HarperBusiness, 1995.

Castro, Janice. "Disposable Workers." *Time,* 29 March 1993, 40–47.

Chandler, Alfred D., Jr. *Scale and Scope: The Dynamics of Industrial Capitalism.* Cambridge: Harvard University Press, 1990.

Chandler, Alfred D., Jr., and Richard S. Tedlow. *The Coming of Managerial Capitalism.* Homewood, Ill.: Richard D. Irwin, 1985.

Chandler, Susan. "United We Own." *Business Week,* 18 March 1996, 96–100.

Chernow, Ron. *The House of Morgan: An American Banking Dynasty and the Rise of Modern Finance.* New York: Atlantic Monthly Press, 1990.

Chilcote, Ronald H. *Theories of Development and Underdevelopment.* London: Westview Press, 1984.

Church Almanac, 1975. Salt Lake City: Deseret News, 1975.

Church Almanac, 1995. Salt Lake City: Deseret News, 1995.

Church of Jesus Christ of Latter-day Saints, The. *Providing in the Lord's Way.* Salt Lake City: The Church of Jesus Christ of Latter-day Saints, 1990.

"Church's Humanitarian Efforts Provide Relief around the World." *Church News,* 13 August 1994, 3.

Clark, J. Reuben, Jr. "Demand for Proper Respect of Human Life." *Improvement Era* 49 (November 1946): 688–89, 740.

———. "Private Ownership under the United Order." In *J. Reuben Clark: Selected Papers,* edited by David H. Yarn, Jr. Provo, Utah: Brigham Young University Press, 1984. The original address appears in *Improvement Era* 45 (November 1942): 688–89, 752–54. Citations are from the Yarn collection.

Clarke, Thomas. "Democracy, Integration, and Commercial Survival: The Webbs on Associations of Producers." In *Ownership and Participation,* vol. 2 of *International Handbook of Participation in Organizations,* edited by Raymond Russell and Veljko Rus, 123–34. Oxford: Oxford University Press, 1991.

Clawson, David L. "Religious Allegiance and Economic Development in Rural Latin America," *Journal of Interamerican Studies and World Affairs* 26 (1984): 499–524.

Clayre, Alasdair, ed. *The Political Economy of Co-operation and Participation: A Third Sector.* Oxford: Oxford University Press, 1980.

Clifford, Donald K., Jr., and Richard E. Cavanagh. *The Winning Performance: How America's High Growth Midsize Companies Succeed.* New York: Bantam Books, 1985.

Cohen, Roger. "Europe's Recession Prompts New Look at Welfare Costs." *New York Times,* 9 August 1993, A1, A8.

Collins, Clare. "Families That Do Good Together Enjoy It." *New York Times,* 6 June 1991, C10.

Collins, Lois M. "Portrait of Homeless In Utah Is Changing." (Salt Lake City) *Deseret News,* 30 January 1993, A10.

Commission of the European Communities. *Programme of Research and Actions on the Development of the Labour Market: Forms of Organisation, Type of Employment, Working Conditions, and Industrial Relations in Cooperatives, Any Collectiveness or Other Self-managing Structure of the EEC* (Luxembourg: Office for Official Publications of the European Communities; Washington, D.C.: European Community Information Service, 1986).

Conan Doyle, Arthur. *A Study in Scarlet.* 1887. Reprint, London: John Murray and Jonathon Cape, 1974.

Cook, Lyndon W. *Joseph Smith and the Law of Consecration.* Provo, Utah: Grandin Book, 1985.

Cornforth, Chris. "Can Entrepreneurship Be Institutionalized? The Case of Worker Co-operatives." *International Small Business Journal* 6 (July-September 1988): 10–18.

Cornforth, Chris, et al. *Developing Successful Worker Co-operatives.* London: Sage, 1988.

Cotton, John L., David A. Vollrath, Kirk L. Froggatt, Mark L. Longnick-Hall, and Kenneth R. Jennings. "Employee Participation: Diverse Forms and Different Outcomes." *Academy of Management Review* 13 (January 1988): 8–22.

"Couples Enter Vietnam to Teach English." *Church News*, 30 January 1993, 3.

Covey, Stephen R. *Principle-Centered Leadership*. New York: Simon & Schuster, 1991.

Cowan, Alison Leigh. "Unclear Future Forced Board's Hand." *New York Times*, 7 August 1993, 37, 49.

Cramer, James J. "Confessions of a Limousine Neoliberal." *New York*, 11 March 1996, 34–38.

Crosby, Cherill. "U.S. Aid to Utah for Food $200 Million and Rising." *Salt Lake Tribune*, 8 April 1993, A1.

Crowley, Brian Lee. *The Self, the Individual, and the Community: Liberalism in the Political Thought of F. A. Hayek and Sidney and Beatrice Webb*. Oxford: Clarendon Press, 1987.

Crucy, Thierry. "Cecile Pelous: Love and Friendship in India." *Tambuli* (March 1992): 8–15.

Crystal, Graef S. *In Search of Excess: The Overcompensation of American Executives*. New York: W. W. Norton & Company, 1991.

Currie, Robert, Alan Gilbert, and Lee Horsley. *Churches and Churchgoers: Patterns of Church Growth in the British Isles since 1700*. Oxford: Clarendon Press, 1977.

Danner, Peter L. "Sympathy and Exchangeable Value: Keys to Adam Smith's Social Philosophy." *Review of Social Economy* 34 (December 1976): 317–31.

Darnton, John. "In Poor, Decolonized Africa, Bankers Are New Overlords." *New York Times*, 20 June 1994, A1, A8.

———. "'Lost Decade' Drains Africa's Vitality." *New York Times*, 19 June 1994, A1, A10.

Davidson, Joan, and Dorothy Myers with Manab Chakraburty. *No Time to Waste: Poverty and the Global Environment*. Oxford: Oxfam, 1992.

Davis, Ray Jay. "Antipolygamy Legislation." In *Encyclopedia of Mormonism*, edited by Daniel H. Ludlow, 52–53. New York: Macmillan, 1992.

Day, Kathleen. *S&L Hell: The People and the Politics behind the $1 Trillion Savings and Loan Scandal*. New York: W. W. Norton, 1993.

Deane, Phyllis. *The First Industrial Revolution*. 2nd ed. Cambridge: Cambridge University Press, 1979.

Decoo, Wilfried. "Mormonism in a European Catholic Region: A Contribution to the Social Psychology of LDS Converts." *Brigham Young University Studies* 24 (winter 1984): 61–77.

Dentzer, Susan. "The Wealth of Nations." *U.S. News & World Report*, 4 May 1992, 54.

DePalma, Anthony. "Economy Reeling, Mexicans Prepare Tough New Steps." *New York Times*, 26 February 1995, A1, A8.

DeParle, Jason. "Sharp Increase Along the Borders of Poverty." *New York Times*, 31 March 1994, A18.

De Pree, Max. *Leadership Is an Art*. New York: Doubleday, 1989.

De Soto, Hernando. *The Other Path: The Invisible Revolution in the Third World*. New York: Harper & Row, 1989.

Dew, Sheri L. *Ezra Taft Benson: A Biography.* Salt Lake City: Deseret Book, 1987.

Dobrzynski, Judith H. "Assessing the Value of Family." *New York Times,* 18 June 1995, F1.

———. "Should I Have Left An Hour Earlier?" *New York Times,* 18 June 1995, F12.

Dos Santos, T. "The Structure of Dependence." *American Economic Review* 60 (May 1970): 231–36.

Draper, Richard D. "*Hubris* and *Ate:* A Latter-day Warning from the Book of Mormon." *Journal of Book of Mormon Studies* 3 (fall 1994): 12–33.

Drucker, Peter F. *Managing for the Future: The 1990s and Beyond* (New York: Penguin Books, 1993).

Dyer, W. Gibb, Jr. *The Entrepreneurial Experience: Confronting the Career Dilemmas of the Start-up Executive.* San Francisco: Jossey-Bass Publishers, 1992.

Egan, Timothy. "Montana's Sky and Its Hopes Are Left Bare after Logging." *New York Times,* 19 October 1993, A1, A26.

Eichenwald, Kurt. *Serpent on the Rock.* New York: HarperBusiness, 1995.

Ellerman, David P. *The Democratic Worker-Owned Firm: A New Model for East and West.* London: Unwin Hyman, 1990.

Elmer-Dewitt, Philip. "Summit to Save the Earth." *Time,* 1 June 1992, 40–59.

Embry, Jessie L. *Mormon Polygamous Families: Life in the Principle.* Salt Lake City: University of Utah Press, 1987.

———. "Ethnic Groups and the LDS Church" and "Speaking For Themselves: LDS Ethnic Groups Oral History Project." *Dialogue* 25 (winter 1992): 81–110.

"Employee Morale Is Getting Worse." *Incentive* 168 (January 1994): 5.

Encel, Sol. "Reflections on a Visit to Mondragon." *Bulletin of the International Communal Studies Association* 8 (fall 1990): 4–6.

"Erasing Illiteracy." *World Monitor Magazine* 4 (March 1991): 6–7.

Erlanger, Steven. "In Russia, Success Isn't Such a Popular Idea." *New York Times,* 12 March 1995, E4.

———. "Russia's New Dictatorship of Crime." *New York Times,* 15 May 1994, E3.

Esper, George. "LDS Medical Volunteer Recounts Somalia's Horrors." *Provo (Utah) Daily Herald,* 28 March 1993, A9–10.

Estrin, Saul, and Derek C. Jones. "The Viability of Employee-Owned Firms: Evidence from France." *Industrial and Labor Relations Review* 45 (January 1992): 323–38.

Fairbank, John King, and Edwin O. Reischauer. *China: Tradition and Transformation.* Rev. ed. Boston: Houghton-Mifflin, 1989.

Fales, Susan L. "Artisans, Millhands and Laborers: The Mormons of Leeds and Their Nonconformist Neighbors." In *Mormons in Early Victorian Britain,* edited by Richard L. Jensen and Malcolm R. Thorp. Salt Lake City: University of Utah Press, 1989.

Faltermayer, Edmund. "Is This Layoff Necessary?" *Fortune,* 1 June 1992, 71–86.

Fanning, Connel M., and Thomas McCarthy. "A Survey of Economic Hypotheses Concerning the Non-Viability of Labour-Directed Firms in Capitalist Economies." In *Labor-Owned Firms and Workers' Cooperatives,* edited by Sune Jansson and Ann-Britt Hellmark, 7–50. Aldershot, U.K.: Gower Publishing, 1986.

Farnsworth, Clyde H. "Experiment in Worker Ownership Shows a Profit." *New York Times,* 14 August 1993, 33, 46.

Fefer, Mark D. "How Layoffs Pay Off." *Fortune,* 24 January 1994, 12.

Ferguson, Isaac. "Freely Given." *Ensign* 18 (August 1988): 10–15.

———. "Humanitarian Service." In *Encyclopedia of Mormonism,* edited by Daniel H. Ludlow, 661–63. New York: Macmillan, 1992.

Fillmore, Shellie. "LDS Mission Will Aid in Restoring Peace." *(Brigham Young University) Daily Universe,* 9 December 1992, 1.

Finch, John. *The Millennium, The Religion of Jesus, and the Foolery of Sectarianism.* Birmingham, U.K.: F. B. S. Flindell, 1838.

———. *Moral Code of the New Moral World.* Corrected, revised, and approved by Robert Owen. Liverpool: James Stewart, 1840.

Finley, M. I. *The Ancient Economy.* 2nd ed. London: Hogarth Press, 1985.

Flanders, Robert Bruce. *Nauvoo: Kingdom on the Mississippi.* Urbana: University of Illinois Press, 1965, 144–50.

Florence, Giles H., Jr. "Called to Serve." *Ensign* 21 (September 1991): 13–16.

Frank, Andre Gunder. *Capitalism and Underdevelopment in Latin America: Historical Studies of Chile and Brazil.* New York: Monthly Review Press, 1967.

Freudenheim, Milt. "A Doting Uncle Cuts Back, And a City Feels the Pain: Kodak Rethinks Its Civic Duties in Rochester." *New York Times,* 8 October 1995, F1, F9.

Freund, William C., and Eugene Epstein. *People and Productivity.* Homewood, Ill.: Dow Jones—Irwin, 1984.

Friedman, Milton. *Capitalism and Freedom.* Chicago: University of Chicago Press, 1962.

Fox, Feramorz. "United Order: Discrimination in the Use of Terms." *Improvement Era* 47 (July 1944): 432.

Fox, Frank W. *J. Reuben Clark: The Public Years.* Provo, Utah, and Salt Lake City: Brigham Young University Press and Deseret Book, 1980.

Fuchsberg, Gilbert. "Why Shake-Ups Work for Some, Not for Others." *Wall Street Journal,* 1 October 1993, B1, B4.

Fukuyama, Francis. *Trust: The Social Virtues and the Creation of Prosperity.* New York: Free Press, 1995.

Gall, Lothar. *Bismarck: The White Revolutionary.* Trans. J. A. Underwood. London: Allen & Unwin, 1986.

Gardner, Hamilton. "Cooperation among the Mormons." *Quarterly Journal of Economics* 31 (1917): 461–99.

Gardner, Marvin. "Philippine Saints: A Believing People." *Ensign* 21 (July 1991): 32–37.

Geddes, Joseph A. "The United Order among the Mormons (Missouri Phase)." Ph.D. diss., Columbia University, 1922. Later published as *The United Order among the Mormons: An Unfinished Experiment in Economic Organization.* Salt Lake City: Deseret News Press, 1924.

Gilder, George. *Wealth and Poverty.* New York: Basic Books, 1981.

Giles, Jayne Crosby. "Microbusiness Lending: Bank Services for the Smallest Companies." *Journal of Commercial Lending* 76 (November 1993): 21–31.

Gleick, James. "Making Microsoft Safe for Capitalism." *New York Times Magazine*, 5 November 1995, 50–57, 64.

Golitsyn, Anatoliy. *New Lies for Old: The Communist Strategy of Deception and Disinformation.* New York: Dodd, Mead & Co., 1984.

Gonzalez, David. "The Computer Age Bids Religious World to Enter." *New York Times*, 24 July 1994, 1, 38.

Gorey, Thomas H. "Food Requests in S.L. Rose 20–25% in '90, Report Says." *Salt Lake Tribune*, 20 December 1990, B3.

Goodwyn, Lawrence. *Democratic Promise: The Populist Moment in America.* New York: Oxford University Press, 1976.

Gordon, Barry. "Biblical and Early Judeo-Christian Thought: Genesis to Augustine." In *Pre-classical Economic Thought*, edited by S. Todd Lowry. Dordrecht: Kluwer Academic Publishers, 1987.

Gottlieb, Robert, and Peter Wiley. *America's Saints: The Rise of Mormon Power.* New York: G. P. Puttman's Sons, 1984.

Gould, Lewis L. *Reform and Regulation: American Politics from Roosevelt to Wilson.* 2nd ed. New York: Alfred A. Knopf, 1986.

Gracon, Helen, and Maureen Clark. "Layoffs Should Come Last." *IEEE Spectrum* 31 (May 1994): 52–55.

Graham, Ellen. "Their Careers: Count on Nothing and Work Like a Demon." *Wall Street Journal*, 31 October 1995, B1, B10.

Grant, Heber J. "Message of the First Presidency to the Church." *Conference Report* (October 1936): 2–6.

Greeley, Horace. "An Overland Journey: Two Hours with Brigham Young." *New York Daily Tribune*, 20 August 1859, 5–6.

Green, Lee. "Jungle Doctors." *American Way* (15 April 1993): 58–100.

Grover, Mark L. "Relief Society and Church Welfare: The Brazilian Experience." *Dialogue* 27 (winter 1994): 29–38.

Gunn, Christopher. *Workers' Self-Management in the United States.* Ithaca, N.Y.: Cornell University Press, 1984.

Gutierrez, Gustavo. *A Theology of Liberation.* Maryknoll, N.Y.: Orbis, 1973.

Haberman, Clyde. "Reluctantly, a Kibbutz Turns to (GASP!) the Stock Market." *New York Times*, 8 July 1993, A1, A6.

Hacker, Louis M. *The World of Andrew Carnegie 1865–1901.* Philadelphia: J. B. Lippincott Company, 1968.

Hacker, Sally L. "Gender and Technology at the Mondragon System of Producer Cooperatives." *Economic and Industrial Democracy* 9 (May 1988): 225–43.

Halvorson-Quevedo, Raundi. "The Growing Potential of Micro-Enterprises." *OECD Observer* 173 (December 1991/January 1992): 7–11.

Hammond, Scott and Barbara. "Reworking the Workplace." *BYU Today* (October 1985): 21–24.

Hansell, Saul. "Banks Learning to Make Loans to Help Poor Areas." *New York Times*, 9 January 1994, A1, A18.

Harrington, Michael. *Socialism.* New York: Saturday Review Press, 1972.

Harrison, Bennett. "The Failure of Worker Participation." *Technology Review* 94 (January 1991): 74.

Hart, John L. "Gospel's influence spreads from temple." *Church News*, 24 June 1995, 8–10.

———. "'No poor among them' Is ultimate goal in Peru." *Church News*, 7 November 1981, 12.

———. Over Half LDS Now Outside U.S." *Church News*, 2 March 1996, 3, 6.

Hartley, William G. "Bishop, History of the Office." In *Encyclopedia of Mormonism*, edited by Daniel H. Ludlow, 119–22. New York: Macmillan, 1992.

Hayek, Friedrich A. *The Road to Serfdom.* Chicago: University of Chicago Press, 1944.

Heald, Morrel. *The Social Responsibility of Business: Company and Country, 1900–1960.* Cleveland: The Press of Case Western University, 1970.

Heaton, Tim B. "Vital Statistics." In *Encyclopedia of Mormonism*, edited by Daniel H. Ludlow, 1518–37. New York: Macmillan, 1992.

Heilbroner, Robert L. *The Making of Economic Society.* 8th ed. Englewood Cliffs, N.J.: Prentice-Hall, 1989.

Heinerman, John, and Anson Shupe. *The Mormon Corporate Empire.* Boston: Beacon Press, 1985.

Hemlock, Doreen. "I.P.O.'s: When Employee-Friendly=Investor-Friendly." *New York Times*, 25 February 1996, F4.

Hengel, Martin. "Property and Riches in the Old Testament and Judaism." In *Earliest Christianity.* London: SCM Press, 1986.

Hermanson, Roger H., Daniel M. Ivancevich, and Dana R. Hermanson. "Corporate Restructuring in the 1990s: The Impact of Accounting Incentives." *The Corporate Growth Report* 10 (February 1992): 14–18.

Hewlett, Sylvia Ann. *When the Bough Breaks: The Cost of Neglecting Our Children.* New York: Basic Books, 1991.

Hill, Greg. "Benson Institute Program Enhances Lives of Struggling People." *Church News*, 3 June 1995, 8–10.

Hill, Marvin, Keith Rooker, and Larry Wimmer. "The Kirtland Economy Revisited: A Market Critique of Sectarian Economics." *Brigham Young University Studies* 17 (summer 1977): 391–475.

Hilts, Philip J. "Cigarette Makers Debated the Risks They Denied." *New York Times*, 16 June 1994, A1, D22.

———. "Tobacco Company Was Silent on Hazards." *New York Times*, 7 May 1994, A1, A11.

Hinckley, Bryant S. *The Faith of Our Pioneer Fathers.* Salt Lake City: Deseret Book, 1956.

Hinckley, Gordon B. "Out of Your Experience Here." *BYU Today* (March 1991): 18–21, 35–37. From an address at BYU, 16 October 1990.

———. "The State of the Church." *Ensign* 21 (May 1991): 51–54.

Hinton, Wayne K. "The Economics of Ambivalence: Utah's Depression Experience." *Utah Historical Quarterly* 54 (summer 1986): 268–85.

Hirschman, Albert O. *Getting Ahead Collectively: Grassroots Experiences in Latin America.* New York: Pergamon, 1984.

History of The Church of Jesus Christ of Latter-day Saints. Edited by B. H. Roberts. 3rd ed. Salt Lake City: Deseret News, 1961.

Hoe, Susanna. *The Man Who Gave His Company Away.* London: Heinemann, 1978.

Hofer, John. *The History of the Hutterites.* Elie, Manitoba: James Valley Book Centre, 1982.

Hofstadter, Richard. *Social Darwinism in American Thought*. Rev. ed. New York: George Braziller, 1959.

Holland, Jeffrey R. "A Handful of Meal and a Little Oil." *Ensign* 26 (May 1996): 29–31.

Holloway, Marguerite, and Paul Wallich. "A Risk Worth Taking." *Scientific American*, November 1992, 126.

Holusha, John. "Eastman Kodak Chief Is Ousted by Directors." *New York Times*, 7 August 1993, 37, 49.

———. "Kodak Chief Offers a New Vision." *New York Times*, 29 October 1993, D1, D17.

———. "Kodak Joins Others in Scaling Back Expectations." *New York Times*, 16 December 1993, D1, D6.

Horne, Alistair. *The Terrible Year: The Paris Commune, 1871*. New York: Viking Press, 1971.

Hossain, Mahabub. *Credit for the Rural Poor: The Experience of the Grameen Bank in Bangladesh*. Dhaka, Bangladesh: The Bangladesh Institute for Development Studies, 1985.

Hostetler, John A. *Hutterite Society*. Baltimore: Johns Hopkins University Press, 1974.

House, Karen Elliott. "Malaysian Premier Says U.S. Policies Hurt Chance for Global Growth, Stability." *Wall Street Journal*, 29 March 1993, A8.

Hovenkamp, Herbert. *Enterprise and American Law 1836–1937*. Cambridge: Harvard University Press, 1991.

"How to Keep Your Career from Dominating Your Life." *Church News*, 30 July 1988, 15.

Huff, Kent W. *Joseph Smith's United Order: A Non-communalistic Interpretation*. Orem, Utah: Cedar Fort, 1988.

"Hungry World." *U.S. News and World Report*, 21 October 1991, 18.

Hunter, Milton R. *Will A Man Rob God?* Salt Lake City: Deseret News Press, 1952.

Hunter, Howard W. "All Are Alike unto God." *Ensign* 9 (June 1979): 72–74.

———. "Being a Righteous Husband and Father." *Ensign* 24 (November 1994): 49–51.

———. "The Gospel—A Global Faith." *Ensign* 21 (November 1991): 18–19.

———. "Prepare for Honorable Employment." *Ensign* 5 (November 1975): 122–24.

International Enterprise Development Foundation. Internal Enterprise Mentors Organization Documents, "Case Statement." St. Louis, Mo.: Enterprise Mentors/IEDF, March 1993.

"In True Fashion." *Ensign* 21 (September 1991): 66–67.

Israelsen, L. Dwight. "An Economic Analysis of the United Order." *Brigham Young University Studies* 18 (summer 1978): 536–62.

———. "United Orders." In *Encyclopedia of Mormonism*, edited by Daniel H. Ludlow, 1493–95. New York: Macmillan, 1992.

Jackall, Robert, and Henry Levin, eds. *Worker Cooperatives in America*. Berkeley: University of California Press, 1984.

Jacobson, Cardell K., Tim B. Heaton, E. Dale LeBaron, and Trina Louise Hope. "Black Mormon Converts in the United States and Africa: Social Characteristics and Perceived Acceptance." In *Contemporary Mormonism:*

Social Science Perspectives, edited by Marie Cornwall, Tim B. Heaton, and Lawrence A. Young. Urbana: University of Illinois Press, 1994.

Jacobson, Louis, Robert LaLonde, and Daniel Sullivan. *The Costs of Worker Dislocation.* Kalamazoo, Mich.: W. E. Upjohn Institute for Employment Research, 1993.

James, John A. *Money and Capital Markets in Postbellum America.* Princeton, N.J.: Princeton University Press, 1978.

Janofsky, Michael. "On Cigarettes, Health and Lawyers." *New York Times,* 6 December 1993, D1, D8.

Jansson, Sune, and Ann-Brit Hellmark, eds. *Labor-Owned Firms and Worker Cooperatives.* Aldershot, U.K.: Gower Publishing, 1986.

Jenkins, Carri P. "Cecile Pelous: Rubbing away the Hurt." *BYU Today* (July 1992): 23–28.

———. "Empowering the People: Expanding the Role of Followers." *BYU Today* (September 1990): 28–32, 60–63.

Jensen, Kenneth E. *Utah Personal Income 1929–1985.* Salt Lake City: Utah Department of Employment Security, 1986.

Jensen, Richard L., and Malcolm R. Thorp, eds. *Mormons in Early Victorian Britain.* Salt Lake City: University of Utah Press, 1989.

Johnson, Dirk. "Economies Come to Life on Indian Reservations." *New York Times,* 3 July 1994, A1, A18.

Jones, Derek, and Jan Svejnar, eds. *Participatory and Self-Managed Firms.* Lexington, Mass.: Lexington Books, 1982.

Jones, Derek. "Historical Perspectives on Worker Cooperatives." In *Worker Cooperatives in America,* edited by Robert Jackall and Henry Levin. Berkeley: University of California Press, 1984.

Jones, Derek C., and Jeffrey Pliskin. "The Effects of Worker Participation, Employee Ownership, and Profit-Sharing on Economic Performance: A Partial Review." In *Ownership and Participation,* vol. 2 of *International Handbook of Participation in Organizations,* edited by Raymond Russell and Veljko Rus, 43–63. Oxford: Oxford University Press, 1991.

Journal of Discourses. Liverpool and London: Latter-day Saints Book Depot, 1854–86. Reprint, Salt Lake City, 1964.

Judson, George. "Some Indians See a Gamble with Future In Casinos." *New York Times,* 15 May 1994, E5.

Kahn, Joseph, and Miriam Jordan. "Women's Banks Stage Global Expansion." *Wall Street Journal,* 30 August 1995, A8.

Kalish, Gerald, ed. *ESOPs: The Handbook of Employee Stock Ownership Plans.* Chicago: Probus Publishing, 1989.

Kamm, Henry. "Even in the Kibbutz, Socialism Is under Challenge." *New York Times,* 10 September 1991, A3.

Kanter, Rosabeth Moss. *Commitment and Community: Communes and Utopias in Sociological Perspective.* Cambridge: Harvard University Press, 1972.

———. *When Giants Learn to Dance: Mastering the Challenge of Strategy, Management and Careers in the 1990s.* New York: Simon & Schuster, 1989.

Kardas, Peter, Katrina Gale, Richard Marens, Paul Sommers, and Gorm Winther. "Employment and Sales Growth in Washington State Employee Ownership Companies: A Comparative Analysis." *Journal of Employee Ownership Law and Finance* 6 (spring 1994): 83–135.

Kay, Jeffrey. "An Invisible Empire: Mormon Money in California." *New West,* 8 May 1978, 36–41.

Keller, Bill. "A South African Mall That Black Know-how Built." *New York Times,* 12 September 1993, L3.

Kelso, Louis O., and Mortimer J. Adler. *The Capitalist Manifesto.* New York: Random House, 1958.

———. *The New Capitalists.* New York: Random House, 1961.

Kelso, Louis O., and Patricia Hetter Kelso. *Democracy and Economic Power: Extending the ESOP Revolution.* Cambridge, Mass: Ballinger Publishing, 1986.

Keynes, John Maynard. *The General Theory of Employment, Interest, and Money.* New York: Harcourt Brace, 1936.

Kilborn, Peter T. "Labor Day Message No One Asked to Hear." *New York Times,* 5 September 1993, E1, E4.

———. "Scrapping 'Us Versus Them,' Industry Is Giving Workers a Say and a Stake." *New York Times,* 22 November 1991, A23.

Kimball, Spencer W. "Becoming the Pure in Heart." *Ensign* 8 (May 1978): 79–81.

———. "The False Gods We Worship." *Ensign* 6 (June 1976): 3–6.

———. "Keep Your Money Clean." *Improvement Era* 56 (December 1953): 948–50.

———. "The Stone Cut without Hands." *Ensign* 6 (May 1976): 4–9.

———. "Welfare Services Meeting Address," 7 April 1974,*Conference Report* (Salt Lake City: Church of Jesus Christ of Latter-day Saints, 1974), 183–85.

———. "Welfare Services: The Gospel in Action." *Ensign* 7 (November 1977): 76–79.

"The Kindness of Strangers." *Economist,* 7 May 1994, 11, 19–22.

Klein, Katherine, and Corey Rosen. "Job Generation Performance of Employee Owned Companies." *Monthly Labor Review* 8 (August 1983): 15–19.

Klein, Joe. "We Can Do It for Ourselves." *Newsweek,* 29 March 1993, 31.

Knowlton, David. "Missionaries and Terror: The Assassination of Two Elders in Bolivia." *Sunstone* 13 (August 1989): 10–15.

Kotkin, Joel. *Tribes: How Race, Religion, and Identity Determine Success in the Global Economy.* New York: Random House, 1992.

Krause, Paul. *The Battle for Homestead 1880–1892: Politics, Cultures, and Steel.* Pittsburgh: University of Pittsburgh Press, 1992.

Krimerman, Len, and Frank Lindenfeld, ed. *When Workers Decide: Workplace Democracy Takes Root in North America.* Philadelphia: New Society Publishers, 1992.

Kristol, Irving. *Reflections of a Neoconservative* (New York: Basic Books, 1983).

Krugman, Paul. *The Age of Diminished Expectations.* Boston: MIT Press, 1990.

Kuehl, Charles, and Peggy Lambing. *Small Business Planning and Management.* 2nd ed. Chicago: Dryden Press, 1990.

Lamb, Robert Boynton. "Adam Smith's System: Sympathy, Not Self-Interest." *Journal of the History of Ideas* 35 (1974): 671–82.

Lamm, Richard D., and Michael McCarthy. *The Angry West: A Vulnerable Land and Its Future.* Boston: Houghton-Mifflin, 1982.

Larmer, Brook, and Mac Margolis. "Dead End Kids." *Newsweek,* 25 May 1992, 38–40.

Larson, Gustive O. *The "Americanization" of Utah for Statehood.* San Marino, Calif.: The Huntington Library, 1971.

Lasch, Christopher. *The Revolt of the Elites and the Betrayal of Democracy.* New York: W. W. Norton & Company, 1995.

Lauck, W. J. *Political and Industrial Democracy.* New York: Funk & Wagnalls, 1926.

Lawler, Edward E., III. *High Involvement Management.* San Francisco: Jossey-Bass, 1986.

"LDS Church Officials Dispute Finance Report." *Provo (Utah) Daily Herald,* 30 June 1991, A1–2.

"LDS Financial Empire Puts Church at Fortune 500 Level." *Arizona Republic.* Reprint, *Salt Lake Tribune,* 30 June 1991, A1–5; 1 July, A1–5; 2 July, A1–5.

Lee, Harold B. *Stand Ye In Holy Places.* Salt Lake City: Deseret Book, 1974.

———. "Unity for the Welfare of the Church and Nation." *Improvement Era* 45 (May 1942): 297.

Leete-Guy, Frederick. "Federal Structure and the Viability of Labour-Managed Firms in Mixed Economies." In *Ownership and Participation,* vol. 2 of *International Handbook of Participation in Organizations,* edited by Raymond Russell and Veljko Rus, 64–79. Oxford: Oxford University Press, 1991.

Leibenstein, Harvey. *Beyond Economic Man: A New Foundation for Economics.* Cambridge: Harvard University Press, 1976.

———. *General X-Efficiency Theory and Economic Development.* Oxford: Oxford University Press, 1978.

Lemann, Nicholas. "The Other Underclass." *Atlantic Monthly,* December 1991, 96–110.

Leone, Mark P. "An Anthropological View of *Great Basin Kingdom.*" In *Great Basin Kingdom Revisited: Contemporary Perspectives,* edited by Thomas G. Alexander, 77–95. Logan, Utah: Utah State University Press, 1991.

"Letter of the First Presidency Concerning Military Training." *Improvement Era* 49 (February 1946): 76–77.

Leuck, Thomas J. "Save the Business, Keep It in Brooklyn." *New York Times,* 17 July 1994, CY4.

Levin, Henry. "Employment and Productivity of Producer Cooperatives." In *Worker Cooperatives in America,* edited by Robert Jackall and Henry Levin. Berkeley: University of California Press, 1984.

Levine, David. "Participation, Productivity and the Firm's Environment." *California Management Review* 32 (summer 1990): 86–100.

Levinson, Marc. "Thanks. You're Fired." *Newsweek,* 23 May 1994, 48–49.

Lewis, Michael. *Liar's Poker: Rising Through the Wreckage on Wall Street.* New York: W. W. Norton, 1989.

Lewis, John P., ed. *Strengthening the Poor: What Have We Learned?* New Brunswick, N.J.: Transaction Books, 1988.

Lewis, Paul. "U.N. Lists Four Nations at Risk Because of Wide Income Gaps." *New York Times,* 2 June 1994, A6.

Lewis, Peter H. "Drawing on Family Values to Fight the Software Wars: Alan Conway Ashton." *New York Times,* 3 October 1993, F8.

Livesay, Harold C. *Andrew Carnegie and the Rise of Big Business.* New York: Little, Brown and Company, 1975.

Livingstone, Ian. "A Reassessment of Kenya's Rural and Urban Informal Sector." *World Development* 16 (June 1991): 651–70.

Lockwood, Maren. *The Oneida Community: A Study in Organizational Change.* Ph.D. diss., Harvard University, 1962.

Lohr, Steve. "Economic Recovery: Manhandle with Care." *New York Times,* 13 February 1994, E2.

Logue, John, and Cassandra Rogers. *Employee Stock Ownership Plans in Ohio: Impact on Company Performance and Employment.* Kent, Ohio: Northeast Ohio Employee Ownership Center, 1989.

Lownestein, Roger. "Will Flat Wages Beget Future Trouble?" *Wall Street Journal,* 12 October 1995, C1.

Lublin, Joann S. The Great Divide." *Wall Street Journal,* 11 April 1996, R1, R4, R15–17.

———. "Ranks of Unemployed Couples Multiply, Devastating Double-Income Households." *Wall Street Journal,* 7 May 1993, B1.

Ludlow, Daniel H., ed. *Encyclopedia of Mormonism.* New York: Macmillan, 1992.

———. *Latter-day Prophets Speak.* Salt Lake City: Bookcraft, 1948.

Macfie, A. L.. "Adam Smith's *Moral Sentiments* as Foundation for his *Wealth of Nations.*" *Oxford Economic Papers* 11 (October 1959): 209–28.

Machiavelli, Niccolo. *The Prince.* 1513. Reprint, New York: Mentor Books, 1962.

Mackenzie, Norman, and Jeanne Mackenzie. *The Fabians.* New York: Simon & Schuster, 1977.

Madrick, Jeffrey. *The End of Affluence: The Causes and Consequences of America's Economic Decline* (New York: Random House, 1995).

Magnet, Myron. *The Dream and the Nightmare: The Sixties' Legacy to the Underclass.* New York: Morrow, 1993.

Magraw, Roger. *France 1815–1914: The Bourgeois Century.* London: Fontana, 1983.

Main, Jackson Turner. *The Social Structure of Revolutionary America.* Princeton, N.J.: Princeton University Press, 1965.

Manes, Stephen, and Paul Andrews. *Gates: How Microsoft's Mogul Reinvented an Industry and Made Himself the Richest Man in America.* New York: Doubleday, 1993.

Mangum, Garth L., and Bruce D. Blumell. *The Mormons' War on Poverty.* Salt Lake City: University of Utah Press, 1993.

Mann, S. A. *Message of S. A. Mann, Acting Governor, January 11, 1870. Journals of the Legislative Assembly of the Territory of Utah, Nineteenth Annual Session.* Salt Lake City: Joseph Bull, Public Printer, Deseret News Office, 1870.

Marcus, Amy Dockser. "Israeli Kibbutz's New Free-Market Style Defies Socialist Ideals, Sparks Debate." *Wall Street Journal,* 26 May 1993, A15.

Marsh, Thomas, and Dale McAllister. "ESOP's Tables." *Journal of Corporation Law* 3 (spring 1981): 613–17.

Marshall, Ray. *Unheard Voices: Labor and Economic Policy in a Competitive World.* New York: Basic Books, 1987.

Martin, Douglas. "Hiring Welfare Recipients and Making Them Management." *New York Times,* 21 May 1994. 26.

Marx, Karl, and Friedrich Engels. *The Communist Manifesto.* In *The Marxist Reader,* edited by Emile Burns, 21–59. 1848. Reprint, New York: Avenel Books, 1982.

Marx, Karl. *Kapital: A Critique of Political Economy.* Trans. Ben Fowkes and D. Fernbach. New York: Vintage Books, 1977–81.

Mason, Jerry. "Family Economics." In *Utah in Demographic Perspective,* edited by Thomas K. Martin, Tim B. Heaton, and Stephen J. Bahr. Salt Lake City: Signature Books, 1986.

Mathur, Purushottam Narayan. *Why Developing Countries Fail to Develop.* London: Macmillan, 1991.

Mauss, Armand L. *The Angel and the Beehive: The Mormon Struggle with Assimilation.* Urbana: University of Illinois Press, 1994.

Max-Neef, Manfred A. *From the Outside Looking In: Experiences in "Barefoot Economics."* Uppsala, Sweden: Dag Hammarskjold Foundation, 1982.

Maxwell, Neal A. "The Church Can Now Be Universal with Priesthood Revelation of 1978." *Church News,* 5 January 1980, 20.

———. *Of One Heart: The Glory of the City of Enoch.* Salt Lake City: Deseret Book, 1979.

———. "Settle This in Your Hearts." *Ensign* 22 (November 1992): 65–67.

May, Dean L. "Brigham Young and the Bishops: The United Order in the City." In *New Views of Mormon History: A Collection of Essays in Honor of Leonard J. Arrington,* edited by Davis Bitton and Maureen Ursenbach Beecher. Salt Lake City: University of Utah Press, 1987.

———. "A Demographic Portrait of the Mormons, 1830–1980." In *The New Mormon History: Revisionist Essays on the Past,* edited by D. Michael Quinn. Salt Lake City: Signature Books, 1992.

———. "The Economics of Zion." *Sunstone* 14 (August 1990): 15–23.

———, ed. *A Dependent Commonwealth: Utah's Economy from Statehood to the Great Depression.* Provo, Utah: Brigham Young University Press, 1974.

May, Frank O., Jr. "Correlation of the Church Administration." In *Encyclopedia of Mormonism,* edited by Daniel H. Ludlow, 323–25. New York: Macmillan, 1992.

McBrien, Dean D. "The Economic Content of Early Mormon Doctrine." *Southwestern Political and Social Science Quarterly* 6 (September 1925): 179–91.

McConkie, Bruce R. "Come: Let Israel Build Zion." *Ensign* 7 (May 1977): 115–18.

———. *Mormon Doctrine.* 2nd ed. Salt Lake City: Bookcraft, 1966.

McGovern, Arthur F. *Liberation Theology and Its Critics: Toward an Assessment.* Maryknoll, N.Y.: Orbis Books, 1989.

McGraw, Dan. "The Christian Capitalists." *U.S. News & World Report,* 13 March 1995, 53–62.

McKay, David O. *Gospel Ideals.* Salt Lake City: Improvement Era, 1953.

McNiff, William J. *Heaven on Earth: A Planned Mormon Society.* Oxford, Ohio: The Mississippi Valley Press, 1940.

McRobie, George. *Small Is Possible.* New York: Harper and Row, 1981.

Meek, Christopher B., and Warner P. Woodworth. "Technical Training and Enterprise: Mondragon's Educational System and Its Implications for other Cooperatives." *Economic and Industrial Democracy* 11 (November 1990): 505–28.

Meek, Christopher B., Warner P. Woodworth, and W. Gibb Dyer, Jr. *Managing by the Numbers: Absentee Owners and the Decline of American Industry.* Reading, Mass.: Addison-Wesley, 1988.

Meyer, Richard L. "Financial Services for Microenterprises." In *Microenterprises in Developing Countries,* edited by Jacob Levitsky. London: Intermediate Technology Publications, 1989.

Milbank, Dana. "Here Is One LBO Deal Where the Workers Became Millionaires." *Wall Street Journal,* 27 October 1992, A1, A12.

Milford, Peter. "Worker cooperatives and consumer cooperatives: can they be combined?" In *Labor-Owned Firms and Worker Cooperatives,* edited by Sune Jansson and Ann-Brit Hellmark, 117–39. Aldershot, U.K.: Gower Publishing, 1986.

Mill, John Stuart. *On Liberty.* 1859. Reprint, Indianapolis, Ind.: Bobbs-Merrill, 1956.

———. *Collected Works.* Edited by J. M. Robson. Toronto: University of Toronto Press, 1965.

Miller, James P. "Some Workers Set Up LBOs of Their Own And Benefit Greatly." *Wall Street Journal,* 12 December 1988, A1, A7.

Mishel, Laurence, and Jared Bernstein, eds. *The State of Working America, 1992–1993.* Armonk, N.Y.: Sharpe, 1993.

Monroe, Sylvester. "The Gospel of Equity." *Time,* 10 May 1993, 54–55.

Monson, Thomas S. "My Brother's Keeper." *Ensign* 24 (November 1994): 43–46.

———. "A Royal Priesthood." *Ensign* 21 (May 1991): 47–51.

———. "A Sacred Duty to Help the Poor, Needy." *Church News,* 15 December 1990, 7.

Morgan, Arthur E. *The Philosophy of Edward Bellamy.* New York: King's Crown Press, 1945.

———. *Plagiarism in Utopia: A Study of the Continuity of the Utopian Tradition.* Yellow Springs, Ohio: Arthur E. Morgan, 1944.

"'Mormon' Women's Protest: An Appeal for Freedom, Justice and Equal Rights." Full account of proceedings at the Great Mass Meeting, Salt Lake City, 6 March 1886.

Morrison, Alexander B. *The Dawning of A Brighter Day: The Church in Black Africa.* Salt Lake City: Deseret Book, 1990.

———. *Visions of Zion.* Salt Lake City: Deseret Book, 1993.

Morrow, Lance. "The Temping of America" *Time,* 29 March 1993, 40–47.

Mostert, Mary. "Planting with Humble Faith, Devoted Effort." *Church News,* 4 December 1992, 3–4.

Muller, Jerry Z. *Adam Smith in His Time and Ours: Designing the Decent Society.* New York: The Free Press, 1993.

Murray, Matt. "Amid Record Profits, Companies Continue to Lay Off Employees." *Wall Street Journal,* 4 May 1995, A1, A6.

Nasar, Sylvia. "Defending the Father of Economics: Adam Smith Was No Gordon Gekko." *New York Times,* 23 January 1994, E6.

———. "Fed Gives New Evidence of '80s Gains by Richest." *New York Times,* 21 April 1992, A1, A17.

———. "Friedrich von Hayek Dies at 92; An Early Free Market Economist." *New York Times,* 24 March 1992, A15.

———. "The 1980s: A Very Good Time for the Very Rich." *New York Times*, 5 March 1992, A1, D24.

———. "Third World Embracing Reforms to Encourage Economic Growth." *New York Times*, 8 July 1991, A1, D3.

National Center for Employee Ownership. *Employee Ownership Report.* Oakland, Calif.: National Center for Employee Ownership.

———. *Privatization and Employee Ownership: The International Experience.* Oakland, Calif.: National Center for Employee Ownership, 1992.

National Industrial Conference Board. *Special Report No. 32, The Growth of Working Councils in the United States: A Statistical Summary.* New York: National Industrial Conference Board, 1932.

"A 1945 Perspective." *Dialogue* 19 (spring 1986): 35–39.

Nevins, Allan. *The War for the Union: War Becomes Revolution.* Vol. 2. New York: Charles Scribner's Sons, 1960.

Newman, Katherine S. *Falling from Grace: The Experience of Downward Mobility in the American Middle Class.* New York: The Free Press, 1988.

Nibley, Hugh W. *Approaching Zion.* Vol. 9, *The Collected Works of Hugh Nibley*, edited by Don E. Norton. Salt Lake City: Deseret Book; Provo, Utah: Foundation for Ancient Research and Mormon Studies, 1986.

———. "Leadership versus Management." *BYU Today* 38 (February 1984): 16–19, 45–47.

———. "Subduing the Earth." In *Nibley on the Timely and Timeless: Classic Essays of Hugh W. Nibley.* Provo, Utah: Religious Studies Center, Brigham Young University, 1978, 85–99.

Noble, Barbara Presley. "Questioning Productivity Beliefs." *New York Times*, 10 July 1994, F21.

———. "Retooling the 'People Skills' of Corporate America." *New York Times*, 22 May 1994, F8.

Nolan, Barbara E. *The Political Theory of Beatrice Webb.* New York: AMS Press, 1988.

Norris, Floyd. "You're Fired. (But Your Stock Is Way Up.)" *New York Times*, 3 September 1995, E3.

North, Douglass C. *Structure and Change in Economic History.* New York: W. W. Norton, 1981.

Nowak, Martin A., Robert M. May, and Karl Sigmund. "The Arithmetics of Mutual Help." *Scientific American*, June 1995, 76–81.

Nulty, Peter. "Kodak Grabs for Growth Again." *Fortune*, 16 May 1994, 76–78.

Oaks, Dallin H. *The Lord's Way.* Salt Lake City: Deseret Book, 1991.

———. *Pure in Heart.* Salt Lake City: Bookcraft, 1988.

Oakeshott, Robert. *The Case for Workers' Cooperatives.* 2nd ed. London: Macmillan, 1990.

O'Brian, Joan. "Utah Ranks 48th in Per Capita Income." *Salt Lake Tribune*, 28 April 1993, B1.

O'Brien, Timothy L. "Making Entrepreneurs of the Poor May Lift Some off Federal Aid." *Wall Street Journal*, 22 January 1993, A1, A5.

"Officials in Peru Receive Supplies from Church for Community Kitchens." *Church News*, 15 December 1990, 6.

Ostrow, Ronald J. "Mormon Merchants," *Wall Street Journal*, 20 December 1956, A1, A8.

Otero, Maria, and Elisabeth Rhyne, eds. *The New World of Microenterprise Finance: Building Healthy Financial Institutions for the Poor.* West Hartford, Conn.: Kumarian Press, 1994.

Overman, Stephanie. "The Layoff Legacy." *HRMagazine* 36 (August 1991): 28–32.

Pace, Glenn L. "Infinite Needs and Finite Resources." *Ensign* 23 (June 1993): 50–55.

Pack, Spencer J. *Capitalism as a Moral System: Adam Smith's Critique of the Free Market Economy.* Aldershot, U.K.: Edward Elgar Publishing, 1991.

Packer, Boyd K. "The Edge of the Light" *BYU Today* (March 1991): 22–24, 38–43. (Address at Brigham Young University, 4 March 1990.)

Palmer, Spencer J. *The Expanding Church.* Salt Lake City: Deseret Book, 1978.

Palmer, William R. "United Orders in Utah." *Improvement Era* 46 (January 1943 and February 1943): 24–25, 86–87, 116.

Parrella, Adilson. "Featherstone Speaks at Fireside." *(Brigham Young University) Daily Universe,* 2 March 1988, 1.

Passell, Peter. "The False Promise of Development by Casino." *New York Times,* 12 June 1994, F5.

Pasztor, Andy. *When the Pentagon Was for Sale: Inside America's Biggest Defense Scandal.* New York: Scribner, 1995.

Pear, Robert. "Poverty in U. S. Grew Faster than Population Last Year." *New York Times,* 5 October 1993, A20.

———. "The Picture from the Census Bureau: Poverty 1993: Bigger, Deeper, Younger, Getting Worse." *New York Times,* 10 October 1993, 5.

Peel, J. D. Y. *Herbert Spencer: The Evolution of a Sociologist.* New York: Basic Books, 1971.

Perlez, Jane. "Welcome Back, Lenin." *New York Times,* 31 May 1994, A1, A9.

Peters, Thomas J., and Robert H. Waterman, Jr. *In Search of Excellence: Lessons from America's Best-Run Companies.* New York: Harper & Row, 1982.

Peterson, Kathleen Lubeck. "The Ward Family: Pulling Together." *Ensign* 25 (July 1995): 22–26.

Phillips, Joseph D. "The Self-Employed in the United States." *University of Illinois Bulletin* 59 (1962, 91): 1–100.

Pinchot, Gifford and Elizabeth. *The End of Bureaucracy and the Rise of the Intelligent Organization.* San Francisco: Berrett-Koehler Publishers, 1993.

Pollack, Andrew. "Japan's Companies Moving Production to Sites Overseas." *New York Times,* 29 August 1993, A1, A16.

Pollard, John. "Students Helped by Homeless." *(Brigham Young University) Daily Universe,* 9 June 1993, 1.

Portes, Alejandro, Manuell Castells, and Lauren A. Benton, eds. *The Informal Economy: Studies in Advanced and Less Developed Countries.* Baltimore: Johns Hopkins University Press, 1989.

Pratt, Orson. *Masterful Discourses and Writings of Orson Pratt.* Compiled by N. B. Lundwall. Salt Lake City: Bookcraft, 1962.

Pratt, Parley P. *Writings of Parley Parker Pratt.* Edited by Parker Pratt Robinson. Salt Lake City: Deseret News Press, 1952.

Pratte, Alf. "Good Nutrition More Important Than Cholesterol." *Utah County Journal,* 23 February 1993, 1–2.

Prokesch, Steven. "Labor Policy Aids Miller Furniture." *New York Times*, 14 August 1986, D1, D5.

Quail, J. *Mr. Andrew Carnegie on Socialism, Labour and Home Rule: An Interview.* Aberdeen: Northern Newspaper, 1892.

Quarles van Ufford, Philip, Dirk Kruijt, and Theodore Downing, eds. *The Hidden Crisis in Development: Development Bureaucracies.* Amsterdam: Free University Press, 1988.

Quarrey, Michael, and Corey Rosen. *Employee Ownership and Corporate Performance.* Berkeley, Calif.: National Center for Employee Ownership, 1986.

———. *Employee Ownership and Corporate Performance.* Oakland, Calif.: National Center for Employee Ownership, 1994.

Quinn, D. Michael. *J. Reuben Clark: The Church Years.* Provo, Utah: Brigham Young University Press, 1983.

Quinn, Michelle. "Job Crunch: The Slamming Doors of Silicon Valley." *New York Times*, 23 January 1994, F5.

Quint, Michael. "Change Worries Kodak's Hometown." *New York Times*, 9 August 1993, D1, D8.

Radice, Lisanne. *Beatrice and Sidney Webb: Fabian Socialists.* London: Macmillan, 1984.

Raines, John C., and Donna C. Day-Lowen. *Modern Work and Human Meaning.* Philadelphia: Westminster Press, 1986.

Rand, Ayn. *Atlas Shrugged* (1957; Reprint, New York: Penguin Books, 1992).

———. *The Virtue of Selfishness.* New York: New American Library, 1964.

Rehfeld, John E. "In Japan, Personnel Has a Corner Office." *New York Times*, 1 May 1994, F9.

Richards, Bill. "Investigators Sort Out a Mess from the Days of Alternative Energy." *Wall Street Journal*, 15 December 1994, A1, A6.

Richards, Stephen L. "The Gospel of Work." *Improvement Era* 43 (January 1940): 10–11, 60–61, 63.

Richardson, Sir William. *The CWS in War and Peace: 1938–1976.* Manchester, U.K.: Co-operative Wholesale Society, 1977.

Riding, Alan. "In a Time of Shared Hardship, the Young Embrace Europe." *New York Times*, 12 August 1993. A1, A11.

Rimlinger, Gaston V. "Smith and the Merits of the Poor." *Review of Social Economy* 34 (December 1976): 333–44.

Robison, Lindon J. *Becoming a Zion People.* Salt Lake City: Hawkes Publishing, 1992.

———. "Economic Insights from the Book of Mormon." *Journal of Book of Mormon Studies* 1 (fall 1992): 35–53.

Rogers, Joel, and Wolfgang Streeck. "Workplace Representation Overseas: The Works Councils Story." In *Working under Different Rules*, edited by Richard B. Freeman, 97–156. New York: Russell Sage Foundation, 1994.

Romney, Marion G. "The Celestial Nature of Self-Reliance." *Ensign* 12 (November 1982): 91–93.

———. "The Purpose of Church Welfare Services." *Ensign* 7 (May 1977): 92–95.

———. "The Role of Bishops in Welfare Services." *Ensign* 7 (November 1977): 79–84.

———. "Socialism and the United Order Compared." In Romney, Marion G., *Look to God and Live,* edited by George J. Romney. Salt Lake City: Deseret Book, 1971. (Address at Brigham Young University, January 1966.)

———. "Welfare Services." *Ensign* 5 (November 1975): 124–28.

Rose, R. B. "John Finch, 1784–1857: A Liverpool Disciple of Robert Owen." *Transactions of the Historic Society of Lancashire and Cheshire* 109 (1957): 159–84.

Rosen, Corey. "Ownership, Motivation and Corporate Performance: Putting ESOPs to Work." In *ESOPs: The Handbook of Employee Stock Ownership Plans,* edited by Gerald Kalish, 271–89. Chicago: Probus Publishing, 1989.

Rosen, Corey, Gianna Durso, and Raul Rothblatt. *International Developments in Employee Ownership.* Oakland, Calif.: National Center for Employee Ownership, 1990.

Rosen, Corey, and Michael Quarrey. "How Well Is Employee Ownership Doing?" *Harvard Business Review* 65 (September–October 1987): 126–30.

Rosen, Corey, and Karen M. Young, eds. *Understanding Employee Ownership.* Ithaca, N.Y.: ILR Press, 1991.

Rosenberg, Nathan. "Adam Smith and *Laisser Faire* Revisited." In *Adam Smith and Modern Political Economy,* edited by Gerald P. O'Driscoll, Jr. Ames, Iowa: Iowa State University Press, 1979.

Rosenberg, Nathan, and L. E. Birdzell, Jr. *How the West Grew Rich: The Economic Transformation of the Industrial World.* New York: Basic Books, 1986.

Roth, William. "The Dangerous Ploy of Downsizing." *Business Forum* (fall 1993): 5–7.

Rothschild, Joyce, and J. Allen Whitt. *The Cooperative Workplace.* Cambridge: Cambridge University Press, 1980.

Rowland, Mary. "Why Small Businesses Are Failing." *New York Times.* 11 August 1991, F16.

Rudd, Glen L. *Pure Religion: The Story of Church Welfare Since 1930.* Salt Lake City: The Church of Jesus Christ of Latter-day Saints, 1995.

Rust, Richard Dilworth. "The Book of Mormon, Designed for Our Day." *Review of Books on the Book of Mormon* 2 (1990): 1–25.

Russell, Raymond. *Sharing Ownership in the Workplace.* Albany, N.Y.: State University of New York Press, 1985.

St. Clair, Larry L., and Clayton C. Newberry. "Consecration, Stewardship and Accountability: Remedy for a Dying Planet." *Dialogue* 28 (summer 1995): 93–99.

Salowsky, Heinz. "The Decline of Self-Employment in Industrial Countries." *Intereconomics* 1978: 306–8.

Sanger, David E., and Steve Lohr. "A Search for Answers to Avoid the Layoffs." *New York Times,* 9 March 1996, A1, A12–A13.

Sanyal, Bishwapriya. "Organizing the Self-Employed: The Politics of the Urban Informal Sector." *International Labour Review* (1991): 39–56.

Scarlet, Peter. "Mormons Unite with Other Faiths to Solve Social Problems of the World." *Salt Lake Tribune,* 3 April 1993, D1, D2.

Schor, Juliet B. *The Overworked American: The Unexpected Decline of Leisure.* New York: Basic Books, 1991.

Schumacher, E. F. *Small Is Beautiful.* New York: Harper and Row, 1973.

Schuman, Michael. "The Microlenders." *Forbes*, 25 October 1993, 164–66.

Seidman, L. William. *Full Faith and Credit: The Great S&L Debacle and Other Washington Sagas.* New York: Random House, 1993.

Selz, Michael, and Udayan Gupta. "Lending Woes Stunt Growth of Small Firms." *Wall Street Journal*, 16 November 1994, B1, B2.

Senge, Peter M. *The Fifth Discipline: The Art and Practice of the Learning Organization.* New York: Doubleday, 1990.

Serrill, Michael S. "Banker to the Poor." *Time*, 27 May 1991, international edition, 66.

Sethuraman, S. V., ed. *The Urban Informal Sector in Developing Countries: Employment, Poverty, and Environment.* Geneva: International Labour Office, 1981.

Seymour-Jones, Carole. *Beatrice Webb: A Life.* Chicago: Ivan R. Dee, 1992.

Shallenbarger, Sue. "Work-Force Study Finds Loyalty Is Weak, Divisions of Race and Gender Are Deep." *Wall Street Journal*, 3 September 1993, B1, B8.

Sher, Richard B., and Jeffrey R. Smitten, eds. *Scotland and America in the Age of the Enlightenment.* Edinburgh: Edinburgh University Press, 1990.

Sheffield, G. and Sheridan R. "Botanist's Studies Motivated by Desire to Help Sick, Afflicted." *Church News*, 5 September 1992, 7.

Sheffield, Sheridan R. "Aim of Gospel Literacy Effort: Enrich Lives." *Church News*, 30 January 1993, 3, 5.

"A Short Sketch of the Rise of the Young Gentlemen and Ladies of the Relief Society of Nauvoo." *Times and Seasons*, 1 April 1843, 154–57.

Shover, John. *First Majority, Last Minority: The Transforming of Rural Life in America.* DeKalb, Ill.: Northern Illinois University Press, 1976.

Sillito, John R., and John S. McCormick. "Socialist Saints: Mormons and the Socialist Party in Utah, 1900–1920." *Dialogue* 18 (spring 1985): 121–31.

Simons, Marlise. "Gold in Streets (Some Call It Trash)." *New York Times*, 4 January 1994, A4.

Sims, Calvin. "Family Values as a Las Vegas Smash." *New York Times*, 3 February 1994, D1, D7.

Singer, Hans. "Lessons of Post-War Development Experience 1945–1988." In *A Dual Economy*, edited by Willem L. M. Adriaansen and J. George Waardenburg. Rotterdam: Wolters-Noordhof, 1989.

Sloan, Allan. "The Hit Men." *Newsweek*, 26 February 1996, 44–48.

Smart, Tim. "Let the Good Times Roll—and a Few More Heads." *Business Week*, 31 January 1994, 28–29.

Smiley, Robert W., Jr., and Ronald J. Gilbert, eds. *Employee Stock Ownership Plans: Business Planning, Implementation, Law and Taxation.* New York: Prentice-Hall, 1989 (with annual Yearbook updates).

Smith, Adam. *The Correspondence of Adam Smith.* Edited by Ernest Campbell Mosner and Ian Simpson Ross. Oxford: Clarendon Press, 1977.

———. *An Inquiry into the Nature and Causes of the Wealth of Nations.* Edited by R. H. Campbell, A. S. Skinner, and W. B. Toad. 1776. Reprint, Oxford: Clarendon Press, 1976.

———. *Lectures on Jurisprudence.* Edited by R. L. Meek, D. D. Raphael, and P. G. Stein. Oxford: Clarendon Press, 1978.

———. *The Theory of Moral Sentiments.* Edited by D. D. Raphael and A. L. Macfie. 1759. Reprint, Oxford: Clarendon Press, 1976.

Smith, Geri, and Elisabeth Malkin. "Surveying the Wreckage." *Business Week,* 23 January 1995, 58–59.

Smith, Joseph, Jr. *An American Prophet's Record: The Diaries and Journals of Joseph Smith.* Edited by Scott H. Faulring. Salt Lake City: Signature Books, 1989.

———. *A Compilation Containing the Lectures on Faith.* Comp. N. B. Lundwall. Salt Lake City.

———. *Teachings of the Prophet Joseph Smith.* Compiled by Joseph Fielding Smith. Salt Lake City: Deseret Book, 1977.

———. *The Words of Joseph Smith: The Contemporary Accounts of the Nauvoo Discourses of the Prophet Joseph.* Compiled and edited by Andrew F. Ehat and Lyndon W. Cook. Provo, Utah: Religious Studies Center, Brigham Young University; Salt Lake City: Bookcraft, 1980.

Smith, Joseph F. *Gospel Doctrine.* Salt Lake City: Deseret Book, 1977.

———. "The Message of the Latter-day Saints on Relief for the Poor." *Improvement Era* 10 (August 1907): 831–33.

———. "The Truth about Mormonism." *Out West* 23 (1905): 239–55.

Smith, Joseph Fielding. *Answers to Gospel Questions.* Vol. 4. Salt Lake City: Deseret Book, 1963.

Snow, Donald R. "Models Used in Projecting Mormon Growth," Presentation at the annual meeting of the Mormon History Association, Ogden, Utah, May 1982.

Snow, Lorenzo. "Mormonism, By Its Head." *Land of Sunshine* 15 (October 1901): 252–59.

Snyder, Neil H., James J. Dowd, Jr., and Dianne Morse Houghton. *Vision, Value, and Courage: Leadership for Quality Management.* New York: Free Press, 1994.

Sowell, Thomas. "A Road to Hell Paved with Good Intentions." *Forbes,* 17 January 1994, 60–65.

Specter, Michael. "Russia's Declining Health: Rising Illness, Shorter Lives." *New York Times,* 19 February 1995, A1, A12.

Spencer, Herbert. *Social Statics.* New York: D. Appleton, 1866.

Stack, Jack. *The Great Game of Business.* New York: Doubleday, 1992.

Stack, Peggy Fletcher. "Famine, Flood? LDS Humanitarian Agency Supplies International, Local Helping Hand." *Salt Lake Tribune,* 31 August 1991, A10.

———. "Senior Couples Lend Skills to Mormon 'Peace Corps.'" *Salt Lake Tribune,* 23 January 1993, D1, D2.

Stanley, Alessandra. "Mission to Moscow: Preaching the Gospel of Business." *New York Times,* 27 February 1994, F4.

Stark, Rodney. "The Rise of a New World Faith." *Review of Religious Research* 26 (1984): 18–27.

Steiner, Sue. *Employee Ownership: Alternatives to ESOPs.* Oakland, Calif.: National Center for Employee Ownership, 1990.

Stephen, Frank H. *The Economic Analysis of Producer Cooperatives.* London: Macmillan, 1984.

Stern, Gabriella. "Kid's Homework May Be Going the Way of the Dinosaur." *Wall Street Journal,* 11 October 1993, B1, B8.

Sternberg, William, and Matthew C. Harrison, Jr. *Feeding Frenzy.* New York: Henry Holt, 1989.

Sterngold, James. *Burning Down the House: How Greed, Deceit and Bitter Revenge Destroyed E. F. Hutton.* New York: Simon & Schuster, 1990.

Stevenson, Richard W. "Barings Knew of Big Gamble, Officials Assert." *New York Times,* 5 March 1995, A1, A8.

Stout, Mary Kay. "Russian Members Distribute Bales of Clothes and Shoes among LDS, Others." *Church News,* 4 September 1993, 3, 10.

Stover, John F. *American Railroads.* Chicago: University of Chicago Press, 1961.

Sutton, Antony C. *Western Technology and Soviet Economic Development.* 3 vols. Stanford, Calif.: Hoover Institution on War, Revolution, and Peace, 1968–73.

Swoboda, Frank, and Kathleen Day. "U.S. to Fine Coal Companies $5 Million for Safety Violations on Dust Samples." *Washington Post,* 5 April 1991, A9.

Talmage, James E. *The Articles of Faith.* Salt Lake City: Deseret News, 1899. Reprint, Salt Lake City, The Church of Jesus Christ of Latter-day Saints, 1975.

Taylor, Frederick Winslow. *The Principles of Scientific Management.* 1911. Reprint, New York: Norton, 1967.

Taylor, James C., and David F. Felten. *Performance by Design: Sociotechnical Systems in North America.* Englewood Cliffs, N.J.: Prentice-Hall, 1993.

Taylor, John. "Address to the Annual Conference of the New York Conference, November 2, 1856." *The Mormon* (January 31, 1857): 1.

———. *The Government of God.* Liverpool: S. W. Richards; London: Latter-day Saint Book Depot, 1852.

Taylor, P. A. M. *Expectations Westward: The Mormons and the Emigration of their British Converts in the Nineteenth Century.* Edinburgh, U.K.: Oliver & Boyd, 1965.

Taylor, Stanley. "Economic Aid." In *Encyclopedia of Mormonism,* edited by Daniel H. Ludlow, 434–35. New York: Macmillan, 1992.

"Technology in Utah: Software Valley." *Economist* (23 April 1994): 69–70.

Tedlow, Richard S. *The Rise of the American Business Corporation.* Chur, Switzerland: Harwood Academic Publishers, 1991.

Temin, Peter. *Lessons from the Great Depression.* Cambridge: MIT Press, 1989.

Thomas, Henk, and Christopher Logan. *Mondragon: An Economic Analysis.* London: George Allen & Unwin, 1982.

Thomas, Henk. "The Performance of the Mondragon Cooperatives in Spain." In *Participatory and Self-Managed Firms,* edited by Derek Jones and Jan Svejnar. Lexington, Mass.: Lexington Books, 1982.

———. "The Dynamics of Social Ownership: Some Considerations in the Perspective of the Mondragon Experience." *Economic Analysis and Workers' Management* 19 (1985): 147–60.

Thompson, E. P. *The Making of the English Working Class.* London: Victor Gollancz, 1963.

Thorp, Malcolm R. "The Setting for the Restoration in Britain: Political, Social and Economic Conditions." In *Truth Will Prevail: The Rise of The Church of Jesus Christ of Latter-day Saints in the British Isles 1837–1987,* edited by V. Ben Bloxham, James R. Moss, and Larry C. Porter. Solihull, U.K.: The Church of Jesus Christ of Latter-day Saints, 1987.

Tomasko, Robert M. *Rethinking the Corporation: The Architecture of Change.* New York: American Management Association, 1993.

Top, Brent L. "'Thou Shalt Not Covet.'" *Ensign* 24 (December 1994): 22–26.
"Top 20 Languages Spoken in the Church." *Church News*, 30 November 1991, 7.
Tracy, Jack. *Conan Doyle and the Latter-Day Saints.* Bloomington, Ind.: Gaslight Publications, 1979.
Tullis, F. Lamond. "Church Development Issues among Latin Americans—Introduction." In *Mormonism: A Faith for All Cultures*, edited by F. Lamond Tullis. Provo, Utah: Brigham Young University Press, 1978.
———. *Mormons in Mexico.* Logan, Utah: Utah State University Press, 1987.
———, ed. *Mormonism: A Faith for All Cultures.* Provo, Utah: Brigham Young University Press, 1978.
Turpin-Forster, Shela C. "Mondragon's Message for Employee Ownership." Paper in possession of authors.
Tyler, Alice Felt. *Freedom's Ferment.* New York: Harper and Brothers, 1962.
Uchitelle, Louis. "Job Extinction Evolving into a Fact of Life in U.S." *New York Times*, 22 March 1994, A1, D5.
———. "Male, Educated and Falling Behind." *New York Times*, 11 February 1994, D1, D4.
———. "Newest Corporate Refugees: Self-Employed and Low-Paid." *New York Times*, 15 November 1993, A1, D2.
———. "Strong Companies Are Joining Trend to Eliminate Jobs." *New York Times*, 26 July 1993, A1, D3.
———. "Temporary Workers Are on the Increase in Nation's Factories." *New York Times*, 6 July 1993, A1, D2.
———. "Trapped in the Impoverished Middle Class." *New York Times*, 17 November 1991, D1, D10.
Uchitelle, Louis, and N. R. Kleinfield. "On the Battlefields of Business, Millions of Casualties." *New York Times*, 3 March 1996, A1, A26–A29.
Uhrban, Alfred W. "Welfare in the Church." *Improvement Era* 59 (November 1956): 810.
"U.N. Says Half the World Yearns for Basic Rights." *Salt Lake Tribune*, 18 April 1993.
United Nations Department of International Economic and Social Affairs. *World Economic Survey 1992: Current Trends and Policies in the World Economy.* New York: United Nations, 1992.
United States General Accounting Office. *Employee Stock Ownership Plans: Little Evidence of Effects on Corporate Performance.* Washington, D.C.: United States General Accounting Office, 1987.
Uphoff, Norman. "Paraprojects as New Modes of International Development Assistance." *World Development* 18 (October 1990): 1401–11.
Ure, Jon. "Sons of Industrialist Aid Armenians." *Salt Lake Tribune*, 11 April 1993, B1–2.
"Utah Workplace Deaths Twice National Average." *Provo (Utah) Daily Herald*, 22 March 1993, C3.
Vanek, Jaroslav, ed. *Self-Management: Economic Liberation of Man.* Baltimore: Penguin, 1975.
Vobejda, Barbara. "Education Is No Protection from Wage Squeeze, Report Says." *Washington Post*, 4 September 1994, A20.
Wagner, Gordon E. *Consecration and Stewardship: A Socially Efficient System of Justice.* Ph.D. diss., Cornell University, 1977.

———. "Stewardship in the Southern Sudan." Paper presented at the Plotting Zion conference sponsored by Sunstone Foundation and National Historic Communal Societies Association, Provo, Utah, 3–5 May 1990.

Wahid, Abu N. M., ed. *The Grameen Bank: Poverty Relief in Bangladesh* (Boulder, Colo.: Westview Press, 1993).

Walker, Ronald W. "Brigham Young on the Social Order." *Brigham Young University Studies* 28 (Summer 1988): 37–52.

Wall, Joseph Frazier. *Andrew Carnegie.* 2nd ed. Pittsburgh: University of Pittsburgh Press, 1989.

Wallerstein, Immanuel. *The Capitalist World Economy.* New York: Cambridge University Press, 1979.

Wallich, Paul, and Marguerite Holloway. "More Profitable to Give Than to Receive?" *Scientific American,* March 1993, 142.

Walton, Charles C. *Ethos and the Executive: Values in Managerial Decision Making.* Englewood Cliffs, N.J.: Prentice-Hall, 1969.

Walton, Sam, with John Huey. *Made in America: My Story.* New York: Doubleday, 1992.

Webb, Beatrice Potter. *Beatrice Webb's American Diary, 1898.* Edited by David A. Shannon. Madison: University of Wisconsin Press, 1963.

———. *The Cooperative Movement in Great Britain.* London: Swan Sonnenschein; New York: Charles Scribner, 1891. Reprint, London: London School of Economics and Political Science, 1987.

———. *Diary of Beatrice Webb 1873–1943.* Original in British Library of Political and Economic Science. Available on microfiche from Cambridge, U.K.: Chadwyck-Healey; Teaneck, N.J.: Somerset House.

———. *My Apprenticeship.* London: Longmans, Green & Co., 1926.

———. *Our Partnership.* Edited by Barbara Drake and Margaret I. Cole. London: Longmans, Green & Co., 1948.

Webb, Sidney and Beatrice. *The Truth About Soviet Russia.* London: Longmans, Green & Co., 1942.

Webb, Marilyn. "How Old Is Too Old?" *New York,* 29 March 1993, 66–73.

Weisbord, Marvin R. *Productive Workplaces.* San Francisco: Jossey-Bass, 1987.

Werhane, Patricia H. *Adam Smith and His Legacy for Modern Capitalism.* Oxford: Oxford University Press, 1991.

Werner, Walter, and Steven T. Smith. *Wall Street.* New York: Columbia University Press, 1991.

"What in the World Is Happening to Workers?" *CWA News* (November 1991): 6–8.

White, Jean Bickmore. "Dr. Martha Hughes Cannon: Doctor, Wife, Legislator, Exile." In *Sister Saints,* edited by Vicky Burgess-Olson. Provo, Utah: Brigham Young University Press, 1978.

Whitman, David. "The Rise of the 'Hyper-Poor.'" *U.S. News and World Report,* 15 October 1990, 40–42.

Whitney, Craig R. "Western Europe's Dreams Turning to Nightmares." *New York Times,* 8 August 1993, A1, A16.

Whitson, Robbey Edward. *The Shakers: Two Centuries of Spiritual Reflection.* New York: Paulist Press, 1983.

Whyte, William Foote, and Kathleen King Whyte. *Making Mondragon: The*

Growth and Dynamics of the Worker Cooperative Complex. Ithaca, N.Y.: ILR Press, 1988.

———. "Mondragón: A Vision Lives On." *National Catholic Reporter* 25 (3 March 1989): 2.

Widtsoe, John A. "Evidences and Reconciliations: Are Communism and Its Related 'Isms' Preparatory to the United Order?" *Improvement Era* 43 (October 1940): 609, 633–34. Reprint, *Evidences and Reconciliations.: Aids to Faith in a Modern Day*. First collector's edition. Salt Lake City: Bookcraft, 1987, 374–77.

———. "Evidences and Reconciliations: Should Church Doctrine Be Accepted Blindly?" *Improvement Era* 51 (July 1948): 449, 478. Reprint, *Evidences and Reconciliations*, 226-228.

———. *Joseph Smith: Seeker after Truth, Prophet of God*. Salt Lake City: Bookcraft, 1957.

———. *Priesthood and Church Government*. Salt Lake City: Deseret Book, 1950.

———. *A Rational Theology: As Taught by The Church of Jesus Christ of Letter-day Saints*. 1915. Reprint, Salt Lake City: Deseret Book, 1965.

Wiener, Hans, with Robert Oakeshott. *Worker-Owners: Mondragon Revisited*. London: Anglo-German Foundation for the Study of Industrial Society, 1987.

Williams, Robert Chadwell. *Klaus Fuchs, Atom Spy*. Cambridge: Harvard University Press, 1987.

Wilson, James Q. "Adam Smith on Business Ethics." *California Management Review* 32 (fall 1989): 59–72.

Wilson, William J. *The Truly Disadvantaged: The Inner City, the Underclass, and Public Policy*. Chicago: University of Chicago Press, 1987.

Winters, Charlene Renberg. "AIDS Knowledge May Get Boost from Samoan Rainforest." *BYU Today* (September 1992): 2–3.

———. "Building a Business beyond Accounting Ledgers and Elbow Grease." *BYU Today* (July 1990): 8–9.

———. "Project Manila Helps Third World Entrepreneurs." *BYU Today* (September 1992): 14, 16.

Witham, Craig. "Provo Woolen Mills: A Cooperative Enterprise." *Utah County Journal*, 23 September 1987, 1, 14, 22.

Wood, Steven. "City Wards and Branches in the LDS Church." Paper presented at 1993 Washington Sunstone Symposium, Washington, D. C., 13 March 1993.

Woodruff, Wilford. *The Discourses of Wilford Woodruff*. Edited by G. Homer Durham. Salt Lake City: Bookcraft, 1969.

———. *Wilford Woodruff's Journal*. Edited by Scott G. Kenney. Midvale, Utah: Signature Books, 1983.

Woodworth, Warner P. "Brave New Bureaucracy." *Dialogue* 20 (fall 1987): 25–36.

———. "Capitalism with a Human Face: Social Responsibility in the Steel Industry." Paper presented at the International Association of Business and Society, Sundance, Utah, 22–24 March 1991.

———. "Developing Innovations for Global Transformation." Keynote speech for International Week, Brigham Young University, Provo, Utah, 25 January 1993.

———. "Hard Hats in the Boardroom: New Trends in Workers' Participation." In *Organization and People,* edited by J. B. Ritchie and Paul Thompson, 362–71. St. Paul: West, 1988.

———. "The Informal Economy and Micro-Entrepreneurs in the Philippines: Research Analysis." Technical report, Brigham Young University, 1990.

———. "Israeli Hi Tech Co-ops Challenge Popular Myths." *Workplace Democracy* 12, no. 2 (fall 1985): 10–19.

———. "Steel Busting in the West." *Social Policy* 18, no. 3 (1988): 53–56.

———. "Third World Strategies Toward Zion." *Sunstone* 14 (October 1990): 13–23.

———. "Weirton Steel: An ESOP Conversion." In *Worker Empowerment: The Struggle for Workplace Democracy,* edited by Jon D. Wisman, 117–30. New York: Bootstrap Press, 1991.

Woodworth, Warner P., and Vernon Dillenbeck. "A New Strategy: Combining Manufacturing and Management." *Journal of Engineering Technology* 7, no. 2 (fall 1990): 32–34.

Woodworth, Warner P., and Christopher B. Meek. *Creating Labor-Management Partnerships.* Reading, Mass.: Addison-Wesley, 1995.

Worden, Andrew. "A Prophet Touched My Life." *Ensign* 7 (February 1977): 59.

Worthy, James C. *Shaping an American Institution: Robert E. Wood and Sears, Roebuck.* Urbana: University of Illinois Press, 1984.

Wright, John W., ed. *The Universal Almanac 1995.* Kansas City: Andrews and McMeel, 1994.

Young, Brigham. *Letters of Brigham Young to His Sons.* Edited by Dean C. Jessee. Salt Lake City: Deseret Book, 1974.

Young, Lawrence A. "Confronting Turbulent Environments: Issues in the Organizational Growth and Globalization of Mormonism." In *Contemporary Mormonism: Social Science Perspectives,* edited by Marie Cornwall, Tim B. Heaton, and Lawrence A. Young. Urbana: University of Illinois Press, 1994.

Yunus, Muhammad. "Credit as a Human Right: A Bangladesh Bank Helps Poor Women." *New York Times,* 2 April 1990, A17.

Zehr, Mary Ann. "Imported from Bangladesh." *Foundation News* (November–December 1992): 28–32.

Zey, Mary. *Banking on Fraud: Drexel, Junk Bonds, and Buyouts.* New York: Aldine de Gruyter, 1993.

Zwerdling, Daniel. *Workplace Democracy.* New York: Harper & Row, 1980.

Index